Cases in
Financial Management

Cases in Financial Management

Second Edition

JERRY A. VISCIONE

Ph.D.

GEORGE A. ARAGON

D.B.A.

Both of Boston College

HOUGHTON MIFFLIN COMPANY   BOSTON
Dallas   Geneva, Illinois   Hopewell, New Jersey   Palo Alto

DEDICATION

Jerry Viscione wishes to dedicate this book to
his mother and father, and sister and brother.

George Aragon wishes to dedicate this book to
his mother and father, and Mummoo.

Cover design by Jill Haber.

Printed in the U.S.A.

Library of Congress Catalog Card Number: 83-81685

ISBN: 0-395-34267-8

BCDEFGHIJ-BP-8987654

Contents

Preface   vii

Note on Case Analysis   1

Part I
Financial Statements   7

Fulton Flying Lessons, Inc.   9
Capitol Corporation   18

Part II
Financial Analysis and Forecasting   23

Valu-Hi Drug Stores (A)   25
Valu-Hi Drug Stores (B)   33
Ankh Corporation   37
Hollowville National Bank   39
ChemCo, Inc.   56
Super Sounds   58
Breau Company (A)   60
Breau Company (B)   70
Xenon, Inc.   71
Tesco, Inc. (A)   77
Tesco, Inc. (B)   83
Winston College   88
Paducah Portrait   96
Carroll Company Incorporated   100
Bolton College Food Service   105
Budin Company (A)   112

Part III
Working Capital Management   127

Gansett Furniture Company (A)   129
Fund for Government Investors   144
Children's Memorial Hospital (A)   154
Brown Furniture Company, Inc.   171
National Credit Company   174
J. H. Company   184
Budin Company (B)   188
Addison Electric Company   196
Midwest Grain Company   209
Swanson Corporation   236
Etech, Inc.   265

Part IV
Capital Budgeting   285

Chou Canning Company   287
The Daily Ledger   292
United Chemical Company   294
Thermo Rubber, Inc.   296
Jenkins Plumbing Company   308
Note on the Capital Asset Pricing Model (CAPM)   310
Valuation Exercise   322
Javits Company   324
Filtron Corporation   334
Metchler Corporation   340
Gansett Furniture Company (B)   350
Palazolo Manufacturing Company   363
Teague Corporation   370

Part V
Long-Term Financing and Dividends   375

Delicious, Inc.   377
Cost-of-Capital Illustrations   390
American Forge Corporation   400
Children's Memorial Hospital (B)   408
Hammond Publishing Company   433
PODER Industries   446
Frecter Company   464
Brenco Corporation   469
Quality Hardware, Inc.   477
Basic Industries, Inc.   486
Dunkin' Donuts Incorporated   492

Part VI
Comprehensive Cases   511

Megansett Corporation   513
Winco Distribution Company   521
Electricircuit, Inc.   537
Incoterm Corporation   549
Phillips Bakeries, Inc.   563
Meditronics, Inc.   569

APPENDIXES   575

A. Present Value of $1 at Discount Rate k for n Years   577
B. Present Value of an Annuity of $1 at Discount
   Rate k for n Years   579

INDEX OF CASES   581

Preface

The case method of instruction has long proved to be a useful vehicle for teaching financial management. Cases provide an opportunity for students to develop the ability to implement financial training by learning to do the following:

1. Identify problems in unstructured contexts
2. Resolve multi-issue problems
3. Formulate options
4. Make decisions and develop plans of action

Many students accustomed to courses that focus on lectures, discussion of readings, and/or homework problems have difficulty adjusting to the case method, particularly if they have had little or no management experience. To help students with the adjustment process and to increase the benefits gained from this useful method of instruction, we provide three types of cases. This range enables students to bridge the gap between end-of-chapter problems and exercises and unstructured cases.

The first type of case is similar to the more extended end-of-chapter problems and exercises. Because these are the most structured cases in the book, they are tailored to emphasize skill development rather than problem identification and decision making. However, in almost all these cases the student will be required to do some issue specification and decision making. These cases will be guided and will have something close to a "right" answer or a narrow range of "right" answers. Approximately 40 percent of the cases in this book are of this type, and many are based on our work or on consulting experiences.

The second type, comprising about 25 percent of the cases in the book, provides the central span of the bridge and is more open-ended than is the first type. In these cases, emphasis shifts from technique development to identifying problems, formulating alternatives, choosing the appropriate analysis, and reaching a decision. The situations are presented more in context than are the cases of the first type; however, these cases are structured to some extent to help the student apply concepts and techniques to decision making and to demonstrate to students that problems and decisions are interdependent. For example, often the solution to one particular problem has problematic implications for other issues confronting the manager; the second case type demonstrates this kind of situation.

The third type, approximately 35 percent of the cases in this book, presents the situations in contexts similar to those that confront managers in reality. These cases emphasize the importance of defining issues clearly, of making and defending a decision, and of designing a program of action to implement the decision. These resemble the more traditional type of cases, and they are sometimes referred to as Harvard Cases.

The fifty-eight cases are divided into six parts—Financial Statements, Financial Analysis and Forecasting, Working Capital Management, Capital Budgeting, Long-Term Financing and Dividends, and Comprehensive Cases. As in the first edition, we include in each section, except for the last, some of each of the three types of cases. The Financial Analysis and Forecasting and the Capital Budgeting sections include a larger proportion of type one cases because of the importance of learning techniques such as the preparation of cash budgets; however, a number of type two and three cases are also included in these two sections.

We noted in the preface to the first edition that many users would appreciate the large number and the great variety of cases on financial analysis and working capital. This edition strengthens that feature. We should mention that this emphasis has not been at the expense of other vital areas, such as capital budgeting and long-term financing. Indeed, there are now more cases that provide an opportunity to discuss the application of capital markets theory and to rely on computer applications. Moreover, we continue to include a number of cases that expose students to financial management in not-for-profit organizations.

ACKNOWLEDGEMENTS

In writing the two editions of this book, we received help from many kind and competent people. We were fortunate to have the encouragement of our families and friends, the cooperation of many busy executives, and the assistance of reviewers, editors, student assistants, and others.

We are grateful to Kenneth Frantz who wrote the Hammond Publishing case and to Richard Fisher and Harry Dickinson who wrote the Midwest Grains case. We are grateful to John Preston and Frank Campanella, who assisted in the preparation of the cases on hospitals and on the Winston College case, respectively. Stephen Barrett, Diane Bauman, and Deborah Buckley, research assistants, performed research and helped with the initial drafts of cases. The following graduate assistants also helped with the writing of cases and accompanying teaching notes and/or with other aspects of the casebook: Rod Brown, Brian Donahue, Kevin Dziwulzki, James Fitzgerald, Carol Gordon,

Ellen Goss, Steven Kwiatkowski, Maria Provenzano, Susan Rudolph, David Santom, and Steven Tibbets.

We owe a substantial debt to the following managers: Robert Aragon, John Balboni, John Bitner, David Breslin, William Brett, Karen Chalmers, Kenneth Clark III, Anita DeSanto, Richard Driscoll, Richard Garvey, Richard Hart, Elaine Kiuber, Gary Koenig, Robert Linden, David March, Robert J. Pink, Sr., Ronald Porter, Joseph Raimo, Jeff Randall, John Rees, Al Roitfarb, Robert Rosenberg, Philip Smith, Mark Steinkrauss, and Robert Tyhurst.

The following academic reviewers provided numerous constructive comments: Severin Carlson, University of Rhode Island at Kingston; Peter Ewald, Long Island University; John Ford; Anthony Herbst, University of Texas at Arlington; David Higgins, University of Wisconsin at La Crosse; J. B. Ludtke, University of Massachusetts at Amherst; Edward Maher, University of New Brunswick; Joseph Moosally, Mankato State University; Gordon Roberts and R. G. Storey, Dalhousie University; Donald Thompson, Georgia State University; and Ben Trykowski, California State University at Los Angeles.

We are grateful to Dean John Neuhauser and to our colleagues at Boston College, who provided helpful comments. Professors David Murphy, Peter Olivieri, and Ron Porter helped write cases or teaching notes. The following assisted with class testing or provided help in other ways: Gail Chu, Tom Downs, William Horne, Walter Greaney, Jr., Mya Maung, Hassan Tehranian, and Ruben Trevino. We also appreciate the patience and skills of Anne Shenkman and Mary Sullivan, who provided secretarial, editorial, and administrative support.

Jerry A. Viscione

George A. Aragon

Note on Case Analysis

The purpose of this note is to provide an overview of the case method of instruction and to address several issues that are especially relevant to students unaccustomed to this educational technique. The case method of instruction has two distinct and important aspects: *case analysis*, which involves the identification of relevant issues and problems for resolution, the design of solutions that are both workable and theoretically proper, and the phased implementation of the proposed solution or plan of action; and *case presentation*, which involves the cogent reporting of the analysis, the "selling" of the case analysis publicly, anticipating and rebutting criticisms and questions, modifying the preliminary analysis and solution when necessary, and building an effective consensus in support of the proposed plan of action.

The two aspects of the case method are interrelated, the second being a verbal presentation and defense of the first. However, the second aspect involves a separate, crucial characteristic of the case method: the process of synthesizing counterarguments, criticisms, and concerns. This is a political process of building a consensus around the most workable solution, which may not be the solution initially proposed. Indeed, the case method is not usually concerned with the "correct" or "ideal" solution to case issues and problems: such a solution may never be discovered or may be impossible to implement. Since case presentation is essentially an oral and evolutionary process, this note is concerned with the first, analytical, aspect of the case method.

Case analysis should begin with a clear specification of objectives and goals. This permits a systematic approach to the collection and classification of relevant evidence,[1] and, by logical inference, relates case facts to their probable impacts. Out of the process of relating facts to probable impacts emerge working hypotheses about what is "wrong" or "right" about the company's financial management. The working hypotheses represent an interpretation of case facts and the identification of problems or issues. Consider, for example, a case in which the corporate objective is specified as the maximization of shareholder wealth. Some of the case facts are the following:

---

1. Evidence in a case context comes in a variety of forms: deductions, opinions, and calculations. With *all* case evidence, the student should consider the source: the evidence is only as reliable as the source. Thus, if project manager X has consistently overestimated the profitability of past projects, his or her future estimates of profitability should not be taken at face value.

1. The firm does not use analytical capital budgeting techniques (deduction).
2. The firm's president is quoted as saying he wants to have the "largest company in the industry" (opinion).
3. Return on investment is 8 percent, whereas typical rivals are earning 15 percent (calculation).

Logical inference may be used to identify these as being relevant facts in the following manner:

1. If the firm does not use analytical capital budgeting, it may make unprofitable investments (although not necessarily).
2. Becoming the "largest" firm may take the company into large-scale but unprofitable activities.
3. The low return on investment is likely to be reflected in a relatively low price-earnings multiple and thus lower share prices for every given level of profits.

Out of these case facts emerges the working hypothesis that the capital budgeting system is a relevant problem area. This is still a working hypothesis because it may in fact turn out that the real problem is poor management of profitable investments or simply a poor year with phenomenal future profitability. Case analysis attempts to construct those particular hypotheses that are most likely to identify the real problems.

Once the problem areas or issues in need of resolution are identified, a case analysis should design workable solutions. This involves the development of a plan of action that will both facilitate the effective pursuit of objectives and be practical in the context of real-world constraints. Students unaccustomed to the case method will often latch onto the design stage as a place to demonstrate familiarity with theory (or assigned readings). This is usually a mistake. Theoretical discussion should be built into the development of working hypotheses and the design of realistic solutions, but explicit theory is out of place in case analysis. Everything should relate *directly* to the unique facts of the particular case. It follows that unworkable solutions, however theoretically elegant ("Fire the president"), are useless in a case situation. Likewise, workable plans of action ("Buy a computer") are worse than useless if they lead to greater problems.

When the design of workable solutions has been accomplished, case analysis should take up explicitly the implementation of the solution. This stage will normally include direct concern for behavioral and organizational factors. In the short run, few substantive changes can be implemented in any but the most urgent circumstances. In the long run, substantive changes are more likely: key personnel may be educated to the virtues of various changes, trust and confidence in the proposed direction of solutions (if not specific solutions) may develop, and organizational resistance may diminish. Thus a plan of action should propose workable solutions with both short- and long-run perspectives.

In summary, case analysis involves the general stages of *investigation*, *design*, and *implementation*. Investigation results in the identification of problems and issues in need of resolution by relating various facts to their impacts on the pursuit of established objectives. The design stage considers workable answers that are theoretically valid. The implementation stage is primarily concerned with the management of proposed solutions. Finally, proposed solutions should explicitly incorporate both short- and long-run perspectives. The completion of a case analysis then leads to its presentation and defense.

ADJUSTING TO STUDYING BY THE CASE METHOD

Students new to the case method, especially those with little or no prior work experience, frequently encounter problems in making the transition from a lecture course to a case method course. This section addresses some of the issues and problems that often arise.

Incomplete Information

Students frequently conclude that the first few cases they study share one common feature: they do not include enough information to enable one to solve them. Although the reaction is understandable, it is an incorrect inference. The fact is that in some situations there is enough information, whereas in others the reader is given all the information available to the manager at the time.

Managers seldom have all the information they would like. Even if it exists, the manager may not have the time and/or the resources to gather it. Cases simply reflect this basic fact of life.

Unfortunately, the only advice available to students is to do the best analysis possible and to be sure to make a recommendation. The good news is that the uncomfortable feeling will diminish.

Facts vs. Opinions

Cases include facts and opinions; the former should be accepted at face value but the student should scrutinize opinions. Suppose, for example, that a case states: "Last year was the most profitable in the firm's history." The student should not question this statement. Now, suppose that a case includes the following: "Ms. Joan Jones, president of the XYZ Company, thought that last year's profit level was fabulous." Her view is important information in terms of what decision she might accept. However, it is an opinion, not a fact, and the reader should not automatically agree that the profit level was fabulous.

Assumptions

To perform many kinds of financial analysis, one must make assumptions. Very often the reasonableness of assumptions is a key concern. Thus, if the case presents an analysis, the student should evaluate the reasonableness of the underlying assumptions. Naturally, the student should exercise care in making assumptions for any analysis he or she performs and also should be prepared to defend them during a class discussion.

Time

A typical question students ask is: "How long does it take to prepare a case?" To do an adequate job on the cases in this book, one generally must spend between two and five hours. (Students usually spend more time on written case assignments.) Expect to feel frustrated at first; it is not possible to be as thorough as one would like within a limited time. The time constraint is just another reflection of the managerial environment. Decision makers typically are pressed for time, and thus, they learn to set priorities and to perform tasks in less time.

Unfortunately, there is no magic formula for dealing with the time constraint problem. One needs practice and experience to learn how to cope with the pressures of time. Realize, however, that the impossibility of doing a thorough job in a limited time is intrinsic to the case method and is not due to any deficiency in one's background or ability. More importantly, perhaps, the student should not deal with the sense of frustration by spending enormous amounts of time on the cases. This approach may ease the initial frustration but it will not help one to adjust to the case method and learn how to cope with the time pressure of a manager's job.

Library Research

Most cases use disguised companies, but sometimes the actual name is disclosed. If it is, the students wonder if they should look up information about the company in a library. Unless the instructor asks the class or certain members to gather these data, the student should not do so on his or her own initiative. The reason for this is that such information often harms the case discussion by discouraging participation.

Preparing a Case

There is no one best way to prepare a case because so much depends on the individual. Below are comments designed to provide the reader with ideas to consider in developing a suitable approach.

Many instructors provide suggested questions which are intended to guide the student. They are not meant to limit the nature or scope of the student's analysis. Also, in most instances it is not wise to view the goal of a case assignment to be to answer the questions.

Most cases are issue cases, which means that there are one or several decisions to make and/or problems to solve.[2] Thus, one must define the issue(s) and develop feasible alternatives. It's usually a good idea to write the issue(s) in one or two sentences and to list the options. Although this is the initial task, one must recognize that the definition of issue(s) and the list of options are somewhat tentative. This is because once the student performs the analysis, new light might be shed on what the real issue is, and he or she might find that some of the alternatives are not as feasible as they had seemed and others may become feasible.

The final task is the recommendation. This involves selecting an option, including a plan of implementation, and preparing to present it to others.

Many efficient case preparers begin by reading the case very quickly. They actually skim it to obtain a general picture. They then read it carefully, making marginal notes, underlining key points, and noting certain items on a separate piece of paper. Next they think about the problem, possible options, and what kind of analysis might be appropriate. Notice that they do not "push numbers" until after they think about the task. This point is stressed because many novices ignore this crucial step.

---

2. Some cases are appraisal cases which means that the decision(s) has been made or the problem(s) solved and that the task is to evaluate what was done.

PART I
FINANCIAL STATEMENTS

Fulton Flying Lessons, Inc.

In early November, Joseph Zampanti, president of Fulton Flying Lessons, Inc., was preparing for a second meeting with Joan Lestille, whom he hoped would invest in his company. At a meeting held in October, Ms. Lestille indicated interest but noted that she could not rely on the firm's financial statements to make a sound investment decision.

BACKGROUND

Joseph Zampanti had always wanted to own and manage a small business, and in August he decided to form Fulton Flying Lessons, Inc., in Silver Spring, Maryland. His plan was to sell flying lessons, which would be given by pilots retained on a contract basis. His investigation revealed that he could charge $25 for a lesson. The fee for the pilot would be $10, and he estimated that other lesson-related expenses would be $3.25.

On September 1 Zampanti started the business by investing $200,000 and borrowing $125,000 at an annual interest rate of 9 percent. The loan was to be repaid in five equal annual installments of $32,136, commencing in one year. (These installments include interest and principal.) On September 1 he purchased, for cash, two airplanes for $150,000 each and office equipment for $6,000. He estimated that the useful life of the airplanes would be ten years and that the useful life of the office equipment would be five years. Moreover, he estimated that the salvage value of these fixed assets would be negligible at the end of their useful lives. His final transactions on September 1 were to pay an annual rental fee of $12,000 for office space and a hangar and $6,000 for a one-year insurance policy.

To generate business, Zampanti decided to place weekly advertisements in a local newspaper, commencing September 3. The cost would be $50 per month. He was also able to sign a contract with a local country club for 1,000 lessons. The country club agreed to pay $25,000 on September 5, for which Zampanti agreed to provide 200 lessons during September and 200 lessons in each of the four subsequent months. Although he did not give a discount for this large order, he did agree to give free airplane rides to children of country club members on a Sunday morning during September.

Business boomed. During September he gave 1,000 lessons (including 200 to country club members). The price of each lesson was $25; all customers paid with cash. The pilots were happy with the $10-per-lesson fee arrangement, especially since Zampanti paid them at the end of each day. His estimate of other costs related to giving lessons proved high: actual costs per lesson were $2.95. Of the $2,950 total, only $2,800 had been paid by the end of September. Bills for the remaining $150 had been received but were not due until October. The only other expenditures for the month were $2,000 for Zampanti's salary,[1] $250 to organize the corporation, and $150 to give the free rides to the children of country club members.

Although Zampanti was pleased with the first month, he realized that he could have sold 2,000 to 3,000 lessons. However, with two airplanes he could sell only 1,000 lessons per month. He decided to buy two more airplanes and contacted the bank that had lent him $125,000. He was told that if he was able to raise $150,000 of equity capital, the bank would consider lending him an additional $150,000. Since Zampanti used all his personal resources with his original investment, he had to search for an investor. He was willing to give up 35 percent of the ownership of the firm for an investment of $150,000. A friend informed him that Joan Lestille represented many wealthy individuals who invested in new business ventures. He called her and arranged a meeting. She asked him to bring his financial statements (see Table 1).

Zampanti was surprised that Ms. Lestille did not want to begin by reviewing the financial statements. When he gave them to her, she put them aside and asked him questions concerning what motivated him to start his own business and what his long-range personal goals were. She then asked questions about the competitive environment in which the firm operated. She seemed very impressed, but her attitude changed as soon as she saw the financial statements. She understood that Zampanti had no prior experience with accounting, but she stressed that she just could not make a decision to invest based on the financial statements he gave her. She suggested that he obtain assistance and that they meet again when the accounting records were in order. Since she was going to be out of town for two weeks, she suggested that they meet again during the first week of November.

During October Zampanti sold only 800 lessons because he was committed to giving 200 lessons to country club members. Pilot fees were $10,000, his salary was $2,000, and the advertising expense for the month was $50. Other lesson-related expenses totaled $3,000, including the $150 owed from last month. Not included in the $3,000 were bills for $200, which had been received but for which payment was not due until November.

---

1. The reader may ignore payroll taxes in preparing this case.

TABLE 1
Fulton Flying Lessons, Inc.
Income Statement
Month of September

Sales (1,800 @ $25)	$45,000
Pilot fees	10,000
Lessons expenses	2,800
President's salary	2,000
Rent	12,000
Insurance	6,000
Depreciation expense	2,600
Organization expense	250
Advertising	50
Promotion	150
	$ 9,150

Fulton Flying Lessons, Inc.
Balance Sheet
At September 30

Cash		$ 30,750	Notes payable	$125,000
Office equipment	$ 6,000			
Less accum. deprec.	100	5,900		
Airplanes	$300,000		Common stock	200,000
Less accum. deprec.	2,500	297,500	Retained earnings	9,150
Total		$334,150	Total	$334,150

With respect to putting his accounting records in order, Zampanti had a long meeting with Bill Vargas, a close personal friend who was a CPA. He took notes at the meeting; a summary of them is presented in Exhibit 1.

Demand during October was even greater than it was in September. Each day Zampanti was turning away, because of lack of capacity, three or four customers for every one he served. He was convinced that this information, coupled with properly prepared financial statements, would persuade Ms. Lestille to invest.

EXHIBIT 1
Summary of Notes Taken at Meeting with Bill Vargas

I had a long meeting with Bill Vargas today. I told him that I purchased a simplified bookkeeping guide in a stationery store to help me prepare the financial statements. I explained that I thought the problem was that I deducted depreciation expense and that, had I not done this, Ms. Lestille would not have objected.

Bill began by stating that I handled depreciation properly. He believed that Ms. Lestille probably objected because I prepared my statements according to the cash basis of accounting rather than the accrual basis. He began this explanation by pointing out the difference between an income statement and a balance sheet. An income statement is a summary of revenues and expenses for a specific period of time. A balance sheet, on the other hand, is a statement of assets (what a company owns), liabilities (what a company owes), and equities (what the owners have invested) at a specific point in time. Preparing these statements according to the accrual basis of accounting makes them more useful for decision making than statements prepared according to the cash basis. Moreover, statements prepared according to the cash basis can be misleading.

As Bill began to explain the accrual basis, I could not believe what I was hearing. According to the accrual basis, the figure reported for net income for the period is normally not equal to the amount of cash generated during the period. In fact, it will often be very different from the amount of cash generated. I told him that I might not understand accounting, but that I did understand that I took in $45,000 during September and spent $33,250 on expenses, leaving $11,750. This is how much cash I have. I can spend cash but I cannot spend the other academic concepts Bill was proposing.

He responded by saying that, while it is indeed important for a manager to know how much cash came into and left the firm during a period, this information does not indicate how profitable the firm was during the period. He finally convinced me with the following example. Suppose we form a business to produce and sell widgets. We hire laborers for $2,000 per month and pay them at the end of each month. These laborers can produce 1,000 widgets per month, so the labor cost is $2 per widget. The cost of the materials needed for the widgets is $1 per widget. Since we plan to produce 1,000 widgets per month, we will purchase $1,000 worth of materials each month, and we will assume that we pay cash for these materials. There would obviously be other costs involved, but to keep the example simple we will assume that we have no other costs. To continue, let us assume that during the first month we produce 1,000 widgets and sell them for $10 each. We agree to receive payment in the subsequent month. During the second month we produce 1,000 widgets and sell them for $2 each. These are cash sales; that is, we receive payment during the second month. During the third month we produce 1,000 widgets. We sell 500 of them for $10 each during the third month, and these are also cash sales. We expect to sell the 500 extra that we produced in a subsequent month.

Given the preceding information, we can construct income statements for each of the first three months. We will begin by preparing them according to the cash basis of accounting. Accordingly, revenues are recognized and recorded when payment for them is received. Expenses are recognized and recorded when payment for them is made. The cash basis statements appear at the top of page 13.

According to these statements, the second month was the best and the first month was the poorest. We know that this is not true; in fact, we know that the opposite is true. During the first month we sold 1,000 units at $10 each and it

	Income Statements		
	For Month 1	For Month 2	For Month 3
Sales (revenues)	$ 0	$12,000	$5,000
Labor	2,000	2,000	2,000
Materials	1,000	1,000	1,000
Net income	$(3,000)	$ 9,000	$2,000

cost us $3 each to make them. Thus we made $7 on each unit, for a total profit of $7,000. It is true that we have not received payment, and we are certainly interested in the pattern of our firm's cash flow. However, the people who purchased the widgets from us are legally committed to pay for them, and this commitment was made in the first month. In other words, the revenue was generated during the first month and hence we should recognize it in the first month. On the other hand, during the second month we sold 1,000 units at $2 each and it cost us $3 each to make them. We can conclude that month 1 was much better in terms of profits than month 2. However, since we used the cash basis of accounting, the opposite is shown. Had we relied on the accrual basis, this distortion would not have occurred.

Accrual accounting relies on the realization concept to deal with revenues. The realization concept states that revenues (that is, sales) are recognized and recorded on the books when they are earned (that is, when the transaction takes place) regardless of when the cash is received. The amount recorded is the amount that was or is expected to be received. For example, suppose our firm sells $1,000 of goods or services during December and intends to receive payment in January. The accrual basis, relying on the realization concept, would record the $1,000 as revenues during December, whereas the cash basis would record the $1,000 as revenues during January. (Note that a balance sheet at the end of December prepared according to the accrual basis would include the $1,000 as an asset called accounts receivable. The cash basis balance sheet at the end of December would not include this asset.)

Bill continued by restating the preceding income statements, incorporating the realization concept.

	Income Statements		
	For Month 1	For Month 2	For Month 3
Revenues	$10,000	$ 2,000	$5,000
Labor	2,000	2,000	2,000
Materials	1,000	1,000	1,000
Net income	$ 7,000	$(1,000)	$2,000

The distorted view for the first two months is eliminated. However, there is still a problem. Look at month 3. During month 3 the firm sold 500 units and it cost $3 to make each of these units. In other words, the firm earned $3,500 (500 × $7 per unit). Yet the statement shows $2,000. What happened? Is there a distorted view?

Before answering this question, assume that the firm sells the extra 500 produced during month 3 for $8 each in month 4. Moreover, assume that the firm ceases operations for month 4. The income statement for month 4 would be as follows:

Income Statement
For Month 4

Revenues	$4,000
Expenses	0
Net income	$4,000

Did the firm earn a $4,000 profit in month 4? No. During month 4 the firm sold 500 at $8 each, which cost $3 each to produce. Thus the firm earned a $2,500 profit during month 4. We can avoid this distortion by following the matching concept, which means that the cost of producing a product or the cost of providing a service is recognized and recorded as an expense in the same period in which the revenue from this product or service is recognized. (This distortion did not occur in months 1 and 2 because we sold the amount produced in each of these months. Thus we recorded the revenues for 1,000 units in each of these months and matched the costs of producing these products to the revenues.) Restating months 3 and 4, incorporating both the realization concept and the matching concept, produces the following:

	Income Statements	
	For Month 3	For Month 4
Revenues	$5,000	$4,000
Labor costs in products sold	1,000	1,000
Material costs in products sold	500	500
Net income	$3,500	$2,500

I told Bill that I understood his point, but I wondered how to recognize that we produced 1,000 units during month 3. The cost of producing the products not sold is shown as an asset called inventory on the firm's balance sheet at the end of month 3. It makes sense because the firm owns these products until it sells them. Putting it another way, the cost of producing a product becomes an asset, and this asset becomes an expense when the product is sold. In a retailing firm, the language is different but the principle is the same. A retailing firm purchases products and resells them. The cost of these purchases is an asset (that is, inventory), and this asset becomes an expense when it is sold. Stated alternatively, the costs of purchases are recorded as expenses in the same period in which the revenues from these purchases are recorded.

Bill went on to explain that the matching concept often confuses people. As noted, the costs of producing products are recorded as expenses in the same period in which the revenues are recognized. However, there are other costs, called period costs, that are not related directly to sales but rather are used up simply by the passage of time. These costs are recorded as expenses in the period during which they are consumed. Bill used as an example my salary from Fulton Flying Lessons, Inc. I am not directly involved in giving lessons. Moreover, my salary is the same each month regardless of the number of lessons given. Thus this cost should be recorded as an expense in the period used. That is, the $2,000 cost for the month should be charged as an expense for the month. I asked him when during the month my salary becomes an expense. Since I am paid on the thirtieth of each month, does my salary become an expense on the thirtieth? He responded that expenses are recognized when they are incurred, regardless of when payment is made. For example, if I were preparing an income statement for one week during the month, then I would recognize the portion of my salary applicable to that week—$500, which is one-fourth of the total—as an expense for that week. Moreover, this amount would appear as a liability, called accrued wages or accrued expenses, on the balance sheet as of the end of that week.

To explain the opposite situation—paying for expenses before they are used—Bill used fire insurance as an example. Suppose a firm buys a three-year fire insurance policy for $3,600. This is a period cost because it will be used up with the passage of time. However, since the cost will provide coverage for three years, one-third of this cost ($1,200) must be charged as an expense for each of the three years. Actually, the $3,600 would be recorded as an asset when the policy is purchased (regardless of whether payment is made at the time of purchase or prior to or subsequent to the time of purchase). Then one-third of this asset would be charged as an expense for each of the next three years. Naturally, if an income statement were being prepared for one month, $100 would be charged as an expense for that month ($3,600 ÷ 36 months).

At this point, I told Bill that I had several questions concerning depreciation. The book I used as a guide explained that fixed assets (such as land, buildings, and equipment) are tangible economic resources that provide service for more than one year. Other than land, these assets are subject to physical deterioration, and hence they are written off as an expense over a period of time. The expense is called depreciation. Several methods for depreciating an asset are available. I chose straight-line depreciation, which is calculated by taking the original cost of the fixed asset, subtracting the asset's estimated salvage value (that is, estimated value at the end of its useful life) and dividing this amount by the number of years that the asset will provide service (that is, useful life).

$$\text{Yearly depreciation charge} = \frac{\text{Original cost} - \text{Estimated salvage value}}{\text{Number of years that asset will provide service}}$$
$$\text{(Useful life)}$$

My first question concerned the reliability of my depreciation expense numbers. Since I estimated the salvage value and the number of years that the assets would provide service, my numbers for depreciation expense were estimates. I wondered if there were a way to obtain an exact figure. Bill said no, and he explained that accountants have to rely on estimates in a number of situations. There is just no way around it. Thus the readers of financial statements must realize that the numbers presented on these statements are not as precise as they look.

Bill added that one would expect that accountants would attempt to obtain estimates that are as reasonable as possible. Whether or not this is the case is debatable. Accountants exercise a great deal of care in arriving at estimates, but they tend to rely on conservative estimates. For example, if it is estimated that a fixed asset will provide service for 10 to 12 years, many accountants would choose 10 years in calculating depreciation. Many people applaud accountants for relying on conservative estimates, while others argue that a conservative estimate is not necessarily the best estimate.

I then asked about accumulated depreciation and book value. The guide I relied on defined accumulated depreciation as the cumulative sum of depreciation charges from the date of the purchase of the fixed asset to the balance sheet date. It also defined book value of a fixed asset as original cost less accumulated depreciation. The guide suggested that both the original cost of the fixed asset and the accumulated depreciation on the fixed asset be shown on the balance sheet. It emphasized, however, that only the difference—that is, the book value—is added to the other assets to calculate total assets. For example, I should show my airplanes on my balance sheet at the end of the first month as follows:

Airplane	$300,000	
Less accum. deprec.	2,500	297,500

The book value at the end of the first month is $297,500, and it is this amount that is added to other assets in calculating total assets. The guide went on to explain that a firm with many fixed assets would not list each of them on the balance sheet. Rather, all the fixed asset accounts and all the accumulated depreciation accounts would be combined, and only one amount for each would be shown. Some firms report only the net amount—that is, the difference between the total of the fixed asset accounts and the total of the accumulated depreciation accounts. My question was how to calculate accumulated depreciation at other points in time. Bill said it was simple. Every time I record depreciation expense, I should add this amount to accumulated depreciation. To illustrate this point, he made the calculations for the first three months for the two airplanes.

Month	Depreciation Expense	Accumulated Depreciation End of Month	Book Value End of Month
0	0	0	$300,000
1	$2,500	$2,500	$297,500
2	$2,500	$5,000	$295,000
3	$2,500	$7,500	$292,500

I thanked Bill for his help and told him that I should now be able to prepare my financial statements. He suggested that I prepare a separate income statement for September and October and balance sheets as of the end of each of these months. This would be preferable to just one income statement and one balance sheet, because it would enable Ms. Lestille to make comparisons.

After the meeting we went for a cup of coffee. I told him about an article I had read in the financial section of the newspaper. The article was about a company that purchased a piece of equipment for $500,000 five years ago. It noted that the current depreciation reserve was $300,000, producing a book value of $200,000. The author claimed that the asset could not be sold for $200,000. The author also noted that the reserve at the end of the asset's life would be $500,000, and that this amount would not be sufficient to replace the equipment.

Bill groaned and noted that many people misinterpret depreciation, even those who should know better. Book value is defined as original cost less accumulated depreciation, and it is the fixed asset's book value that is added to other assets to calculate total assets. That is what book value is and that is all it is. Unfortunately, people confuse it with market value. The book value of a fixed asset does not indicate what the fixed asset is worth, what it could be sold for, or what it would cost to replace it. (Bill added as a footnote that book value is important for determining gains and losses on the sale of fixed assets. When a fixed asset is sold, it is the difference between the selling price and the book value that determines gain or loss on the sale.)

With respect to depreciation reserve, Bill explained that at one time accumulated depreciation was called reserve for depreciation. This older term should no longer be used, though, because it confuses people. Depreciation is simply and only a procedure for allocating a portion of the cost of a fixed asset to the periods during which the fixed asset is expected to provide service. As noted previously, when depreciation is charged, accumulated depreciation is increased. This does not mean that the firm has set aside funds to replace the fixed asset. Perhaps a fund should be established, but this has nothing to do with the procedure for charging depreciation. (If a firm sets aside funds to replace a fixed asset, the amount set aside will be listed as an asset on the firm's balance sheet. However, it has nothing to do with depreciation expense, accumulated depreciation, or book value. Also, note that if a firm decides to set aside a certain amount of funds each year to replace a fixed asset, depreciation expense charged on this fixed asset each year does not indicate how much should be set aside each year.)

Capitol Corporation

Cynthia Lathem, manager of the credit department of the Capitol Corporation, was anxious to see the results of an experiment she and five analysts were conducting on the usefulness of ratio and flow of funds analyses. The purposes of the experiment were to test the usefulness of these analyses in (1) judging the ability of a firm to pay its liabilities, and (2) helping one to distinguish between strong and marginal credits.

The Capitol Corporation sold a variety of food products to supermarkets. Most of its customers owned at least two supermarkets and many purchased more than $50,000 of merchandise per month from Capitol. One of the responsibilities of the credit department was to monitor the creditworthiness of these large credits on a regular basis. The analyst usually computed ratios and prepared a sources and uses of funds statement. The latter statement, also known as a funds statement or a statement of changes in financial position, was prepared even though customers supplied them along with income statements and balance sheets, because Ms. Lathem preferred a statement which included in its body the change in each balance sheet item.[1] The analysis often included information gained from other sources (for example, an article on the customer that appeared in a business publication such as the *Wall Street Journal*). After performing the analysis, the analyst prepared a report for Ms. Lathem. The report typically included ratios, a flow of funds statement, a narrative indicating strengths and weaknesses, and the analyst's recommendation.

Ms. Lathem frequently talked shop with her analysts over a drink after work on Fridays. One Friday, when two junior analysts and three senior analysts were present, she asked what they thought about the techniques employed. She was surprised at the differing viewpoints. Some felt that ratios and flow of funds statements were excellent tools. Others expressed the view that these techniques were not very helpful for making credit decisions. After further discussion they decided to conduct an experiment.

---

1. Casewriter's note: Many published statements show a change in (net) working capital in the body of the statement. If this format is employed, changes in each current asset and current liability are reported in a separate tabulation accompanying the statement.

Ms. Lathem would provide them with financial statements for two firms. Each analyst would compute ratios and a sources and uses of funds statement and address the following two issues:

1. For each firm, they would answer the question: Can the firm pay its current liabilities when due?
2. They would compare the two firms and make a judgment regarding which was financially stronger.

Although analysts normally reviewed quarterly data for two years and annual data for the previous five years, they decided to rely on annual data for only two years.

Ms. Lathem picked two supermarket chains that had done business with Capitol in the past. Data on the first firm, called Company X, are shown in Exhibits 1 and 2, and Exhibits 3 and 4 present the information on Company Y. The amounts on the statements were not changed other than for some minor rounding. Also, Ms. Lathem took the liberty of altering the format somewhat.

The exhibits do not show the actual dates. This was done to help Ms. Lathem disguise the identity of the two firms. The two years were consecutive, with year 2 being the later year and year 1 being the year before it. For example, suppose statements were from 1983 and 1982. Year 2 would be 1983 and year 1 would be 1982. (These were not the actual years selected.) Finally, the same two years were selected for each firm.

EXHIBIT 1
Company X
Income Statements
(000 omitted)

	For Year 2	For Year 1
Net sales	$319,845	$327,231
Cost of goods sold	239,721	245,076
Gross profit	$ 80,124	$ 82,155
Selling, general, and administrative	73,689	75,959
Depreciation	4,605	3,650
Operating profit	$ 1,830	$ 2,546
Other income	2,416	618
Total income	$ 4,246	$ 3,164
Interest expense	3,513	2,252
Earnings before taxes	$ 733	$ 912
Income taxes	268	262
Income from continuing operations	$ 465	$ 650
Discontinued operations		
Operating loss	91	349
Disposal loss	314	—
Net income	$ 60	$ 301

EXHIBIT 2
Company X
Balance Sheets
(000 omitted)

	End of Year 2	End of Year 1
Cash	$ 1,941	$ 2,229
Receivables net	3,682	3,018
Tax claims	963	270
Inventories	32,858	28,528
Prepaid expenses and other current	1,813	1,058
Total current	$41,257	$35,103
Net property, plant and equipment	47,766	44,951
Other assets	690	900
Good will	2,087	2,087
Deferred charges	1,364	1,450
Total	$93,164	$84,491
Notes payable	$ 5,817	$ 4,548
Accounts payable	28,490	23,466
Accruals	4,769	3,734
Total current	$39,076	$31,748
Long-term debt	29,716	29,870
Deferred income taxes	2,182	1,353
Other long-term liabilities	715	315
Preferred stock	86	96
Common and paid-in capital	9,646	9,420
Retained earnings	11,864	11,810
Less: Treasury stock	121	121
Total	$93,164	$84,491

EXHIBIT 3
Company Y
Income Statement
(000 omitted)

	For Year 2	For Year 1
Net sales	$2,528,013	$2,109,738
Cost of goods sold	2,031,144	1,694,529
Gross profit	$ 496,869	$ 415,209
Selling, general and administrative*	416,205	350,722
Operating profit	$ 80,664	$ 64,487
Other income	18,161	14,766
Total income	$ 98,825	$ 79,253
Interest	530	633
Earnings before taxes	$ 98,295	$ 78,620
Federal income taxes	46,795	35,900
Cumulative accounting change	(3,877)	—
Net income	$ 47,623	$ 42,720

*Includes depreciation and amortization expenses of $30,467,492 in year 1 and $25,038,079 in year 2. (Note that the last three zeros are omitted from figures on the statement but not from the depreciation and amortization amounts listed in this footnote.)

EXHIBIT 4
Company Y
Balance Sheets
(000 omitted)

	End of Year 2	End of Year 1
Cash	$ 24,225	$ 18,276
Marketable securities	32,398	24,288
Receivables net	5,822	6,720
Inventories	187,295	144,275
Prepaid expenses	4,825	3,306
Construction advances	1,632	4,973
Total current	$256,197	$201,838
Net property, plant and equipment	116,303	105,676
Life insurance—cash value	1,364	1,265
Investments	2,978	2,019
Deferred charges	103	103
Total	$376,945	$310,901
Notes and accounts payable	$ 71,693	$ 52,561
Accrued expense	30,108	23,386
Federal income taxes	11,579	6,819
Total	$113,380	$ 82,766
Installment purchase obligation	3,810	2,990
Self-insurance reserve	2,150	2,012
Deferred income tax	4,650	—
Common stock and paid-in capital	19,337	19,322
Retained earnings	238,383	207,068
Less: Treasury stock	4,765	3,257
Total	$376,945	$310,901

PART II
FINANCIAL ANALYSIS AND FORECASTING

Valu-Hi Drug Stores (A)

In early October 1976, Joan Laski, president of the Valu-Hi Drug
Stores, was preparing for an upcoming meeting with the firm's banker.
Ms. Laski was not looking forward to the meeting since she would have
the unpleasant task of informing the bank's loan officer, Mr. Smith,
that Valu-Hi would not be able to meet the first installment on its
$200,000 loan. Indeed, she was going to have to ask Mr. Smith for addi-
tional credit. Once the bank knew about the impending default, it might
demand immediate payment of the loan in full, possibly even forcing
the retail chain to liquidate.

LOAN

On December 1, 1973, Valu-Hi borrowed $200,000 from the Cleveland
National Bank at a variable interest that was 1 percent above the prime
rate. (The prime rate is usually the lowest rate charged on business loans
to the bank's most creditworthy borrowers. Valu-Hi's interest rate was
tied to the prime rate and hence was variable. For example, on December 1, 1975, when the prime rate was 7¼ percent, Valu-Hi's loan rate
was 8¼ percent; and in January 1976, when the prime rate was 7 percent, the interest rate on Valu-Hi's loan was 8 percent.) Interest was
payable quarterly, commencing March 1, 1974, and the first of four
equal annual principal payments of $50,000 was scheduled to begin
December 1, 1976.

In early October it became obvious to Ms. Laski that insufficient
cash would be available to make the first principal payment on the loan.
Moreover, she believed that an additional loan would be needed to support the build-up in working capital that the anticipated increase in
sales volume would produce. Alternatively, Ms. Laski had also considered asking for fewer additional funds and a waiver of interest payments
for the next five quarters. She had decided against that alternative,
however, believing that the bank would probably look more favorably
on a request that included timely payment of interest.

BACKGROUND OF THE COMPANY

Valu-Hi was formed by Ms. Laski and two other people in 1951 in
Cleveland, Ohio. Currently, the firm had 12 stores, all located within

the city. This concentration enabled Valu-Hi to realize significant savings in many areas, especially in advertising and salary expenses. These savings allowed the firm to earn returns in excess of the industry average throughout the early 1970s and played a significant role in persuading the Cleveland National Bank to extend a sizable loan.

Unfortunately, Valu-Hi's profitability had been adversely affected by 1974-1975 economic recession; and although the region was still experiencing some recovery, the pace of improvement was considerably behind that of the rest of the country. As a consequence of the slack economic environment, Valu-Hi had been unable to pass on continuing cost increases. For example, since 1972 the cost of products sold had increased by 5 percent per year, while other expenses—such as labor, utilities, and supplies—had risen by more than 2 percent per year. In contrast, the firm had been able to increase prices by an average of only 2 percent per year. The cost-price squeeze began to impair Valu-Hi's operating performance seriously, and the firm experienced losses for the first time in 1974. The deterioration of the financial condition necessitated additional infusions of long-term capital, so the owners invested their remaining savings. (See Exhibits 1 and 2.)

During the summer of 1976, the pace of the region's economic recovery accelerated, and hopes were raised that 1977 would be a very good year. If so, Ms. Laski believed that the improving situation could be sustained only by an additional infusion of funds. Since the 1976 equity investment had exhausted the owners' financial resources, and because the owners were unwilling to dilute their ownership of the firm, additional funds would probably have to come from the bank.

Ms. Laski knew that it would not be easy to convince the bank to go along with her proposal. She knew that the bank would compare Valu-Hi's performance during the last several years with the performance of other drug companies. The comparison would probably be based on the business data compiled by various organizations. For example, Dun & Bradstreet and the Robert Morris Associates regularly publish data on a number of financial ratios for a large number of industries each year. (An example is shown in Exhibit 3.) Ms. Laski, however, thought that there was a real danger in this type of comparison. For instance, the Cleveland region had been affected by the recession more severely than had the country as a whole. Moreover, recovery had proceeded at a substantially slower pace than it had in the country overall. Thus industry averages representing all economic regions were bound to understate Valu-Hi's performance relative to its particular adversity.

Ms. Laski was also bothered because the industry average ratios were likely to include a tremendous variety of operations. Thus single-store operations would be combined with chain-store operations. In fact, some firms probably would have other retailing and even manufacturing operations. How could the relatively small-margin but high-turnover operations of Valu-Hi, for example, be compared with the high-margin but low-turnover operations of a firm with substantial manufacturing activity? Ms. Laski thought that a fairer comparison would be between Valu-Hi and other small drug stores in the Cleveland area. But such data did not exist.

The alternative of comparing Valu-Hi's recent performance against its previous experience seemed even less satisfactory to Ms. Laski: the essence of the problem was the deep and protracted economic downturn. True, the firm had encountered recessions in the past, but the 1974–1975 experience, coupled with rapid cost inflation, had been the worst since the Great Depression. Ms. Laski thought that there just was not a comparable experience against which valid comparisons could be made.

Her reservations notwithstanding, Ms. Laski knew that the bank would apply some ratio analysis. She remembered that the loan officer, Mr. Smith, had informed her at the time of the initial loan that, whether or not ratio comparisons were made in evaluating performance, ratios could in an absolute sense (that is, without need for comparisons) often reveal the fundamental soundness of the company and thus the security of the loan.

To help prepare for the Monday meeting, she asked her assistant to perform a ratio analysis as the bank probably would for the period 1973 through 1976. She suggested that the assistant be as hard-nosed as the bank would be but to pinpoint areas of strength that could be used to reassure the bank.

EXHIBIT 1
Valu-Hi Drug Stores
Income Statements
(000 omitted)

	Years Ended			9 Months Ended
	12/31/73	12/31/74	12/31/75	9/30/76
Net sales	$8,500	$8,650	$8,850	$6,743
Cost of goods sold	5,746	6,020	6,346	4,983
Gross margin	$2,754	$2,630	$2,504	$1,760
Advertising and promotion	500	530	575	450
Salaries, officers and management	750	757	765	580
Salaries, other	975	1,034	1,096	872
Other expenses*	340	354	368	287
Profit before taxes	189	(45)	(300)	(429)
Taxes	76	(18)	(120)	(172)
Profit after taxes	$ 113	$ (27)	$ (180)	$ (257)

* Includes depreciation expense of $20,000 in 1973, $22,000 in 1974, $23,000 in 1975, and $18,000 in 1976.

EXHIBIT 2
Valu-Hi Drug Stores
Balance Sheets
(000 omitted)

	12/31/73	12/31/74	12/31/75	9/30/76
Cash	$ 220	$ 200	$ 190	$ 170
Accounts receivable	335	340	350	355
Due from income taxes	0	0	0	96
Inventory	1,564	1,643	1,700	1,710
Other current	27	28	30	31
Total current	$2,146	$2,211	$2,270	$2,362
Net fixed assets	410	415	431	435
Other	127	119	110	121
Total assets	$2,683	$2,745	$2,811	$2,918
Due to stockholders	$ 187	$ 100	$ 40	$ 0
Due to trade	650	661	676	688
Other current	402	410	469	475
Total current	$1,239	$1,171	$1,185	$1,163
Long-term debt	229	229	179	179
Common stock	449	606	888	1,274
Retained earnings	766	739	559	302
Total	$2,683	$2,745	$2,811	$2,918

EXHIBIT 3
Robert Morris Industry Ratios

This exhibit presents selected financial ratios for the retail drug industry. Robert Morris Associates prepares and publishes this type of information annually for many industries. Although most of the information is self-explanatory, detailed descriptions are provided in the introduction to the publication, which is titled *Annual Statement Studies.*

Average ratios are provided for firms within the industry and for various size categories within each industry. The first set of ratios is a conversion of balance sheet amounts into percentage amounts. For example, cash was an average of 6.8 percent of total assets for the 94 reporting firms in the retail drug industry with assets of less than $250,000. The income data section presents 100-percent statements. That is, net sales is set equal to 100 percent, and each expense is calculated as a percentage of net sales.

The next section of ratios presents three different numbers in each size category for every ratio. These numbers, which are not averages, were calculated in the following fashion. First, Robert Morris Associates (RMA) computes all the ratios for each company in a particular size category that has submitted its financial statements for analysis. Second, for any given ratio, RMA arrays all that ratio's numerical values in what is considered a "strongest-to-weakest" order. For an illustration, check the three quick ratio values presented for companies with total assets under $250,000. Ninety-four drug retailers of this size submitted financial data. The quick ratio was computed for every company, and these 94 ratios were then placed in order from the strongest one ("the best quick ratio") to the weakest ("the poorest quick ratio"). The figure falling in the middle of this list of ratios, .5, is the median, meaning 47 quick ratios were higher (considered better) than .5 and 47 were lower. The figure halfway between the median and the best (in this case, highest) of the ratios is the upper quartile figure, in this case .9. The figure halfway between the median and the weakest ratio, .2, is the lower quartile figure.

By presenting the ratios in this fashion, RMA mollifies the undue influence of extreme ratio values. Note that all three figures for each ratio in every size category are ordered from the strongest to the weakest: upper quartile—median—lower quartile. For example, RMA considers a high current ratio to be stronger than a lower one, and a high debt to worth ratio to be weaker than another ratio with a lower value. A brief description of each ratio follows:

1. *Quick.* (Cash + Marketable securities + Net receivables)/Current liabilities
2. *Current.* Current assets/Current liabilities
3. *Fixed/Worth.* Net fixed assets/Tangible net worth
4. *Debt/Worth.* Total debt/Tangible net worth
5. *Unsubordinated debt/Capital funds.* (Current + Senior long-term debt)/ (Tangible net worth + Long-term subordinated debt)
   This ratio records debt leverage in relation to the capital base, also known as the borrowing base. Using subordinated debt capital provides an extra cushion for senior creditors, who can then view leverage from this ratio.
6. *Sales/Receivables.* Net annual sales/Trade accounts and Bills receivables
   Days' sales (in bold print). 360/Sales/Receivables
   Average time (in days) that sales are uncollected.
7. *Cost sales/Inventory.* Cost of sales/Inventory
   Days' sales (in bold print). 360/Cost of sales/Inventory
   Average length of time (in days) that inventory remains in the company before it is sold.
8. *Sales/Working capital.* Net annual sales/(Total current assets − Total current liabilities)
   This is a turnover ratio; a low ratio may indicate unprofitable use of working capital.
9. *Sales/Worth.* Net annual sales/Tangible net worth
10. *Profit before taxes/Worth.* Net profit before taxes/Tangible net worth
11. *Profit before taxes/Total assets.* Net profit before taxes/Total assets

EXHIBIT 3–A
Retailers of—Drugs*
86 Statements
Ended on or about June 30, 1975, and
92 Statements
Ended on or about December 31, 1975

Asset Size	Under $250M	$250M & Less than $1MM	$1MM & Less than $10MM	$10MM & Less than $50MM	All Sizes
Number of Statements	94	47	26	11	178
Assets	%	%	%	%	%
Cash	6.8	7.7	7.1	5.1	5.6
Marketable securities	.1	.0	.3	.9	.7
Receivables net	14.6	12.9	7.8	7.6	8.1
Inventory net	52.8	56.9	59.6	56.1	56.6
All other current	1.6	1.2	1.4	.3	.6
Total current	75.9	78.7	76.2	69.9	71.6
Fixed assets net	17.5	13.8	17.8	20.7	19.7
All other non-current	6.6	7.5	6.0.	9.4	8.6
Total	100.0	100.0	100.0	100.0	100.0
Liabilities					
Due to banks—Short-term	5.8	5.5	6.6	.8	2.2
Due to trade	24.7	23.4	24.4	22.6	23.0
Income taxes	1.2	.9	1.6	3.6	3.0
Current maturities LT debt	2.9	3.5	3.6	1.4	1.9
All other current	8.8	8.8	7.0	5.5	6.0
Total current debt	43.4	42.1	43.2	33.9	36.2
Non-current debt, unsub.	15.3	16.9	17.3	11.8	13.1
Total unsubordinated debt	58.7	59.0	60.5	45.7	49.3
Subordinated debt	.7	.1	1.0	.1	.2
Tangible net worth	40.6	40.9	38.5	54.2	50.4
Total	100.0	100.0	100.0	100.0	100.0
Income data					
Net sales	100.0*	100.0*	100.0	100.0	100.0*
Cost of sales	67.4	67.6	72.3	71.5	71.3
Gross profit	32.6	32.4	27.7	28.5	28.7
All other expense net	30.1	30.5	25.9	24.9	25.6
Profit before taxes	2.6	1.9	1.8	3.5	3.1
Ratios					
Quick	.9	.7	.6	1.1	.7
	.5	.6	.3	.4	.4
	.2	.2	.2	.2	.2
Current	2.8	2.7	2.4	2.8	2.6
	1.8	2.0	1.8	2.1	1.9
	1.4	1.5	1.3	2.0	1.4
Fixed/Worth	.2	.2	.3	.2	.2
	.4	.3	.4	.4	.4
	1.0	.6	1.0	.5	.8

*See the disclaimer following the table.

EXHIBIT 3–A (continued)

Asset Size	Under $250M	$250M & Less than $1MM	$1MM & Less than $10MM	$10MM & Less than $50MM	All Sizes
Number of Statements	94	47	26	11	178
Ratios (cont.)					
Debt/Worth	.8	.9	1.1	.5	.8
	1.4	1.6	2.1	.8	1.5
	4.5	2.3	3.2	1.3	3.2
Unsub. debt/Capital funds	.7	.8	1.0	.5	.8
	1.3	1.6	2.1	.8	1.5
	4.2	2.3	3.0	1.3	3.0
Sales/Receivables	6 56.6	5 66.8	1 394.0	3 133.6	4 91.9
	13 27.4	15 24.2	5 73.7	5 69.1	11 33.4
	26 14.0	25 14.5	8 43.7	8 43.3	21 17.1
Cost sales/Inventory	67 5.4	75 4.8	72 5.0	80 4.5	74 4.9
	88 4.1	95 3.8	80 4.5	95 3.8	90 4.0
	116 3.1	113 3.2	95 3.8	109 3.3	113 3.2
Sales/Working capital	14.8	13.9	13.9	10.2	13.5
	8.3	7.5	10.2	8.1	8.1
	4.5	5.9	6.8	6.6	5.4
Sales/Worth	15.3	13.7	15.8	7.8	13.3
	7.3	7.3	10.2	5.6	7.6
	4.2	5.5	8.2	4.3	4.9
% Profit bef. taxes/Worth	48.7	27.1	33.1	27.6	38.4
	18.5	15.9	15.4	21.8	17.7
	5.8	7.7	3.7	15.3	6.4
% Profit bef. taxes/Tot. assets	17.2	11.0	12.4	12.9	13.5
	8.3	6.3	6.1	11.5	7.4
	1.7	3.4	.9	10.3	2.1
Net sales ($)	**38772M**	**74579M**	**256549M**	**912971M**	**1282871M**
Total assets ($)	**11516M**	**22586M**	**72226M**	**312497M**	**418825M**

Copyright 1976 Robert Morris Associates. Current data are available from Robert Morris Associates, 1616 Philadelphia National Bank Building, Philadelpha, PA 19107.
M = $ thousand
MM = $ million

DISCLAIMER STATEMENT

RMA cannot emphasize too strongly that their composite figures for each industry may *not* be representative of that entire industry (except by coincidence), for the following reasons:

1. The only companies with a chance of being included in the study in the first place are those for whom their submitting banks have recent figures.
2. Even from this restricted group of potentially includable companies, those which are chosen, and the total number chosen, are not determined in any random or otherwise statistically reliable manner.
3. Many companies in their study have *varied* product lines; they are "mini-conglomerates," if you will. All they can do in these cases is categorize them by their *primary* product line, and be willing to tolerate any "impurity" thereby introduced.

   In a word, don't automatically consider their figures as representative norms, and don't attach any more or less significance to them than is indicated by the unique aspects of the data collection.

Valu-Hi Drug Stores (B)

While Ms. Laski was waiting for her assistant's report [See Valu-Hi Drug Stores (A)], she decided to review some notes on financial analysis that she had collected while attending a management seminar in 1975. In the context of her impending visit to the bank and the unpleasant prospect of having to advise the bank that Valu-Hi would default on its first loan installment payment and require an increase in its borrowing from the bank, Ms. Laski was encouraged to find something in her notes that might be useful in preparing for her bank visit. In applying the financial techniques discussed in her notes to her own particular situation, she was disconcerted to realize that her estimated need of an additional loan of $75,000 might be in serious error.

BACKGROUND

In 1975 Ms. Laski attended a three-day seminar at a leading business school in the Midwest. Several sessions had been spent covering techniques of financial management. Two sessions in particular, which focused on the estimation of financial requirements, seemed especially relevant now, and she reviewed the notes with intense interest. The introductory session had dealt with the relationship between sales and a firm's need for funds. Ms. Laski recalled that the instructor had shown how increasing sales levels typically create a need for funds. When sales increase, accounts receivable, inventory, and working cash also increase. The increased assets must be matched (that is, financed) by an increase in liabilities and/or owners' equity. Moreover, if the firm's existing capacity is insufficient to support the higher sales and operating level, sources are also needed to acquire additional fixed assets. The instructor had stressed that these considerations of increased working capital investment and fixed asset investment, however obvious they might appear, are very often overlooked, with disastrous consequences.

A second session had then gone into the formal systematic techniques of financial planning. Ms. Laski's notes contained a detailed description of two techniques—cash budgeting and pro forma statements. Both techniques can be used to determine the magnitude and timing of funds needs, but Ms. Laski was aware that the usefulness of such statements heavily depends on the ability to obtain reasonable estimates, the proper selection of the forecast period, and the detail with which the statements are prepared.

FINANCIAL FORECASTS

Ms. Laski preferred to work with pro forma statements. She first had to decide which time interval and which terminal date were best. Since sales were not seasonal, she decided that annual forecasts would suffice. She was not sure what the ideal terminal date should be, and thus she decided initially to prepare annual pro forma statements for 1976 and 1977. If the data indicated that a longer-term forecast was necessary, she would extend the forecast period.

Ms. Laski then turned her attention to developing estimates. To obtain reasonable estimates for the great variety of items to be forecast, she called a meeting of the firm's functional managers. She began by asking the marketing manager, Mr. Harold, for his estimates of sales and gross margin levels for 1976 and 1977. He said that a sales level of $9 million for the current year (ending December 31, 1976) was virtually certain within a range of plus or minus 1 percent. He thought that sales for 1977 would increase by 13 percent. Moreover, since the firm would finally be in a position to pass on some of the previous price increases, he expected that the average gross margin would be 30 percent for the final quarter of 1976 and 31 percent for 1977. After a brief discussion, the group concluded that these estimates were reasonable.

Ms. Laski then asked Mr. Grey, manager of purchasing and inventory, for his estimates regarding purchases, payables, and inventory levels. He began by noting that, unlike many competitors, Valu-Hi had managed to control inventory carefully during the recessionary period. He believed that the turnover (that is, cost of goods sold divided by ending inventory) target of 3.7 would be achieved for 1976 and 1977. He then noted that purchases for the remainder of the year would be evenly distributed throughout the quarter and that monthly purchases for 1977 would be level. Purchases were estimated to be level because it was expected that monthly sales would be level during 1977. Regarding payables, he reminded the managers that credit terms from suppliers were net 30 days. Because of tightened liquidity conditions, the firm was currently taking slightly more than 30 days to pay. He hoped that this situation would be rectified by the end of 1976.

At this point, Mr. Harold said that he realized that Mr. Grey used the inventory turnover target to monitor purchases, but that he had really never quite understood how it was done. Mr. Grey explained that once he estimated cost of goods sold expense, he could calculate what purchases should be to achieve the inventory target. For example, suppose that inventory were $2 at the beginning of year 1 and that cost of goods sold expense were estimated at $11.10 for the year. To be on target, inventory at the end of year 1 should be $3. (Cost of goods sold expense of $11.10 divided by ending inventory of $3 equals 3.7, which is the target.) For a retail firm like Valu-Hi, cost of goods sold expense is calculated as follows:

Beginning inventory + Purchases − Ending inventory = Cost of goods sold

Since three of the four variables in the equation are now available, the estimate of purchases, $12.10, can be obtained by solving the equation.

Operating expenses were the next major items to be estimated. Ms. Laski turned to Mr. Bradler, the general manager, to shed what light he could on all other expense categories. He began by reviewing how cutbacks in personnel were made during the recent economic slump and how salaries were raised by only minor increments during the past three years. He was confident that management salaries would be $770,000 and that other salaries would be $1.1 million for 1976. Because of low increments in the recent past, he believed that annual increases of 6 percent should be expected for the next several years. In addition, he was confident that he could hold the line on personnel and not add people during the next year. Mr. Bradler then noted that the advertising budget of $600,000 for 1976 would be realized and that it would increase by 5 percent during 1977.

"Other" expenses were the most difficult to estimate, but they would be about $380,000 for the current year, including a depreciation expense of $24,000. Mr. Bradler thought that an estimated 5-percent increase in "other" expenses for 1977 was reasonable.

The discussion then turned to the company treasurer, Ms. Matterese, who began by noting that one of the bright spots during the recession was the firm's ability to manage receivables and inventory levels. Because of the careful monitoring by the individual store managers, there had been no change in the collection period. Thus Ms. Matterese felt comfortable in relying on historical experience to estimate receivables. She then praised Mr. Grey for his ability to control inventories carefully. In fact, she noted that there had been an improvement and suggested that a turnover of 3.7 was too conservative. She believed that 3.8 or 3.9 was more reasonable. Mr. Grey thanked her for the compliment but disagreed with her recommendation to change the estimate for inventory. He noted how the store managers had objected to his strict inventory policies and recommended that inventory levels be increased. Ms. Laski understood Ms. Matterese's point but decided to rely on Mr. Grey's judgment.

The treasurer then noted that the approved capital budget would produce an expenditure of $5,000 on fixed assets during the final quarter of 1976 and $35,000 for 1977. Depreciation expense would be

$24,000 in 1976 and $28,000 in 1977. Ms. Matterese believed that a working cash balance of $175,000 would be sufficient through 1977. She then turned to long-term financing and noted that stockholders could not be counted on for additional funds. However, the owners had agreed to a prohibition on dividend payments for the next several years. The long-term debt included $150,000 of the bank loan and a $29,000 note due in December 1977. The remaining $50,000 due on the bank loan was included in "other" current liabilities. Ms. Matterese suggested that Ms. Laski assume no change in the remaining portion of "other" current liabilities, in "other" assets, and in "other" long-term assets.

With respect to taxes, Ms. Matterese said that the firm's effective income tax rate had been 40 percent and suggested that Ms. Laski use this rate in her forecasts. She reminded her that as of September 30, 1976, the firm had $96,000 of tax credits that would apply to future periods. She explained that when a firm incurs a loss, the tax laws permit the firm to use this loss to offset taxable income for the previous three years. If the loss is not completely used up, the firm can carry the remainder of the loss forward for up to five years. This was the case with Valu-Hi. The loss for the first nine months of 1976 created a tax shield of $172,000. For the three years prior to 1976, the firm paid taxes of $76,000. Thus this amount was refunded to the firm and the remaining $96,000 could be used to offset future taxes. For example, if profits before taxes were $50,000 for the last quarter of 1976, tax expense would be $20,000. Thus $20,000 of the credit would be used up, and the remaining $76,000 would be available to offset income taxes in subsequent years.

Ms. Laski thanked each of the managers for their estimates and returned to her office. She hoped that the estimates, however rough, would provide her with enough information to determine Valu-Hi's real funds needs through 1977.

Ankh Corporation

Jack Williams, controller of the Ankh Corporation, strode confidently down the hall towards the president's office. When president Tony Roberts wanted a "private word" you could count on a challenge.

"Hi, Jack," Roberts said, "how's the audit going?" "Suspiciously smooth," joked Jack. "Frankly, I expected a load of questions on the allocations to the FRX board assembly; but, so far, not a peep, thank God!"

"I'm not surprised. You've got that operation running itself," said Roberts reassuringly. "I admire that in a manager. . . . Which brings me to the point of this meeting. I had breakfast with Sam Newman from Citizens'. Sam told me that Morgan Company has run into severe financial problems and the Company may be available." "I'm familiar with the Company," interjected Jack. "Nielsen's president, isn't he?" Roberts nodded in agreement. "In fact," added Jack, "they use our 'FRIX' assembly in their 95-10 work stations. I thought the 95-10 was a big success story for them. What happened?"

"Too much success, I think; but I'd like to get your opinion once you've had a chance to go over the financials. Sam says they're falling over each other trying to get those 95-10's out the door. There's been a complete breakdown of financial controls; they've had something like three controllers in the last two years. Still, I think there is a good fit from a product line standpoint and, frankly, I'm impressed with their technical strength and the forward integration potential we could gain through their distribution."

"Anyway, Jack, could you look over these statements? That's all Sam is authorized to provide at this point," Roberts said, handing him a thin folder. "I promised to give Sam an idea as to whether we'd be interested in a closer look. Can you let me know in about an hour?" Jack took no time responding. "No sweat," he said confidently.

As Jack returned to his own office he noticed that his door was closed, his secretary standing outside waiting for him. "Jack," she said quickly, "the auditors are waiting to see you. They said it's urgent; something to do with the FRX project." Without losing stride, Jack marched into the office, beaming, "Hi guys! I'll give you 20 minutes."

Morgan Company
Income Statement
For the Year Ending 12/31/81
($000)

Sales	$12,400
Cost of goods sold	9,440
Gross profit	$ 2,960
Selling, general and administrative	2,040
Operating profit	$ 920
Interest expense	625
Profit before taxes	$ 295
Federal income taxes (40% rate)	118
Net income	$ 177

Morgan Company
Balance Sheet
At 12/31/81
($000)

Assets	
Cash and marketable securities	$ 260
Receivables	3,100
Inventory	2,380
Current	$5,740
Net fixed assets	2,260
Total assets	$8,000
Liabilities and equity	
Accounts payable	$ 900
Notes payable (@ 15%)	2,760
Other current	560
Current	$4,220
Long-term debt	1,760
Total liabilities	$5,980
Net worth	2,020
Total liabilities and equity	$8,000

Industry ratios

Current ratio	2.2 X	Net profit on sales (PM)	3.19 %
Total debt/assets (D.R.)	50.00 %	Return on total assets (ROA)	5.90 %
Sales/inventory (INV X)	7.00 X	Return on equity (ROE)	10.80 %
Avg. collect. pd. (ACP)	52 days	Gross margin (GM)	18.00 %
Fixed assets turn. (FAX)	3.25 X	Selling, gen'l. & adm. (SG&A)	12.30 %
Total assets turnover (TAX)	1.85 X	Price/earnings ratio	6.0 X

Hollowville National Bank

In June 1982, Ms. Andrea West, an analyst in the credit department of the Hollowville National Bank, was about to perform a credit analysis of the Bamm Corporation. Bamm had a $110,000 line of credit secured by accounts receivable. The policy of the bank was to analyze existing accounts at least once each year, and that was the purpose of this review.

Ms. West joined the commercial lending training program of the Hollowville National Bank after earning her MBA degree in January, 1982. Trainees spent 12 to 18 months in the credit department of the bank and after that joined a lending group as an officer. During this time, trainees performed credit analyses and also attended classes one afternoon each week.

CREDIT ANALYSIS

All credit analyses called for the preparation of a "spread sheet" which included the following three elements:

1. Information from the firm's financial statements
2. Standard ratios
3. Sources and uses of funds statements

The spread sheet standardized for all bank customers the presentation of financial statements; translating a variety of formats to one in-house form was its most important function. The spread sheet also accomplished three other goals. First, it encouraged the loan officer to gather what the bank considered the right kind of information from the client. For example, it was considered important to know the salaries of a firm's officers, whenever possible. This information was not always reported separately on an income statement issued by the firm, but the loan officer tried to obtain it from the customer. Second, ratios that the bank considered essential for a credit analysis would be computed. Of course, analysts were permitted and encouraged to calculate whatever other ratios they deemed to be appropriate in a given situation. Third, it required the preparation of annual sources and uses of funds statements on a cash basis, which means that the change in each account is shown in the body of the statement.

Exhibit 1 presents the spread sheet used by Hollowville. Instructions accompanying this document, which are not presented, indicated that ratios were to be computed for at least three years and a minimum of two annual sources and uses of funds statements were required. The instructions also noted that comparisons to industry average ratios were helpful wherever possible. Finally, they noted that the spread sheet was not intended to limit the scope of the financial analysis performed and encouraged the analyst to utilize other appropriate sources of information.

The spread sheet and any additional financial analyses, financial projections, for example, became the exhibits for the final report. The exhibits were to be preceded by a narrative of no more than two or three pages which summarized the financial analysis and other relevant information and presented the analyst's recommendation(s). Exhibit 2 contains the format and guidelines for the narrative.

BAMM CORPORATION'S CREDIT FILE

A file was maintained for each customer that included previous credit reviews and other pertinent information. Ms. West's first step was to review the file. The information she considered relevant for her analysis and report is summarized below.

The Bamm Corporation was founded in 1938 by Mr. Henry Bamm. His son, John, assumed the presidency in 1963 and in 1982 he was the president and sole owner of the company.

The firm was a distributor of small and medium-sized water boilers designed for commercial use. Although there were some residential users, most sales, which were made by the company's salespeople and independent dealers, were to commercial concerns such as restaurants. In 1982 the firm had exclusive distribution rights for two manufacturers in three states.

The Bamm Corporation could point with pride to its record of earning a profit in every year of its history. When John Bamm assumed the presidency in 1963, the firm was operating in a portion of one state. By the middle of 1981, the firm had complete control over three states. Although there was opportunity for growth to other states and for expanding its product line, Mr. Bamm decided that growth would cease to be an objective. He was satisfied with his current level of income and he was anxious to devote more time to several avocations.

Previous credit reviews stressed the firm's excellent reputation. Dealers were quite loyal because they always received excellent service and fair treatment. The two manufacturing firms were also quite enthusiastic. They had noted that the marketing abilities of Mr. Bamm and his key personnel were enviable and that the firm had never paid a bill late. Indeed, Mr. Bamm was more proud of and concerned about his credit record than about the firm's profit history.

The two suppliers produced a variety of products. They were leaders in most areas in which they competed and were financially strong. Even if one of them should develop problems, which was highly unlikely, the firm would easily be able to establish a relationship with other suppliers. Indeed, other manufacturers had frequently asked the firm to establish a relationship.

HISTORY WITH HOLLOWVILLE

The Bamm Corporation had been a customer of the bank since 1952 and borrowed for the first time in 1968 when a $10,000 line of credit was arranged. The line was increased on several occasions and reached $40,000 by 1977. Terms included a 90-day clean-up provision and a personal guarantee by Mr. John Bamm.

In 1977 Mr. Bamm and his controller visited the bank to request a $75,000 working capital line to finance seasonal needs. (Up to this point the firm had dealt with the manager of a branch but because of the size of this request a loan officer attended the meeting.) The loan officer visited Mr. Bamm and his controller the next week and proposed the following:

1. A line of credit for one year secured by accounts receivable. The limit of the line would be the lesser of $75,000 or 80 percent of accounts receivable. It was understood that the line might be renewed annually.

2. The interest rate would float and would be ¾ percent above Hollowville's prime lending rate.

3. The firm would provide a listing of accounts receivable each month by customer and a detailed aging schedule. Unaudited financial statements would be provided on a quarterly basis. Annual statements also would be supplied and for these a review[1] by an independent CPA was required for 1977 and audits in subsequent years.

4. Mr. Bamm would personally guarantee the loan.

5. There would be no compensating balance requirements, no commitment fees, and no clean-up provision. Moreover, the firm could borrow and repay the loan at any time. In other words, the firm did not have to borrow for a specified period of time. The only requirement was that the amount borrowed or repaid be in multiples of $5,000.

---

1. Casewriter's note: A review consists of an evaluation of the firm's accounting procedures based primarily on inquiries of a firm's personnel. The scope is much less than that of a full audit. The fee also is much less.

Mr. Bamm's controller reacted strongly to the personal guarantee. He said that because of the firm's history, there should be no personal guarantee. He concluded his comment on this point by stating that he would urge Mr. Bamm to reject the offer if this was a condition of the loan. Mr. Bamm then said that he agreed but, if necessary, he would "sign for the note." On hearing this remark, the controller repeated the above statement and was even more forceful. The loan officer said he would get back to them.

The controller then mentioned the interest rate but in a much calmer fashion. He said that he thought the prime rate was in order. The loan officer responded that the firm was receiving an excellent rate and that as much as 1 or 2 percent above prime had been charged to similar customers. After some discussion, the controller agreed that this rate was reasonable, at least for the first year. However, he thought that this issue should be reviewed the next year. The loan officer agreed.

Mr. Bamm said that he was opposed to a review or an audit. In his opinion, the firm did not need it, and so he viewed the fee as an additional interest charge. The loan officer said he would have to get back to him on this point.

The prior credit analysis had rated Bamm as a very satisfactory risk. People at the bank had only praise for Mr. Bamm. After the meeting, the loan officer inquired about the role of the controller. He learned that he was quite capable. Moreover, he learned that he had been with the firm a long time. Mr. Bamm had total confidence in him and he "called the shots" on financial decisions.

The loan officer called the controller the next week to say that a personal guarantee would not be necessary. Also, if the loan amount did not exceed $50,000 during 1977, a CPA review would not be necessary. He added that a review would be required for 1978 and a full audit would be necessary for years beyond 1978.

In reviewing the history subsequent to 1977, Ms. West found that the line was increased to $110,000 in 1980. Also, there were numerous memoranda in the file that included considerable praise for Mr. Bamm and the controller. The reason for so many memoranda was that the controller visited the bank at least twice each year to discuss progress. He was definitely willing to discuss weaknesses and problems in an open manner. Moreover, issues like modifications in strategy and proposed capital expenditures were always discussed with the loan officer before a decision was made, and it was apparent that the bank's advice was heeded.

Each year the controller mentioned the interest rate but never complained too much. Although the rate had never been changed and the loan officer felt that the matter was not that serious, the controller did indicate that competing banks might be willing to offer a lower rate "to obtain the business." (Mr. Bamm and several of his key personnel had transferred much of their personal business to Hollowville in the last several years.) As she read about this issue, Ms. West was happy that she did not have to make a recommendation on this point. That is, a credit analyst did not make a pricing suggestion.

Each year the controller requested that the requirement for a CPA review (followed in the subsequent year by a full audit) be waived. The request was granted each year until 1981 and there was a review that year. (The review fee in 1981 was $1,800 and the anticipated fee for an audit was $5,000.) In early June 1982, the controller called to request a permanent alteration in this requirement so that only a review would be needed. The request was granted. (The controller called at 1:00 P.M. on that day and the loan officer called back 20 minutes later to grant the request.)

There was one additional point that Ms. West noted. Previous analyses did not include industry comparisons. It was reported that most firms that distributed these kinds of boilers also sold many other products. Thus, comparisons to these firms were not considered useful.

Ms. West reviewed the receivables securing the loan. Although some distributors took 60 to 90 days to pay or even longer, bad debts were not a problem. The controller had reported that some of these firms were small and relied heavily on trade credit. The firm's terms were net 30 days but it was understood that these customers would not pay within 30 days. However, these firms always eventually paid. Moreover, they paid for the credit facility provided by Bamm. The price schedule for purchases of different volumes was such that the gross margin for these accounts was higher. These dealers realized this and considered it fair.

As noted above, this was the annual credit analysis for the Bamm Corporation (that is, the firm was requesting a renewal but not a change in the size of the line). Exhibits 3 and 4 contain income statements and balance sheets for 1979 and 1980, respectively. Exhibit 5 presents three pages from the 1981 CPA review—the income statement, the balance sheet, and the auditors' statement.

EXHIBIT 1
Hollowville National Bank
Spread Sheet
Fiscal Year (Note 1)[1]

Assets
  Cash and marketable securities
  Trade accounts receivable
  Inventory

  _____ (Note 2)

  _____

  _____

Total current assets
  Land and buildings
  Net land and buildings
  Leasehold improvements
  Net leasehold improvements
  Machinery and equipment
  Net machinery and equipment
Net fixed assets
  Prepaid expenses

  _____

  _____

  _____

Total assets

Liabilities and Net Worth
  Notes payable
  Accounts payable—trade
  Accrued liabilities
  Accrued income taxes

  _____

  _____

  _____

  Current maturities of long-term debt

_____

1. All notes are shown in Exhibit 1-A, which follows this exhibit.

EXHIBIT 1 (continued)

Total current liabilities
   Long-term senior debt: secured
   Long-term senior debt: unsecured
   Deferred income taxes

   _____

   _____

   _____

Total liabilities
   Common stock
   Retained earnings
      Less: Treasury stock
Total net worth
Total liabilities and net worth

Working capital (Note 3)
Current ratio
Quick ratio (Note 4)
Sales/receivables (Note 5)
Cost of goods sold/inventory (Note 6)
Total debt/net worth

   _____

   _____

   _____

Net sales (Note 7)
   Cost of goods sold
Gross profit
   Selling and delivery
   General and administrative
   Research and development
Operating profit
   Other expense (income)—net
   Interest expense
   Profit-sharing
Pretax profit
   Income taxes
Net profit
   Change in sales (%)

EXHIBIT 1 (continued)

Officers' salaries
Lease payments
Cash earnings (Note 8)
Cash earnings/current maturities of long-term debt
Interest coverage (Note 9)
Sales/fixed assets (Note 10)
Purchases/accounts payable (Note 11)

_____

_____

_____

Sources:

_____

_____

_____

_____

_____

Total sources

Uses:

_____

_____

_____

_____

_____

Total uses

Increase (decrease) in cash

EXHIBIT 1-A
Notes Accompanying Exhibit 1

Note 1—Data were gathered and ratios were computed for at least three fiscal years. At a minimum, two annual sources and uses of funds statements were prepared. For ratios there is a column for industry averages for the most recent fiscal year.

Note 2—Lines represent spaces for other accounts. The reader will also see lines after groups of ratios. These spaces are for additional ratios the analyst might want to compute.

Note 3—Refers to net working capital which is equal to current assets minus current liabilities.

Note 4—Cash plus marketable securities plus trade receivables divided by current liabilities.

Note 5—Net sales for the year divided by the trade receivables balance at the end of the year. (Can also convert to day's sales outstanding by dividing result into 360 days.)

Note 6—Cost of goods sold expense for the year divided by the inventory balance at the end of the year. (Can also convert to day's inventory by dividing result into 360 days.)

Note 7—Next to each column for the income statement accounts is a column for percents. Net sales is set equal to 100 percent and every other item is listed as a percentage of net sales.

Note 8—Cash earnings equals net income plus depreciation and amortization expenses.

Note 9—Operating profit divided by interest expense.

Note 10—Net sales for the year divided by the net fixed asset balance at the end of the year.

Note 11—Purchases for the year divided by the accounts payable trade balance at the end of the year. (Can also convert to day's purchases outstanding by dividing the result into 360 days.)

EXHIBIT 2
Hollowville National Bank
Guidelines for Narrative Section of Credit Report

The narrative portion should be no longer than two to three pages and should include the following five sections:

1. Introduction and Risk Assessment
2. Purpose of Loan
3. Operations and Financial Position
4. Security for Loan
5. Comments and Recommendations

A brief description of the five sections follows.

   1. *Introduction and Risk Assessment.* In one or two paragraphs the analyst should highlight the firm's operations and financial condition and then conclude with an evaluation of risk. Risk assessment should range from very unsatisfactory to very satisfactory or nominal credit risk. Included should be a brief statement describing the firm's history, its basic operations, its marketing strategy, and the loan officer's opinion of the quality of management.

   2. *Purpose of Loan.* Here the amount and terms of the loan are described along with a discussion of how and when the firm will use the proceeds. Collateral is mentioned but not discussed in detail here. Finally, if another party is guaranteeing the loan, this fact should be noted. The financial strength of the guarantor(s) should be appraised in section 4.

   3. *Operations and Financial Position.* Here the analyst should expand on the financial data highlighted in section 1. The analyst may discuss what he or she considers appropriate, but the following should be included.

   a. An explicit discussion regarding how the firm's financial position has improved, deteriorated, or remained unchanged.
   b. If a review or audit by an independent CPA is required, note any qualifications in the auditor's report. Also, if there has been a change in CPA, this point should be mentioned along with the analyst's or loan officer's opinion(s) regarding the implication of the change.
   c. For analyses that include financial projections, the analyst must state explicitly the assumptions used in preparing them.

   4. *Security for Loan.* In this section the collateral securing the loan, if any, should be described in detail including a statement regarding the quality and adequacy of the collateral.

   5. *Comments and Recommendations.* This part allows the analyst to discuss issues and/or information not addressed in previous sections. A relevant article about the firm appearing in a newspaper or magazine is an example of the type of information to include here. The final paragraph of this section presents the

analyst's recommendation. For new or renewal loan requests, a specific recommendation must be provided including whether the loan should be granted and what the provisions should be. These provisions might include an amount different from the one requested. Finally, if changes are in order for existing credits, these should be clearly indicated.

EXHIBIT 3
The Bamm Corporation
Income Statement
For the Year Ended December 31, 1979
(In thousands)

Sales revenue	$1,165.8
Less: Sales returns and allowances	.8
Net sales	$1,165.0
Cost of goods sold	773.7
Gross profit	$ 391.3
Other expenses:	
Officers' salaries	$ 77.5
Other salaries	99.6
Selling and delivery	10.5
Administrative	151.9
Profit before taxes and bonuses	$ 51.8
Less: Executive bonuses	13.6
Profit before federal taxes	$ 38.2
Less: Federal taxes	7.4
Net income	$ 30.8

EXHIBIT 3 (continued)
The Bamm Corporation
Balance Sheet
December 31, 1979
(In thousands)

Assets
Current assets:

Cash and marketable securities	$ 13.5
Accounts receivable—net	174.8
Inventory	267.0
Other current	10.1
Total current	$465.4

Fixed assets:

Equipment and furniture—net	$ 15.5
Total fixed	$ 15.5

Other assets:

Life insurance—cash value	$ 37.0
Deferred charges	5.0
Total other	$ 42.0
Total assets	$522.9

Liabilities and Stockholders' Equity
Current liabilities:

Accounts payable—trade	$ 71.3
Notes payable (Hollowville)	15.0
Accrued federal income taxes	.9
Other payables and accrued expenses	24.8
Total current	$112.0

Long-term liabilities:

Loans payable—life insurance	$ 37.0
Deferred income taxes	15.8
Total long-term	$ 52.8

Stockholders' equity:

Common stock (100 shares, no par)	$131.0
Retained earnings	227.1
Total stockholders' equity	$358.1
Total liabilities and stockholders' equity	$522.9

EXHIBIT 4
The Bamm Corporation
Income Statement
For the Year Ended December 31, 1980
(In thousands)

Sales revenues	$1,250.1
Less: Sales returns and allowances	37.2
Net sales	$1,212.9
Cost of goods sold	830.1
Gross profit	$ 382.8
Other expenses:	
Officers' salaries	$ 83.3
Other salaries	118.8
Selling and delivery	11.0
Administrative	116.7
Profit before taxes and bonuses	$ 53.0
Less: Executive bonuses	3.3
Profit before state and federal taxes	$ 49.7
Less: State income taxes	6.4
Profit before federal taxes	$ 43.3
Less: Federal taxes	9.3
Net income	$ 34.0

EXHIBIT 4 (continued)
The Bamm Corporation
Balance Sheet
December 31, 1980
(In thousands)

Assets

Current assets:

Cash and marketable securities	$ 19.8
Accounts receivable—net	167.5
Inventory	278.6
Other current	3.0
Total current	$468.9

Fixed assets:

Equipment and furniture—net	$ 17.1
Total fixed	$ 17.1

Other assets:

Life insurance—cash value	$ 41.0
Deferred charges	5.3
Total other	$ 46.3
Total assets	$532.3

Liabilities and Stockholders' Equity

Current liabilities:

Accounts payable—trade	$ 51.6
Notes payable (Hollowville)	15.0
Accrued federal income taxes	1.6
Other payables and accrued expenses	14.7
Total current	$ 82.9

Long-term liabilities:

Loans payable—life insurance	$ 41.0
Deferred income taxes	16.3
Total long-term	$ 57.3

Stockholders' equity:

Common stock (100 shares, no par)	$131.0
Retained earnings	261.1
Total stockholders' equity	$392.1
Total liabilities and stockholders' equity	$532.3

EXHIBIT 5
The Bamm Corporation
Income Statement
For the Year Ended December 31, 1981
(In thousands)

Sales revenues	$1,444.9
Less: Returns and allowances	46.3
Net sales	$1,398.6
Cost of goods sold	958.3
Gross profit	$ 440.3
Other expenses:	
Officers' salaries	$ 88.7
Other salaries	124.9
Selling and delivery	14.0
Administrative	139.1
Profit before taxes and bonuses	$ 73.6
Less: Executive bonuses	5.0
Profit before federal and state taxes	$ 68.6
Less: Federal and state income taxes	23.5
Net income	$ 45.1

EXHIBIT 5 (continued)
The Bamm Corporation
Balance Sheet
December 31, 1981
(In thousands)

Assets

Current assets:

Cash and marketable securities	$ 22.3
Accounts receivable—net	183.1
Inventory	317.3
Other current	3.6
Total current	$526.3

Fixed assets:

Equipment and furniture—net	$ 17.3
Total fixed	$ 17.3

Other assets:

Life insurance—cash value	$ 45.5
Total other	$ 45.5
Total assets	$589.1

Liabilities and Stockholders' Equity

Current liabilities:

Accounts payable—trade	$ 65.7
Notes payable (Hollowville)	5.0
Accrued federal income taxes	2.3
Other payables and accrued expenses	16.3
Total current	$ 89.3

Long-term liabilities:

Loans payable—life insurance	$ 45.5
Deferred income taxes	17.1
Total long-term	$ 62.6

Stockholders' equity:

Common stock (100 shares, no par)	$131.0
Retained earnings	306.2
Total stockholders' equity	$437.2
Total liabilities and stockholders' equity	$589.1

EXHIBIT 5 (continued)

BENOIT and COOKE
CERTIFIED PUBLIC ACCOUNTANTS

Board of Directors
Bamm Corporation

We have reviewed the accompanying balance
sheet of Bamm Corporation as of December 31, 1981,
and related statements of income, and of changes in
financial position for the year then ended, in accordance with standards established by the American
Institute of Certified Public Accountants. All information included in these statements is the representation of the management of the Bamm Corporation.

A review consists principally of inquiries of
company personnel and analytical procedures
applied to financial data. It is substantially less
in scope than an examination in accordance with
generally accepted auditing standards, the objective of which is the expression of an opinion
regarding the financial statements taken as a whole.
Accordingly, we do not express such an opinion.

Based on our review, we are not aware of any
material modifications that should be made to the
accompanying financial statements for them to be
in conformity with generally accepted accounting
principles.

Benoit and Cooke
(signature)

April 1, 1982

ChemCo, Inc.

As Sally, the bookkeeper, hurried out of his office, Bob Brown stared out the window in disbelief. Sally's update on the small company's cash balance was 50 percent higher than the figure she had given him the day before.

The rapidly rising cash balance was both comforting and troublesome to Bob. "I just wish I knew if the bottom is going to drop out again," he said to himself.

Fifteen months earlier, as Bob began his first day as ChemCo's general manager, the bookkeeper informed him that the company was out of cash. No cash for bills, no cash for payrolls, no cash for coffee, no cash, period.

But cash began to flow in the very next day and the trauma passed. As Bob's successful management took hold, the cash balance began to build. By the end of the fiscal year (June 30), the firm's balance sheet showed cash and savings accounts in excess of $130,000. By the end of September the balance was up to $250,000.

Despite the upward trend in cash, there was volatility. From one week to the next, the cash account swung by as much as $50,000. The more closely Bob tried to track the cash balance, the wider it seemed to swing.

So Bob and Sally worked out a rudimentary cash budget for the next three months. He had a copy of the budget, and he received a daily cash report. They prepared a new three-month budget each month, and the system was working well. But still—volatility.

AN UNEXPECTED PROFIT OPPORTUNITY

Bob was jotting down the assumptions for a new cash budget covering the October to December quarter when the telephone rang.

"Bob," said Ted Davis, ChemCo's largest supplier, "I'm going to have some extra feedstock in November. Would you be interested in taking it at a 25% discount?"

"How much feedstock are you talking about?"

"Your December order," said Davis. "If you'll take it the first week in November with immediate payment you can have the discount. I have a temporary storage problem, and I'm going to have to make room for three more carloads arriving at the end of November."

"I've got a copy of the order," Bob replied. "It's for $50,648. We'd accelerate delivery by 30 days and payment by 60 days, right?"

"Right."

"O.K., can I get back to you? We have the capacity, but I want to check our cash position."

"Sure. But I'll have to know definitely by the end of the day," Davis answered.

Bob turned back to his assumptions for the new cash budget.

1. Opening cash October 1: $250,000
2. Accounts receivable: equal to 50 days sales
3. Feedstock payment: 28% of current month sales
4. Salaries, total: $70,950 per month
5. Employee insurance: $730 per month
6. Payroll tax: 5.77% of salaries
7. Insurance: $17,000 due December
8. Rent and utilities: $5,951 per month
9. Telephone: $2,214
10. Legal, advertising and other: $10,643 per month
11. Debt service: $3,880 per month
12. Taxes: $95,446 due end of October
13. Miscellaneous capital items: $713 per month

Bob considered that all the cash outlays for the three-month period were fixed. In addition, he expected delivery of two new trucks on November 1, requiring a cash payment of $40,000.

Payments from customers would arrive in equal amounts on the 15th and 30th. Rent and utilities were paid on the first. Salaries were paid on the 15th and 30th of the month. All other cash outlays occurred on the 30th.

ChemCo kept a $50,000 operating cash balance. Excess funds earned 14% interest payable at the end of the quarter. The monthly sales are as follows:

August (actual)	$166,521
September (actual)	194,705
October (estimate)	231,571
November (estimate)	160,857
December (estimate)	180,884

Super Sounds

True Gallo, senior vice-president for a national supermarket chain, was explaining a new business possibility to his friend, Brenda Sweda, manager for an investment company. "The basic idea is that we will sell pre-recorded music cassette tapes through supermarkets, with the tapes displayed on a revolving rack near the check-out counter. We will buy the tapes from a major record company like Capitol or Columbia Records, with our selections of artists and titles for each tape. Then we'll contract with major supermarket chains for distribution."

"Sounds interesting," remarked Brenda. "What kind of volume do you think is possible?" "I've got the crucial assumptions laid out here," responded True, as he handed Brenda a sheet of paper (Exhibit 1). "I'm no financial genius," continued True, "but I do know something about marketing, and I think we could get distribution through about 6,500 stores fairly quickly. I think we could sell an average of 50 tapes per month per store. Our cost would be $1.50 per tape, plus 5% for freight. The price to the store would be $2.994, with a retail price of $4.99. We would use commission brokers to place the tapes with the chains and about 5% of the gross would go to the brokers."[1]

"What kind of trade terms do you think you'd have?" asked Brenda. "We'd have to buy on net 30 terms but I think we'd have to give about 45 days on receivables to the stores. Also, I've assumed an allowance for returns of 20%. The delivery time from the record manufacturer to the stores would be about 30 days and the store stock would be 72 tapes per store. We would expect to service the racks weekly, adding new titles, transferring or selling off slow moving tapes to jobbers and restocking popular titles."

"What kind of selection do you think you'd be able to get?" asked Brenda, "and how much flexibility would you have in packaging artists and titles on a tape?" "Good question," noted True, "tentative conversations I've had with the record companies I've approached suggest that the entire 'MOR' (middle-of-the-road) catalogue would be available; after all, as far as the record companies are concerned, it's all

---

1. Casewriter's note: Although Super Sounds would be responsible for maintaining the store's tape inventory, sales and brokers' commissions would be recorded only at the time of purchase by the store's customers.

'gravy.' That's good for us, too, because we'd rather not gamble with new stuff. The standards, you know, the 'Golden Oldies' are higher percentage picks. On the other hand, we could be a little creative since we could package titles in brand new ways. You know, like, "Barbra Streisand Sings Broadway."

"Interesting *idea*," Brenda commented. "Yeah, *idea*," True emphasized discouragingly, "that's my problem. I'm stymied because I can't get the numbers together in a way that bankers, and venture capitalists, like yourself, can relate to. That's where I hope you can help me." "Well," responded Brenda, "as you know, True, this is not the kind of deal we'd be interested in, simply because we're unfamiliar with the entertainment field and we don't usually get involved in pure start-ups . . ." "I realize that," interjected True, "but what about helping me scratch out some financials as a personal favor?" "Of course," Brenda answered quickly, "but, frankly, I can't give you more than a few hours here and there over the weekend." "From you that's plenty," True remarked appreciatively. "Anything you can do with the financials will at least get the ball rolling." "Well, why don't I just try to get a feel for the overall profitability and financial requirements. Later, if it makes sense, you can get someone to do a more detailed analysis. I'll draw up some quarterly pro forma income statements and balance sheets for the first year."

EXHIBIT 1
Super Sounds
Assumptions

- Sales volume of 50 units per month per store at 6,500 stores achieved at beginning of month 1. No growth in volume during 12-month period.
- Store inventory equal to 72 units
- Billing price of $2.994 per unit with 20% return allowance
- Terms of sale expected to average 45 days collection
- Delivery time from manufacturer to store is 30 days
- Purchase terms are net 30 days
- Cost per unit is $1.50 plus 5% for freight
- Brokers' commissions are 5% of gross billings
- Salaries are $10,000 per month
- General and Administrative expenses are $7,500 per month
- Racks and organizational expenses prior to the first month, paid in cash, expenses in first month of operation, $125,000
- Bank line-of-credit available for 50% of net receivables
- Corporate federal, state and local taxes of 50%. One-fourth of estimated annual tax liability paid in March, June, September and December
- Minimum cash balance desired equal to three months of salaries and G&A, total of $52,500

Breau Company (A)

In mid-June 1977, Roland Sterle was about to prepare a monthly cash budget for the Breau Company for the fiscal year ended May 31, 1978. Gathering the estimates had been quite a task, certainly very different from what he had expected. He hoped that the information contained in the budget would be useful to Mr. Breau, the firm's president.

BACKGROUND

In September 1976, Roland Sterle entered a two-year MBA program at a university in Portland, Oregon. Since he had just graduated from college the previous May, he was one of the youngest members of the class. To offset partially his relative lack of experience, he planned to obtain a good summer job between his first and second years. Locating opportunities proved frustrating and time consuming. Most available jobs would not provide the experience he desired, and competition was intense for those that would.

In early April 1977, Roland obtained an interview with Christian Breau, the president and major stockholder of the Breau Company. Located in Portland, the Breau Company was a wholesale distributor of hotel supplies and equipment. Mr. Breau, an alumnus of the university, hired a student each summer to work in the firm's accounting department to fill in for employees on vacation. Roland made quite an impression on Mr. Breau. A half-hour interview turned into a three-hour discussion. The result was that Roland was hired to work primarily but not solely in the accounting department. In addition, Mr. Breau would have him work on several finance-related projects.

Roland began work in late May and spent his first two weeks in the accounting department. On the Friday afternoon of the second week, Mr. Breau called him into his office. He told him that he wanted him to spend the next week working on the preparation of a monthly cash budget for fiscal 1978. Up to this point, the firm had never relied on cash budgeting. Management realized that it was an important tool, but there just never seemed to be enough time to implement the technique properly. It was not just a matter of preparing the budget. To be useful, a cash budget must be continuously monitored and updated. The president then told Roland that recent circumstances indicated that the company could no longer postpone the use of this management tool.

He concluded by scheduling a meeting for 8:00 A.M. on the subsequent Monday, at which time they would discuss the project at greater length.

THE LONG WEEKEND

Roland was really excited about the project. He spent Friday evening in the library and considerable time the rest of the weekend reading books he had obtained there. He learned that most large firms prepared both short- and long-range forecasts. A short-range forecast was typically prepared for 1 year or less, and long-term forecasts were those extending beyond 1 year. Although some firms prepared projections (that is, forecasts) for 10 years or even longer, 5 years into the future was generally the longest planning horizon for the majority of firms.

Roland was surprised to find that there was considerable variation in making short-term forecasts. He had thought that most firms simply prepared a monthly cash budget for the subsequent 12 months, but this was not the case at all. Daily, weekly, monthly, and quarterly time intervals were used, with some combination of these intervals being the most common. For example, one firm he studied prepared a daily cash budget for the subsequent 30 days, a monthly budget for the next 5 months, and quarterly forecasts for the remainder of the year.

MONDAY MORNING MEETING

Roland arrived at the office at 7:30 A.M. on Monday. Mr. Breau was also there, but he was meeting with the firm's sales manager, so Roland reviewed his notes. When the meeting began, Roland told the president about his weekend activity and suggested that they rethink whether a monthly forecast was best. The president was pleased with Roland's initiative but said that he wanted a monthly forecast for the next 12 months. At a later point he would consider longer-term forecasts and different time intervals for the one-year forecast. For now, however, it would be enough of a chore to update and monitor a monthly forecast for one year. Until the monthly budget was operating smoothly, he would not consider refinements and/or extensions.

The president then told Roland that the firm currently had a $325,000 line of credit with its commercial bank. In June 1976 a $275,000 line of credit was negotiated, but it was not enough and subsequently he had to request an increase. The line would be renegotiated in two weeks, and, while he thought that $400,000 would be sufficient, he was really not that confident in his estimate. Moreover, because of the compensating balance requirements, he did not want to request $400,000 if this amount was not needed. Although the firm paid interest only on the amount actually borrowed, there was a 10–20-percent compensating balance requirement. That is, the firm had to maintain demand deposit balances equal to at least 20 percent of the amount borrowed plus 10 percent of the unused portion of the line. For example, if $100,000 of a $400,000 line were being borrowed, the firm would have to maintain a deposit balance of at least $50,000 (20 percent times $100,000 plus 10 percent times $300,000).

Compensating balance requirements had never been a problem, since the firm typically maintained large cash balances in its checking account. This practice was going to change, however, for two reasons. First, the firm had never invested in marketable securities because of the lack of proper cash planning. If Mr. Breau thought that there was a temporary cash surplus, he would put some money into a savings account. While some interest income was earned by doing this, he believed that the amount earned would increase substantially if he were to institute a program of investing in marketable securities; and he hoped that effective cash budgeting would enable him to develop such a program.

The second reason was a change in the company's commercial bank's policy of charging for its services. Through the end of 1976, firms used deposit balances to compensate the bank for its services. As of January 1, 1977, the bank began to charge its commercial clients a fee for many of its services. Under the new pricing policy, the Breau Company would have to maintain compensating balances only for its line of credit, and would pay cash for all other bank services that it used. Thus the firm intended to reduce its demand deposit balance to the minimum necessary to support operations. (Naturally, if the amount required to meet the 10–20-percent compensating balance requirement on the line of credit were larger than the minimum cash balance required to support operations, then the larger cash balance would be maintained. For example, if $1 were needed to support operations and a $2 balance were needed to satisfy the compensating balance requirement, then the firm would have to maintain a cash balance of $2.)

Mr. Breau then noted that it would not be easy to estimate the minimum cash level needed to support operations. Given an adequate line of credit and access to other external sources that the firm indeed had, he believed that the cash balance at the end of each month should equal $5,000 plus half of the payroll for the subsequent month. (As will be explained later, annual salaries were estimated at $759,490, giving a monthly payroll of $63,291.)

Mr. Breau then noted that they would not be starting completely at ground zero. The firm did have a projection of sales by month for the next 12 months and an operating expense budget for the year. He told Roland to obtain a copy of each of these and a copy of the firm's recent financial statement from Mr. Goldfine, the firm's vice-president. He concluded by suggesting that they meet again Friday morning, but he

encouraged Roland to see him anytime during the week if he had any
questions.

GATHERING ESTIMATES

Mr. Goldfine was the number-two person in the company. One of his
numerous duties was to supervise the accounting department. When
Roland approached him after his meeting with Mr. Breau, he told
Roland that he was also very interested in the project and that he would
be available to help answer the many questions that would arise. He
then gave Roland copies of the firm's fiscal 1977 financial statements
(Exhibit 1), the fiscal 1978 monthly projections of sales (Exhibit 2),
and the fiscal 1978 operating expense budget (Exhibit 3).

Roland spent the rest of that day and the next three days studying
data and talking to various employees. These people were all very cooperative and took the time to give him the help he needed; they all knew
that Mr. Breau and Mr. Goldfine strongly endorsed the project.

Roland's starting point was sales. He learned that the $9.15 million
target for fiscal 1978 (Exhibit 2) was a reasonable estimate. Management set a target for sales each year, based on discussions with salespeople. Actual sales were generally close to the goal. The monthly
breakdown was another matter. The projections shown in Exhibit 2
were based on previous experience. It was not that these estimates were
unreasonable. Rather, operational problems in the warehouse frequently
resulted in sales for one month being pushed to the subsequent month.
For example, sales were $483,309 in April 1977 and $640,897 in May
1977. Had there not been a bottleneck in the warehouse, April's sales
would have been $513,309 and May's would have been $610,897. A
$30,000 order scheduled to be shipped during April was delayed until
May because of a problem in the warehouse.

Regarding collections, all sales were on terms of 2/10 net 30 days,
which were the terms offered by the firm's competitors. Although some
customers took advantage of the discount, the majority paid on approximately the thirtieth day, and a significant number paid in 60 or 90
days. Because of competitive pressures, the firm could not enforce the
30-day limit. When Roland asked what portion of the customers each
month paid in 10, 30, 60, and 90 days, he was told that this information was not readily available and that it would be a time-consuming
task to gather it. He decided to look at past data on month-end accounts
receivable balances and compare them with monthly sales. His analysis
revealed that the accounts receivable balance at the end of each month
was usually approximately equal to sales for that month plus one-third

of the previous month's sales. Thus he decided to rely on a day's sales outstanding ratio of 40 days to project collections.[1]

Roland's next step was to examine purchases. He was surprised to learn that monthly purchases were kept at a stable level. He was told that this was done to insure timely deliveries. Commencing in June 1977, monthly purchases were increased from $540,000 per month to $575,000 per month. It was expected that this level would be maintained through the end of May 1978. Finally, he learned that all the goods purchased in one month were paid for in the subsequent month.

Roland then turned his attention to operating expenses. He was told that the figures contained in the expense budget (Exhibit 3) were reasonable estimates, since management worked very hard at keeping operating expenses within budget. The firm had been relying on a formal operating expense budget for the past four years. Although individual expense items had varied considerably from the budgeted amount, operating expenses in total had never varied more than 5 percent from the total amount budgeted. As shown in Exhibit 3, each operating expense item was budgeted on an annual basis, and thus Roland had to find a way to arrive at monthly estimates. He was advised to analyze previous years' worksheets, which listed actual expenses by month for each item. Since most items were paid for in the month of incurrence, these worksheets were a useful starting point. After reviewing the worksheet and talking to the people responsible for the various expense items, Roland arrived at the following monthly estimates:

1. *Advertising.* An advertisement was purchased in a trade journal for September, October, and November of each year. The entire amount was paid in September.

2. *Repairs and gasoline.* This amount represented gasoline and services for the firm's vehicles. Approximately 20 percent of the $117,500 total was expended in September, when needed new tires were normally purchased. The remainder was spread evenly over the remaining 11 months.

3. *Bad debts.* Roland was told that it was reasonable to assume that collections would be reduced by $800 each month because of bad debts.[2]

---

1. The reader may assume 30-day months and assume that sales are spread out evenly during each month. These assumptions will reduce the figure work involved in preparing the cash budget.
2. The reader will note that there is no allowance for "doubtful accounts" on the balance sheet. The reason is that the firm used the direct charge method in accounting for bad debts. That is, when the firm determined that a customer would not pay, the expense was recorded.

4. *Health and accident.* This amount represents insurance premiums, which would be paid in 12 equal monthly installments. Management was looking into alternative health programs because of skyrocketing costs. Mr. Breau hoped that he could find a plan that would save $10,000 to $15,000 for fiscal 1978. However, he instructed Roland not to count on any savings and to use the $110,000 figure in the cash budget.

5. *Maintenance.* This figure represented a contract that called for 12 equal payments of $600 per month.

6. *Auto leases.* Mr. Breau was experimenting with leasing, and the $2,600 amount represented one contract. The firm would pay $400 in June and $200 in each subsequent month.

7. *Outside commissions.* The $32,000 would be paid in 12 equal monthly installments.

8. *Consulting and legal.* This amount represented retainers and payments and would be spread evenly throughout the year.

9. *Donations.* The firm would expend $10,000 during August and the remainder during November.

10. *Freight.* Freight expense represented shipping charges for purchases and would be paid in equal amounts each month. (The firm treated freight as an operating expense rather than adding it to the cost of purchases in calculating cost of goods sold expense.)

11. *Interest.* This amount was relatively minor, for two reasons: (1) the term debt would be eliminated in September, and (2) the firm followed the practice of netting interest income against interest expense. (The budgeted amount included interest expense on the line of credit and assumed that there would be a substantial increase in interest income.) It was difficult to pinpoint when the inflows and outflows would occur. Roland was told to be conservative and assume five monthly outflows of $1,000 each, commencing in June.

12. *Memberships.* This amount represented membership fees for various trade and professional organizations. One-half of the total would be paid in August and the remainder in September.

13. *Miscellaneous labor.* This amount represented the person added for the summer plus temporary help hired during May to help take the inventory. The firm would spend $1,000 per month during June, July, and August of 1977 and $2,000 during May 1978.

14. *Office supplies.* This item represented forms, stationery, envelopes, postage, and so on. It was estimated that $10,000 would be disbursed in November and December and that the remaining $62,000 would be expended at the rate of $6,200 per month.

15. *Heat, light, and power.* November, December, January, and February would each require $5,000, and the remaining $16,000 would be paid in equal monthly installments over the other eight months.

16. *Salaries.* Salaries, which were paid twice each month, would be spread evenly throughout the year.

17. *Payroll taxes.* These tax expenses were incurred in 12 equal monthly amounts. However, they were paid in the month subsequent to incurrence.

18. *Taxes, other.* In June, September, December, and April, $36,000 of the total would be paid in four equal installments. The remaining $14,000 would be expended in September.

19. *Sales discounts.* These represented cash discounts taken by customers who paid within 10 days. It was estimated that monthly collections would be reduced by the following amounts because of discounts:

	Reduced Collections
June 1977	$ 5,800
July	5,800
August	7,700
September	6,700
October	7,700
November	8,100
December	10,300
January 1978	11,000
February	8,800
March	5,300
April	5,000
May	5,800
	$88,000

(The firm treated a sales discount as an operating expense rather than as a deduction from gross sales.)

20. *Telephone.* This was a cash expense that normally varied very little from month to month. Thus it was decided to assume 12 equal amounts.

21. *Selling.* This item consisted primarily of expense accounts for salespeople. The firm would expend $7,000 in December and $3,000 in all other months.

22. *Depreciation.* This expense would be incurred in 12 equal monthly amounts.

23. *Insurance.* This expense represented all insurance policies except for the health and accident plan. It was estimated that $40,000 would be spent in September, $20,000 in December, and $8,000 in March.

24. *Rent.* Rent was $6,750 per month.

25. *Contingency.* This amount was budgeted to protect against overages for other operating expenses. If the total of all other operating expenses excluding the contingency were on or below target, then Mr. Breau would probably expend this amount on additional bonuses. Roland was told to assume two equal expenditures of $10,000 for April and May.

26. *Federal income taxes.* Estimated payments of $55,000 each would be made in April, June, September, and December.

At the Friday morning meeting, Roland briefly reviewed what he had done, and he said that he just needed a little more information regarding fixed assets, accrued expenses, long-term debt, and dividends. The president told him that he planned to expend $50,000 on fixed assets in September. Although no other expenditures were planned, unexpected fixed asset purchases were frequently required; thus he told Roland to assume another $5,000 expenditure for January. Of the accrued expenses at May 31, 1977, $4,900 represented payroll taxes incurred during May, which would be paid during June. The remaining $5,100 represented special legal services rendered during May, which would be paid in June.

The final principal payment of $20,000 on the term debt would be made during September. Finally, Mr. Breau expected to declare and pay dividends of $120,000 during December.

Roland told the president that he had all the information he needed and that he should be able to complete the budget by 3:00 or 4:00 P.M. They scheduled a meeting for 4:00 to go over the budget. The president concluded by saying that he would be negotiating the line of credit during the next week and would appreciate Roland's recommendation regarding how much to request.

EXHIBIT 1
Breau Company
Income Statement
Year Ended 5/31/77
(000 omitted)

Net sales	$8,484,019
Cost of goods sold	6,360,016
Gross profit	$2,124,003
Selling, general, & administrative	1,725,700
Profit before taxes	$ 398,303
Federal income taxes	173,220
Net income	$ 225,083

EXHIBIT 1 (continued)
Breau Company
Balance Sheet, 5/31/77
(000 omitted)

Cash	$	86
Accounts receivable		802
Inventory		2,387
Fixed assets (net)		399
Total assets	$	3,674
Accounts payable	$	540
Accrued expenses		10
Long-term debt		20
Common stock		1,542
Retained earnings		1,562
Total liabilities & stockholders' equity	$	3,674

EXHIBIT 2
Breau Company
Monthly Sales Targets, Fiscal 1978
(000 omitted)

June 1977	$ 600
July	600
August	800
September	700
October	800
November	850
December	1,050
January 1978	1,150
February	950
March	550
April	500
May	600
	$9,150

EXHIBIT 3
Breau Company
Operating Expense Budget, Fiscal 1978

Sales	$9,150,000
Gross margin @ 25%	2,287,500
Operating expenses	
Advertising	2,750
Repairs & gasoline	117,500
Bad debts	9,600
Health & accident	110,000
Maintenance	7,200
Auto leases	2,600
Outside commissions	32,000
Consulting & legal	42,000
Donations	12,500
Freight	48,500
Interest	5,000
Memberships	4,000
Misc. labor	5,000
Office supplies	82,000
Heat, light, & power	36,000
Salaries	759,490
Payroll taxes	61,518
Taxes, other	50,000
Sales discounts	88,000
Telephone	66,000
Selling	40,000
Depreciation	40,000
Insurance	68,000
Rent	81,000
Contingency	20,000
Total operating	$1,790,658
Profit before taxes	496,842
Federal income taxes	220,000
Net income	$ 276,842

Breau Company (B)

At 3:30 P.M. Roland Sterle arrived at the president's office with the cash budget and his recommendation concerning the size of the line of credit that should be requested. Mr. Breau told him that he unfortunately could not discuss the matter with him at that time. He was expecting a call any minute from an important customer, which would tie him up for the remainder of the afternoon. He said that he would study the budget over the weekend and that they would discuss it first thing Monday morning.

On Monday morning the president began by telling Roland that he had done an excellent job. Since the meeting with the bank was not until the next week, he wanted to study it some more and have Mr. Goldfine study it before finalizing a strategy for the meeting. In the meantime, he had another task for Roland. He wanted him to prepare monthly pro forma income statements and balance sheets for fiscal 1978.

Mr. Breau continued by saying that, as expected, he found the cash budget useful for many purposes. For example, not only would it help him decide how much of a line to request and how to plan his marketable securities purchases, but it also indicated that he should try to reduce the compensating balance requirements. He had never fully appreciated how much of a burden these requirements could be. There was also, however, a benefit that he had not expected: the cash budget organized information well, and this benefit led him to want pro forma statements.

The president then said that, in his opinion, a major purpose of any budget was to motivate performance. As Roland knew, the firm had operating expense budgets, sales targets, targets regarding receivables levels, and so on. However, these targets were not treated as a unit; in fact, they were always discussed as separate agenda items at management meetings. He thought that pro forma statements would help in two ways: (1) they would organize data for managers, and (2), more importantly, they would clearly show how all targets related to the return-on-investment (ROI) target on which bonuses were based. Hence the managers would be better motivated to achieve those targets.

Mr. Breau concluded by telling Roland to ignore the compensating balance requirements in preparing the pro forma statements because he was confident that he could negotiate a substantial reduction in these requirements.

Roland said that he thought preparing pro forma statements was a good idea, especially since little additional effort would be required. He concluded by saying that he believed he would be able to complete the task by the end of that day.

Xenon, Inc.

In early April 1984, Mr. Timothy Fitzgerald, assistant to the president of Xenon, Inc., had just completed the task of gathering estimates and was ready to prepare projections for April to June, 1984. He knew the president, Mr. James Walsh, was anxious to receive his recommendation regarding how great a line of credit should be requested for the remainder of the second quarter.

BACKGROUND

Xenon, Inc. was formed in February 1974 by Mr. James Walsh. The firm sold office and maintenance supplies primarily to small and medium-sized industrial firms. All goods were purchased ready for sale. Relationships with customers and suppliers were excellent.

Through June 1983 growth had been steady but not spectacular. At that time new marketing policies were implemented that were designed to increase the firm's market share. The new policies were quite effective and sales grew rapidly in the last half of 1983.

By December 1983, Mr. Walsh concluded that further increases in market share were likely and that the higher level could be maintained. However, to achieve this growth he would need additional external financing. His plan was to find equity investors and, if necessary, to rely on his bank for funds until the equity was invested. His search for equity capital began in October 1983. By December he had reached an agreement with a reputable group of private investors. On July 2, 1984, they would invest $1.5 million. The funds would be allocated as follows: $1.1 million for the purchase of new fixed assets; $400,000 for working capital.

To fund the sales growth during the last half of 1983, the firm relied on its own liquidity balances which at June 30, 1983, consisted of a cash balance of $20,000 plus $165,000 invested in marketable securities. The cash balance was viewed as the minimum necessary to handle day-to-day transactions and to compensate the bank for its services. Mr. Walsh had hoped that $115,000 of the marketable securities would be sufficient for growth so the firm could maintain a liquidity reserve of $50,000. However, by mid-December, the balance in marketable securities was only $25,000. Since this was less than he desired and since it seemed obvious that $25,000 would not be enough for the next six months, he decided to seek a line of credit at his commercial bank.

On December 21, 1983, Mr. Walsh met with Ms. Catherine Russell, a senior loan officer at the bank. He explained what had occurred over the past six months and requested a line of credit of $50,000 through July 1984.

Ms. Russell knew Xenon, Inc., quite well. She had always been very impressed with the administrative and marketing abilities of Mr. Walsh and his key managers. Moreover, the firm had always pursued conservative financial policies and always paid its bills on time. Because of Walsh's excellent reputation, she knew that many banks in the area would be delighted to lend him $50,000. Her only concern was that it appeared that the size of the request was a subjective guess by Mr. Walsh and not based on any analysis. She expressed this concern by asking if $50,000 would be enough. He said he was confident that it would be. She decided not to pursue the issue. The next day she called to notify Mr. Walsh that his request was approved.

FIRST QUARTER OF 1984—GOOD NEWS AND BAD NEWS

Sales and profits during the first quarter were much higher than anticipated. By the end of March, it was clear that sales for the quarter would be almost twice the level of the first quarter of 1983 and profits would be more than twice as large. It was equally clear that a $50,000 line of credit would not be enough to finance the firm through the end of June. By the middle of February, the loan balance reached $50,000, and after that it was necessary to sell marketable securities and this resource was exhausted on March 5, 1984. By the third week of March, the cash balance fell below $20,000 and the firm was struggling to pay its bills on time.

Mr. Walsh called Ms. Russell on March 27 to discuss the problem. He told her that he thought that an increase in the line to $75,000 would be sufficient, but he was not at all sure. She suggested that they meet for lunch the next day. Ms. Russell began the meeting by noting that she had arranged for the limit on the line to be increased so that Mr. Walsh could meet the obligations that were maturing in the next few days. She proposed that this increase be viewed as a stopgap measure to give Mr. Walsh time to think about how much was needed. She urged him to do some sort of analysis, such as cash budgeting, to help him make the choice. She concluded by offering to help in any way she could.

Mr. Walsh thanked her and said that he agreed that some kind of analysis was necessary. The cash flow gyrations over the last six months had convinced him that he must pay more attention to this important part of the business. He explained that when sales growth had accelerated during the second half of the previous year he had decided to hire an assistant, and because of the increasing importance of financial management, he had decided to hire a person with finance expertise and experience. The problem was that it had taken several months to locate a good person. Fortunately, the issue was resolved; Timothy Fitzgerald had joined the firm on March 1. The president concluded by saying that he would ask Mr. Fitzgerald to work on this analysis right away.

TASK DEFINITION

When Mr. Walsh returned to his office he met with Mr. Fitzgerald and explained what had happened at the meeting with Ms. Russell. He then asked Mr. Fitzgerald how he thought they should proceed. Mr. Fitzgerald noted that there were three issues: (1) forecast period, (2) interval within the period, and (3) technique.

With respect to the forecasting period, Mr. Fitzgerald said that for the purpose of estimating short-term requirements it probably made sense to prepare projections one year ahead. Mr. Walsh understood his point but suggested that for this first effort they focus on April to June. After a brief discussion, they agreed on this time horizon.

The second issue—interval—referred to the choice of time periods within the forecasting cycle. A forecast could be prepared on a weekly basis, a monthly basis, or for some other interval. Mr. Fitzgerald suggested that a monthly basis was probably what was needed at Xenon and the president quickly agreed.

Regarding technique, Mr. Fitzgerald explained that one option was to prepare a monthly cash budget. Alternatively, he could prepare pro forma (projected) income statements and balance sheets. Mr. Walsh asked about the difference, and after a brief discussion, he requested that Mr. Fitzgerald prepare both. Mr. Walsh concluded the meeting by saying that he would rely heavily on Mr. Fitzgerald's recommendation on what line of credit the firm should request for the next three months.

DERIVING ESTIMATES

Mr. Fitzgerald spent the next three days reviewing historical data and talking to various managers. Everyone was most cooperative. For example, quarterly financial statements were normally compiled no sooner than ten days after the end of the quarter. However, recognizing the importance of this task, the firm's accountant worked all day Saturday, March 31, to complete the statements by April 2 (see Exhibit 1).

Because of capacity limitations, the growth in sales for the next several months was expected to be low. The marketing manager, after considerable thought, estimated sales for each of the next four months. These are presented below along with actual sales for the three previous months.

Actual		Estimated	
January	$286,750	April	$366,900
February	$318,293	May	$374,200
March	$359,671	June	$381,700
		July	$389,300

Xenon's products were priced to provide a gross profit of 30 percent and Mr. Fitzgerald concluded that it was reasonable to use this figure for each month. Operating expenses were estimated at 15 percent of sales each month. This estimate included interest on the line of credit and the long-term debt and depreciation expense of $16,000 per month. The amount of federal and state income taxes the firm would have to pay was difficult to determine since it was not clear what impact the new facilities would have on taxes. The firm's accountant advised him to use a rate of 43 percent for total state and federal taxes.

With respect to balance sheet accounts, Mr. Walsh told Mr. Fitzgerald that a cash balance of $20,000 would be necessary to support sales for the next three months. The president noted that he was anxious to replenish the liquidity reserve but felt it was best to wait until the equity infusion. Thus, he suggested he use a zero balance for marketable securities in his projections.

Approximately 90 percent of the firm's sales were on credit and the remainder were for cash, and Mr. Fitzgerald decided to use this breakdown for each month. The firm's credit terms were net 60 days but the average collection period was 75 days. Although Mr. Walsh hoped to get the average down to 65 days in the near future, he agreed with his assistant that it was best to use 75 days for the forecasts. Mr. Fitzgerald concluded that it was reasonable to assume that sales would be spread evenly during each month and that there would be no bad debts.

Inventory was purchased one month prior to sale on terms of net 45 days. Xenon always paid its bills on time, so Mr. Fitzgerald planned to use 45 days in the projections. Since receiving deliveries on a timely basis was no problem, he concluded that a safety stock of $5,000, the amount on hand at March 31, would be sufficient, so he decided to assume that this amount would be on hand at the end of each of the next three months. Finally, he decided that it was reasonable to assume that purchases would be evenly distributed throughout each month.

The firm's accountant had a schedule of planned capital expenditures for April to June. Based on this schedule, Mr. Fitzgerald derived the following estimates for this account.

End of Month	Property, Plant, and Equipment—Net
April	$2,398,554
May	2,418,967
June	2,404,967

These figures took into account estimated purchases of equipment, depreciation, and the planned retirement of fully depreciated fixed assets.

Mr. Fitzgerald discussed prepaid expenses and the "other" assets account with the firm's accountant. After some analysis, both agreed that there likely would be only minor changes in these accounts, and so Mr. Fitzgerald decided to assume that they would remain constant at their March 31 levels for the next three months.

The notes payable account represented the line of credit and Mr. Fitzgerald planned to use it as a plug figure. Accounts payable—trade was for purchases of inventory. Accrued expenses represented the unpaid portion of operating expenses and generally the balance at the end of each month equalled 20 percent of the total operating expenses for the month. An estimated income tax payment had been made on March 15 and the next payment would be for $50,000 on June 15.

Interest expense on the long-term debt, which was included in the estimate of operating expenses, was paid each month. Principal payments were due quarterly, and the next payment would be for $25,000 on June 30. Finally, no change was expected in the common stock and paid-in capital accounts, and dividends of $8,000 would be paid each month.

Mr. Fitzgerald was now ready to construct the statement and to prepare his recommendation. He realized that the president would rely heavily on his advice.

EXHIBIT 1
Xenon, Inc.
Income Statement
Quarter Ending March 31, 1984

Net sales	$964,714
Cost of goods sold	675,299
Gross profit	$289,415
Operating expenses	146,781
Earnings before taxes	$142,634
Income taxes	59,821
Net income	$ 82,813

EXHIBIT 1 (continued)
Xenon, Inc.
Balance Sheet, March 31, 1984

Cash	$ 17,620
Accounts receivable	739,206
Inventory	261,830
Prepaid expenses	197,124
Total current	$1,215,780
Property, plant, and equipment—net	2,383,452
Other assets	325,616
Total	$3,924,848
Notes payable	$ 61,700
Accounts payable—trade	382,715
Accrued expenses	10,790
Income taxes payable	14,821
Long-term debt—current portion	100,000
Total current	$ 570,026
Long-term debt	545,000
Common stock	100,000
Paid-in capital	479,122
Retained earnings	2,230,700
Total	$3,924,848

Tesco, Inc. (A)

In early October 1983, Ms. Stephanie Barret, treasurer of Tesco, Inc., had just finished the task of developing the necessary estimates and was ready to prepare a set of monthly pro forma (projected) financial statements and a monthly cash budget for the last three months of 1983. She was performing this task in response to a concern expressed by the firm's president.

BACKGROUND

Tesco, Inc. was formed in January 1970 by Mr. Louis Abrik in St. Paul, Minnesota. The firm manufactured a variety of consumer products that were sold through discount department stores. The business had been profitable from the beginning through the first nine months of 1983. (Exhibit 1 presents an income statement for the first nine months of 1983 and a balance sheet as of September 30, 1983.) Although an expansion program had been completed during 1981, the firm was rapidly approaching capacity. Another expansion was planned for 1984 which would be financed primarily by equity. Mr. Abrik and Ms. Barret were currently negotiating with a group of reputable investors who were interested in providing the desired capital for a percentage of the company's equity. Negotiations were proceeding smoothly, and Mr. Abrik was anxious to have the equity put into the business.

Mr. Abrik was concerned about the firm's recent bank borrowings. Tesco had a credit arrangement with a commercial bank which enabled the firm to borrow up to the lesser of $450,000 or 80 percent of its accounts receivable balance. All borrowings under this credit arrangement were secured by accounts receivable. Typically the firm would borrow much less than this limit around the tenth of each month. The firm would begin to repay the loan soon after the fifteenth of the month, and in most months the loan balance would be zero by the end of the month. This pattern changed during 1983. The maximum amount borrowed in any month was approximately $150,000, which was expected. However, the loan had not reached a zero level at any point during 1983.

Mr. Abrik talked to Ms. Barret about the situation. Ms. Barret reminded the president that the failure to attain a zero balance at any point had not been totally unexpected. When the firm financed the expansion in 1981, long-term debt was employed to finance the acquisition of fixed assets. A two-year term loan, which was paid in monthly intervals through June, 1983, was employed to finance working capital. Ms. Barret thought two years would be sufficient time for operations to provide the needed funds. If a longer period was necessary, the firm could rely on its credit line.[1] Ms. Barret added that the bank had been informed about this possibility when the term loan was arranged. Moreover, she had talked to the lending officer about this matter on several occasions and she was assured that there would be no problem.

The treasurer then suggested that she prepare a monthly cash budget for the rest of 1983. She had been meaning to formalize existing procedures for some time and this was probably a good time to start. She noted that it would be a good idea to share the information with the prospective investors. However, since they likely would prefer an alternative format, she proposed to prepare the following for them:

1. Pro forma income statements by month for the remainder of 1983
2. Pro forma balance sheets as of the end of each month for the remainder of 1983

The president agreed that the preparation of a monthly cash budget and a set of pro formas would be a good idea. He concluded the discussion by thanking Ms. Barret, and saying that he looked forward to reviewing the information.

EXISTING PROCEDURES

The firm's procedures for forecasting cash requirements were quite informal. Ms. Barret would merely forecast at the end of each month how much the firm would have to borrow on the tenth of the next month. Ms. Barret had always wanted to do some cash budgeting but never had found the time. Revenues and expenses for the year were budgeted as part of the firm's control system along with capital expenditures. However, the treasurer never took the time to prepare a cash budget. Cash budgeting was not a high priority item for the following reasons:

1. The firm's sales were not seasonal and so monthly borrowings did not vary much. Further, the treasurer's predictions regarding the

---

1. Casewriter's note: The firm's credit facility should not be confused with a line of credit which is an informal arrangement. The latter typically requires that borrowings on the line be "off the books" for a certain period which means that the balance be zero for a stipulated period such as 30, 60, or 90 days. Moreover, generally, a line of credit must be renewed each year. Tesco's arrangement was called a credit line but it was a more permanent source. More importantly, there was no requirement that the loan be off the books for a certain period each year.

maximum amount that would have to be borrowed were quite accurate.

2. The firm's credit arrangement provided a substantial borrowing reserve. As noted previously, for example, during 1983 the maximum amount borrowed in any month was about $150,000 and the credit limit was $450,000.

3. There was a liquidity reserve of $60,000 which was invested in Treasury securities. Although the relationship with the bank was excellent, this reserve ensured that the firm would not be too dependent on that source.

GATHERING ESTIMATES

Exhibit 2 presents the sales estimates for October through February and actual sales for the previous three months. The firm's products were priced to give a gross margin of 40 percent. Although occasionally there were variations from this figure, Ms. Barret expected none during the next three months and decided to use 60 percent for cost of goods sold. Selling, general, and administrative expenses were expected to be $115,000 per month for the rest of the year. Included in this figure are interest expense on the credit line and the long-term debt, and depreciation expense of $5,000 per month on office furniture and company vehicles. Finally, the income tax rate was 40 percent.

Ms. Barret was quite confident in her revenue and expense estimates. As noted, they were derived from the firm's operating budget. Moreover, it was early October, and the treasurer had a good grasp of what October's results would be and expected no major surprises in the subsequent two months. She was less sanguine, however, about certain asset and liability levels.

The cash balance would be $15,000 at the end of each month. This amount was maintained in a demand deposit at all times to compensate the bank for services. A liquidity reserve of $60,000 was invested in marketable securities as mentioned above. Tesco did not expect to sell any of these securities and would rely on additional bank borrowings, if necessary, to fund cash needs. Thus, the balance in cash plus marketable securities would be at least $75,000 at the end of each month. (If there were surpluses, they would be used to repay the bank debt. If there were surpluses over and above the amount needed to pay off the bank debt, they would be invested in marketable securities.)

The firm recently had been experiencing some difficulties with collections. Although some of the effects were still being felt, Ms. Barret was confident that the problem would be solved by year-end. Given these targets and the sales estimates, the accounts receivable balance at the end of the next three months would be as follows:

End of Month	Accounts Receivable Balance
October	$633,500
November	638,750
December	625,000

Goods sold in one month were produced in the preceding month and manufacturing costs consisted of the following:

Raw materials used	20%
Direct labor	60%
Overhead (including depreciation expense of $12,500)	20%

These percentages represented approximate proportions. Because a significant segment of overhead includes fixed costs like depreciation, the actual proportions may vary slightly. For example, overhead might represent 22 percent in one month and direct labor 58 percent. However, for the quarter as a whole the proportions would be 20 percent, 60 percent, 20 percent, and if there were variations they would be small. Thus, Ms. Barret decided to use these percentages for each month.

Raw materials needed for one month were purchased toward the end of the preceding month, and because service from suppliers was excellent, the firm maintained a safety stock of only $5,000. For example, the raw material balance at September 30, 1983, was $54,320. During October, goods needed for sales in November would be produced, so manufacturing costs in October would be 60 percent of November's sales estimate of $411,000 or $246,600. The raw materials component would be 20 percent of this figure or $49,320. Hence, this amount was purchased during the latter part of September and was on hand at the end of the month. This amount plus the safety stock of $5,000 gives the total on hand at the end of September, $54,320.

The production cycle was short; thus work in process inventory was generally a minor amount. Ms. Barret did not think it was worth the effort to derive a detailed estimate and decided to assume that work in process inventory would be $4,400 at the end of each month.

The balance in finished goods represented the goods produced during September (for October's sales) plus a safety stock. Management was considering altering the level of the finished goods buffer. The treasurer believed that no decision on this issue would be made during the final quarter and so she decided to assume that the safety stock of finished goods inventory on hand at September 30 would be the amount on hand at the end of the three subsequent months.

Expenditures for fixed assets were expected to be $30,000 per month for the next three months. No fixed assets would be sold or retired during the period. Finally, no change was anticipated for "other assets."

The note payable—bank account represented borrowings on the credit line. Accounts payable was for purchases of raw materials. Terms for raw material purchases were net 30 days and invoices were paid when due. The firm had made an estimated tax payment during September, and a final estimated payment of $55,000 would be made during December.

Accrued production costs represented the unpaid portion of direct labor and overhead, primarily payroll taxes related to direct labor and the salary portion of overhead. In other words, some of the direct labor and overhead costs incurred in one month were paid in the next month, and this liability represented the unpaid portion of these costs. Ms. Barret estimated that this liability would be $21,000 at the end of October, $22,500 at the end of November, and $19,400 at the end of December.

Other accruals were for selling, general, and administrative expenses incurred during the month but not paid as of the end of the month. Generally, the balance of this liability was equal to $4,000 plus unpaid interest on the long-term debt. (Interest on both short- and long-term debt is included in the estimates of selling, general, and administrative expense discussed earlier.) Interest on short-term debt is paid on the last day of each month and interest on long-term debt is explained below.

The interest rate on the long-term debt was 14 percent. Interest due plus a principal payment of $50,000 was made once each quarter on the last day of the quarter. For example, on September 30, 1983, a payment of $114,750 was made which consisted of interest of $64,750 plus principal of $50,000. The next payment would be made at the end of December 1983.

No change was expected in the common stock and paid in capital accounts. Finally, dividends would be $10,000 per month.

Ms. Barret now had the estimates needed to prepare the cash budget and pro forma statements. She knew that Mr. Abrik would appreciate her views on what the information contained in the reports implied for the firm's financing requirements, and especially for its credit line. Thus, Ms. Barret decided that she would carefully analyze the statements and prepare a brief report for the president.

EXHIBIT 1
Tesco, Inc.
Income Statement
For the nine months ended 9/30/83

Net sales	$3,727,800
Cost of goods sold	2,236,700
Gross profit	$1,491,100
Selling, general and administrative	969,200
Profit before taxes	$ 521,900
Income taxes	208,700
Net income	$ 313,200

Tesco, Inc.
Balance Sheet, 9/30/83

Cash and marketable		Notes payable—bank	$ 42,500
securities	$ 75,000	Accounts payable	49,320
Accounts receivable	637,500	Income taxes payable	41,650
Inventories:		Accrued production costs	19,575
Raw materials	54,320	Other accruals	4,000
Work in process	4,400	Long-term debt—current	
Finished goods	271,380	portion	200,000
Total current	$1,042,600	Total current	$ 357,045
Property, plant and		Long-term debt	1,600,000
equipment—net	3,161,500	Common stock	100,000
Other assets	217,000	Paid-in capital	441,500
		Retained earnings	1,922,555
Total	$4,421,100	Total	$4,421,100

EXHIBIT 2
Tesco, Inc.
Actual and Estimated Sales

Actual		Estimated	
July 1983	$405,300	October 1983	$408,000
August 1983	427,800	November 1983	411,000
September 1983	409,500	December 1983	420,000
		January 1984	408,000
		February 1984	415,000

Tesco, Inc. (B)

In early October 1983, Ms. Stephanie Barret, treasurer of Tesco, Inc., was about to prepare a monthly cash budget and a set of pro forma statements for the rest of 1983. (See Tesco, Inc. (A).) She decided that this would be a good time to analyze the impact of inflation on the firm's financing requirement.

Each year the firm would hold a planning meeting in the fall. To help the executives prepare for the meeting, Ms. Barret would compile annual forecasts for the subsequent five years under various sets of assumptions. For example, last year one set consisted of annual income statements and balance sheets based on the assumption of an annual sales growth of 10 percent.

Over the past several years, Ms. Barret wondered what influence high and varying inflation rates were having on the firm. It was never an urgent concern because the firm had ready access to capital. Moreover, despite the fact that in several previous years the inflation rate was higher than expected, the firm was always able to achieve its net profit margin target. In other words, the firm was able to raise prices to compensate for unexpected increases in costs. Nevertheless, the treasurer thought that it was important to isolate the impact of inflation.

Since this was the first attempt, she thought it would be best to keep the analysis as simple as possible. If the results showed that such an analysis provided useful information, she would ask her assistant to dig into the matter. Thus, for this effort she would prepare two sets of annual pro forma (projected) financial statements for each of the next five years. Both sets would assume zero real sales growth for the firm for the next five years. That is, the number of units sold by Tesco in 1983 would be the number sold for each of the next five years. The first set would assume a zero inflation rate and the second would assume an inflation rate of 7 percent. Moreover, the dollar level of sales would increase by the inflation rate. Thus, for the first set, annual sales would remain constant (at 1983's level) for each of the next five years; annual sales would increase by 7 percent for the second set.

With the basic guidelines established, Ms. Barret turned her attention to estimating the net profit margin and balance sheet items.

NET PROFIT MARGIN

As noted above, the firm had always been able to achieve its net profit margin despite varying inflation rates. Ms. Barret wondered if this had been the experience of most firms and so she looked into the matter. She learned that Tesco's experience was not at all typical and that inflation could easily wreak havoc on a firm's net profit margin for two basic reasons. First, the effect of inflation on the cost of raw materials, labor, and other items like electricity might not be uniform. For example, if the consumer price index increased by 7 percent, wage rates might increase by this amount but the impact on an item like raw materials might be very different. Second, it was not at all certain that a firm could recoup inflationary cost increases by raising prices. Indeed, her research showed that unlike Tesco, many firms had been unable to increase their prices enough to offset the impact of inflation on costs, and consequently, their net profit margins had declined.

In thinking about interest expense, Ms. Barret considered the firm's two existing debt instruments—the credit line and the long-term debt. (See Tesco, Inc. (A).) Interest expense on the credit line was very difficult to predict because it was a function of the amount borrowed and the interest rate, and inflation affected both of these factors. Inflation affected the dollar level of sales which in turn affected the dollar level of current assets and these assets had to be financed. The interest rate on the credit line floated with the prime rate, which meant that the interest rate changed when the prime rate changed. And an important determinant of the prime rate of interest was the anticipated inflation rate.

Tesco's interest rate on its long-term debt outstanding was fixed at 14 percent. Many financial officers that Ms. Barret knew told her that she had been fortunate to obtain long-term debt at a fixed interest rate because at the time lenders were reluctant to offer fixed-rate financing. Ms. Barret did not feel "so lucky" because she had to pay a price for it. When the rate was set at 14 percent, the lender took inflation into account and the amount included for inflation was the market's expectation regarding inflation for the life of the loan. If the actual inflation rate was greater than what was anticipated, then Tesco would gain at the lender's expense. On the other hand, if the actual inflation was less than the expected amount, the lender would gain at Tesco's expense because the debt did not have a call option and this was why Ms. Barret did not feel "so lucky."

Very often, a borrower is granted the right to retire the debt prior to maturity (a call option). Thus, if interest rates decline by a sufficient amount, it pays the borrower to refinance. Tesco did not have this option because it had to give it up in order to obtain fixed-rate debt. Ms. Barret had realized that she was foregoing a valuable option but she had thought it was worth it to resolve uncertainty regarding future interest costs on this debt.

There was no uncertainty regarding depreciation expense on existing fixed assets because this expense was based on the cost of these assets which, of course, was already known. However, depreciation on new fixed assets, purchased either for expansion or to replace existing assets, depended on the prices of these fixed assets and inflation affected these prices.

Further complicating the analysis was the pleasant prospect of further improvements in productivity. As Tesco's volume expanded, it had been able to justify more sophisticated equipment which enabled it to produce more units for each direct labor hour. The increased volume also enabled the firm to reap economies in certain marketing and warehouse expenses. Although this analysis assumed no growth in volume over five years, further gains in these areas were expected for two reasons. First, as will be discussed below, new fixed assets were to be acquired in 1984 and these would boost productivity. Second, new systems were installed in the latter part of 1983 which were expected to produce further economies in warehousing and marketing activities.

Ms. Barret concluded from her review that if inflation had any impact on Tesco's net profit margin, it would be positive. This view was based on the belief, supported by considerable historical evidence, that the prices for the firm's products would increase by at least the inflation rate. Inflation also would affect costs, but such inflationary increases in costs would be offset partially by the productivity and efficiency gains discussed above. Despite her confidence that this would happen, the treasurer decided to take a conservative stance in the projections and assume the following: for the set of pro formas that assumes a zero inflation rate, the net profit margin in 1984 would be one percentage point higher than the actual rate for 1983 and then remain at the 1984 level for 1985, 1986, 1987, and 1988. For the set that assumes a 7 percent inflation rate, the net profit margin each year would be the same as the actual rate for 1983.[1]

BALANCE SHEET ITEMS

For current assets, accounts payable, and accrued expenses, Ms. Barret thought it was reasonable to assume that these assets and liabilities would bear the same relationship to sales in each subsequent year as

---

1. To reduce the calculation time, the reader should round the net profit margin and all other items that involve percentage computations to the nearest tenth of 1 percent. For example, if the net profit margin was 2.34 percent, use 2.3 percent; if it was 2.35 percent, use 2.4 percent.

they did in 1983. For example, she planned to divide the accounts receivable balance at December 31, 1983, by annual sales for 1983. She
would then multiply the annual sales estimates for 1984, 1985, 1986,
1987, and 1988 by this fraction to derive the accounts receivable
estimates for the end of each of these years.

With respect to fixed assets, the firm was planning a major expansion
during 1984. A group of private investors would invest $2 million of
equity, and the money would be used to expand the plant and purchase
new equipment. These additions would provide sufficient capacity for
the next five years and so only replacements would be necessary. Ms.
Barret thought it was reasonable to assume for the zero inflation set
that expenditures for replacement each year would equal the amount
of depreciation each year. Thus, for this scenario, she would derive the
net fixed asset balance as follows: the $2 million of additions would be
added to the net fixed assets balance at December 31, 1983, and this
would be the amount used for the December 31, 1984, and all subsequent pro forma balance sheets.

Developing net fixed asset estimates for the set which assumed 7 percent inflation was more complex. Inflation would not impact existing
fixed assets. However, when worn out fixed assets were replaced, the
prices for replacements might be higher. After performing some analysis,
Ms. Barret decided to proceed as follows: she would use the same procedure to derive the December 31, 1984, balance that was employed for
the set assuming zero inflation—that is, $2 million would be added to
the December 31, 1983, balance to derive the figure for December 31,
1984. For each subsequent year the balance would increase by
½ of 1 percent per year.

The final asset was "other." For the set which assumed a zero inflation rate, she would keep this asset at the December 31, 1983, level
for each of the next five years. The asset would increase at 7 percent
per year for the other set of pro formas.

The notes payable—bank account, which represented the firm's
credit arrangement, would be used as the "plug" figure in the analysis.
In other words, this account would be set at an amount to balance the
total of the assets and the total of the liabilities plus equities.

The long-term debt required principal payments of $200,000 per
year, so this liability would be reduced by this amount each year.
(Interest on this debt was accounted for in the discussion of the net
profit margin.) Other than the $2 million equity issue in 1984, no
further issues of common or preferred stock were contemplated for the
next five years. Moreover, she did not anticipate that the firm would
repurchase any of the outstanding shares for the next five years. Finally,
the treasurer estimated that the firm would pay out dividends each year
equal to 25 percent of its earnings.

Ms. Barret was anxious to see what the analysis showed. She realized that some of the estimates were based on somewhat arbitrary assumptions. Nevertheless, she believed that overall they were reasonable and that the pro formas would provide a good view of the impact of an inflation rate of 7 percent.

Winston College

In late December 1976, Sidney Turon, financial vice-president and chief business officer of Winston College, was about to prepare a monthly cash budget for January through August 1977. He had spent the past three days speaking with department heads to obtain the necessary estimates. He was confident that cash budgeting would enable him to use cash and manage payables more efficiently.

BACKGROUND

In December 1976, Sidney Turon assumed the position of financial vice-president and chief business officer of Winston College. Although he had no prior experience in higher education, he came to Winston after twenty-five successful years with a major industrial firm. His background included many years of experience in accounting, cost analysis, production control, and financial management at the highest corporate level. Initially, Turon had high hopes of bringing some of the discipline of corporate financial practices to academe. The information he gleaned from his hiring interviews, his inspection of Winston's financial reports, and his intuitive sense that colleges and universities were "way behind the times" led him to conclude that such discipline was long overdue.

No sooner was Turon moved into his office than he was faced with his first problem. Tom O'Brien, a local business executive, prominent alumnus, and volunteer leader of the development effort to improve donations to Winston from the business community, telephoned to "let off steam" about his immediate problem. O'Brien had contracted with Winston to furnish and install 5,000 square yards of carpeting in various locations on campus. O'Brien's firm completed the work and billed Winston in September. Repeated calls to physical plant, the purchasing department, and most recently to the accounts payable department had not resulted in payment. Moreover, the accounts payable department had just informed O'Brien that they were instructed to hold payment on all invoices in excess of $1,000 until January 15. It was this that prompted O'Brien to call Turon.

Turon had just reviewed the most recent bank statement, which indicated minimal cash balances with the Lexton Bank. Puzzled by the prospective shortage of cash, Turon requested copies of the current year's cash budget and those for the prior three years, for comparison purposes. However, Tom Wills, the controller, informed him that Winston had never had "cash problems" in the past and therefore had never bothered to waste valuable time preparing cash budgets that would never be used. Occasionally a supplier would complain about slow payment, but such complaints were normally limited to summer months and December. Wills had heard of investing excess cash in short-term securities but figured the risk and management time involved were not worth the few dollars of potential interest income. If Winston College were to have a serious cash flow problem, it could always appeal to the Lexton Bank to expand the line of credit temporarily to accommodate the problem. After all, Winston had banked with Lexton for the past 72 years, and Phil Jamison, Lexton's vice-president for operations, was a member of the class of '36.

Turon gently placed the telephone receiver on the hook after his call to Wills and decided to gather the information required to assemble a cash budget for the next eight months.

After three days of discussions with department heads, he had the following information.

Tuition

Registration for the fall of 1976 was as follows: 8,000 undergraduate students; 700 Law School students; 6,000 student credit-hours in the Graduate School of Management; and 25,000 student credit-hours in the Graduate School of Arts and Sciences. Normally, a portion of the students enrolled for the fall term did not return for the spring term. The estimated attrition for the current academic year (students registered for fall 1976 who would not return for spring 1977) was as follows: 400 undergraduate students; 15 Law School students; 120 student credit-hours in the Graduate School of Management; and 2,500 student credit-hours in the Graduate School of Arts and Sciences.

To provide academic and financial balance, Winston pursued an active spring transfer program, which produced new students for the spring term to offset the loss from the fall term. The "transfers in" for the spring 1977 term were estimated as follows: 200 undergraduate students; 5 Law School students; 45 student credit-hours in the Graduate School of Management; and 180 student credit-hours in the Graduate School of Arts and Sciences.

Tuition rates were as follows: $1,750 per semester for undergraduates; $1,800 per semester for Law School students; $95 per student credit-hour for the Graduate School of Management; and $110 per student credit-hour for the Graduate School of Arts and Sciences. Only 70 percent of tuition revenue was due directly from students. (The remaining 30 percent is explained later.) The billing date for undergraduates and the law students for the spring term was December 20, 1976. Graduate students in management and arts and sciences would be billed on February 7, 1977. Based on past experience, it was estimated that collections from tuition would be as shown in Table 1. The uncollected percentages in the table refer primarily to refunds given to students who withdraw prior to a certain date after the start of the semester. Turon decided that he would treat these refunds as offsets to collections rather than disbursements in the preparation of the cash budget.

Contracts and Grants

Winston was very aggressive in seeking funds to support research. These funds normally came in the form of contracts and grants from government agencies, private businesses, and foundations. Generally, the contract or grant would permit the college to charge a price that would enable it to cover the total of the direct and indirect costs connected with the contract or grant. Total contract and grant revenue for the year ending August 31, 1977, was budgeted at $8 million, detailed as follows:

Direct salaries	$4.5 million
Other direct costs	.8 million
Indirect costs	2.7 million

On the 25th of each month, Winston would invoice the sponsoring sources for actual direct costs and indirect costs incurred during the month. Normally, payment was received 45 days after the invoice date. Except for December, June, July, and August, monthly billings averaged 7 percent of total budgeted revenue (that is, $8 million). During those four months, billings averaged 11 percent of the total budgeted for the year. Winston paid all direct costs for contracts and grants in the month of incurrence. (Indirect costs were overhead items related to the contracts and grants. These costs are included in the various expense categories, which are discussed subsequently.)

TABLE 1
Winston College
Estimated Collection Periods

Student Category	Month of Billing	Month of Billing + 1	Month of Billing + 2	Uncollected
Undergraduate	10%	85%	4%	1%
Law School	5%	85%	7%	3%
Graduate SOM	95%	4%	—	1%
Graduate A&S	93%	5%	1%	1%

Budget Office

Jennifer Moore in the Budget Office reminded Turon that over the past six months $5 million had been spent to finance phase 1 of the Riverside Dormitory Project. In June, when interest rates were high, the decision was made to finance phase 1 from current operations rather than to rely on debt financing. Now that mortgage rates had come down, it was expected that Turon would seek a commercial mortgage of $5 million to replenish operating funds. Since most of the paperwork, title searches, and so forth had already been completed and since the Eastern Federal Savings and Loan Company had committed the funds, Turon believed he would have the $5 million in hand sometime during January

Development Office

Total pledges from all sources for unrestricted gifts for operations were expected to be $3 million for both the 1976–1977 and 1977–1978 fiscal years. Based on previous experiences, it was expected that monthly collections would be as follows:

July–September	$150,000 per month
October–November	210,000 per month
December	630,000
January–June	210,000 per month

The remainder would never be realized. (There were two types of gifts: restricted and unrestricted. "Restricted" meant that the donor specified how the gift should be used. "Unrestricted" meant that the donor left the use of the gift to the college's discretion. Winston used unrestricted gifts to support operating expenditures.)

Housing

Campus housing owned by Winston currently amounted to 5,000 student beds. Revenues from housing affected cash flow from September through May. After examining current rates and past experiences, Turon estimated that housing revenues would have the following impact on receipts and disbursements for January through May 1977:

Month	Collections	Refunds
January	$2,125,000	$25,000
February	100,000	25,000
March		25,000
April		25,000
May		25,000

(Unlike tuition, Turon decided to include these refunds among the disbursements in the cash budget.)

Student Aid

Overall, about 20 percent of student tuition revenue was financed by external federal, state, and local government aid sources. Some 10 percent was financed through two major restricted gifts. Government aid for the spring was received in two equal payments in February and March. Winston typically received the full amount of the private donors' gifts in September.

Debt Service

Principal and interest on mortgages and bonds was $2.4 million, paid out to various lenders and trustees in equal monthly amounts. The first debt service payment on the new $5 million mortgage would not be made until February 1978.

Endowment Income

The market value of Winston's Endowment Fund was approximately $16 million. This was usually invested in a balanced portfolio, that is, 50 percent invested in common stock and 50 percent in high-grade bonds. Annual dividend income on the stock typically ran at a 3-percent rate. Interest on the bonds averaged 9 percent. Winston received both in two equal installments in September and March. Although realized capital gains were reinvested, Winston followed the practice of applying all the endowment income to operating purposes.

Food Service

Thirty-two hundred students were on the board plan. The rate was $450 per semester; bills for the semester were mailed during December. Generally, 11 percent of the total board revenue for the semester was collected during December, 85 percent during January, and 4 percent during February. Turon estimated that this collection pattern would continue.

In addition to board revenues, it was estimated that from January through May the cafeterias would have cash sales of $50,000 per month. During June, July, and August, cash sales would drop to $20,000 per month.

Book Store

Book store sales of $1.92 million for September 1976 through August 1977 were expected to generate a gross profit of 20 percent. Here again the sales pattern was highly seasonal. Sales were expected to be $40,000 for each of the three summer months. Fifty percent of the remaining $1.8 million in sales were textbook sales, which would be divided evenly between September and January. The remaining sales, for general book store items, were evenly distributed over the nine months of the academic year (September through May). All sales were for cash and were made approximately 30 days after the book store received the merchandise from suppliers. Winston followed the practice of paying book store suppliers 30 days after the receipt of merchandise. Although gross profit margins varied greatly by product line, Turon decided to use 20 percent for each month in preparing the budget.

Other Revenue

Cash receipts from other revenue sources—such as the infirmary, organized activities, vending machines, and other miscellaneous sources—were estimated at $400,000 for January and $100,000 for each of the remaining months through June. (There were no receipts from these sources during July and August.)

Summer Session

Tuition and fees for the summer session were estimated at $800,000; they would be received in June. Salaries for summer session faculty would be $200,000 in both July and August. (These salaries were not included in the $18 million for faculty salaries, discussed later.)

Payroll Office

Annual salaries of $30 million were made up of faculty salaries ($18 million) and salaries for all other employees ($12 million). Faculty salaries were paid in equal monthly payments from September through May, while all other salaries were disbursed over the full fiscal year.

Fringe Benefits

Fringe benefits for retirement, medical insurance, and other insurance amounted to $4.5 million. These were paid in equal monthly payments over the fiscal year.

Student Aid

Institutional student aid provided by Winston for the current year was $1.5 million for September, $1.5 million for January, and $100,000 for June. Although a substantial portion of this aid was in the form of tuition remission, the entire amounts would be treated as disbursements on the cash budget.

Energy and Utilities

The director of physical plant provided Turon with the following estimates of cash expenditures for heat, light, water, and gas:

Month	Expenditure
January	$235,000
February	235,000
March	235,000
April	75,000
May	75,000
June	75,000
July	225,000
August	225,000

Computer Center

Winston leased its computer from a major computer manufacturer for $50,000 per month.

Dining Department

Purchases of food were projected at $160,000 per month for the nine months of the current academic year for the board plan. Food purchases for the cash cafeterias were estimated at $25,000 per month except for December and the summer months, when they were expected to be $10,000 per month. Food purchases were spread out evenly during each month, and all purchases were on terms of 2/10 net 30. Winston followed the policy of taking advantage of all cash discounts.

All Other Operating Costs

All other operating costs were expected to amount to $9 million. They would be expensed during the summer months at the rate of $300,000 per month and during the months of the academic year at $900,000 per month. Almost all such expenses were for goods and services purchased from various vendors. Normally, vendor invoices were dated in the month following Winston's actual incurrence of the expense. Terms were net 30; Winston followed the practice of taking full advantage of these terms.

DEVELOPING A CASH BUDGET

At this point Turon believed he had sufficient information to develop a monthly cash budget for January through August. He had a nagging concern about O'Brien's call, however, and wondered how many other vendors were affected by the delayed-payment policy. He called the Accounts Payable Office and learned that bills totaling $440,000 were past due. Turon wanted to be on a current basis with all vendors by the end of January; thus he planned to pay this past due amount during January.

Prior to beginning to work on the cash budget, Turon estimated that the cash balance would be $200,000 on January 1, 1977. He believed this balance to be much too low. Whereas he had little hands-on experience in managing cash in a university environment, he thought it would be prudent to maintain an end-of-month cash balance at no less than 20 percent of the following month's projected cash outlays (for convenience, rounded to the next highest $100,000).

As Turon began his work, he wondered just how much income he could generate for Winston by investing excess cash in short-term marketable securities. Moreover, while he expected that maximum borrowings would occur in August, particularly since invoices for the fall semester would not be mailed until August 29, he was anxious to know just how much Winston would need to borrow from the Lexton Bank.

Paducah Portrait

Early one morning in February 1984, Fred Martin, the marketing manager of the American Jigsaw Puzzle Company, walked into the office of Allen Jones, the firm's president. "Boss," Martin said, "the Rhinegold Museum won't budge. If we don't do the Paducah portrait, they might go to someone else."

Jones was frustrated. He didn't think there was much of a market for the Paducah. But he couldn't afford to lose the museum's business. Rhinegold had given him an exclusive contract to market puzzles from prints of paintings in its collections. Losing Rhinegold's business meant locating another museum, and this was an unpleasant prospect because Rhinegold had many excellent paintings and did not charge royalties. Accepting the order was, in his opinion, equally troublesome. If demand was insufficient, and he felt it was, the firm would suffer a loss. Moreover, he realized that if he relented on this order, Rhinegold would make similar requests in the future.

BACKGROUND

After receiving a degree in fine arts in 1969, Allen Jones began a successful career in sales. However, he continued to spend most of his free time on his real love, art; and although he was happy with his job, he wanted to work for himself in a business dealing with his avocation. Consequently, in 1973 he began to investigate various possibilities.

After a thorough search which consumed almost one year, he concluded that the distribution of commercial puzzles based on fine art prints would most suit his talents and limited capital. In late 1974, he persuaded the Rhinegold Museum to give him an exclusive contract to market puzzles from its prints. There was no fee involved. The museum was interested primarily in fostering an interest in art in children and, secondarily, in publicizing its collections. Rhinegold did insist, however, that a member of its staff sit on the firm's board of directors and it reserved the right to cancel the contract on 90 days' notice.

Upon completion of negotiations with Rhinegold, Jones started the American Jigsaw Puzzle Company, operating on a part-time basis from his house. The firm was basically a marketing organization. Jones would negotiate with a manufacturer to transfer the print onto good quality cardboard, which would then be cut with a precision die into quality puzzles. The puzzles would then be sold to gift shops, bookstores, and stationers.

Although the puzzles would be sold in small quantities to retailers, Jones believed that he had to order in lots of 2,500 in order to charge a competitive price and still earn a satisfactory profit. This was because the unit cost charged by the manufacturer decreased rapidly as the order size increased. Thus, a key ingredient for success was to select prints that would sell.

The firm prospered. By 1983, Jones was devoting full time to the business and he had several full-time employees. Sales and profits had increased every year. Except for the Rhinegold Gift Shop which typically ordered 200 to 300 units of a puzzle, customers usually ordered 25 to 50 units. Fortunately, Jones had displayed an uncanny sense for selecting paintings that would make successful commercial puzzles. This ability created excellent relations with customers, enabled the firm's capable sales force to open new accounts, and allowed the firm to earn higher than expected profits because the amount of inventory written off each year was substantially below the industry average.

BUDGET FOR 1984

In early December 1983, Jones began to develop the firm's operating budget for the year ended December 31, 1984. Based on discussions with the manufacturer, Jones concluded that the price schedule (that is, the cost per unit for American) then in effect would not change throughout 1984. The schedule was as follows:

Order Size	Per Unit Cost
625	$2,920
1,250	1,536
2,500	1,325
5,000	1,104

An order size of 625 was the minimum the manufacturer would accept. (The manufacturer always quoted a schedule of prices but the firm had never deviated from an order size of 2,500 units for a puzzle.)

Jones estimated that operating expenses for 1984 would be $140,000, an increase of 10 percent over the previous year. Sales were estimated at 200,000 units, which was 20,000 units higher than the 180,000 units expected for 1983. Given a selling price of $2.50 per unit and an order size of 2,500 units, pretax profits would be $95,000 as shown below.

Sales—200,000 units @ $2.50	$500,000
Cost of goods—200,000 units @ 1.325	265,000
Operating expenses	140,000
Pretax profits	$ 95,000

Salaries accounted for the major share of operating expense and most of the remainder was for rent, utilities, and auto expenses. Mr. Jones viewed operating expenses as overhead which could not easily be reduced. Thus, he found it useful to compute per unit cost based on sales projections for the year. This schedule is shown next.

Per Unit Cost at 200,000 Units				
Order Size	625	1,250	2,500	5,000
Manufacturer's cost	2.920	1.536	1.325	1.104
Overhead	.700	.700	.700	.700
Total	3.620	2.236	2.025	1.804

PROBLEMS WITH RHINEGOLD

Recently, the Rhinegold Museum had begun to insist that American use certain of its prints other than those selected by Jones. This reflected the museum's desire to promote its unique collection and lesser-known paintings.

In January 1984, Rhinegold made a specific request. The director called Mr. Martin, the firm's marketing manager, and asked that the Paducah portrait be used for a puzzle. Mr. Jones and Mr. Martin visited the director. Mr. Jones explained that it was necessary to order in lots of 2,500 units to maintain a price of $2.50 and he was convinced that there would not be sufficient demand for the Paducah. Thus, there was a good chance that the firm would have to write off a large portion of the inventory. The director explained that it was quite important to the museum and asked Jones and Martin to reconsider.

A week later, Mr. Martin called the director to suggest that Rhinegold order 625 units of the Paducah. American would order this quantity from the manufacturer and charge Rhinegold its cost of $3.62 per unit. The director said that he would think about it and call back.

The next day, the director called Mr. Martin. He said that Rhinegold was willing to order 625 units of the Paducah. However, he believed that it was unfair to charge a price higher than $2.50. Martin said that he would have to get back to him.

Jones was dismayed by the director's position. If he ordered 625 units of the Paducah and sold it at $2.50 per unit, he would lose money. Ordering a larger quantity also would produce a loss, because he doubted that there would be much of a market for this product.

The president was even more concerned about the long-term implications of this decision. If he accepted the order, Rhinegold would make similar requests. Indeed, the director had clearly indicated a desire for lesser-known paintings on puzzles. On the other hand, rejection could mean the loss of the Rhinegold's business and the loss of the exclusive contract. Although he might be able to locate another museum, this outcome was not certain. Moreover, those museums he thought might be interested did not have the quality collections possessed by Rhinegold and they likely would want royalties.

Carroll Company Incorporated

"I wish I had never opened my big mouth," Robert Banter mused as he prepared for a meeting that afternoon with the other members of the Carroll Company management group. He realized that it could be a stormy session and that he could find himself in the middle of a bitter argument.

COMPANY BACKGROUND

The Carroll Company, which was founded by the late Robert Carroll in 1936, was engaged in the wholesale distribution of supplies, mechanical devices, and other types of equipment to dentists, physicians, and similar professional groups. The warehouse and offices were located in a two-story building in Birmingham, Alabama. The firm currently employed eight people. John Carroll, the president, along with three others, handled the sales effort and managerial duties; there were also two secretaries and two warehouse employees.

John Carroll, who assumed the presidency in 1960, owned 50 percent of the common stock, and other members of the Carroll family owned the remaining 50 percent. No other member of the Carroll family was employed by the firm. The company had been profitable in every year through 1973, but adverse economic conditions caused the firm to experience its first loss in 1974. As a result, the company had to eliminate dividends and borrow from the bank to meet expenses. The loss was a real shock to the Carroll family because the firm had known only success. The elimination of dividends proved to be a real hardship for certain members of the family, and all the owners were dismayed by the firm's need to rely on borrowed funds for the first time in its history.

To deal with these problems, Mr. Carroll did the following:

1. He reduced the number of employees from nine to eight. (The slot eliminated was a secretary/administrative assistant.)
2. He reduced other expenses as much as possible.
3. He froze his salary and the salaries of the three salespeople.
4. He instituted a new scheduling approach, which was expected to increase the number of sales calls per day per salesperson.

These actions dramatically changed the profit picture. Sales and profits increased in each year subsequent to 1974, and 1977 was a record year for both (see Exhibit 1). The bank debt was repaid during 1976 and the salary freeze was lifted for everyone but Mr. Carroll in 1977. He intended to resume dividends in 1978 and raise his own salary by 10 percent. Moreover, at the present time, he and his staff were considering the addition of several new employees.

MANAGEMENT MEETING

Mr. Carroll and the three salespeople constituted the firm's management team. Monthly meetings were held to discuss sales and other managerial problems. Robert Banter, who had been an employee in the warehouse for three years before being promoted to the sales staff, was attending the management meeting for the first time on February 8, 1978. He had also just completed a degree program in business administration at an evening college. For Robert's benefit, Mr. Carroll reviewed the firm's sales and profit targets for 1978:

1. An 8-percent increase in sales. (Mr. Carroll also noted that the five-year goal was to increase sales by 9 percent per year following 1978.)
2. Profits before taxes of $60,000. (Mr. Carroll explained that a $60,000 level would permit the payment of $20,000 in dividends after allowing for income taxes, increases in working capital, and the purchase of a car.)

Mr. Carroll then turned the discussion to the creation of new positions. All agreed that morale was low because everyone was working too hard. It was not that employees were working too many hours, but rather that they were under constant pressure. All agreed that this working environment could not continue. Although refilling the slot eliminated in 1975 would relieve the pressure, three new people were needed to solve the problem—one salesperson, one warehouse employee, and one secretary/administrative assistant. The increased sales volume called for by the current five-year plan would come primarily from increasing the size of the customer base. Some of the higher volume might be generated by increased sales to existing customers, but most would come from new customers. The size of the customer base could be increased only by an increase in the number of sales calls. It was unrealistic to expect the existing sales force to make more sales calls. The number of sales calls per person was already higher than the industry average, and no further efficiency could be expected in this area. There was some discussion of whether the company could achieve 1978's sales target by focusing on increased sales to existing customers. All agreed that it would be very difficult, if not impossible.

One point on which there was no debate was that adding only a salesperson would be horrendous. The clerical and warehouse employees were already working at capacity and there was no way that the increased workload created by the incremental sales could be accommodated without one new person in each of these areas.

One of the salespeople suggested that they should contact the firm's commercial banker to obtain advice on how to go about resolving the problem. Mr. Carroll thought that the suggestion was good, but that it would not help with the decision that would have to be made on the following day. He told them that over the weekend he had met someone, Joseph Harwell, who had broad industry experience and was considered a brilliant salesperson. When Mr. Harwell mentioned to Mr. Carroll that he was considering a job change, Mr. Carroll scheduled an interview for February 9 at 4:00 P.M. He knew that Mr. Harwell would not be available long and was convinced that if he postponed the interview or did not make a firm offer at the interview, Mr. Harwell would be lost to a competitor.

ROBERT BANTER VOLUNTEERS

As Mr. Carroll proceeded, Robert could tell that the president was leaning, albeit reluctantly, toward postponing the interview. The others had not really commented, but they did agree as Mr. Carroll recounted how serious errors had been made in the past when major decisions were made without proper study. Yet as he listened, the nature of the problem struck Robert as being very similar to breakeven analysis. He recalled that he had covered this topic in various courses and that it was a relatively simple analysis. In fact, he never understood why it was covered in three of his core courses since it was indeed so simple. Thus he excitedly interrupted Mr. Carroll and told the group that a simple breakeven analysis would provide them with the information they needed. All he needed was revenue and expense data and the projected salary levels of each of the three potential employees.

Mr. Carroll listened with interest and told Robert that he would have the firm's income statements for the past five years on his desk at 7:00 A.M. the next day. In addition, he told him to rely on the following annual salary figures:

1. Salesperson—$15,000 base salary
2. Warehouse employee—$12,000
3. Secretary/administrative assistant—$11,000

Robert told the president that he would have the analysis ready by noon the next day.

EXPLOSION

At this point, one of the salespeople said, "We are all anxious to achieve our sales goal of an 8-percent increase in 1978 and 9 percent in subsequent years. What if Robert recommends that we should not hire three additional people? Will we abandon our sales goals?" (All the salespeople were paid a fixed salary plus a commission of 1 percent of total firm sales in excess of $45,000 per month. This amount is included in selling expenses in Exhibit 1. Thus each salesperson's compensation was influenced by the firm's total sales level each month.)

Mr. Carroll responded that he, too, wanted sales growth. However, his family members needed and deserved dividends and he thought that this should receive priority. A heated argument followed, which at times became bitter and personal. Mr. Carroll finally agreed to consult with them before reaching a final decision and scheduled a meeting at noon the next day to discuss Robert's analysis and recommendation.

Robert Banter was speechless. He had volunteered to perform a simple analysis. He did not understand how he had been roped into making a recommendation. He quickly realized that he was in the middle of a bitter argument.

Even though he stayed up until 2:00 A.M. studying, he arrived at 6:30 the next morning. He found the income statements for the past five years on his desk (see Exhibit 1). He quickly realized that he would need some more information and went to see Mr. Carroll to ask for some additional estimates of operating expenses for the coming year.

The president understood and was willing to help. He told Robert that rent would be $7,700 for the year and that the gross margin target of 29.5 percent was reasonable for 1978. He told Robert to call the firm's accountant, who could help with the other numbers. The accountant was quite helpful. She told him that, with raises granted during 1977 and with the increase Mr. Carroll intended to take for himself, total salaries would be $123,000 for the year (not including the salaries for the three potential positions). In addition, she told him that fringe benefits plus payroll taxes would be about 9 percent of total salaries. She then indicated that depreciation expense would be $3,100 for the year and estimated that 90 percent of "other" expenses, 50 percent of selling expenses, and 50 percent of office supply expenses were fixed. She guessed that the fixed portion of these expenses would increase in 1978 by about 5 percent over 1977's level. The variable portions of these expenses would bear a similar relationship to sales as 1977's relationship to sales.

With this information, Robert was ready to make the necessary calculations. He wondered how he would respond to the question he knew he would be asked: "What do you recommend, Bob?"

EXHIBIT 1
Carroll Company Incorporated
Income Statement

			Years Ended		
	12/31/73	12/31/74	12/31/75	12/31/76	12/31/77
Net sales	$593,703	$585,753	$649,431	$677,689	$840,821
Cost of goods sold	435,701	435,765	478,444	484,044	598,720
Gross margin	$158,002	$149,988	$170,987	$193,645	$242,101
Other expenses					
Salaries	$ 89,371	$ 96,641	$ 83,796	$ 87,871	$105,295
Fringe benefits & payroll taxes	5,448	6,732	7,265	9,863	9,593
Selling expenses	19,055	24,213	22,078	28,352	32,604
Office supplies	6,507	7,516	5,693	5,407	7,087
Rent	6,600	6,600	6,930	6,930	7,590
Depreciation	4,528	4,781	3,725	3,262	2,719
Other	13,447	11,748	10,150	17,382	22,592
Profit before taxes	$ 13,046	($ 8,243)	$ 31,350	$ 34,578	$ 54,621

Bolton College Food Service

In late January 1976, Dr. Bell, executive vice-president of Bolton College, realized that a tough decision regarding the food service had to be made. Students were expecting a board rate of $750. However, given the existing level of service, a $750 rate would most likely not enable the food service to break even for the fiscal year ending June 30, 1977.

BOLTON COLLEGE

Bolton College was a well-known private university located in Walnut Valley, North Carolina. Founded in 1863, it catered primarily to the local community until 1960. During the sixties, however, there was a dramatic change in the student population; by 1972 one-half of the 10,000 undergraduates and one-quarter of the 4,000 graduate students were residents. The reason for the shift was in part a response to Bolton's growing national reputation and in part a result of its desire to increase both the quality and the size of the student population. There had been no growth since that time, and none was planned for the next five years. Moreover, the proportion of resident students had remained the same since 1972, and Bolton planned to maintain this proportion for the next five years.

The significant increase in resident students created a severe housing problem, which could not be accommodated by constructing facilities in the space adjacent to the university. Thus, in 1968, an area called Crestview, located 1½ miles south of the campus, was purchased, and housing for 500 students was constructed. In 1971 an area called Lakeview, located 2 miles north of campus, was purchased, and housing for 1,500 students was constructed. A shuttle bus service was installed to transport students living in these areas to and from the Walnut Valley campus.

FOOD SERVICE

The increase in the total student population and the increasing proportion of resident students produced a spectacular growth in the food service. In 1960 there had been two units, with total annual revenue of $.5 million. By 1976 there were seven units, with an expected total revenue of over $3.3 million. In the early sixties an outside food service firm was retained. However, a number of problems arose and dissatisfaction became so great that, when the contract expired in 1968, Bolton decided to assume the operation of all the food service units.

The growth would have been even greater, but all the new housing constructed on the main campus since the mid-1960s had been apartment-type housing. There were two types of housing: apartments and dormitories. All graduate residents and approximately 40 percent of undergraduate residents lived in apartments, which had kitchen facilities. These students were not required to be on the board plan, but resident students in dormitory housing (that is, without kitchens) were required to be on the board plan.

Five of the units were located on the campus, one was at Crestview, and one was at Lakeview. Through 1974, three of the units—Joshua, Crestview, and Lakeview—were strictly board operations; that is, they serviced only resident students on the board plan. The other four units—Hale, Barry, Crandell, and Tower—were cash operations. As will be explained, a decision made in 1974 blurred the distinction between the board and cash operations.

Unfortunately, growth brought problems. Through fiscal 1970, the Bolton College Food Service (dining department) operated at about breakeven. In fiscal 1971, the first of a series of significant annual losses occurred. The board of trustees took a dim view of this situation, and in January 1974, when it appeared that the loss for the fiscal year ended June 1974 would hit a record $500,000, the trustees directed Dr. Bell to take whatever actions were necessary to achieve a breakeven level on a fully costed basis by fiscal 1977. The only constraint placed on him was that he could not contract an outside food service for either the board or cash operations. (In addition to its own fixed expenses, each department was charged with a portion of the university's expenditures for maintenance. The allocation was determined by the space the department used. Breaking even on a fully costed basis meant that revenues had to be sufficient to cover not only the department's fixed and variable expenses but also its charge for maintenance. If a department were to reduce its space requirements, its charge for maintenance would be reduced. However, the university's expenditures on maintenance would most likely not be reduced.)

In February 1974, Dr. Bell hired John Rendo, who had an excellent reputation in the food service industry, to manage the Bolton College Food Service. Soon after he was hired, Mr. Rendo told Dr. Bell that the food service had two major problems. The first was the lack of proper control of costs. He explained in detail the new system that he intended to implement. Dr. Bell was pleased and agreed with Mr. Rendo's approach to controlling costs. The second major problem was that there was insufficient volume for seven units, and Mr. Rendo proposed two policy changes to eliminate this problem. First, he wanted to allow commuter students, faculty, and administrators to purchase meals for cash at Joshua, Crestview, and Lakeview. He guessed that most of this market did not eat breakfast or dinner at the Bolton College Food Service. He argued that opening the board units to these people would increase volume at these units. Second, he wanted to institute a point plan as an option to the regular board plan. (The price for the point plan would be the same as for the regular board plan.) Students choosing this option would be able to purchase food with coupons (that is, points) at all seven units. In addition to the greater variety, students would have more flexible dining hours. Joshua, Crestview, and Lakeview served breakfast from 7:00 A.M. to 9:00 A.M., lunch from 11:00 A.M. to 1:00 P.M., and dinner from 5:00 P.M. to 7:00 P.M. (Although the hours of the other units varied, at least one was open between 7:00 A.M. and midnight.) Mr. Rendo believed that this option would encourage more students in apartment housing to purchase the board plan. Dr. Bell was impressed with Mr. Rendo's enthusiasm and accepted both recommendations.

In March 1974, Dr. Bell announced an increase from $600 to $650 in the board rate (that is, the annual charge for the board plan) and implied that annual increases of $50 would continue. At the same time, he announced that prices at the cash units would be raised an average of 8 percent. These higher prices and careful control of costs reduced the loss to $250,000 for the fiscal year ended June 30, 1975. Had volume increased, as expected, the loss would have been even lower; unfortunately, however, the anticipated increase in volume did not materialize. There was, though, a significant reallocation of existing volume among the seven units because a large number of resident students on the regular board plan switched to the point plan. Mr. Rendo told Dr. Bell that he was not disappointed because he believed it would take more than one year for the policies to produce the desired effect.

For the academic year 1975–1976, the board rate was increased to $700 and cash prices were raised an average of 5 percent. Although the new policies again did not produce the desired increase in volume, by December 1975 it appeared that the loss for fiscal 1976 would be $150,000. The improvement was a result of the higher prices and further reductions of costs.

Despite the positive trend, three factors caused Dr. Bell to doubt that a breakeven level for fiscal 1977 would be achieved with a $750 board rate. First, in January 1976, the board of trustees announced an 8½-percent salary increase for all departments. Second, Mr. Rendo insisted that, despite favorable economic news to the contrary, food costs would continue to increase rapidly. Third, Dr. Bell doubted that the point plan or the sale of board meals to commuters, faculty, and administrators would produce an increase in volume. As a starting point,

Dr. Bell asked Mr. Rendo to prepare a budget for 1976–1977 and to recommend action for achieving a breakeven level. He directed Mr. Rendo to use the following assumptions in the forecast:

1. A board rate of $750 with no increase in volume
2. A 5-percent increase in cash prices with no increase in volume
3. An 8½-percent increase in salaries
4. A 5-percent increase in food costs, operating expenses, and maintenance charges

Mr. Rendo's report is contained in Exhibits 1 and 2. Included in this report were recommendations to increase the board rate to $800 for the 1976–1977 academic year and to close the Crestview facility.

Mr. Rendo had always wanted to close Crestview (see Exhibit 1). However, this idea continued to receive sharp criticism from the housing staff, who argued convincingly that the Crestview dining facility helped create a spirit of community among the students who lived there. This was especially important since these students were separated from the campus. Dr. Bell sympathized with this point of view, but he knew that a proposal to close any of the other units would also produce a strong negative reaction.

Dr. Bell realized that an unpopular decision had to be made to carry out the breakeven policy. However, he was not convinced that Mr. Rendo's recommendation should be accepted. Unless it could be demonstrated that the board plan was the primary cause of the loss, how could he in fairness raise board prices by an additional $50 to $800? This would mean a total increase of 14 percent, versus 5 percent for cash prices. Even if Mr. Rendo's views regarding the 5-percent limit on cash prices were correct, why not close one or more of the cash units? Dr. Bell realized that further analysis was necessary to evaluate these or other options properly. He decided first to estimate the break-even point for each unit. He would then calculate a separate profit-and-loss statement for the combined cash operations and estimate a break-even point for these. The same procedure would be followed to determine the breakeven point for the three board operations combined.

To obtain reasonable estimates for the preceding analyses, Dr. Bell met with Mr. Rendo and the university's able budget director, Donald Flora. They agreed that, at the existing level of volume, all board plan customers could be serviced at Joshua and Lakeview. Moreover, the elimination of the point plan would not produce a noticeable reduction in volume. Finally, they agreed that no more than two units could be closed. Turning to costs, Mr. Flora advised that food costs as a percentage of revenue would be the same for the board and cash operations, assuming a 5-percent increase in food costs, a 5-percent increase in cash prices, and a board rate of $750. With respect to other expenses, Mr. Flora began by noting that estimating the fixed and variable portions was not simple. He then said that, after analyzing the direct operating expenses and direct salaries and discussing them with Mr. Rendo, he "guesstimated" that the following amounts were fixed at each location:

	Type of Operation	Fixed Portion of Direct Salaries (000 omitted)	Fixed Portion of Direct Operating Expenses (000 omitted)
Joshua	Board	$200	$120
Crandell	Cash	65	23
Hale	Cash	65	22
Crestview	Board	18	14
Barry	Cash	25	8
Lakeview	Board	80	35
Tower	Cash	10	1
		$463	$223

With respect to the variable portions, Mr. Flora noted that it would probably be safe to assume that the variable rate was the same regardless of whether the revenue was from the board plan or from the cash operation.

The last item to estimate was indirect salaries. They all agreed that these salaries were fixed, provided that the number of units remain at seven. The elimination of one or more units would produce a decrease in indirect salaries of $15,000 per unit, except for Joshua, which would produce a reduction of $25,000. Joshua, however, was the only unit that could not be closed, since it was the main facility.

Dr. Bell realized that the estimates were uncertain. All he was certain of was that a decision had to be made soon. He was determined to meet the board of trustees' mandate that the food service break even on a fully costed basis by fiscal 1977.

EXHIBIT 1

University of Bolton College

Walnut Valley Campus

January 31, 1976

Dr. Paul Bell
Executive Vice President
Bolton College

Dear Paul:

I am enclosing the budget you requested. The allocations of revenues and expenses are based on this year's experience. As you can see, the loss will increase. In order to achieve our break-even mandate, I recommend that we close Crestview and increase the board rate to $800 for the 1976-77 academic year.

I am confident that by closing Crestview we can accomplish a substantial reduction in expenses without losing any volume. (The Crestview volume will flow to the other locations.) I estimate the following reduction in expenses.

Direct Salaries	$ 18,000
Operating Expenses	14,000
Food	10,000
Maintenance	13,000
Indirect Salaries	15,000
	$ 70,000

The reason for the savings in food costs is due to the elimination of waste. As you know there has always been an abnormally high level of waste at this unit. These savings and the $800 board rate will enable us to operate the food service at a slight surplus.

Paul, a comment is in order regarding cash prices. The students have correctly observed that board rates have been increasing at a greater rate than cash prices. I would like to increase cash prices by more than 5% but it is impossible given the competitive environment. The independent sandwich shops adjacent to the campus already underprice us. I maintain that they can do this because they operate at a loss! They are Ma and Pa shops and the entire family works in them for little or no salary.

I will be happy to discuss my recommendations with you at your convenience.

Cordially,

John Rendo, Food Service Manager

EXHIBIT 2
Bolton College Food Service
Preliminary Budget for Fiscal Year Ended 6/30/77
(000 omitted)

	Joshua	Crandell	Hale	Crestview	Barry	Lakeview	Tower	Total
Revenues								
Board	$1,566	$ 74	$ 12	$172	$120	$547	$ 1	$2,492
Cash[1]	323	190	301	1	103	91	80	1,089
	$1,889	$264	$313	$173	$223	$638	$81	$3,581
Percent of total	52.8%	7.4%	8.7%	4.8%	6.2%	17.8%	2.3%	
Direct expenses								
Salaries	$ 612	$123	$133	$ 56	$ 73	$219	$28	$1,244
Food cost	871	106	145	108	117	339	36	1,722
Operating expense	239	40	42	25	22	75	6	449
Total direct	$1,722	$269	$320	$189	$212	$633	$70	$3,415
Indirect expenses								
Indirect salaries[2]	$ 69	$ 10	$ 11	$ 6	$ 8	$ 23	$ 3	$ 130
Maintenance[3]	115	26	38	13	20	31	13	256
Total indirect	$ 184	$ 36	$ 49	$ 19	$ 28	$ 54	$16	$ 386
Excess (deficit)	$ (17)	$(41)	$ (56)	$ (35)	$(17)	$ (49)	$ (5)	$ (220)

[1] Cash sales include $400,000 of catering business, which is operated at Joshua and Lakeview.

[2] Indirect salaries are allocated according to revenue.

[3] Maintenance is allocated according to space. For example, Joshua uses 45 percent of the total space allocated to the food service, and hence it is charged with 45 percent of the total maintenance charges allocated to the food service.

Budin Company (A)

On May 4, 1976, Fred Mosher, a financial consultant, was preparing for a meeting the next week with the management of the Budin Company. The purpose of the meeting was to discuss the firm's goals and to work on the development of a five-year financial plan. Mr. Mosher believed that, while he should help prepare a financial plan, Budin's management should set the goals. However, since management was having difficulty with this task, he agreed to provide guidance.

BACKGROUND

The Budin Company was founded by Joseph Budin in 1934. The founder remained active in the day-to-day operations of the firm until his death in 1964, even though his son, Robert, assumed the presidency in 1958. The firm was a distributor of plumbing supplies, with offices and warehouse located in Massachusetts, where the firm did 90 percent of its business. In fiscal 1975, the firm had sales of $935,000 on assets of approximately $450,000.

The plumbing supply industry grew rapidly during the sixties, and the Budin Company shared in this growth. By concentrating its marketing strategy on certain specialty items, the firm was able to outperform the industry with respect to gross margin. But since the strategy also involved greater service costs, the higher gross margin was eroded and the firm's profit before taxes margin on sales was only slightly higher than the industry average through 1970. (Exhibit 1 presents information on average sales and profits for firms with less than $1 million in sales. Exhibits 2 and 3 present annual financial statements for the Budin Company for 1970 through 1975.)

In 1971 a combination of marketing problems caused the firm to experience its first sales decline in more than a decade and its first loss in more than two decades. These problems were handled quickly and were resolved by the end of the year. A new marketing strategy implemented in the latter part of 1971 proved most effective. By March 1972, it appeared that sales could average between $65,000 and $70,000 per month for the remainder of the year. Moreover, the firm was able to increase its gross margin level at the same time. The rapid growth in sales necessitated a corresponding building of accounts receivable and inventory. These investments resulted in a substantial cash drain. During April the firm was unable to take advantage of cash discounts. By the end of May, it was 30 days late on its payables. By the end of June, Budin was borrowing $30,000 on its $50,000 line of credit with its bank.

During June, Mr. Budin had a long talk with the bank's loan officer, Mr. James. Mr. James began by acknowledging the long and open relationship the two had had. Because of the close relationship, he felt he could speak frankly with Mr. Budin. Mr. Budin responded that he had a great deal of respect for Mr. James's judgment and that his father had held Mr. James's business acumen in high regard. Mr. Budin then said that he would be happy to listen to any advice Mr. James might give regarding the company's financial problems, since he honestly had been unable to understand or control the firm's deepening cash shortage. Mr. James said he believed that Mr. Budin's emphasis on recruiting and developing a strong marketing team had been at the expense of financial control. In fact, it appeared to Mr. James that marketing and distribution were the only areas under control. Because of the absence of proper financial control, these functions were causing the company to exhaust one source of financial flexibility after another with no advance warning. In fact, Mr. James concluded that Budin had no financial policy at all. Mr. James advised Mr. Budin that the problem seemed so severe that Budin should forgo additional marketing initiatives until proper financial controls were implemented. Mr. Budin thanked Mr. James and asked him how he could go about obtaining help to solve his immediate financial problem and implement proper financial controls. Mr. James suggested that Mr. Budin contact Fred Mosher, a financial consultant who specialized in small wholesaling companies. Mr. James concluded by noting that, if necessary, his bank would be willing to increase the firm's line of credit above $50,000. Mr. Budin thanked him but said that he hoped borrowings above the existing amount ($30,000) would not be necessary.

CONSULTANT'S ANALYSIS

Mr. Mosher's first step was to analyze the situation and to gather information on the industry. (A summary of the industry information, which was updated in 1976, is presented in Exhibit 4.) He was very impressed with the marketing ability of Mr. Budin and his four-person sales staff. Given the competitive situation in the region, he believed that it was indeed unique to increase sales this rapidly and also to increase gross margins. This was in large part the result of effective control of cost of goods sold. Mr. Mosher concluded that the firm's liquidity problems could be traced directly to the surge in sales and proposed to explain this in a formal presentation to Mr. Budin and his

senior staff. He then planned to array a set of financial options open to
the company as a way out of the liquidity problem.

FINANCING OPTIONS

When Mr. Mosher completed his analysis, he called Mr. Budin to
schedule the meeting. Mr. Budin, two members of his staff, and the
firm's attorney attended. Mr. Mosher first gave a detailed presentation
of the causes of the liquidity crisis. He then explained that since sales
were expected to remain at the $65,000–$70,000 level for at least the
next year, the liquidity crisis would not become more severe. (Knowing
their ability and desire to generate sales, he emphasized how the situation could become much worse if sales were to increase further without
proper financing.)

The consultant then discussed options for resolving the existing crisis.
One possibility was debt. The firm was currently using $30,000 of the
$50,000 revolving line of credit. He thought that the bank would prob-
ably be willing to increase the $50,000 limit on the line of credit. Mr.
Budin opposed this idea and indicated that he did not like to rely on
borrowed money. He noted that the firm had had to borrow a significant amount of money for the first time in 1970. However, he viewed
this loan as temporary and looked forward to paying it off.

But new equity, the second option proposed, was also out of the
question, and Mr. Budin went on to explain why. He owned 60 percent
of the common stock and other members of the Budin family owned
the remainder. Neither he nor other members of the family wanted to
invest additional money in the company. The owners were also firmly
opposed to admitting other investors.

The president then noted that prior to 1970 the firm was a Subchapter S corporation. (A Subchapter S corporation is a corporation
taxed as a partnership. Thus each owner includes on his or her own tax
return a percentage of the firm's earnings, the percentage being determined by the individual's relative ownership. For example, suppose
John Doe owns 20 percent of the common stock of a Subchapter S
corporation that earns $100,000. On his personal tax return, he would
include $20,000 of these earnings. Note that this is the amount he
would include regardless of whether the firm paid all or none of its
earnings in dividends. If the firm did pay dividends, John Doe would
not also have to pay taxes on these dividends.) At one time all earnings
were paid out in dividends. In the early sixties, the level was reduced to
an amount that was approximately high enough to enable the owners
to meet their income taxes created by their share of the firm's earnings.
The difference between total earnings and the amount distributed was
considered as a loan due to the stockholders. For example, if the firm

earned $30,000 and $10,000 was paid out in dividends, the $20,000 difference became a debt due to stockholders. This debt reached $110,000 by the end of 1969. In that year, the owners elected to drop the Subchapter S status. In addition, they agreed that a 100-percent dividend payout policy was unrealistic and that a smaller payout would commence after their loans were repaid. In 1972, when the firm increased its revolving line of credit from $15,000 to $50,000, the bank insisted that the loans due to stockholders be converted to common stock. (The statements in Exhibit 3 are restated to show conversion during 1970. The firm's actual statements were not restated.) Mr. Budin noted that he planned to reconvert the $110,000 to debt due to stockholders as soon as the bank loan was paid off.

Seeing that external sources were not feasible, Mr. Mosher suggested a third plan, which would require cutting back on the firm's marketing effort to a sales target of $55,000 per month. He asserted that if expenses as well as receivables and inventory were properly managed, the liquidity crisis would quickly disappear. Although it was a bitter pill for marketing people to swallow, particularly after their competitive successes, they selected this option. It worked. The liquidity crisis disappeared, and by the end of 1972 bank debt was reduced to $10,000 and the firm was again taking advantage of cash discounts.

As part of his final report, Mr. Mosher recommended targets for various expense categories. These targets were intended to produce a pretax profit margin of 6 percent of sales. In addition, he recommended that they aim for receivables and inventory goals of 10.8 percent and 25.5 percent of sales, respectively. He concluded that these should be viewed as short-range goals only and that Mr. Budin should give serious thought to developing a five-year business plan. When Mr. Budin received the final report, he telephoned Mr. Mosher. He said that he liked the idea of developing a business plan and noted that he would give thought to longer-term objectives while working on the short-range targets.

ADMINISTERING THE PLAN, 1973-1975

Mr. Budin and his two key salespeople worked hard to meet the profit and working capital targets. They met regularly each month to check on progress.

In 1973, Mr. Budin called Mr. Mosher to announce happily that he had eliminated the bank debt. He advised Mr. Mosher that he was considering a large salary increase for himself and his two key employees. Since the three of them had not had a raise for two years, he thought that a 20-percent salary increase was justified but wanted Mr. Mosher's opinion. Mr. Mosher said he would review Budin's monthly financial statements and advise him of the impact of such an increase. After reviewing the financial statements for the first six months of 1973, Mr. Mosher told Mr. Budin that the large increases would most likely prevent the firm from meeting its profit objective. Accordingly, Mr. Budin decided to give small increases to his two key employees but to take no raise for himself.

During the same discussion, Mr. Mosher asked him how the development of the longer-term objectives was progressing. Mr. Budin said that he had decided on some but was still uncertain about others. He really wanted to get rid of the loans due to the stockholders and he hoped that the company could do so over the next five years. He then noted that, because of the salary freeze, his salary and the salaries of his two key employees were out of line. He could earn almost as much by working as a sales manager for his competitors. While his two key employees were earning a little more than they could earn as salespeople elsewhere, they really deserved much larger salaries because of the managerial duties they performed. In addition to rectifying their unfair compensation levels, something had to be done about their work load. Each worked more than 70 hours per week, and all three of them were over 50 years old. For health reasons alone, this situation could not continue, and it appeared that this problem could be resolved only by hiring additional employees.

The president then noted that the receivables and inventory targets recommended by Mr. Mosher were reasonable as permanent goals. Mr. Mosher suggested that it might be possible to lower the inventory target as sales increased. Mr. Budin replied that while it might be possible, it was probably not a good idea since inventory was such an important part of the firm's marketing strategy.

The only area in which he was still undecided was sales and profits. He was confident that he and his two key people, together with an expanded sales staff, could produce dramatic increases in sales. He noted that he really wanted to go after sales, but that the experience of 1972 was making him hesitant. Mr. Budin concluded by saying that he would just have to give it some more thought. Mr. Mosher indicated that he was concerned because the failure to specify objectives was preventing the development of the plan. However, he understood Mr. Budin's position.

In early 1974, the firm began to build large cash balances, largely because inventory levels were reduced. Rather than use the excess funds to reduce the loans due to stockholders, Mr. Budin decided to go after higher sales. During the latter half of 1974, when it was obvious that sales and profits would set new records and that the profit target would be exceeded, he gave substantial raises to his two key employees and moderate increases to himself and all other employees. He also increased benefits for all employees.

The 1974 stockholders' meeting, held in February 1975, proved to be a stormy session. The stockholders were quite upset because the loans could not be reduced after a year of record profits. Mr. Budin explained that he took advantage of the opportunity to increase sales because he thought it was best for everyone in the long run. They agreed that the president had always had their best interests in mind and appreciated his efforts. However, they emphasized that they needed the money that was tied up in these loans. (These loans did not require interest payments. No one had ever suggested that they should, and there was no discussion of this point at the meeting.) Mr. Budin promised that he would give the elimination of the loans high priority. After the meeting, he decided that 1975's goal would be to keep sales at approximately 1974's level. Thus sufficient cash would be available to enable a substantial reduction of the loans due to the stockholders. Two factors prevented this goal from being achieved: (1) the reduction of inventory levels proved to be short-lived, and (2) the decisions Mr. Budin made during the latter half of 1974, together with rapid inflation, had a dramatic effect on operating expenses. Mr. Budin realized that another liquidity crisis would have occurred had it not been for the temporary change in income tax rates.[1]

MR. MOSHER RETURNS

Mr. Budin thought it best to contact Mr. Mosher. After hearing about the stockholders' meeting, the consultant suggested that the specification of objectives and the development of a plan should be postponed no longer. The president indicated that he was still uncertain about sales growth but realized that a decision had to be made. He told Mr. Mosher that, although he wanted to go after 20 to 30 percent per year, he would select 10 percent per year as the goal for the next five years. He asked Mr. Mosher to recommend a plan based on this goal as well as on the objectives specified during previous discussions. Mr. Mosher said that he needed more information regarding expenses, especially salaries, since Mr. Budin had previously indicated that new people would be

---

1. Corporation income taxes consist of a normal tax plus a surtax. The normal tax was 22 percent on the first $25,000 of taxable income, and the surtax was 26 percent on taxable income over $25,000. In other words, the income tax rate was 48 percent on taxable income above $25,000. As part of a temporary tax law, the income tax rates for corporations for 1975 were as follows:

  Normal tax—20 percent on first $25,000 of taxable income; 22 percent on taxable income over $25,000

  Surtax—26 percent on taxable income over $50,000

  This change in rates was for 1975 only. In early 1976, opinions varied as to whether the lower effective tax rates would be extended beyond 1975.

needed to eliminate the 70-hour and longer work weeks for himself and his two key employees. The consultant suggested that they meet in one week to discuss these matters. He also suggested that Mr. Budin specify priorities for the various goals. Finally, he noted that he would also have to contact the firm's accountant to obtain information regarding depreciation rates on fixed assets as well as accounts payable. Mr. Budin agreed to meet in one week to discuss expenses, and he said that he would instruct the firm's accountant to provide Mr. Mosher with the necessary information.

When they met, Mr. Mosher first noted how the accountant had been quite helpful. The accountant put in a great deal of effort to determine that, if inventory was 25.5 percent of sales, trade payables would be 5.2 percent of sales. The accountant could only guess at fixed asset purchases over the next five years. Mr. Mosher noted that since the amount was so small he was going to assume that annual fixed asset expenditures would equal depreciation charges. He then asked Mr. Budin about expenses. The president began by saying that a 30-percent gross margin was a reasonable objective. He then noted that, although it would be difficult, he planned to limit annual increases to 5 percent in operating expenses other than salaries. Mr. Budin had learned his lesson in 1974 and had finally instituted the budget system that Mr. Mosher had previously recommended. Moreover, he was studying various ways to reduce these operating expenses and discussed his efforts in this regard. For example, he had just established a policy that was expected to reduce telephone expense by about 15 percent. Mr. Mosher was convinced that these operating expenses were finally under control.

The discussion then turned to salaries. Mr. Budin said he believed that annual 6-percent increases were reasonable. He reminded Mr. Mosher that he was the only one who had not received adequate increases in the past five years. Thus, in addition to the 6-percent increases, he would like to increase his own salary by $5,000 or $10,000. However, he quickly added that, if necessary, he would not make this adjustment. He then told Mr. Mosher that the firm had to add three new people and that each would command a salary of $15,000. Although he needed these people immediately, he would agree to hiring one in early 1977 and the other two in early 1978.

The president then solicited Mr. Mosher's views regarding tax rates. Mr. Mosher noted that he believed that the lower effective tax rates would remain in effect at least for 1976. Moreover, he was confident that these lower rates would become permanent. Mr. Mosher was surprised at Mr. Budin's reaction. The president not only strongly disagreed with the consultant, but he also instructed Mr. Mosher to use the higher tax rates for planning purposes, even for 1976.

The consultant then asked Mr. Budin about priorities. Mr. Budin said that all the goals were important. If he had to establish priorities, he would. However, he was not sure how he would go about it, so he would have to rely on Mr. Mosher for assistance. They then agreed that Mr. Mosher would make a presentation the next week at a meeting with the president, his two key employees, and the firm's attorney.

EXHIBIT 1
Plumbing and Heating Wholesalers
Industry Averages for Wholesalers with Less Than $1 Million of Sales

	1969	%	1970	%	1971	%	1972	%	1973	%	1974	%
Average net sales	675,666		685,106		701,676		767,148		666,799		659,967	
Average gross margin*	161,022	24	165,638	24	168,061	24	191,125	25	157,052	24	166,703	25
Average income before taxes*	13,205	2	12,464	2	13,491	2	17,738	2	12,509	2	29,046	4

Note: Plumbing and heating wholesalers net sales range from less than $1 million to greater than $6 million.
* Percentage of net sales.
SOURCE: National Supply Association (formerly Central Supply Association), *Reports of Operating Costs—Plumbing, Heating, Cooling and Piping Wholesalers.*

EXHIBIT 2
Budin Company
Income Statements

	1970	1971	1972
Sales	$644,585.66	$630,383.60	$703,467.33
Cost of goods sold	475,310.60	475,380.85	521,938.91
Gross profit	$169,275.06	$155,002.75	$181,528.42
Less operating expenses			
Advertising	132.00	327.66	309.00
Automotive Rep. & gasoline	4,676.28	5,311.22	5,418.68
Freight in	3,111.43	3,241.27	4,151.86
Commissions	—	—	—
Heat, light, power	2,358.29	2,207.80	2,146.52
Insurance	3,456.52	5,401.40	5,143.02
Legal	16.44	—	—
Professional fees	—	—	—
Office cleaning	540.00	1,350.00	300.00
Office supplies	7,098.58	8,199.00	6,209.89
Salaries	97,495.92	105,425.40	91,413.56
Outside commissions	1,119.26	587.63	—
Payroll taxes	4,358.10	4,613.06	5,458.64
Rent	7,200.00	7,200.00	7,560.00
Taxes	6,089.32	501.98	10.19
Telephone & telegraph	2,827.96	3,751.46	3,782.08
Travel & trade	3,607.79	3,292.67	3,023.17
Truck & car rental	9.98	120.71	2,408.45
Depreciation	4,938.93	5,215.42	4,470.28
Other	1,391.32	1,655.97	1,654.61
Bad debt	2,535.62	1,188.54	147.36
Blue Cross Insurance	1,586.63	2,732.27	3,259.04
Misc. labor	491.18	1,671.30	474.60
	$155,041.55	$163,994.76	$147,340.95
Profit before income tax (loss)	$ 14,233.51	$ (8,992.01)	$ 34,187.47
Income tax	3,131.37	—	7,174.98
Net income	$ 11,102.14	$ (8,992.01)	$ 27,012.49

EXHIBIT 2 (continued)

	1973	1974	1975
Sales	$729,073.40	$906,542.38	$935,396.44
Cost of goods sold	528,047.98	653,149.81	656,019.55
Gross profit	$201,025.42	$253,392.57	$279,376.89
Less operating expenses			
Advertising	205.56	204.00	200.18
Automotive rep. & gasoline	6,091.60	7,117.43	11,292.48
Freight in	4,268.70	4,457.68	6,236.64
Commissions	—	91.69	2,202.79
Heat, light, power	2,846.68	2,988.74	3,444.80
Insurance	3,829.49	4,131.47	6,368.40
Legal	—	—	—
Professional fees	304.24	480.00	2,490.00
Office cleaning	262.57	1,116.00	1,050.00
Office supplies	5,897.64	7,730.98	9,989.14
Salaries	95,863.90	114,868.14	131,373.37
Outside commissions	—	—	—
Payroll taxes	7,494.35	8,129.14	9,190.37
Rent	7,560.00	8,280.00	8,280.00
Taxes	7,142.15	7,202.70	8,818.25
Telephone & telegraph	4,147.02	5,718.04	7,292.33
Travel & trade	2,378.00	3,659.90	5,512.43
Truck & car rental	3,612.67	3,693.74	3,859.44
Depreciation	3,915.11	2,967.50	4,242.89
Other	3,127.97	4,236.32	3,753.92
Bad debt	—	1,604.03	—
Blue Cross Insurance	3,265.45	3,382.96	7,670.34
Misc. labor	1,087.85	1,746.30	1,011.06
	$163,300.95	$193,806.76	$234,278.83
Profit before income tax (loss)	$ 37,724.47	$ 59,585.81	$ 45,098.06
Income tax	10,306.80	20,544.31	9,402.28
Net income	$ 27,417.67	$ 39,041.50	$ 35,695.78

EXHIBIT 3
Budin Company
Balance Sheets

	1970	1971	1972	1973	1974	1975
Current assets						
Cash	$ 18,483	$ 30,418	$ 26,237	$ 30,278	$ 35,557	$ 40,126
Accounts receivable	94,069	63,038	93,561	78,740	111,505	109,441
Inventory	184,352	176,507	188,529	205,599	213,038	243,203
Other current	19,164	22,997	26,830	30,662	34,495	49,786
Total current	$316,068	$292,960	$335,157	$345,279	$394,595	$442,556
Fixed assets, net	14,800	12,917	9,339	8,764	12,480	9,545
Total assets	$330,868	$305,877	$344,496	$354,043	$407,075	$452,101
Current liabilities						
Notes payable, bank	$ 12,000	$ 10,000	$ 10,000	$ —	$ —	$ —
Accounts payable	37,874	24,181	35,797	27,418	40,783	48,911
Other current	2,233	1,927	1,918	2,426	3,051	4,253
Total current	$ 52,107	$ 36,108	$ 47,715	$ 29,844	$ 43,834	$ 53,164
Common stock	$233,077	$233,077	$233,077	$233,077	$233,077	$233,077
Retained earnings	45,684	36,692	63,704	91,122	130,164	165,860
Total liabilities & equity	$330,868	$305,877	$344,496	$354,043	$407,075	$452,101

EXHIBIT 4
Summary of Information on Plumbing Supply Industry

The plumbing supply industry has grown rapidly during the post–World War II period. Although there are large firms in the industry, no single firm or group of firms dominates. From 1951 to 1962, industry sales displayed a cyclical pattern with two major peaks, the first in late 1954 and early 1955 and the second in 1959. Unlike the fifties, the decade of the sixties was a period of steady growth. Sales increased in every year from 1963 to 1972. Moreover, gross and net margins remained stable throughout this period.

The majority of plumbing supplies produced are used in new residential construction, especially one-family homes. (The second largest segment of the market is for repairs and remodeling.) Consequently, factors affecting the construction industry also affect the plumbing supply industry, though with a time lag of about six months, since plumbing supplies tend to be used toward the end of construction projects. Two key factors affecting housing, and hence the sale of plumbing supplies, are inflation and mortgage rates. From 1956 to 1976, mortgage rates doubled, increasing from 4½ percent to 9 percent. This increase, together with the rapid inflation of the mid-seventies, produced a substantial slowdown in construction activity. Exhibit 4-A provides data on housing starts for the period 1950 through 1975. Analysts labeled the severity of the recent decline as a "depression," and substantial concern was raised in congressional hearings on the state of the industry. There was widespread belief that a resurgence of inflation in the latter seventies could destroy the industry.

Because of widespread recognition of the need to assist the construction industry and substantially improved economic conditions in 1976, optimism toward industry prospects began to return. Economic analysts, for example, considered a revival in the industry to be the key to overall economic recovery. For this reason, it was believed that the presidential administration and Congress would take measures to assure that the recovery of the construction industry was not impeded. Some observers even saw signs of an emerging boom in pent-up demand for single-family housing that would carry through the 1980s with an average of total housing starts between 2.1 and 2.5 million units per year for at least a decade. The refurbishing of existing housing was also projected to increase strongly. A Citicorp survey, for example, estimated that 15 percent of all homeowners would make major improvements in 1977 and 1978, an increase of 11 percent over 1975's level.

Thus, given the relationship between the plumbing supply and construction industries, the future appeared bright in 1976 for manufacturers and distributors of plumbing supplies, like Budin, provided the economy did not return to the 1973–1975 conditions.

Source: Industry background is drawn from "Building Analysis," *Standard & Poors Industry Survey*, August 1975; and "Is the One-Family House Becoming a Fossil? Far From It," *Fortune*, April 1976.

EXHIBIT 4-A
Housing Starts
(In thousands)

Years	Total Starts	One-Family Starts
1950	1,396	1,154
1955	1,329	1,154
1960	1,296	995
1961	1,365	975
1962	1,492	992
1963	1,642	1,021
1964	1,561	970
1965	1,510	964
1966	1,196	780
1967	1,322	845
1968	1,546	901
1969	1,500	811
1970	1,469	815
1971	2,085	1,153
1972	2,379	1,309
1973	2,058	1,132
1974	1,353	889
1975	1,172	896

SOURCES: *Statistical Abstracts of the United States: Construction Review*, 1974.

PART III
WORKING CAPITAL
MANAGEMENT

Gansett Furniture Company (A)

In mid-June 1976, Marshall Smith, chief financial officer of the Gansett Furniture Company, was trying to determine what financial action to pursue with respect to the firm's projected working capital requirements. These projections indicated a surge in needed funds, but Mr. Smith was uncertain how much of this increase should be viewed as a "permanent" increase—and thus financed with high-cost, long-term funds. Compounding his uncertainty was the fact that Gansett had only recently experienced a substantial reversal of working capital needs in a relatively short period. Mr. Smith was reluctant to undertake long-term financing that would turn out to be in excess of long-term requirements.

BACKGROUND OF THE COMPANY

Gansett Furniture Company, founded in 1940, manufactured upholstered furniture and fixtures.[1] By 1970, the company was in its second generation of management, under the presidency of John Gansett.

Under Mr. Gansett's leadership, the company revamped its antiquated production system; established a royalty-basis relationship with a nationally prominent furniture designer; narrowed and focused the product line; completed a long-needed move to a larger, more efficient facility; and, in the restaurant furniture division, sought and captured a part of the "chain" business.

Sales were concentrated in three principal product/market areas. Major among these was a proprietary line of quality leather-upholstered furniture, which the company manufactured and sold to high-end retailers in the western states through a network of commissioned sales representatives. This "Home Line" accounted for between 45 and 50 percent of Gansett's total sales.

Gansett also manufactured a line of office and institutional furniture in various fabrics, in vinyls, and in leather. This line, also sold through commissioned sales representatives in the western states, accounted for 15 to 20 percent of total company sales.

Gansett's third principal product market was custom-fabricated booths, cabinets, chairs, countertops, and other fixtures for restaurant

---

1. For additional background on ownership, see Gansett Furniture Company (B).

and coffee shop chains, sold on a nationwide basis. This activity represented about 35 percent of Gansett's total sales.

RESULTS FROM 1970 THROUGH 1973

Between 1970 (when Gansett's current president assumed complete control over management) and 1973, Gansett's sales grew rapidly, as shown:

Year	Total Sales (000)
1970	$1,400
1971	1,965
1972	2,430
1973	3,500

The growth in Gansett's Home Line had resulted from a broadening of the company's market area and customer base. Although sales were still largely centered in California, continued increases had been achieved in other western states and in national distribution. The company's customer base, once centered on a small number of local accounts, had grown to the point where, by the end of 1973, the Home Line was sold to more than 400 accounts, with roughly 10 percent of the accounts representing 65 percent of its sales. The success of the Home Line could be attributed to a more stylized, focused product line, broader market coverage, and greatly improved merchandising and promotion. And although most of the growth was in upholstered leather furniture sales, sales in fabrics were becoming increasingly important. In July 1973, for example, the company introduced Gansett Denims, a line of quality upholstered blue denim furniture. By December the denim line had already produced $250,000 in sales to dealers, even though it was just beginning to reach the retail floor.

The growth in the Fabrication Division resulted from increased sales to a small number of restaurant and coffee shop chains. Up until 1970, much of the Fabrication Division's sales consisted of "one-of-a-kind" restaurants. At that time—and coincident with the management reorganization noted earlier—Gansett sought and penetrated the "chain" business. For example, by 1973 the company was fabricating the booths, cabinets, countertops, and chairs for all the new restaurants of a fast-growing national family restaurant. A number of other national restaurant chains were also firm customers of the Fabrication Division.

Gansett's sales growth, however, was not matched by profit growth.

Year	Net before Taxes	% Sales
1970	$(62,000)	(4.4)
1971	44,500	2.3
1972	49,500	2.0
1973	68,100	1.9

One major reason for this was that the company's growth quickly out-stripped the effectiveness of its largely informal controls and procedures. Management, preoccupied with the sales growth and generally overex-tended, was forced to improvise along the way. What it ended up with was an overly complicated, jerry-built system that was limited in its ability to control costs. For example, until mid-1973, as many as eight different people were handling the company's purchasing.

A second reason for the low profitability was that weaknesses in the costing and pricing systems and the absence of profit analysis made it difficult for the company to identify with any consistency specific items in the Furniture Division, and entire jobs in the Fabrication Divi-sion, that might be losing money.

A third reason was that, up until its move to the new 78,000-square-foot facility in January 1973, the company operated out of a five-building, 45,000-square-foot complex, at the cost of significant material-handling and production inefficiencies.

NEW FINANCIAL MANAGER IN 1973

The firm's management group was strengthened in 1973 by the addition of Marshall Smith as chief financial officer. Mr. Smith implemented a system of tight cost controls almost immediately, and overhead costs increased little during the year, while sales increased by more than 40 percent. In addition, a cost analysis of the product line identified un-profitable or marginally profitable items. These items were substantially increased in price or dropped altogether.

1974 PROJECTIONS AND PERFORMANCE

Although 1973 had been a good year for the industry, the outlook for 1974 was mixed. The general uncertainty over economic conditions in 1974 tempered management's optimism. Mr. Smith prepared two sub-stantially different sales and cash flow forecasts for the year, based on alternative economic assumptions.

The more optimistic forecast projected sales of $4 million, or an in-crease of roughly 14 percent over 1973.

Division	1974 Sales Forecast
Home Line	$1,800,000
Office-Institutional	800,000
Fabrication	1,400,000
Total	$4,000,000

In support of the optimistic forecast, management recognized that a substantial part of the Fabrication Division's current production capacity was already committed for 1974. Two accounts alone could generate $1 million in sales volume. The forecast for the Home Line assumed an increase of only $100,000 over 1973's level of $1.7 million, and it made no assumptions about the performance of the new denim line.

The pessimistic forecast assumed sales of $2.8 million, or a 20-percent decline from 1973. Should such a deterioration begin to develop, the company would implement a contingency budget reflecting a substantial and immediate reduction in certain highly discretionary advertising and market development expenses that were currently planned. These reductions could cut as much as $175,000 from the operating budget and still keep the company profitable. Further, although the pessimistic forecast did not reflect it, the company would break even, even if its cost of goods increased to 65 percent.

As it turned out, the economy in 1974 began to decline sharply. Even so, Gansett's sales in the year totaled $3,859,000, just slightly below the $4 million optimistic forecast. Profit before taxes dropped to $36,000. However, in a letter to the company's banker, Mr. Smith noted that the reduced profitability reflected a number of discretionary accounting treatments intended by management to reduce tax liability and promote the firm's liquidity. Perhaps the most significant of these changes was a switch in inventory valuation method from FIFO to LIFO. The net impact was a substantial decrease in ending inventory, which increased cost of goods sold and consequently decreased profit before taxes by $107,000. Second, the company decided to write off as "obsolete" inventory many items purchased for use on subsequently discontinued models. This further reduced before-tax profit by another $35,000. Third, the company chose to expense marketing and advertising costs that it reasonably could have capitalized. This reduced income before taxes by another $40,000. Also, the company's management increased the bad debt reserve to $14,000 from $6,000 (which management felt more clearly reflected historical experience). Along with miscellaneous other writeoffs, management estimated that income before taxes— although reported as $36,000—could have been shown as high as $253,000.

1975 PROJECTIONS AND PERFORMANCE

As a consequence of the substantial "noncash" writeoffs against 1974 income, Gansett found itself with strong cash flow. For example, whereas the cash balance at the end of 1973 had totaled $1,213, by the end of 1974 it had swollen to $151,375, and Gansett's financial officer was actively involved in money market investments. Furthermore, since

Mr. Smith anticipated a drop in sales as the economic recession deepened in 1975, he expected continued net inflows of cash. A reduction in sales would decrease accounts receivable and force production cutbacks.

As 1975 began to unfold, the prospects for a sales drop began to materialize. Sales for the first quarter of 1975 were already below what they were in the same period in 1974. In April 1975, Mr. Smith projected total sales of only $3.7 million for the year, and profit before taxes of $150,000. The estimated before-tax profit was based on the cost structure shown in Table 1.

Rather than decreasing, sales for 1975 turned out to be just slightly ahead of 1974, a total of $3.9 million. Profit before taxes amounted to $51,000, also ahead of 1974's unadjusted estimate, but substantially below the previous year's adjusted figure. (See Exhibits 1 and 2 for financial statements for 1974 and 1975.)

FINANCING ARRANGEMENTS

In August 1973, Gansett had entered into a term loan agreement with the American National Bank in an attempt to restructure a high level of short-term borrowings. The borrowings, in the form of a revolving credit line, had grown in response to working capital requirements, which rose quickly between 1970 and 1973. Sales, as noted earlier, increased from $1.4 million to $3.5 million during the period—a compound growth rate of more than 35 percent per year.

Gansett obtained a $250,000 term loan to pay down the estimated permanent working capital portion of the current accounts receivable revolving credit line of $250,000. However, subsequent experience indi-

TABLE 1
Cost and Profit Projections

Sales	100.0%
Less variable sales expenses (cash discounts; design royalties; commissions; overrides; incentives)	9.0%
	91.0%
Less direct costs	60.0%
Available for overhead and profit	31.0%
Current overhead levels	(In $ thousands)
Factory	$ 505
Sales	241
General and administrative	251
Total overhead	$ 997
Breakeven point	$3,200
Profit before taxes on sales of $3,700	$ 150

cated that the revolving line of credit was still being used to meet long-term requirements. For example, during the 15-month period from August 1973 to October 1974, the average monthly borrowing from the accounts receivable loan was around $90,000, and the daily balance was seldom less than $50,000. In short, Mr. Smith concluded that the accounts receivable loan had been part of the "permanent" working capital.

However, several developments between November 1974 and April 1975 changed the character of Gansett's short-term borrowing requirements:

1. Decrease in working capital requirements
   A. Gansett greatly improved the efficiency of its inventory management. For example, leather, which averaged $160,000 during the first eight months of 1974, had been brought down to a $40,000 to $50,000 level as a result of a very favorable single-sourcing agreement with a major quality supplier.
   B. Accounts receivable, which averaged about 38 days during 1974, averaged only about 27 days in the first quarter of 1975. Two factors contributed. (1) The collection period for Contract Division sales was much shorter than it was for the furniture factory. Since contract sales represented 45 percent of sales during the first quarter (as opposed to the more normal 35 percent), the overall collection period dropped. (2) Watching these accounts more carefully reduced the collection period for the furniture company.
2. Internal cash generation.
   A. Profits were retained in the company as a matter of corporate policy.
   B. Accounting policies, recounted elsewhere, shielded substantial income from taxes.
3. External funds sources. John Gansett invested additional long-term capital in the form of a $120,000 subordinated loan. The loan agreement was executed July 30, 1974.

These three factors combined to improve the company's cash flow dramatically. Gansett's cash flow "turned around" in August 1974 after having been predominantly positive during each of the eight months through April 1974. During this period, inflows exceeded outflows by nearly $480,000. The company had average accumulated cash in the general vicinity of $100,000 to $150,000 in excess of its "permanent" working balance requirements. This cash was invested in 30-day certificates of deposit and commercial paper. In April the company had $200,000 in these investments.

Thus, although Gansett was still borrowing from its accounts receivable line, the character of the borrowings had changed markedly.

Borrowings from the line were no longer functioning as part of the "permanent" working capital. Instead, they served mainly to balance the cash flow during that part of the month when outflows exceeded inflows. Even though the company's daily loan balance from November 1974 through March 1975 exceeded $75,000 on several occasions and $100,000 on one, it *averaged* only $13,000 (Exhibit 3) and was *zero* roughly two-thirds of the time.

Because of its strong cash position, the company requested that its bank replace the current accounts receivable line with a lower-cost unsecured line in the general range of $100,000 to $150,000 for the remainder of the year. The bank agreed with this analysis and granted a one-year line of unsecured credit with a $150,000 limit as of May 1, 1975. The purpose of the unsecured line was to allow the company to "balance" its cash flow during the month. In April 1976, in anticipation of the approaching renegotiation of the unsecured line, Mr. Smith reviewed borrowing experience with the line. He noted that, on the basis of internal figures (shown in Table 2), the line had effectively served its purpose.

However, Mr. Smith believed that the figures also suggested that by March 1976 the size and possibly even the character of the company's needs might be changing once again. In April the loan balance was never below $60,000 and had, for the first time, reached its maximum limits of $150,000 before the end of the month. He believed that the increased borrowing activity could be traced to two principal factors:

1. Gansett's cash outlays for a significant expansion in capacity and working capital in December 1975 had absorbed $90,000. During March and April, Gansett had invested an additional $80,000 in cash for raw materials for expanded operations. Mr. Smith estimated that it would be several weeks before the increased inventory would begin to convert into cash.

2. Gansett's main inventory had built up approximately $170,000 since the first of the year. But Mr. Smith did not view the entire increase as permanent. For example, the leather inventory alone had

TABLE 2
Line Usage

Month	Days of 0 Balance	Daily Average Balance	Range of Loan Balance	Daily Average Net Cash Position
December 1975	30	$ 1,300	$0–$40,000	$180,500
January 1976	25	9,000	0– 45,000	44,200
February	24	3,500	0– 20,000	(2,400)
March	9	23,200	0– 65,000	(40,900)

increased from $47,000 on December 31 to $141,000 on March 31. However, the major reason for that had been the company's decision to forward-buy in anticipation of a price increase scheduled for April 15.

The combined impact on working capital approximated $350,000 when increases of nearly $5,000 in accounts receivable and prepaid expenses from December 31, 1975, to March 31, 1976, were added.

Offsetting these funds uses during the period had been a $100,000 reduction in accounts receivable; a $108,000 reduction in the cash account; $35,000 in increases in customer deposits; and $60,000 in borrowings against the unsecured line.

Mr. Smith concluded that the current unsecured line was not only allowing the company to balance its cash flow during the month but helping finance some of its temporary working capital increases. To accommodate these increases fully, the company wanted to raise its borrowing power to the general range of $250,000 to $300,000 for 90 to 120 days. Over that period, the liquidation of its forward-bought position, a return of the total inventory to a more normal level, and the gradual conversion of the expansion inventory to accounts receivable and ultimately to cash could be expected to reduce the company's short-term borrowing needs at the current sales level.

In late April 1976, Mr. Smith wrote to the firm's bank with respect to the firm's line of credit, which was due to expire May 1. He requested a temporary increase in the line to $300,000 for a 120-day period. He noted that within that period of time the company should be able to identify the part of the surge in working capital that was likely to be permanent and thus to determine how it should be financed over the longer term. The banker agreed to the adjustment and authorized an increase in the line of credit until June 1, 1976, with maximum unsecured borrowing of $250,000.

RECENT DEVELOPMENTS

During April and May 1976, Gansett's working capital requirements clarified somewhat. The company was averaging sales volume at an annualized level of just under $6 million, dramatically above the pace earlier in the year.

As a result of these gains, the company had achieved historical highs in several key areas:

1. As of May 31, the company's total backlog stood at $950,000.
2. Accounts Receivable as of May 31 was $540,000.
3. Inventory as of May 31 was $880,000.

From December 31, 1975, to May 31, 1976, Accounts Receivable and Inventory increased from $1,043,000 to $1,420,000, or $377,000.

TABLE 3
Analysis of Borrowings against Unsecured Line

Month	Days of 0 Balance	Daily Average Balance	Range of Loan Balance
December	30	$ 1,300	$ 0-$ 40,000
January	25	9,000	0- 45,000
February	24	3,500	0- 20,000
March	9	23,200	0- 65,000
April	0	107,800	40,000- 150,000
May	0	182,400	130,000- 220,000

That amount was provided by two major sources: the company's excess cash and, particularly over the last three months, its borrowing against the unsecured line (see Table 3).

WORKING CAPITAL PROJECTIONS

By the end of May 1976, the company was booking business at an annualized sales level of approximately $6 million. Mr. Smith believed that, as shipments began to approximate these levels, accounts receivable and four "true" inventory turns[2] could require a wide range of working capital investments, as shown in Table 4.

TABLE 4
Capital Projections
(in $000)

	Low	Probable	High
Sales	$5,000	$5,500	$6,000
Accounts receivable (45 days)	625	690	750
Inventory (4 true turns)	900	990	$1,080
	$1,525	$1,680	1,830
May 31 levels	1,420	1,420	1,420
Required increases	$ 105	$ 260	$ 410

---

2. "True" inventory turns equal ending inventory divided into cost of goods sold.

Exhibit 4 projects profits before taxes and interest on the term loan, and Exhibit 5 projects cash flows before taxes and existing term loan payments based on a sales level of $6 million for the 12 months ending June 30, 1977. These estimates, prepared by Mr. Smith for the banker, were based on an assumed average collection period of 45 days and four true inventory turns. Any improvements in these ratios that the company might achieve would obviously yield lower working capital requirements at any given level of sales.

Beyond the working capital increases, Gansett would need capital to pay off a three-year note. A payment of $43,500 would be due August 31, 1976, and a liquidating payment of $17,000 would be due December 31, 1976.

Mr. Smith believed that, even though projections were by their very character limited, they could suggest the general size of the working capital increases that might be required. His projections strongly suggested that the company would require additional capital. He was unsure, however, how much, if any, of these requirements should be financed with long-term capital.

The importance of accurately determining Gansett's permanent working capital requirement went beyond the loss of financial flexibility that an under estimation of permanent needs could mean. The current differential between short- and long-term rates meant that overstating permanent needs could lock Gansett into redundant cash and unnecessarily high rates for a long time. Mr. Smith expected term debt cost to be at least a full percentage point higher than a revolving credit line. For these reasons he wanted to develop the best possible estimate of permanent working capital requirements.

EXHIBIT 1
Gansett Furniture Company
Statement of Income and Retained Earnings

	Year Ended December 31	
	1975	1974*
Sales, net of cash discounts of $66,460 and $78,746	$3,904,848	$3,859,227
Cost of sales	3,031,121	2,836,853
	$ 873,727	$1,022,374
Selling, general, and administrative expenses		
Selling	432,541	584,286
General and administrative	370,644	372,019
	803,185	956,305
Income from operations	$ 70,542	$ 66,069
Other		
Interest expense	36,320	42,127
Other income, principally interest	(16,550)	(12,431)
	19,770	29,696
Income before taxes on income	$ 50,772	$ 36,373
Provision for taxes on income	14,000	12,200
Net income	$ 36,772	$ 24,173
Retained earnings at beginning of year	81,949	57,776
Retained earnings at end of year	$ 118,721	$ 81,949
Net income per common share	$2.28	$1.50

* Reclassified to conform with 1975 presentation.

EXHIBIT 2
Gansett Furniture Company
Balance Sheet

	December 31	
	1975	1974
Assets		
Current assets		
Cash, including short-term investments of $50,000 in 1975 at cost, which approximates market, and $150,000 of certificates of deposit in 1974	$ 114,267	$ 151,375
Accounts receivable, less allowance for doubtful accounts of $10,000 and $14,000 (pledged)	430,068	295,787
Inventories (pledged)	613,238	599,605
Prepaid expenses and other current assets	31,772	29,273
Total current assets	$1,189,345	$1,076,040
Property and equipment, net (pledged)	102,594	81,657
	$1,291,939	$1,157,697
Liabilities and shareholders' equity		
Current liabilities		
Accounts payable	$ 373,506	$ 283,994
Accrued expenses	76,105	100,843
Customer deposits	20,257	25,598
Current portion of notes payable	95,912	31,774
Income taxes	10,330	
Deferred income taxes	20,704	22,380
Total current liabilities	$ 596,814	$ 464,589
Notes payable, less current portion	200,502	237,433
Subordinated long-term debt	120,000	120,000
Deferred income taxes	4,072	1,896
Commitments	$ 324,574	$ 359,329
Shareholders' equity		
Common stock, $8 par value		
Authorized—125,000 shares		
Outstanding—16,136 shares	129,088	129,088
Capital in excess of par value	122,742	122,742
Retained earnings, per accompanying statement	118,721	81,949
	$ 370,551	$ 333,779
	$1,291,939	$1,157,697

EXHIBIT 3
Gansett Furniture Company
Accounts Receivable Borrowing Line: Average Monthly Balance
(Rounded to Nearest 000)

8/73	$118,000
9/73	116,000
10/73	87,000
11/73	70,000
12/73	0
1/74	23,000
2/74	45,000
3/74	39,000
4/74	143,000
5/74	100,000
6/74	103,000
7/74	144,000
8/74	117,000
9/74	136,000
10/74	89,000
11/74	26,000
12/74	0
1/75	19,000
2/75	5,000
3/75	15,000

EXHIBIT 4
Gansett Furniture Company
Projection of Sales and Profit and Loss (000)

	July/76	Aug.	Sept.	Oct.	Nov.	Dec.	Jan./77	Feb.	Mar.	Apr.	May	June	Total
Sales	$375	$475	$460	$470	$505	$515	$515	$515	$530	$530	$555	$555	$6,000
Less Var. sales exp. (10.5%)	40	50	48	49	53	54	54	54	56	56	58	58	630
Cost of Sales (72%)													
Direct labor	94	118	115	118	126	129	129	129	132	132	137	137	1,500
Mat. & fac. ovhd.	176	224	214	220	238	242	242	242	250	250	261	261	2,820
	310	392	377	387	417	425	425	425	438	438	458	458	4,950
Gross margin after var. exp.	65	83	83	83	88	90	90	90	92	92	97	97	1,050
Less Sales & del. exp.	35	35	35	35	35	35	35	35	35	35	35	35	420
Gen. & adm.	25	25	25	25	25	25	25	25	25	25	25	25	300
Earnings before interest and taxes	$ 5	$ 23	$ 23	$ 23	$ 28	$ 30	$ 30	$ 30	$ 32	$ 32	$ 37	$ 37	$ 330

EXHIBIT 5
Gansett Furniture Company
Projection of Cash Flows (000)

	July/76	Aug.	Sept.	Oct.	Nov.	Dec.	Jan./77	Feb.	Mar.	Apr.	May	June
Cash inflows												
(A/R = 45 days)	$390	$ 362	$ 425	$ 468	$ 465	$ 487	$ 510	$ 515	$ 515	$ 523	$ 530	$ 542
Cash outflows												
Add. to inventory	386	306	354	416	385	371	371	404	382	436	400	400
Var. sales exp.	40	50	48	49	53	54	54	54	56	56	58	58
Sales, gen., & adm.	60	60	60	60	60	60	60	60	60	60	60	60
Other		44				17						
Total outflows	$486	$ 460	$ 462	$ 525	$ 498	$ 502	$ 485	$ 518	$ 498	$ 552	$ 518	$ 518
Net cash flow	(96)	(98)	(37)	(57)	(33)	(15)	25	(3)	17	(29)	12	24
Cum. net cash flow	$ (96)	$(194)	$(231)	$(288)	$(321)	$(336)	$(311)	$(314)	$(297)	$(326)	$(314)	$(290)

Gansett Furniture Company
Projection of Inventory and Accounts Receivable

	July/76	Aug.	Sept.	Oct.	Nov.	Dec.	Jan./77	Feb.	Mar.	Apr.	May	June
Ending A/R												
(A/R = 45 days)	$ 550	$ 662	$ 698	$ 700	$ 740	$ 768	$ 773	$ 773	$ 787	$ 795	$ 820	$ 832
Inventory available during month	910	1,026	990	1,014	1,092	1,113	1,113	1,113	1,146	1,146	1,200	1,200
Less use this month	270	342	330	338	364	371	371	371	382	382	400	400
	$ 640	$ 684	$ 660	$ 676	$ 728	$ 742	$ 742	$ 742	$ 764	$ 764	$ 800	$ 800
Invent. req. next month	1,026	990	1,014	1,092	1,113	1,113	1,113	1,146	1,146	1,200	1,200	1,200
Add to inv. this month	$ 386	$ 306	$ 354	$ 416	$ 385	$ 371	$ 371	$ 404	$ 382	$ 436	$ 400	$ 400

Note: Inventory calculated assumes four true turns per year.

Fund for Government Investors

At approximately 11:30 A.M. on Monday May 25, 1977, Richard Garvey, vice-president of the Fund for Government Investors, was informed by the company's accountant that roughly $500,000 would be available for investment that day. Since investments had to be made by noon, Mr. Garvey quickly huddled with Don Conner, president, to finalize security purchases that day.

BACKGROUND

The Fund for Government Investors was incorporated in Maryland in October 1974 and in 1977 had 200 million shares authorized with a par value of $.001. As of March 1977, 36.8 million shares were outstanding. The fund was an open-end, no-load, investment company specializing in short-term investments in marketable debt securities issued by the U.S. government, its agencies and instrumentalities. (See Exhibit 1 for a list of typical securities.) The fund's sole objective was stated to be the achievement of current income with safety of principal.

Since beginning operations, the fund had grown rapidly. From 1975 to 1976, it increased its assets from $9 million to $34 million. Earnings distributed during the year approximated the returns available on short-term Treasury Bills, repurchase agreements, and 30-day certificates of deposit. The rate of return for the year (1976) averaged 5.1 percent. (See Exhibits 2 and 3 for recent financial statements.)

The most active users of the fund's services were professional money managers. Additionally, investment advisers, bank trust departments, trade associations, and business people moved hundreds of thousands of dollars in and out daily. The fund's principal services to these investors were convenience and flexibility. It eliminated a great deal of paperwork for many managers handling a large number of small accounts. Instead of having to develop and manage a number of portfolios geared to the maturity and income requirements of a wide clientele, the fund permitted money managers to participate in high-yielding investments without regard to maturity. For example, Mr. Garvey noted that a bank trust custodian might manage $20 million representing 200 different accounts. Close management of such accounts was likely to involve substantial administrative expenses. Keeping track of maturities and yield opportunities (and risks) made the task uneconomical. More-

over, since account investments had to be made on an individual basis
and since the average account size was small, the trust officer would be
closed out of higher-denomination, more profitable securities and the
possibility for profitable diversification would be diminished. The fund
proposed to remedy these burdens by permitting "no-penalty" withdrawals, participating in higher-yield securities (by pooling individual
accounts), and reducing the restrictions on investment portfolios by
investing in a broad range of securities. The fund also permitted the
custodian to keep track of individual accounts with relative ease and
would relieve the trust administrator of the responsibility and risks of
security selection.

FUND MANAGEMENT

The fund received investment advice and management services from
Money Management Associates. Under an agreement with Money Management Associates, the fund paid a fee at an annual rate of .5 percent
of the fund's average net assets. Other expenses of the fund, excluding
interest and extraordinary legal expenses, could not exceed .5 percent
of the average daily net assets per annum.

INVESTMENT POLICY

The fund invested in short-term U.S. government securities, consisting
primarily of Treasury Bills, and short-term notes of the Federal National
Mortgage Association, Federal Home Loan Banks, and the Federal Farm
Credit Agencies. In addition, the fund invested in bonds, debentures,
and notes of these issuers and other federal agencies that matured within
two years and were guaranteed by the U.S. government. It also purchased
U.S. government securities under "repurchase" agreements.

By investing primarily in short-term securities, the fund hoped to
minimize fluctuations in the market value of its portfolio. Under no circumstances was the fund permitted to invest in securities that matured
in more than two years. The average maturity of the fund's portfolio
reflected the managers' expectations of yield-rate trends over the next
12 months. When interest rates were expected to rise over the 12-month
period, there was a desire to keep the portfolio relatively short-term to
have the liquidity to partake of higher future yields. Conversely, when
the fund's managers anticipated a decline in market yields, they attempted to lengthen the average maturity of the portfolio.

INVESTMENT RESTRICTIONS

The fund, aside from being explicitly restricted with respect to maturity and type of investments, was not permitted to borrow money except as a temporary measure to facilitate redemptions (in such cases, borrowings were restricted to 30 percent or less of total assets at current value). Additionally, it was not permitted to sell securities short; write options; underwrite securities of other issuers; purchase or sell real estate, commodities, or commodity contracts; or loan money to others (excepting repurchase agreements). It was not permitted to purchase a security while borrowing was outstanding.

DIVIDENDS

The fund distributed all its net income on a daily basis. Dividends were declared on each day that the fund was open for business. Shareholders received dividends in additional shares unless they elected to receive cash. Payment was made monthly in additional shares at the net asset value (discussed later) of the fund on the payable date or in cash, if preferred.

The fund's net income consisted of all interest income accrued and discounts earned plus or minus any realized gains or losses, less estimated expenses of the fund.

The fund was not expected to realize any long-term capital gains or losses; however, if any were realized, they were distributed once every year.

NET ASSET VALUE AND AMORTIZED COST BASIS

Net asset value per share was determined by adding the market or appraised value of all securities and all other assets, deducting liabilities and dividing by the number of shares outstanding.

United States government securities maturing within one year were valued at amortized cost. Amortized cost was the purchase price of the security plus accumulated discount or accrued interest from the date of the purchase. This method of valuation did not take into account unrealized gains or losses due to short-term market fluctuations, and it tended to stabilize the price of the fund's shares. Securities with maturities over one year were valued at market.

The amortized cost basis of valuation could often lead to a net asset value different from market value. When interest rates declined, the fund's market value would rise; when interest rates rose, its market value would decline (owing, of course, to the inverse relationship

TABLE 1
Impact on Value Per Share and Shareholder Position of Amortized Cost Basis Compared with Market Value
Effect of Amortized Cost Bases

	Declining Interest Rates	Rising Interest Rates
Fund net redemptions	Improve existing shares	Dilute existing shares
Fund net seller	Dilute existing shares	Improve existing shares

between yield and security price changes). To the extent that the fund's adjusted cost calculation of the short-term securities differed from the actual liquidation value, the price at which a shareholder purchased or redeemed shares would correspondingly differ from the per-share liquidation value of the portfolio. Thus, when interest rates were declining and purchases of fund shares exceeded redemptions, the interest of existing shareholders could be diluted. Declining interest rates and net redemptions of fund shares or rising rates and net purchases of fund shares could enhance the interests of existing shareholders. When interest rates were declining, the fund's valuation method tended to understate the percentage rate of net investment income per share. When interest rates were rising, the reverse was true. (These relationships are shown in Table 1.)

The fund's managers believed that the amortized cost basis offered the most consistent and conservative method of valuing short-term investments.

INVESTMENT STRATEGY

Aside from its overall investment policy, the fund's investment strategy was built around a conception of the trend of interest rates over the next 12 months. Expectation of higher interest rates implied shorter-term investments; lower interest rates suggested longer-term investments.

In developing a sense for the trend of interest rates, Mr. Garvey paid close attention to actions and pronouncements of the Federal Reserve, which might reveal intentions with respect to monetary policy. Normally the Fed's intentions were purposely disguised and, if revealed, were formulated in terms of general policy targets to preserve maximum flexibility. It was particularly difficult to predict interest rate movements when it seemed that the Fed might be changing policy. For example, Fed policy of monetary ease had been pursued since the fall of 1976 to encourage and support the economic recovery. By May 1977, the recovery had developed momentum and there was renewed concern over the pace of inflation. Many observers wondered whether the Fed would attempt to moderate the expansion to keep inflation from accelerating again. However, the premature moderation of the economic recovery might stall it and possible even reverse it. Because of the uncertainty, Mr. Garvey thought a shift in monetary policy might be near, and he followed statements by Federal Reserve Chairman Arthur Burns with particular scrutiny. He was especially intrigued by recent testimony by Dr. Burns before a congressional committee (Exhibit 4), in which the prospect for higher interest rates was raised.

Even with insights into monetary policy, forecasting of near-term interest rate changes was subject to considerable uncertainty. Mr. Garvey noted, for example, that rapid and substantial investment of "petrodollars" by Arab countries in short-term Treasury securities had recently added a new dimension to the volatility of short-term rates. For such reasons, the fund's management had decided against purchasing the services of various economic consulting firms that attempted to project interest rate movements with the use of sophisticated econometric models. The fund's managers were simply not convinced that predictive accuracy was high enough to warrant the expense. According to Mr. Garvey, the fund's managers basically relied on an analysis of Federal Reserve statements and actions along with market "intuition" to estimate the trend of short-term rates.

SECURITY CHOICE

Throughout the morning, the fund managers had been receiving phone calls from banks and investors who were calling to inform them of cash deposited or of requests for withdrawal (share redemption). Under the fund's terms, a request for cash withdrawal had to be made by noon on the day desired. Conversely, new money invested in the fund had to be in the form of federal funds (that is, collected bank balances) before it would begin earning money for the investor. Moreover, such deposits had to be recorded by noon to earn interest for that day.

As the fund managers were informed of intended deposits or withdrawals for that day, they relayed the information to their accountant, who recorded the amounts. In addition, the accountant was responsible for determining which portfolio securities would mature that day and what their denominations were. Throughout the morning the collection of data generated a running total indicating the net cash position anticipated by noon that day. By 11:30, the fund managers typically expected the bulk of transactions to have been recorded and thus used the calculated net cash position as of that time to estimate investible funds.

As noted previously, on this particular morning the fund's accountant advised the fund managers that $500,000 would be available for investment. Within minutes, Mr. Conner and Mr. Garvey had narrowed the

choice of securities to three: (1) a discount one-year Treasury Bill
selling at 94.340; (2) a six-month Federal Intermediate Credit Bank
Note with a 5.6-percent coupon selling at par; and (3) a nine-month
Bank for Cooperatives Note with a 5½-percent coupon selling at 99.856.
Aside from the immediate considerations of relative yields, the fund
managers were also uncertain how long they should commit their
investment.

EXHIBIT 1
Fund for Government Investors
Portfolio of Investments
December 31, 1976

Payable at Maturity			Amortized Cost & Value*	Yield on Date of Purchase (%)
United States Treasury Bills				
$ 500,000	Due	January 6, 1977	$ 499,598	6.02
50,000	Due	February 8, 1977	49,736	5.13
500,000	Due	February 10, 1977	497,282	5.02
500,000	Due	February 17, 1977	496,808	5.02
500,000	Due	February 24, 1977	496,553	4.71
430,000	Due	March 3, 1977	426,745	4.58
7,725,000	Due	April 21, 1977	7,621,007	4.58
1,000,000	Due	May 12, 1977	981,671	5.25
500,000	Due	May 19, 1977	490,381	5.22
700,000	Due	May 26, 1977	686,809	4.86
500,000	Due	June 2, 1977	490,358	4.74
500,000	Due	June 9, 1977	490,027	4.68
500,000	Due	June 16, 1977	489,605	4.68
1,000,000	Due	June 28, 1977	970,085	6.53
1,000,000	Due	October 18, 1977	961,414	5.07
$15,905,000			$15,648,079	
United States Treasury Notes				
$ 1,032,500	Due	June 30, 1977	$ 1,000,446	6.50
Federal Farm Credit Bank				
1,500,000	Due	January 27, 1977	1,495,179	4.53
300,000	Due	January 28, 1977	298,972	4.73
2,000,000	Due	February 22, 1977	1,987,144	4.55
700,000	Due	March 15, 1977	692,903	5.16
$ 4,500,000			$ 4,474,198	

EXHIBIT 1 (continued)

Payable at Maturity			Amortized Cost & Value*	Yield on Date of Purchase (%)
Federal National Mortgage Association				
200,000	Due	January 27, 1977	199,350	4.53
200,000	Due	January 28, 1977	199,083	6.44
1,500,000	Due	January 31, 1977	1,493,733	6.32
1,390,000	Due	February 1, 1977	1,382,805	6.36
80,000	Due	February 2, 1977	79,655	4.96
1,125,000	Due	February 3, 1977	1,118,863	6.22
350,000	Due	February 7, 1977	347,822	6.39
3,000,000	Due	February 15, 1977	2,983,238	4.56
144,510	Due	March 10, 1977	142,995	5.62
$ 7,989,510			$ 7,947,544	
Federal Land Banks				
$ 414,900	Due	January 20, 1977	$ 413,687	5.96
Federal Intermediate Credit Banks				
1,046,089	Due	January 3, 1977	1,045,816	4.77
104,169	Due	February 1, 1977	103,717	5.18
791,056	Due	April 4, 1977	779,265	6.22
1,043,875	Due	June 1, 1977	1,019,607	5.87
521,831	Due	July 5, 1977	507,012	5.80
$ 3,507,020			$ 3,455,417	
Farmers Home Administration				
$ 1,006,495	Due	March 31, 1977	$ 1,054,332	6.30
Government National Mortgage Association				
$ 154,088	Due	April 1, 1977	$ 152,141	5.20
$34,509,513			$34,145,844	

Average Maturity of Portfolio   89 days

* Same cost is used for federal income tax purposes.

EXHIBIT 2
Fund for Government Investors
Financial Statements

Statement of operations
For the year ended December 31, 1976

Investment income		$947,878
Expenses		
Investment advisory fee	$ 83,600	
Custodian fee	15,376	
Data processing	7,048	
General & administrative	36,940	
Total		-142,964
Deduct		
Waiver of investment advisory fee	32,959	
Expenses assumed by investment adviser	13,163	
Total		46,122
Net expenses		96,842
Net investment income		$851,036

Statement of assets and liabilities
December 31, 1976

Assets		
Investments in United States government securities at value		$34,145,844
Cash in custodian bank		24,323
Total assets		$34,170,167
Liabilities		
Dividends payable	$81,066	
Expenses payable & accrued	10,856	
Subscriptions for shares	24,822	
Total liabilities		116,744
Net assets (equivalent to $1 per share)		$34,053,423

151

EXHIBIT 3
Fund for Government Investors
Statement of Changes in Net Assets

	For the Year Ended December 31, 1976	January 22, 1975 (Commencement of Operations) to December 31, 1975
Net investment income		
Distributed to shareholders	$ 851,036	$ 130,121
From capital share transactions (at constant net asset value of $1 per share)		
Proceeds from sale of shares	$99,472,702	$16,472,422
Dividends reinvested	351,980	102,856
Total	99,824,682	16,575,278
Cost of shares redeemed	(74,891,259)	(7,555,278)
Increase in net assets	$24,933,423	$ 9,020,000
Net assets—beginning of period	9,120,000	100,000
Net assets—end of period	$34,053,423	$ 9,120,000

EXHIBIT 4
Fund for Government Investors

Excerpts from statement by Arthur F. Burns, Chairman, Board of Governors of the Federal Reserve System, before the Committee on Banking, Housing and Urban Affairs, U.S. Senate, May 3, 1977

The Federal Open Market Committee was well aware of its heavy responsibility to encourage economic expansion and yet help to curb inflation when it met last month to discuss the longer-run growth of the monetary aggregates. The Committee decided to leave unchanged over the year ending in the first quarter of 1978 the previous growth range of 4½ to 6½ percent in M-1, which is a monetary measure confined to currency and demand deposits. For M-2, and likewise for M-3, the upper boundary of the growth range was reduced, however, by ½ of a percentage point. Consequently, the growth ranges projected for the coming year are 7 to 9½ percent for M-2 and 8½ to 11 percent for M-3. As the committee may recall, M-2 includes savings and consumer-type time deposits at commercial banks besides currency and demand deposits, while M-3 is a still more comprehensive aggregate—since it also includes the deposits at savings banks, savings and loan associations, and credit unions.

. . . .

Events during the past several months have again demonstrated quite clearly that the twists and turns that occur in financial markets often are dominated by developments unrelated to Federal Reserve actions. For instance, from late in 1976 to late April, the Federal funds rate—the one interest rate over which the Federal Reserve has close control—traded within a narrow range between $4\frac{5}{8}$ percent and $4\frac{3}{4}$ percent; yet, other market rates of interest in that period fluctuated over ranges as wide as a full percentage point. Those fluctuations in interest rates in large part reflected changing public perceptions of the outlook for the Federal budget. Thus, interest rates moved upward sharply when the administration proposed a new fiscal policy, including the so-called rebate program; and they fell markedly when the President announced that he had dropped the rebate plan.

Children's Memorial Hospital (A)

On March 23, 1976, Allan Karas, chairman of the Finance Committee of Children's Memorial Hospital, was deliberating a possible change in the hospital's long-standing liquidity policy and banking arrangements. He had been concerned that the hospital had relatively little near-term financial flexibility and had been asked to present his recommendations to the hospital's board of directors the following day.

BACKGROUND

Children's Memorial Hospital was founded in Springfield, Massachusetts, in 1949 as a nonprofit voluntary corporation, specializing in the treatment and rehabilitation of severely handicapped children and teenagers. In 1976 the hospital had a capacity of approximately 110 patient beds and almost 400 employees. On September 30, 1975, at the end of the fiscal year, the hospital had assets of $5.7 million in unrestricted funds and assets of $211,000 in restricted funds (Exhibit 1-B). Total patient revenues for the year were approximately $4.6 million, and the hospital experienced a net loss of more than $750,000 for the year (Exhibit 1-A).

Fiscal year 1975 had been a year of crisis for the hospital; a series of financial shocks had had a profound impact on profitability and liquidity. Apart from these unexpected setbacks, the hospital had also been adversely affected by delays and interruptions in payment for services typical of the health care industry.

OPERATING DIFFICULTIES

Operating losses of almost $360,000 and $780,000 were incurred in fiscal years 1974 and 1975, respectively. A further difficulty for management had been the improper recording of financial transactions, which had the effect of understating the magnitude of losses as they were being incurred and thus taking longer to alert management of trouble. Operating losses constituted an important drain on working capital.

As a consequence of the drain from operations, net working capital plunged from $228,000 at fiscal year-end 1974 to a negative $284,000 at fiscal year-end 1975. The auditor's letter to the board of directors of the hospital (Exhibit 1) noted that Children's Memorial was in arrears on payment of withheld employee payroll taxes and on principal and interest payments on a sizable construction loan payable to a bank. Because of the loan's default, the bank had the option to declare the entire loan due and payable, although as of March 23, 1976, the bank had not done so.

As noted before, complicating the operating difficulties was the improper treatment of certain transactions and events, which seriously understated the magnitude of the hospital's financial difficulties. For example, in contrast to the audited loss of $761,000 from operations reported by the outside accountants, internal records had shown a loss of only $243,000 for fiscal year 1975. Several of the adjustments required by the auditors are summarized here:

1. *Free Service and Bad Debt Allowance* $165,000
   Although budgeted, a sufficient amount had not been set up in the reserve on a monthly basis to offset the necessary writeoffs. The auditors strongly recommended further investigation of outstanding accounts receivable balance due from both welfare and parents, to determine whether they were collectible or whether a larger reserve should be set up in sufficient amounts to cover their possible writeoff.

2. *Interest Adjustment* $130,000
   An adjustment to interest expense was necessary since the hospital accountant had capitalized interest rather than expensing it.

3. *Accounts Payable* $75,000
   A large number of purchases were made directly by department heads without advising the director of financial control. When the bills arrived for payment, the director simply stuffed them into a drawer unless he had approved the purchase request. This obscured substantial hospital liabilities.

4. *Depreciation Adjustment* $20,000
   The hospital accountants had used a useful life estimate of 50 years rather than the more appropriate $33\frac{1}{3}$-year basis.

5. *Other Adjustments* $56,000
   The hospital should have expensed $10,000 to adjust prepaid insurance and $25,000 to record additional liabilities discovered during the audit, and in addition, a $21,000 adjustment necessary for work that was done on the main building.

As a consequence of these discoveries, stringent financial controls were implemented, and a new, more competent accounting and financial staff was hired. The hospital's director also ordered more frequent and extensive internally developed financial reports.

PAYMENT SYSTEM

Children's Memorial, like other health care providers, rarely received payment for health services directly from patients. More typically, patients had medical care insurance or were protected by state welfare programs. In either case, Children's Memorial received payment from these "third parties" upon submission and review of claims. Not only did this create a payment lag, but the practice also involved other uncertainty since hospital claims were subject to adjustment in cases where the "allowable costs" as contractually defined by the third party differed from hospital claims.

State Programs

State welfare payments were generally more unpredictable in timing and amount than private insurance plans such as Blue Cross/Blue Shield, since welfare payments were strongly affected by state budget policies. Because of the hospital's specialization in intensive care and long-term rehabilitation, its patients were to a large extent covered by joint state/federal welfare programs. For example, in 1975 roughly 56 percent of all Children's Memorial revenues were from the state welfare department, with another 22 percent paid by Blue Cross.

In September 1975, the state legislature had seriously considered drastic cutbacks in welfare funds for health care. Among the reported proposals were: (1) the elimination of all in-hospital care for 45,000 General Relief recipients; (2) a 6-percent reduction in state reimbursement for all welfare patient categories; (3) cancellation of a 9-percent cost-of-living increase that was scheduled to go into effect on October 1, 1975; (4) wholesale cutbacks for medically indigent (Medicaid) recipients (largely children of poor families and elderly patients); and (5) a massive cutback in nursing home services, which would force patients to stay in hospitals longer than necessary.

The hospital's executive director viewed the impact of these changes on the hospital as catastrophic. She announced that, to survive, the hospital would have to close its new wing,[1] close 46 percent of its beds, reduce outpatient visits by 44 percent, eliminate nine departments, and lay off about 40 percent of the hospital staff.

As a result of organized and intensive appeals by health care providers, the final version of the health care cuts that went into effect differed from earlier proposals but resulted in considerable uncertainty about impacts on specific patients. In late December 1975, the executive director of the hospital wrote to the commissioner of human

---

1. For further background, see Children's Memorial Hospital (B).

services seeking clarification in order to plan hospital operations; she was advised that the hospital's patients would not be affected. However, she learned from a state senator in February 1976 that the governor had (once again) proposed a bill to control hospital costs, and that it was the highest-priority item in the governor's program for the state fiscal year beginning July 1, 1976.

Apart from possible severe swings in state health care spending, institutions like Children's Memorial encountered another financial difficulty. In recent years state funds had become depleted before the end of the fiscal year, generally in the spring. In consequence, Children's Memorial lost cash flow from the state for two or three months until supplemental funds were acquired. This seriously eroded the hospital's liquidity and raised financial requirements.

Private Plans

Private medical insurance plans were also a source of uncertainty in the hospital's liquidity management. Rising medical care costs and usage were outstripping increases in insurance premiums. As a consequence, private health care insurance providers were also experiencing adverse financial shocks. The State Blue Cross Association, for example, had recently written to hospital administrators advising them of the effects of rising health care costs. The association noted, for example, that if the current rate of costs were to continue, health insurance premiums would have to double by 1980. Between January 1, 1974, and March 1, 1976, the Blue Cross Association had already lost $50 million. While subscription premiums were raised substantially to meet rising costs, the letter stated, "Our financial results will be closely monitored in the months ahead. If hospitals do not operate within projected budgets, it will seriously impair our operating results and may require Blue Cross to institute emergency action to assure its financial integrity."

EXISTING LIQUIDITY ARRANGEMENTS

To meet payment lags and other liquidity requirements, Children's Memorial had a $500,000 line of credit at the Mountain National Bank and a $100,000 line with the Landview National Bank. The hospital had had a long-standing deposit relationship with both banks. The Mountain National line was at prime rate plus 2 percent. Draw-down from the line was evidenced by either 90-day or demand notes. As of March 23, 1976, Children's Memorial was borrowing $500,000 from Mountain plus another $100,000 from the Landview National Bank on the following basis:

Bank	Borrowing	Amount
Mountain	90-day due 4/26/76 @ 7¾%	$350,000
Mountain	Demand—29 days @ 7¾%	150,000
Landview	Demand—29 days @ 7¾%	100,000

Offsetting its borrowing, Children's Memorial also had a sizable investment in marketable securities and other deposits. In part, these securities were needed as collateral for the credit line, but they also provided investment income to the hospital. For example, the Mountain line of credit was completely collateralized with $500,000 worth of certificates of deposit at the bank, and the Landview National Bank line was collateralized by savings deposits of $100,000. These accounts and investment were as follows:

Cash accounts	$ 312,345
Savings account	201,559
Certificate of deposit (@ 5%)	500,000
Securities (@ market)	179,238
Total	$1,193,142

FINANCIAL PROJECTIONS

The single most difficult estimate to develop was the timing of receipts from third-party payers. This uncertainty, in fact, was the major reason for the hospital's lines of credit. A cash flow forecast prepared for the March 24 to April 30 period indicated that the hospital's liquidity would be depleted by the end of the period. The cash balance at the end of April was projected to be less than $1,500. The full lines of credit, totaling $600,000, would be completely used. At March 24 the hospital had approximately $1.3 million in Accounts Receivable and $1 million in Accounts Payable. Approximately $500,000 in Accounts Receivable were over 90 days old. Of the hospital's Accounts Payable, almost $600,000 were more than 90 days past due.

Completely using up all the hospital's lines of credit disturbed Mr. Karas greatly. Aggravating his concern was the interest differential between credit cost and interest earnings on collateral. At the December meeting of the board, he had raised the general problem. He had reported that as of November 30, 1975, the hospital had $177,000 in operating cash and savings, $260,000 in certificates of deposit, and $356,000 in capital market securities. Mr. Karas had estimated that interest costs on the line of credit exceeded income earned on the securities used for collateral by $15,000 on an annual basis.

A board member had then suggested that the securities be sold to pay off the line and thus save financing costs. Mr. Karas readily acknowledged the logic of this suggestion, but thought that it did not go to the heart of the problem, namely, insufficient financial flexibility. Perhaps it *would* be best to pay off the line to save the financing costs, but this option, he believed, could not be considered until the larger problem was resolved. Mr. Karas then noted that his preference was to attempt to collateralize the lines of credit with the hospital's accounts receivables and to keep the marketable securities as financial reserve. He advised the board that the banks would probably not be receptive to such a proposal since current collateral was safer, but he requested and was authorized permission to pursue the matter.

An exploratory discussion Mr. Karas had with one of Mountain's senior loan officers revealed that, as a matter of bank policy, a line of credit could not be collateralized by accounts receivable. Thus, if the marketable securities were sold, the line would have to be paid off. The loan officer further advised Mr. Karas that the Landview National Bank was likely to respond similarly.

Mr. Karas was disappointed and upset that the hospital's long-standing bank was unwilling to consider an alternative arrangement, particularly one widely available to other types of corporations. For years, Children's Memorial had kept its principal operating and payroll accounts at the bank. The average balances were quite large in these accounts. Moreover, the hospital deposited withheld payroll taxes at the bank. Mr. Karas thought that a more acceptable option should be available in the hospital's banking relationship, particularly if the hospital were willing to make do with a smaller line of credit. For example, if Children's Memorial were to liquidate its marketable securities and pay off its line of credit, the hospital would develop a peak anticipated cash shortage of $200,000. If Children's Memorial were to secure a $250,000 line of credit with its accounts receivable, the bank would certainly be protected and the hospital would have increased financial flexibility and reduced financing costs. In short, he believed that Children's Memorial could do better.

BANK SEARCH

At the January meeting of the board, Mr. Karas reported his dissatisfaction with the hospital's existing bank arrangements and obtained approval to explore alternatives. He was asked to head a search committee composed of several members of the Finance Committee.

After some investigation, Mr. Karas developed a list of banks to approach (balance sheets are shown in Exhibits 2, 3, 4, 5, and 6). In the discussion with each bank, he indicated that Children's Memorial would be willing to switch all accounts at its existing banks to the new bank. In return, Children's Memorial would request a reserve line of credit of approximately $250,000, secured by third-party receivables.

The four banks he contacted indicated varying degrees of interest in the proposal. Following an initial discussion with officers at each of the banks, Mr. Karas sent further financial data to each bank.

Landview National Bank

The largest of the banks contacted appeared lukewarm to the proposal. The bank's loan officer (at a branch office) raised certain concerns the bank had with respect to the dependability of the third parties involved. As noted before, in the hospital's case, these were principally the State Welfare Department and Blue Cross, which accounted for 56 percent and 22 percent of all receivables, respectively. The loan officer recounted to Mr. Karas the crisis that had hit all hospitals in November, when the state legislature had voted to curtail medical benefits covered by the welfare program substantially.

The role and support of these third-party payers was substantially uncertain, and the loan officer thought they did not leave much room for optimism. But the loan officer promised to send the hospital's preliminary request to the senior officer at the headquarters office. However, following the discussion, Mr. Karas concluded that further discussion would probably be unproductive and decided to concentrate on other prospects.

Valley National Bank

The meeting with the loan officer at Valley National Bank (VNB) was pleasant and productive. Mr. Karas thought that the bank was seriously interested in the possibility of a banking relationship with Children's Memorial. At the end of the two-hour discussion, the bank's loan officer promised to call Mr. Karas, although he had not done so as of March 23.

Following the meeting, Mr. Karas and other members of the Search Committee met to evaluate and discuss the possibility of a relationship with VNB. After some discussion, committee members decided not to pursue the possibility, for the following reasons:

1. A review of the published financial statements revealed that the bank had been only marginally profitable in the last two years.
2. The bank's total equity and cumulative undivided profits were considerably less than those of any of the other banks considered.
3. Because of the first and second points, the bank was probably not in a position to take any meaningful risk if Children's Memorial should encounter future unpredictable problems.
4. The bank did not have a branch near the hospital for check-cashing purposes.

Other Proposals

These considerations eventually narrowed the list of banking candidates to two: the Glen Trust and the Meadow Bank. In several important ways, these two banks were very similar:

1. Both were solid, middle-sized banks.
2. Both banks had been prudent insofar as increasing loan loss reserves and so forth before closing the previous year's books.
3. Both banks gave the hospital in-depth attention at the senior officer level, and both had obviously done their homework in reviewing the financial data given.
4. Both made it abundantly clear that they were very interested in developing a long-term relationship with Children's Memorial, starting as soon as practical.
5. Both had branches very near Children's Memorial for payroll cashing and other purposes.
6. Both banks indicated that, circumscribed by responsibilities to depositors and stockholders, as responsible bankers they would always tend to be as supportive as possible should a "good client" develop problems.
7. Although Glen Trust had a larger capital account balance, Meadow Bank had been more profitable during the past year.

After several discussions with each bank, Mr. Karas received the following proposals:

Summary of Glen Trust Proposal

1. A $250,000 revolving line of credit fully secured by accounts receivable, not including Welfare Department accounts receivable
2. Interest charged at 3¼ percent over prime (the bank's executive vice president pointed out that about two percentage points of the rate simply reflected the bank's administrative expense associated with a receivable loan)
3. No requirement for compensating balances

The bank's internal auditors would spend a week analyzing the hospital's receivables and other records.[2] In addition, the bank would expect weekly updated accounts receivable reports, which it would

---

2. Children's Memorial would be expected to put up a $1,000 deposit to cover the cost of the audit, which would be completely refundable except if at the completion of the audit and home office review the bank were to make a firm offer and Children's Memorial were to refuse it.

audit periodically. The bank estimated that it would take about three weeks to conclude a firm arrangement.

Summary of Meadow Bank Proposal

1. A $250,000 unsecured line of credit
2. Interest charged at 1 percent over prime
3. No fee charges for the unused portion of the credit line
4. No requirement for compensating balances

The senior vice president of the bank pointed out that the standard type of receivables loan agreement used by all banks had many onerous terms, all favoring the lender. While he indicated that the bank would reserve the right to convert to a secured basis if Children's Memorial's financial condition were to become significantly worse than projected, he hoped that such a need would never arise, as such loans were more costly and burdensome to administer for both the hospital and the bank.

The senior vice president also stated that he had reviewed the hospital data with the bank's president. In his opinion, if Children's Memorial wanted to proceed, all that remained was for him to visit the hospital and possibly meet some of the senior management. He mentioned that the entire arrangement could be easily concluded in the next several days.

MARCH BOARD MEETING

As Mr. Karas prepared for the March board meeting, two things concerned him. First, while a relationship with the Meadow Bank would be less costly, he had greater confidence in the willingness of Glen Trust to stick by Children's Memorial if financial difficulties developed. Moreover, he thought the difference in rates might not be critical, since his ultimate goal was to use the line only as a reserve. The line would have to be used in early 1976, but beyond that point Mr. Karas hoped that further borrowing from the line would not be necessary. Also, he had second thoughts about his initial recommendation to liquidate the hospital's marketable securities and pay off the existing lines. He believed that the present banks would be willing to maintain the lines of credit even if the hospital were to withdraw its operating accounts. He thought that the current arrangement, while costly, resulted in a type of "forced savings" by the hospital, since management was more inclined to budget funds for a reduction of borrowings than for a deposit into a savings account.

EXHIBIT 1
Children's Memorial Hospital
Summary of Auditor's Statement

To the Governing Board of Children's Memorial Hospital, Inc.:

. . . .

As reflected in the accompanying financial statements, the hospital incurred net losses of $761,630 in 1975 and $252,890 in 1974. Unaudited information subsequent to September 30, 1975 indicates that losses are continuing. . . .

At September 30, 1975, the hospital was in arrears on payment of withheld employee payroll taxes and on principal and interest payments on its 8½-percent construction loan payable to a bank. As a result, the bank has the option to declare the entire sum due and payable. As of November 7, 1975, the bank had not exercised this option. Realization of the investment in plant and equipment . . . is dependent upon the success of future operations.

In view of the magnitude of the matters discussed in the preceding paragraph, we are unable to express, and we do not express, an opinion on the accompanying financial statements of Children's Memorial Hospital, Inc.

November 7, 1975

EXHIBIT 1-A
Children's Memorial Hospital
Statement of Operations
For the Years Ended September 30, 1975 and 1974

	1975	1974
Patient revenues		
Inpatient routine care	$2,297,745	$1,800,136
Outpatient charges	239,384	184,845
Ancillary charges	1,999,707	1,299,166
Day care program	416,880	413,592
	$4,953,716	$3,697,739
Less		
Contractual adjustments on agencies, municipalities, and Blue Cross accounts	$ 58,768	$ 76,318
Provision for doubtful accounts and free service to patients	260,170	60,876
	$ 318,938	$ 137,194
Net patient revenues	$4,634,778	$3,560,545

EXHIBIT 1-A (continued)

	1975	1974
Operating expenses		
Salaries and wages (less physician-returned fees of $153,580 in 1975 and $170,567 in 1974)	$3,482,386	$2,859,006
Supplies and expenses	1,538,070	876,535
Depreciation	225,814	149,718
Interest expense	165,549	31,625
	$5,411,819	$3,916,884
Operating loss	$ (777,041)	$ (356,339)
Other income (expense)		
Cafeteria revenue	$ 33,253	$ 12,805
Unrestricted gifts, bequests, and contributions	20,193	34,468
Unrestricted investment income	36,719	71,049
Other	9,669	14,626
Fundraising expenses	(43,704)	(29,499)
Loss on sale of investments	(40,719)	—
	$ 15,411	$ 103,449
Net loss	$ (761,630)	$ (252,890)

EXHIBIT 1-B
Children's Memorial Hospital
Balance Sheet at September 30, 1975 and 1974
Unrestricted Funds—Assets

	1975	1974
Current assets		
Cash in checking accounts	$ 66,959	$ 74,025
Cash in savings accounts	104,685	127,646
Certificates of deposit	260,000	200,598
Accounts receivable—patient care, less allowance of $166,100 in 1975 and $99,400 in 1974	992,952	707,862
Interest and other receivables	28,371	17,045
Inventories, at the lower of cost (first-in, first-out) or market	46,637	45,236
Prepaid expenses	36,683	35,033
Total current assets	$1,536,287	$1,207,445
Investments, at cost	$ 348,293	$ 461,611
Plant and equipment, at cost	$6,744,110	$6,436,406
Less accumulated depreciation	2,921,214	2,695,400
	$3,822,896	$3,741,006
	$5,707,476	$5,410,062

EXHIBIT 1-B (continued)
Liabilities

	1975	1974
Current liabilities		
Notes payable to a bank due on demand ($150,000) or by January 26, 1976 ($369,000), interest payable at 1% above prime rate	$ 519,000	$ 250,332
Current maturity of 8½% construction loan	43,700	—
Accounts payable, including construction payables of $110,000 in 1975 and $171,000 in 1974	1,020,329	587,339
Accrued expenses	237,584	141,340
Total current liabilities	$1,820,613	$ 979,011
8½% construction loan payable, in 240 equal monthly installments, less current maturity	$1,414,681	$1,484,014
Due to Provincial House	548,703	479,530
Due to restricted funds	58,053	11,919
Commitments and contingencies		
Fund balance	1,865,426	2,455,588
	$5,707,476	$5,410,062

Restricted Funds—Assets

	1975	1974
Cash	$ —	$ 40,967
Cash in savings banks	32,970	32,970
Certificates of deposit	120,000	113,533
Accrued interest	—	1,028
Due from unrestricted funds	58,053	11,919
	$211,023	$200,417

Liabilities

	1975	1974
Research fund balance	$192,370	$184,669
Special Purpose Fund balance	18,653	15,748
	$211,023	$200,417

EXHIBIT 2
Landview National Bank
Balance Sheet
As of December 31, 1975

	1975	1974
Resources		
Cash and due from banks	$3,157,400	$2,199,851
Investment securities		
U.S. government	402,714	404,357
State and municipal	466,888	859,777
Other	131,666	136,057
Total investment securities	1,001,268	1,400,191
Trading account securities	107,353	151,632
Loans and discounts	4,455,074	5,136,298
Federal funds sold	202,620	153,754
Customer acceptance liability	193,883	201,673
Equipment and banking houses	138,323	133,032
Other real estate	18,284	498
Other assets	292,939	336,341
Total assets	$9,567,144	$9,713,270
Liabilities		
Capital stock ($15 par)	$ 90,240	$ 90,240
Surplus	233,760	233,760
Undivided profits	204,208	186,471
Total capital accounts	$ 528,208	$ 510,471
Borrowed funds	99,710	95,124
Federal funds purchased	604,225	543,127
Mortgage indebtedness	424	469
Acceptances executed	194,524	202,843
Possible loan loss reserve	91,369	83,100
Other liabilities	259,184	323,975
Deposits		
Demand	2,160,152	2,131,718
Saving and time	2,351,114	2,742,061
Foreign offices	3,278,234	3,080,382
Total deposits	7,789,500	7,954,161
Total liabilities	$9,567,144	$9,713,270

EXHIBIT 3
Mountain National Bank
Balance Sheet
As of December 31, 1975
(000 omitted)

	1975	1974
Resources		
Cash on hand and in banks	$ 248,003	$ 278,793
U.S. government securities	111,176	71,442
State and municipal securities	188,843	181,495
Other investment securities	144,768	110,388
Trading account securities	8,248	7,939
Investments in unconsolidated subsidiaries	15,639	13,803
Loans	911,316	999,904
Federal funds sold	83,314	13,200
Bank premium	24,596	22,008
Customer acceptance liability	23,163	23,717
Other assets	33,726	30,900
Total assets	$1,792,792	$1,753,589
Liabilities		
Demand deposits	$ 724,979	$ 697,633
Time deposits	560,273	643,093
Foreign deposits	65,825	38,493
Total deposits	1,351,077	1,379,219
Federal funds purchased	209,292	174,841
Borrowed funds	23,030	2,842
Acceptances executed	24,633	25,399
Other liabilities	41,131	36,257
Reserve for loan losses	16,820	14,099
Capital notes	20,032	20,032
Common stock ($11)	22,089	22,089
Surplus	49,411	49,411
Undivided profits	35,277	29,400
	$1,792,792	$1,753,589

EXHIBIT 4
Valley National Bank
Balance Sheet
As of December 31, 1975
(000 omitted)

	1975	1974
Assets		
Cash on hand and in banks	$ 8,240	$ 5,483
U.S. government securities	22,747	1,920
Federal agency securities	2,405	5,461
Other securities	8,195	10,260
Federal Reserve stock	71	71
Loans and discounts	26,365	24,718
Securities purchased	23,350	49,212
Bank building and equipment	1,223	1,435
Other assets	614	853
Total assets	$93,210	$99,413
Liabilities		
Capital stock	$ 1,786	$ 1,786
Surplus	600	600
Undivided profits	794	763
Deposits	82,160	77,220
Securities sold	5,856	17,182
Interest unearned	1,432	1,087
Other liabilities	582	775
Total liabilities	$93,210	$99,413
Book value per share	$ 21.38	$ 21.17

Capital stock $1,785,000, par $12
No dividend paid
Traded OTC
Price range 1975, 28$^{1}/_{8}$–13$^{1}/_{8}$; 1974, 15$^{2}/_{8}$–14$^{3}/_{8}$

EXHIBIT 5
Glen Trust
Balance Sheet
As of December 31, 1974
(000 omitted)

	1974	1973
Assets		
Cash on hand and in banks	$ 15,290	$ 14,687
U.S. government securities	5,853	7,139
Other securities	24,003	27,545
Federal funds sold	12,100	19,910
Loan and discounts	77,017	69,934
Bank equipment and building	1,064	1,078
Other assets	3,464	3,313
Total assets	$138,791	$143,606
Liabilities		
Capital stock ($3.85 par)	$ 3,080	$ 3,080
Surplus	5,004	4,730
Undivided profits	1,728	1,712
Federal funds purchased	7,662	12,310
Deposits	117,800	118,831
Reserve for loan losses	661	636
Other liabilities	2,856	2,307
Total liabilities	$138,791	$143,606
Book value per share	$ 12.27	$ 11.91

Capital stock $3,080,000, par $3.85

EXHIBIT 6
Meadow Bank
Balance Sheet
As of December 31, 1974
(000 omitted)

	1974	1973
Assets		
Cash on hand and in banks	$ 6,448	$ 6,472
U.S. government securities	5,554	5,066
Municipal securities	9,270	6,440
Other securities	1,015	1,033
Federal funds sold	3,600	3,840
Loans and discount	46,474	46,183
Bank building and equipment, etc.	1,579	1,418
Other assets	1,307	1,188
Total assets	$75,247	$71,640
Liabilities		
Debentures and capital notes	$ 648	$ 648
Capital stock	1,955	1,955
Surplus	1,963	1,963
Undivided profit	720	410
Reserves	658	598
Dividends payable	38	38
Deposits	64,415	64,739
Other liabilities	4,850	1,289
Total liabilities	$75,247	$71,640

6% convertible debentures: 12/31/74, $648,240 due 2/1/88
Capital stock: Authorized $2,700,000, outstanding $1,954,558, par $13.50.

Brown Furniture Company, Inc.

In early 1983, William Smith, financial vice president of Brown Furniture Company, Inc., ran into Michael Senters, an old friend, while waiting for a flight at O'Hare International Airport. They had not seen each other since they graduated from a well-known western business school in 1965. Over a drink, Mr. Smith recounted the growth of Brown and the financing policies that had developed in response to the firm's rapid growth. Mr. Senters, who was a senior lending officer at a leading commercial bank, was particularly intrigued by the firm's relatively low use of bank borrowing. Mr. Smith told Mr. Senters that financial management of credit policy had been vital to the firm's capital self-sufficiency.

"The key to our low cash requirement, and thus our low bank borrowing cost, Mike, is the fact that we insist on good credit terms from our suppliers. In fact, they have relatively little choice in the matter, since extending credit is pretty standard policy in the industry. On the other hand, we encourage fast payment from our customers by offering slightly more liberal discounts than is standard practice for our industry. But look at the days receivables we have compared with the industry average. On the average, we are getting paid off 30 days earlier than our competitors. By speeding inflows and taking advantage of supply credit available, we are pretty much self-financing and thus we have relatively little need for bank borrowing. And when you start talking about borrowing rates of 13 percent, that's important. Some months, of course, we are a little short and we have to borrow, but as soon as we get surplus we pay off the debt and put any left over into certificates of deposit."

BROWN FURNITURE COMPANY

Brown's sales had grown at a compound annual rate of 17 percent over the last five years, reaching a peak of $3.2 million on assets of $2.3 million in 1982. (See Exhibits 1 and 2 for 1982 financial statements.) The company had been purchased in 1976 by a group of three investors, two of whom had been employed in various management positions in the forest products industry, most recently with Waite Timber Company, where they met. The two managers decided jointly to purchase a company of their own. They had, with a mutual friend (a professional investor), negotiated a deal with Gilliam Industries to acquire its furniture manufacturing division, which then became Brown Furniture Company. The three owners assumed key managerial positions, with Mr. Smith taking charge of finance and accounting. Mr. Smith knew that the firm would have to be as self-sufficient as possible because the owners were reluctant to invest additional equity capital except for the most urgent purposes, and because long-term debt capacity had been exhausted in the purchase of the firm. Moreover, because of the high debt to equity ratio, the firm's commercial banker told Mr. Smith that $40,000 to $50,000 was the maximum the bank would be willing to lend on a line of credit. Mr. Smith, realizing that this amount was the total of the young firm's financial flexibility, decided to rely on it as little as possible.

CREDIT POLICY

Long before, Mr. Smith decided that the firm would have to manage its credit policy aggressively if the firm were to minimize additional outside financing. Specifically, he undertook a program to pass up trade discounts and to favor suppliers who offered the longest repayment terms even though, in some cases, the suppliers had slightly higher priced items. He told Mr. Senters, "In a sense, I saw all these small suppliers as a group of small banks, each of them giving us a little but collectively enough to finance most of our purchases. In fact, the competition among suppliers on some products is so keen that they're almost begging us for business. Most give us terms of 2/10 net 30, but with some searching I've got terms of 2/10 net 45, and even 2/10 net 60 in some cases. I pay as late as possible without risking a bad credit rating.

"On the other hand, with respect to our receivables, I've done whatever possible to speed them up. If you look at our financial statements, you'll see that our average collection period is about 30 days faster than the industry overall. [See Exhibit 3.] Sure, we have to give up a little on discounts, 3/10 net 30 compared with 2/10 net 60 for our competitors, but we want and need to get our hands on cash faster."

EXHIBIT 1
Brown Furniture Company
Income Statement
Year Ended 12/31/82
($000)

Sales	$3,200
Cost of goods sold	2,360
Gross profit	$ 840
Selling & advertising	290
Other expenses	150
Interest expense	160
Profit before taxes	$ 240
Taxes (50% rate)	120
Profit after taxes	$ 120

EXHIBIT 2
Brown Furniture Company
Balance Sheet
12/31/82
($000)

Assets		Liabilities & net worth	
Cash	$ 100	Accounts payable	$ 295
Market securities*	150	Accrued expenses	200
Accounts receivable	130	Current portion long-term debt	100
Inventory	708	Current	$ 595
Current	$1,088	Long-term debt	900
Net plant & equipment	1,212	Net worth	805
Total assets	$2,300	Total liabilities & net worth	$2,300

*Average yield: 10 percent per annum.

EXHIBIT 3
Brown Furniture Company
Selected Ratio Comparisons

	Industry Average	Brown
Inventory/cost of goods	34%	30%
Average collection period*	45 days	15 days
Days purchases outstanding*	20 days	45 days
Return on net worth	15%	15%

*Based on 360-day year.

National Credit Company

In 1974, Ronald Allen, executive vice president of the National Credit Company, was reviewing a study prepared at his request on the company's credit-scoring system, which was used to evaluate consumer loan applications. Mr. Allen had shared a widespread feeling that the existing credit-scoring system had never worked properly and should be reviewed to determine its current effectiveness and problem areas.

The study represented the first in-depth look at the company's credit-scoring system since 1967, when it was placed in operation. The completed study identified important weaknesses in the existing system and proposed certain changes. This was the study Mr. Allen was now considering. Lately, however, he had also begun to develop some strong reservations about credit scoring in general. Thus, even as he studied the proposal to revise the current system, he wondered whether a more fundamental alternative might be preferable.

BACKGROUND

National Credit Company was primarily involved in granting large business credits. However, in 1965, in search of more loan activity, National had focused attention on the lucrative personal loan market. Its intention had been to seek personal loans aggressively through its 17 branch offices in southern California.

To facilitate the review of loan applications and in line with a corporate desire to decentralize retail loan decisions, National announced to its branch managers and 54 lending officers that branch loan officers would have authority to accept or reject loan applications.

THE EXISTING SYSTEM

Since credit analysis and decisions were new to the branch officers and since there was insufficient time to provide in-depth training, National established three broad criteria for the credit decision: (1) a credit-scoring system; (2) a Credit Bureau report; and (3) policy guidelines for the consideration of qualitative and quantitative factors absent from the loan application.

Credit Scoring

The first step in evaluating a credit application was assigning a numerical "score" to the data filled in by the applicant. The determination of how many points to assign particular types of answers was itself based on a statistical technique known as discriminant analysis. In essence, the technique tried to estimate the importance of various types of borrower characteristics (see Exhibit 1 for some typical questions) to help predict whether the loan would be good or bad (hence discriminating between good and bad borrower characteristics).

When a loan application was completed and submitted, the intention was that the branch loan officer would "score" and total the points for the application. He or she would then evaluate the total point score, according to the plan. Applications with total scores of 87 or better would be automatically accepted. Total scores below 52 would be automatically rejected. Scores between 52 and 86 would be classified as "judgment calls" and would be approved or denied by the loan officer on the basis of his or her assessment of the applicant's overall creditworthiness.

Credit Bureau Report

If a credit application fell into the judgment call group, a Credit Bureau report was to be used. However, such reports involved additional out-of-pocket costs to the company.

Policy Guidelines

A third information source consisted of policy guidelines reflecting the qualitative and quantitative considerations absent from the application and bureau report, such as the borrower's character or extenuating circumstances resulting in poor credit scores or ratings. This information source, too, was to be used in judgment call applications.

DISSATISFACTION WITH CURRENT SYSTEM

In practice, Mr. Allen believed that loan officers had relied too heavily on the credit-scoring plan and Credit Bureau report. This was particularly true with the judgment calls, for which the loan officer's own assessment was supposed to play an important role. In essence, the loan officers were using the credit score and the bureau report as a means of avoiding the difficult and uncomfortable task of putting their judgment "on the line." In fact, they often used the bureau report even when applications clearly should have been accepted or rejected.

The almost complete reliance on the applicant's score in conjunction with a Credit Bureau report seriously concerned top management in several ways. For one thing, changes in demographic factors had importantly affected the scoring system's accuracy. For example, two types of employment that received relatively high scores in 1967 were brokerage and engineering. And although in 1974 these professions were very severely affected by the economic downturn, such changes had not been routinely incorporated in the system. Moreover, the recent and impending reforms in consumer credit prohibited the use of certain questions, such as those dealing with marital status, which were believed to explain a great deal about the applicant.

In light of all these factors, Mr. Allen noted that there was almost common recognition that the credit-scoring system was not only out of date but also leading to undesirable credit performance. In 1974 he ordered a study to reconsider variables and weights in the existing credit-scoring plan and to propose other options.

1974 Study

The current system was evaluated through a statistical analysis of 1,500 applications. Exhibit 2 illustrates the effectiveness of the current system. If the current credit-scoring system were used to evaluate applications whose histories were known (that is, applications that subsequently proved to be good loans or bad loans or that had been rejected), the following decisions would have been signaled. With respect to loan applications that were approved and subsequently went sour ("bads"), the current system would have indicated automatic rejection of 21 percent, automatic approval of none, and judgment calls for 79 percent. With respect to loans that were approved and turned out to be good, the current system would have automatically rejected 15 percent, automatically accepted only 1 percent, and placed 84 percent in the judgment call category.

Based on this analysis, the study recommended the deletion of four categories from the current system: "age," "marital status," "other income," and "monthly debt payments." It recommended that all other categories be maintained, although with changes in their point values.

The reason for dropping the four categories were that three of them ("age," "other income," and "debt payment") were judged irrelevant in discriminating between good and bad applications. The fourth category, "marital status," was illegal, as noted previously.

Proposed System

Aside from the deletions and revisions recommended for various categories and weights in the existing system, the study recommended the incorporation of other categories. The various categories and numerical weights proposed are shown in Exhibit 3. For example, the report proposed including the questions "Is the applicant a current borrower?" and "How long has the applicant been at the current address?" It was also suggested that the "account balance" category have four ranges instead of the current three and that the Credit Bureau rating be directly incorporated into the overall score.

Other Administrative Problems

The study also noted that, in some cases, potential customers were confused by terminology in the loan application. For example, household bills were included as debts while department store and charge card balances were omitted, and the specification of mortgage payments did not include real estate taxes. The salary category was also believed to be misleading since it was a pretax amount. Administrative problems also arose in scoring the applications since the loan officer had the tedious task of checking the application line by line against a scorecard. This tedium was believed to discourage the proper use of the credit-scoring system. The study also found that competence in evaluating the credit reports varied considerably from loan officer to loan officer.

The report noted that the "mortgage/rent," "bank account," and "job" categories had weights that did not agree with intuition. The report stressed, however, that all the weights had been confirmed statistically.

The proposed system would also decrease the score on the highest "mortgage/rent" category, indicating that a high mortgage/rent payment diminished capacity to pay rather than being positively correlated with liquid wealth.

The proposed system also gave dominant, explicit consideration to the "Credit Bureau" category. Increasing importance was also given to "bank account balance" and "years on the job." "Telephone" and "monthly salary" diminished in importance.

Under the proposed system, the cutoff score would be 81. Those with scores equal to or above 81 would be automatically accepted. Score totals of 54 or less would be unconditionally refused. Those from 55 to 80 would be viewed as judgment calls. The effectiveness of the proposed system was then evaluated by applying it to the 1,500 applications whose histories were known. On the basis of the statistical analysis, the study estimated that 15 percent of all applications would be automatically accepted. Thirty percent would be unconditionally rejected, and 55 percent would be judgment calls (Exhibit 4).

MR. ALLEN'S GENERAL RESERVATIONS

Mr. Allen thought the 1974 report had done a good job of updating the 1967 system and of raising some of the "people" problems associated with the system's operation. Yet he wondered whether a deeper question should be addressed: namely, were credit-scoring plans generally the best way to analyze "creditworthiness"?

Mr. Allen believed that creditworthiness encompassed both a willingness to pay and an ability to pay. He thought scoring mixed such factors together, along with other characteristics, such as whether the person was a current customer. What bothered Mr. Allen was that the use of characteristics in the scoring system dealt with the "willingness" and "ability" to pay questions indirectly. In other words, applicants in "poor" job categories were presumably less willing and able to pay than those in "fair" job categories. But the method did not tell the lending officer whether the applicant would be unwilling or unable to pay legal debts. Thus credit scoring dealt with categories rather than people, and Mr. Allen believed that the direction of consumer-oriented legislation was such as to make class exclusions harder to implement and justify. A case in point was the prohibition of credit denial on the basis of marital status, even though it had proved useful in determining probability of loss. According to Mr. Allen, society was coming to view credit as a "right" rather than a "privilege," and, consequently, credit decisions would have to be made on the basis of the individual's particular financial status rather than on the basis of statistical classifications. If so, then credit decisions would have to be made as objectively as possible while incorporating the individual applicant's unique financial situation.

Mr. Allen thought that a way to meet these requirements would be to use the same general methods of credit analysis used in granting business credit. An applicant's willingness to pay could be inferred to some extent from his or her previous credit relationships. Ability to pay, however, would entail an examination of committed and available cash flows, similar to a debt service/cash flow analysis used in business credit. A measure of willingness to pay could incorporate a Credit Bureau report (although, operationally, credit reports would be relatively rare). A consumer-oriented cash flow analysis would compare net monthly earnings (cash inflows) with the total of monthly cash expenses (outflows) and debt repayment. If the ratio of committed cash flow to available cash flow were below a preset cutoff point, the applicant would be considered a good credit risk. If committed cash relative to available cash were above the preset level, she or he would be considered "fully obligated" and thus a poor credit risk. Mr. Allen thought such a method could have several advantages over a credit-scoring system. For one thing, it could lead to a more equitable allocation of credit. Indeed, he believed that even welfare recipients could qualify for some credit. Second, it provided a more explicit measure of debt capacity, a measure missing from the credit-scoring plan. With credit scoring, a person's financial requirements could vary widely without substantially affecting the decision, whereas the cash flow approach would reveal exactly how much debt capacity the borrower had. Third, the potential borrower could evaluate his or her position privately and, where a rejection would be implied, save the company the time and trouble of scoring the application. Fourth, there were ways to check the reasonableness of applicants' figures easily. For example, the Bureau of Labor Statistics provided estimates of living costs in various parts of the country for different numbers of dependents. (See Exhibit 5 for an example.)

A related question to be addressed in such a system was the specification of free cash "margin" or, alternatively, the cutoff ratio of committed to available cash. As a working approximation, Mr. Allen thought the cutoff might be usefully put at 75 percent of available cash flow, although he was not sure whether this figure would be too high or too low. He believed, however, that this approach to credit analysis could be superior to the credit-scoring plan, but he wondered what counterarguments could be made in favor of credit-scoring plans.

EXHIBIT 1
National Credit Company
Credit-Scoring Questions

1. How much does applicant want to borrow?
2. Does applicant have a telephone?
3. Does applicant own a home?
4. How much mortgage/rent does applicant pay per month?
5. How many years has applicant been at current job?
6. What is applicant's monthly salary?
7. What is applicant's balance of other debt?
8. Is applicant a current customer?
9. What type of job does applicant have?

EXHIBIT 2
Current System's Performance

A. Best profit results for a cutoff score of __87__ .
  1. Assumption leading to above result is that profit on 16 goods accounts are needed to compensate for one chargeoff.
  2. Sixty-seven percent of all rejects are assumed to be chargeoffs.
B. Best cutoff score gives loans to __1.2__ percent of total applicants.
C. Best cutoff score gives loans to
  1. __1__ percent of total goods
  2. __0__ percent of total chargeoffs
  3. __0__ percent of total rejects
D. Judgment area of __52__ to __86__ points produces:

	Unconditionally Refuse	Judgment	Unconditionally Accept
Goods	15%	84%	1%
Bads	21%	79%	0%
Rejects	41%	59%	0%
Total Population	25%	74%	1%

EXHIBIT 3
Proposed Discriminant Weights

1. Amount of credit requested

0–500	501–1,000	1,001–1,500	1,501–2,000	Over 2,000
17	14	8	6	0

2. Telephone

Yes	No
5	0

3. Home ownership

Yes	No
5	0

4. Mortgage/rent per month

0–90	91–150	151–225	Over 225
0	1	6	3

5. Years at current address

0–3	4–6	Over 7
0	2	5

6. Years on the job

0–3	4–5	Over 6
0	2	8

7. Monthly salary

0–600	601–800	801–1,100	Over 1,100
0	5	6	7

8. Other debt balance

0–200	201–800	801–1,500	Over 1,500
9	8	4	0

9. Bank account

None	Savings	Checking	Both
3	0	4	5

10. N.C.C. customer

Yes	No
9	0

11. Bank account balance

0–100	101–500	501–1,000	Over 1,000
0	1	8	11

12. Job category

Poor	Fair	Good	Excellent
4	0	7	14

13. Credit Bureau

Poor	Inquiries only	Fair	Excellent	No check
0	11	23	34	0

EXHIBIT 4
Proposed System's Performance

A. Best profit results for a cutoff score of __81__ .
    1. Assumption leading to above result is that profits on 16 good accounts are needed to compensate for one chargeoff.
    2. Sixty-seven percent of all rejects are assumed to be chargeoffs.
B. Best cutoff score gives loans to __15__ percent of total applicants.
C. Best cutoff score gives loans to
    1. __22__ percent of total goods
    2. __2__ percent of total chargeoffs
    3. __4__ percent of total rejects
D. Judgment area of __55__ to __80__ points produces:

	Unconditionally Refuse	Judgment	Unconditionally Accept
Goods	16%	62%	22%
Bads	50%	48%	2%
Rejects	51%	45%	4%
Total Population	30%	55%	15%

EXHIBIT 5
Low-Budget Average Expenses*

Expenses	No. of Dependents					
	0	1	2	3	4	5
1. Rent	$ 40	$ 56	$ 87	$123	$ 145	$ 162
2. Utilities						
Renters	13			25		
Owners	—			78		
3. Food & clothing						
Food	97	130	196	260	300	330
Clothing	24	33	50	65	76	84
Total (F&C)	$121	$163	$246	$325	$ 376	$ 414
Income level	$340	$458	$681	$902	$1,040	$1,147

1. Check homeowner's mortgage payments to insure that real estate taxes are included. Real estate taxes average about 3 percent per year (.0025 per month) on the market value. A $35,000 house will be taxed at approximately $87.50 per month.
2. Utilities should include monthly expenses for telephone ($10–20), electricity ($15–40), heat (average of $53), and water (negligible). A person who rents may have heat included in the rental payment.
3. Food and clothing are difficult for most applicants to estimate, and many may substantially underestimate. Refer to the low-budget food and clothing as a guide to the minimum amount. If the expense listed appears too low, use low-budget expense for the appropriate number of dependents.

* Low-budget average expenses are taken from data supplied by the U.S. Department of Labor for a standard of living that is lower than their standard "modest but adequate" standard of living for a family of four. These expenses are as of autumn 1975 for the southern California area. These numbers are only guides to the reasonableness of an applicant's expenses.

J. H. Company

In late December 1978, Linda Goldman, president of the J. H. Company, was considering a proposal submitted by the Fidelity Business Group (FBG) to purchase a portion of the firm's inventory. Included in the firm's inventory was a supply of various types of labels that the firm put on its products. The offer from FBG pertained to the supply of one type, which had a book value of $250,000. If the offer were accepted, FBG would purchase these labels and then resell them to the firm at their book value as they were needed. Ms. Goldman was seriously considering the proposal because she was concerned that current inventory levels were excessive.

BACKGROUND

The J. H. Company was formed in 1956 by James Herzog to manufacture a full line of toppings, syrups, and flavorings for restaurants and the food services of large organizations. The firm was immediately profitable, and sales and profits grew steadily. When sales hit $2.3 million (and profits, $90,000) for the fiscal year ended June 30, 1967, Mr. Herzog was confronted with a major investment decision. Since $2.3 million of sales represented maximum plant capacity, further growth would require new capacity and working capital investment, and hence additional financing. Because of the firm's excellent track record and its debt-free balance sheet, he was confident that the firm's commercial bank would supply the funds to finance expansion. He didn't know, however, whether he should pursue further growth. He was then forty-eight years old and for the last thirty years had known nothing but hard work. If he did not pursue growth, he believed that he could begin to relax more. On the other hand, the challenge of further growth enticed him.

The siren song of expansion won out, and Mr. Herzog began planning for additional capacity. His first step was to meet with the loan officer of the firm's commercial bank. The officer expressed some concern that the firm's inventory to sales ratio was substantially above the industry average. He quickly added, however, that this factor was offset by many positive indicators, and that consequently the bank would welcome a loan request from the J. H. Company.

A sizable loan was requested and granted during December 1967, and the J. H. Company continued on a growth path. The expansion program

was successful. By fiscal 1973, sales increased by 350 percent and profits increased by 400 percent over fiscal 1967's levels. Debt payments were being met easily, and the firm possessed substantial liquidity. However, management was still concerned about the inventory level, which was still significantly above the industry average. In addition, a new and very serious problem developed. Mr. Herzog was no longer happy. His job was now quite different from what it was when the firm's sales were in the $2 million range. Although he was quite effective as the president of a larger company, he just did not like his new role. It was no longer fun. After considerable thought and many discussions with friends and family, he decided to retire and offered his assistant, Ms. Goldman, the presidency. She would receive a substantial increase in salary and a bonus based on profits. Moreover, new common shares, equal to 50 percent of the outstanding amount, would be authorized, and she would be given the option of purchasing these new shares. Mr. Herzog estimated that her bonuses would enable her to purchase all these shares over the next five years. Ms. Goldman accepted the offer.

The new arrangement worked quite well. Although Mr. Herzog was an active member of the board of directors, he did not meddle in the day-to-day operations of the business or attempt to hinder proposals to make changes in the firm's financial policies. For example, he had always been averse to using debt capital, but he acceded to Ms. Goldman's proposal to use debt on a continuing basis. Moreover, he agreed to a low dividend payout ratio and to a goal to go public by 1980.

Sales and profits continued to grow, and they set a record high of $18 million and $1 million, respectively, for the fiscal year ended June 30, 1978. Unfortunately, the inventory to sales ratio was also at the highest level in the firm's history. Ms. Goldman just did not know what to do about the problem. Since she had become president, she hired several consultants and implemented many of their recommendations, all of which failed to reduce inventory levels substantially. Not only was the high level of inventory depressing the firm's rate of return and rate of growth, but it was also depressing her.

FIDELITY BUSINESS GROUP

One evening while Ms. Goldman was reading a trade publication, she learned about the Fidelity Business Group, which was in the business of maintaining inventory levels for firms. After her investigation revealed that FBG was a reputable organization, she decided to arrange a meeting with a representative of the organization. Mr. Fitzgerald, a vice president of FBG, told her that his firm had the financial resources necessary to maintain inventory levels for firms and the expertise required to manage

inventory at the lowest cost possible. He suggested that he examine the firm's inventory to determine whether a relationship was possible that would be beneficial to both firms.

Mr. Fitzgerald found that the firm's $2.6 million inventory consisted primarily of the various ingredients necessary to produce toppings, syrups, and flavorings. In addition, there were various types of cans and labels. Since for most types of cans and labels the firm maintained a 1-month supply, Mr. Fitzgerald was surprised that the firm had approximately 250,000 units of one type and used only 6,945 of these per month. Ms. Goldman told him that although a 1-month supply of these labels was sufficient to support production, the firm normally purchased a 36-month supply to take advantage of quantity discounts offered by suppliers. (Exhibit 1 presents a typical pricing schedule.) She went on to say that, given the four different prices, the firm could purchase in quantities for 1 month, 4 months, 12 months, or 36 months. Since the savings could be attained without additional costs and risks, the firm normally purchased a 3-year supply. Except for capital costs, the incremental carrying costs for a 3-year supply (versus a 1-month supply) were negligible. Moreover, these labels were used on the firm's most stable products. Whereas unit sales of these products had not grown for the past several years, demand for the existing volume of production was solid. Thus there was virtually no risk of obsolescence.

When his investigation was complete, Mr. Fitzgerald made the following offer regarding the labels discussed:

1. FBG would purchase labels having a book value of $250,000 on January 1, 1979, hold title, and resell them to the J. H. Company.
2. FBG would pay the J. H. Company $80,000 on January 1, 1979, $60,000 on January 1, 1980, and $60,000 on January 1, 1981.
3. FBG would bear all carrying costs and guarantee delivery within two days.
4. J. H. would buy back the labels as production required for $250,000.

(It was estimated that these labels would be used up evenly over the next three years.)

Ms. Goldman was intrigued by the offer. If it were accepted, the inventory to sales ratio would be below the industry average for the first time in the firm's history. Moreover, if the transaction were considered a taxable exchange—and she was not sure that it would be—then a significant tax shield would be created, given the firm's 48-percent income tax rate.

Ms. Goldman did not know what type of analysis was appropriate to evaluate the proposal. The firm normally analyzed divestment decisions in a capital budgeting context and used a cutoff rate of 10 percent in evaluating these decisions. She was not convinced, however, that this was the appropriate way to analyze this proposal.

EXHIBIT 1
Price Schedule for Labels

Order Size	Price per Unit
0–24,999	$1.32
25,000–79,999	1.20
80,000–249,999	1.10
250,000 and up	1.00

Budin Company (B)

The Budin Company was a distributor of plumbing supplies located in Massachusetts. Sales in 1975 were $935,000 on assets of approximately $450,000. (See Exhibits 1 and 2 for financial data.) The firm employed ten people. Three worked in the warehouse, which was located on the first floor of a two-story building rented by the firm. There were three outside salespeople, including Robert Budin, the president of the firm. Philip Collins was in charge of inside sales and was also responsible for various administrative functions. In performing these duties, he was assisted by Patrick Dole, plus a bookkeeper and a secretary.

Mr. Budin, Mr. Collins, and Bruce Boyd, an outside salesperson, constituted the firm's management team. They met once each month to discuss various managerial matters. A marketing meeting was also held each month. These three people, the other outside salespeople, and Mr. Dole attended these meetings, which were devoted to discussing various aspects of the firm's marketing effort.

As explained in the Budin Company (A) case, Fred Mosher, a financial consultant, was retained to help the firm develop a five-year financial plan. The plan was to be based on various goals and targets established by management. Mr. Budin was especially concerned about one aspect of the plan: the inventory target. The president told Mr. Mosher that an inventory to sales ratio of 25½ percent was a reasonable goal. However, given the existing system for managing inventory, there was no way to insure that this level would be attained. If this target were not achieved, the firm could not achieve its objectives for the next five years. For example, the firm owed its stockholders $110,000. Mr. Budin wanted to eliminate this debt over the next five years, and he was counting on operations to provide the funds. If inventory were significantly above 25½ percent, a substantial portion of funds from operations would be tied up in inventory, and hence these funds would not be available to retire the debt.

Mr. Budin decided to use the procedure that led to a reduction of the firm's telephone expenses. At one of the management meetings in late 1975, the alarming increase in the firm's telephone expenses was discussed. One of the managers agreed to study the matter and to make a recommendation at a subsequent management meeting. This person analyzed the telephone bills and investigated the systems and policies of other firms. The result was a new policy, which produced an average reduction of 15 percent in monthly telephone bills. Mr. Budin knew that

developing a more efficient inventory system without creating significant new expenses was a much more difficult problem, but he thought
that a study by one of the managers was the best starting point. Thus
he asked Mr. Collins to perform the investigation.

After work that evening, Mr. Collins met his daughter, who was attending a graduate school of business, for a drink. When he told her
about his new assignment, she offered to help, since she had studied
inventory control systems in several of her courses. Mr. Collins thanked
her and then noted that he had read several books and articles about inventory control systems. He found that the theories and procedures
recommended by the various authors were totally unrealistic, at least
for the Budin Company. His daughter disagreed and asked her father to
explain the firm's existing system to her. A summary of his explanation
follows.

The Budin Company maintained an inventory of more than 9,000
different items, ranging in value from a few cents to several dollars each.
Given the size of the work force, there was no way that detailed records
could be maintained.[1] It was enough of a chore to count and value the
inventory once each year.

It was unrealistic to consider reducing the number of different items,
since this breadth was the heart of the firm's marketing strategy. Although the plumbing supply business was very competitive, approximately one-quarter of Budin's volume was obtained from customers
who were never contacted by a Budin salesperson. This situation was
unique in the area, and it was caused by Budin's reputation for being
able to give a customer what he or she needed when it was needed. A
large portion of the sales generated by the firm's salespeople was also
the result of the firm's reputation for service. Since Budin's emphasis
on service created operating expenses higher than the industry average,
its average gross margin had to be higher than the industry average in
order to achieve adequate profitability. Thus, when a salesperson
quoted prices to a potential customer, they were rarely lower than
those quoted by competitors. In fact, other than for Budin's three
major product lines—which accounted for approximately 50 percent
of total volume—they were often higher. What enticed the customer to
choose Budin was the firm's reputation for service. Not only would
Budin have the product, but it would also make special deliveries. For
example, suppose a customer placed an order and received shipment on
a Monday. Subsequent to receiving shipment, the customer realized that
a product, not originally ordered, was needed that week. Budin would

---

1. As noted in the Budin (A) case, management hoped to add three employees over
   the next two years—a salesperson, a bookkeeper, and a secretary. It was expected
   that existing functions would fully occupy the bookkeeper and secretary, and
   that neither would have the time to maintain detailed inventory records.

make every effort to get the item to the customer. It was not unusual for a salesperson to pick the item up at the warehouse and personally deliver it.

To justify its reputation, Budin not only maintained a large inventory but also pursued an active "buy-out" policy. That is, if Budin did not carry or had run out of an item requested by a customer, it would purchase the product from a competitor. There were an average of 40 buy-outs each week; and, although they produced only about 15 percent of the dollar volume of sales, five people were directly involved in these purchases—the three outside salespeople, Mr. Collins, and Mr. Dole. (Naturally, the warehouse and clerical employees were involved in receiving, shipping, and accounting for these purchases.) Suppose a salesperson were to take an order that required a buy-out. She or he would ask Mr. Dole to take care of it. Mr. Dole would place the order and instruct the warehouse people to pick it up and add it to the customer's order. He would also see to it that the paper flow created was properly directed. Since it was not always obvious where to place an order, this procedure would take anywhere from 10 minutes to one hour of Mr. Dole's time.

Unfortunately, when a salesperson asked Mr. Dole to take care of a buy-out, he would often reply that because of other buy-outs or other pressing matters, he would be unable to handle it until the next day or two days later. If the salesperson judged that the buy-out could not wait that long, he would take care of it himself. Not only did it create additional work for already overburdened salespeople, but since buy-outs were usually handled between 9:00 A.M. and 5:00 P.M., the salespeople lost from 10 minutes to one hour of prime selling time for each buy-out. On average, the salespeople handled 10 buy-outs each week.

With respect to items carried in stock, as noted previously the inventory contained more than 9,000 different items, ranging in value from a few cents to several dollars each. Approximately 60 percent of the dollar volume of purchase for stock were made from three manufacturers located in the Midwest. Usually, weekly orders were placed with each of these manufacturers, and Mr. Budin personally handled these purchases. To obtain information to help him decide what to purchase, he would have a physical count of approximately 100 key items taken each week, which collectively accounted for about 20 percent of total sales. This task, performed by one of the warehouse employees, took about two hours. In addition, a "want list" was maintained for these products. Mr. Budin, the two outside salespeople, Mr. Collins, and Mr. Dole were frequently in the warehouse (for example, to check on the status of an order). When they were there, they would spot-check certain items. If they saw that they were out of stock of an item supplied by these three manufacturers, they would note this fact on Mr. Budin's want list. If they saw that they were running low on an item—and this

situation was much more usual than a zero level—they would add it to Mr. Budin's want list. These spot-checks were nothing more than quick glances. These people just did not have the time to stop and take a count. Thus usually all that would appear on the want list was the name of the item and perhaps information regarding orders. For example, if a salesperson expected a customer to place a large order for one of these items, he would note this information on the want list. When Mr. Budin reviewed the list prior to placing the order, he would frequently find between 100 and 150 items on it. Although he was frequently concerned about certain items on the list and would like to have gone downstairs to the warehouse to check on them personally, he rarely had the time to do it.

In addition to reviewing the physical count and the want list, Mr. Budin had to deal with three factors before deciding what and how much to order: (1) estimated demand, (2) delivery time, and (3) price trends. With respect to estimating demand, Mr. Budin relied totally on his "feel" for the market and used no analytical procedures to help estimate demand. Fortunately, his "feel" for the market was quite good and actual demand was usually close to what he had estimated.

Estimating delivery time was the most frustrating part of the process. It normally took between three weeks and two months to receive delivery, but it could take as long as six months. Although these firms were large, they had many problems, some administrative and others related to production. The administrative problems were usually blamed on the computer. For example, on one occasion, when Mr. Budin called to check on the status of an order, he was told that the delay was due to a new computer system that would not permit partial shipments. That is, if Mr. Budin were to order 100 items and one was unavailable, the entire order would be held up until it was available. Mr. Budin shocked the manufacturer's representative when he asked to speak to the computer programmer. He was told that computer programmers do not deal with customers. The final result was that the program was altered to allow items to be cancelled. That is, if certain items were unavailable when Budin placed an order, they would be removed from the order.

If the manufacturer was having production problems with certain products, it could take as long as six months to receive shipment of these products. Mr. Budin was in constant contact with manufacturers' representatives, who would tell him whether production problems were developing for certain items. If these products were an important part of his stock, he had no choice but to order more of them.[2] For about

2. Attempted buy-outs for the products of these three manufacturers were often unsuccessful. Budin was the major supplier of these products in the Boston area. Many competitors did not carry these products; and of those that did, it was likely that if Budin was out of stock, they also would be. Moreover, substitution was often not an alternative because customers frequently requested specific brand names.

three-quarters of these increased orders, it turned out that there was no delay because the manufacturer was able to correct the production problems. Mr. Budin had investigated the matter and found that he was receiving honest estimates from the manufacturers' representatives. The information was often poor because, when production problems began to develop, there was just no way to predict whether delayed shipments would result. Thus Mr. Budin believed that he had to continue the policy of increasing the order size of key products when he was cautioned by the representatives, even though he realized that if there were no increased orders because of potential delays he could reduce his inventory by approximately 15 percent.

Many people asked Mr. Budin why he did not switch suppliers. There were three reasons. First, despite their production problems, the suppliers produced quality products. Budin's customers recognized and wanted this quality, and thus they often specifically requested these manufacturers' brands. Second, the arrangement Budin had with these suppliers enabled him to achieve the higher gross margins that were necessary for his firm. Third, the Budin Company had done business with these suppliers for many years. Whenever the firm experienced difficulties, these suppliers were always helpful. Now that they were having problems, Mr. Budin thought that he should stick by them.

From reading various trade journals, Mr. Budin kept abreast of costs borne by the manufacturers. When he felt that a significant price change was in the wind, he would adjust his order size, determining the extent of the increase by analyzing his current cash position. Since he did not believe in borrowing to do this and since he was mindful of the necessity for achieving an inventory target, he did not speculate very much even though his predictions were quite good. Overall, the firm saved between $3,000 and $4,000 per year by speculating, and the inventory was only about $15,000 higher because of it.

Five percent of the remaining purchases for stock were from local suppliers. The warehouse manager handled these purchases according to guidelines established by Mr. Budin. Since these items were usually readily available, it was not necessary to maintain a large stock of them.

The remaining 35 percent of purchases for stock were from 30 manufacturers, and these were handled by Mr. Dole. Since there was a minimum order size required to avoid paying freight, the frequency of orders would vary. For example, sometimes an order would be placed with a manufacturer every week, and at other times an order would not be placed with this manufacturer for as long as a month. During an average week, Mr. Dole would place 10 orders.

To perform this task, Mr. Dole also maintained a want list, and items were put on this list as they were on Mr. Budin's list. That is, five people placed items on the list based on quick glances when they were in the warehouse. There was one important difference between the two want lists, however. Whereas only a few items on Mr. Budin's list would be at a zero level, approximately 50 percent of the items on Dole's list were at zero level.

Each morning Mr. Dole reviewed the list. (Although he would have preferred to go downstairs to count and/or eyeball certain items, he usually did not have time to do so.) He then decided what to order from which manufacturers. Next, he would check with Mr. Budin, who would frequently tell him to make changes. If Mr. Budin was on the road, Mr. Dole would check with Mr. Collins, who would also frequently tell him to make changes.

The possibility of adding or dropping an item from stock was discussed at the monthly marketing meetings. If an item carried in stock was not moving very well, they would discuss eliminating it. Although all of them were supposed to be alert to such items, generally Mr. Budin was the only one who suggested items for elimination, and he was often overruled. (Naturally, since Mr. Budin was the president and owned a majority of the common shares, he could not be overruled. For this type of decision, however, he generally went along with the majority.)

With respect to adding items, if someone wanted to propose carrying a new product or product line, he or she would make a presentation at a meeting. For example, in late 1975 one of the salespeople proposed adding a line from a new manufacturer. He estimated that an inventory investment of $4,000 would be required and that this inventory level would support annual sales of $20,000. All agreed that sales of $20,000 per year could be generated, but the proposal was rejected because the average gross margin on the line was only 29 percent. (The firm's gross margin target was 30 percent. However, since the average gross margin on buy-outs was 20 percent, the average margin on stock items had to be higher.)

In evaluating the inventory system there were two questions to answer:

1. Does the existing system get the job done? That is, does it produce an ideal level of inventory?
2. Does the existing system minimize the cost and time required to do the job?

Management had never been able to answer either question satisfactorily. With respect to the first, all that could be done to judge whether too little was purchased was to keep track of buy-outs for items normally carried in stock. Management estimated that there were five such buy-outs each week, totaling $200. In addition to the lower gross margin on these purchases, there were additional transportation costs and clerical costs associated with them.

Judging whether there was too much stock could be done only once each year, when inventory was counted and valued. At that time,

Mr. Budin and Mr. Collins spent a weekend reviewing the records. They concluded each year that inventory could be 15 to 20 percent lower without impairing the marketing effort. There was really no easy solution, however, since there was no consistency with respect to which items were overstocked. In other words, each year they found that several hundred items were overstocked, but the overstocked items would be different each year. What really bothered Mr. Budin was that he was not at all confident that the system would maintain overstocking at this level.

With respect to the second question, management was convinced that the existing system was cheaper than the alternatives proposed at previous management meetings. One alternative was to hire a person to handle purchasing and inventory records. Mr. Budin did not think that this option was feasible, at least not for the next several years. He was not sure whether he could afford the three new people they planned to hire, never mind adding a fourth salary. Mr. Budin also thought that the second alternative, which was to computerize the system, was unrealistic. In his view, since a computer could not place orders, computerizing the system actually meant keeping better records. In other words, it would provide better information, but it would not significantly reduce the time that he, Mr. Dole, and others would have to spend. Moreover, there would be the cost of the computer plus the cost of the person who would maintain the records.

Although Mr. Budin thought that the task could not be performed at a lower cost, he was not sure whether the existing system could be altered to reduce the time that he and his employees had to spend.

EXHIBIT 1
Budin Company[1]
Income Data, 1970–1975

Year	Sales	Gross Margin[2]	Profit before Taxes	Total Assets
1970	$644,586	$169,275	$14,234	$330,868
1971	630,384	155,003	(8,992)	293,086
1972	703,467	181,528	34,188	338,300
1973	729,073	201,025	37,725	361,108
1974	906,542	253,393	59,586	434,489
1975	935,396	279,377	45,098	458,032

[1] Complete financial statements for 1970 through 1975 are presented in Budin (A) case. Also, the firm's targets for accounts receivable and accounts payable are 10.8 percent of sales and 5.2 percent of sales, respectively.

[2] Target is 30 percent of sales.

EXHIBIT 2
Budin Company
Ending Inventory Levels, Inventory to Sales Ratios, Purchases, 1970–1975

Year	Ending Inventory	Ending Inventory/Sales (%)	Purchases
1970	$184,352	28.6	$437,589
1971	176,507	28.0	467,536
1972	188,529	26.8	533,961
1973	205,599	28.2	545,118
1974	213,038	23.5	660,589
1975	243,203	26.0	686,185

Addison Electric Company

In early January 1974, Addison Electric Company financial managers were considering whether to continue their commercial paper financing program. Although commercial paper financing had been successful in slowing the rapidly increasing rate of financing costs over the past five years, the managers were wondering whether the program could be continued in view of projected credit market conditions, and if so, whether they should continue it.

Addison Electric supplied power to the Madison metropolitan area. Operating revenues were generated primarily by the sale of electric power to commercial, industrial, and residential users. In fiscal year 1973, operating revenues totaled $850 million on assets of $2.95 billion. (See Exhibit 1.) From 1968 to 1973, revenue growth reached an 8-percent annual compounded rate. This was primarily caused by rapidly increasing demand and cost-price increases. Net operating income and income before interest charges grew at an average annual rate of 16 percent and 15 percent, respectively, during the 1968–1973 period. Unfortunately, operating performance was offset by rapidly increasing interest charges, which rose at a compound rate of 30 percent per year from 1968 to 1973. The formidable financing costs of 1973 were kept from rising even higher only through astute financial management. Because of the rapid cost increases, however, net income over the period increased only 5 percent per annum.

FINANCING ACTIVITIES

Substantial capital expansion led Addison Electric to engage in an active financing program. From 1968 to 1973, construction expenditures increased by approximately 16 percent per year and totaled $1.4 billion for the six-year period. Net internal generation of funds provided $427 million of these requirements (see Exhibit 2).

The external funds requirements were met by a combination of basic security types. A series of bond issues accounted for $580 million (net of repayments). Another $107 million was raised with an issue of preferred stock in 1970, and two common equity issues contributed $173 million. Short-term borrowings increased by $193 million. As noted, the rapid growth in construction financing requirements forced an increased use of short-term borrowings. Since major construction programs took several years, total program financing was normally spent out gradually. Typically, such construction programs were financed with short-term bank borrowing until completion, at which time the borrowings were refinanced with more permanent capital. The company thus minimized the amount of idle funds by using borrowings only as needed.

FINANCING COSTS

Aggravating Addison's substantial need for debt financing was a rise in borrowing costs. In part, this increase reflected a gradual deterioration in Addison's bond rating from Aaa to A (according to Moody's rating system) between 1968 and 1973. To a larger extent, however, the escalation in financing costs reflected a general rise in interest rate levels (see Exhibit 3). This translated into higher interest costs.

COMMERCIAL PAPER PROGRAM

In light of its heavy use of short-term bank borrowing, the rapid rise in bank loan rates caused Addison's management to seek cheaper financing options whenever possible. One important option was commercial paper ("paper").

Although the firm was eligible for prime-rate borrowing from its banks, Addison's financial managers recognized that, with a compensating balance requirement of 10 percent of the line of credit plus 10 percent of borrowings under the line, the effective borrowing cost was in excess of the prime rate. In comparison, consideration of commercial paper rates suggested that paper would be a cheaper short-term financing option even if the paper issues had to be backed up 100 percent with an available bank line of credit.

Commercial paper, like corporate bonds, was rated by major agencies. Paper ratings were closely tied to bond ratings but more conservatively valued. Generally, commercial paper was automatically downgraded relative to the corporation's bonds. Moody's rated commercial paper as P–1, P–2, or P–3, in descending order of quality. As would be expected, the cost of commercial paper was inversely related to quality rating.

Addison first undertook commercial paper financing in mid-1968. In issuing commercial paper, the commercial paper dealer would advise the company about the security's maturity, yield, and face amount. (See Exhibit 4 for a specimen of a commercial paper security.) Frequently, the commercial paper dealer requested that a commercial paper issue be tailored to various maturity dates on projected funds requirements.

The cost of commercial paper financing to Addison was "market plus an eighth, discounted." The $\frac{1}{8}$-percent surcharge represented the commercial paper dealer's commission. Thus, if the market rate were $4\frac{1}{8}$-percent, Addison's issue cost would be $4\frac{1}{4}$ percent, discounted. The rates were quoted on a per-annum basis. To calculate the amount of discount, interest cost first had to be converted to a daily basis and then multiplied by the number of days to maturity. For example, if Addison wanted to issue $5 million principal amount, 36-day commercial paper at $4\frac{1}{4}$ percent per annum discounted, total annual interest would be $212,500, or about $590.28 per day. Total interest for 36 days would be about $21,250. The 36-day interest amount would be deducted from the $5 million (since the commercial paper is on a discounted basis), yielding $4,978,750 to Addison.

$$(\$5,000,000)(.0425) = \$212,500 \text{ per annum}$$

$$\$212,500/360 = \$590.2777 \text{ per day}$$

$$(\$590.2777)(36) = \$21,250 \text{ interest total}$$

$$(\$500,000,000) - \$21,250 = \$4,978,750 \text{ proceeds to Addison}$$

Following initial success with the security, in 1968 Addison gradually developed its commercial paper financing. By year-end 1971, the company had more than $60 million outstanding in such debt, compared with almost $34 million that it was borrowing from its bank line of credit.

Although Addison gradually reduced commercial paper borrowings during 1972, the magnitude of paper activity was large. Commercial paper issues during the year totaled nearly half a billion dollars (Exhibit 5).

The company's financial managers estimated that the paper activity saved almost $600,000 in interest charges during 1972 alone (Exhibit 6). This estimate assumed that, without the use of paper financing, Addison Electric would have had to borrow from its banks at prime plus 10 percent compensating balances. However, ignoring compensating balance costs, Addison's paper activity during 1972 was estimated to have saved more than $300,000 in interest charges. Exhibit 7 contains a breakdown of estimated savings by month and borrowing rate differentials (commercial paper rate versus prime rate).

As shown in Exhibit 7, the interest rate differential dropped continuously during the year as the average paper rate increased substantially faster than the prime rate. The monthly figures obscure the fact that during February the differential had peaked at 98 basis points[1] and dropped to half that level by December. In fact, savings in dollars amounted to only $13,000 in December, down from almost $50,000

---

1. There are 100 basis points in 1 percent of interest.

per month in February and March. By December 31, the differential had dropped to 32 basis points.

During January 1973, the commercial paper–prime-rate differential decreased from 32 basis points at the start of the month to 15 basis points on January 31, and by the end of March the spread was 1 basis point. From February 18, 1972, to March 31, 1973, the differential had dropped 100 basis points. While the prime rate had increased from 4.77 percent to 6.25 percent (148 basis points), the paper rate had risen from 3.76 percent to 6.24 percent (248 basis points). (See Exhibit 8 for a monthly summary.)

In April the spread began to reopen because of a decline in the paper rate. By April 10, the differential had increased to 7 basis points. During the month, however, Standard & Poor's downgraded the company's bond rating to A, although Moody's did not immediately follow suit. In expectation that Moody's would in fact probably follow once Addison's planned mortgage issue was announced and in light of the relatively low differential between paper and prime-rate borrowing, Addison paid off the last of its paper borrowings on April 18 and temporarily left the paper market. Estimated savings on interest during April were roughly $20.

In September 1973, Moody's downgraded Addison's commercial paper to P–2 but kept the corporation's bonds at an Aa rating.

Although Addison's paper rate increased significantly in consequence of its downgrading and overall tightening credit markets, by late October the commercial paper–prime spread had once again widened to a significant level, and the company re-entered the paper market. On October 29, Addison's 9.08-percent paper rate was 42 basis points below the company's prime rate, and the company issued $3 million worth of paper.

During November the spread began to narrow again and had dropped to one basis point by the end of November.

During December Moody's followed Standard & Poor's earlier action and downgraded the corporation's bonds from Aa to A. Shortly after December, the commercial paper rate for Addison moved ahead to its prime borrowing rate. On December 6 the paper rate was 26 basis points higher than the prime borrowing rate. The differential persisted through the month. By December 31, the company's paper rate was 10 percent.

For fiscal year 1973, overall, total new notes issued represented slightly over $100 million, compared with retirements of $98 million (Exhibit 9). On-balance commercial paper outstanding increased by slightly less than $3 million for the year. Addison ended 1973 with a commercial paper balance of slightly over $35 million.

Estimated savings for the year ranged from under $6,000 when compared with prime-rate borrowing to more than $80,000 when compared with prime rate plus 10-percent compensating balance. (See Exhibit 10.)

DECISION PROBLEM

At year end, the company's financial managers were looking toward 1974 with considerable misgivings. Additional long-term external financing was definitely going to be necessary. Increased fixed financial charges would almost certainly result in a further downgrading in bond and commercial paper ratings. A decline to P–3 would make paper borrowing difficult and probably much more expensive.

Projected construction expenditures for 1974 were over $266 million, of which possibly $106 million would be generated internally. The remainder, of course, would have to come from outside funds. Because common stock had been issued in 1972 and 1973, it was almost certain that the shortfall would have to be raised with preferred stock or long-term debt—either of which would reduce financial coverage and undoubtedly lead to a further downgrading of the company's bonds and commercial paper.

Moreover, credit market conditions appeared to be tightening. If so, Addison Electric's financial managers were concerned about the strength of their banking relationships. The use of commercial paper, while saving the company money, also reduced the bank's profitability on the line of credit and perhaps diminished the bank's sense of loyalty to the arrangement. If money did get tighter, would the bank see the commercial paper program as a reasonable cause for rationing credit to the firm? Or, if unaffecting the availability of credit, would the decline in commercial paper rating justify a line of credit cost above the prime rate?

Furthermore, if Addison Electric did want to continue with its commercial paper activity, would it be able to do so in view of the possible further deterioration of financing coverage ratios?

In short, given the uncertain future credit environment, was this an appropriate time to pursue a credit policy that would only minimally involve the firm's banks?

EXHIBIT 1
Addison Electric Company
Selected Financial Data
Fiscal Year 1973 ($ Thousands)

Revenues	$ 849,776
Net income	81,437
Balance sheet items	
Current assets	277,490
Plant and equipment	2,675,788
Total	$2,953,278
Current liabilities	$ 532,639
Long-term debt	1,393,519
Preferred stock	221,063
Common equity	$2,953,278

EXHIBIT 2
Addison Electric Company
Sources and Uses of Funds
1968-1973 ($ Thousands)

Sources	
Funds from operations	$ 403,452
Depreciation	370,690
Short-term debt	192,649
Long-term debt	578,599
Preferred stock	106,666
Common stock	171,347
Total	$1,823,403
Uses	
Additions to plant	$1,396,428
Working capital and other	81,957
Dividends	345,018
Total	$1,823,403

EXHIBIT 3
Bond Yields and Interest Rates, 1929–1973
(Percent per Annum)

Year or Month	U.S. Government Securities 3-month Treasury Bills	U.S. Government Securities 3-5 Year Issues	U.S. Government Securities Taxable Bonds	Corporate Bonds (Moody's) Aaa	Corporate Bonds (Moody's) Baa	High-grade Municipal Bonds (Standard & Poor's)	Average Rate on Short-term Bank Loans to Business—Selected Cities	Prime Commercial Paper, 4-6 Months	Federal Reserve Bank Discount Rate	Federal Funds Rate	FHA New Home Mortgage Yields
1929	—	—	—	4.73	5.90	4.27	—	5.85	5.16	—	—
1933	0.515	2.66	—	4.49	7.76	4.71	—	1.73	2.56	—	—
1939	.023	.59	—	3.01	4.96	2.76	2.1	.59	1.00	—	—
1940	.014	.50	—	2.84	4.75	2.50	2.1	.56	1.00	—	—
1941	.103	.73	—	2.77	4.33	2.10	2.0	.53	1.00	—	—
1942	.326	1.46	2.46	2.83	4.28	2.36	2.2	.66	1.00	—	—
1943	.373	1.34	2.47	2.73	3.91	2.06	2.2	.69	1.00	—	—
1944	.375	1.33	2.48	2.72	3.61	1.86	2.6	.73	1.00	—	—
1945	.375	1.18	2.37	2.62	3.29	1.67	2.4	.75	1.00	—	—
1946	.375	1.16	2.19	2.53	3.05	1.64	2.2	.81	1.00	—	—
1947	.594	1.32	2.25	2.61	3.24	2.01	2.1	1.03	1.00	—	—
1948	1.040	1.62	2.44	2.82	3.47	2.40	2.1	1.44	1.34	—	—
1949	1.102	1.43	2.31	2.66	3.42	2.21	2.5	1.49	1.50	—	4.34
1950	1.218	1.50	2.32	2.62	3.24	1.98	2.68	1.45	1.59	—	4.17
1951	1.552	1.93	2.57	2.86	3.41	2.00	2.69	2.16	1.75	—	4.21
1952	1.766	2.13	2.68	2.96	3.52	2.19	3.11	2.33	1.75	—	4.29
1953	1.931	2.56	2.94	3.20	3.74	2.72	3.49	2.52	1.99	—	4.61
1954	.953	1.82	2.55	2.90	3.51	2.37	3.69	1.58	1.60	—	4.62
1955	1.753	2.50	2.84	3.06	3.53	2.53	3.61	2.18	1.89	1.78	4.64
1956	2.658	3.12	3.08	3.36	3.88	2.93	3.70	3.31	2.77	2.73	4.79
1957	3.267	3.62	3.47	3.89	4.71	3.60	4.20	3.81	3.12	3.11	5.42
1958	1.839	2.90	3.43	3.79	4.73	3.56	4.62	2.46	2.15	1.57	5.49
1959	3.405	4.33	4.07	4.38	5.05	3.95	4.34	3.97	3.36	3.30	5.71
1960	2.928	3.99	4.01	4.41	5.19	3.73	5.00	3.85	3.53	3.22	6.18
1961	2.378	3.60	3.90	4.35	5.08	3.46	5.16	2.97	3.00	1.96	5.80
1962	2.778	3.57	3.95	4.33	5.02	3.18	4.97	3.26	3.00	2.68	5.61

1963	3.157	3.72	4.00	4.26	4.86	3.23	5.01	3.55	3.23	3.18	5.47
1964	3.549	4.06	4.15	4.40	4.83	3.22	4.99	3.97	3.55	3.50	5.45
1965	3.954	4.22	4.21	4.49	4.87	3.27	5.06	4.38	4.04	4.07	5.46
1966	4.881	5.16	4.66	5.13	5.67	3.82	6.00	5.55	4.50	5.11	6.29
1967	4.321	5.07	4.85	5.51	6.23	3.98	6.00	5.10	4.19	4.22	6.55
1968	5.339	5.59	5.25	6.18	6.94	4.51	6.68	5.90	5.17	5.66	7.13
1969	6.677	6.85	6.10	7.03	7.81	5.81	8.21	7.83	5.87	8.21	8.19
1970	6.458	7.37	6.59	8.04	9.11	6.51	8.48	7.72	5.95	7.17	9.05
1971	4.348	5.77	5.74	7.39	8.56	5.70	6.32	5.11	4.88	4.67	7.78
1972	4.071	5.85	5.63	7.21	8.16	5.27	5.82	4.69	4.50	4.44	7.53
1973	7.041	6.92	6.30	7.44	8.24	5.18	8.30	8.15	6.44	8.74	8.08
1972: Jan.	3.403	5.33	5.62	7.19	8.23	5.25	—	4.08	4.50	3.50	7.59
Feb.	3.180	5.51	5.67	7.27	8.23	5.33	5.52	3.93	4.50	3.29	7.49
Mar.	3.723	5.74	5.66	7.24	8.24	5.30	—	4.17	4.50	3.83	7.46
Apr.	3.723	6.01	5.74	7.30	8.24	5.45	—	4.58	4.50	4.17	7.45
May	3.648	5.69	5.64	7.30	8.23	5.26	5.59	4.51	4.50	4.27	7.50
June	3.874	5.77	5.59	7.23	8.20	5.37	—	4.64	4.50	4.46	7.53
July	4.059	5.86	5.57	7.21	8.23	5.39	—	4.85	4.50	4.55	7.54
Aug.	4.014	5.92	5.54	7.19	8.19	5.29	5.84	4.82	4.50	4.80	7.54
Sept.	4.651	6.16	5.70	7.22	8.09	5.36	—	5.14	4.50	4.87	7.55
Oct.	4.719	6.11	5.69	7.21	8.06	5.20	—	5.30	4.50	5.04	7.56
Nov.	4.774	6.03	5.50	7.12	7.99	5.03	6.33	5.25	4.50	5.06	7.57
Dec.	5.061	6.07	5.63	7.08	7.93	5.03	—	5.45	4.50	5.33	7.57
1973: Jan.	5.307	6.29	5.94	7.15	7.90	5.05	—	5.78	4.77	5.94	7.56
Feb.	5.558	6.61	6.14	7.22	7.97	5.12	6.52	6.22	5.05	6.58	7.55
Mar.	6.054	6.85	6.20	7.29	8.03	5.30	—	6.85	5.50	7.09	7.56
Apr.	6.289	6.74	6.11	7.26	8.09	5.16	—	7.14	5.50	7.12	7.63
May	6.348	6.78	6.22	7.29	8.06	5.12	7.35	7.27	5.90	7.84	7.73
June	7.188	6.76	6.32	7.37	8.13	5.15	—	7.99	6.33	8.49	7.79
July	8.015	7.49	6.53	7.45	8.24	5.39	—	9.18	6.98	10.40	7.89
Aug.	8.672	7.75	6.81	7.68	8.53	5.47	9.24	10.21	7.29	10.50	8.19
Sept.	8.478	7.16	6.42	7.63	8.63	5.11	—	10.23	7.50	10.78	—
Oct.	7.155	6.81	6.26	7.60	8.41	5.05	—	8.92	7.50	10.01	9.18
Nov.	7.866	6.96	6.31	7.67	8.42	5.17	10.08	8.94	7.50	10.03	8.97
Dec.	7.364	6.80	6.35	7.68	8.48	5.12	—	9.08	7.50	9.95	8.86

SOURCE: *Economic Report of the President* (Washington D.C.: U.S. Government Printing Office, 1974).

EXHIBIT 4
Addison Electric Company
Commercial Paper Specimen

No. **1600**

$ ~VOID~ ____

Madison Wisconsin _____ 19____

On _____ for value received ADDISON ELECTRIC CO. promises to pay to the order of bearer

the sum of _____ DOLLARS

payable at the principal office of THE FIRST UNITED BANK, Madison, Wisconsin.

Countersigned for authentication of signature of maker only.

THE FIRST UNITED BANK   ADDISON ELECTRIC COMPANY

By _____   By _____
    AUTHORIZED SIGNATURE   AUTHORIZED OFFICER

EXHIBIT 5
Addison Electric Company

COMMERCIAL PAPER ANNUAL PROGRAM SUMMARY
JANUARY 1, 1972–DECEMBER 31, 1972

BEGINNING OUTSTANDINGS		$61,500,000
TOTAL VALUE OF NOTES ISSUED	$462,199,000	
TOTAL VALUE OF NOTES MATURED*	491,099,000	
NET INCREASE (DECREASE)		(28,900,000)
ENDING OUTSTANDINGS		$32,600,000
MAXIMUM OUTSTANDINGS	$62,600,000	
MINIMUM OUTSTANDINGS	$22,200,000	
AVERAGE DOLLARS OUTSTANDING		$50,055,000
MAXIMUM MATURITY ISSUED	99 DAYS	
MINIMUM MATURITY ISSUED	·2 DAYS	
AVERAGE MATURITY ISSUED		39 DAYS

*INCLUDES NOTES REPURCHASED.

EXHIBIT 6
Addison Electric Company

COMMERCIAL PAPER ANNUAL COST OF BORROWING SUMMARY
JANUARY 1, 1972–DECEMBER 31, 1972

YOUR COMMERCIAL PAPER BORROWING RESULTED IN AN EFFECTIVE BORROWING RATE OF	4.47%	
AT A TOTAL COST OF		$2,260,722

HAD YOU OBTAINED THE SAME FUNDS THROUGH BANK BORROWING AT PRIME THE RESULTS WOULD HAVE BEEN: AN EQUIVALENT EFFECTIVE BORROWING RATE OF	5.12%	
AT AN EQUIVALENT COST OF		$2,589,856
WHICH EXCEEDS YOUR ACTUAL COST BY		$329,134

HAD YOU OBTAINED THE SAME FUNDS THROUGH BANK BORROWING AT PRIME +10% COMPENSATING BALANCES THE RESULTS WOULD HAVE BEEN: AN EQUIVALENT EFFECTIVE BORROWING RATE OF	5.63%	
AT AN EQUIVALENT COST OF		$2,848,840
WHICH EXCEEDS YOUR ACTUAL COST BY		$588,118

EXHIBIT 7
Addison Electric Company
Monthly Commercial Paper Summary
January 1, 1972–December 31, 1972

	Starting Outstandings ($000)	Repurchase Prior to Maturity ($000)	Redemption at Maturity ($000)	New Issues ($000)	Average Daily Outstandings ($000)
Jan.	61,500.0	0.0	58,500.0	59,000.0	59,903.2
Feb.	62,000.0	0.0	17,000.0	16,500.0	61,517.2
Mar.	61,500.0	0.0	52,500.0	46,500.0	59,274.2
Apr.	55,500.0	0.0	54,500.0	54,500.0	55,353.3
May	55,500.0	0.0	42,250.0	48,050.0	57,209.7
June	61,300.0	0.0	45,400.0	46,250.0	61,695.0
July	62,150.0	0.0	53,250.0	36,100.0	57,658.1
Aug.	45,000.0	0.0	25,400.0	20,050.0	43,116.1
Sept.	39,650.0	0.0	34,050.0	33,350.0	39,158.3
Oct.	38,950.0	0.0	35,850.0	50,700.0	42,501.6
Nov.	53,800.0	0.0	47,800.0	24,000.0	31,783.8
Dec.	30,000.0	0.0	24,600.0	27,200.0	31,832.3
Year	61,500.0	0.0	491,099.0	462,199.0	50,054.8

EXHIBIT 7 (continued)

	Cost of Borrowing ($000)	Equivalent Cost at Prime ($000)	New Issues Average Maturity (Days)	Average Maturity (Days)	Effective Borrowing Rate (%)	Equivalent Rate at Prime (%)
Jan.	222.84	266.92	46.9	22.8	4.34	5.20
Feb.	189.02	237.32	46.3	24.3	3.83	4.81
Mar.	185.98	233.30	38.5	20.8	3.66	4.59
Apr.	192.70	219.71	36.6	19.5	4.20	4.78
May	216.90	245.04	43.0	23.0	4.43	5.00
June	225.55	255.82	41.3	25.1	4.41	5.00
July	231.36	252.08	39.4	24.1	4.69	5.11
Aug.	173.37	192.62	41.0	24.8	4.70	5.22
Sept.	159.09	174.54	34.6	21.3	4.91	5.38
Oct.	185.11	204.74	30.4	21.1	5.09	5.63
Nov.	135.30	150.86	36.5	19.0	5.14	5.73
Dec.	143.51	156.89	39.4	21.4	5.27	5.76
Year	2,260.72	2,589.86	39.3	22.5	4.47	5.12

EXHIBIT 8
Addison Electric Company
Monthly Commercial Paper Summary
January 1, 1973–December 31, 1973

	Starting Outstandings ($000)	Repurchase Prior to Maturity ($000)	Redemption at Maturity ($000)	New Issues ($000)	Average Daily Outstandings ($000)
Jan.	32,600.0	0.0	26,600.0	24,200.0	31,040.3
Feb.	30,200.0	0.0	20,850.0	3,050.0	23,058.9
Mar.	12,400.0	0.0	9,350.0	1,000.0	6,648.4
Apr.	4,050.0	0.0	4,050.0	0.0	1,591.2
May	0.0	0.0	0.0	0.0	0.0
June	0.0	0.0	0.0	0.0	0.0
July	0.0	0.0	0.0	0.0	0.0
Aug.	0.0	0.0	0.0	0.0	0.0
Sept.	0.0	0.0	0.0	0.0	0.0
Oct.	0.0	0.0	0.0	8,000.0	4,666.7
Nov.	8,000.0	0.0	4,150.0	27,000.0	24,728.3
Dec.	30,850.0	0.0	32,950.0	37,450.0	31,524.2
Year	32,600.0	0.0	97,950.0	100,700.0	20,901.5

EXHIBIT 8 (continued)

	Cost of Borrowing ($000)	Equivalent Cost at Prime ($000)	New Issues Average Maturity (Days)	Average Maturity (Days)	Effective Borrowing Rate (%)	Equivalent Rate at Prime (%)
Jan.	148.85	156.00	34.6	20.9	5.60	5.87
Feb.	104.58	106.62	39.7	16.7	5.87	5.98
Mar.	34.47	34.62	35.0	17.6	6.07	6.10
Apr.	4.64	4.66	0.0	6.9	6.22	6.25
May	0.0	0.0	0.0	0.0	0.0	0.0
June	0.0	0.0	0.0	0.0	0.0	0.0
July	0.0 0.	0.0	0.0	0.0	0.0	0.0
Aug.	0	0.0	0.0	0.0	0.0	0.0
Sept.	0.0	0.0	0.0	0.0	0.0	0.0
Oct.	3.52	3.66	36.1	35.5	9.13	9.50
Nov.	191.24	194.04	35.0	21.3	9.36	9.50
Dec.	265.58	258.89	33.4	24.0	9.89	9.64
Year	752.88	758.50	34.5	20.8	7.65	7.70

EXHIBIT 9
Addison Electric Company
COMMERCIAL PAPER ANNUAL PROGRAM SUMMARY
JANUARY 1, 1973–DECEMBER 31, 1973

BEGINNING OUTSTANDINGS		$32,600,000
TOTAL VALUE OF NOTES ISSUED	$100,700,000	
TOTAL VALUE OF NOTES MATURED*	97,950,000	
NET INCREASE (DECREASE)		2,750,000
ENDING OUTSTANDINGS		$35,350,000
MAXIMUM OUTSTANDINGS	$35,350,000	
MINIMUM OUTSTANDINGS	$0	
AVERAGE DOLLARS OUTSTANDING		$20,901,000
MAXIMUM MATURITY ISSUED	113 DAYS	
MINIMUM MATURITY ISSUED	5 DAYS	
AVERAGE MATURITY ISSUED		35 DAYS

*INCLUDES NOTES REPURCHASED.

EXHIBIT 10
Addison Electric Company
COMMERCIAL PAPER ANNUAL COST OF BORROWING SUMMARY
JANUARY 1, 1973–DECEMBER 31, 1973

YOUR COMMERCIAL PAPER BORROWING RESULTED IN AN EFFECTIVE BORROWING RATE OF	7.65%	
AT A TOTAL COST OF		$752,875
HAD YOU OBTAINED THE SAME FUNDS THROUGH BANK BORROWING AT PRIME THE RESULTS WOULD HAVE BEEN:		
AN EQUIVALENT EFFECTIVE BORROWING RATE OF	7.70%	
AT AN EQUIVALENT COST OF		$758,496
WHICH EXCEEDS YOUR ACTUAL COST BY		$ 5,621
HAD YOU OBTAINED THE SAME FUNDS THROUGH BANK BORROWING AT PRIME +10% COMPENSATING BALANCES THE RESULTS WOULD HAVE BEEN:		
AN EQUIVALENT EFFECTIVE BORROWING RATE OF	8.47%	
AT AN EQUIVALENT COST OF		$834,346
WHICH EXCEEDS YOUR ACTUAL COST BY		$81,471

Midwest Grain Company

INTRODUCTION

In the summer of 1980 the executive group of Midwest Grain Company was reviewing the preliminary profit and loss figures for the most recent fiscal year ended June 30, 1980. Although final audited figures would not be available until sometime in September, the preliminary financial data clearly indicated that the 1979–1980 fiscal year's profitability had been dramatically affected by the high cost of money, the overall effect of which was accentuated by the high level of inventories which a large grain merchandising firm had to maintain in order to remain competitive in the world marketplace. Alarmed by the fact that short-term interest rates had reached an unprecedented level over the prior fiscal year and by the fact that wide fluctuations in such rates had been experienced from time to time (Exhibits 1–4), Midwest's management was in the process of reviewing its working capital policies in an attempt to devise a strategy for the coming years which would maintain or increase Midwest's financial flexibility while at the same time reduce the company's overall cost of funds.

One strategy which seemed somewhat promising was the possibility of Midwest entering the commercial paper (or "corporate IOU") market. Management was unsure what opportunities for issuing commercial paper, if any, might be available, particularly given the fact that at present there were very few privately held companies who were issuing commercial paper. Furthermore, after "going private" in 1977 Midwest had experienced very little visibility in the public financial markets. Although certain members of top management were somewhat unsure as to how the various factors affecting such a major financial decision should be evaluated, all were of the opinion that if a commercial paper issue of any sort were floated it would be imperative that the issue be marketed by a commercial paper dealer of national prominence so that access to the various commercial paper markets across the country would be assured.

Of six or so major commercial paper dealers in the United States, management was of the opinion that Caldwell & Simonton, an investment banking firm with extensive commercial paper dealings, was in the best position to provide marketing and administrative services to a newcomer to the commercial paper marketplace like Midwest. Caldwell & Simonton had been contacted and asked to submit, by August 1, a formal proposal detailing the pros and cons of a commercial paper issue for Midwest. The proposal had been received on a timely basis, and after analyzing the preliminary June 30, 1980 financial statements, management had decided to very seriously consider the terms detailed in the Caldwell & Simonton presentation.

BACKGROUND OF THE COMPANY

By the summer of 1980 Midwest Grain Company (headquartered in Chicago) had come to be considered one of the ten largest grain merchandising firms in the world.[1] Formed in the late 1940s as a small family partnership, the firm's initial operations consisted of purchasing wheat from small Midwestern farmers and subsequently selling the wheat to a selected group of American mills. Wheat continued to be the primary grain merchandised by the firm until 1951, at which time the firm hired additional management personnel and decided to venture into the merchandising of various additional grains, including soybeans, milo, and corn. Throughout the 1950s the firm's operations grew rapidly and in 1959 Midwest's five partners incorporated the business.

During the early 1960s Midwest was able to expand its domestic merchandising operations by opening additional offices in strategic locations throughout the United States, and several small grain storage facilities were acquired in 1965. In 1966 international operations were expanded through the opening of permanent export sales offices in several European cities. The opening of these offices was very instrumental in allowing Midwest to establish a firmer foothold in the various export markets for grain, all of which had seen a general strengthening in the late 1960s. Export market demand continued to be strong on into the early 1970s, and in 1972 Midwest was able to participate in several large grain sales to the Soviet Union and to several European countries.

Midwest's large-scale participation in the 1972 and subsequent sales placed certain new financial burdens on the company which, in manage-

---

1. It should be noted that virtually all of the large international grain companies (including Midwest Grain Company) are privately held. For confidentiality reasons, detailed information useful in ranking such firms on a relative basis is not generally available.

ment's opinion, ultimately needed to be alleviated with permanent debt or equity financing. With the completion of several highly profitable fiscal years (primarily attributable to favorable price movements in the wheat and soybean futures markets) and the national exposure gained through the large sales previously mentioned, Midwest's management began to strongly feel that the badly needed injection of permanent capital might most advantageously come through an issue of common stock. Although board of director support for a common stock issue was not unanimous initially, the majority opinion of the board was that the stock market was ripe for an issue of the size contemplated by Midwest, and the issue was successfully floated in 1973. Most of the capital raised was used to finance permanent working capital needs and to acquire additional grain storage facilities located in strategic export shipping locations. Midwest's management felt that acquisition of the particular facilities purchased would provide additional vertical integration to the firm by providing assured access to export ports while at the same time facilitating in the management of grain inventories.

As early as 1976, however, the administrative burdens of public ownership were beginning to wear on Midwest's management. The legal and accounting fees associated with the various required SEC filings were becoming an administrative as well as a financial burden; more importantly, however, management began to feel that public ownership was undermining much of the confidentiality of the merchandising operation which had heretofore been considered critical to the company's success. In particular, the disclosures required by the SEC of inventory positions, hedging operations, and the like were troublesome to Midwest's management, and stockholder sensitivity to real or perceived exposure positions seemed to be of increasingly major concern at annual stockholder meetings.

In response to the situation, management decided to purchase the outstanding common stock and take the company private in the spring of 1977. At such time stockholdings became consolidated in the executive group of Midwest's management which consisted of approximately twenty individuals.

CURRENT WORKING CAPITAL FINANCING

At present Midwest's working capital needs (Exhibit 6) are financed through the utilization of various lines of credit totaling approximately $675 million spread among a credit pool of some fifteen commercial banks located in major financial centers coast to coast. For some years now Midwest has enjoyed mutually profitable banking relationships with foreign as well as domestic banks, and in recent years Midwest has been able to capitalize on the more competitive interest rates often quoted by foreign banks.

Virtually all outside borrowing is channeled through Midwest's corporate headquarters in Chicago, with funds being distributed to subsidiary merchandising companies as required. On a day-to-day basis cash needs are primarily dependent upon the timing of collections from both domestic and international sales, payments for purchases of grain, and transfers to/from clearing houses of the margin money required to maintain Midwest's hedge positions in all major grain futures markets. Daily cash needs for the parent corporation as well as for each subsidiary are determined each morning, hopefully before twelve o'clock. Once aggregate daily cash needs have been determined as accurately as possible, Midwest's management incorporates them into overall estimates of near-term financing requirements. Depending upon the level of such requirements and management's evaluation of potential interest rate movements, working capital loans of varying maturities are entered into. Although overnight borrowings on regular lines of credit are not uncommon when management feels that short-term rates are going to ease in the near future or working capital needs are somewhat soft, loans are generally entered into for maturities of 7 to 90 days. Excess funds, when available, are invested in corporate money market funds or overnight investment pools, particularly when an aberration in the borrowing and investing rates occurs and an arbitrage opportunity presents itself. Midwest has not generally followed a policy of hedging present or anticipated borrowings with financial futures market instruments.

Although regular lines of credit at or near prime are maintained with virtually all members of Midwest's credit pool, the vast majority of Midwest's working capital needs are met utilizing "domestic storage" bankers' acceptances (BA's). Quotations of "all inclusive" BA rates are obtained each morning from those banks with whom Midwest has lines of credit, and the level of such rates as well as anticipated movements in such rates are evaluated by management in conjunction with the periodic assessment of anticipated near-term working capital requirements. Regular lines of credit are not utilized nearly as much as BA lines; however, the regular lines do provide an additional means of obtaining funds when the level of BA rates or the maturities offered on BA loans are considered unsatisfactory.

All working capital loans are collateralized by warehouse receipts evidencing ownership of grain. A common collateral pool is maintained at Midwest's lead bank in Chicago, and appropriate collateral is segregated in favor of creditors as loans are made. As a general rule Midwest has excess collateral on hand with its lead bank, so under collateralization is not a practical problem even when taking into account the fact that banks discount the market value of underlying collateral in the determination of the amount of collateral required to be segregated for a particular working capital loan.

OVERVIEW OF THE INVESTMENT BANKING
FIRM'S PROPOSAL

The proposal submitted by Caldwell & Simonton contained a brief
financial profile of those companies whose paper was currently being
sold in the various commercial paper markets, the aggregate size of
which was estimated to exceed $125 billion. Of approximately 1,000
industrial firms, public utilities and finance companies active in the
markets, many were among the largest and most prominent of U.S.
corporations. The commercial paper issued by those companies was
generally issued on a "stand alone" basis, or more specifically, backed
solely by the financial integrity of the underlying company.

During the initial discussion of the proposal, Midwest's financial
condition was analyzed and compared to that of a sample of firms currently issuing commercial paper (Exhibit 8). This was done in order to
provide a preliminary estimate of Midwest's financial strength relative
to that of the firms against whose commercial paper the proposed Midwest issue might compete. The results of the comparison indicated that
although Midwest's working capital position was strong (Exhibit 7), it
did not appear that Midwest's equity base was substantial enough (on a
"stand alone" basis) to command the highest quality rating for its
paper. This was potentially problematic since, in Caldwell & Simonton's
opinion, a rating of A-1, P-1, or F-1[2] would be critical in order for
Midwest to maximize the potential benefits of an entry into the commercial paper market (Exhibit 5). In addition to potential rating problems, potential distribution problems also existed. Given the fact that
Midwest had previously been publicly owned for only a relatively short
time, it was unclear how widespread investor familiarity with Midwest
might be. Although Midwest's strong position within the grain industry
gave the firm a certain amount of national and international exposure
(particularly in the Chicago area), it was Caldwell & Simonton's opinion
that it would be difficult to market Midwest "stand alone" paper, particularly in the nongrain financial centers.

In order to address and circumvent potential rating and distribution
problems, Caldwell & Simonton advocated a "bank-supported" commercial paper program for Midwest. Reported by the Federal Reserve
to approximate $2 billion of the total dollar amount of commercial
paper outstanding, bank-supported commercial paper programs (although substantially fewer in number than "stand alone" offerings) had
become increasingly popular in recent years. It appeared that a bank-
supported issue could very easily be integrated with Midwest's existing

---

2. These are the designations assigned by Standard & Poor's Corporation, Moody's
   Investors Service, and Fitch Investors Service, respectively, to commercial paper
   considered by them to be of the highest quality.

banking arrangements, and a $60 million initial issue (designed to represent approximately 10 percent of Midwest's existing bankers' acceptance and regular lines of credit) was proposed. This amount was considered large enough to give Midwest a prominent entry into the commercial paper market while at the same time providing potential commercial paper coverage for a portion of Midwest's annual cash needs. Should the results of the issue be favorable, it was contemplated that the amount of the issue would be raised at some point in the future, perhaps to a level of $100 to $200 million.

One of the primary advantages to Midwest of a bank-supported program would of course be the ability to shift the primary underlying credit support of the issue to a commercial lending institution, and away from Midwest as a "stand alone" entity. Although such a shifting could be accomplished in several ways, Caldwell & Simonton advocated that an irrevocable letter of credit issued by a commercial bank be used to guarantee investor security, with Midwest providing collateral for the letter of credit in the form of unconditional pledges of its inventory, accounts receivable, and other assets. As such, investors would look to the commercial bank's letter of credit for primary protection of their investment, and the commercial bank issuing the letter of credit would look to Midwest for collateral sufficient to protect the bank's guarantee to investors via the letter of credit.

Due to the nature of this particular guarantee process, it was customary for the various commercial paper rating agencies to assign ratings to bank-supported paper on the basis of the supporting bank's commercial paper rather than on the basis of that which would be assigned to the respective underlying company on a "stand alone" basis.[3] In essence, then, Midwest would step into the commercial paper rating of the bank providing credit support, thus substantially reducing or eliminating the effect of potential rating and/or distribution problems. Structuring a program in the above fashion would have the further advantage of maintaining the confidentiality of Midwest's financial condition. This would be possible because although in the usual case detailed financial information about Midwest would have to be provided to the commercial paper rating agency(ies) chosen to rate the issue (as well as to other participants in the program), the rating agencies only

---

3. It is conceivable that a commercial paper rating agency would assign to a bank-supported issue a rating higher or lower than that of the commercial bank providing primary credit support of the issue; this might be done based upon the rating agency's assessment of underlying guarantees, the quality of security, and the financial integrity of each participant in the program. In Midwest's case it was contemplated that, if possible, a commercial bank having an acceptably high commercial paper rating would be selected to provide primary credit support and that the rating ultimately assigned to the Midwest issue would be the same as that of the institution so selected.

published detailed financial information relating to the institution providing the primary guarantee to investors, which in Midwest's case would be a commercial bank.

The commercial bank initially contacted to provide primary credit support was Chicago National. Midwest's banking relationship with Chicago National had grown over a number of years to the point that an aggregate line of credit of $100 million had been negotiated for the current fiscal year. Chicago National had participated in several other bank-supported commercial paper programs in the past, and had agreed in principle to issue the irrevocable letter of credit called for in the Midwest proposal. Chicago National's commercial paper was presently considered to be of excellent quality and carried the highest rating from the major commercial paper rating agencies. Preliminary contact with the various rating agencies indicated that if a bank-supported program for Midwest was adopted, Chicago National's commercial paper rating of A-1, P-1 would be assigned to the Midwest issue.

STRUCTURAL DETAILS OF THE PROGRAM

Among other documents submitted with the Caldwell & Simonton proposal was an outline for a credit agreement in which the legal structure of the proposed program was detailed.[4] Under the proposed arrangement a division of the investment banking firm would establish a free-standing corporation named Midwest Commercial Paper, Inc. This corporation (incorporated and controlled by Caldwell & Simonton) would be responsible for issuing Midwest's commercial paper to outside investors. In return for investment funds such investors would receive a promissory note issued by Fidelity Guaranty Trust Company of Illinois (the "Issuing Agent Bank"). The note would be co-executed by Midwest Commercial Paper, Inc. as "Maker," and would be secured by an irrevocable letter of credit issued by Chicago National (the "Letter of Credit Bank"). With Caldwell & Simonton's prominent position as a national dealer in commercial paper, it was anticipated that Midwest's paper could be sold in most major commercial paper markets. Caldwell & Simonton was of the firm opinion that with a bank as substantial as Chicago National providing primary credit support, investor interest and confidence in Midwest paper would initially be strong, and would increase with time as the issue's presence in the commercial paper markets matured.

---

4. A major portion of the proposed credit agreement addressed various legal ramifications in the event that any or all participants in the program defaulted on the terms of the agreement. Although critical in order to provide adequate protection to all parties, the details of that portion of the credit agreement are not discussed herein.

In order to provide additional custodial security to investors, funds generated from the issuance of Midwest's paper would be deposited in a special bank account maintained at Fidelity Guaranty (the Issuing Agent Bank). In addition to the initial receipt of funds from each issue, a major responsibility of the bank would be to ascertain that all promissory notes and other legal documents associated with each respective issue of commercial paper were in order and that no defaults on the terms of the credit agreement had occurred. Prior to release of the funds to Midwest, the bank would also be responsible for ascertaining that the letter of credit issued by Chicago National was outstanding in good form and adequately collateralized by assets segregated by Midwest's lead bank in Chicago. After all necessary verification, Fidelity Guaranty would be responsible for transferring the net proceeds[5] of each respective issue to Midwest. Repayment of loan proceeds would follow the same basic funds flow pattern, of course in reverse order.

FEES ASSOCIATED WITH THE PROPOSED ISSUE

Also presented in the Caldwell & Simonton proposal was a discussion of quantitative considerations relating to the issue. Of particular note to Midwest's management were the various "front end" or nonrecurring costs usually associated with a financial package of such magnitude. Foremost among these costs would be the legal, printing, and documentation fees charged by the Manhattan law firm which Caldwell & Simonton retained for commercial paper offerings of this nature. In addition, it was anticipated that Midwest would be required to underwrite the legal fees of the outside counsel retained by Chicago National and Fidelity Guaranty to review all documents associated with the issue. The amount of the above fees was estimated to be approximately $125,000 and $5,000, respectively. Compensation to Caldwell & Simonton for preparing the initial proposal and incorporating its special purpose corporation to issue the paper would consist of a nonrecurring arrangement fee of $25,000.

Anticipated annual recurring fees would generally be of two major kinds—those based upon a flat annual charge and those based upon a function of the level of commercial paper activity. The most substantial of the anticipated fees to be paid once a year would be the fee to be paid to the special purpose corporation established to issue the paper to investors. This fee, assessed in order to offset the costs of annual filings

---

5. The reader will recall that interest expense on most bankers' acceptances and commercial paper is deducted from the gross proceeds of each issue prior to transfer of funds to the debtor, and at maturity the gross amount of the debt is remitted to the lender. Such interest is typically calculated using a 360-day year.

and various administrative expenses, was estimated to be $15,000 annually. Annual fees would also be payable to the commercial paper rating agency from whom rating of the issue would be desired. It was anticipated that rating from only one of the accepted agencies (see footnote 2 above) would be necessary; regardless of the particular rating agency chosen or the quality of the rating ultimately assigned to the issue, an annual fee of $8,500 was usually charged.

Variable annual fees associated with the proposed issue would also be payable to the various commercial banks participating in the issue. The most substantial of such fees would be payable to the commercial lending institution providing primary credit support. Preliminary discussion with Chicago National indicated that on a negotiated basis it would charge various commitment and support fees, as well as an outstanding loan fee based upon a function of the amount of commercial paper outstanding during a given period of time. Specifically, Chicago National was proposing to assess such fees in the following manner:

1. A commitment fee of 1/8 of 1 percent would be charged for making the commercial paper line of credit available; this fee would be assessed on the full $60 million line, *regardless of utilization*.
2. A support fee of 1/8 of 1 percent would be charged on the full $60 million letter of credit issued, *regardless of usage*; that is, the support fee would be assessed without regard to the actual amount of commercial paper outstanding and "backed" by the letter of credit.
3. In addition to the foregoing, an outstanding loan fee of 1/8 of 1 percent would be charged on the gross amount of monies owed in the commercial paper market.

In light of the above proposed fee structure, it was understood that Chicago National would not require that compensating bank balances be maintained.[6]

Fees to be charged by Fidelity Guaranty as the Issuing Agent Bank would be based upon the amount of commercial paper outstanding on the first day of each month. Specifically, it was proposed that the gross dollar amount of commercial paper outstanding on the first day of each month be averaged each quarter, with the resulting fees based upon the following schedule:

---

6. This concession was granted by Chicago National in order to be consistent with existing banking arrangements whereby Midwest was not required to maintain compensating balances under either its regular or BA lines of credit.

Charges per quarter based upon a *quarterly average* amount of commercial paper outstanding of:

$ 1 million to $20 million	$80 per million
$21 million to $30 million	$55 per million
$31 million to $50 million	$40 per million
$51 million to $60 million	$35 per million
Basic annual charge (to be prorated each quarter)	$5,000

It was anticipated that certain other minor fees associated with the issue (such as those relating to the cost of tombstone announcements, etc.) might be encountered; however, the potential amount of such charges was not anticipated to be material.

EXHIBIT 1
Midwest Grain Company
Interest Rate Movements
1978–1980

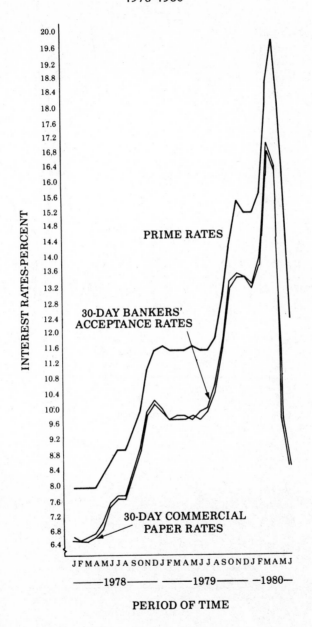

See Exhibit 3 for source of graphical information.

EXHIBIT 2
Midwest Grain Company
Interest Rate Movements
1978–1980

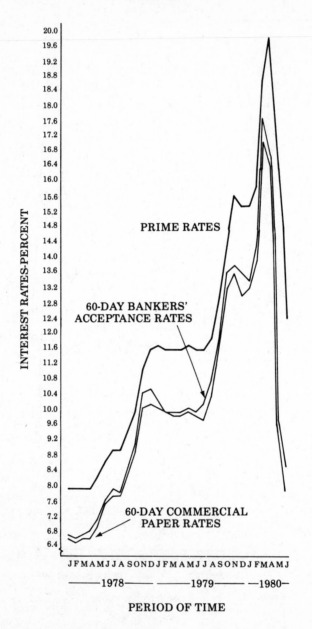

See Exhibit 4 for source of graphical information.

EXHIBIT 3
Midwest Grain Company
Average Monthly Interest Rates
1978–1980

Month	30–Day Bankers' Acceptance Rates[1] (Percent)	30–Day Commercial Paper Rates[2] (Percent)	Prime Rates[3] (Percent)
Jan 78	6.7	6.6	8.0
Feb 78	6.6	6.6	8.0
Mar 78	6.7	6.6	8.0
Apr 78	6.8	6.7	8.0
May 78	7.1	6.9	8.3
Jun 78	7.6	7.5	8.7
Jul 78	7.8	7.7	9.0
Aug 78	7.8	7.7	9.0
Sep 78	8.4	8.3	9.5
Oct 78	9.0	8.9	10.0
Nov 78	10.0	9.9	11.0
Dec 78	10.3	10.2	11.6
Jan 79	10.1	10.0	11.7
Feb 79	9.8	9.8	11.6
Mar 79	9.9	9.8	11.6
Apr 79	9.9	9.8	11.6
May 79	9.8	9.9	11.7
Jun 79	10.0	9.8	11.6
Jul 79	10.1	10.0	11.6
Aug 79	10.7	10.5	11.9
Sep 79	11.8	11.6	13.0
Oct 79	13.4	13.2	15.5
Nov 79	13.6	13.5	15.2
Dec 79	13.5	13.5	15.2
Jan 80	13.3	13.2	15.7
Feb 80	14.0	13.8	18.5
Mar 80	17.0	16.8	19.6
Apr 80	16.4	16.3	16.3
May 80	9.8	9.7	12.4
Jun 80	8.7	8.6	11.3

[1] Bankers' acceptance rates illustrated are composite offered rates quoted to investors in prime bankers' acceptances of the indicated maturity. They are shown without regard to the amount of various administrative fees charged by banks, BA dealers or other intermediary parties. Such fees (estimated to be approximately 7/8 of 1 percent, or 87½ basis points) are incorporated into the "all inclusive" interest rates quoted to the ultimate borrower of funds, and consequently are absorbed by the borrower.

[2] Commercial paper rates illustrated are composite offered rates quoted to investors in the commercial paper of industrial firms whose commercial paper carries an A-1, P-1 rating and whose long-term debt instruments carry a AA, Aa rating. They are shown without regard to the amount of various administrative fees charged by commercial paper dealers or other intermediary parties. Such fees (estimated to be approximately 1/8 of 1 percent, or 12½ basis points) are incorporated into the "all inclusive" interest rates quoted to the ultimate borrower of funds, and consequently are absorbed by the borrower.

[3] Prime rates illustrated are composite rates quoted by commercial banks located in major financial centers coast to coast.

See Exhibit 1 for a graphic illustration of movements in the above interest rates.

NOTE: All interest rates are presented on an annualized, interest rate equivalent basis.

EXHIBIT 4
Midwest Grain Company
Average Monthly Interest Rates
1978–1980

Month	60–Day Bankers' Acceptance Rates[1] (Percent)	60–Day Commercial Paper Rates[2] (Percent)	Prime Rates[3] (Percent)
Jan 78	6.8	6.7	8.0
Feb 78	6.7	6.6	8.0
Mar 78	6.8	6.7	8.0
Apr 78	6.9	6.7	8.0
May 78	7.2	7.0	8.3
Jun 78	7.7	7.6	8.7
Jul 78	8.0	7.8	9.0
Aug 78	7.9	7.8	9.0
Sep 78	8.5	8.4	9.5
Oct 78	9.2	9.0	10.0
Nov 78	10.5	10.1	11.0
Dec 78	10.6	10.2	11.6
Jan 79	10.3	10.1	11.7
Feb 79	10.0	10.0	11.6
Mar 79	10.0	9.9	11.6
Apr 79	10.0	9.9	11.6
May 79	10.1	10.0	11.7
Jun 79	10.0	9.9	11.6
Jul 79	10.2	9.8	11.6
Aug 79	10.8	10.4	11.9
Sep 79	11.9	11.7	13.0
Oct 79	13.6	13.2	15.5
Nov 79	13.8	13.6	15.2
Dec 79	13.6	13.0	15.2
Jan 80	13.4	13.2	15.7
Feb 80	14.3	13.9	18.5
Mar 80	17.5	16.9	19.6
Apr 80	16.5	16.2	16.3
May 80	9.9	9.6	12.4
Jun 80	8.6	8.0	11.3

[1] Bankers' acceptance rates illustrated are composite offered rates quoted to investors in prime bankers' acceptances of the indicated maturity. They are shown without regard to the amount of various administrative fees charged by banks, BA dealers or other intermediary parties. Such fees (estimated to be approximately 7/8 of 1 percent, or 87½ basis points) are incorporated into the "all inclusive" interest rates quoted to the ultimate borrower of funds, and consequently are absorbed by the borrower.

[2] Commercial paper rates illustrated are composite offered rates quoted to investors in the commercial paper of industrial firms whose commercial paper carries an A-1, P-1 rating and whose long-term debt instruments carry a AA, Aa rating. They are shown without regard to the amount of various administrative fees charged by commercial paper dealers or other intermediary parties. Such fees (estimated to be approximately 1/8 of 1 percent, or 12½ basis points) are incorporated into the "all inclusive" interest rates quoted to the ultimate borrower of funds, and consequently are absorbed by the borrower.

[3] Prime rates illustrated are composite rates quoted by commercial banks located in major financial centers coast to coast.

See Exhibit 2 for a graphic illustration of movements in the above interest rates.

NOTE: All interest rates are presented on an annualized, interest rate equivalent basis.

EXHIBIT 5
Midwest Grain Company
Comparison of Yields on High-Grade
and Medium-Grade Commercial Paper

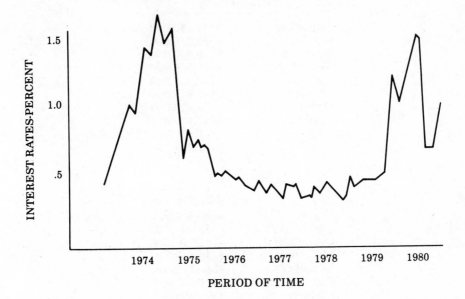

Rate spread is the rate on medium-grade less the rate on high-grade commercial paper calculated from rates charged by two major dealers for dealer-placed 30- to 59-day paper; ratings for medium-grade, A–2, or P–2, and for high-grade, A–1 or P–1.

Source: *Federal Reserve Bulletin*, Washington, D.C., June 1982, page 332.

EXHIBIT 6
Midwest Grain Company
Consolidated Outside Bank Borrowings for the Periods Indicated

Fiscal 1977–78

September	$ 11,250,000
October	$ 20,250,000
November	$ 36,900,000
December	$ 60,965,000
January	$160,665,000
February	$183,345,000
March	$179,610,000
April	$143,100,000
May	$131,500,000
June	$115,235,000

Fiscal 1978–79

July	$ 86,790,000
August	$ 87,400,000
September	$ 69,000,000
October	$161,150,000
November	$249,960,000
December	$276,165,000
January	$293,086,000
February	$295,950,000
March	$264,450,000
April	$216,450,000
May	$172,050,000
June	$157,225,000

Fiscal 1979–80

July	$ 95,250,000
August	$ 60,022,000
September	$ 43,800,000
October	$ 39,900,000
November	$213,760,000
December	$399,450,000
January	$561,001,000
February	$550,703,000
March	$476,145,000
April	$315,975,000
May	$292,220,000
June	$135,466,000

EXHIBIT 7
Midwest Grain Company
Consolidated Balance Sheets as of the Dates Indicated

	June 30, 1978	June 30, 1979	June 30, 1980
Assets			
Cash and marketable securities, at lower of cost or market	$ 16,459,000	$ 17,981,000	$ 23,258,000
Trade accounts and notes receivable	7,934,000	9,377,000	11,722,000
Inventories (Note 1)	163,086,000	219,609,000	218,110,000
Other current assets	885,000	1,784,000	1,920,000
Total current assets	$188,364,000	$248,751,000	$255,010,000
Property, plant, equipment, and other assets, net (Note 2)	37,204,000	39,839,000	36,036,000
Total assets	$225,568,000	$288,590,000	$291,046,000
Liabilities and Stockholders' Equity			
Notes payable to banks (Note 2)	$115,235,000	$157,225,000	$135,466,000
Accounts payable and other current liabilities	11,492,000	11,830,000	24,070,000
Deferred gains on hedge transactions (Note 3)	220,000	3,412,000	695,000
Federal and state income taxes payable (current and deferred), net	4,870,000	8,871,000	8,447,000
Current maturities of long-term debt	3,414,000	2,327,000	2,820,000
Total current liabilities	$135,231,000	$183,665,000	$171,498,000
Long-term debt (Note 2)	15,275,000	12,850,000	12,992,000
Stockholders' equity, net (Note 4)	75,062,000	92,075,000	106,556,000
Total liabilities and stockholders' equity	$225,568,000	$288,590,000	$291,046,000

Note 1—Inventories. Grain inventories are valued at current market prices and have been adjusted in order to reflect the value of current grain crop year purchase and sale commitments as well as the amount of accrued charges relating to inventory on hand as of the balance sheet dates indicated. Open futures market hedge positions relating to such inventory are reflected in inventory at the current market value of the open contracts as of the respective balance sheet dates.

Note 2—Short-term and Long-term Debt. Total interest expense relating to all outside borrowings was $24,800,000 and $41,900,000 in the fiscal years ended June 30, 1979 and June 30, 1980, respectively. A corresponding figure for the fiscal year ended June 30, 1978 was not available.

Long-term debt relates primarily to permanent financing obtained subsequent to the purchase of grain storage facilities and other fixed assets.

Note 3—Deferred Gains on Hedge Transactions. Such amounts relate to futures market transactions entered into in order to hedge purchase and sale commitments relating to subsequent grain crop years.

Note 4—Stockholders' Equity. The amounts shown for stockholders' equity include common stock, retained earnings, and treasury stock (at cost).

As a matter of company policy Midwest Grain Company does not distribute dividends, and no treasury stock has been purchased since May 31, 1977; accordingly the indicated changes in stockholders' equity may be attributed to net income for the respective periods of time.

EXHIBIT 8
Midwest Grain Company
Selected Issuers of Commercial Paper

Company Name/Business	Commercial Paper/Bonds As of 4/23/80			Fiscal Year Ended	Financial Highlights (000 omitted)		
	Moody's	S & P	Fitch		Total Assets	Long-term debt	Shareholders' Equity
Bay State Gas Co.* Canton, Massachusetts Gas utility	P–2/Baa	A–2/BBB	–/–	12/31/79	$ 218,592	$ 70,600	$ 74,512
Big Three Industries, Inc.* Houston, Texas Diversified	P–1/A	A–1/A+	–/–	12/31/79	700,052	133,706	404,137
Chessie System, Inc.* Baltimore, Maryland Railroad, coal, real estate	P–2/–	A–2/–	–/–	12/31/79	3,418,781	910,267	1,303,934
Consolidated Freightways, Inc.* San Francisco, California Freight carrier and mfg.	P–1/A	A–1/AA	–/–	12/31/79	769,171	115,388	344,190
Grace & Co., W. R.* New York, New York Chemicals	P–2/Baa	A–2/BB	–/–	12/31/79	3,728,853	839,802	1,572,282
Heileman Brewing Co., Inc., G.* La Crosse, Wisconsin Brewer	–/–	A–1/–	F–1/–	12/31/79	225,537	31,506	99,675
Marriot Corporation* Washington, D.C. Food service and lodging	P–2/–	–/–	–/–	12/28/79	1,080,365	370,877	413,503

226

Issuer				Date			
McDonnell Douglas Finance Corporation* Long Beach, California Captive equipment, finance	P-2/-	A-1/A	F-1/-	12/31/79	545,909	223,011	110,072
Milton Bradley Co.* Springfield, Massachusetts Mfg. toys and games	P-2/-	-/-	-/-	12/31/79	257,531	26,970	138,102
Miss. River Transmission Corporation* St. Louis, Missouri Gas transmission	P-2/Baa	A-1/A	-/-	12/31/79	322,632	65,056	123,220
Plessey, Inc.* Melville, New York Industrial	-/-	A-2/-	-/-	3/31/79	113,797	34,047	46,678
Trailmobile Finance Co.* Chicago, Illinois Captive finance	P-2/A	A-1/A	-/-	12/31/79	361,150	145,000	71,341
Armstrong Co., Inc., A. J.** New York, New York Commercial finance	P-2/-	A-2/-	-/-	12/31/79	282,857	54,000	47,897
Industrial National Corporation** Providence, Rhode Island Bank holding company	P-2/A	A-2/A	-/-	12/31/79	3,224,684	105,049	168,331
International Harvester Credit Corporation** Chicago, Illinois Captive finance	P-2/A	-/-	F-1/A	10/31/79	4,149,072	1,551,164	553,316

*Denotes issuer whose commercial paper is regularly sold to investors through the use of commercial paper dealers.
**Denotes issuer whose commercial paper is generally placed directly with investors.

APPENDIX A
Midwest Grain Company
Commercial Paper and Bankers' Acceptance Financing

Commercial paper and bankers' acceptances are used very extensively within today's business environment since they both provide a source of the short-term credit which businesses so desperately need on a continuing basis. This note will highlight the similarities and differences in the ways that the two debt instruments function while familiarizing the reader with aspects of commercial paper and bankers' acceptances as primary sources of short-term credit.

COMMERCIAL PAPER

The use of commercial paper (commonly referred to as a short-term promissory note or a "corporate IOU"—see Attachment 2) enables a borrower to raise short-term funds from investors either through direct placement or through the use of commercial paper dealers as intermediary parties. Since in most cases commercial paper represents an unsecured obligation of the borrower, strong financial standing is a prerequisite in order for a company to be able to issue commercial paper; as a result, only selected companies are capable of doing so. Assuming that the maturity of a commercial paper issue is less than 270 days, the issue is generally not required to be registered under the various federal securities acts; however, even without formal registration constraints, the establishment of a viable commercial paper program is likely to require a great deal of legal work on the part of highly specialized attorneys.

The ability to issue commercial paper allows a company to borrow a certain amount of money (generally denominated in $100,000 increments) at a specified rate of interest for a given period of time. In the usual case a company's commercial paper is sold[1] by a firm (such as A. G. Becker or Merrill Lynch)[2] specializing in the marketing of commercial paper; for that service the marketing firm extracts a negotiable fee which is usually quoted in terms of a portion of a percent or perhaps in terms of "basis points" (1 percent equals 100 basis points). Commercial paper

---

This technical note was prepared by Richard L. Fisher, formerly of the McIntire School of Commerce of the University of Virginia, in conjunction with Kenneth F. Clark, III, of Wachovia Bank and Trust Company, N.A.

1. The terms "issued" and "sold" are used somewhat interchangeably within this discussion. As a practical matter, however, commercial paper is considered to be "issued" by the borrower (or by a separate legal entity associated therewith) when funds are borrowed using commercial paper, and commercial paper is considered to be "sold" to investors when their funds are invested in commercial paper.

2. As reported by the Federal Reserve, approximately 60 percent of all commercial paper issuers are able to place their paper directly with investors without utilizing the services of commercial paper dealers. Although in such circumstances the customary dealer commission is avoided, the issuing company will generally incur additional internal operating expenses associated with the maintenance and processing of commercial paper transactions.

dealers usually quote commercial paper rates to borrowers on an "all inclusive" basis with the understanding that the all inclusive rate includes not only the interest rate dictated in the commercial paper marketplace, but that it also includes the amount of any direct fees or commissions charged by the firm marketing the commercial paper. It should be noted, however, that the all inclusive rate does not generally include the costs associated with other financial intermediaries which may be involved in guaranteeing the commercial paper obligations or providing custodial, depositary, or funds transfer services. Also excluded from the all inclusive rates quoted by commercial paper dealers are the potential costs associated with support lines of credit which may be required to be maintained with commercial banks at levels equal to or greater than the amount of commercial paper potentially issuable; such costs often take the form of required compensating bank balances equal to 10 to 20 percent of the amount of the supporting lines (depending upon utilization).

Commercial paper is issued in varying lengths of maturity (for example, 30 to 90 days), with the most common maturity probably being 30 days. It is not uncommon, however, for commercial paper to be issued in maturities of less than 30 days depending upon overall interest rate or money market conditions. As a practical matter the firm marketing an issue generally informs the potential borrower as to which maturity levels are considered to be the most competitive from an interest cost standpoint, and the borrower then attempts to integrate the resulting availability of funds into its overall borrowing posture.

Proceeds from the issuance of commercial paper are generally remitted to the borrower on a net basis after interest expense for the given maturity of the loan has been calculated and deducted from the loan principal using the agreed upon all inclusive rate quoted to the borrower. For purposes of such calculation it is assumed that the all inclusive rate is an annual one, and that a 360-day year is to be used for calculation purposes (see Attachment 1). Since interest expense on commercial paper borrowings is deducted from the principal amount of the loan prior to transfer of the net proceeds to the borrower, it should be noted that the "effective rate" of interest charged to the borrower is actually higher than the all inclusive rate initially quoted by commercial paper dealers when transactions are entered into. Also instrumental in raising the effective rate of interest charged to the borrower are the amount of additional direct or indirect costs associated with financial intermediaries and banking arrangements incidental to the process of issuing commercial paper.

The level of commercial paper rates dictated in the marketplace at any point in time will be influenced by a number of factors; foremost among these factors is the supply and demand for commercial paper loans and investments. Other prominent factors include the perceived quality of the commercial paper based upon the integrity (financial and otherwise) of the company issuing the commercial paper, the integrity of the firm guaranteeing the issue (though many times the same as the issuing company), and the integrity of the firm(s) marketing the issue. The quality of commercial paper issues is rated by several independent rating agencies, with the more common ones being Standard & Poor's Corporation, Moody's Investors Service, and Fitch Investors Service. The official quality designation assigned to an issue by one or more of the recognized rating agencies will have a direct impact on the interest rates generated in the commercial paper marketplace. Another factor likely to influence the market rates of interest is the amount of recurring visibility which an issue receives; the more often a company's commercial paper is seen in the marketplace, the more likely are investors to be familiar with the issuing company's background and stability. As investors become more familiar and comfortable with a particular company's issue, the resulting interest rates generated in the commercial paper markets and ultimately quoted to the borrower should soften on a relative basis.

The above notwithstanding, however, it should be noted that the commercial paper markets are at times very sensitive and they may react unfavorably to general economic adversity or to undesirable publicity surrounding a particular company. In the worst case, investor interest in a given company's commercial paper may "dry up" completely due to a loss of investor confidence. "Stand alone" commercial paper offerings (as opposed to bank-supported programs) are particularly sensitive to such a situation.

BANKERS' ACCEPTANCES[3]

Bankers' acceptance (BA) markets also provide a means by which businesses are able to obtain short-term credit in order to meet working capital needs. Although the originating party in a bankers' acceptance transaction is a commercial bank, loans granted under bankers' acceptance agreements differ in several important respects from loans granted under normal line of credit arrangements. One primary difference relates to the fact that regulations of the Federal Reserve impose restrictions on the types of underlying transactions which may be financed with bankers' acceptances. Thus, depending upon the particular trade or business of a given company, bankers' acceptance financing may or may not be a viable borrowing alternative. In the general case acceptance financing is available to companies engaged in the financing of current transactions associated with:

1. The importation or exportation of goods between countries, or
2. The storage or shipment of readily marketable goods, provided that the participating bank is secured at the time of acceptance (see explanatory tab on the left side of Attachment 3).

Another primary difference relates to the fact that in a bankers' acceptance transaction the bank is generally not committing its own funds (except on a contingent basis) for the life of the loan; rather the bank (and very possibly a BA dealer) is in essence serving as a middleman between an investor and a borrower. As a prerequisite to such an arrangement, however, there is generally an under-

---

3. This discussion will primarily be concerned with "domestic storage" acceptances which are bankers' acceptances associated with the financing of readily marketable goods stored in warehouses. "Trade" acceptances associated with the financing of imports or exports will not be discussed herein.

standing between the bank and the borrower that acceptance financing is feasible under the terms of the existing banking relationship. Assuming that the bank's acceptance portfolio is within legal limits[4] it will probably make the BA borrowing medium available to its customers. In the typical case the commercial bank involved in a bankers' acceptance transaction advances to the borrower a certain amount of money at a specified "all inclusive" rate of interest for a given period of time not to exceed 180 days. As with commercial paper borrowings, the interest expense for the life of the bankers' acceptance is calculated and deducted from the principal amount of the loan, with the resulting net amount of funds being remitted to the borrower (see Attachment 1 and the discussion of effective interest rates above). In exchange for such funds the borrower transfers to the bank a draft (see Attachment 3)[5] signed by an authorized officer of the borrowing company. The draft (through its interaction with various credit agreements) ultimately gives the bank the right of offset with respect to company assets accessible to the bank (in the event that the borrower defaults on the loan). As a practical matter, however, the borrower usually contacts the bank and wires the principal amount of the loan to the bank at maturity; the right of offset merely provides additional protection to creditor parties.

Upon receipt of a signed draft the bank will examine its propriety and assuming that it finds everything in order the bank will officially "accept" it by so noting on the face of the draft (hence the term "bankers' acceptance"). Having advanced funds to the borrower and having received and accepted a properly executed draft, the bank may choose to transfer the draft to a BA dealer who in turn will likely discount the draft and sell it via the BA markets to an investor (alternatively a division of the accepting bank may invest its own funds thereby avoiding discounting of the instrument with a BA dealer). Just as a borrower is quoted an "all inclusive" rate of interest when he borrows on a bankers' acceptance, so too is the investor (or purchaser) in a BA quoted an all inclusive rate of interest which is used to determine the net amount of funds to be invested (see Attachment 1). The difference between the net amount of funds advanced by the investor, and the net amount of funds received by the borrower represents the dollar amount of the commissions charged by the bank and any other financial intermediaries participating in the transaction. This difference is often quoted in terms of an interest rate or basis point differential through an appropriate comparison of the all inclusive rates of interest quoted to the investor and the borrower (see Attachment 1).

The level of all inclusive rates quoted to a borrower using bankers' acceptances will depend upon a number of factors. The starting point for determination of a rate is of course the base rate of interest determined in the marketplace for a

---

4. Banking regulations stipulate that the total amount of a bank's portfolio of bankers' acceptance loans which have subsequently been discounted and sold to investors may not exceed, at any given point in time, the amount of the bank's "capital" (broadly defined as stockholders' equity).

5. As a practical matter presigned drafts are often kept on hand by banks with whom BA loan agreements are in effect. This procedure facilitates paperwork processing at the time that loans are made.

bankers' acceptance of given quality;[6] this rate is primarily dependent upon the supply and demand for bankers' acceptance loans and investments. Once a base rate of interest has been determined, the various commissions charged by the BA dealer, the accepting bank, and any other financial intermediaries must be established. Of such commissions, the commission charged by the accepting bank (usually between 40 and 200 basis points) is likely to be the most flexible. Major determinants of the amount of the bank's commission are likely to be the overall financial strength of the borrower, the quality of the existing banking relationship, the adequacy of the underlying collateral used to secure the bankers' acceptance, and the extent to which the bank is able to participate in new bankers' acceptance business based upon capital constraints at any given point in time (see footnote 4).

Although bankers' acceptance markets may at times be quite volatile, it should be reiterated that the commercial bank participating in a bankers' acceptance transaction (having "accepted" the company's draft) is the primary guarantor to the investor. As such, even in the face of economic adversity or undesirable publicity surrounding a given company, investor interest in a company's acceptance obligations may not be severely diminished if the financial condition of the accepting bank is stable. Further alleviating potential loss of investor confidence is the tendency of commercial banks to "work with" a borrower in order to avoid contraction of credit scources.

Such circumstances are to be contrasted with a similar situation involving a company's commercial paper. As has previously been mentioned, loss of investor confidence in a given company's commercial paper (for whatever reason) may be extremely problematic, particularly with respect to "stand alone" offerings. If other favorable borrowing mediums (such as acceptance financing) are not available, a company previously taking advantage of competitive commercial paper borrowing rates may find itself having to borrow under regular bank lines of credit at interest rates which, relative to commercial paper rates, may be unfavorable.

---

6. In contrast to the assignment of quality ratings to commercial paper, bankers' acceptance obligations are not officially rated by organizations such as Moody's or Standard & Poor's. In an attempt to ascertain the relative financial integrity of an accepting bank, investors often refer to ratings assigned to the bank's other debt obligations (if any), to comparative measures of size (deposits or capital), and to relative measures of asset quality and liquidity.

MIDWEST GRAIN COMPANY
Attachment 1 to Appendix A
Analysis of Loan/Investment Proceeds

	Borrower	Investor
Factual setting assumed:*		
Principal amount of loan/investment	$1,000,000	$1,000,000
Maturity period	30 days	30 days
All inclusive rate of interest quoted*	15.625%	14.75%

A. Calculation of the net proceeds to be advanced to the *borrower*:

Principal amount of loan	$1,000,000
Less: Interest *expense* for the term of the loan:	
$1,000 000 × .15625 × 30/360	13,021
Net amount of loan	$ 986,979
Principal to be repaid at maturity	$1,000,000

B. Calculation of the net amount to be advanced by the *investor*:

Principal amount of investment	$1,000,000
Less: Interest *income* for the term of the investment:	
$1,000,000 × .1475 × 30/360	12,292
Net amount of investment	$ 987,708
Principal to be received at maturity	$1,000,000

C. Calculation of commissions or fees:

	Absolute Dollars	All Inclusive Rate of Interest
Discount/Rate to borrower	$13,021	15.625%
Discount/Rate to investor	12,292	14.75 %
Differential (Commission)	$ 729	.875%
		(or 87½ basis points)

---

*The above scenario would be applicable to either a commercial paper or a bankers' acceptance transaction. However, depending upon the type of transaction (i.e., commercial paper or bankers' acceptance), the level of all inclusive rates of interest quoted to the investor and the borrower (as well as the size of the spread between such rates) would likely differ.

MIDWEST GRAIN COMPANY
Attachment 2 to Appendix A
Sample Promissory Note Evidencing Bank-Supported
Commercial Paper Indebtedness

MIDWEST COMMERCIAL PAPER, INC.
PROMISSORY NOTE

No._____
Chicago, Illinois
_____, 19____

$_____

On _____, for value received, MIDWEST COMMERCIAL PAPER, INC., a Delaware corporation (the "Maker"), promises to pay to the order of BEARER, the sum of $_____, payable at the Corporate Trust Office of Fidelity Guaranty Trust Company of Illinois, Chicago, Illinois (the "Issuing Agent Bank").

This Note has been issued by the Issuing Agent for the account of the Maker, pursuant to a certain Depositary Agreement dated _____, as from time to time amended (the "Depositary Agreement"), between the Maker and the Issuing Agent, to which a certain company referred to therein (the "Company") and Chicago National (the "Letter of Credit Bank") have joined as consenting parties.

This Note is entitled to the benefits of a Letter of Credit issued to the Issuing Agent by Chicago National, Chicago, Illinois pursuant to a certain Credit Agreement dated as of _____ as from time to time amended (the "Credit Agreement"), among the Maker, the Company, the Letter of Credit Bank, and a certain bank for certain limited purposes thereunder, provided that this Note is presented to the Issuing Agent for payment, at its aforesaid Corporate Trust Office, not later than the Issuing Agent's close of business on the 15th day following the above-stated maturity date or, if such 15th day is not a Business Day, on the next succeeding Business Day. As used herein, the term "Business Day" means a day on which the aforesaid Corporate Trust Office of the Issuing Agent is open for business and the letter of Credit Bank is open at its address specified in the Credit Agreement for the purpose of conducting a commercial banking business.

The Credit Agreement, the Depositary Agreement, and said Letter of Credit are on file with the Issuing Agent at its aforesaid Corporate Trust Office, and reference is made to those documents for the terms upon which said Letter of Credit and this Note have been issued and the procedures governing drawings thereunder by the Issuing Agent.

This Note shall be governed by and construed in accordance with the laws of the State of Illinois.

MIDWEST COMMERCIAL PAPER, INC.

By _____
        Authorized Signature

Countersigned for Authentication only:
FIDELITY GUARANTY TRUST
COMPANY OF ILLINOIS
            as Issuing Agent

By _____
        Authorized Signature

This Note is not valid for any purpose unless countersigned by Fidelity Guaranty Trust Company as Issuing Agent.

MIDWEST GRAIN COMPANY
Attachment 3 to Appendix A
Sample "Domestic Storage" Bankers' Acceptances

Swanson Corporation

In late May 1971, Mr. Corrie Jackson, vice president finance of the
Swanson Corporation, was considering what action he should take with
regards to the company's credit arrangements at five banks. In May,
Swanson's lines of credit totaled $18.5 million, of which the company
was borrowing $5.5 million. Compensating balances required to support
this credit totaled $3.3 million, more than $1.3 million above Swanson's
transaction balance needs at these banks.[1] According to Mr. Knight,
Swanson's treasurer, this excess cost $73 thousand per year at the cur-
rent prime rate of 5.5%. Mr. Jackson considered this expense high relative to the company's reduced current borrowings and low most likely
future requirements.

On the other hand, for a number of reasons Mr. Jackson was unsure
whether this was the appropriate time to seek a change in Swanson's
lines of credit and, if so, what type of arrangements he might propose
to Swanson's banks. Mr. Jackson believed that caution was called for
because of financial difficulties recently experienced by the company
and because of the considerable uncertainty still underlying Swanson's
forecasted cash needs. Moreover, the company had recently been involved in disputes with two of its banks, one of which was Swanson's
oldest and "lead" bank. These difficulties were as yet unresolved.
Swanson still had a $7.5 million line of credit at the lead bank, but had
communicated its intention not to use this line until the bank relented
in its demand that Swanson pay ½% above the prime rate on any borrowings. The other dispute involved the adequacy of Swanson's balances as compensation for the services and the line of credit provided
by a small bank. Although the amount at stake in this case was not in
itself of major importance, Mr. Jackson was concerned because he had
thought he might be able to reduce Swanson's total compensating balance requirements by shifting some lines of credit from certain large
banks to this and several other of Swanson's small banks. Since the

Copyright © 1972 by the President and Fellows of Harvard College.

This case was prepared by George Aragon under the direction of Michael L.
Tennican as a basis for class discussion rather than to illustrate either effective or
ineffective handling of an administrative situation. Reprinted by permission of the
Harvard Business School.

1. Swanson currently also had over $800 thousand in working balances at banks
   from which it was not borrowing.

dispute now troubling him stemmed from the initial attempt to see how this overall plan might work out, Mr. Jackson was particularly interested in resolving it favorably.

Secondly, since some of Swanson's bank balances served both to support lines of credit and to compensate banks for cash collection and disbursement services, Mr. Jackson wanted to ensure that any changes in Swanson's borrowing arrangements would not adversely affect the cost of bank participation in the company's collections and disbursement system.

Further complicating Mr. Jackson's decision was the fact that he had only recently (in January) been promoted to his present position. Although he had been with the company for the 20 years since his graduation from Harvard Business School, Mr. Jackson's work experience had been with Swanson's Altoona, Pennsylvania, division, most recently as its controller. Lacking the context of long, established working relationships with the company's major bankers, Mr. Jackson knew that his decisions might substantially influence the tenor if not the substance of his future relationships with them.

BACKGROUND OF THE COMPANY

The Swanson Corporation, headquartered in Lodi, California, manufactured a wide range of heavy custom-made industrial process equipment in production centers around the world. Consolidated world-wide sales for fiscal year ending September 1970 totaled $150 million, approximately 67% of which total was generated by domestic subsidiaries. Swanson's domestic subsidiaries reported profits in 1970 of about $2.4 million, resulting in a 2.5% return on total assets of almost $95 million and a 4.0% return on stockholders' equity of almost $60 million. Other pertinent financial data for the period 1966–1970 and a recent balance sheet are shown in Exhibits 1 and 2.

Prior to late 1967, Swanson had five wholly owned domestic subsidiaries, six foreign subsidiaries, and two domestic joint ventures. Each of the subsidiaries, many acquired as going concerns in the period from 1955 to 1967, had operated essentially as a separate company. Despite these acquisitions, however, the original business of the company (now the Lodi division) still accounted for over 60% of domestic sales and 75% of profits. The domestic subsidiaries were widely dispersed, with locations in California, Illinois, Pennsylvania, Oregon and Utah.

During 1967, while completing a major expansion program which included acquisitions of a pump manufacturer in Skokie, Illinois, and a boiler fabricator in Salt Lake City, Utah, Swanson experienced a severe dropoff in an important source of current financing for the Lodi division, namely progress payments. These progress payments (or customer advances) were a form of construction financing traditionally required by heavy equipment manufacturers, such as the Lodi division, during the construction of specialized process equipment—which construction could take up to 22 months. In 1967, however, progress payments dropped almost $16 million, requiring immediate and extensive bank borrowings. The precipitous drop in progress payments also portended a severe sales decline.

To relieve Swanson's sudden funds shortage, the First National Bank of San Francisco, Swanson's only major bank at that time, agreed to organize and manage a credit syndicate to provide up to $18 million in lines of credit. The large share, $7.5 million, committed by the First of San Francisco helped secure commitments from the Bank of Brooklyn ($5 million), the Bank of the Bronx ($3 million), and the First National Bank of Sacramento ($2.5 million).

At the insistence of its lenders, Swanson extensively reorganized its domestic operations and instituted tight domestic operational and financial controls. In October 1967, though the five domestic subsidiaries remained as profit centers, the financial and other staff activities of these operating units were largely taken over by a new "corporate division," a headquarters group comprising the senior line executives and the supporting staff groups. Swanson's foreign subsidiaries and joint ventures were also put under more direct corporate control.

The anticipated sales decline materialized in 1968. World-wide sales dropped from $182 million in 1967 to $156 million in 1968. Domestic operations accounted for virtually all this decrease, dropping from $146 million to less than $119 million. In response, Swanson pressed to curb cash outflows through operating cutbacks, reduction of capital expenditures, tight controls on inventories and accounts receivable, and slowing of payments to suppliers.

These measures served to generate substantial amounts of cash from domestic operations in 1968 and the following two years. As shown in Exhibit 1, inventory liquidations by domestic subsidiaries generated almost $18 million of cash from 1968 through 1970; reduction of receivables generated another $4 million in the same period. Liquidations of fixed assets accounted for another $1 million. For the three-year period, depreciation on domestic assets exceeded $9 million, while gross additions to plant for the domestic subsidiaries totaled less than $6 million. Swanson's policy of delaying payment on trade payables succeeded in keeping the decrease in this liability to less than $2 million from 1968 through 1970. Dividend payments were sharply reduced from $453 thousand in 1968 to $75 thousand in 1969 and 1970. Thus, although profits totaled only about $5.1 million for the period and although customer advances continued to decrease, from $28 million in 1968 to less than $8 million in 1970, Swanson had been able to reduce bank debt by almost $7 million and long-term debt by almost $2.5 million.

The operating cutbacks and tight cash controls throughout the corporation were, in 1971, continuing to generate substantial amounts of cash. The second quarter of fiscal year 1971, ending March 28, 1971, resulted in cash generation well ahead of year-earlier figures—and ahead of projections for the quarter. Part of this improvement was due to the decision in January 1971 to close down the Skokie, Illinois, division, which division had sustained operating losses ever since its acquisition in 1967. Primarily because of the liquidation of accounts receivable and inventory, Skokie generated over $700 thousand of cash in the first six months in contrast with earlier forecasts of roughly $1 million in cash absorption for the period.

The primary source of Swanson's second quarter cash generation was the Lodi division. As a consequence of an unanticipated buildup in customer advances, Lodi generated almost $8 million in cash during the fiscal quarter against forecasts of less than $3 million. Moreover, updated forecasts as of early May indicated that cash generation by the Lodi division was likely to exceed $1 million for the third quarter 1971 in contrast with the earlier forecast of about $0.5 million.

On the 24th of May 1971, Swanson's board of directors voted to close down the Salt Lake division, another division which had been unprofitable since its acquisition in 1967. It was anticipated that this action would generate an additional $2 million to $3 million in cash during the third and fourth quarters of fiscal year ending September 1971. The closing at Salt Lake, as at Skokie, produced sizable "nonrecurring" charges against income.

The bulk of Swanson's cash generation had been going toward debt repayment. Bank borrowings were reduced from $15 million in February to $5.5 million in May. Mr. Jackson anticipated further reductions, to possibly less than $1.5 million in bank debt by September 1971.

ELEMENTS OF SWANSON'S CASH MANAGEMENT SYSTEM

From the time of its reorganization in 1967, Swanson had constantly pursued ways to increase the efficiency of cash use throughout the corporation. According to Mr. Jackson, the need to monitor cash use closely during the company's recent business decline had greatly augmented the attention devoted corporate-wide to cash collection, reporting, disbursement, and investment. In 1970, Swanson's corporate treasurer, Mr. Knight, formalized the consolidation of domestic cash responsibilities by establishing a corporate cash management department, managed by Mr. Bishop. For the most part, the cash management system currently concentrated on domestic rather than foreign operations.

"In all areas of cash management," noted Mr. Jackson, "we have been fortunate in having the assistance and cooperation of our banks. They have been instrumental to the implementation and daily operation of our cash management system—even though increasing the productivity of our cash has meant reduced bank balances."

THE COLLECTION SYSTEM

In late 1967, Swanson had accelerated collection of customer payments by a week or more by adopting a lock box collection system.[2] With the help of the First National Bank of San Francisco, Swanson had analyzed the geographical distribution of its customers and found that, with current mail delivery times and check clearance times, 95% of all payments could be received and collected within two days if a total of 18 lock boxes were opened in San Francisco, Portland (Oregon), Cleveland, Chicago, and New York.

The system was restudied in March 1971. Having been notified of postal schedule changes, Mr. Jackson asked Mr. Bishop to study what effect these changes might have on the company's lock box system. Mr. Bishop's study revealed that the postal changes would have little effect, but that the lock boxes in New York and San Francisco were increasingly affected by congestion within those cities and within the banks themselves. In fact, the study revealed that if all the lock boxes in San Francisco and New York were relocated in Lodi, cash collection could be speeded by two to four days. Thus, although Swanson continued to maintain balances at the San Francisco and New York banks, the lock boxes were moved to the First National Bank of Lodi.

DISBURSEMENT POLICY AND PROCEDURES

Swanson's disbursement policies were designed to use suppliers' funds so long as such funds were, on average, "less expensive" than bank funds. Currently, Swanson's general policy was to hold up payments on invoices less than 45 days old[3] and to "play the percentages" by taking

---

2. Lock boxes are post office boxes to which customers are instructed to mail payments. Banks collect deposits from the boxes several times per day and begin processing any checks immediately. Accompanying invoices and other details are also forwarded at daily intervals to the division or company using the particular lock box. Strategically located lock boxes can sometimes reduce payment transit times substantially.

3. Other than "required" or "urgent" invoices, such as payments to governmental agencies and local utilities, and "minor" payables under one thousand dollars.

discounts even if the invoice was paid after the discount deadline. The corporate division authorized the payment of invoices on the basis of weekly disbursement requests submitted by the operating divisions. When approved, disbursement checks were mailed by the operating divisions on the last mail pickup at the end of the accounting week, giving the corporate division use of the bank balances behind the checks over the weekend. "By delaying our disbursements, we have built up our trade payables about as much as we can," noted Mr. Jackson. "Since we have used this cash to retire bank debt, you might say we consider payables a substitute for loans. So long as the average amount of discounts we lose is below our bank borrowing cost, it's cheaper for us to 'borrow' from our suppliers." Swanson also delayed the date on which suppliers would have the use of Swanson's payment (and thus created "float") by paying them with checks drawn on remote banks. As an example, most of the Lodi division's suppliers were located in the southwest and were paid with checks drawn on the Bank of Brooklyn.

Some of Swanson's banks were also sources of float. The Altoona National Bank, for instance, was used by the Altoona division primarily to meet the plant payroll. The day payroll checks were issued, a check drawn on the First National Bank of San Francisco was deposited in the Altoona bank. To clear the deposit, the Altoona bank had to send the check to the Federal Reserve Bank in Philadelphia in order to use the Federal Reserve's clearing system. As a consequence, Swanson's San Francisco account was not reduced until about two days after Altoona received the check—and perhaps had cashed most of the payroll checks.

CASH REPORTING AND FORECASTING

Weekly cash reports and monthly forecasts submitted by Swanson's divisions helped to keep Swanson's top management up to date on the firm's cash position. In addition, Swanson had in 1970 instituted regular cash management meetings attended by the firm's top general and financial managers. These meetings, held at monthly intervals in 1971, permitted quick action on corporate-wide cash flow trends or problems. As an example of one such problem, Mr. Jackson noted that a recent meeting had revealed a large buildup in accounts receivable from foreign subsidiaries. The meeting resulted in actions that reduced the amount from $7 million in March 1971 to $3 million in early May 1971. According to Mr. Jackson, this type of problem would not have been recognized until much later, if at all, absent the cash meetings and the thorough cash reporting procedures only recently established.

In hopes of further improving its cash system, Swanson was currently attempting to develop more accurate forecasts of divisional receipts and disbursements. Forecasts currently prepared by the divisions were still considered weak; forecasts beyond two months were considered extremely unreliable. Swanson hoped to enter division purchase orders directly into its computer-based information system and thus to eliminate processing of these orders by the under-manned divisional accounting departments. Such a system would, it was believed, enable headquarters to foresee payment needs emerging before they actually appeared on the weekly requests for disbursement authorization and ultimately to make such requests unnecessary.

According to Mr. Bishop, forecasting errors were not yet a problem because Swanson's current bank balances, required to support its lines of credit, were substantially in excess of transaction needs. Thus, Swanson had a cash "buffer" which absorbed temporary deviations from anticipated operating cash requirements. However, if Swanson took action to reduce these balances, the problem of forecasting error was likely to become much more acute.

DOMESTIC INTRA-COMPANY PAYMENTS

Until early 1971, payments between divisions were not identified as such on disbursement requests and consequently were authorized as if to outside companies. Internal disbursements and collections were, however, channelled through only two banks. All operating divisions used the First of San Francisco bank for disbursing and receiving internal payments. The corporate division used the First of Sacramento for disbursing and receiving internal payments. Thus, if operating division A wanted to pay some amount to operating division B, A would draw a check on the First of San Francisco and send the check to B's lock box at the First of San Francisco. If A wanted to transfer funds to the corporate division, A would draw a check on the First of San Francisco and send it to the corporate division's lock box at the First of Sacramento. Conversely, when the corporate division paid A, it drew on the First of Sacramento and sent the check on A's lock box to the First of San Francisco. Thus, although the distribution of Swanson's bank balances between the First of San Francisco and the First of Sacramento banks would fluctuate in response to payments between the corporate and the operating divisions (which payments accounted for 60% of all the intra-company payments in 1970), Swanson's overall level of corporate funds was unaffected by the internal payments. One problem, according to Mr. Bishop, was that the internal transactions generated excess working balances at the banks totaling almost one-fifth ($500,000) of all working balances in 1970.

These excess working balances arose primarily from the corporate division's inability to distinguish "inside" from "outside" payables on the weekly disbursement requests submitted by the operating divisions.

To see the problem, consider a situation where division A owed $1 million to division B. When the payment to division B came due, division A would request authorization to disburse $1 million, without indicating that the funds were to be used to pay division B. Division B, on the other hand, might not be anticipating receipt of division A's payment in the week division A had planned to make it. Thus, on its own weekly request, B would not indicate an anticipated receipt as an offset to its own cash needs. The corporate division would thus authorize A to disburse $1 million from its account and, to support this authorization, would transfer sufficient funds to A's account. Similarly, funds would be transferred to division B in amounts to cover a net cash flow estimate that did not reflect the $1 million cash payment by division A. Thus, if corporate balances overall happened to be low for that week, the corporate division might even have to borrow from one of its banks to ensure that divisions A and B had funds to meet their authorized disbursements. A few days later, of course, when A's payment to B had cleared B's lock box and had been matched with supporting documents, the corporate division would know that the payment had been made internally.

To resolve its internal payments difficulties, Swanson's financial managers decided, early in 1971, to phase out of the two-bank system and to channel all internal payments through a single, intra-company clearing account at the First National Bank of Lodi. Under this system, all domestic divisions were to pay invoices to other domestic divisions with special checks drawn on the clearing account, containing only nominal balances, at the First National Bank of Lodi and were to send these checks to the receiving division's lock box at Lodi. As part of the arrangement with the bank, these special transactions would be reported daily to Mr. Bishop as simple accounting transfers between the divisions. Since no funds flowed into or out of the bank as a result of checks written on this intra-company account (though individual divisions might show large net accounting inflows or outflows), there was no need for the divisions to seek disbursement authorization for internal transactions and hence no need to hold up intra-company payables.

THE ROLE OF BANK BALANCES

Deposits as Compensation for Services

The size of its bank cash balances was central to Swanson's banking relationships. As a matter of policy, the company had never paid directly for bank services, such as processing payroll checks, maintaining the company's lock boxes, and rendering financial counsel. Swanson instead compensated its banks for services by maintaining demand deposits which the bank could then lend or otherwise invest.

In order to determine fair levels of balances to leave on deposit, Mr. Knight had recently requested and begun to receive "account analyses" from its banks. These analyses indicated the volume of services provided by the bank during the month and the value of such services in terms of deposit balances.[4] (Two account analyses are shown as Exhibits 3 and 4).

Deposits as Compensation for Lines of Credit

A second important role played by bank balances was to compensate for lines of credit extended by Swanson's banks. Minimum compensating balances for this purpose typically were stated as a percentage of the unborrowed line of credit ("the availability") plus a percentage of Swanson's current borrowings. Swanson's financial managers looked upon these compensating balances as akin to "borrowing insurance," though Mr. Jackson believed that the "borrowing insurance" analogy was imperfect. As recent inquiries had confirmed, a bank was not in fact legally bound to lend money against a line of credit and could legally terminate a line at any time.

Swanson's policy was to leave on deposit the larger of the balances required for services provided or the line of credit. Some of Swanson's deposit requirements were met by deposits it had to keep on hand for normal operating purposes, so that these working, or transaction, balances served a number of purposes. However, Swanson's working balance needs were currently averaging only $2 million per day at its credit banks, considerably below the company's current compensating requirements of $3.3 million.

Monitoring of Balances

Previous to 1970, little attention had been given at Swanson to the size of its bank balances in relation to its compensating requirements. In fact, these requirements had not even been broken down by bank at the corporate level. Thus, Swanson often had excess balances in some banks and shortages in others.[5] At year end, any shortfall was charged to the corporation as a "de facto" loan during the year. At year end 1969, Swanson had received shortfall charges totaling $20,000.

---

4. In calculating this value, the bank typically would place a dollar value (including profit) on services rendered and, given its earnings rate (e.g. the 91-day Treasury Bill rate), determine the required investible balance (collected deposits less reserve requirements) to compensate for the services.
5. As described more fully later, Swanson's required balances were calculated on a yearly, moving average basis.

In 1970, with the formation of the cash management department Swanson had begun to monitor and use its bank balances more aggressively. By tracking deposit balances and compensating requirements on a corporate-wide basis, Swanson was able to pin-point balance shortages or excesses among its banks and transfer balances to bring these more into line. This had been of special importance during the recent cash buildup since Swanson's bank balances would, if not used elsewhere, often exceed requirements. Any excess balances anticipated in a given bank were used for meeting deposit shortages in another bank, for repayment of bank loans, or for very short-term investment in the overnight or weekend funds market. According to Mr. Bishop, Swanson did not hold a marketable securities portfolio per se since it made no sense to hold relatively low-yielding assets as long as the company had short-term debt.

Although shortfall charges totaled $4,000 in 1970, all of the shortfall was attributed to unanticipated miscellaneous charges added on at year end by the First of San Francisco bank. However, this charge was offset by earnings from weekend and overnight investments during the year totaling more than $5,000.

CREDIT ARRANGEMENTS

In May 1971, Swanson had lines of credit totaling $18.5 million at five banks, including two in New York City, two in California, and one in Pennsylvania. With the exception of a recent agreement negotiated with the Altoona National Bank, Swanson's existing credit arrangements dated back to the company's 1967 liquidity crisis. As mentioned earlier, the First National Bank of San Francisco had at that time organized a syndicate to provide up to $18 million in credit. The lines arranged then, $7.5 million at San Francisco, $5.0 million at the Bank of Brooklyn, $3.0 million at the Bank of the Bronx, and $2.5 million at the First National Bank of Sacramento, were still in effect in May 1971. All these agreements called for loans to be on an unsecured, prime rate basis, with the understanding that Swanson would maintain compensating balances in varying amounts at each of the banks. In return for the credit assistance, Swanson had agreed to reorganize its domestic operations from affiliated companies to operating divisions, to institute tight operating and financial controls, and to accept one of the San Francisco's senior vice presidents as vice president finance of the company's newly created corporate division. This vice president, Mr. Jackson's immediate predecessor, retired in late 1970.

The credit arrangement with the Altoona National Bank was more recent and had been negotiated at the request of Mr. Jackson. While controller of the Altoona division, Mr. Jackson had suggested to

Swanson's top management that more intensive use of working balances kept at banks for local plant and office use might permit reductions in the firm's total credit expense. Besides Altoona, Swanson currently had approximately 18 other banks around the country which served local plants and offices but which provided no credit. Working balances in these 18 banks exceeded $800 thousand per day on average.

Swanson's top management decided to explore Mr. Jackson's suggestion on an experimental basis, and shortly before leaving the controllership of the Altoona division, Mr. Jackson was authorized to seek a $500,000 line of credit on a 90-day, unsecured, prime rate basis. This was accomplished in November 1970. The total line was then borrowed and used to pay down borrowings from the Bank of the Bronx. After negotiating the line of credit, Mr. Jackson received an invitation, which he accepted, to join the Altoona's board of directors. He was currently still a member of the board.

Recently, Swanson had been involved in disputes over credit arrangements with both the First of San Francisco and the Altoona National banks. Since the disputes raised issues basic to Swanson's credit arrangements at all its banks, Swanson was particularly concerned that they be resolved in the best long-run interests of the company.

First National Bank of San Francisco

As Swanson's oldest bank, the First of San Francisco had developed a special relationship with the company. This relationship became oppressively intimate, in the view of Swanson's top management, in 1967 when the bank insisted that one of the bank's senior vice presidents, Mr. Warburg, be installed as Swanson's vice president finance. Swanson's management generally felt uncomfortable with the bank's overly protective attitude which at times constrained management decisions. As Swanson's cash position steadily improved during 1968, 1969, and 1970, Swanson's management became increasingly restive.

As the relationship between Swanson and the First of San Francisco became increasingly strained, the bank for its part began to show signs of taking a harder stance vis-à-vis Swanson, particularly with regard to the prime rate it granted on the company's borrowings. In several conversations related to other matters, the bank's representatives inserted comments to the effect that the bank was disposed to restrict its prime rate to "short term" borrowings, defined to be those for a period of a year or less. The bank noted that although Swanson's borrowings were in the form of 90 day notes, they were in fact being used to finance the company's production cycle, which cycle at times stretched to 22 months. The bank's representatives therefore argued that these borrowings were more properly classed as intermediate-term, rather than short-term, loans, and were thus ineligible for the bank's prime rate. Swanson's management, on the other hand, was proud of the company's prime rate, believing this rate to be an important indicator of "credit-worthiness." Thus Swanson's executives responded that the bank's definition of short-term was arbitrary and inconsistent with the practice of all of Swanson's other banks. Discussions between the bank and Swanson as to whether the borrowings were short- or intermediate-term never resolved the disagreement.

In early 1971, shortly after Mr. Warburg's retirement, the bank issued its usual annual statement of credit commitment to Swanson. Unlike previous notifications, however, the 1971 document stated that Swanson would be charged 0.5% above the bank's prime rate "to reflect the longer term nature" of the corporation's borrowing. Swanson's management considered the higher rate totally unacceptable and was particularly disturbed that it had received no notice beforehand. Although there was no official break in the relationship, the bank was paid off. Soon thereafter Swanson accepted the line of credit, but advised the bank that it would not borrow until granted the prime rate.

Believing the bank would not alter its position, Mr. Jackson decided to explore the possibilities of finding an amenable bank of equal size and stature to replace the First of San Francisco. During April 1971, Mr. Knight approached the Los Angeles National Bank. Mr. Knight expressed Swanson's interest in opening a $6 million domestic line of credit on a 90-day, unsecured, prime rate basis. Mr. Knight also inquired as to whether either of Swanson's two major competitors had banking relationships with the Los Angeles bank. The bank promptly notified him that it currently had no outstanding borrowing relationships with either of Swanson's competitors and that it would within a month give Swanson a firm response to the company's request for a line of credit. The bank added that the Bank of the Bronx, one of Swanson's major New York banks, was the lead bank for one of Swanson's major competitors.

Problem with Altoona National Bank

In early May 1971, Mr. Jackson was notified by the Altoona National Bank that Swanson's average deposit balances were roughly half of what they should be for compensating balance purposes. The bank stated that Swanson's balances were just about sufficient to meet services rendered, such as payroll transactions, with nothing left over to meet requirements of its line of credit. The bank's letter suggested that Swanson's major banks were not treated in this manner and that the company should be fair to its "country cousins."[6] The Altoona bank believed that its services and credit extension should be compensated for separately, contrary to Swanson's practice of compensating only for the larger of the two requirements.

Accompanying its letter was an account analysis, Exhibit 3, showing a collected balance of $91,560, required balances of $100,000 to support the $500,000 line of credit, and required balances of $88,593 to support bank services. The calculated shortfall was thus $97,053 for the month. The Altoona bank requested another $100,000 in compensating deposits.

Mr. Jackson asked Mr. Bishop to respond to the Altoona's complaints and to keep him apprised of further developments. In his response, Mr. Bishop pointed out that Altoona's calculation of balance requirements was at variance with methods used by all of Swanson's other banks in at least three respects. First, he noted that the relatively low (.15%/month) earnings credit imputed to Swanson's collected balances was substantially below that of, for example, the Bank of Brooklyn, which used a .442%/month earnings credit. (An accounting analysis for the Bank of Brooklyn is shown as Exhibit 4.)

Secondly, Mr. Bishop noted that Swanson's policy was to compensate for only the larger of credit line or service requirements, but not for both as the Altoona appeared to require. He stated that this "double counting" of balances was Swanson's policy at all banks.

Thirdly, Mr. Bishop pointed out that the Altoona appeared to be calculating required balances on a monthly rather than a moving average basis, again contrary to company policy at all other credit banks. This arrangement was considered particularly important since the seasonality of working balance levels at the Altoona division made a monthly requirement more expensive than a moving average policy. Exhibit 5 illustrates the difference between the two methods with respect to balances at the Bank of Brooklyn.

The Altoona bank countered Swanson's criticism of the relatively low earnings credit by pointing out that the bank deducted only 8% of gross deposits as "uncollected." The bank stated that, in fact, uncollected deposits in Swanson's account had in the past been closer to 30%. The bank stated it would raise Swanson's earnings credit to .25%/month, but would calculate collected deposits at only 70% of gross deposits.

Mr. Bishop responded that the 30% uncollected figure was inappropriate because it excluded allowance for income tax withholding and social security deposits placed at the bank. These deposits together averaged about $50,000 per day. If these deposits were included in the calculations, Swanson's collected deposits would have averaged $108,950

---

6. This refers to Altoona's status as a "country bank," i.e., a member of the Federal Reserve System not headquartered in a Federal Reserve city.

per day on a 30% uncollected basis over the previous six-month period, indicating an excess over requirements.

These exchanges having consumed nearly a month, Mr. Jackson was in late May still awaiting a response from the bank concerning Mr. Bishop's tax and social security withholding proposal. Since he was coming to doubt that the bank's officers would accede to this or comparable proposals without strong urgings, Mr. Jackson had to decide whether to press his points further and, if so, whether simply to state that Swanson would repay the loan when due in June and relinquish its line of credit unless the bank capitulated.

THE EFFECTIVE COST OF BORROWING

The Analysis of Current Costs

In addition to the Altoona and San Francisco bank problems, Mr. Jackson also spent considerable time during his first months on the job in attempting to devise ways to reduce the company's credit expense. Because Swanson's banks required compensating balances to support the unborrowed portion of a line of credit ("the availability") as well as the borrowed portion, Swanson's reduced borrowing had the effect of increasing the firm's credit expense. Swanson's arrangements at the Bank of the Bronx, the Bank of Brooklyn, and the First of Sacramento required compensating balances equal to 20% of the borrowing plus 20% of the availability.[7] The requirement at the First of San Francisco was 15% of the availability plus 15% of the borrowing. Thus, as shown below, Swanson's compensating requirements remained at $3.325 million during February and March 1971 even though borrowings had decreased from $15 million to $9.5 million. According to Swanson's calculation, its effective interest rate on borrowings had increased from 7.39% to 8.84% during this time span:

	2/10/71	3/5/71
Lines of credit	$18,500,000	$18,500,000
Borrowings	15,000,000	9,500,000
Compensating balances required	3,325,000	3,325,000
Funds for use	11,675,000	6,175,000
Interest cost on borrowing at 5.75%	863,000	546,000
Actual interest rate	7.39%	8.84%

---

7. This was, of course, equivalent to a constant requirement of 20% of the total line. The practice of quoting two rates, one for the unused line and one for the usage, was a carryover from past periods in which banks had specified different rates on the availability and the use.

As an alternative way of viewing its credit expense, Mr. Knight suggested that Swanson might focus on the balances required by these credit agreements over and above what Swanson would keep on deposit to meet normal transaction needs. He reasoned that since Swanson would maintain $2 million in deposits for operating purposes anyway, only $1.325 of its compensating requirements might be viewed strictly as "borrowing insurance." Seen this way, he calculated that Swanson's borrowing insurance was costing the company about $73,000 per year at the prime rate. As shown in Exhibit 6, $33,000 of this expense was being incurred at the Bank of the Bronx, where Swanson currently maintained required balances of $600,000, but made no use of the bank for either collections or disbursements. Another $21,000 in credit expense was being incurred at the First of San Francisco Bank, where Swanson's $7.5 million line of credit was not being used due to the dispute concerning Swanson's loss of the bank's prime rate on borrowing.

Due to his concern over the cost of Swanson's credit and the likelihood that the cost would continue, Mr. Jackson asked Mr. Knight to review the situation and to explore the effects of alternative credit arrangements.

Alternative Credit Arrangements

Mr. Knight's review first stated that Swanson had unused credit capacity at a number of country banks at which company plants maintained working balances, but with which the company currently had no credit arrangements. He estimated that balances at four banks alone (Exhibit 7) could support lines of credit totaling $2 million. Secondly, with regard to Swanson's current credit arrangements, Mr. Knight suggested that Swanson explore with its current lenders three alternative combinations of lines and rates that would reduce Swanson's costs. As shown in Exhibit 6, alternative 1 assumed no reduction in total lines, but assumed a change in compensating balances to a policy of 10% of the availability plus 20% of the use (10–20) as opposed to the current 15–15 and 20–20 requirements. This revision alone, it was estimated, could save Swanson $53,625 per year at the current prime rate. (The prime rate dropped from 5.75% to 5.5% during March 1971.) The second alternative assumed a reduction in total lines from $18.5 million to $13 million while leaving current compensating rates unchanged. The $5.5 million reduction in lines envisioned decreases of $1 million each at the Bank of the Bronx, the Bank of Brooklyn, and the First of Sacramento, and a $2.5 million reduction at the First of San Francisco. Although more expensive than alternative 1, this alternative would save more than $45,375 per year at the prime rate. The third alternative was based on a combination of reduced lines and rates and a redistribution of working balances. It assumed a reduction in total lines from $18.5 million to $15 million and a reduction in balances to 10% of the availability plus 20% of the use. This $3.5 million reduction in lines was based on decreases of $1 million each at the Bank of the Bronx and the Bank of Brooklyn, and a $1.5 million reduction at the First of San Francisco. This alternative was estimated to be the least expensive, reducing the corporation's "borrowing insurance" costs to $13,750 per year at the 5.5% prime rate.

In addition to these possible arrangements, Mr. Knight speculated that there might be some advantages to Swanson in a "compromise" requirement of a straight 15% on both availability and borrowings rather than the 10–20 policy he had recommended or the 20–20 policy Swanson currently had at several banks. According to Mr. Knight, the 15% required balance against borrowings of a 15–15 policy would result in a lower effective interest cost (prime/.85) than the 20% requirement on borrowings of either the 10–20 or 20–20 policies. Since interest rates were likely to be high when Swanson's borrowings were high the dollar cost savings, he thought, might be substantial. On the other hand, Mr. Knight noted that when borrowings were low, as currently, the 15–15 policy would require greater balances than a 10–20 policy (though less than the 20–20 policy). In this event, however, Swanson would, he believed, have sufficient cash, associated with reduced operations, to meet such requirements.

EXPLORATION OF ALTERNATIVES

Discussion with First Vice President of Sacramento Bank

In order to gauge possible bank reactions to alternative credit arrangements, Mr. Jackson explored the situation informally with a senior vice president at the Sacramento bank who was familiar with Swanson and its history. Mr. Jackson brought the banker up to date by noting that the company's future cash needs continued to be uncertain, but that Swanson's most recent operating plans indicated a continuing buildup of cash.

With regard to seeking changes in required compensating balance rates or the size of credit lines, the banker stated his belief that frequent changes were not advisable but that Swanson's banks would, in all probability, graciously accept changes based on a sincere and carefully developed projection of cash needs. Furthermore, the banker stated, should unforeseen events change the projections dramatically, the banks would probably be willing again to extend credit if needed. He emphasized, however, that if Swanson was perceived as having tried to save a couple of "short-run" dollars with the full intention of rebuilding lines again soon, Mr. Jackson could have a difficult time finding bank funds.

Mr. Jackson then sought the banker's view on the probable reaction of Swanson's major banks should the company shift a portion of its credit lines from its major banks to several country banks. Mr. Jackson explained that he thought the company's average working balances at four country banks alone could support $2 million in lines of credit. He added that Swanson was currently exploring the practicability of such an arrangement with a $500,000 loan at the Altoona bank. He stated that some "misunderstandings" with the bank were still being worked out but that if this exploratory arrangement ultimately proved satisfactory, he would like to implement similar credit agreements with Swanson's other country banks. The banker responded that such arrangements were frequent and "understandable" on the part of the big city banks. On the other hand, he emphasized that it would be most undesirable to enter into further such arrangements without advising the big banks of his plans and giving them the reasons behind such plans. The banker further strongly advised against using borrowings from the country banks to pay off any one of the principal banks while still borrowing from the others. He explained that, judging from his experience, the banks still lending to Swanson might become fearful that the bank which had been paid off would not return. "In fact," he stated, "most multibank arrangements are made formal not so much to control the borrower as to keep all the lenders involved."

Commenting further on Swanson's current banking relationships, Mr. Jackson's informant expressed some concern about the company's use of both the Bank of the Bronx and the Bank of Brooklyn. He said that the Bank of the Bronx, with a line less than that of the Bank of Brooklyn, probably felt "uncomfortable." He thought that one bank in New York would be enough and that both banks were of excellent quality. The banker added that, given the evident cooling in Swanson's relationship with its traditional "lead" bank, Swanson's other banks were unclear which bank was currently viewed by Swanson's management as the company's "lead" bank—or whether Swanson had even selected one of the banks as its prime contact.

In closing, the banker commented that it was always a mistake for either side to try to adhere too rigidly to a formula calculation of required balances or to be too rigid in requesting the prime rate on bank loans. He added that little favors are long remembered by bankers. As an illustration, he related that an important corporate client of his bank had asked to be charged one-quarter above the prime rate in light of the fact that the bank at that time was having to raise funds, at a cost above the loan rate, in the Euro-dollar market. The banker said that this gesture had cost the corporate client less than $10,000, but had created lasting goodwill.

Bank of the Bronx

In mid-May, Mr. Jackson asked Mr. Knight to get another reading on possible bank reactions by raising the issue of credit expense with the Bank of the Bronx. In a letter to the bank, Mr. Knight stated that Swanson's cash generation had been greater than anticipated and that the company was currently using only $5.5 million of total credit availability of $18.5 million. Mr. Knight added that Swanson's board of directors was likely to decide in favor of closing the Salt Lake division soon, which would mean additional cash generation of almost $3 million in the current year alone. Mr. Knight also noted that the company was seeking to use working balances at country banks more intensively by negotiating lines of credit and borrowing from them. The added lines and borrowings would permit reductions in current arrangements with major banks. He concluded that in view of all the above, Swanson felt its current balance requirements at the bank were too high.

Mr. Knight asked the banker for reactions to two alternatives to the current situation. The first would change the balance requirements from 20% of the total line to 10% of the available line and 20% of the use, but would make no change in the current amount of the line, $3 million, or current borrowings, $1 million. The second alternative would reduce the line to $2 million, but would not change the 20% balance requirement. (According to Mr. Knight's analysis, the first alternative would save Swanson $16,500 in credit expense per year; the second, $11,000.)

The response from the Bank of the Bronx was prompt. After noting its "delight" that Swanson's cash needs were declining below those of previous years, the bank advised that "consistent with your ability to do so, it would be wise to maintain the maximum given amount of availability." The letter suggested that Swanson maintain its current $3 million line, which the bank believed to be "more nearly in line with the most conservative set of circumstances from a sources and uses of funds standpoint." If this line were maintained, the bank suggested a reduction in the required balance from 20% of use plus 20% of availability to 20% of use plus 15% of availability "with the understanding that your average usage could be in the 50% range." In a later telephone discussion with the bank, Mr. Knight surmised that "past services" could be translated as the willingness of the bank to stand by Swanson during the difficult period of 1967 and 1968. Mr. Jackson was, in late May, still trying to formulate a final response to the bank's communications.

Los Angeles National Bank

In early May 1971, the Los Angeles bank, which had been approached in April, informed Swanson of its "pleasure in being able to extend to Swanson a $4 million line of credit, available until September 30, 1971." Borrowings would be permitted on a 90–day, unsecured basis, at the bank's prime rate. The commitment was subject to a variety of conditions, including:

1. Out of debt to the Los Angeles National Bank for 60 consecutive days annually;
2. Commercial deposit balances of not less than the greater of 10% of the commitment or 20% of the use;
3. Total outstanding bank debt (Swanson Corporation and U.S. subsidiaries) not greater than $17 million;
4. Total bank line of credit at least $4 million greater than total usage;
5. Notes and accounts receivable from foreign subsidiaries and affiliated companies not to exceed $6 million;
6. Designation of one of Swanson's major credit banks to serve as agent for all credit banks.

Mr. Jackson was disappointed with these terms for a number of reasons. First, given the relatively short-term extension of the line, Swanson would have to seek renewal in a matter of a few months. Mr. Jackson was secondly concerned with the requirement that Swanson maintain credit lines at least $4 million in excess of usage. He believed the requirement was designed to allow the Los Angeles bank to be "rotated out" relatively quickly if it so chose. He further believed that Swanson's other banks might fear that, once rotated out, the Los Angeles bank would not return. Thirdly, Mr. Jackson believed the appointment of an agent bank would impair the bilateral understandings he and his predecessor had developed with each of the company's credit banks. Under an agent bank arrangement, all of Swanson's credit banks would be represented by a single bank. Swanson's bank borrowings or debt repayment would be channelled through the agent bank which would, in turn, "farm out" the loans or repayments to Swanson's individual credit banks. Although Swanson would still be responsible for actually negotiating the individual lines of credit and would set conditions on the borrowing or repayment policy of the agent bank (e.g., borrow only from the bank offering the lowest rate), Mr. Jackson felt the agent arrangement would reduce his flexibility in dealing with the banks. Primarily for these reasons, Mr. Jackson decided to postpone either an acceptance or rejection of the offer.

Thus, in late May, Mr. Knight wrote to the bank to reaffirm Swanson's desire to establish a borrowing relationship with the bank. In addition, he indicated Swanson's desire to open a corporate checking account, to establish three lock boxes[8] and to open a payroll disbursing account for the Altoona division at the bank. Mr. Knight informed the bank of Swanson's recent decision to shut down the Salt Lake division, which he indicated could have an important impact on the company's short-term credit needs. Thus, the treasurer concluded that Swanson preferred to hold off committing itself on the bank's credit offer until Swanson's situation was clarified. The Los Angeles bank stated its understanding of Swanson's position and indicated its willingness to reconsider the company's request when Swanson's situation was more definite.

SUMMARY OF DECISION PROBLEMS AND OBJECTIVES

According to Mr. Jackson, a number of factors indicated continued low usage of bank credit at least until the end of the fiscal year in September. At current levels of borrowing, the current compensating balance requirements resulted in a total credit expense that seemed to him unduly high. Moreover, he noted that should operating cutbacks continue, this credit expense would increase even further. Working balance needs could, he felt, drop as low as $1.5 million over the next 12 months. Current domestic sales were at a rate of $82 million, down from $100 million in fiscal 1970, and were anticipated to decline further in the remainder of the year. As working balances decreased, the portion of compensating balances kept purely for "borrowing insurance" would of course increase, making the burden of Swanson's credit arrangements more difficult to justify.

Beyond the immediate future, however, a number of fundamental uncertainties clouded all of Swanson's projections. Since 1968, depreciation had exceeded gross additions to plant in every year; planned outlays for the current fiscal year were less than half of projected depreciation. Therefore Mr. Jackson felt it likely that increased investments in plant would be required in the near future, particularly if the scale of operations were greatly increased. The exact timing of such needs was, however, still subject to considerable uncertainty. Mr. Jackson was also aware that a new product line developed by one of Swanson's domestic joint ventures showed great potential for market acceptance and that Swanson's board of directors was considering investing several million dollars in the venture during fiscal year 1972.

Swanson's uncertainties with regard to the timing and magnitudes of future cash needs were reflected in a recent 3-year forecast of sales and cash flows prepared by the operating divisions and the corporate finance

---

8. The three lock boxes at the Portland (Oregon) National Bank would be transferred to the Los Angeles bank.

department. Taking the divisions' sales forecasts as given, the finance department developed a set of "best," "likely," and "worst" outcomes in terms of cash requirements by 1974 by varying its assumptions with regard to several key financial and operating ratios. The "best" forecast assumed a 4% after-tax earnings rate on sales and the lowest assets/sales and highest current liabilities/sales ratio actually experienced by the company during the previous five years. The "likely" forecast assumed a continuation of current performance for the period. The "worst" forecast assumed only 2% after-tax earnings on sales and used the highest assets/sales ratio and lowest current liabilities/sales ratio actually experienced in the previous five years of operations.

Thus, with overall sales of the domestic subsidiaries projected to increase 50% from $82 million to $125 million between 1971 and 1974, the finance department's cash projections showed a range of total debt of almost $39 million under the "worst" forecast to a cash *surplus* of more than $12 million under the "best" outcome. The "likely" forecast was for almost no change in total borrowings from year end 1972 to 1974.

If the $39 million need should materialize, Mr. Jackson believed that a major portion would probably have to be financed by banks. Mr. Jackson knew that Swanson's board was strongly opposed to any issue of common stock and had in the past always shown great reluctance to assume long-term debt.

For these reasons, Mr. Jackson had reservations about introducing what might prove to be very temporary reductions in the dollar amount of Swanson's credit lines. His concerns about the possible level of future credit needs also complicated the decision concerning possible rearrangements in the portions of Swanson's total needs obtained from specific banks.

If he could count on future needs being at or below current levels, the cheapest sourcing pattern would seem to call for replacing the lines at the Bank of the Bronx with lines at Swanson's country banks. Mr. Jackson thought that, if it were important to do so, he could pressure the Altoona bank into accepting compensating balance requirements comparable to those regarded as standard by Swanson's major banks. This plan would not only reduce credit expenses; it would also eliminate some rather less tangible problems. Mr. Jackson recalled the statement by the bank officer at the First of Sacramento that both of Swanson's New York banks probably felt uncomfortable under the current arrangement and that it might be wise for Swanson either to retain only one of the banks or to clearly designate one of the two as its main New York bank. Moreover, Mr. Jackson remained concerned about the revelation that the Bank of the Bronx was the lead bank of a major competitor.

Eliminating the Bank of the Bronx, however, was not without its drawbacks. Mr. Jackson was fearful that this elimination might both reduce Swanson's costs in the short run and reduce the company's access to a large credit line should this later prove necessary. Swanson's country banks would clearly be unable to match the potential lending power of the Bank of the Bronx.

The appropriate decisions concerning arrangements, actual or potential, with the Los Angeles and San Francisco banks were also, in Mr. Jackson's view, dependent on the magnitude of Swanson's future borrowing needs. The relationship with the First of San Francisco was both expensive and irritating, but the bank seemed fully willing to continue lending to Swanson as in the past. Mr. Jackson was unclear whether the Los Angeles bank would be a completely satisfactory replacement in the event Swanson again encountered a major funds need. And even if he could count on the Los Angeles bank as a reliable member of Swanson's group of banks, the bank's desire for an agent arrangement would force a fundamental change in Swanson's past policy of bilateral negotiations. Nonetheless, even if he did not accede to the agent bank concept, Mr. Jackson was beginning to feel that it would be necessary to decide upon and at least informally to designate one of Swanson's banks as its lead bank.

Mr. Jackson was also concerned about the process by which the changes decided upon would be put into effect. He noted that a number of changes in the company's banking relationships had already been introduced in the past year, two of which had resulted in important disputes. He was concerned that Swanson's bankers might feel he was trying to move too quickly and without due concern for past relationships. He knew he would be reminded by Swanson's bankers that they had stood by the company in the past and that the company ought not to disregard old friends now that it was no longer so much in need of them. In addition, almost none of the bankers yet knew Mr. Jackson very well and were still trying to get a "feel" for the type of relationship they should have with the new financial vice president. Mr. Jackson believed they would thus be particularly sensitive to any changes he suggested. On the other hand, Mr. Jackson felt the absence of a long personal relationship gave him some degree of freedom for introducing new arrangements. He believed strongly in using the company's cash as efficiently as possible and wondered if this was a proper time to relay that conviction to Swanson's banks.

EXHIBIT 1
Swanson Corporation

Swanson Corporation and Domestic Subsidiaries
Sources and Uses of Funds 1966–1970
(000)

	1970	1969	1968	1967	1966
Sales	$100,636	$122,702	$118,712	$145,931	$112,300
Sources					
Net income*	$ 2,404	$ 2,018	$ 730	$ 105	$ 1,109
Depreciation	2,897	3,040	3,479	3,281	2,810
Dividends from subsidiaries	1,000	1,000	1,500	—	—
Liquidations	—	—	956	111	459
Total	$ 6,301	$ 6,058	$ 6,665	$ 3,497	$ 4,378
Uses					
Investment in plant and equipment	$ 2,387	$ 1,317	$ 2,316	$ 7,806	$ 7,117
Dividends paid	75	75	453	453	907
Investment in subsidiaries	1,909	(214)	(614)	(2,756)	882
Long-term debt repayment	976	511	1,075	(3,473)	1,929
Total	$ 5,347	$ 1,689	$ 3,230	$ 2,030	$ 10,835
Increase (decrease) in working capital					
Cash	$ 2,270	$ (2,932)	$ 2,082	$ (1,543)	$ 2,334
Accounts receivable	2,396	865	(7,289)	9,135	654
Inventories	(6,333)	(10,989)	(456)	178	7,648
Trade payables	(1,793)	1,126	2,435	(2,152)	(1,278)
Customer advances	5,753	13,537	383	15,887	(16,220)
Notes to banks	(2,006)	3,018	5,811	(19,002)	(656)
Accruals and other liabilities	667	(256)	469	(1,034)	2,061
Total	$ 954	$ 4,369	$ 3,435	$ 1,469	$ (5,457)
* Annual Interest Charges	$ 2,026	$ 1,661	$ 1,665	$ 987	$ 467

EXHIBIT 2
Swanson Corporation
Swanson Corporation and Domestic Subsidiaries
Consolidated Balance Sheet
March 31, 1971
(000)

Assets

Current

Cash	$ 894	
Net receivables, current	22,382	
Receivables due after one year	2,810	
Inventories	18,109	
Total current assets		$44,195

Other

Prepaid expenses	$ 463	
Deferred tax benefits	7,000	
Investments	23,895	
Other	148	
Total other assets		$31,506

Fixed

Net plant & equipment	$20,441	
Plant in liquidation	2,879	
Less Salt Lake reserves	(1,388)	
Total fixed		$21,932
Total		$97,633

Liabilities & shareholders' investment

Current

Bank loans	$ 5,500	
Customer advances	7,799	
Current loan maturities	1,100	
Accounts payable	7,606	
Accrued expenses	1,114	
Accrued income tax	1,579	
Dividend payable	453	
Total current liabilities		$25,151
Long-term debt	$ 4,900	
Deferred taxes	4,255	
Deferred compensation	590	
Shareholders' investment	62,737	
Total long-term capital		$72,482
Total		$97,633

EXHIBIT 3
Swanson Corporation
Altoona National Bank Account Analysis

ACCOUNT: <u>SWANSON CORPORATION</u>

FOR MONTH ENDING
<u>APRIL 30, 1971</u>

Average daily ledger balance   <u>$99,740</u>
Less--Average uncollected balance   <u>8,180</u>
  Collected balance   <u>$91,560</u>
Less--Balance required to support
      line of credit   <u>$100,000</u>
Available balance for services   <u>($ 8,440)</u>

SERVICES

			Unit Charge	Balance Req.
<u>1</u>	Maintenance	@	<u>$.60</u>	<u>$ 400</u>
<u>1,648</u>	Ledger transactions	@	<u>.08</u>	<u>87,893</u>
	Account reconciliation	@		
	Collections	@		
	Wire transfers	@		
	Mail transfers	@		
	Lock boxes	@		
<u>5</u>	Items deposited	@	<u>.02</u>	<u>67</u>
	Returned items	@		
<u>5</u>	Deposits	@	<u>.07</u>	<u>233</u>
		@		
		@		
		@		
		@		

Total earning balance required for services   <u>($88,593)</u>
Balances remaining for other bank services
  (deficiency)   <u>($97,033)</u>

EXHIBIT 4
Swanson Corporation
Bank of Brooklyn Account Analysis

ACCOUNT: <u>SWANSON CORPORATION</u>

FOR MONTH ENDING:
<u>DECEMBER 31, 1970</u>

Average daily ledger balance	$781,100
Less--Average uncollected balance	$ 57,100
Collected balance	$724,000

Services Rendered	Price Per Item	Activity	Available Balance Needed* Per Item	In Total
Account Maintenance	$ 2.60	1	$ 747.40	$ 747
FDIC Assm't. (Per $1000 Coll. Bal.)	.035	724	10.06	7,283
Checks Paid	.09	1528	25.87	39,529
Check Reconcilement	54.00	1	15,522.84	15,523
Checks Recon.	.015	1528	4.31	6,586
Lock Box Activity Account Maintenance	150.00	1	43,119.00	43,119

Total Available Balance Needed To Support Account Activity	$112,787
Additional Available Balance Needed To Support Account Activity	_____
Balance Available To Support Credit, Advisory And Other Services	$611,213

*Balances, net of reserves, are given an earnings credit of
__.442%__ per month, based on the current moving average of the 91
day Treasury Bill Rate. Balances needed to support account activity
reflect balances including required reserves.

EXHIBIT 5
Swanson Corporation
Swanson Corporation Analysis Sheet Re Credit-Supporting Balances
Bank of Brooklyn
(Dollar figures in thousands)

	20-20 Agreed (%)		Total Line	Moving Average Line	Loan	Required Balance Monthly	Moving Average Requirement	Monthly Collected Balance[1]	Monthly Deficit[2]	Moving Average Balance	Moving Average Deficit[2]
	Line	Loan									
Jan.	20%		$5,000	$5,000	$4,000	$1,000	$1,000	$1,240		$1,240	(240)
Feb.	20		5,000	5,000	4,000	1,000	1,000	1,286		1,263	(263)
Mar.	20		5,000	5,000	2,500	1,000	1,000	741	259	1,089	(89)
Apr.	20		5,000	5,000	4,000	1,000	1,000	961	39	1,057	(57)
May (est.)	20		5,000	5,000	3,500	1,000	1,000	1,000		1,045	(45)
June (projected)	20		5,000	5,000	3,000	1,000	1,000	700	300	988	12
July (projected)	20		5,000	5,000	2,500	1,000	1,000	500	700	918	82
Aug. (projected)	20		5,000	5,000	1,250	1,000	1,000	1,200		954	46
Sept. (projected)	20		5,000	5,000	—	1,000	1,000	900	100	948	52
Oct. (projected)	20		5,000	5,000	—	1,000	1,000	900		953	47
Nov. (projected)	20		5,000	5,000	—	1,000	1,000	1,000		957	43
Dec. (projected)	20		5,000	5,000	—	1,000	1,000	1,500	—	1,002	(2)
											(2)

[1] Obtained from bank—daily average for each month
[2] Calculated by HBS researcher.

NOTE: Shortage (overage) 1,398
Cost @ 5½% $6.4

EXHIBIT 6
Swanson Corporation
Alternative Bank Credit Arrangements
($000's)

	Totals	First of San Francisco	Bank of Brooklyn	Bank of Bronx	First of Sacramento	Altoona National
Present arrangement						
Present line	18,500	7,500	5,000	3,000	2,500	500
Comp. bal. %		15%	20%	20%	20%	20%
Amount	3,325	1,125	1,000	600	500	100
Less working balances	2,000	750	950	—	200	100
Balance	1,325	375	50	600	300	—
Cost @ 5½%	72.875	20.625	2.75	33.0	16.5	—
Alt. I—Change to 10–20 policy						
Line	18,500	7,500	5,000	3,000	2,500	500
Comp. bal. %		10%	10%	10%	10%	10%
Amount	1,850	750	500	300	250	50
Less working balances	2,000	750	950	—	200	100
Balance		—	—	300	50	—
Cost @ 5½%	19.250	—	—	16.5	2.75	—
Alt. II—Reduce lines						
Line	13,000	5,000	4,000	2,000	1,500	500
Comp. bal. %		15%	20%	20%	20%	20%
Amount	2,350	750	800	400	300	100
Less working balances	2,000	750	950	—	200	100
Balance	500	—	—	400	100	—
Cost @ 5½%	27.500	—	—	22.0	5.5	—
Alt. III—Combination						
Line	15,000	6,000	4,000	2,000	2,500	500
Comp. bal. %		10%	10%	10%	10%	10%
Amount	1,500	600	400	200	250	50
Less working balances	2,000	750	950	—	200	100
Balance		—	—	200	50	—
Cost @ 5½%	13.750	—	—	11.0	2.75	—

EXHIBIT 7
Swanson Corporation
Possible Lines of Credit at Country Banks

Bank	Possible Line	20% Compensating	3 Months Average Balance
Lodi State	$ 600,000	$120,000	$305,106
First National of Lodi	300,000	60,000	93,138
Fresno State Bank	600,000	120,000	20,230
Reno National	500,000	100,000	43,000
	$2,000,000	$400,000	$461,474

Etech, Inc.

In early September 1982, Mr. Stephen Smith, manager of the Investment Department of Etech, Inc. was preparing for a full-day meeting with the other three members of the Department. It had been one year since the Investment Department had been formed as a separate unit in the Treasurer's Department to manage Etech's portfolios of marketable securities. The purpose of the meeting was to resolve a number of issues that had arisen and to establish an agenda of tasks to perform during the coming year.

BACKGROUND

In 1945 three engineers, who were close personal friends, began to work evenings and weekends on the development of a new type of electronic measuring device. After two years of hard work, the product was ready for use and the engineers obtained a substantial contract from the Department of Defense. At that point, they left their respective positions to form Etech, Inc.

Over the years, numerous products were introduced and the firm attained an excellent reputation for producing quality products. Top management cherished this reputation and believed that the firm's success was due primarily to the policy of allocating substantial sums to research and development and to the ability to attract and retain excellent engineers.

Through 1965, sales and profit growth had been steady but the rate of growth had been much lower than many firms producing similar products. At that time, new marketing policies were instituted which were designed to accelerate the rate of growth. For each of the next ten years, sales grew by more than 20 percent per year. Unfortunately, higher growth brought problems. In 1973 and 1974 profits declined and the firm incurred its first loss in 1975.

An in-depth review was conducted during the first two months of 1976 to determine the causes of the deterioration in profitability. The review indicated that weakness in management was the primary cause of the deterioration. More specifically insufficient attention had been paid to the following functional areas: strategic planning, finance, and control. The review also noted that product quality was still considered excellent and the firm had no fundamental problem in this area.

Many changes were implemented to correct these management problems including a reorganization into two product divisions: the Analytical Instrumentation Products Group and the Electronics Test and Measurement Products Group. Each division was managed by an Executive Vice President who reported directly to Etech's President. Within each division, product managers were given total responsibility for the success of their products. This was a significant departure from previous practice. Up to that time, product managers had responsibility only for production, engineering and quality control. Other aspects, notably marketing, were handled by two different centralized departments. The Marketing Department had managed domestic sales and the International Department had been responsible for sales outside the United States of America. (Approximately 25 percent of Etech's sales came from overseas business: 60 percent from Europe; 10 percent from Canada and Latin America; 15 percent from Asia; and 15 percent from other areas.)

Etech returned to profitability during 1976. From 1976 to 1981 sales grew by 20 percent per year and growth in net income exceeded 25 percent each year. For the year ended December 31, 1981 management proudly reported that annual sales passed the $1.5 billion mark for the first time; net income of almost $150 million was also a new record.

FINANCIAL POLICY

The 1976 review indicated that the firm had no clear policy with respect to the use of long-term debt. The final report recommended that once normal profitability was restored, Etech's target level for long-term debt should be 40 percent of total capital (i.e., the sum of long-term debt plus net worth). This recommendation was accepted and although the level had been evaluated on several subsequent occasions, no change had been made to the 40 percent target.

A more serious problem uncovered was the lack of adequate financial planning. On numerous occasions Etech had to postpone or cancel projects because of the lack of capital. Additionally, several times Etech had borrowed short term to finance projects which were ultimately funded by long-term debt. (This was viewed as a problem because at these times short-term interest rates had been substantially higher than long-term rates.) Improvements in the financial planning process was a major part of the reorganization and in addition, the following financial policies were established.

1. Etech would raise funds ahead of need. No specific time was established but it was understood that generally external capital requirements would be raised 6 to 12 months before the funds were actually needed for capital expenditures.

2. To minimize transaction costs, Etech would enter the capital markets no more than once each year.
3. The firm would maintain ample liquid balances (i.e., cash plus marketable securities). Although exact amounts would vary depending on business conditions, generally it would equal operating requirements for the subsequent three months plus approximately $15 to $20 million. In addition, a line of credit would be maintained but it would be used primarily as a reserve.

The above policies produced a substantial increase in liquidity. By September 1982, cash plus marketable securities was slightly more than $700 million and this total was divided into three portfolios: (1) the Short-Term Portfolio (approximately $100 million); (2) the Investment Portfolio (about $200 million); (3) the International Portfolio (approximately $400 million).

INVESTMENT DEPARTMENT

In September 1981 management formed an Investment Department to manage the three portfolios and the firm's pension funds. Mr. Stephen Smith was hired to manage the Department which reported to Mr. Harold Jones, the Treasurer. The Department was given four functions:

• Manage the day-to-day operations of the Short-Term and Investment Portfolios (i.e., purchases and sales, recordkeeping, etc.).
• Develop, implement and monitor a policy for selecting investments for the Short-Term and Investment Portfolios.
• Oversee the management of the International Portfolio.
• Manage the various Pension Portfolios. (These were different from the three portfolios described above.)

Mr. Smith decided to manage the Pension Portfolios along with an assistant. Ms. Theresa Beal was given responsibility for the Investment Policy and Mr. Thomas Dukes was in charge of the day-to-day operations of the Short-Term and Investment Portfolios. Although each person assumed leadership for a specific area, they worked as a team.

The full-day meeting mentioned in the first paragraph of the case would focus on issues pertaining to the first two functions. Before describing these, however, a few remarks are in order regarding the International Portfolio and the pension funds.

Investments in the International Portfolio were based primarily on tax and exchange rate considerations. Since these required considerable expertise in tax and currency matters, this portfolio had always been managed by an outside investment firm. When the Investment Department was formed, Mr. Smith and Mr. Jones discussed this arrangement and agreed that it should continue because they could not gain the required expertise at an acceptable cost. Of course, the Department was responsible for providing general guidelines for these investments and for monitoring the activities of the outside investment firm.

A major function of the Investment Department was the direct management of domestic pension portfolios. The overseas pension portfolios were managed by investment firms in the respective countries. The Investment Department's role with respect to the overseas portfolios was to be sure that managers of these investment firms were being prudent in their investment strategies and to develop a consistent World Pension Administration Policy. As noted above, Mr. Smith and an assistant performed these tasks.

MANAGING DAY-TO-DAY OPERATIONS

As noted, Mr. Thomas Dukes was responsible for the Short-Term and Investment Portfolios. What follows is a description of the policies he inherited, the changes he made, and the issues he wished to address at the upcoming full day meeting.

Short-Term Portfolio

The Short-Term Portfolio was the firm's cash balance for transaction needs and the size, $100 million in early September 1982, was determined by Mr. Jones, the Treasurer. Because of the pattern of collections of receivables and payments of trade credit and operating expenses, there were times during each month when a large part of the transaction balance was not needed. This temporary surplus of cash was used to compensate the firm's banks for services. However, generally, these surpluses were much larger than what was needed for compensating balances. Thus, the policy was to invest all surpluses above the amount needed for compensating balances. The policies and procedures that were in place when the Investment Department was formed are described next.

Each morning the cash supervisor would compute the cash balance to determine whether there was a shortage or a surplus (over and above the amount needed for compensating balances). If there was a shortage, securities would be sold. If there was a surplus, and this was much more common, the supervisor would determine how long the surplus would be available. He would then invest the surplus in an instrument whose maturity matched the expected duration of the surplus.

In selecting securities for the Short-Term Portfolio low priority was given to marketability (i.e., ability to sell an asset quickly for an amount close to its recently quoted price). To understand why, one must appreciate how the cash supervisor estimated the duration of the surplus. When the cash supervisor computed the cash balance and found a surplus, he would first review an updated schedule of estimated daily disbursements for the next 30 days. Since most items on the list were for purchases already made and for known expenses (e.g., payroll), generally there was only a small difference between the estimates and the actual amounts. The cash supervisor would then review an updated schedule of estimated daily cash receipts for the next 30 days. Generally, the major items were expected collections of receivables from sales already made. A receivable could be due in 10 days and the customer could actually pay in 15 days. However, the schedule of collections listed expected collection dates, not due dates, and given the credit history of customers, good estimates could be derived. In summary, estimates of receipts and disbursements for the next 30 days, and hence the estimate of the duration of cash surpluses, generally were quite accurate. Consequently, marketability was not a major concern when investing these temporary cash surpluses.

Default risk was the dominant factor in selecting investments for all the portfolios.[1] Mr. Jones and other members of senior management believed that, given the nature of Etech, default risk should be minimized. Given this view, Mr. Jones instructed the cash supervisor to limit investments for the Short-Term Portfolio to time deposits, high-quality commercial paper, repurchase agreements, and Treasury Bills.

As noted above, then there was a cash shortage, and this did not occur often, the cash supervisor would sell securities to cover the shortage. When Mr. Dukes assumed responsibility he changed this policy. What he did was compare the following three options.

- Sell securities in the Short-Term Portfolio.
- Borrow on the line of credit.
- Sell securities in the Investment Portfolio and temporarily transfer these funds to the Short-Term Portfolio.

He considered the two additional options because it could be profitable to select one of them. For example, sometimes it was cheaper to borrow for a few days to meet a temporary shortage instead of liquidating a security prior to maturity.

---

1. All the financial instruments discussed in the case are described in Exhibit 1. As explained below, Exhibit 1 is a summary of some of Ms. Beal's analysis. Most of these securities are short-term debt instruments issued or backed by financial institutions or industrial concerns. Default risk refers to the borrower's ability to meet interest and principal payments on the debt when they are due.

With respect to the composition of the portfolio, Mr. Dukes shifted more funds to Eurodollar time deposits.[2] These provided a higher yield than domestic time deposits and, in his opinion, there was not a significant risk differential. Moreover, he believed they possessed much less (default) risk than commercial paper. Indeed as the economy worsened he became quite concerned about the degree of default risk inherent in commercial paper and in April 1982 he stopped investing in commercial paper. In his view, the difference in yield between commercial paper and Treasury Bills was not worth the additional risk. (In September 1982, investments in the Short-Term Portfolio were allocated as follows: 25 percent in Eurodollar time deposits, 55 percent in domestic time deposits, and 20 percent in Treasury Bills and repurchase agreements.)

With respect to financial institutions to choose for time deposits, Mr. Dukes had been uncomfortable with the way the selections had been made. Up to September 1981, the cash supervisor would select well-known banks and purchase time deposits with these banks subject to limits described later. This concern was one of the motivations for a study by Ms. Beal, described below, that resulted in an approved list of banks.

At the full-day meeting, Mr. Dukes planned to discuss the possibility of including other financial instruments in the Short-Term Portfolio. He was particularly interested in discussing commercial paper. As noted, he had stopped investing in commercial paper. Perhaps this prohibition was no longer necessary, especially in light of the list of approved firms developed by Ms. Beal (discussed below). Finally, although he had the discretion to change the 25 percent limit on Eurodollar time deposits established by the Treasurer, he had never done so. He wanted to discuss with his colleagues the possibility of increasing the limit.

Investment Portfolio

The Investment Portfolio, $200 million in September 1982, was the result of the policy described earlier of raising capital before the funds were actually needed. It was difficult to predict the exact timing of the uses of these funds and so no attempt was made to match the maturity of the securities in the Investment Portfolio with the expected date that funds would be needed. However, there was a one-year limit—that is, securities had to have a maturity of one year or less. Moreover, unlike the Short-Term Portfolio, marketability as well as default risk was an important factor in selecting investment for this portfolio.

---

2. The Treasurer had instructed the cash supervisor to invest no more than 25 percent of the total Short-Term Portfolio in Eurodollar time deposits. However, the cash supervisor had never come close to this limit.

Up to September 1981, the Investment Portfolio had been managed by the Treasurer with the assistance of a clerical person. Most of this portfolio had been invested in Eurodollar certificates of deposit and domestic certificates of deposit. (The Treasurer had limited Eurodollar certificates to 30 percent of the total portfolio.) With respect to maturity, the Treasurer would target the average maturity at 45 days if he thought interest rates were going to increase and a longer maturity if he thought interest rates would decline. For the two years up to September 1981, the Treasurer believed that interest rates would increase and so the maturity had been kept at about 45 days. Thus for all practical purposes, the portfolio had been managed by a clerical person who would simply roll over the certificates as they matured subject to the following guidelines.

- Invest no more than $50 million in any one money center bank.
- Invest no more than $15–$20 million in any one regional bank.

(These limits applied to the total of time deposits and certificates of deposit.)

Mr. Dukes believed that maturity selection should be more flexible than the one used by the Treasurer. Moreover, he believed that there should be specific guidelines. Thus, the first task undertaken by Ms. Beal was to develop guidelines for selecting maturities. She completed this task in November 1981 and Mr. Dukes began to rely on them at that time. He had been quite pleased with the results.

He continued to focus on Eurodollar and domestic certificates of deposit. However, he occasionally invested in T Bills when he thought the yield differential was small enough to justify the improvement in risk. The enhanced liquidity was an added bonus.[3]

Mr. Dukes described the process used for selecting investments for this portfolio.[4]

I first look at the approved list of financial institutions that is derived by a screening process developed by Terry Beal. These are primarily U.S. Money Center Banks, strong foreign banks, and strong regional banks. I then consider the marketability of the instrument. Marketability is particularly important for this portfolio since we often ride the yield curve.[5]

---

3. Treasury Bills have no credit risk. For this reason and because the market is so large, they are easily converted to cash.
4. Mr. Dukes refers several times to projects of Ms. Beal which are explained later.
5. A yield curve is a graphical display of yields available at a given time on securities of identical risk but varying maturities. Sometimes the shape of the yield curve is such that a portfolio manager can improve the yield of the portfolio by trading one maturity for another. Trading to take advantage of the slope of the yield curve is called riding the yield curve.

We want to be sure we are able to sell the instrument if we think it is appropriate. Next, I review the maturity guidelines. Trends in the Treasury Bill rate influence my decision on how long or how short to make the investment. I also have to consider the maximum exposure policy—that is, the maximum amount I can invest in any one institution. Finally, I review what is available in the marketplace by which institution. For example, I may want to purchase a CD from Citibank, however, if Citibank believes that rates will decline, they may not be issuing CDs that day and so I will have to pick up another institution or another investment. Within these parameters, I also must think of the economy, the money supply and the political situation, all of which have an effect on the market and interest rates.

I have a computer terminal at my desk that displays market rates for all of the money market instruments for a variety of maturities. On the screen, I am also able to access the inventory of "what's available" from the major brokerage houses such as Merrill Lynch. After reviewing these rates and "what's available" I make specific decisions for the day and convey the instructions to my banker.

Mr. Dukes was looking forward to discussing at the meeting the 30 percent limit on Eurodollar deposits. He was also anxious to discuss the maturity guidelines and eligible investments for this portfolio. Both of these issues were based on Ms. Beal's activities which are described next.

INVESTMENT POLICY

Ms. Beal assumed leadership for the development of investment policies. During the first year she worked on four tasks in the order presented below:

- Guidelines for selecting maturities
- Approved list of countries
- Approved list of financial institutions and industrial concerns
- Analysis of various investment alternatives

A summary of each is presented below.

Maturity Guidelines

Ms. Beal consulted with economists and investment professionals, researched the finance literature, and performed considerable analysis which consisted of tests of the performance of alternative maturity strategies. Her study was completed in November 1981 and the final report included the following:

1. The interest rate on three-month Treasury Bills is a useful indicator for interest rates on marketable securities and so this rate should be our benchmark for considering levels and trends in interest rates.

2. No single set of guidelines will work in all environments because so much depends on economic conditions, fiscal and monetary policy, etc. In other words, a maturity strategy that will work well in one environment may produce suboptimal results in a different environment.

3. Given the caveats noted above and assuming a continuation of volatile interest rates, the guidelines shown in Table 1 should be followed.

As the full-day meeting approached, Ms. Beal wondered if it might be time to alter the guidelines. The guidelines in Table 1 assume an environment of volatile interest rates and an average rate on three-month Treasury Bills of 13 percent. Many economists were predicting lower and more stable interest rates, though views did vary. (Exhibit 2 presents a summary of statements that appeared in various business publications.)

If interest rates did continue to decline during the next 12 months and were more stable, then perhaps the existing guidelines should be discarded. Table 2 (on page 274) presents a set of guidelines for a stable environment with an average rate on three-month Treasury Bills of less than 11 percent. The problem with these guidelines is that they assumed the average of the three-month Treasury Bill rate would be 9–11 percent

TABLE 1
Maturity Guidelines
High and Volatile

When Rate on Three-Month Treasury Bills Is:	Investment Maturities Should Be:
Less than 12%	Short; sell everything with maturity of more than six months and invest short (0 to 14 days)
12–13%	14–45 days
13–14%	45–60 days
14–16%	90 days
16–17%	120 days
17–18%	180 days
Greater than 18%	One year—sell everything with a maturity of less than six months and invest for one year

TABLE 2
Maturity Guidelines
Low and Stable

When Rate on Three-Month Treasury Bills Is:	Investment Maturities Should Be:
Less than 10%	Short; sell everything with maturity of more than six months and invest short (0 to 14 days)
10–11%	15–45 days
11–12%	45–60 days
12–14%	90 days
14–15%	120 days
15–16%	180 days
Greater than 16%	One year—sell everything with a maturity of less than six months and invest for one year

and many people were predicting a much lower average. Thus, she planned to present the following three options.[6]

1. Retain guidelines in Table 1.
2. Adopt guidelines in Table 2.
3. Develop new guidelines for a lower interest rate environment (i.e., average three-month Bill rate of less than 9 percent). In the meantime, lock in existing rates.

Approved List of Countries

Ms. Beal's next task was to prepare an approved list of countries. As noted above, a substantial portion of the investments in the two portfolios were in Eurodollar time and certificates of deposit. These were dollar-dominated deposits of commercial banks located outside the United States. (These were foreign-based banks or subsidiaries of U.S. commercial banks. Thus, Etech was exposed to political risk—that is, a foreign government could restrict the flow of capital or expropriate the funds.) After an in-depth investigation, Ms. Beal concluded that by restricting investments to the following countries, there would be ample investment opportunities and the firm would be exposed to minimal

---

6. Exhibit 3 presents historical data on interest rates for the previous 12 months on selected money market instruments. Data on the prime lending rate are also included. The prime rate is the interest rate banks charge their most creditworthy customers.

political risk: Switzerland, West Germany, the United Kingdom, the Netherlands, and Japan.

In September 1982, Ms. Beal believed that the countries selected had served Etech well and would continue to do so in the future. Thus, she did not plan to raise this item at the full-day meeting.

Approved List of Financial Institutions and Industrial Firms

As noted above, credit risk was the dominant factor in selecting investments. Analyzing the financial institutions and industrial concerns backing the instruments was the key factor in judging risk. Ms. Beal developed a series of "screens" which led to formalizing an approved list of financial institutions and industrial firms that was frequently revised. The "screens" included relying on a quality rating from an outside consultant, performing ratio analysis, and assessing the quality of management. Assessing the quality of management was very difficult and so Ms. Beal relied primarily on the rating from the outside consultant and supplemented it with her own observations.

As the full-day meeting approached, Ms. Beal planned to report that the method of selecting firms and financial institutions needed no alteration. She was concerned, however, about the limits. As noted earlier, Mr. Jones had placed a limit of $50 million for money center banks and $15–$20 million for regional banks. These limits had been retained by the Investment Department. Given that there was so much talk about banks in trouble, she wondered if it might be wise to lower the limits. (Exhibit 4 gives summaries of statements appearing in the news regarding difficulties banks were having.)

The trouble with lowering the limits substantially was that given the list of approved countries and the list of approved financial institutions, the firm could not continue its focus on Eurodollar and domestic time and certificates of deposit. They might decide to change the focus anyway but reducing the limits substantially would force them to do so.

Eligible Investments

When the Investment Department was formed, the four members believed that it probably made sense to expand the variety of instruments selected. They all agreed that there were options available that would improve the yields of the two portfolios without altering risk levels in an appreciable way. Although they were anxious to make the change right away, they decided to wait until Ms. Beal performed an investigation of the options. They did this knowing that Ms. Beal would first tackle the three tasks described above. (They also agreed that Mr. Dukes should select others in the meantime if he uncovered an unusual opportunity.)

Ms. Beal performed a thorough literature search and consulted with professionals. She then analyzed the performance of various instruments over time. Since credit risk and marketability were so important, she paid particular attention to how each instrument fared during a crisis.

Ms. Beal's analysis was completed in early September 1981. (A summary of some of the securities she studied is presented in Exhibit 1.) When she sent her report to her colleagues, she noted that bankers' acceptances, Yankee CDs, and repurchase agreements deserved special attention. Also, because of Etech's marginal federal income tax rate of 46 percent, municipal notes should be given serious consideration.

MR. SMITH'S TASKS FOR THE FULL-DAY MEETING

In preparing for the full-day meeting, Mr. Smith worked with Mr. Dukes and Ms. Beal in specifying the issues described above. His only separate tasks were to review transaction costs and the size of the two portfolios. With respect to the latter he spoke with the Treasurer and reviewed capital investment and financing plans for the next 12 months. He concluded that each portfolio would grow by about 10 percent over the next year.

One of Etech's lead banks handled most of the firm's security transactions. The bank was paid for this service through compensating balances and the required amount in September 1981 was $100,000. There had been no change during the year even though the number of transactions increased because of the maturity guidelines. However, he thought an increase would be forthcoming. Etech's policy was to compensate its banks (via maintaining demand deposits) fairly for services performed and it did not negotiate hard. Indeed, often it would increase the level even though a bank did not ask. Thus, given this policy and the increased transactions, Mr. Smith thought an increase to $120,000 would be in order. He estimated that if the firm invested more because of the increased size of the two portfolios and because of the increased variety of instruments being considered, then a further increase to $130,000–$140,000 would be in order.

Mr. Smith was looking forward to the full-day meeting. There were many issues to discuss and resolve.

EXHIBIT 1
Selected Money Market Instruments

INTRODUCTION

Below are brief descriptions of various money market instruments. Ms. Beal developed the information by consulting with specialists and researching a variety of publications. Keep in mind that comments, especially those on marketability and default risk, are opinions expressed by the sources relied upon to develop this summary.

Commercial Paper

Definition:	Unsecured promissory notes of corporations
Minimum Size:	$100,000—generally size is much larger
Maturity:	Average is under 30 days—maximum is 270 days
Marketability:	Very limited
Default Risk:	Generally viewed as minimal risk but depends on issuer

Domestic Certificates of Deposit

Definition:	Negotiable short-term debt instrument issued by banks
Minimum Size:	$100,000—generally minimum for secondary market trading is about $1 million
Maturity:	14 days–12 months; average approximately 3 months
Marketability:	Very liquid
Default Risk:	Generally viewed as minimal risk but depends on issuer

Eurodollar Certificates of Deposit

Definition:	Dollar-denominated certificate of deposit issued by foreign branch of a U.S. bank or by a foreign bank outside the United States
Minimum Size:	$250,000—generally issue size is larger
Maturity:	One week and up; three-month maturity is common
Marketability:	Very liquid
Default Risk:	Generally viewed as minimal but depends on issuer

Yankee Certificates of Deposit

Definition:	Dollar-denominated certificate of deposit issued by U.S. branch of a foreign bank
Minimum Size:	Generally $1 million is minimum but often larger
Maturity:	Varies but three months is common
Marketability:	Very liquid
Default Risk:	Depends on creditworthiness of parent bank

EXHIBIT 1 (continued)

U.S. Treasury Bills

Definition:	Short-term obligation of U.S. Government
Minimum Size:	Generally $10,000
Maturity:	Up to one year
Marketability:	Most liquid marketable security
Default Risk:	None

Bankers' Acceptances

Definition:	Note issued by a purchaser of goods, usually an importer, accepted by a bank which in effect substitutes the bank's credit for that of issuer
Minimum Size:	Varies
Maturity:	30–180 days
Marketability:	Very liquid
Default Risk:	Generally viewed as minimal but it depends on bank

Time Deposit

Definition:	Non-negotiable fixed-rate deposits placed in a commercial bank. (Usually not considered a money market instrument)
Minimum Size:	Varies
Maturity:	14 days and up
Marketability:	Not marketable
Default Risk:	Depends on bank

Eurodollar Time Deposit

Definition:	Dollar-denominated time deposit issued by foreign branch of U.S. bank or by a foreign bank outside the United States
Minimum Size:	Varies
Maturity:	Overnight to several years; 7–180 days quite common
Marketability:	Not marketable
Default Risk:	Depends on bank

Repurchase Agreements

Definition:	Sale of securities with the simultaneous agreement of seller to repurchase securities at a specific date and price. Typically backed by U.S. securities
Minimum Size:	Generally $1 million
Maturity:	Overnight to a few days is most common
Marketability	Not marketable
Default Risk:	Minimal

EXHIBIT 1 (continued)

Municipal Notes

Definition:	Short-term debt instruments of local governments or other tax-exempt organization; interest is free from federal taxes. Some "munis" are guaranteed by U.S. Government or by insurance companies.
Minimum Size:	Varies, but often minimum is $10,000 or more
Maturity:	Several months
Marketability:	Generally very liquid
Default Risk:	Generally considered minimal but depends on issuer

EXHIBIT 2
Information on Interest Rates

INTRODUCTION

Below in outline form is a sample of information appearing in business publications.

1. "Econometric Forecast," *The Wharton Magazine*, Spring, 1982, p. 49+. It was reported that although the rate on three-month Treasury Bills exceeded 14 percent during February 1982, there had been a decline during the second quarter of 1982. A forecast for the remainder of 1982 through the end of 1983 indicated that there would be a gradual increase in the three-month Treasury Bill rate to about 14 percent in the third quarter of 1983. After that the rate would decline and would once again be in the 12 percent range.

2. *Predicasts*, April 26, 1982, No. 87, p. B-40. Forecasts from six different sources predicted rates on three-month T Bills ranging from 9.7 percent to 12.1 percent for remainder of 1982. The average of these short-term predictions was 11.4 percent.

3. "T-Bills in the Rain," by Richard Phalon, *Forbes*, April 26, 1982, p. 174+. This article suggested that there might be a change in the trend that interest rates were taking. While during April there had been about a .5 percent difference between the rate on T Bills and taxable money market funds, the difference could widen as investors become more willing to pay a higher price to accept the lower risk T Bills provide.

4. *Budget of the United States Government*, Fiscal Year 1982, p. 3. The budget is based on various assumptions, the interest rate on three-month T Bills being one of them. The assumption was an average rate of 11 percent for three-month T Bills for fiscal 1982 (i.e., year ended September 30, 1982).

5. "A Break in Interest Rates," *Newsweek*, August 30, 1982, p. 16+. It was reported that on August 20, 1982, the 90-day T Bill rate was 7.3 percent. *Newsweek* asked six economists to predict what the rate would be by the end of 1982. All but one indicated that the rate would increase. The highest was 11.25 percent and the second highest was 10.5 percent. The one economist who predicted a lower rate estimated that it would be 7 percent by the end of 1982.

EXHIBIT 3
Prime Rates and Selected Money Market Rates (September, 1981–August, 1982)*

	Prime Rate	Commercial Paper			Bankers' Acceptances		Certificates of Deposit		
		1 month	3 months	6 months	3 months	6 months	1 month	3 months	6 months
1981									
September	20.08	15.95	16.09	15.93	16.11	15.80	16.31	16.84	17.19
October	18.45	14.80	14.85	14.72	14.78	14.62	14.97	15.39	15.71
November	16.84	12.35	12.16	11.96	12.00	11.84	12.45	12.48	12.65
December	15.75	12.16	12.12	12.14	12.13	12.27	12.27	12.49	13.07
1982									
January	15.75	12.90	13.09	13.35	13.06	13.31	13.03	13.51	14.25
February	16.56	14.62	14.53	14.27	14.47	14.09	14.78	15.00	15.12
March	16.50	13.99	13.80	13.47	13.73	13.33	14.12	14.21	14.25
April	16.50	14.38	14.06	13.64	13.95	13.49	14.44	14.44	14.42
May	16.50	13.79	13.42	13.02	13.29	12.90	13.95	13.80	13.77
June	16.50	13.95	13.96	13.79	14.00	13.76	14.18	14.46	14.66
July	16.26	12.62	12.94	13.00	12.90	12.91	12.88	13.44	13.80
August	14.39	9.50	10.15	10.80	10.34	10.90	10.07	10.61	11.53

*See Exhibit 3 A for accompanying notes.

EXHIBIT 3 (continued)
Prime Rates and Selected Money Market Rates (September, 1981–August, 1982)*

| | Eurodollar Certificate of Deposit | U.S. Treasury Bills | | | Municipal Notes | Federal Funds |
	3 months	3 months	6 months	1 year	AAA	Rate
1981						
September	17.80	14.70	14.92	14.53	11.55	15.87
October	16.34	13.54	13.82	13.62	12.05	15.08
November	13.33	10.86	11.30	11.20	11.05	13.31
December	13.24	10.85	11.52	11.57	11.70	12.37
1982						
January	14.29	12.28	12.83	12.77	12.30	13.22
February	15.75	13.48	13.61	13.11	12.20	14.78
March	14.90	12.68	12.77	12.47	11.95	14.68
April	15.18	12.70	12.80	12.50	11.66	14.94
May	14.53	12.09	12.16	11.98	11.05	14.45
June	15.45	12.47	12.70	12.57	11.55	14.15
July	14.37	11.35	11.88	11.90	11.47	12.59
August	11.57	8.68	9.88	10.37	10.68	10.12

*See Exhibit 3 A for accompanying notes.

EXHIBIT 3A
Notes for Exhibit 3

1. The data were taken from Federal Reserve Bulletins. The Fed gathers this information from a variety of scources. Most figures represent some form of average for the month. See Bulletins for further details.

2. There was no published series for Yankee Certificates of Deposit. Rates tend to be slightly higher than and to move with Eurodollar CD rates. The difference in rates between the two instruments is seldom more than 10 basis points.

3. The rate on repurchase agreements secured by federal securities is about the same as the federal funds rate, but very often it is a little lower.

4. Rates on Eurodollar time deposits are generally higher than rates on Eurodollar certificates of deposit. Rates on domestic time deposits may be higher or lower than rates on domestic certificates of deposit.

5. Rates on bankers' acceptances may be higher or lower than rates on domestic certificates of deposit.

EXHIBIT 4
Information on Weak State of Banking Industry

INTRODUCTION

Below in outline form is a sample of information appearing in business press.

1. "Call In the Reserves? The FDIC Is Handling a Rash of Bank Failures," Shirley Hobbs Scheibla, *Barrons*, March 8, 1982, pp. 48–49. It was reported that many banks were in weak condition and the FDIC had to help facilitate mergers. The FDIC had to spend more to rescue banks during the last eight weeks of 1981 than it had spent on bank failures in the previous 47 years.

2. "Banking on Oil," Priscilla Meyer and Ellyn Spragins, *Forbes*, April 26, 1982, p. 39+. This article focused on the problems created by oil loans. It reported one estimate of total oil production and drilling loans outstanding through all types of financing vehicles, including foreign banking, of about $70 billion. Many bankers were worried about their loans because most of these loans assumed rising oil prices. Some loans were based on the assumption that the price would rise to $75 to $90 per barrel by 1987. The article also discussed other frightening aspects of energy lending and some specific problems.

3. "Reverberations; After the Penn Square Collapse," *Fortune*, August 9, 1982, p. 7+. Toward the end of the summer of 1982, the Penn Square Bank failed. The FBI was investigating the bank's collapse in cooperation with the FDIC. It appeared that the failure was due to an unbalanced loan portfolio, which consisted mostly of risky energy loans. Many other banks had participated in Penn Square's loans and so were expecting large losses. For example, Continental Illinois, the nation's sixth largest bank, had participated in about $1 billion in Penn Square loans.

4. "Three Banks Fail; Forced Closings Reach 24 for 1982," *Wall Street Journal*, August 30, 1982, p. 6. It was reported that by the end of the summer, the banking industry looked even more bleak. By then 24 commercial banks had failed including 3 small banks that were closed by state banking commissions. Failures were attributed primarily to large loan losses.

5. "A Brush with Bankruptcy," *Newsweek*, August 30, 1982, p. 54+. Another problem that appeared was poor economic conditions in Mexico and the request to international creditors for help. Mexico was the largest debtor of developing countries with $81 billion in foreign borrowing. It was estimated that about $22 billion of this total was owed to U.S. banks. A massive rescheduling of debt would affect the earnings outlook for all the banks involved.

PART IV
CAPITAL BUDGETING

Chou Canning Company

In July 1984, Cynthia Chou, president of the Chou Canning Company, was reading a trade association journal and noticed an advertisement announcing the invention of a new piece of vacuum equipment. The major feature of the new equipment was an automatic self-adjusting control device, which eliminated the need for continual manual adjustment. The ad claimed that the equipment, which cost $110,000 (including installation costs), would produce significant labor savings and would also reduce the spoilage rate of raw materials. Ms. Chou decided to request a demonstration of the new equipment.

After talking with a sales representative and observing a demonstration of the new equipment, the president became even more interested. She estimated that the machine would produce annual labor and raw materials savings of $24,000 and $3,500, respectively, over its five-year life. Although a used market likely would develop for this kind of equipment, Ms. Chou decided that it was safest to assume a zero salvage value.

Despite the advantages, Ms. Chou was uncertain whether it would be economical to sell the existing machine and buy the new one. The machine currently in use had been purchased five years ago for $60,000. It was being depreciated at a rate of $5,000 per year over a useful life of ten years to a $10,000 salvage value. Ms. Chou estimated that she could sell the machine now for $20,000, an amount substantially less than its $35,000 book value. When she learned that it would sell for only $20,000, she checked to see if the salvage value estimate of $10,000 (i.e., estimate of market value five years from now) was still reasonable; she found that it was.

In evaluating capital investments, Ms. Chou typically calculated an internal rate of return, net present value, and payback. Her after-tax required rate of return was 12 percent for most replacement type investments. To help derive the cash flows for this investment, she talked to the firm's tax accountant about the investment tax credit (ITC) and depreciation. A summary of this conversation is presented in Exhibit 1, and as explained there the ITC on the new equipment, which would be purchased on January 1, 1985, was $11,000. Depreciation expense for tax purposes for each of its five years of life would be as follows:

Year	Depreciation
1	$15,675
2	22,990
3	21,945
4	21,945
5	21,945

Ms. Chou was confident that the labor and materials savings estimates discussed above were reasonable. She was much less sanguine about the firm's marginal tax rate. The firm's operating budget indicated a marginal tax rate of 46 percent for 1984. The rate for 1985 was hard to predict. Ms. Chou had been trying unsuccessfully for two years to sell a bottling operation that was losing money. The only offer she had received was for an amount significantly less than the book value of the assets. If the offer was accepted, the transaction would produce a tax loss large enough to eliminate not only the taxes paid during the last three years but also those due for the next two or three years as well. Moreover, she was considering purchasing a firm that—although it had been incurring losses and was currently incurring a loss—she believed she could turn into a profitable operation. Since these losses might also shield future profits, it was conceivable that the firm could have a zero effective tax rate for the next five years or even longer. To deal with this uncertainty, the president decided first to perform the calculations using a 46 percent tax rate for each of the next five years and then to redo the calculations, assuming a zero tax rate for each of the next five years.[1]

After performing these calculations, Ms. Chou planned to explore the impact of another factor. There was the possibility that the new equipment would require an increase in inventory of raw materials of $10,000. (If this increase did occur there would be no offsetting increase in current liabilities.) This might be necessary to ensure that the machine would attain its maximum operating efficiency. To account for this possibility, Ms. Chou decided that she would redo the analysis, incorporating the possible increase in inventory.

---

1. The carryback/carryforward provisions of the tax law enables a firm to carry losses back 3 years and forward for 15 years. Thus, even if Chou Canning has a zero tax rate for the next 5 years, the ITC and depreciation on the proposed equipment could be used to offset profits for the 10 years after that, assuming, of course, that the firm has taxable income during that time. To simplify the analysis, the reader may ignore these potential tax shields. In other words, for the zero tax rate scenario, the reader may assume that unused tax shields over the 5-year period will *not* be used in subsequent years.

EXHIBIT 1
Memorandum

TO: File
FROM: Cynthia Chou
RE: Conversation with tax accountant

I spoke with Henry De Sisto about the investment tax credit (ITC) and depreciation expense. My primary purpose was to learn how to make the calculations necessary to analyze capital investments. Henry emphasized at the start of the conversation that changes in the tax laws could occur in the future, so in subsequent years I should check with him before relying on the following guidelines.

INVESTMENT TAX CREDIT

A firm is entitled to a tax credit when it purchases fixed assets, except real property (e.g., building). Examples are machinery, computer equipment, automobiles and trucks, and office furniture. The amount of the credit depends on the useful life of the assets. If the useful life is 2 years or less, there is no credit. It is 6 percent of the cost of asset (including installation charges) if the life is 3 or 4 years and 10 percent for assets with a life of 5 years or longer. To illustrate, below is the dollar credit allowed for a $50,000 piece of equipment assuming lives of 2, 3, 5, and 10 years.

Life	ITC—%	ITC—Dollars
2 years	0%	$ 0
3 years	6%	3,000
5 years	10%	5,000
10 years	10%	5,000

A credit is a direct reduction of taxes. For example, if the $50,000 equipment has a 5-year life, the credit is $5,000, which means that the firm's tax liability will be reduced by $5,000 in the year the asset is placed in service.

There is a recapture provision which means that if the credit is not actually earned, part or all of it must be repaid. In our example, the credit allowed is $5,000 and may be taken in the year the asset is placed in service. If it turns out that the firm owns the asset for less than 5 years, it would have to pay back part of the credit since the firm was not really entitled to the full amount. In other words, although a firm is permitted to take the credit right away, it must actually earn the amount taken to keep it. The credit is earned according to the following schedule.

Years Owned	% Credit
1	2%
2	4%
3	6%
4	8%
5	10%
6	10%
etc.	10%

To continue with our example, if a credit of $5,000 was taken because a 5-year life was assumed and the firm owned it only two years as the schedule shows, only 4 percent is earned. Thus, the firm is entitled to $2,000 and would have to repay $3,000.[1]

DEPRECIATION

The depreciation deduction allowed for tax purposes depends on the type of fixed asset. Most machinery, like the one the firm is contemplating, is depreciated over a 5-year life. The annual amount is derived by multiplying the depreciable base each year by the following percentages.

Year	Percentage
1	15%
2	22%
3	21%
4	21%
5	21%

The depreciable base is derived by subtracting one-half the ITC from the cost of the asset (including installation costs).

We will illustrate with the equipment the firm is considering. Its cost is $110,000, and since its life is 5 years the ITC will be $11,000. The depreciable base is $104,500, which is the cost of $110,000 less one-half the $11,000 ITC. Depreciation is computed by multiplying the depreciable base by the percentages as shown below.

Year	Depreciable Base	X	%	=	Depreciation Expense
1	$104,500	X	15%	=	$15,675
2	104,500	X	22%	=	22,990
3	104,500	X	21%	=	21,945
4	104,500	X	21%	=	21,945
5	104,500	X	21%	=	21,945

---

1. When the existing equipment Ms. Chou is considering replacing was purchased, the tax law was different. Because of that law a portion of the ITC taken on that equipment would have to be repaid. The reader may ignore this amount in preparing the case.

The tax basis at the end of 5 years will be zero. If the asset is sold for a positive amount at that time, the amount will be a taxable gain. For example, if the salvage value is $5,000, the gain will be $5,000 and the firm would pay taxes on this gain. If the asset has a zero salvage value, there will be no taxable gain or taxable loss. As noted previously, the estimated salvage value for the new equipment is zero.

The Daily Ledger

In late November 1984, Mr. Joseph Curran, owner of *The Daily Ledger*, was deciding which of two pieces of equipment he should purchase to replace a machine that would be disposed of in early 1985.

THE DAILY LEDGER

Founded in 1970 by Mr. Joseph Curran, *The Daily Ledger* was a prominent local paper in a medium-sized city in Georgia. Although the two competing papers were established prior to World War II, *The Daily Ledger* surpassed them in circulation in 1980. The circulation advantage widened each year after that, and by 1984 the firm had a comfortable margin over its nearest rival.

In mid-October 1984, the *Ledger* began having serious problems with its packaging machine. The machine was constantly breaking down and on several occasions the malfunction resulted in the late distribution of papers. Mr. Curran talked to Mr. Paul Selheim who was responsible for the operation of the machine. Mr. Selheim explained that the automatic adjuster had worn out. It had recently been replaced but several other parts were starting to wear out and he expected continual problems. Mr. Selheim's view was that the machine was no longer functional and, while he could get by for the rest of the year, the machine should be replaced as soon as possible and certainly no later than January 1, 1985. Further discussion convinced Mr. Curran that replacement was essential. It seemed clear that maintenance costs would increase substantially and that even with these larger expenditures operating problems would continue.

Mr. Curran immediately began a search for new equipment. He and his assistant gathered data from various vendors and observed 12 demonstrations. By the middle of November he had narrowed the choice to two similar machines and was assured by each manufacturer that their machine could be delivered and operational by the first week of January 1985.

FINANCIAL DETAILS

The existing machine would have a book value of $20,000 on December 31, 1984. Because of the serious mechanical problem, Mr. Curran estimated that its market value would equal its disposal costs in January 1985, when it would be replaced. Cash operating costs for this machine for 1984 would total $33,500—$19,000 for labor and $14,500 for other cash operating costs. Finally, had the decision not been made to retire this machine, depreciation expense would have been $4,000 per year for the next five years.

Each of the two replacements being considered had an estimated useful life of five years and an estimated salvage value of zero five years from now. Moreover, Mr. Curran estimated that the cash operating costs (i.e., labor and other cash operating costs) discussed below would increase by 6 percent per year for years subsequent to 1985.

The first replacement would cost $105,000, including installation costs. For 1985, labor costs to operate this machine were estimated at $20,500 and the estimate for other cash operating cost was $15,250 for the year. The second replacement had more sophistication than the first and thus would cost $130,000 including installation costs. Cash operating costs would be lower, however. Mr. Curran estimated that for 1985 labor costs to operate this machine would be $17,200 and other cash operating costs would be $14,000 for the year.

An inventory of paper and other supplies was needed to operate the existing machine. Mr. Curran estimated that the same amount would be required to operate either replacement.

With respect to income taxes, both machines would qualify for the 10 percent Investment Tax Credit. The firm's marginal income tax rate was 46 percent. Mr. Curran thought that this marginal rate might be lower in subsequent years but he decided that it was best to use 46 percent for each of the next five years.

In evaluating investments, Mr. Curran typically employed the net present value and internal rate of return methods. Finally, for investments like these he used a hurdle rate of 14 percent.

United Chemical Company

Margaret Simpson's first day as financial analyst at United Chemical Company began with a summons to the office of Clive Knowland, the assistant controller.

"Margaret," Clive began even before she had a chance to sit, "the Consumer Products Division gave me this proposal last week," he said holding up a sheaf of papers.

"It's a new product called the Personal Security System. It's a miniature siren that can be heard for several blocks, something like those anti-theft devices for cars. Top management has a lot of interest in this.

"According to the summary," Clive continued, "the rate of return exceeds the 22 percent hurdle rate for new products."

"Sounds interesting," Margaret volunteered.

"Yes," Clive conceded, "but I notice that Oscar Jones prepared the proposal, and he's notorious for leaving important things out.

"And that worries me, because if people get an incorrect proposal, things can get mighty uncomfortable around here. Would you look it over carefully? Don't hesitate to call Oscar, but as a rule he doesn't give much help."

Margaret went back to her desk, and it didn't take her long to note two items of concern.

1. There didn't seem to be any adjustment for inflation in the figures.
2. No adjustments were made to cash flows for working capital.

She placed a call to Oscar.

"Oscar," she started, "I have a couple of questions about the proposal."

"Go ahead," Oscar replied impatiently.

"Well, do the sales and expense figures have any inflation in them?"

"Yes and no," responded Oscar. "We didn't inflate the numbers, if that's what you're getting at; but inflation won't be a problem because we plan to pass on any cost increases through higher prices. Our profit margin will stay the same."

"But do you have a feel for what kind of inflation you might experience in, say, raw materials or labor expenses?" persisted Margaret.

"Well, your guess is as good as mine, but if it will make you happy,"

Oscar said wearily, "the paper this morning said inflation's down to 7 percent. Anything else I can help you with?"

"Yes," said Margaret, "one more thing. Did you include the working capital requirements in the cash flow projections?"

"We didn't forget them," Oscar replied sharply. "See, right on page 3, in the 'working capital' section, in black and white."

"Yes, of course," Margaret answered. "I just wanted to make sure they're not included in the $5 million equipment category. Thanks for your help, Oscar."

Margaret studied the cash flow projections and the working capital requirements (Table 1) and knew that she should make some changes and discuss them with Knowland.

TABLE 1
Cash Flow Projections
($000)

Gross investment	$5,000				
Less: Tax credit	500				
Net investment	$4,500				
Year					
Sales	$5,000	$10,500	$12,500	$11,750	$7,000
Cash expenses	3,500	8,350	9,750	9,000	5,000
Depreciation	750	1,100	1,050	1,050	1,050
Profit before taxes	$ 750	$ 1,050	$ 1,700	$ 1,700	$ 950
Taxes (46% rate)	345	483	782	782	437
Net income	$ 405	$ 567	$ 918	$ 918	$ 513
Depreciation	750	1,100	1,050	1,050	1,050
Cash flow	$1,155	$ 1,667	$ 1,968	$ 1,968	$1,563
Working capital	$ 500	$ 2,100	$ 2,500	$ 2,300	$ -0-

Thermo Rubber, Inc.

In late March 1976, Robin Porter, a senior financial analyst at Thermo Rubber, Inc., was working on an interesting capital budgeting assignment. The techniques the company used to evaluate capital investments were in the process of being upgraded, and Ms. Porter was assigned the task of recommending to what extent more sophisticated techniques should be used for investments classified as normal replacements.

Thermo Rubber, Inc., founded in 1924 in Idaho, manufactured a complete line of rubber- and plastic-coated products for household, garden, and office and other institutional needs. These products were sold in the United States and in four foreign countries through factory salespeople, primarily to department stores and mail order houses. In addition, products were sold directly through the sales force to certain large institutional customers. In 1975 sales were almost $180 million on assets of $123.6 million. (See Exhibits 1 through 5 for financial data.) During 1975 consumer products accounted for approximately 65 percent of the company's sales, and institutional sales accounted for the remainder.

EXISTING CAPITAL BUDGETING REQUIREMENTS

Up through 1975, the company's procedures for screening capital investments were not very different from what they were in the 1930s, even though by 1975 the level of capital expenditures was quite large (Exhibit 5). Capital requests were approved at either the divisional level or the corporate level, depending on the size and the type of investment. The general managers of the various divisions had the authority to make decisions on replacement requests up to $50,000. Replacement requests over $50,000 and all strategic investment requests had to be approved by the finance committee of the board of directors. (The president of the company was a member of the board of directors and head of its finance committee.)

When a request was submitted to headquarters, it was first classified as either normal replacement or strategic. The first referred to the replacement of existing assets and to investments for which no return was anticipated (for example, a cafeteria for employees). Strategic investments included everything else. However, these requests were primarily for the expansion of facilities for existing products and for new products. For normal replacements, which accounted for approximately 45 percent of the capital budget, no formal financial analysis was performed and the decision was based on need. If the replacement request was greater than $50,000, a member of the financial analysis staff would check that the cost of the investment, as specified in the request, was correct. Moreover, the analyst would then verify as best as he or she could that the need was legitimate. For replacement requests under $50,000, the financial analysis department would become involved only if the general manager asked for assistance. If no assistance was requested, presumably the general manager or a member of his or her staff evaluated the request.

For strategic investments, a thorough analysis was performed. During the first phase of the analysis, the firm's legal, marketing, and finance staffs would be involved. The legal department would make sure that the investment would create no insurmountable legal problems. The marketing staff would render an opinion regarding the investment's "fit" in the firm's overall marketing strategy, and the finance people would determine whether the investment promised adequate profitability. A 12-percent after-tax rate of return was considered "adequate." Rate of return was defined as average expected net income divided by the original cost of the investment.

If the first phase indicated that the investment was promising, the payback period would be calculated for the investment, payback being defined as the number of years required for the cumulative net income after taxes from an investment to cover its cost. For investments judged to possess average risk, a payback of from 6 to 10 years was required. If the investment involved above-average risk, a 3- to 4-year payback was required. (The degree of risk was subjectively assessed.)

ADVENT OF PRESENT VALUE TECHNIQUES

The motivation to consider altering capital budgeting procedures was the result of a change in recruitment policies in the late sixties. Prior to 1967, a bachelor's degree was required to become a management trainee at Thermo Rubber, Inc. An applicant to the accounting department was required to have a bachelor's degree in accounting, but no specific major was required of applicants to other departments. In fact, management was proud that it was able to train liberal arts and science majors to become effective managers. Moreover, since the firm sought balance and since virtually all the accounting trainees, who represented the majority of trainees, were from business schools, most of the trainees for the other departments had liberal arts or science backgrounds.

In 1967 the firm altered its recruitment policies and began to hire MBAs for some of the trainee positions. Many of the new finance trainees were surprised to find that the firm did not use present value techniques to screen capital investments. They had learned in school that present value techniques were clearly superior to the techniques the company used, and they began to question openly the firm's procedures for evaluating capital investments.

These young managers had thought that senior management just did not understand present value techniques, but this was simply not the case. Not only did senior managers understand present value techniques, but many of them had read about analytical methods for incorporating risk in capital budgeting. The fact was that top management understood but rejected the use of these techniques, believing that management is more like an art than a science and that the use of these "sophisticated" techniques leads to mechanical decision making. Putting it another way, top management thought that young managers would not develop properly if they relied too heavily on quantitative decision-making methods.

Despite the negative attitude, top management was open to discussing the matter. Indeed, such discussions were encouraged. In late 1975, top management decided to give present value techniques a chance. Nicholas Gulateri, assistant controller and manager of the financial analysis department, was given the task of instituting present value analysis as an adjunct to existing procedures; that is, current procedures would continue and the present value analysis would be added to them. Mr. Gulateri was authorized to hire two financial analysts because of the additional work. Top management also considered implementing analytical methods for evaluating risk, but decided to wait and see how the present value techniques would work out.

Mr. Gulateri decided that he would focus his attention on strategic investments. Therefore he asked Robin Porter to work on replacements and to recommend the extent to which present value techniques should be used to evaluate these investments.

Ms. Porter vigorously attacked this exciting assignment. She had numerous discussions with colleagues on the finance staff as well as colleagues in other staff positions. She also sought the opinions of senior managers at headquarters as well as managers in the field. Although most people's initial reaction was that the present value analysis was not necessary for most replacement-type investments, she was able to show them that it was indeed appropriate. (A summary of her notes of these discussions is presented in Exhibit 6.) These discussions convinced her that her report must include an illustration. She thought that it would be best to select one with which most people would be familiar; and, after investigating several possibilities, she concluded that the purchase of cars for salespeople would provide an excellent example.

Requests to purchase autos came from the regional sales managers. There was no set schedule for car replacement. For example, one regional manager believed that it was best to replace cars every three years, and his capital requests reflected this belief. Another manager, who relied on the judgment of his assistant managers, would request the replacement of some cars that were less than two years old while maintaining others that were four or five years old. This type of procedure was followed even though financial data were readily available on which to make a more informed decision. For example, in one region Ms. Porter found that the cost of a new car was $6,000. Expenditures for repairs and maintenance increased as a car aged. Moreover, the amount of gas used also increased since miles per gallon decreased. On the other hand, expenses such as insurance and excise taxes decreased. After careful study, she concluded that, given the extent of use by the salespeople in this region, a car normally could be maintained for no more than four years, and she arrived at the following operating expense estimates:

Year	Operating Expenses (Excluding Depreciation Expense)
1	$3,650
2	4,275
3	4,690
4	5,100

Obtaining reasonable estimates for trade-in values was difficult, and Ms. Porter concluded that it would be best to rely on two sets of estimates:

Year	Trade-In Value (Optimistic Estimate)	Trade-In Value (Pessimistic Estimate)
1	$4,000	$3,500
2	2,000	1,000
3	0	0
4	0	0

Ms. Porter was concerned about the treatment of income taxes. The firm's normal income tax rate was 48 percent, but she was not sure that this rate was applicable to the gains and losses that might be incurred when the old cars were traded in for new cars. Moreover, since the firm depreciated its cars using the sum-of-the-years' digits method over a three-year life to a zero salvage value, she wondered whether and how the 10-percent investment tax credit would affect the depreciation rate as well as the calculation of gains and losses.

Her investigation revealed that, when a car was traded in for a new car, the transaction was considered a nontaxable exchange. That is, no gain or loss was recognized for income tax purposes. The depreciable base of the new car would be equal to the net price plus the book value of the car that was traded in.[1]

With respect to the 10-percent investment tax credit, Ms. Porter learned that the property had to have a useful life of at least three years to qualify for the credit. If the useful life was at least three years but less than five years, only one-third of the net price paid entered into the calculation of the credit. For example, suppose a firm were to purchase a car for $9,000 with a useful life of three years. The investment credit would be $300 ($9,000 $\times$ $^1/_3$ $\times$ 10%). Suppose the car were traded in at the end of three years and that the net price for the second car were $7,500 ($9,000 less assumed trade-in value of $1,500). The investment credit on the second car would be $250 ($7,500 $\times$ $^1/_3$ $\times$ 10%). With respect to depreciation, she learned that the amount of the investment credit did *not* affect the depreciation that could be charged.

There was one further complication: the recapture of the investment credit. If property with a useful life of three (or four) years were disposed of prior to the third year, the investment tax credit taken on that property would have to be paid back in the year of disposition. Moreover, if the firm were to adopt a policy of trading in cars every year or every two years, the Internal Revenue Service would probably rule that the useful life was in effect less than three years and would disallow the credit altogether.[2] Moreover, using the sum-of-the-years'-digits method (or double-declining balance method) of depreciation required a useful life of at least three years. Thus such a ruling would mean that straight-line depreciation would have to be used. Because of this possibility, Ms. Porter decided to use straight-line depreciation over a three-year life to a zero salvage for the alternatives of trading the auto in every year and every two years, and to use the sum-of-the-years'-digits method over a three-year life to a zero salvage for the alternatives of trading the auto in every three years and every four years.

Although Ms. Porter considered gathering data on autos for other regions as well as analyzing other types of fixed asset investments, she concluded that this one example would be sufficient to make her point. She considered this assignment to be a great opportunity. Although the report would be prepared for Mr. Gulateri, he had told her that many members of top management would read it. Thus she would obtain a great deal of exposure from this assignment.

---

1. Net price is defined as list price minus trade-in allowance. Exhibit 7 presents an example of how depreciation will vary when equipment is frequently replaced and the transactions are nontaxable exchanges.
2. At the time this case was written, the IRS had recently made such rulings, and these rulings were upheld by the courts.

EXHIBIT 1
Thermo-Rubber, Inc.
Income Statement for Years ended December 31
(000 omitted)

		1975		1974
Net sales		$179,551		$153,788
Other income (net)		381		734
Total net income		$179,932		$154,522
Cost of goods sold		121,854		110,837
Gross profit		$ 58,078		$ 43,685
Selling expenses	$27,682		$23,530	
Depreciation and amortization expense	7,129		6,191	
Interest expense	617	35,428	710	30,431
Profit before taxes		$ 22,650		$ 13,254
Income taxes		10,600		6,243
Net income		$ 12,050		$ 7,011

EXHIBIT 2
Thermo-Rubber, Inc.
Balance Sheets as of December 31
(000 omitted)

	1975	1974
Assets		
Cash	$ 649	$ 709
Temporary cash investments	14,617	569
Net accounts receivable	21,461	16,054
Inventories	24,140	26,436
Prepayments	821	1,733
Total current assets	$ 61,688	$ 45,501
Net property	56,090	55,239
Land	1,538	1,767
Addition in progress	2,428	2,252
Excess cost investment in subsidiary over book value assets acquired	1,403	1,406
Investments	336	325
Other assets	121	117
Total assets	$123,604	$106,607
Liabilities		
Notes payable	$ 205	$ 1,258
Current debt	836	843
Accounts payable	10,451	8,364
Accruals	5,486	4,077
Income taxes	6,414	—
Total current liabilities	$ 23,392	$ 14,542
Long-term debt	6,560	7,330
Deferred income taxes	4,506	3,569
Deferred investment credit	1,800	1,777
Common stock	8,607	8,607
Capital surplus	18,696	22,785
Retained earnings	60,043	47,997
	$123,604	$106,607

EXHIBIT 3
Thermo-Rubber, Inc.
Income Data, 1966–1975
(000 omitted)

Year	Sales	Operating Income	Depreciation & Amortization	Income Taxes	Net Income
1966	$ 54,812	$11,446	$2,286	$ 4,354	$ 4,033
1967	61,563	12,378	2,616	4,983	4,550
1968	68,708	12,076	2,853	6,339	3,899
1969	70,691	14,620	3,107	4,077	5,039
1970	76,707	15,706	3,337	5,385	6,363
1971	85,880	17,430	3,586	6,817	7,769
1972	112,972	28,396	4,443	7,441	9,323
1973	125,711	25,300	5,014	10,017	11,661
1974	153,788	20,240	6,191	6,243	7,011
1975	179,551	30,198	7,129	10,600	12,050

EXHIBIT 4
Thermo-Rubber, Inc.
Common Stock Data

Year	Earnings per Share ($)*	Dividend per Share($)*	Price Range
1966	.62	.23	$13^6/8 – 9^3/8$
1967	.65	.25	$11^4/8 – 6^2/8$
1968	.57	.27	$11^3/8 – 9^1/8$
1969	.71	.28	$13^5/8 – 9^1/8$
1970	.79	.30	$17^4/8 – 9^2/8$
1971	.93	.31	$33^2/8 – 17^3/8$
1972	1.26	.32	$44^4/8 – 30^2/8$
1973	1.42	.34	$51^4/8 – 32$
1974	.88	.37	$38^3/8 – 10^5/8$
1975	1.46	.42	$27^7/8 – 14^2/8$

* Adjusted for 2-for-1 stock splits in November 1970 and August 1973 and a three percent stock dividend in March 1965.

EXHIBIT 5
Thermo-Rubber, Inc.
Capital Expenditures
Years Ended December 31
(000 omitted)

1966	$11,280
1967	11,849
1968	12,447
1969	13,074
1970	13,733
1971	14,624
1972	15,151
1973	15,913
1974	16,948
1975	8,472
1976*	14,213

*Estimated

EXHIBIT 6
Memorandum
March 1976

TO: File
FROM: Robin Porter
RE: Analysis of replacement-type investments

Most people initially argued that it was not necessary to perform a present value for normal replacements. A typical response was the following: "For most of these investments, no analysis is necessary because the decision is really already made. If a secretary's typewriter breaks down, for example, don't we have to replace it?" These people did agree, however, that present value analysis was appropriate when there were significant cost differences among possible replacements for a specific piece of equipment. For example, suppose it would cost $40,000 to replace a current piece of equipment, but that a more efficient model was available. The better model would cost much more, perhaps $70,000 or $80,000 more, but promised to produce significant savings in labor and/or materials. All agreed that, in this type of situation, it was no longer a replacement investment but rather a strategic investment, and that hence an analysis was appropriate. However, these people suggested that most replacement decisions were not of this type and thus that no analysis was needed.

I was able to convince these people by pointing out that, while a variety of replacements might not be available, there was still the issue of how often to replace various types of equipment, and that we could use present value analysis to help resolve this issue. I relied on the following example.

Suppose a firm were going to purchase a piece of equipment for $5,000 and had the options of replacing it every year or every two years. If the firm decided to replace it every year, the net cash outflow would be $6,000 at the end of each year. If it decided to replace the equipment every two years, the net cash outflow would be $1,000 at the end of the first year subsequent to purchase and $10,000 at the end of the second year. The cash flows for each alternative can be displayed as follows:

Year	Every Year
0	5,000
1, 2, 3, 4, ... ∞	6,000

Year	Every 2 Years
0	5,000
1, 3, 5, 7, ... ∞	1,000
2, 4, 6, 8, ... ∞	10,000

The present value factor for a perpetual annuity assuming annual compounding can be calculated for varying intervals by means of the following formula:

$$\frac{1}{[(1 + i)^n - 1]}.$$

where

$$i = \text{discount rate}$$
$$n = \text{interval}$$

Assuming a 10-percent discount rate, the factor for a perpetual annuity of $1 at the end of each year is 10.0000. The factor for a perpetual annuity of $1 at the end of every second year is 4.7619. We can now calculate the present value of the cash flows for each alternative.

Every Year

Year	Amount	X	PV Factor @ 10%	=	PV
0	5,000	X	1.0000	=	5,000
1, 2, 3, 4, ... ∞	6,000	X	10.0000	=	60,000
			Total	=	65,000

To simplify the calculation of the second option, it would be helpful to restate the cash flows as follows:

Year	Amount	=	Revised		
0	5,000	=	5,000		
1	1,000	=	1,000		
2	10,000	=	1,000	+	9,000
3	1,000	=	1,000		
4	10,000	=	1,000	+	9,000
5	1,000	=	1,000		
6	10,000	=	1,000	+	9,000
•	•		•		•
•	•		•		•
•	•		•		•
∞	∞		∞		∞

We can now calculate the present value.

Every Two Years

Year	Amount	X	PV Factor @ 10%	=	PV
0	5,000	X	1.0000	=	5,000
1, 2, 3, 4, . . . ∞	1,000	X	10.0000	=	10,000
2, 4, 6, 8, . . . ∞	9,000	X	4.7691	=	42,922
					57,922

Replacing the equipment every two years has a lower total cost.

EXHIBIT 7
Illustration of Depreciation Calculations

Assume that Firm A is going to purchase a piece of equipment for $9,000 and that it intends to replace the equipment at the end of each year. The trade-in value of the equipment at the end of one year will be $5,500, so each subsequent purchase will require an outlay of $3,500. The transaction will be a nontaxable exchange. Finally, this equipment will be depreciated on a straight-line basis over a three-year life to a zero salvage value.

Depreciation expense for the first year is calculated as follows:

$$\frac{\text{Cost} - \text{Salvage value}}{3} = \text{Depreciation expense}$$

$$\frac{9{,}000 - 0}{3} = 3{,}000$$

For each subsequent year, depreciation expense is calculated as follows:

$$\frac{\text{Net price} + \text{Book value of old}}{3} = \text{Depreciation expense}$$

For year 2:

$$\frac{3{,}500 + 6{,}000}{3} = 3{,}167$$

Book value end of year 2:

$$3{,}500 + 6{,}000 - 3{,}167 = 6{,}333$$

For year 3:

$$\frac{3{,}500 + 6{,}333}{3} = 3{,}278$$

Book value end of year 3:

$$3{,}500 + 6{,}333 - 3{,}278 = 6{,}555$$

Depreciation expense will increase each year until it reaches $3,500. At that point, it will remain at an annual level of $3,500.

Jenkins Plumbing Company

Jenkins Plumbing Company decided to computerize its accounting and billing operations. The computerization was expected to save significant clerical costs and thus was classed as a cost-reducing investment. Such investments had to provide a minimum return of 8 percent per year.

After talking with various computer manufacturers, Jenkins's president, Clark Jones, narrowed the choices down to two. The manufacturer for system A offered to install a complete operating system including programming, personnel orientation, and equipment installation for a total cost of $170,000. The manufacturer for system B suggested a more gradual, phased-in, approach. For $170,000, the manufacturer would provide continued operating support for two years, after which all the "bugs" would be out of the system and full benefits could be realized. Both manufacturers indicated that a five-year system life was appropriate. Jones decided to ignore any salvage value.

Jones asked Bob to determine which system would produce the maximum return on investment. Bob shared Clark's concern for maximum ROI but he remembered that the last capital budgeting analysis he did also involved two mutually exclusive investments; but, while one had higher internal rate of return, the other had a higher present value. Bob felt uneasy rejecting the higher ROI project in favor of the "textbook correct" higher net present value project. The recommendation didn't sit well with Mr. Jones and Bob was unable to defend his recommendation.

Somehow, Bob could feel in his bones that this was going to be another one of those situations. He was still convinced that present value analysis was the proper approach, but he was not about to suggest it again unless he could conclusively show Jones that he was "getting the ROI message."

Investment Summary

	System A	System B
Net investment	$170,000	$170,000
Salvage value	-0-	-0-
Economic life	5 years	5 years
Operating savings		
Years 1–2	60,000	12,000
Years 3–5	60,000	100,000
Corporate tax rate	40%	40%

ACRS depreciation

Year	% Investment		
1	15%	$ 25,500	$ 25,500
2	22%	37,400	37,400
3	21%	35,700	35,700
4	21%	35,700	35,700
5	21%	35,700	35,700

Note on the Capital Asset Pricing Model (CAPM)

The Capital Asset Pricing Model (CAPM) is both a theoretical and an empirical framework for measuring the risk of an investment and relating this risk to an appropriate rate of return. A forceful feature of the CAPM is that it provides a basis for comparing the relative attractiveness of any number of investment alternatives even though such alternatives may vary substantially with respect to either risk or return or both. Thus, the CAPM permits the comparative valuations of investment alternatives.

RETURN

The return from an investment is measured by dividing the cash received plus any change in investment value by the amount of the investment.

Assume that you pay $100 for a share of common stock. The stock pays a dividend of $2.00 during the year, and at the end of the year the stock price has risen to $120. Your return on the stock for the year is 22 percent.

$$\text{Return on investment} = \frac{\text{Cash} + \text{Change in value}}{\text{Beginning investment}}$$

$$\text{Return on investment} = \frac{\$2.00 + \$20.00}{\$100} = .22 = 22\%$$

Table 1 shows a series of returns realized from annual investments in common stock for Vaxon Company.

TABLE 1
Vaxon Company Common Stock

Year	Beginning Stock Price	Dividends Paid	Ending Stock Price	Return
19x1	$100	$2.00	$120	22.00%
19x2	120	2.10	115	2.42
19x3	115	2.20	100	11.13
19x4	100	2.30	105	7.30
			Total return	15.75%
			Average return	3.94%

RISK FOR A SINGLE INVESTMENT

At the time an investment is made, returns are not predictable because the returns are to be generated in the future. This unpredictability is inherent in all investment decisions since the essence of investment is to pay out cash today for the promise or expectation of more cash in the future. Sometimes the future is favorable, as it was in the year 19x1 for Vaxon stockholders; sometimes the future turns out to be unfavorable, as it was in year 19x2 for Vaxon stockholders. Risk is the degree to which actual future returns may differ from expected returns.

When we consider a single investment in isolation, we can measure its risk by calculating its variance or, more usually, the standard deviation, which is the square root of the variance. The standard deviation of an investment's returns provides a measure of its dispersion of possible returns from its expected returns. The greater the dispersion of returns, the greater the risk. For example, Figure 1 shows the dispersion of returns for two investments, A and B. A has a greater dispersion and hence more risk.

To calculate an investment's standard deviation, we first compute its variance, and then take the square root of the variance. Table 2 (on page 312) shows how the variance and standard deviation of returns are calculated for the Alton Company.

We first calculate the average return over the 10-year period (column 2). Then, in column 3, we calculate the deviation of each annual return from the overall average. The deviation for each year is then squared (column 4) and summed. The variance is calculated by dividing the sum of column 4 by the number of periods minus 1 (i.e., 9). Dividing by 9 rather than 10 is necessary because we have lost 1 degree of freedom in

Figure 1   Probability Distributions—Investments A and B

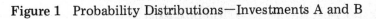

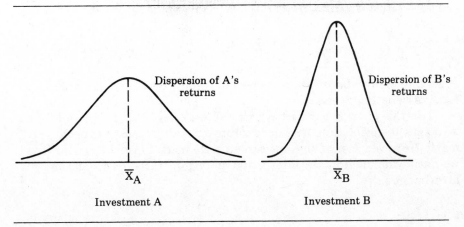

TABLE 2
Calculation of Standard Deviation of Returns
of Alton Company Stock

(1) Year	(2) Return	(3) Deviation		(4) Deviation Squared
19x1	25.00%	(25.00 − 8.45) =	16.55	273.90
19x2	0.58	(.58 − 8.45) =	−7.87	61.94
19x3	20.00	(20.00 − 8.45) =	11.55	133.40
19x4	10.30	(10.30 − 8.45) =	1.85	3.42
19x5	3.00	(3.00 − 8.45) =	−5.45	29.70
19x6	9.50	(9.50 − 8.45) =	1.05	1.10
19x7	16.25	(16.25 − 8.45) =	7.80	60.84
19x8	−8.13	(−8.13 − 8.45) =	−16.58	274.90
19x9	15.00	(15.00 − 8.45) =	6.55	42.90
19x10	−7.00	(−7.00 − 8.45) =	−15.45	238.70
Average	8.45%		Variance	1120.81/9 = 124.53
			Standard deviation	11.16%

the calculation of the average that is used to calculate the annual deviations. Dividing by the number of periods minus 1 gives us an average squared deviation, which is the same as the variance. The sum of squared deviations in Table 2 is 1120.81 and the average squared deviation is 124.53. In other words, the variance is 124.53 and the standard deviation is 11.16 percent.

Since the standard deviation is sensitive to the unit of measure, it is useful to "standardize" it by dividing it by the average return. This gives the *coefficient of variation*.

$$\text{Coefficient of variation} = \frac{\text{Standard deviation}}{\text{Average return}}$$

$$= \frac{11.16\%}{8.45\%}$$

$$= 1.32$$

As the relative dispersion of expected returns decreases, the coefficient of variation decreases.

Up to this point, what we have said about investment risk is valid for investments in isolation, that is, ignoring any other investments we make. However, few, if any, investments are made in isolation, and thus we must examine how the interaction among investments affects an investment's risk.

PORTFOLIO RISK

A portfolio of investments refers to the entire collection of investments we have made. In the unlikely event that we have made only one investment, that investment is in fact our portfolio.

The actual returns we get from each investment in the portfolio may differ from what we expected to get. From the standpoint of a portfolio, the key idea is that better-than-expected outcomes on some investments help offset less-than-expected outcomes on others.

In Table 3 the actual returns from two different shares of common stock are shown for the years 19x1 to 19x4. The average annual return for Jones Company stock is 3.94 percent and its standard deviation is 12.30 percent, producing a coefficient of variation of 3.12. Kalman Company common stock over the same period had average returns of 16.06 percent, a standard deviation of 12.30 percent, and a coefficient of variation of 0.77.

Notice in Table 3 that whenever Jones's stock returns were below average, Kalman's returns were above average; and whenever Jones's stock returns were above average, Kalman's were below average. For example, in 19x1, Jones's stock returns were 22 percent, considerably above its average return of 3.94 percent. In the same year, Kalman's stock returns were a negative 2.00 percent, considerable below its average of 16.06 percent. In 19x3, Jones's stock returns were considerably below average, but Kalman's were considerably above average. In other words, relative to their average returns, the annual returns for each company moved in opposite directions. This can be seen in 19x4 also. Even though the returns for Jones and Kalman were both positive in 19x4, Jones's returns were above average and Kalman's were below average. Thus the returns to Jones and Kalman are *negatively correlated.*

Because the returns of Jones and Kalman stocks are negatively correlated, it is possible to create a portfolio of stocks, made up of both stocks, that is entirely risk-free. In Table 4 are shown the returns to a

TABLE 3

Year	Jones Company Stock Returns	Kalman Company Stock Returns
19x1	22.00%	−2.00%
19x2	−2.42	22.42
19x3	−11.13	31.13
19x4	7.30	12.70
Average	3.94%	16.06%
Standard deviation	12.30%	12.30%
Coefficient of variation	3.12	0.77

TABLE 4

Year	Jones Co. Return	X	Weight	Kalman Co. Return	X	Weight	Portfolio Return
19x1	22.00%		.50	−2.00%		.50	10.00%
19x2	−2.42		.50	22.42		.50	10.00
19x3	−11.13		.50	31.13		.50	10.00
19x4	7.30		.50	12.70		.50	10.00
Average	3.94%		.50	16.06%		.50	10.00%

portfolio comprising half Jones and half Kalman. Notice that the portfolio return is a weighted average of the individual stock returns. Equally important, notice that the risk, or dispersion of returns of the portfolio, has been eliminated. In other words, two risky investments have been combined to create a risk-free investment. Although the return on the portfolio is the weighted average of the returns from both stocks, the standard deviation of the portfolio is *not* equal to the weighted average of the standard deviations of the underlying investments. In fact, the standard deviation of the portfolio is zero since there is no deviation in any year from the average 10 percent return. Except in unusual cases (when the stocks are perfectly positively correlated), the standard deviation of a portfolio is less than the weighted average of the standard deviations of the investments in the portfolio. The reason is that when some investments are doing well, other investments are doing poorly, and vice versa. These offsetting effects mean that risk is being eliminated. This important result means that the "true" risk of an investment is not its total dispersion of returns but rather, only the part of its dispersion that cannot be diversified away.

Since risk reduction depends on the offsetting interactions of investments, portfolios which contain many diverse investments are preferable to portfolios which are less diversified. Although in the hypothetical example above only two securities were needed to produce a zero-risk portfolio, this was intended for expositional purposes only. Investments that perfectly offset one another are rare.

The most diversified portfolio available at a given point in time is known as the *market portfolio*. Since it is maximally diversified, all possible opportunities for risk elimination will have been exploited in it. In practice, most available opportunities for risk reduction will be realized in randomly selected portfolios with as few as 50 stocks. Thus, almost any large, diversified collection of stocks will resemble the market portfolio. The Standard and Poor's Index of 500 Common Stocks is generally considered to be representative of the market portfolio.

Unlike the Jones/Kalman portfolio, the S&P Index is not completely risk-free even though it has 500 different securities. That is because, realistically speaking, there are certain investment risks which cannot be diversified away completely, even in the market portfolio. These undiversifiable risks are known as *market risks*. Market risks reflect broad, fundamental factors such as the state of the economy (e.g., boom, recession, inflation); the political and social environment (e.g., war, change in political orientation of the federal government, social unrest); and investor psychology (e.g., general optimism or pessimism about the future). These market risk factors affect all investments in the same way (i.e., positively or negatively), though to varying degrees. For example, some companies are less sensitive to economic recessions (e.g., companies in the health care industry) than are other companies, even though all companies are adversely affected.

THE BETA COEFFICIENT

Since market risks cannot be avoided (by definition) even in a widely diversified portfolio, it is important to determine the relative sensitivity of particular investments to such market risks. The average responsiveness of an investment's returns to changes in market risk factors is estimated by examining the behavior of the investment's returns relative to changes in returns for the market portfolio (remember that the returns on the market portfolio reflect market risks). The average responsiveness of an investment's returns to market risk factors is known as the *systematic risk* of the investment.

The systematic risk of a stock is measured by its covariance of returns with the market—the degree to which the returns from both the particular stock and the market move together. The covariance is calculated in a manner analogous to the variance. In order to compare the covariances of different investments on a common basis, we standardize the covariance by dividing by the variance of the market's returns. This produces an index of relative systematic risks for investments that is called the *beta* of the investment.

$$\text{Beta} = \frac{\text{Covariance of returns of investment and market}}{\text{Variance of the market}}$$

Table 5 (see page 316) calculates the market variance using the same method used for calculating Alton's variance (see page 312).

To calculate the covariance between Alton's returns and the S&P (i.e., the market), we multiply their joint deviations and take the average, as shown in Table 6 (see page 316). With this information, we can now calculate Alton's beta.

$$\text{beta}_{\text{Alton}} = \frac{88.27}{142.98} = 0.62$$

TABLE 5
Calculation of Market Returns Variance
(Hypothetical S&P Data)

(1) Year	(2) Return	(3) Deviation	(4) Deviation Squared
1	26.47%	(26.47 – 10.97) = 13.50	182.25
2	–6.36	(–6.36 – 10.97) = –17.33	300.33
3	16.02	(16.02 – 10.97) = 5.05	25.50
4	2.50	(2.50 – 10.97) = –8.47	71.74
5	26.25	(26.25 – 10.97) = 15.28	233.48
6	20.18	(20.18 – 10.97) = 9.21	84.82
7	7.37	(7.37 – 10.97) = –3.60	12.96
8	–6.11	(–6.11 – 10.97) = –17.08	291.73
9	18.94	(18.94 – 10.97) = 7.97	63.52
10	6.44	(6.44 – 10.97) = –4.53	20.52
Average	10.97%	Variance	1286.85/9 = 142.98
		Standard deviation	11.96%

TABLE 6
Calculation of Covariance of Alton Co. and Market Returns

(1) Year	(2) Alton Co. Deviation	(3) S&P Deviation	(4) = (2) × (3)
1	16.55	13.50	223.43
2	–7.87	–17.33	136.39
3	11.55	5.05	58.33
4	1.85	–8.47	–15.67
5	–5.45	15.28	–83.28
6	1.05	9.21	9.67
7	7.80	–3.60	–28.08
8	–16.58	–17.08	283.19
9	6.55	7.97	52.20
10	–15.45	–4.53	69.99
		Covariance	706.16/8* = 88.27

*We divide by 8 rather than 9 on the assumption that two degrees of freedom are lost in calculating the two means.

Alton's beta of .62 indicates that the company's stock is less sensitive to market factors than is the average stock. When the stock market returns go up or down by 10 percent, Alton's returns will vary in the same direction by only 62 percent as much, or 6.2 percent.

Stocks with betas less than 1.0 are considered "defensive" investments because their returns are, on the average, less volatile than the stock market overall. Stocks with betas greater than 1.0 are considered "aggressive" investments because they fluctuate more than the market. Betas of exactly 1.0 indicate that the stock's returns are equally risky as the market overall.

SECURITY MARKET LINE

In our economy, Treasury Bills are considered to be risk-free because they have no possibility of default. If the Treasury had to, it could always print enough money to repay outstanding debts. These risk-free investments provide returns that are considered to be risk-free. Since risk-free Treasury Bills (and federally insured savings accounts) are readily available, risky investments must promise even higher returns to be competitive. The bonus return promised by risky investments is known as the *risk premium*.

The risk premium that should be provided by an investment is related to its market risk (i.e., its beta). The greater an investment's beta, the greater its risk premium should be. This relationship is shown in Figure 2 (see page 318), and is known as the Security Market Line.

The intercept, R_f, corresponds to the return from a risk-free (i.e., zero beta) investment, such as three-month Treasury Bills. The Security Market Line represents the amount of total return (risk premium plus risk-free return) that should be provided from investments of different betas. Notice that investments with betas of 1.0 are just as risky as the market portfolio and, thus, should provide the same risk premium and same total return as the market (R_m). The risk premium (R_p) is the difference between R_m and R_f. Notice also that a stock with a beta of 2.0 is twice as risky as the market and should provide twice as much risk premium as the market.

The Security Market Line links a stock's market risk to its expected rate of return through equation 1.

$$\text{Expected rate of return from stock } x = R_f + (R_m - R_f)B_x \qquad (1)$$

where $(R_m - R_f)$ is the market risk premium and B_x is the relative market risk (i.e. "Beta") of stock x.

Figure 2   Security Market Line (SML)

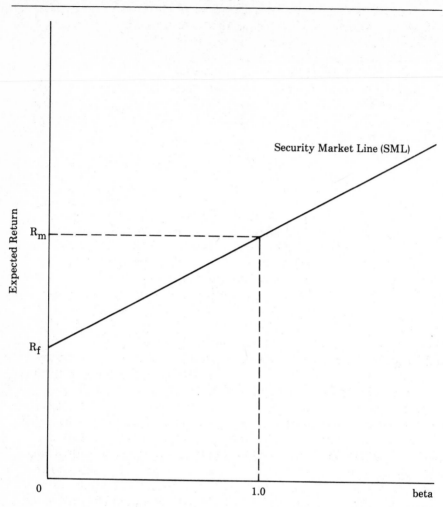

ESTIMATING THE RISK PREMIUM

Although it is usually necessary to estimate a stock's beta from past returns, the amount of return we require from an investment should reflect expected future returns rather than historical returns from the stock market. We clearly can't know with certainty what the expected return on the market is. One procedure for estimating the expected market return is to assume that the historical risk premium (excess of return over the risk-free rate) will persist in the future. Since we do know what the expected risk-free return is, we simply add on the historical risk premium to get an estimate of the expected future return on the market.

One authoritative study estimates that the historical risk premium on the market is 8.8 percent.[1] Using this historical risk premium and an assumed expected risk-free return of 13 percent, Alton stock, with a beta of .62, should provide at least 18.46 percent return.

$$\text{Required return from Alton stock} = R_f + (R_m - R_f)B_{\text{Alton}}$$
$$= 13 + (8.8).62$$
$$= 18.46\%$$

FINANCIAL LEVERAGE AND BETA

Previously, we showed that an investment's total risk is composed of two parts: market risk, which cannot be diversified away, and non-market risk, which is eliminated in well-diversified portfolios.

$$\text{Total risk} = \text{market risk} + \text{nonmarket risk}$$

We can further break down an investment's market risk into two parts: business risk and financial risk. Financial risk is present whenever the company borrows money.

$$\text{Market risk} = \text{business risk} + \text{financial risk}$$

If two companies have the same business risk but use different amounts of debt in their capital structures, they will have different market risks and different betas. Thus, for a given level of business risk, a company's beta will increase with financial leverage as shown in Figure 3 (see page 320).

Although the use of debt increases the beta of a company and, hence, its required rate of return, it also adds to the value of the company by virtue of the tax shield effect of interest paid on the debt.

When we estimate a company's beta, the influence of the added financial risk and interest tax shields are both present. If a company is financially levered, the beta we observe represents both its underlying business risk and the magnifying effect of its debt, less the tax shield

---

1. Roger G. Ibbotson and Rex A. Sinquefield, *Stocks, Bonds, Bills and Inflation: 1926–1978*. (Charlottesville, Va.: Financial Analysts Research Foundation, 1979).

Figure 3   Relationship of Beta to Financial Leverage

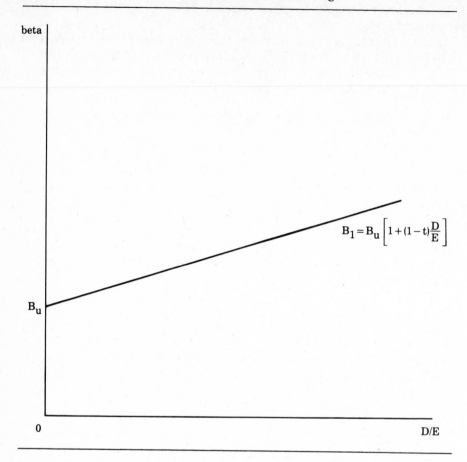

value of its interest deductions. This is shown in equation 2.

$$\beta_1 = \beta_u \left[1 + (1 - t)\frac{D}{E} \right] \tag{2}$$

where β_1 is the company's beta including both business and financial risk; β_u is the business risk beta only; t is the company's tax rate; and D/E is the company's ratio of debt relative to equity.

Although we cannot estimate a company's business risk beta directly, rearranging equation 2 permits an indirect estimate, as shown in equation 2a.

$$\beta_u = \frac{\beta_1}{[1 + (1 - t)D/E]} \tag{2a}$$

Let us assume that Alton's tax rate is 40 percent and its debt to equity ratio is .50; then its business risk beta would be calculated as .48.

$$\beta_u = \frac{.62}{[1 + (1 - .4).5]}$$

$$= .48$$

Knowing Alton's business risk beta and its tax rate, we could estimate what its beta would be under different capital structure alternatives, as shown in Table 7, and using equation 2.

Of course, our reason for computing a stock's beta is to estimate the required rate of return from the stock. Thus, using the Security Market Line equation, the estimates of the expected risk-free rate and risk premium, and the alternative levered betas, we can estimate the company's required rate of return, given its business risk beta and alternative capital structures.

TABLE 7
Relationship of Beta to Financial Leverage
Alton Company

D/E Rate	Beta	Required Rate of Return*
0	.48	17.22%
.50	.62	18.46
1.00	.77	19.78
1.20	.83	20.30

*See equation (1)

Valuation Exercise

Upon graduating from college, John Winters entered the financial management training program of a large industrial concern. The program consisted of one-year assignments in three different departments. In addition, trainees attended class two evenings per week. Below is a problem assigned in one of John's classes.

You were hired on January 1, 1984, by Firm Y. Firm Y was going to make an offer for Firm X that week, and your first task was to determine the maximum price that should be paid for each common share of Firm X. You were given the following information.

1. Firm X is in a different industry than Firm Y.

2.
Firm X
Balance Sheet at 12/31/83
(000 omitted)

Cash	$ 100		
Accounts receivable	250	Long-term debt	$ 500
Inventory	500		
Net fixed assets	1,650	Net worth	2,000
Total	$2,500		$2,500

After the transaction, Firm Y would own all the assets and assume responsibility for the long-term debt.

3. Net sales for Firm X for the year ended December 31, 1983, were $2 million.

4. Firm Y's investigation revealed that there were no excess assets and that all current asset levels would change in direct proportion to sales. For example, if sales increased by 5 percent, cash, accounts receivable, and inventory would each increase by 5 percent.

5. Because of the nature of Firm X's business, current liabilities were zero and would remain at that level in the future.

6. Firm X's beta at December 31, 1983, was 1.8 and this figure assumed that the debt to capital ratio at December 31, 1983, would be maintained in the future. The interest rate on Firm X's long-term debt was 12 percent. An annual interest payment of $60,000 was made on December 31, 1983.

7. Firm Y's management believed that, because of Firm X's business, it should have no debt in its capital structure. Thus, immediately after

the transaction, the $500,000 would be retired. (The reader may assume that there would be no prepayment penalty and may ignore the interest that would be due for the first few days of 1984. In other words, the total cash outlay required to retire the debt would be $500,000.)

8. Firm X had 1 million shares of common stock outstanding at December 31, 1983, and the price per share on that date was $2.00. The market value of its debt at December 31, 1983, was $500,000.

9. The following estimates of sales and EBIT (earnings before interest and taxes) for Firm X were provided.

	Annual Sales	Annual EBIT
Year 1	$2.2 million	$400,000
Years 2 and 3	2.5 million	440,000
Years 4 and 5	2.7 million	460,000
Years 6-10	2.8 million	480,000

In arriving at the EBIT estimates depreciation expense of $100,000 per year was deducted for years 1-3, and depreciation expense of $140,000 per year was deducted for years 4-10.

10. Expenditures on fixed assets would be necessary to replace worn-out equipment and to provide the new capacity needed for growth. No expenditures would be required for year 1. Expenditures in years 2-4 would be $200,000 per year. For years 5-9, fixed asset expenditures would be $50,000 per year, and there would be no fixed asset expenditures in year 10.

11. The terminal value of Firm X at the end of the 10 years would be $2.3 million. (The reader may ignore the potential tax impact of the sale of Firm X in 10 years.)

12. The income tax rate for Firm X and Firm Y was 50 percent, and that rate was expected for each of the next 10 years.

13. Firm Y's cost of equity was 18 percent, and its weighted average cost of capital was 12 percent.

Required. Compute the maximum price that Firm Y should pay for each of Firm X's shares. You may assume the risk-free rate is 8 percent and the required return for the market is 13 percent.

Javits Company

In January 1983, Mark Jones, a recently hired financial analyst for the Javits Company, was looking forward to his first assignment. It presented him with a unique opportunity to "apply some theory to practice," as his boss, Joe Devereaux, had put it. Mark's immediate task was to determine an appropriate minimum rate of return on equity which the Javits Company should require from the possible acquisition of the Bio-Metrics Company. (See Exhibits 1 and 2 for recent selected financial data on both companies.)

CAPITALIZATION AND OWNERSHIP OF JAVITS

The Javits Company had been formed in 1903 to manufacture surgical instruments, drugs, and hospital supplies. A total of 18,000 shares were subscribed by the Javits and Gage Families and a small group of social and business friends. The company was closely held, but transfers of stock, though gradual, took place as various individuals died or sold their interests in the company to others.

During the 1930s, James Gage, a founding shareholder, had increasingly taken active leadership of the company, investing larger and larger amounts of capital through the purchases of various liquidated holdings. Over time, certain company officers had been allowed to participate in the ownership of the company by purchasing modest amounts of stock from the Javits and Gage families.

By the late 1950s, Michael Gage, James's son, had taken over full operational control of the company. The Javits group had increasingly removed themselves from the firm's day-to-day operations. As the two major shareholding groups diverged in their involvement with the company, strains began to develop, with the Gage group favoring more aggressive growth and the Javits group unwilling to assume greater risk.

In 1982, the conflict over the company's future came to a head when the Javits Company was approached by a banking representative of Bio-Metrics, a medium-sized medical supply company, with a merger proposal.

Under the terms of the plan proposed by Bio-Metrics's bankers, the Javits Company would purchase all the outstanding common stock of the Bio-Metrics Company and assume all liabilities in exchange for all assets of the company. The bankers indicated that, while subject to negotiation, a price equal to book value would be acceptable to

Bio-Metrics. A further condition of the sale, as proposed by Bio-Metrics, was that all senior and other key management personnel would be offered three-year employment contracts.

BACKGROUND OF THE BIO-METRICS COMPANY

The Bio-Metrics Company was formed in 1955 by a small group of investors to exploit the discovery of a new drug by a St. Louis physician, Hans Bauer, who became part owner and chief scientist.

The company was originally organized to manufacture and distribute Optexin, a drug for the treatment of glaucoma, a leading cause of blindness. Although developed for treatment of the disease in humans, the drug was also popular in treatment of similar ailments in animals.

The company grew quickly, aided by the continuous introduction of new products discovered by Dr. Bauer and his small staff for the health care industry.

In 1979, the company's pioneering scientist, Dr. Bauer, was killed in a laboratory experiment, and Bio-Metrics was unsuccessful in maintaining the creative momentum it had previously experienced. As a result, some of the major stockholders voiced a desire to reduce their holding of company stock. With the help of the company's investment banking advisor, the desires of the major stockholders were met through a secondary sale of common stock (in other words, the existing shareholders sold some of their own shares rather than the company selling new shares). A secondary offering of 30,000 shares (out of a total of 100,000 shares outstanding) was completed in December 1981, and the shares were traded over-the-counter.

During 1982, the board of directors, which included all major shareholders of the company, became convinced that the prospects for continued development of profitable new products were slim. A consulting study commissioned by the board had predicted a slowing of growth over the next 10 years, as the existing group of products matured, unless significantly large investments in basic research were made. (See Exhibit 3 for the consultant's 10-year projection of sales, profits, cash flows, and assets.) In addition to the forecasts, the consultant had noted the relatively high use of debt by Bio-Metrics relative to other pharmaceutical companies and had recommended a *decrease* in the company's ratio of liabilities to net worth from its current level of 1.0 to a more conservative level of .50. The consultant's projections, upon request from the board, were based on an assumption of this lower liabilities-to-equity ratio. The reduction of liabilities would require the issuance of new stock.

MERGER PROPOSAL

After careful consideration of the consultant's report with which the board strongly concurred in all major respects, several major stockholders voiced their desire to terminate their investments in the company.

The board of the Bio-Metrics Company instructed its bankers to pursue the possible sale of the company to another firm. In consideration of its top management and other loyal employees, the board set as a condition the provision of employment contracts to key employees and the requirement that the purchaser also be in the health care field.

Although Bio-Metrics's board advised its bankers to be flexible on a sale price, it indicated that it considered the book value of the company, $89.17 million, to be a reasonable sale price. Since the purchaser would assume Bio-Metrics's outstanding liabilities of $44.59 million, the shareholders would stand to receive $44.58 million if the sale were made on a book value basis. The sale would be made on a cash basis so that the owners could liquidate their holdings completely. Additionally, Javits would recapitalize Bio-Metrics to reflect a desired liabilities-to-net worth ratio of .50.

DEBATE OVER THE VALUATION OF BIO-METRICS

The Gage group liked the product-market match of the proposed merger and was strongly tempted by the opportunity to run a much larger operation. The Javits group was concerned that the acquisition would result in too rapid an expansion and that it could introduce significant new risks. Moreover, the Javits Company would have to issue new shares to finance the acquisition in a public sale, and the further dilution of ownership was viewed unfavorably by several of the Javits heirs. Although the Javits group was not implacably opposed to the acquisition at the right price, they were understandably concerned that the acquisition might have an adverse impact on the value of their stockholdings if too high a price were paid for the acquisition or if significant problems later arose. As a result, the perceived value of the Bio-Metrics Company was considerably lower among the Javits group than that assessed by the Gage group.

However, the substantially divergent valuations of Bio-Metrics established by the Gage and Javits groups arose from substantially different required rates of return from the acquisition rather than from projections of profits and cash flows to be generated by Bio-Metrics. Indeed, there was no serious disagreement from any of the concerned parties over the projections made by the consultant for Bio-Metrics. While the Javits group thought the estimates reasonable, they felt a substantially greater uncertainty over the possible deviations from the estimates which might develop if competitive and economic conditions varied substantially from expectations.

The debate over the value of Bio-Metrics revolved around the appropriate rate of return to require from the investment, *given* the cash flow projections. The Gage group thought that the complementary features of the two companies would justify using Javits's own after-tax weighted average cost of capital of 13 percent (see Exhibit 4). The Javits group argued that a much higher cost of capital, 19 percent, should be required.

In developing their cost of capital estimates, both groups somewhat remarkably agreed that the capitalization of the acquisition should reflect a liabilities-to-equity ratio of .50 and that the required amount of debt would be available at a pre-tax cost of 12 percent. Thus, the only area of significant disagreement was what the appropriate minimum required rate of return on equity should be. The Gage group felt this rate was equivalent to Javits's own, which it estimated to be 16 percent. The Javits group thought a higher rate, perhaps as high as 25 percent, was more appropriate.

MARK'S ASSIGNMENT

Mark Jones joined the Javits Company in the midst of the debate over the Bio-Metrics acquisition. Mark's boss, Mr. Devereaux, while advocating the position of the Gage group, was intrigued that there should be such a disparity over the appropriate cost of capital for the acquisition. He was interested in having Mark's opinion since the new analyst had just received his MBA.

After listening to Mr. Devereaux briefly describe the arguments on both sides of the question, Mark volunteered that, in general, Bio-Metrics's cost-of-capital rather than Javits's was the appropriate standard. Yet he noted that, in this particular instance, both figures might be roughly equivalent since both companies were in the same industry and would have the same capital structures if the acquisition were effected. Then Mark ventured to speculate that "it would be interesting to see what a 'beta' type analysis might turn up." Mr. Devereaux quickly responded that, while he was familiar with the efficient market concept, any cost-of-capital estimate based on it would probably not be taken seriously by either side unless, of course, it produced an estimate roughly equal to its own. Then, detecting a trace of disappointment in Mark's eyes, Mr. Devereaux added, "Yet, I would like to see how you go about doing that kind of analysis and how the estimate relates to the figures being tossed around here. If nothing else, we may find something of use to us down the road for project analysis. Consider that your first assignment from me, Mark, and let me know what you come up with by five this afternoon. I don't want this to be a major project, just make it 'quick and dirty.'"

ESTIMATES FOR THE COST OF EQUITY
FOR BIO-METRICS

Mark decided that the first thing he had to do was get stock price data for Bio-Metrics in order to calculate its beta. He quickly put in a call to his brother Conrad, who worked in the research department of a brokerage company. After informing Conrad quickly of his assignment, he asked for any available relevant information. Later that afternoon Conrad called back and informed Mark that he had very little data but not much else was available.

Bid-ask prices for Bio-Metrics stock quoted over-the-counter were available only for the last 13 months. (See Exhibit 5 for monthly percentage changes.) While reading the data over the phone, Conrad cautioned, "Be careful with some of these figures; this stock has been thinly traded and sometimes the bid-ask prices don't mean a lot." No dividend information was available.

When Mark suggested he could probably get it from other records, Conrad advised, "Don't waste your time. We've found that just using stock price data gives you as good an estimate of beta. Anyway, this is 'quick and dirty' right?"

Mark then asked Conrad for market return data. Conrad suggested using the closing index of the Standard and Poor's 400 Industrial Stocks for the same period as an estimate of market returns, again ignoring dividend information. (Percentage changes in the monthly closing index are shown in Exhibit 5.)*

Mark was extremely uncomfortable with only 12 months of price information and the absence of dividend data. He thought it ironic that as advanced an idea as the capital asset pricing model should be restricted to such crude data. It made him feel no easier to recall that the idea had been his and that this would be his first assignment. "Conrad, I don't want to come up with something that's going to make me the laughingstock of this place," he said nervously.

"Not to worry. I just happen to have some beta information we've calculated for eight New York Stock Exchange companies in the health care industry. Pick one you like or, better yet, just take an average," he said, laughing. (See Exhibit 6 for information on betas, capital structures, and principal lines of business for eight firms in the health care industry.)

"Cut the sarcasm," Mark said impatiently. "I need estimates of expected market returns and the Treasury Bill rate."

"You don't want much," teased Conrad. "All I can tell you is that we normally assume that the stock market returns will be 9 percentage

---

*Casewriter's note: S & P data are hypothetical.

points above the three-month Treasury Bill rate, which is 13 percent as of this morning. That suggests an expected market return of about 22 percent."

"Twenty-two percent?" Mark said in surprise.

"What's the matter, too high? Then try 20 percent. Look, if I could predict the market, I would have retired already."

EXHIBIT 1
Javits Company
Selected Financial Data

Income Statement Data
For the Year Ended 12/31/82
($ millions)

Sales	$362.30
Operating profit	57.64
Interest	9.10
Profit before taxes	48.54
Taxes	24.27
Net income	$ 24.27

Balance Sheet Data at 12/31/82
($ millions)

Assets		Liabilities & Net Worth	
Working capital	$100.10	Total liabilities	$ 75.82
Fixed assets (net)	127.38	Net worth	151.66
Total assets	$227.48	Total	$227.48

EXHIBIT 2
Bio-Metrics Company
Selected Financial Data

Income Statement Data
For the Year Ended 12/31/82
($ millions)

Sales	$148.61
Operating profit	18.44
Interest	5.35
Profit before taxes	13.09
Taxes	6.54
Net income	$ 6.55

Balance Sheet Data at 12/31/82
($ millions)

Assets		Liabilities & Net Worth	
Working capital	$30.56	Total liabilities	$44.59
Fixed assets (net)	58.61	Net worth	44.58
Total	$89.17		$89.17

EXHIBIT 3
Bio-Metrics Company
Financial Projections 1983–1992
($ millions)

	1983	1984	1985	1986	1987	1988	1989	1990	1991	1992
Net sales	160.50	173.34	187.21	202.18	218.36	235.83	247.62	260.00	273.00	286.65
(1) EBIDT	24.08	26.00	28.08	30.33	32.75	35.37	37.14	39.00	40.95	43.00
Depreciation	4.30	5.20	5.70	6.00	6.30	6.70	7.10	7.30	6.80	6.50
(2) Interest	3.85	4.16	4.49	4.85	5.24	5.66	5.94	6.24	6.55	6.88
Profit before taxes	15.93	16.64	17.89	19.48	21.21	23.01	24.10	25.46	27.60	29.62
(3) Taxes	7.96	8.32	8.95	9.74	10.61	11.51	12.05	12.73	13.80	14.81
Net income	7.97	8.32	8.94	9.74	10.60	11.50	12.05	12.73	13.80	14.81
Depreciation	4.30	5.20	5.70	6.00	6.30	6.70	7.10	7.30	6.80	6.50
Cash from operations	12.27	13.52	14.64	15.74	16.90	18.20	19.15	20.03	20.60	21.31
(4) Increases in debt	2.38	2.57	2.77	2.99	3.24	3.49	2.36	2.48	2.60	2.72
Funds available	14.65	16.09	17.41	18.73	20.14	21.69	21.51	22.51	23.20	24.03
Capital expenditures	(11.43)	(12.92)	(14.02)	(14.99)	(16.01)	(17.18)	(14.08)	(14.73)	(14.60)	(14.69)
Free cash flow	3.22	3.17	3.39	3.74	4.13	4.51	7.43	7.78	8.60	9.34
(5) Total assets	96.30	104.00	112.32	121.31	131.02	141.50	148.57	156.00	163.80	171.99
(6) Total liabilities	32.10	34.67	37.44	40.43	43.67	47.16	49.52	52.00	54.60	57.32
Net worth*	64.20	69.33	74.88	80.88	87.35	94.34	99.05	104.00	109.20	114.67

Notes: (1) EBIDT = 15% sales
       (2) Interest = 12% rate; debt = 33% of assets
       (3) Tax rate = 50%
       (4) Increase in debt = 33% increase in assets
       (5) Assets = 60% of sales
       (6) Total liabilities = 33% of assets

*Casewriter's note: Net worth figure reflects recapitalization by Bio-Metrics or by Javits if acquired.

EXHIBIT 4
Javits Company
Alternative Estimates of Cost of Capital for Bio-Metrics Acquisition

	Capital	% Total	Cost Pre-tax	Cost After-tax	Weighted Cost
I. Gage proposal	Debt	.333	.12	.06	.020
	Equity	.667	.16	.16	.107
					.127
II. Javits proposal	Debt	.333	.12	.06	.020
	Equity	.667	.25	.25	.167
					.187

EXHIBIT 5
Monthly Stock Price Changes
S&P 400 Industrial Index and Bio-Metrics Company
January 1982–December 1982

	Change S&P 400	Change Bio-Metrics*
January 1982	+0.72%	− 1.20%
February	+3.57	+2.16
March	− 3.64	−10.54
April	− 0.86	− 7.36
May	+2.10	− 0.28
June	+0.27	− 2.13
July	+2.22	+5.70
August	− 0.41	+0.96
September	+9.11	+8.48
October	− 0.98	+0.16
November	− 2.09	− 3.49
December	− 1.17	+0.31

*Based on average of monthly closing bid-ask prices.

Casewriter's note: S & P data are hypothetical.

EXHIBIT 6
Data on Selected Firms in the Health Care Industry

Company	Principal Market Segment	Debt/Equity	Beta
A	Operation of hospitals	.68	1.35
B	Operation of hospitals	1.87	1.20
C	Operation of hospitals	2.03	1.35
D	Operation of hospitals	1.00	1.40
Average of four hospital firms		1.40	1.33
E	Pharmaceuticals	0	1.00
F	Pharmaceuticals	0.10	0.85
G	Pharmaceuticals	0.04	0.95
H	Pharmaceuticals	0.31	1.10
Average of four pharmaceutical firms		0.11	0.98
Average of eight health care firms		0.76	1.16

Filtron Corporation

In late March 1975, Virginia Woo, manager of financial analysis of the Filtron Corporation, was satisfied that she had put all the pieces together regarding a proposal submitted by the Crantwell Division to spend $149,000 in capital funds for the purchase and installation of the equipment necessary to produce starch from waste bananas. She was now ready to perform the analysis and submit her report.

BACKGROUND

The Filtron Corporation, located in Dallas, Texas, was a diversified company involved in activities ranging from the manufacture of machine tool parts to the importation and sale of bananas. Sales and after-tax profits for the fiscal year ended September 30, 1974, were $900 million and $40 million, respectively. The Crantwell Division, which conducted the firm's banana business, accounted for 14 percent of these sales and 11 percent of the profits.

Bananas were grown on company-owned land in several tropical countries and exported primarily to the United States, Canada, and Great Britain. In addition to growing bananas, the Crantwell Division manufactured the boxes used to ship bananas and owned a fleet of refrigerated cargo ships. The division used 100 percent of the output of the box operations. Space on the refrigerated ships, however, was very often rented to other companies. These rentals accounted for approximately 5 percent of the division's revenues.

PROPOSAL

The Crantwell Division currently purchased corn starch for use in all its box-making operations. The corn starch was purchased in the United States and shipped to the box-making plants, which were located near the banana plantations. Thus the cost to the firm was a function of the price of corn starch in the United States and shipping and handling charges.

The proposal submitted by Crantwell concerned the production of corn starch from waste bananas for one of its box-making plants. If this venture were to prove economically feasible, division management would presumably recommend that corn starch be produced for all its box-making plants. Moreover, since more corn starch could be produced from the available waste bananas than could be used in the division's box-making plants, it was likely that proposals would be made to produce corn starch for other uses.

Uses of Starch

When starch is modified by one of many commercial methods, the potential uses for it are limited only by one's imagination. In fact, over 250 products are made from starch and its derivatives—products that range from baby food to dynamite. (In fact, because of its bland taste, banana starch may be preferable to other starches for food applications.)

Starch is readily converted to sugar, and there is little question that banana syrup and sugars crystallized therefrom could be used in the soft drink, confectionary, mixed syrup, bakery, preserves, ice cream, and canned fruit industries. The conversion of sugar from starch can be continued another step by the addition of yeast to the sugar syrup, thereby producing alcohol for industrial or food use.

Starch has many uses other than for food or adhesives. The largest consumer of starch in the United States is the paper industry, which uses it to increase the strength of the paper sheet and increase its resistance to tearing. Another large user of starch is the textile industry, which uses it to counteract the abrasive action of fibers during weaving.

Technical Considerations

Starch would be recovered from waste bananas by means of a simple, wet milling process developed specifically for this process. This would be the first commercial application of this process. Its feasibility, however, had been tested in a pilot plant operation in the United States by a consultant hired by the Crantwell Division. (Since there was no technical reason for testing the process in the country where the corn starch would be produced, the test was conducted in the United States to minimize the cost of the study.) Moreover, banana starch had undergone successful testing as an adhesive in corrugated cardboard manufacturing by the Institute of Paper Chemistry.

A review of the process for extracting starch from bananas would provide a basis for understanding the technical aspects of the project. The process normally consists of six steps: grinding, screening, washing, filtering, drying, and crushing.

1. *Grinding.* The pulp of a green banana contains over 20 percent starch (30 percent for plantains), which turns to sugar as the banana

ripens. Unfortunately, the banana peels are difficult to separate from the pulp, forcing one to process both the pulp and peel, thus resulting in a net starch content of 14 percent. The first step is to pregrind the bananas and all into a mush containing pieces of bananas up to ¾ inch across. After pregrinding, the bananas are mixed in a slurry of water containing .5 percent sodium hydroxide (NAOH) by weight, resulting in a ph level of 10 (which is very caustic). The sodium hydroxide effects the separation of protein and starch in the slurry. The slurry mix is then put through a disintegrator, which breaks up the banana and causes the solids to disperse uniformly in the water.

2. *Screening.* In the screening operation, the starch granules are separated from the bulk of the other water-insoluble solids (starch in its natural state is water insoluble). Banana starch granules, which range roughly from 5 to 40 microns across, are carried through the small screen openings by the water in which they are suspended. Some finely divided low-density insolubles also pass through. The other solids are coarser and are stopped by the screen. The material that passes through the screen is called starch milk because in the manufacture of other kinds of starch it is white and milky. In the banana starch process, it is dark brown.

3. *Washing.* The solution next goes into a cyclone-type separator designed for liquids, which induces a high-velocity circular motion. This motion throws the relatively high-density starch granules outward and downward, leaving the center portion of the cyclone relatively starch free. Most of the water from this starch-free area is withdrawn and re-cycled to the slurry tank. The concentrated starch suspension is mixed with fresh water and then goes to a filtration unit.

4. *Filtration.* The filtration unit is basically a centrifuge vacuum filter unit. This is a perforated drum covered with filter medium, which rotates partially submerged in the starch suspension. A vacuum is maintained within the drum, which pulls water through the filter, leaving the starch deposited on the outside.

5. *Drying.* Since the starch from the filter contains about 45 percent water, further drying is normally required to produce an easily handled product and also to save the cost of shipping water. This drying can be accomplished by a conveyer belt and heating tunnel.

6. *Crushing.* To break up lumps and produce a starch that can be readily dispersed in water, it is usually desirable to crush the dried starch cake.

The process developed by Crantwell eliminated the drying and crushing steps. Thus no drying equipment or crushing equipment would be needed, no boiler would be needed to heat the drying tunnel, and, of course, there would be no fuel costs. The starch would be moved wet to the adjacent boxing plant in plastic-lined drums. At the boxing plant, starch had to be mixed with water anyway to make the adhesive, so no problems were anticipated.

An additional benefit to eliminating the drying and crushing would be vastly improved safety. Starch dust is extremely explosive, and special precautions and safety equipment are required in its presence. Wet starch presents no such safety hazard.

Economic Considerations

When the proposal was submitted, Ms. Woo was surprised at the size of the request and the suggested location. First, the division was recommending a plant that was neither the optimum size nor the most efficient plant that could be designed. Moreover, division management planned to use only 870,000 pounds of the starch plant's annual capacity of 1.5 million pounds. Finally, the proposed site was an abandoned packing station located 2½ miles from a box manufacturing plant. The drawback of the site was that it was adjacent to a banana plantation, which because of poor soil conditions was not considered a long-life source.

Ms. Woo learned that Crantwell in the past submitted proposals, ranging from $450,000 to $1.6 million, concerning the use of waste bananas. All these proposals were rejected. The division was just unable to convince corporate management of the economics of using waste bananas. Hence this proposal was designed so that it would minimize the investment required, minimize the risks, produce an attractive return on investment, and provide the opportunity to experiment with other uses for waste bananas.

As mentioned, there were drawbacks to the proposed site. There were also advantages, however, the principal one being that it minimized the size of the investment. The proposed site had a building with water supply, electric power, railroad siding, a road, and a drainage system. Although it would cost a great deal to construct a facility with these features, the building had no alternative economic use. Also, the location would permit the manager of the box plant to supervise the starch plant's activities. He had been consulted and said that it would not overly tax his time and that he would be happy to do it. Finally, the box plant, which operated at an even rate throughout the year, normally maintained a two-month supply of corn starch. Because of the short distance between the box and starch plants, the need for this working capital investment would be eliminated. (Division management estimated that the working capital needed to support the starch operation would be negligible.)

The project had a very low technical risk factor. First, the wet milling process for extracting the starch was considered very simple. Second, the capacity of the proposed plant was only 3½ times that of the pilot operation, so no problem in scaling up was anticipated. Third, the boxes made from the starch produced at the pilot operation were thoroughly tested and found to be satisfactory. Finally, the many potential uses of starch reduced the risk of obsolescence.

Since the starch plant's capacity exceeded the box plant's requirement of 870,000 pounds per year, there was the possibility of producing at capacity and shipping the excess elsewhere. Division management was concerned that doing this might create political problems and hence requested that the analysis assume that the plant would produce only 870,000 pounds of starch per year. At this production level, the cost per pound would be $.0456, as detailed in Table 1.

The current cost to Crantwell for corn starch, including freight and handling, was $11.45 per hundredweight, or $.1145 per pound. Since the price of corn starch was critical to the analysis and since its price varied considerably, Ms. Woo asked her assistant to look into the matter. His report is contained in Exhibit 1. In addition to the uncertainty surrounding pearl corn starch prices, Ms. Woo was somewhat concerned about the annual usage by the box plant. Her examination of past quantities revealed that while 870,000 pounds per year was the normal level, annual usage was sometimes as low as 700,000 pounds.

In performing a financial analysis of investment proposals, the analyst calculated the payback period, the net present value at the firm's after-tax cutoff rate of 10 percent, and the internal rate of return. A maximum time horizon of 10 years was used even for investments, like this starch plant proposal, which were expected to generate revenues for more than 10 years. Management set an upper limit of

TABLE 1
Production Costs

	Total Annual Cost	Cost per Pound of Starch
Labor (including fringes)		
1 working supervisor @ $350/month	$ 4,200	$.0048
2 laborers @ $1/hour	5,000	.0058
Electric power @ $.04/kWh	3,147	.0036
Water	—	—
Caustic soda (sodium hydroxide) @ $219/ton	7,368	.0085
Plastic liners (used containers) @ $.35	1,218	.0014
Maintenance	5,500	.0063
Waste collection expense	3,306	.0038
Subtotal	29,739	.0342
Depreciation (straight-line over 15-year useful life to zero salvage value)	9,933	.0114
Total	$39,672	$.0456

10 years for two reasons. First, it had little confidence in estimates beyond 10 years. Second, it was not interested in investments that could not generate a satisfactory return within 10 years. Finally, the effective income tax rate for the firm in the country in which the starch plant would be located was 40 percent.

EXHIBIT 1
Memorandum
March 28, 1975

TO: Virginia Woo
FROM: John Mosely
RE: Corn starch prices

I looked into the variability of corn starch prices as you requested. I examined the period January 1, 1970, through March 1975. A summary of my findings is presented here.

The price of corn starch is principally determined by the price of corn traded on the Chicago Commodity Exchange. Consequently, corn starch price projections are primarily a function of future corn prices. Unfortunately, because of the multitude and complexity of the factors that determine corn prices—e.g., domestic demand, particularly livestock feeders; export demand; acreage in corn; yields; cultivation costs such as fertilizer; availability; and price of substitutes—it is extremely difficult to project future corn prices within the scope of the analysis you requested. I have, however, examined historical data and determined the following:

1. In the three years prior to March 1973, the average price for #3 yellow corn fluctuated between $1.10 and $1.50 per bushel. During the same period, Filtron's cost for corn starch varied from a low of $6.86 per hundredweight to a high of $8.65 per hundredweight and averaged approximately $7.60 per hundredweight.

2. Beginning in early 1973, corn and corn starch prices rose rapidly. By December 1974, corn was selling for $3.50 per bushel and Filtron's cost of corn starch was approximately $12 per hundredweight. Also, adequate supplies of corn starch were difficult to obtain.

3. During the first months of 1975, corn prices have subsided to $2.75 per bushel level. Currently, March 1976 corn futures are selling for $2.58 per bushel. Filtron's current cost of corn starch is still around $11.50 per hundredweight.

Although I believe that corn and corn starch prices will fluctuate significantly from month to month and from year to year—even to the point where they could drop to the pre-1973 levels for short periods—I think that, barring a complete economic collapse, on the average these prices will significantly exceed their pre-1973 levels.

If you have any questions, please let me know.

Metchler Corporation

In December 1973, John Basil, manager of the operations analysis department of the Metchler Corporation, was analyzing a proposal submitted by one of the firm's divisions to invest $4,478,200 in a polystyrene project in Dampa.[1] Mr. Basil was going to meet with the firm's executive group in one week to present his analysis and recommendation.

METCHLER CORPORATION

The Metchler Corporation was formed in the 1940s to manufacture and sell agricultural products. This was the firm's primary activity up through 1961, when the decision was made to diversify into other industries. By 1972, the firm was operating in 11 industries and achieved a sales level of $2.2 billion on assets of $1.2 billion. (See Exhibits 1 and 2 for 1971 and 1972 financial statements.)

The firm operated through seven divisions. The president of each division reported directly to the corporate president, who, together with the corporate vice-presidents of marketing and finance, constituted the firm's executive group. Capital investments in excess of $75,000 had to be approved by the executive group.

When capital requests were submitted, the operations analysis department would perform the financial analyses. The procedures were to calculate the investment's DCF (that is, internal rate of return), net present value using the firm's 12-percent after-tax cutoff rate, and the payback period. The analysts evaluated risk by performing sensitivity analysis. More specifically, they made calculations using the investment's most likely estimates, and then calculated the measures using one or more sets of pessimistic estimates. Cash flow estimates were prepared by the division submitting the proposal, and, with minor modifications, these usually became the most likely estimates. (An analyst in

---

1. Dampa is a foreign country, which at the time this case was written offered a growing population and economy and an abundance of natural resources. Its political life and economy were run by the military, which were demonstrating a pragmatic attitude toward growth and direct foreign investment. On the negative side, there were high tax rates on repatriated earnings, price controls administered by a cumbersome bureaucracy, and the risk of exchange loss owing to continued devaluation of its currency.

the operations analysis department would review the estimates submitted by the division and discuss them with the division's finance staff. Although significant adjustments were sometimes needed, normally this was not the case. In other words, the divisions generally did a fine job in estimating an investment's cash flows.) The analyst would use his or her own judgment in arriving at more pessimistic estimates.

For all investments with an expected life of more than ten years, a ten year horizon was assumed. What usually happened was that detailed estimates were prepared for each of the first five years of an investment's life, and the assumption was made that the level of profitability attained in year five would be maintained for years six through ten.

POLYSTYRENE PROJECT

In the latter part of 1972, the Spoch Division became interested in a polystyrene project in Dampa. After several months of study, Spoch management decided that it wanted to go ahead. It submitted a request in November 1973 for $4,478,200 to develop a polystyrene extrusion and vacuum-forming facility in Dampa.

Project Rationale

The Spoch Division's basic motivation was derived from the fact that in 1973 there was a shortage of polystyrene resin both in Dampa and the rest of the world. This shortage was caused by the lack of petrochemical resources and production facilities. It was the Spoch Division's intention to capitalize on this shortage in Dampa by using a guaranteed supply of resin from Amery, another Metchler division. For the first three years of the project's life, the supply would be provided from Amery's U.S. plant.[2] Thereafter, resin would be supplied from a Dampian joint-venture project in which Amery intended to participate.

At the end of 1972, polystyrene resin was produced in Dampa by four companies having a combined capacity of 46,800 metons (metric tons) per year. Spoch management estimated that the shortage of polystyrene resin in Dampa for 1973 would be 25 percent (12,500 metons) of the projected requirement. Moreover, at that time polystyrene was one of the three thermoplastics that had shown the fastest growth rate in recent years. From 1969 to 1972, consumption increased 13,600 metons to 40,300 metons, an increase of 51 percent over the three-year

---

2. Spoch's annual requirements would be less than 5 percent of Amery's forecasted annual U.S. production of polystyrene resin.

period. The market was expected to grow 29,000 metons to 69,300 metons, or 72 percent, by 1975.

Although polystyrene had several applications, Spoch wanted to enter the most profitable market area, thermoformed packaging and disposables. At the end of 1972, suppliers of resin were giving priority to heavy industry such as automobiles, refrigerators, and construction parts. Consequently, consumption areas, including packaging and disposables, were the areas most affected by the shortage. Therefore several industries had been forced to substitute materials like paper and cardboard for polystyrene in the manufacture of packaging and disposables. Paper materials, however, were also in short supply at that time because of the lack of paper mill capacity, and their prices had recently increased significantly. Thus a new manufacturer with secured outside resin supplies could take advantage of the shortage in the profitable consumer packaging and disposables market. Spoch management was confident that this market would continue to grow, for the following reasons.

Packaging

1. Increase in consumption of dairy products (for example, the use of yogurt cups in the past three years had grown from 0 to 60 million per year)
2. Shortage of paper and cardboard cost increases
3. Tin and aluminum shortages and price increases
4. New products entering the consumer market
5. Switch from paraffined paper to polystyrene (such as for ice cream containers)

Disposables

1. Reluctance to use glass cups and glasses owing to contamination
2. Increased demand by consumers

If the proposal were approved, Spoch would produce disposables, yogurt cups, sheet in rolls, and margarine cups. Spoch's estimate of the size of the market for the next five years and its goal with respect to market share is presented in Table 1.

Obviously, the key to Spoch's successful entry into this market was that it would be able to obtain resin supplies and that there would be a shortage. There were three potential risks: (1) that the U.S. government would impose restrictions on the exportation of domestically produced resin in light of projected U.S. shortages; (2) that resin would be available, but at such a cost as to price the final product out of the market; and (3) that existing polystyrene manufacturers would expand to supply projected requirements.

TABLE 1
Volume Estimates

	1974	1975	1976	1977	1978	1979
Total polystyrene market	60,000	69,000	79,000	91,000	100,000	110,000
Packaging disposables volume	17,143	18,600	21,300	24,600	27,000	29,700
Expected supplies (domestic & imported)	8,500	10,000	15,000	20,000	27,000	29,700
Forecasted shortage	8,643	8,600	6,300	4,600	—	—
Spoch's forecasted volume		2,739	3,080	3,298	3,628	3,958
Spoch's volume as % of shortage		31.8	48.9	71.7	—	—
Spoch's volume as % of packaging & disposable volume		14.7	14.5	13.4	13.4	13.3

It was Spoch's view that these risks were not great. With respect to the first, Spoch believed that a total resin embargo by the U.S. government would be a drastic measure even if the energy crisis were to worsen. Moreover, the commitment from Amery would last only two or three years, since Dampa was expected to be self-sufficient by 1978.

With respect to the cost of resin, the Dampian government had recently reduced the import duties on resin from 55 percent to 10 percent in reaction to the polystyrene shortages. This measure had been put into effect for the six months starting June 6, 1973. Spoch believed that, since the supply situation would continue to be short, the government would extend the application of the low import duty until Dampa became self-sufficient in polystyrene production.

Finally, during 1973 several Brazilian polystyrene manufacturers were projecting expansion of facilities since demand for edible products' packaging and disposables exceeded their production capacity. It was Spoch's view that these intended expansions would not be implemented because of the unavailability of resin supplies. Spoch itself was turned down by Dow Quimica Dampa in October 1973 when it asked Dow to supply it with polystyrene starting in July 1974. Dow stated that its styrene supplier had just reduced its allocation and that it was unable to supply its existing commitments.[3] Thus Dow was not accepting new customers and Spoch believed that other suppliers would follow suit.

In sum, Spoch believed that, since it would be able to import resin supplies from Amery, it would have a competitive edge in the Dampian polystyrene market and would be able to establish a permanent foothold.

---

3. Polystyrene resin can be derived from styrene monomer.

FINANCIAL DETAILS

As noted previously, the cost of the project was estimated at $4,478,200. The funds would be used as follows:

Item	Amount ($000)
Land—6.2 acres	$ 150.0
Building	680.0
Equipment	1,613.6
Installation	247.6
Firefighting equipment	10.0
Office equipment	34.0
Automotive equipment	144.0
	$2,879.2

In addition, working capital of $1,599,000 would be required when the facility began operations.

Mr. Basil discussed these amounts with Spoch and concluded that they were reasonable. Allowance was made for inflation during construction, as well as for cost overruns. He also discussed the timing of these expenditures and future investments that would be required to replace equipment and to support increases in working capital. These discussions enabled him to arrive at the cash flow estimates presented in Table 2.

TABLE 2
Total Capital Requirements
(In $000)

Year[1]	Fixed Assets	+	Working Capital	=	Total
0	$ 927			=	$ 927
1	1,952.2		$ 1,599.0	=	3,551.2
2	—		—		
3	—		34.9	=	34.9
4	—		56.5	=	56.5
5	—		85.3	=	85.3
6	—		79.6	=	79.6
7	66.9		—	=	66.9
8	66.9		—	=	66.9
9	66.9		—	=	66.9
10	66.9		—	=	66.9
11	(627.1)		(1,855.3)	=	(2,482.4)[2]

[1] An 11-year life was used because operations would begin in year 2.

[2] The negative outflows in year 11 were terminal values. It was assumed that working capital would be freed up in total and that fixed assets would be sold at book value. (The 627.1 figure is net of 66.9 of replacement expenditures in year 11.)

With respect to the cash inflows from the investment, Spoch provided the projections shown in Table 3 (on page 346). The net sales figures were based on the market share estimates previously discussed. Mr. Basil's investigation of the expense estimates revealed that the finance people at Spoch were very cautious in estimating expenses. If they were unsure of the magnitude of an expense item, they always used the higher number. Thus the profit figures presented in Table 2 were conservative.

With respect to taxes, two very different tax situations could be applicable, depending on the disposition of the cash generated by the investment. Assuming that funds were reinvested, a 30-percent corporate income tax, a 5-percent distributed profits tax, and a 25-percent withholding tax would be applicable. Thus, for every dollar of pretax profit earned, $.498 would be available for reinvestment in Dampa. However, if funds were remitted to the United States, a remittance tax would be levied on the funds that actually left the country. Mr. Basil estimated that the following rates would apply, assuming management decided to remit 100 percent of the cash flows from the investment.[4]

Effective Remittance Tax Rate	
Year	% of Net Income (After Taxes)
1	20
2	20
3	21
4	22
5	23
6	23
7	23
8	23
9	23
10	23

Mr. Basil was concerned about a critical assumption underlying the estimates presented in Table 3. Spoch management used current price levels and assumed that operating cost increases and any losses incurred because of exchange-rate fluctuations could be passed on through price increases so that profit margins would remain constant. In Mr. Basil's view, the major economic risk of the project, besides that associated with the availability of supplies, was the imposition of price controls to the extent that profit margins begin to deteriorate. According to a

---

4. The remittance of funds would create a U.S. tax liability. However, U.S. taxes would be fully offset by foreign tax credits.

TABLE 3
Dampian Project
Pro Forma Income Statements
(In $000)

	Year 1[1]	Year 2	Year 3	Year 4	Year 5
Net sales	$6,798.0	$7,111.0	$7,615.0	$8,377.0	$9,081.0
Labor					
Administration	(216.8)	(238.5)	(262.3)	(288.6)	(317.4)
Sales	(86.0)	(94.6)	(104.1)	(114.5)	(125.9)
Hourly workers	(171.6)	(197.4)	(232.6)	(281.5)	(335.6)
Benefits (55% of total					
salaries)	(260.9)	(291.8)	(329.5)	(376.5)	(428.4)
Utilities					
Electricity	(150.0)	(156.9)	(168.0)	(184.8)	(200.4)
Water	(4.2)	(4.4)	(4.7)	(5.2)	(5.6)
Raw materials					
Polystyrene resin	(2,605.5)	(2,725.4)	(2,918.9)	(3,210.7)	(3,480.4)
Inks and solvents	(104.2)	(109.0)	(116.7)	(128.4)	(139.2)
Packaging	(91.2)	(95.4)	(102.2)	(112.4)	(121.8)
Other					
Sales office rental	(20.0)	(21.0)	(22.0)	(23.0)	(24.0)
Telephone, cable, mail	(20.0)	(21.0)	(22.0)	(23.0)	(24.0)
Travel, rep. expenses	(20.0)	(21.0)	(22.0)	(23.0)	(24.0)
Fuel and lubricants	(17.0)	(18.0)	(19.0)	(20.0)	(21.0)
Maintenance	(10.0)	(12.0)	(15.0)	(20.0)	(30.0)
Legal fees	(25.0)	(10.0)	(8.0)	(8.0)	(8.0)
Advertising	(25.0)	(25.0)	(25.0)	(25.0)	(25.0)
Depreciation[2]	(232.9)	(232.9)	(232.9)	(232.9)	(232.9)
Insurance	(14.0)	(14.0)	(14.0)	(14.0)	(14.0)
Contingency	(18.0)	(18.0)	(18.0)	(18.0)	(18.0)
Total expenses	$4,092.3	$4,306.3	$4,636.9	$5,109.5	$5,575.6
Taxable profit	2,705.7	2,804.7	2,978.1	3,267.5	3,505.4
Income tax, 30%	811.7	841.4	893.4	980.2	1,051.5
After-tax profit	$1,894.0	$1,963.3	$2,084.7	$2,287.3	$2,453.9
Distributed profits tax, 5%	94.7	98.2	104.2	114.4	122.7
After-tax profit	$1,799.3	$1,865.1	$1,980.5	$2,172.9	$2,331.2
Withholding tax, 25%	449.8	466.3	495.1	543.2	582.8
Net income[3]	$1,349.5	$1,398.8	$1,485.4	$1,629.7	$1,748.4

[1] Year 1 refers to the first year of operations. Since it would take one year to construct and make the plant ready for operation, the first year of operations would be the second year of the investment's life.

[2] Depreciation expense would be $271,000 per year commencing in year 6. This estimate was based on the expenditure estimates presented in Table 2.

[3] Net Income figures were before remittance tax. If funds were remitted to the United States, a remittance tax that varied between zero and 60 percent would be levied.

December 1973 issue of a major trade journal, "firms are now going through a cost-price wringer that is paring profit margins. One roller is inflation, which after years of slowing down shows signs of picking up steam. The other is the powerful Interministerial Price Commission (CIP) charged with keeping the lid on prices."

There was one other factor that concerned Mr. Basil. Spoch management had investigated several financing alternatives and was recommending a specific financing plan. According to this plan, $3,066,000 of the $4,478,200 required would be borrowed from three sources. (Two of the loans would be from U.S. financial institutions, and one would be from a Dampian financial institution.) This amount would be repaid during the first five years of operation. More specifically, repayment terms were as follows:

Year	Principal	Financing Charges[5]
1	—	—
2	$ 480	$790.2
3	1,386	588.9
4	400	366.0
5	400	285.2
6	400	203.2

Payments would begin in the second year because production would begin one year after construction began. (All estimates assumed that production would begin one year after the request was approved. Actually, Spoch estimated that it would take seven or eight months to ready the plant for operation. Since the land was already developed and the plant construction involved no new technology, no delays were expected beyond those included in the seven- to eight-month forecast.)

The Spoch finance people argued that the rate-of-return calculations should be based on Metchler's equity investment in the project. While it was true that Metchler would have to guarantee the debt of the new subsidiary, the proportion of debt used was significantly above that normally employed. Moreover, Metchler's five-year financial plan called for several debt issues over the next five years. It was Spoch's view that the preceding financing arrangement would not affect the cost or availability of the planned debt offerings.

Mr. Basil knew that this point of view had already been communicated to members of the executive group. Consequently, he thought that he should respond to it in his report.

---

5. These charges include a Dampian tax on certain interest payments. The financing charges (including tax on interest) would be deductible for tax purposes according to Dampian income tax laws.

EXHIBIT 1
Metchler Corporation
Consolidated Statement of Income and Income Retained in the Business
(In $000)

	Year Ended December 31	
	1972	1971
Net sales	$2,202,569	$1,763,052
Operating costs and expenses		
Cost of sales	1,924,669	1,558,723
Selling, general, and administrative expenses	160,128	125,191
Depreciation	38,180	33,866
	$2,122,977	$1,717,780
Operating income	$ 79,592	$ 45,272
Interest and amortization of debt expense	(43,509)	(33,061)
Interest and other income, net	10,462	10,152
Income from continuing operations before income taxes and minority interests	$ 46,545	$ 22,363
Estimated U.S. and foreign taxes	28,032	16,216
Income from continuing operations before minority interests	$ 18,513	$ 6,147
Minority interests in net income of subsidiaries	(5,186)	(243)
Income from continuing operations	$ 13,327	$ 5,904
Income from discontinued operations, net of U.S. income taxes	408	1,676
Gain on disposal of discontinued operations, net of U.S. income taxes	8,042	—
Income before extraordinary items	$ 21,777	$ 7,580
Extraordinary items	(383)	8,714
Net income	$ 21,394	$ 16,294
Income retained in the business at beginning of year	91,044	77,130
Dividends	(2,378)	(2,380)
Income retained in business at end of year	$ 110,060	$ 91,044

EXHIBIT 2
Metchler Corporation
Consolidated Balance Sheet
(In $000)

	December 31	
	1972	1971
Assets		
Current assets		
Cash	$ 19,781	$ 19,895
Marketable securities at cost that approximates market	19,353	65,226
Receivables, less allowance for doubtful accounts	172,435	120,848
Inventories	209,689	150,422
Prepaid expenses	10,986	11,998
Total current assets	$ 432,244	$ 368,389
Investments and long-term receivables	50,072	68,418
Deferred charges	12,719	12,198
Property, plant, and equipment, net	403,103	332,019
Trademarks and leaseholds	47,000	51,250
Excess of cost over fair value of net assets acquired	276,838	281,075
Assets held for disposal, at estimated realizable value	10,317	19,173
	$1,232,293	$1,132,522
Liabilities		
Current liabilities		
Notes and loans payable to banks	$ 63,116	$ 43,420
Notes payable and accrued liabilities	123,886	87,691
Long-term debt due within one year	11,427	14,730
U.S. and foreign income taxes	23,410	22,799
Deferred U.S. and foreign income taxes	10,102	10,885
Total current liabilities	$ 231,941	$ 179,525
Long-term debt	397,338	402,484
Accrued severance and other social benefits	54,069	34,600
Other liabilities and deferred credits	9,300	5,544
Minority interests in net assets of subsidiaries	27,500	2,150
Total liabilities	$ 720,148	$ 624,303
Shareholders' equity		
Capital stock and surplus	401,885	417,175
Income retained in business	110,060	91,044
Total shareholders' equity	$ 511,945	$ 508,219
	$1,232,093	$1,132,522

Gansett Furniture Company (B)

In late 1975, Marshall Smith, chief financial officer of the Gansett Furniture Company, was trying to decide what the firm's stance should be with respect to the possible acquisition of Adolph's Furniture Company. In particular, he thought that the determination of an offering price, the form of transaction, and the form of financing should be established in his own mind rather quickly. However, since the approval of Gansett's bank, the American National Bank, would be required, he was mindful of the bank's perspective in regard to these decisions.

BACKGROUND OF THE COMPANY

The Gansett Furniture Company, founded by two brothers in 1940, was in the business of manufacturing upholstered furniture and fixtures. The two brothers ran it profitably for over twenty-five years before giving way to their sons, John and Arnold. The two cousins, however, were unable to work together productively. Since neither family had voting control (each had 46 percent of the stock), internal conflict, coupled with management indecision on matters small and large, paralyzed the company's growth and eroded its profitability. This condition persisted throughout the late 1960s. In late 1970, however, one of the two, John Gansett, mustered voting control through the support of other, previously neutral stockholders, and forced his cousin, Arnold out of the active management of the business. Arnold became unhappy over the arrangement and was able to obstruct numerous initiatives that John tried to undertake. For one thing, Arnold's refusal to guarantee long-term debt personally (along with the other owners) seriously hampered growth plans.

In late 1972, John Gansett initiated a search for an investor who might be willing to buy out Arnold's shareholdings. He was especially interested in an investor who could also become an active principal in the company and strengthen its financial, internal administrative capabilities. One such possibility was the firm's financial management consultant, Mr. Smith, whom Mr. Gansett had brought in to assist the firm as part of his organization-strengthening plan. Over a period of three to four months, the consultant had worked on Gansett's cost accumulation, overhead allocation and pricing system, and various elements of the internal cost control system. He had also organized a full-day retreat for the company's top management, which focused on the analysis of the company's current condition, problems, opportunities, and plans. In May 1973, Mr. Gansett asked Mr. Smith to assume the company's financial function. This involved forming a financial plan and approaching several banks with a specific loan proposal, which included buying out Arnold's stock. These efforts culminated, in August, with a seven-year, 9-percent loan for $250,000 from American National Bank. Shortly afterward, the company, having received prior approval from the bank, used proceeds from the loan to retire the 46-percent dissident stock.

By June, Mr. Smith was devoting full time to Gansett and functioning as a permanent part of the company's management. He was elected secretary-treasurer and member of the board of directors in August. In late September, he proposed, and the company's management accepted, in principle, that Mr. Smith acquire a majority of the outstanding stock in the company and that the acquisition of stock be accompanied by the establishment of voting trust that would assure the company's president, John Gansett, operating control of the company for three years.

Mr. Smith agreed to pay Mr. Gansett approximately $160,000 for 8,200 shares (50.8 percent). Mr. Gansett, in turn, agreed to lend the company $120,000 on a long-term, subordinated basis to improve its financial strength.

The organizational changes and capital infusions permitted greater managerial flexibility and initiative. Sales in 1974 reached an all-time high of $3.9 million. (See Exhibit 1 for 1973 and 1974 income statements and Exhibit 2 for the 1974 balance sheet.)

Gansett was involved in three principal product market areas. It manufactured a proprietary line of quality leather-upholstered furniture sold to high-end (that is, upper-price-range) retailers in the western states through a network of commissioned sales representatives. This "home line" accounted for between 45 and 50 percent of Gansett's total sales.

Gansett also manufactured a line of office-institutional furniture in various fabrics, in vinyls, and in leather. This line, also sold through commissioned sales representatives in the western states, accounted for 15 to 20 percent of total company sales.

Gansett's third principal product market was custom-fabricated booths, cabinets, chairs, countertops, and other fixtures for restaurant and coffee shop chains on a nationwide basis. This activity represented about 35 percent of Gansett's total sales.

In each of Gansett's principal product markets, the company's rivals were predominantly small, often undercapitalized, specialized manufacturers. Many of these businesses were closely held family enterprises.

RESULTS FROM 1970 THROUGH 1973

Growth

Between 1970 (when Gansett's current president assumed complete control over management) and 1973, Gansett's sales grew rapidly, as shown:

Year	Total Sales (000)
1970	$1,400
1971	1,965
1972	2,430
1973	3,500

The growth in Gansett's Home Line had resulted from a broadening of the company's market area and customer base. Although sales were still largely centered in California, continued increases had been achieved in other western states and in national distribution. The company's customer base, once centered on a small number of local accounts, had grown to the point where, by the end of 1973, the Home Line was sold to more than 400 accounts, with roughly 10 percent of the accounts representing 65 percent of its sales. The success of the Home Line could be attributed to a more stylized, focused product line, broader market coverage, and greatly improved merchandising and promotion. And although most of the growth was in upholstered leather furniture sales, sales in fabrics were becoming increasingly important. In July 1973, for example, the company introduced Gansett Denims, a line of quality upholstered blue denim furniture. By December the denim line had already produced $250,000 in sales to dealers, even though it was only then beginning to reach the retail floor.

The growth in the Fabrication Division resulted from increased sales to a small number of restaurant and coffee shop chains. Up until 1970, much of the Fabrication Division's sales consisted of "one-of-a-kind" restaurants. At that time—and coincident with the management reorganization referred to earlier—Gansett went after and captured the "chain" business. For example, by 1973 the company was fabricating the booths, cabinets, countertops, and chairs for all the new restaurants of a fast-growing national family restaurant. A number of other national restaurant chains were also firm customers of the Fabrication Division.

Profitability

From 1970 to 1972, Gansett's profitability did not meet management's expectations.

Year	Net Before Taxes
1970	$(62,000)
1971	44,500
1972	49,500
1973	68,100

One major reason was that the company's growth quickly outstripped the effectiveness of its largely informal controls and procedures. Management, preoccupied with the sales growth and generally overextended, was forced to improvise along the way. What it ended up with was an overly complicated, jerry-built system limited in its ability to control costs. Any possibility of purchasing economies, for example, was dissipated by the fact that up until mid-1973, no fewer than eight different people were handling the company's purchasing.

A second reason for the low profit levels was that weaknesses in the costing and pricing systems and the absence of profit analysis made it difficult for the company to identify with any consistency specific items in the Furniture Division, and entire jobs in the Fabrication Division, that might be losing money.

A third reason was that, up until it move to a new 78,000-square-foot facility in January 1973, the company operated out of a five-building, 45,000-square-foot complex, at the cost of significant material-handling and production inefficiencies.

NEW FINANCIAL MANAGER IN 1973

Several things contributed to the improvement of profitability in 1973. A larger, more adequate facility, coupled with industrial engineering improvements, generated production and material-handling economies. The firm's management group was also strengthened by the addition of Marshall Smith as chief financial officer. Mr. Smith implemented a system of tight cost controls almost immediately, and overhead costs increased little during the year, while sales increased by more than 40 percent. In addition, a shakedown of the product line identified unprofitable or marginally profitable items. These items were substantially increased in price or dropped altogether.

Moreover, the net income before taxes of $57,600 in 1973 actually understated the overall improvement in profitability. For example, nearly $95,000 in nonrecurring expenses were incurred in the move to the new facility. Finally, the firm's conservative accounting treatment of certain marketing expenses further reduced net income before taxes by possibly as much as $40,000 during the year.

1974 PROJECTIONS AND PERFORMANCE

The general uncertainty over economic conditions in 1974 tempered management's optimism. Mr. Smith prepared two substantially different sales and cash flow forecasts for the year, based on alternative economic assumptions.

The more optimistic forecast projected sales of $4 million or an increase of roughly 14 percent over 1973.

Division	1974 Sales Forecast
Home Line	$1,800,000
Office–Institutional	800,000
Fabrication	1,400,000
Total	$4,000,000

In support of the optimistic forecast, management recognized that a substantial part of the Fabrication Division's current production capacity was already committed for 1974. Two accounts alone could generate $1 million in sales volume. The forecast for the Home Line assumed an increase of only $100,000 over 1973's level of $1.7 million, and it included no sales for the new denim line.

The pessimistic forecast assumed sales of $2.8 million or a 20-percent decline from 1973. Should such a deterioration begin to develop, the company would implement a contingency budget reflecting a substantial and immediate reduction in certain highly discretionary advertising and market development expenses which were currently budgeted. These reductions could cut as much as $175,000 from the operating budget and still keep the company profitable. Further, though the pessimistic forecast did not reflect it, the company would break even even if its cost of goods increased to 65 percent.

Actual sales for 1974 totaled $3,859,000, just slightly below the $4 million optimistic forecast. Reported profit before taxes dropped to $36,000. However, in a letter to the company's banker, Mr. Smith noted that the reduced profitability reflected a number of discretionary accounting treatments intended by management to reduce tax liability and promote the firm's liquidity. Perhaps the most significant of these changes was a switch in inventory valuation method from FIFO to LIFO. The net impact was a substantial decrease in ending inventory, which increased cost of goods sold and consequently decreased profit before taxes by $107,000. Second, the company decided to write-off as "obsolete" inventory several items purchased for use on subsequently discontinued models. This further reduced before-tax profit by another $35,000. Third, the company chose to expense marketing and advertising costs that it reasonably could have capitalized. This further reduced income before taxes by $40,000. Also, the company's management increased the bad debt reserve to $14,000 from the $6,000 which management felt more clearly reflected historical experience. Along with miscellaneous other writeoffs, management estimated that income before taxes—although reported as $36,000—could have been shown as high as $253,000.

1975

As a consequence of the substantial "noncash" writeoffs against 1974 income, Gansett found itself with strong cash flow. Whereas the cash balance at the end of 1973 had totaled $1,213, by the end of 1974 it had swollen to $151,375, and Gansett's financial officer was actively involved in money market investments. Furthermore, Mr. Smith expected continued net inflows as prospects for a deepening of the recession grew. A reduction in sales would decrease accounts receivable and force production cutbacks. As 1975 began to unfold, the prospects for a sales drop began to materialize. Sales for the first quarter of 1975 were already below what they were in the same period in 1974. In April 1975, Mr. Smith projected total sales of only $3.7 million for the year, and profit before taxes of $150,000.

The before-tax profit estimate was based on the cost structure shown in Table 1.

TABLE 1
Cost and Profit Projections

Sales	100.0%
Less variable sales expenses (cash discounts; design royalties; commissions; overrides; incentives)	9.0%
	91.0%
Less direct cost	60.0%
Available for overhead and profit	31.0%
Current overhead levels	(In $ Thousands)
Factory	$ 505
Sales	241
General and administrative	251
Total overhead	$ 997
Breakeven point	$3,200
Profit before taxes on sales of $3,700	$ 150

ACQUISITION SEARCH

Mr. Smith believed that the recession economy would not improve, if at all, until the end of 1975. He knew that the industry decline would severely strain the resources of firms that were unprepared for the downturn or that were possibly undercapitalized. According to Mr. Smith, one had to take a long-term perspective if the firm were to be highly successful in the industry. To him, that meant being prepared for adversity in the expectation of being able to exploit significant opportunities. Thus he watched with some satisfaction as Gansett's careful financial planning produced a growing cash balance in the face of the severe industry decline. He believed that Gansett's best opportunity for significant market penetration existed in the midst of the recession, when otherwise well-positioned, efficient firms would need to be "bailed out." Thus in February 1975 he initiated a search for a firm that could help meet Gansett's product/market objectives and might be available at a bargain.

Gansett's growth plan revolved around three objectives.

1. To gain a larger share of the leather-upholstered residential furniture market by stimulating primary demand, increasing its penetration of the market it already served, and building its sales in the eastern states so that it could serve a national rather than a regional market more adequately
2. To broaden the product line to encompass wood occasional living room furniture and thus to provide the company with a more comprehensive and therefore more attractive marketing package
3. To establish a position in the higher-end fabric-upholstered furniture market, which generated more of the volume in the sales of expensive upholstered furniture

IMPORTANCE OF THE EASTERN MARKET

Mr. Smith believed that the eastern market held the most attractive opportunities for the long-term growth of the Gansett product line. The eastern market, loosely defined as the part of the market east of the Mississippi, was estimated to account for roughly two-thirds of the total sales of leather-upholstered furniture. Gansett's efforts to establish a foothold in this market had met only limited success. Eastern dealers were not likely to buy from a West Coast company when sources of supply were available closer to home, even when the landed cost might be the same. This bias against West Coast manufacturers was an attitude that had proved hard to change. The reverse was not true, however: western dealers were often receptive to eastern manufacturers. The existence of discriminatory freight rates (it cost less to ship from east to west than from west to east) strengthened this bias.

Gansett's interest in the eastern market also stemmed from his conviction that it lined up very well in price, quality, and workmanship with the specialized leather-upholstered furniture manufacturing companies that currently served the market. Moreover, the company believed it had a significant advantage over them in design, style leadership, product development, and merchandising skill. In areas such as Texas, where geography was neither an advantage nor a disadvantage to either Gansett or its eastern competitors, the company had demonstrated its ability to compete against them effectively.

In October 1974, the company had decided to exhibit at High Point, North Carolina, the site of the semiannual National Furniture Market, to explore its sales prospects in the eastern market further. The eastern dealers received the Gansett line highly favorably, especially because they believed that the line might soon be available out of the southeast. That expectation also made it possible for Gansett to flesh out its national sales organization by recruiting several outstanding sales reps at the High Point market. Gansett now had coverage in every state.

Sales rep contacts with eastern dealers since the October market had been very positive and had reinforced the company's conviction that it would achieve significant market penetration within a reasonable period if it were able to offer an economical southeastern shipping point.

In the fall of 1974, the company had started to explore systematically the feasibility of a manufacturing operation on the East Coast. While the acquisition of a profitable upholstery company with a market position that would be compatible with Gansett's would have provided the best vehicle for the eastern expansion, Gansett's extensive search yielded no acceptable candidates. Because of the strategic value of an eastern outlet and the importance of timing, Mr. Smith decided to involve himself personally in the search on a full-time basis.

In late 1974, through an introduction from an intermediary, Mr. Smith arranged a discussion of Gansett's acquisition plans with an officer at the Georgia National Bank, Mr. Philips. Mr. Smith took care to emphasize the general nature of the search lest attractive opportunities be missed. He did establish some tentative parameters to the search, however. He said that Gansett was looking for a furniture manufacturing company that met the following criteria:

1. The company should be based east of the Mississippi, preferably in Georgia.
2. It should have an upper-middle- to high-end product line in upholstery and occasional furniture (such as living area tables, cabinets, and so on, though not bedroom or dining room furniture). In descending order of preference, it should be:
   a. already established in these two areas

b. principally engaged in upholstery
c. principally engaged in occasional furniture
3. The company should have a well-established market position with upper-middle- to high-end retailers in the United States.
4. Its sales should range from $5 million to $10 million.
5. The company should be at least modestly profitable. Of particular interest would be a fundamentally sound company that was well positioned in its market but that, although profitable, needed but hadn't been able to raise sufficient working capital.

Mr. Smith assured Mr. Philips that certain private investors had given oral agreement to help finance a significant acquisition, presuming that the candidate were fundamentally sound. He closed by noting his belief that the prevailing economic conditions would place the cash buyer at significant advantage and that the Gansett Company wished to conclude a deal before the year's end.

In the course of the year, Gansett was provided a number of possible acquisitions, but only one firm was identified that manufactured fabric- and leather-upholstered furniture. Mr. Smith rejected the offering price of five times book value as being totally unreasonable.

In November, he began to concentrate his personal search in Georgia. In the course of his search, he came upon Adolph's, Inc., an upper-middle-priced fabric-upholstered furniture manufacturing company literally on the verge of liquidation. Adolph's was started in 1964 by two brothers, Moyer and Elmer Adolph. The company's sales had peaked at slightly over $1 million in 1972 and had been on the decline ever since. (See Exhibits 3 and 4 for financial background.)

Fiscal Year Ended 4/30	Total Sales
1973	$949,000
1974	803,000
1975	529,000

In the last quarter of calendar year 1975, sales were at an annual rate of $400,000. Adolph's sales organization had literally withered on the vine. The Adolph brothers had refused to replace sales reps in two key territories in spite of their incapacitation for nearly two years. Personal considerations of loyalty to the reps apparently overrode business considerations. In addition, the Adolphs had been unwilling to reduce the size of the factory organization to bring it into line with the diminishing sales level; as a result, the company had been overstaffed for some time. It had also lost a substantial amount of money: $89,000 and $74,000 before taxes in fiscal years 1974 and 1975, respectively.

From Gansett's standpoint, Adolph's was not a going concern, but it did have some advantages over a total start-up: it had plant, machinery, equipment, factory management, and a work force capable of producing at the level of quality and workmanship equal to Gansett's standards. The manufacturing assets could not be replaced for their $20,000 book value. In addition, the plant occupied 36,000 square feet of prime industrial space, which was leased to Adolph's. Adolph's had five remaining years on its current lease, with a five-year renewal option at no more than a 15-percent increase for the entirety of the option. The contractual lease rate of 90¢ per square foot compared very favorably with the going rate of $1.10 per square foot for manufacturing space in surrounding areas. And it had the added feature of a fabric-upholstered line in the middle- to upper-price range with a sales base in the general range of $350,000 to $400,000 that could be revitalized. Mr. Smith believed that, by producing the Gansett line at the facility, Adolph's sales could reach $800,000 in the first year of operation. He believed that current manufacturing assets could support such a sales level, although additional working capital investment would probably be needed.

With respect to costs, Mr. Smith thought that substantial improvement would be immediately possible. Direct costs of production, for example, could probably be kept below 65 percent of sales (30 percent labor and 35 percent materials). Variable selling expense could probably be kept below 10 percent. Finally, he also believed that overhead costs could be kept at about $75,000 at the projected level of activity.

In summary, although Mr. Smith was disappointed that a more "ideal" acquisition in terms of sales volume could not be found, he thought that Adolph's could contribute much to Gansett's growth plans. He also believed that Adolph's value depended a great deal on the terms and form of the transaction.

EXHIBIT 1
Gansett Furniture Company
Statement of Income

	Year Ended Dec. 31	
	1974	1973
Net sales	$3,859,227	$3,377,366
Cost of sales	2,836,853	2,539,770
	1,022,374	837,596
Selling, general, and administrative expenses		
Selling	584,286	498,474
General and administrative	372,019	287,422
	956,305	785,896
Income from operations	66,069	51,700
Other expenses, net	29,696	(5,940)
Income before taxes on income	36,373	57,640
Provision for taxes on income	12,200	22,744
Net income	$ 24,173	$ 34,896

EXHIBIT 2
Gansett Furniture Company
Balance Sheet
Dec. 31, 1974

Assets

Current assets

Cash, including short-term investments of $50,000 in 1975 at cost,
which approximates market, and $150,000 of certificates of
deposit in 1974 .... $ 151,375

Accounts receivable, less allowance for doubtful accounts of
$10,000 and $14,000 (pledged) 295,787

Inventories (pledged) 599,605

Prepaid expenses and other current assets 29,273

Total current assets 1,076,040

Property and equipment, net (pledged) 81,657

$1,157,697

Liabilities and Shareholders' Equity

Current liabilities

Accounts payable .... $ 283,994

Accrued expenses 100,843

Customer deposits 25,598

Current portion of notes payable 31,774

Income taxes .... —

Deferred income taxes 22,380

Total current liabilities .... $ 464,589

Notes payable, less current portion 237,433

Subordinated long-term debt 120,000

Deferred income taxes 1,896

Commitments .... $ 359,329

Shareholders' equity

Common stock, $8 par value
Authorized—125,000 shares;
outstanding—16,136 shares 129,088

Capital in excess of par value 122,742

Retained earnings 81,949

$ 333,779

$1,157,697

EXHIBIT 3
Adolph's, Inc.
Income Statements
For the Years Ended 4/30

	1971	1972	1973	1974	1975
Sales	$900,000	$1,020,000	$949,000	$803,000	$529,000
C/S (%)	.75	.70	.72	.77	.75
C/S $	675,000	714,000	683,280	618,310	396,750
GM	$225,000	$ 306,000	$265,720	$184,690	$132,250
Selling, general, and administrative expenses					
Selling	90,000	102,000	104,390	127,740	68,770
Administrative	81,200	143,050	140,530	145,000	136,480
Interest	800	950	800	950	1,000
Other					
Profit before taxes	53,000	60,000	20,000	(89,000)	(74,000)
Tax (48%)	25,440	28,800	9,600	(42,720)	(35,520)
Profit after taxes	$ 27,560	$ 31,200	$ 10,400	$ (46,280)	$ (38,480)

EXHIBIT 4
Adolph's, Inc.
Balance Sheet
As of 10/30/75

Assets		Liabilities and Stockholders' Equity	
Accounts receivable	$ 20,000	Bank debt	$ 10,000
Inventory	120,000	Accounts payable	55,000
Current assets	$140,000	Current liabilities	$ 65,000
Property and equipment	20,000		
Miscellaneous	5,000	Shareholders' equity	$100,000
		Total liabilities and shareholders' equity	$165,000
Total assets	$165,000		

Palazolo Manufacturing Company

In late January 1977, George Cristelle, manager of financial analysis of the Palazolo Manufacturing Company, was about to analyze a capital investment using simulation. This was the first time that simulation was being used in the company, and he was confident that it would provide information that was more useful for making investment decisions than the information generated by the firm's current procedures.

BACKGROUND

The Palazolo Manufacturing Company was formed by Joan Palazolo in January 1964 in Phoenix, Arizona. The firm was profitable until 1969, when its first loss was incurred. (See Exhibit 1.) Fortunately, Ms. Palazolo realized that the losses were caused by the lack of proper financial management and that her existing management team was not capable of solving the problem. Thus in 1969 she persuaded Harold Johnson, a controller of a large manufacturing company, to become the firm's financial vice president. Mr. Johnson quickly instituted financial controls, which helped reverse the trend. By late 1970 the firm was once again operating at a profitable level, and sales and profits grew steadily, reaching all-time highs of $14.7 million and $.95 million, respectively, for the year ended December 31, 1976.

When Johnson was offered the position, he was reluctant to accept it even though he considered it an enticing challenge. The reason was that his investigation revealed that the finance function was carried out in a small accounting department and that the head of the department was not part of top management. Thus he inferred that Palazolo considered finance relatively unimportant and hence would not give him the support he would need. He was assured, however, that this was not the case, but rather that the firm lacked a strong financial management team because of its initial emphasis on marketing and production. Prior to entering this business, Joan Palazolo believed that a firm with less than $5 million in sales could not survive. Since the firm would initially generate sales of about $1.5 million, rapid growth would be needed. In her view, rapid growth could be achieved only by focusing on quality products and a strong marketing effort. Thus, when she recruited and developed managers, she gave priority to production and marketing.

When sales hit $5 million, Ms. Palazolo decided to continue to grow rapidly and to achieve this by strengthening production and marketing. The failure to develop the finance function hurt the company. In the latter part of 1968, the firm had its first losing month. Monthly losses continued into 1969, and the firm began to have cash flow problems. The biggest problem was morale: the managers lost confidence in their own ability. Ms. Palazolo did not, however. She recognized the problem and was determined to build a strong financial management team. She was convinced that this would solve the problem. Fortunately, her bankers agreed with her and decided to support the firm during its retrenchment period.

During his first three years, Mr. Johnson concentrated on implementing a budget system, improving the cost-accounting system and developing planning procedures. When these pressing problems were solved, he turned his attention to other important areas, including the analysis of capital investments. Up through 1972, little financial analysis was performed when potential capital investments were evaluated. All that the financial staff did was estimate how the investment would affect the firm's profitability, and Mr. Johnson believed that the staff did not do this well. He wanted to implement present value techniques, and he hired two financial analysts to handle the additional work.

Under the new procedures, the cash flows from each investment were estimated. The internal rate of return and the net present value were calculated for each potential investment. Mr. Johnson believed that the firm's cost of capital was between 9 percent and 12 percent. Thus two net present value calculations were made, one using 9 percent and one using 12 percent. For investments involving above-average risk, a higher rate was used. When these procedures were designed, Mr. Johnson recognized that techniques were available that would provide information useful for evaluating risk. His intention was to put the procedures into practice and then experiment with these techniques.

Unfortunately, it took longer than planned to put the new procedures into practice, primarily because of a poor hiring decision. Mr. Johnson hired a person with five years of experience to manage the new department. This person had been on the financial analysis staff of a large firm. He had been involved primarily in designing new systems and was considered to be that firm's resident intellectual. The second member of the staff was a recent graduate of a graduate school in business with no prior business experience. The head of the new department was very bright. He knew his finance and was up-to-date on recent developments in the field. In fact, he was a frequent contributor to the academic journals. In addition, he was quite competent in mathematics and management science. Unfortunately, he was also quite arrogant and could get along with no one. The firm's managers disliked him so much that not only would they not cooperate, but they would also try to hinder his work.

Mr. Johnson tried hard to develop him, but after two years he concluded that there was no hope and fired him. Since Mr. Johnson felt that the second person in the department did not have enough experience to manage the department, he hired someone from the outside. The analyst was so upset at being passed over that he quit. The ultimate result of these personnel changes was that the department did not function properly until mid-1976. By that time, George Cristelle was managing the department.

When Mr. Cristelle assumed the position, he found a memorandum written by the first manager of the department (the intellectual), which outlined various possibilities for incorporating risk in capital budgeting. After reviewing the memorandum and performing some additional research, Mr. Cristelle concluded that simulation was best for the Palazolo Company. Simulation enabled one to generate information concerning an investment's rate of return and the dispersion about that rate of return. (To perform this type of analysis, a manager must estimate a range of values for each item affecting the investment's cash flows and assign probabilities to the possible outcomes.) He told Mr. Johnson that he wanted to try it on an investment that the firm was currently considering. Mr. Johnson agreed.

IMPLEMENTING THE NEW TECHNIQUE

The investment proposal that Mr. Cristelle wanted to use to test the technique was the potential replacement of a machine. The new machine would replace an existing machine and would produce savings in labor and materials each year for its 10-year life. Exhibit 2 presents the details regarding the cash flows related to the investment and shows that it promised, based on point estimates, a positive net present value at both 9 percent and 12 percent, and an internal rate of return of 19 percent.

To perform the simulation, the first step was to estimate probability distributions for each variable. After discussions with Ms. Palazolo, Mr. Johnson, and the production manager who submitted the request, Mr. Cristelle arrived at the estimates presented in Exhibit 3.

With respect to the labor savings and the material savings, the same probability distributions were applicable for each of the 10 years, and the distributions were independent over time. For example, the amount of labor saved in any year would be independent of the amount of labor saved in prior or subsequent years. Putting it another way, the amount of labor saved in year 1 would not affect the shape of the probability distributions applicable to subsequent years. Moreover, the amount of labor saved would be independent of the amount of material saved.

Mr. Cristelle believed that his certainty estimates for the cost of the new machine and the selling price of the existing machine were correct. He had some concern about his certainty estimates for zero-salvage-value estimates. However, if the salvage values were different from zero, the amounts would be so small that they would have little effect on the investment's internal rate of return. The tax rate was a bigger problem: the 48-percent effective income tax rate could change over the next 10 years. He decided to proceed in the following manner. He would perform the analysis using the estimates in Exhibit 3. He would then redo the analysis using different assumptions for the tax rate estimate or rely on a range of estimates for the tax rate.

To perform the analysis, Mr. Cristelle would have to write a program to do the simulation. The program would randomly select one labor savings amount for each year and randomly select one material savings amount for each year from the probability distributions and calculate the internal rate of return. It would repeat the process a sufficient number of times to produce a realistic simulation of the potential internal rates of return. Finally, he wanted the program to summarize the internal rates of return in a useful manner.

EXHIBIT 1
Palazolo Manufacturing Company
Financial Data
(In $ Thousands)

Year	Net Sales	Cost of Goods Sold	Other Expenses	Net Income	Total Assets	Total Debt
1964	$ 1,430	$ 887	$ 501	$ 42	$ 1,788	$ 715
1965	2,360	1,463	826	71	2,950	1,181
1966	3,450	2,129	1,242	79	4,312	1,725
1967	4,861	3,070	1,700	91	6,076	2,430
1968	7,203	4,753	2,373	77	9,038	3,796
1969	8,401	5,665	3,160	(424)	10,007	6,004
1970	8,036	5,465	3,054	(483)	10,040	6,024
1971	8,120	5,359	2,758	3	10,150	5,583
1972	8,782	5,533	2,986	263	10,978	5,436
1973	10,240	6,349	3,379	512	12,800	6,081
1974	12,160	7,478	4,013	669	15,170	7,518
1975	13,075	8,041	4,315	719	15,987	7,998
1976	14,700	8,965	4,778	957	18,263	9,085

EXHIBIT 2
Financial Analysis of Proposed Molding Machine

I. GENERAL DESCRIPTION

This machine will replace an existing machine, which was purchased 10 years ago for $40,000. This machine is being depreciated on a straight-line basis over a 20-year life to a zero salvage value. It is estimated that it could be sold now for $5,000. The new machine will cost $50,000, and it is estimated that it will produce annual labor savings of $8,000 and annual material savings of $6,000. It would be depreciated on a straight-line basis over a 10-year life to a zero salvage value. Finally, this investment would have a negligible effect on the firm's level of working capital.

II. CASH FLOWS

Cost of machine		$50,000
Less: Sale of old machine		(5,000)
Tax shield on loss		
($20,000 – $5,000) × 48%		(7,200)
Cash outflow, year Zero		$37,800
Cash inflows		
Labor	$8,000 × 52% =	$ 4,160
Materials	6,000 × 52% =	3,120
Incremental depreciation	3,000 × 48% =	1,440
Years 1–10		$ 8,720

III. MEASURES OF ECONOMIC WORTH

1. Payback   4–5 years
2. Internal rate of return   19%
3. Net present value @ 9% $18,162
4. Net present value @ 12% $11,470

EXHIBIT 3
Probability Estimates

Probability		Amount
Cost of new machine	1.0	$50,000
Selling price, existing machinery	1.0	5,000
Salvage value, new machine	1.0	0
Salvage value, existing machinery	1.0	0
Tax rate	1.0	48
Labor savings, years 1–10	.10	9,500
	.10	9,000
	.40	8,000
	.20	7,000
	.20	5,500
Material savings, years 1–10	.10	6,800
	.20	6,500
	.30	6,000
	.20	5,200
	.20	4,500

Teague Corporation

In early November 1978, Carol Weintraub, manager of the capital invest-ment analysis department of the Teague Corporation, received a copy of a telex sent from the general manager of the Trailo Division requesting immediate approval to dispose of a toolroom. Although the request did not conform to normal capital-budgeting procedures, Teague's top man-agement had agreed to consider the proposal. Trailo had always wanted to sell the toolroom and received approval during 1975 to search for a buyer. Prior to this proposal, Trailo had been unable to obtain a reason-able offer. Now that an offer, which Trailo's general manager considered appropriate, had been received, the division was anxious to sell.

COMPANY BACKGROUND

The Teague Corporation was formed in 1896 in New Jersey to produce machine tool parts for use in the coal industry. Since its inception, the firm had supplemented its original business with additional products, which it either developed internally or acquired. Although the firm had always been involved in several industries, it did not depart from the manufacturing of machinery, equipment, and hand tool business until 1965, when it acquired the Trailo Corporation, a distributor of food products. Management realized that there were problems involved in managing diverse businesses, but it was convinced that it had the capa-bility to do so. In fact, Trailo was only the first move outside the manu-facturing field; subsequent to that point, Teague entered several new businesses, including the production of food products and fast-food franchising. Indeed, the firm would have diversified even more, but de-clining market values of the common stocks for conglomerates affected the price of the firm's stock even though it had not encountered the problems that plagued many conglomerates.

Sales in 1977 were more than $1.7 billion on assets of almost $1.8 billion. (See Exhibits 1 and 2 for financial statements for 1976 and 1977.) Included among the firm's goals was a target to have sales grow by 15 percent per year over the next five years and to have profits grow by at least that rate. Management believed that most of this growth would come from the expansion of existing businesses.

CAPITAL INVESTMENT ANALYSIS DEPARTMENT

The capital investment analysis department was located at corporate headquarters in New Jersey. Although it became involved in various types of studies and analyses for the executives and the general managers of the divisions, its primary function was to review proposals submitted by the divisions, which were usually capital appropriation or disposal requests. Requests for funds generally included a brief description of the investment, how much money would be needed and when, estimated cash flows from the investment, and an estimate of the investment's profitability. When a request was received, it was evaluated by a member of the capital investment analysis department. Included in the evaluation was a careful analysis of the reasonableness of the profit and cash flow estimates, the calculation of the investment's internal rate of return, a comparison of this rate with the firm's 12-percent after-tax hurdle rate, and a calculation of the investment's payback. When the evaluation was completed, a report was prepared for top management. The report contained a summary of the analysis and the analyst's recommendation. Ms. Weintraub, the manager of the department, reviewed all reports before they were presented to management for approval.

The amount of time that an analyst had to spend analyzing a proposal would vary. A routine replacement of equipment might take a few hours. On the other hand, it might take several months to analyze a major investment. For example, in 1973 one of the divisions proposed a major investment in a South American country. It took the analyst six months to prepare the report. Since the firm had not operated in that country, the analyst had to undertake an in-depth study of the country's political and economic climate before analyzing the investment. After the report was completed and had been read by top management, the analyst made a presentation at a meeting of top management. Top management discussed the investment at several subsequent meetings and, after careful consideration, decided to reject the proposal.

DISPOSAL REQUEST

In 1972, the Trailo Division acquired a group of companies in the United Kingdom. These included a fresh produce distributor, a transportation company, a horticultural supplies operation, and a plastic mold manufacturing company (that is, a toolroom). Trailo was not interested in purchasing the toolroom, but it was part of the package. After three years of operating the toolroom, Trailo Division's general manager received approval to search for a buyer.

In early 1978, Trailo received an offer that it wanted to accept immediately. The vice president of finance received a telex (Exhibit 3) requesting approval on November 7, 1978. He sent a copy of the telex to Ms. Weintraub and called to tell her that the request was going to be considered in a couple of days. He asked her to perform whatever analysis she could and make a recommendation by the next afternoon.

Ms. Weintraub called several managers of Trailo to find out more about the situation. She was curious why Trailo was in such a hurry and learned that the purchaser wanted to complete the deal by the end of its fiscal year, November 23, 1978. She also learned that the purchaser was interested in acquiring the toolroom principally because of the expertise of the 18 employees. With respect to profit projections for the next few years, she was told that profits should be significantly less than the average pretax contribution for the previous four years.

EXHIBIT 1
Teague Corporation
Consolidated Statement of Income
For the Years Ended December 31
(000 omitted)

	1976	1977
Sales, less discounts, returns, etc.	$1,424,138	$1,740,000
Cost of goods sold	962,000	1,183,995
Selling, general, and administrative expense	243,759	293,899
Operating profit	$ 218,379	$ 262,106
Other income	6,398	340
Total income	$ 224,777	$ 262,446
Interest expense	23,009	43,158
Federal income tax	91,339	94,685
Net income to retained earnings	$ 110,429	$ 124,603
Retained earnings, beginning of year	529,982	633,982
Other credits	46,995	51,785
Preferred dividends	9,184	8,900
Common dividends	40,542	45,995
Other debits	3,698	1,223
Retained earnings, end of year	$ 633,982	$ 754,252

EXHIBIT 2
Teague Corporation
Consolidated Balance Sheet
(000 omitted)

	12/31/76	12/31/77
Assets		
Cash and demand deposits	$ 51,823	$ 71,543
U.S. Treasury securities	13,405	12,663
Notes and accounts receivable, net	332,297	416,599
Inventories (lower of cost or market)	605,544	769,174
Prepaid expenses	8,711	9,095
Total current assets	$1,011,780	$1,279,074
Investment in and advances to subsidiaries	8,495	6,349
Other investments	4,502	10,649
Property, plant, and equipment (cost)	555,089	690,307
Accumulated depreciation	(236,020)	(255,434)
Property account, net	319,069	434,873
Prepaid expenses and deferred charges	12,445	18,036
Total	$1,356,291	$1,748,981
Liabilities		
Accounts payable, accrued expenses, etc.	$ 179,611	$ 233,578
Advanced payment on orders	28,339	10,134
U.S. federal and foreign income taxes	67,213	67,402
Loans payable	180,354	305,577
Total current liabilities	$ 455,517	$ 616,691
Long-term debt of subsidiaries	161,635	270,650
Pension reserve of subsidiaries	3,056	3,697
Preference stock (no par)	7,835	7,646
Common stock	41,460	41,588
Capital in excess of par value	73,294	72,895
Retained earnings	633,982	754,252
Total stockholders' equity	756,571	876,381
Less Treasury shares at cost	(20,488)	(18,438)
Net shareholders' equity	736,083	857,943
Total	$1,356,291	$1,748,981

EXHIBIT 3

TELEX

VICE–PRESIDENT OF FINANCE   NOVEMBER 7, 1978
AT LAST TRAILO'S EFFORTS TO SELL TOOLROOM CAN BE SUCCESSFUL.
WE HAVE NEGOTIATED SALE WITH HIGHLY REPUTABLE CONCERN TO PUR-
CHASE.   AT 11/23/78

FIXED ASSETS – AT BOOK VALUE	DLRS 19,300
STOCK – AT COST	8,000
WORK IN PROGRESS – AT FACTORY COST ESTD	<u>33,000</u>
	60,300
DISPOSAL EXPENSES MINIMAL SAY	500

IN ADDITION PURCHASER WILL COLLECT RECEIVABLES AND DISCHARGE
PAYABLES FOR OUR ACCOUNT RELEASING WORKING CAPITAL OF DLRS
53,000 SALE WILL RESULT IN NO BOOK LOSS AND SALE PROCEEDS ARE
PAYABLE ON COMPLETION EARLY DECEMBER.   USUAL WARRANTIES TO BE
GIVEN AND RECEIVED.   PURCHASER WILL ASSUME COMPLETE RESPONSI-
BILITY FOR TOOLROOM STAFF (18) ABSOLVING US FROM ANY SEVER-
ANCE ETC LIABILITY.   PURCHASER WILL TAKE OVER LEASE COMMIT-
MENT ON WORKSHOP (I.E. DLRS 3000 PA FOR 21 YRS FROM 1972
REVIEWS 1975, 1982).   TOOLROOM PROFIT RECORD AS FOLLOWS:

1974 DLRS	6,000	)	
1975 "	7,300	)	BEFORE PROPORTION TRAILO
1976 "	23,000	)	HEAD OFFICE
1977 "	12,000	)	COSTS

PROFITABILITY LATTER PART OF 1978 IS DECLINING AND ORDER BOOK
IS NOW VERY LOW.   IN VIEW OF DECLINING PROFITABILITY WORK IN
PROGRESS AGAINST FIXED SELLING PRICES COULD WORK THRU TO GIVE
LOSSES AND SALE OF W.I.P.   AT FACTORY COST WITHOUT PROVISION
TO REDUCE TO NET REALISABLE VALUE IS PLUS FACTOR OFFSETTING
POSSIBILITY THAT BOOK VALUE OF FIXED ASSETS IS MARGINALLY BE-
LOW MARKET VALUE.

STRONGLY RECOMMEND SALE FOR FOLLOWING REASONS:
1. OPERATION DOES NOT FIT WELL WITH TRAILO'S NORMAL ACTIVI-
   TIES.
2. WE HAVE LITTLE MANAGEMENT KNOWHOW IN THIS TYPE OF OPERA-
   TION.
3. PLANT IS RUN DOWN AND NECESSARY REPLACEMENT COULD COST
   DLRS 35,000 NEXT YEAR.
4. R.O.I. HAS NEVER BEEN GOOD AND NO REASON TO ANTICIPATE IM-
   PROVEMENT.
5. HAVE TRIED FOR 4 YEARS TO FIND BUYER WITHOUT SUCCESS – AND
   CAN NOW DISPOSE WITHOUT A BOOK LOSS.
6. FUNDS RELEASED WILL TOTAL DLRS 113,000.

FORMAL DISPOSAL REQUEST FOLLOWS BUT WOULD LIKE URGENT AP-
PROVAL.

                          GENERAL MANAGER TRAILO DIVISION

PART V
LONG-TERM FINANCING AND DIVIDENDS

Delicious, Inc.

In early January 1978, John Hescott, treasurer of Delicious, Inc., was ready to analyze three proposals for financing a $3 million capital improvement program. The firm's board was going to meet in a few days, and at that time he would have to recommend which of the three proposals should be selected.

BACKGROUND

Delicious, Inc., was founded by Harold Steinberg in 1922 to manufacture and sell candy and related products. The firm was immediately profitable, and sales and profits increased each year through 1929. The Great Depression hit the firm quite hard, and three consecutive annual losses were experienced. The firm survived only by stringent cost-cutting efforts and the support of its commercial bank. At that time the firm had a sizable loan with its commercial bank, which agreed to postpone interest and principal payments for four years. This experience convinced Mr. Steinberg of the importance of sound marketing and financial policies. In his judgment, sound policies meant no debt and slow sales growth. Over the years, many of the firm's managers proposed faster growth and/or the use of debt, but Mr. Steinberg would not seriously consider any of these proposals.

Mr. Steinberg also believed in keeping the company private, in order to maintain flexibility in setting policy and maintain control. By 1978, 892,000 common shares were outstanding. Members of the Steinberg family owned 60 percent of these shares, and former and current employees owned the remainder. If a shareholder wished to sell shares, he or she would have to sell them back to the firm at book value. If the firm did not have the funds, then the person would have to wait up to one year to receive the funds. The only exception to this policy was if the shares were being sold for estate tax purposes. In such a situation, Mr. Steinberg would see to it that the shares were repurchased immediately. Although several people criticized this policy, Mr. Steinberg did not believe that it was unfair, for the following reasons. First, employees who took advantage of the firm's stock option plan could have selected an alternative profit-sharing scheme. Second, although the policy was that a seller might have to wait one year, this never happened since the firm maintained a high level of liquidity. Third, the firm paid healthy dividends. Dividends had been paid in every year since 1940, when they were first instituted. Since that time there had never been a dividend cut; on the contrary, small increases in the dividend rate were frequent. Mr. Steinberg thought that the dividend returns the shareholders were earning were fantastic. When dividends per share increased from $1.60 to $1.65 in 1967, he said, "Many people purchased their shares for $1 per share. On these shares they will now earn a return of 165 percent!"

When the founder died in late 1968, his son Richard assumed the presidency. Although the new president also believed in conservative policies, he had long felt that his father had been a bit too conservative. Moreover, he had always disagreed with his father's policy of keeping the company private. These disagreements were not secret, and it was also known that the elder Steinberg had begun to yield on the issue of taking the company public. He had still believed that it was best to keep the company private, but he had realized that, since so many shares were outstanding, a problem could develop if many stockholders decided to sell at the same time. If they were to do so, the firm might have to borrow a substantial sum to repurchase the shares; from the founder's point of view, this was less desirable than taking the company public.

Richard Steinberg spent his first two years as president trying to convince the board of directors to accept a goal of going public and to change its policy on the use of debt. He wanted to use debt to accelerate the rate of expansion so that the firm would be well positioned to become a public company. Convincing the board to accept the idea of going public was not difficult, since, as noted above, it was well known that the founder had been beginning to yield on this matter. Selling the idea of using debt was more difficult. After many discussions, Richard Steinberg succeeded in obtaining agreement to use a moderate amount of debt. He was able to do this by demonstrating that financing expansion with a moderate level of debt was not too risky, and that it would probably permit greater growth in dividends per share because there would be less of a need for raising funds by issuing new common shares.

To position the company to go public, the new president believed that it would be beneficial to increase both sales and profits. He also believed that this could best be accomplished by introducing two new product lines (that is, different types of candy). He had originally planned to introduce both at the same time and to finance the entire expansion program with debt. However, discussions with members of the board convinced him that the board would never approve such a program. While there was a consensus to accelerate growth somewhat and to use some debt, there was strong sentiment that the marketing and financial policies that proved so successful should not be changed too much. Consequently, the president proposed a three-phase program.

The first new product line (hard rock candy) would require $5 million. It would take about five years, until 1975, for this new product line to be fully integrated into the firm's existing operations.

The second phase was a different product line (licorice), which was larger than the product line of phase 1. This phase would begin in 1976 (after the success of phase 1 could be evaluated) and require about $6 million. Three years after the beginning of phase 2 the product line would have to be expanded; this expansion (phase 3) would require about $2 million.

Although phases 2 and 3 were related, the first phase was unrelated to the others. In other words, by accepting the first phase the firm was not committing itself to the remainder of the program. Thus the board voted to accept phase 1 and finance it with debt. A $5 million, five-year term loan was obtained from its commercial bank. Interest and principal payments were required semiannually, commencing six months from the date on which the loan agreement was signed.

Phase 1 proceeded smoothly. Sales and profit targets were achieved. Loan payments were easily met, and dividends were increased to an all-time high of $2 per share in 1975. In early 1976, the board decided to proceed with phases 2 and 3 even though the costs were higher than those originally estimated. (In 1976 it was estimated that phase 2 would require $7 million and that phase 3 would require almost $3 million.) Despite the success with phase 1, the board balked at financing the second phase entirely with debt. After considerable debate, it was decided to finance $5 million with debt and $2 million with preferred stock. In the autumn of 1976, a $5 million five-year term loan was obtained from the firm's commercial bank. The interest rate was 11 percent, and annual principal payments of $1 million were to begin December 31, 1977. (See Exhibits 1 and 2 for financial statements for 1976 and 1977.) A $2 million, 12-percent preferred stock issue was privately placed with a pension fund. The firm had the option of calling $500,000 of the issue each year at par, commencing December 31, 1979. Mr. Steinberg wanted the call privilege to take effect starting December 31, 1977, but he could not obtain this feature without increasing the dividend rate. Both parties had the option of converting the issue to a debenture, which would be subordinated to bank debt on January 1, 1987. If exercised, the loan would be repaid in five equal annual installments, and the interest rate would be 200 basis points above the interest rate on single A industrial bonds at January 1, 1987.

As noted, phase 2 was a new product line. The plan was to introduce most of the line and then expand the line three years later (phase 3). In mid-1977, however, it became apparent that the firm could not compete effectively with a partial product line; thus phase 3 had to begin as soon as possible. In early September, the firm purchased $3 million worth of capital equipment and obtained a short-term loan from its commercial bank. It was understood that more permanent financing would be arranged to retire the $3 million note. Mr. Hescott, the firm's treasurer, was responsible for identifying options and recommending which should be chosen.

FINANCING OPTIONS

Mr. Hescott's first step was to meet with the firm's commercial banker. He was told that, at a recent meeting, the bank's board decided that its loan portfolio was too long; thus, during the next year, efforts would be made to shorten the average maturity. Consequently, the loan officer said that the best he could do was offer a three-year loan at 10½ percent. Principal payments of $1 million would be required at the end of each of the three years.

Since prepaying the existing term loan would involve no penalty, Mr. Hescott recognized that one possibility was to obtain a $7 million term loan from another bank. On many occasions at various social and community activities, he had been approached by the officers of other banks. While most of these discussions focused on the services that their banks could provide, these officers always made clear that the firm would have to do all its banking business with a new bank or at least establish a substantial deposit relationship. Although switching banks might be attractive in terms of cost, Mr. Hescott realized that this option was not feasible. The firm had done business with the same commercial bank since 1922, and this was the bank that had stood by the firm during the difficult Depression years. In short, the board would not consider switching banks.

Mr. Hescott had numerous discussions with investment bankers and financial institutions. He received three offers, but one of these he immediately dismissed. It was from an insurance company, which was willing to lend $3 million but wanted warrants to purchase common stock. The treasurer thought that the number of new shares they wanted the right to purchase was too high, and that the proposed exercise price was too low.

The second offer was from the pension fund that owned the $2 million of preferred stock. This financial institution was willing to purchase an additional $3 million of 12-percent preferred stock. Each year, $500,000 of the new preferred could be called at par, commencing one year after the existing preferred was retired. The option to convert to a five-year term loan commencing on January 1, 1987, would also apply to these shares.

The third offer was from an investment company that had many wealthy clients. It was willing to underwrite class B shares in 10,000 share lots. Each of the 30 lots would be sold for $100,000. The class

B shares would have no voting rights or dividend rights through December 31, 1979. On January 1, 1980, each class B share would be converted into a regular share, and hence at that time there would be only one class of common stock.

At the board meeting that would be held in a few days, Mr. Hescott planned to present as possibilities the three-year term loan from the firm's commercial bank, the new issue of preferred stock, and the class B shares. He would also recommend which of the three he thought was best. To perform the analysis, he obtained a copy of the flow-of-funds estimates presented in Exhibit 3. He also obtained a copy of the notes he had taken at a seminar on financial management that he attended during 1974 (Exhibit 4). "It sure looked easy in that classroom," he thought, as he read over the notes.

EXHIBIT 1
Delicious, Inc.
Income Statements*
Years Ended 12/31
(000 omitted)

	1977	1976
Net sales	$79,388	$77,115
Cost of goods sold	51,476	50,986
Gross profit	$27,912	$26,129
Selling, general, and administrative expense	20,897	20,049
Operating income	$ 7,015	$ 6,080
Interest on term debt	550	140
Profit before taxes	$ 6,465	$ 5,940
Taxes @ 48%	3,103	2,851
Net income	$ 3,362	$ 3,089
Preferred dividends	240	64
Earnings for common	$ 3,122	$ 3,025
No. of common shares outstanding	892	892
Earnings per share	$ 3.50	$ 3.39
Dividends per share	$ 2.00	$ 2.00

* These statements have been restated to simplify the analysis. Interest expense on short-term debt is included in selling, general, and administrative expense. Interest income on marketable securities is treated as a deduction from selling, general, and administrative expense.

EXHIBIT 2
Delicious, Inc.
Balance Sheets—At 12/31
(000 omitted)

	1977	1976
Cash and marketable securities	$ 743	$ 566
Accounts receivable, net	5,640	5,542
Inventories	7,477	7,322
Other current	296	361
Total current	$14,156	$13,791
Property, plant, and equipment, net	18,444	15,219
Other assets	371	462
Total	$32,971	$29,472
Notes payable	$ 3,000	$ —
Accounts payable and accruals	7,853	7,599
Current portion of term debt	1,000	1,000
Other current	91	87
Total current	$11,944	$ 8,686
Term debt	3,000	4,000
Preferred stock	2,000	2,000
Common stock and surplus	7,655	7,655
Retained earnings	8,372	7,131
Total	$32,971	$29,472

EXHIBIT 3
Delicious, Inc.
Projected Sources and Uses of Funds*
Years Ended 12/31
(000 omitted)

	1978	1979	1980	1981	1982
Sources					
Net income after taxes	$4,019	$4,316	$4,414	$4,622	$4,842
Depreciation	300	300	325	325	325
Funds flow	$4,319	$4,616	$4,739	$4,947	$5,167
Accounts payable and accruals	150	140	140	135	130
Total sources	$4,469	$4,756	$4,879	$5,082	$5,297

EXHIBIT 3 (continued)

	1978	1979	1980	1981	1982
Uses					
Working capital	$ 600	$ 600	$ 480	$ 470	$ 460
Fixed asset expenditures	150	150	200	200	200
Debt payments	1,000	1,000	1,000	1,000	—
Preferred sinking fund	—	500	500	500	500
Preferred dividends	240	240	180	120	60
Common dividends	1,784	1,784	1,784	1,784	1,784
Total uses	$3,774	$4,274	$4,144	$4,074	$3,004
Sources less uses	$ 695	$ 482	$ 735	$1,008	$2,293
Cumulative	$ 695	$1,177	$1,912	$2,920	$5,213

* Flow-of-funds estimates include the increase in funds because of the $3 million capital expenditure program but not the financial burden created by the new financing. In other words, new interest charges, new dividend requirements, or new sinking fund payments that will be required are not included. Also, the estimates assume no increases in common dividend rate.

EXHIBIT 4
Memorandum

TO: File
FROM: John Hescott
RE: Notes on Long-Term Financing Session

The session on long-term financing was very interesting. The instructor assigned the following *Harvard Business Review* articles:

1. "Framework For Financial Decisions," by William Sihler, March–April 1971.
2. "New Framework For Corporate Debt Capacity," by Gordon Donaldson, March–April 1962.

In assigning these articles, the instructor noted that, although many other articles were important, they were really beyond the scope of an introductory session. During the class he referred to several articles, especially one by Modigliani and Miller.

Once a firm has determined its external permanent financial requirements, it must decide how to raise these funds. There are three basic security types from which to choose: debt, preferred stock, and common stock. Sometimes a feature is added to the basic security type; for example, debt could be made convertible into common stock in order to make the security more attractive to investors.

Various factors must be considered in making a long-term financing decision. During the class we discussed the following factors:

1. Analysis of suppliers of capital
2. Control

3. Flexibility
4. Income
5. Risk
6. Value

1. ANALYSIS OF SUPPLIERS OF CAPITAL

Individuals, financial institutions, and other organizations purchase securities. The firm must analyze the needs of various types of investors as well as their ability and willingness to purchase certain types of securities in a manner similar to how it analyzes the markets for its products. A firm does not design a product and then analyze the market. Market research is conducted first, and then the product and marketing campaign is designed to capture the identified market. The same principle applies to selling securities. Since many firms do not have the expertise required to perform this market research, they must rely on an outsider, such as an investment banker, for assistance. The responsibility for overseeing this activity rests with the financial manager. Consequently, it is essential that he or she understand the nature of financial markets and the characteristics of the major participants in these markets.

2. CONTROL

Control is concerned with the effect that the financing choice could have on the management of the firm. The common shareholders elect the board of directors of a firm, each share having one vote.[1] When common stock is issued, there are new votes; consequently, it is possible for the composition of the board to change, leading to a change in management. The importance of this factor depends on the number of new shares being considered relative to the existing number outstanding and the degree of ownership concentration. One normally thinks of loss of owner-ship control in the context of new common equity. A firm relinquishes a certain degree of control, however, whenever it raises external funds. If, for example, a covenant on a loan agreement is broken, the degree of control that a lender can exercise will become painfully clear.

3. FLEXIBILITY

This factor is concerned with the effect that the current financing choice will have on future financial decisions. If we raise debt now, will we have to raise equity the

---

1. In some firms there is more than one class of common stock, with one or more not having voting rights. Also, preferred shareholders sometimes have voting rights and/or a stipulation in the preferred stock agreement stating that, under certain conditions, preferred shares have voting rights. The most common condition is that voting rights are obtained if preferred dividends are not paid for a specified period.

next time? If so, what if equity capital is not available? A firm must always be in a position to raise funds, whether the source be external or internal. The more options open to it, the more likely it is that it will be able to raise funds. Flexibility is important for all firms, but it is especially critical for firms that are frequently in need of external capital.

4. INCOME

The income factor is concerned with the effect that the financing choice has on earnings per share. The instructor relied on the following example. Assume that Firm A had $1 million in EBIT (earnings before interest and taxes) for the year ended 19x as shown in the income statement in Exhibit 4-A.

Firm A has decided to undertake an expansion project, which is expected to increase EBIT by $200,000, to $1.2 million. It needs $500,000 of external capital to finance the expansion, and it is considering the following three possibilities:

1. Long-term debt, with an interest rate of 10 percent. Principal payments of $50,000 per year would be required, commencing at the end of the first year.
2. Preferred stock, with a dividend rate of 9 percent.
3. 50,000 shares of common stock to net the firm $10 per share.

If EBIT increases to $1.2 million, earnings per share (EPS) will be $1.50, $1.22, or $1.17, depending on the financing option selected. (See Exhibit 4-B.)

The instructor noted that many people *incorrectly* deduct sinking fund payments in calculating EPS for the debt options. While the level of sinking fund payments is certainly relevant for making the decision, these payments are not expenses and hence do not affect the calculation of EPS.

EXHIBIT 4-A
A Company
Income Statement
Year Ended 19x
(000 omitted)

Net sales	$10,000
Cost of goods sold	7,000
Gross profit	$ 3,000
Operating expenses	2,000
Earnings before interest and taxes	$ 1,000
Interest expense	100
Earnings before taxes	$ 900
Income taxes @ 50%	450
Earnings after taxes	$ 450
Less preferred dividends	200
Earnings available to common stock	$ 250
No. of common shares outstanding	250
Earnings per share	$ 1.00

EXHIBIT 4–B
A Company
EBIT–EPS Analysis
(000 omitted)

	Debt	Preferred	Common
EBIT	$1,200	$1,200	$1,200
Existing interest	100	100	100
New interest	50	0	0
Earnings before taxes	$1,050	$1,100	$1,100
Income taxes @ 50%	525	550	550
Earnings after taxes	$ 525	$ 550	$ 550
Existing preferred dividends	200	200	200
New preferred dividends	—	45	—
Earnings available to common	$ 325	$ 305	$ 350
No. of common shares outstanding	250	250	300
Earnings per share	$ 1.30	$ 1.22	$ 1.17

Why is there a difference among the three choices? Will debt always produce the highest level of EPS? Will common stock always produce the lowest level of EPS? To answer these questions, the instructor began by noting that debt and preferred stock are fixed cost securities. The after-tax dollar cost of debt in the example is $25,000 (interest of $50,000 times 1 minus the 50-percent tax rate). This is the cost regardless of the level of earnings. If earnings are low, the fixed dollar cost will be a high proportion of the earnings. On the other hand, if earnings are high, the fixed dollar cost will be a small proportion of these earnings. Preferred stock is also a fixed cost security. While preferred dividends are not expenses, they must be paid before common shareholders are entitled to any earnings. Thus they reduce the amount of earnings available to common stock, and the amount of the reduction is a fixed dollar amount. In the preceding example, the fixed dollar cost is $45,000. (Unlike interest payments, preferred dividends do not create a tax shield because they are not expenses.) Since, in this example, the fixed after-tax dollar cost of debt is less than that for preferred stock, the debt option will produce a higher level of EPS than preferred stock at any level of EBIT.[2]

Common stock creates a fixed-percentage dilution. That is, the new shareholders are entitled to a fixed percentage of the total earnings available to common stock. In the preceding example, the fixed-percentage dilution is $16\frac{2}{3}$ percent [number of new common shares (50,000) divided by the total number of common shares that will be outstanding (300,000)]. Since the percentage is constant, the dollar amount will vary. Consequently, whether preferred stock and/or debt will produce a higher level of EPS than common stock depends on the level of EBIT. Moreover, there is a level of EBIT at which EPS will be the same for the debt and common

2. This statement assumed that the firm will be in a position to take advantage of the tax shield created by interest.

stock options and another level of EBIT at which EPS will be the same for the preferred stock and common stock options. These EBIT levels are called indifference points.

There are various ways to determine these indifference points. The most common is to rely on algebra. We first restate the EBIT–EPS analysis in equation form:

$$EPS = \frac{(EBIT - i)(1 - T) - P}{n}$$

where EBIT = earnings before interest and taxes
$\quad i$ = total dollars of interest (existing interest plus new interest)
$\quad T$ = tax rate
$\quad P$ = total dollars of preferred dividends (existing preferred dividends plus new preferred dividends)
$\quad n$ = number of common shares outstanding
$\quad$ EPS = earnings per share

Setting the right-hand side of this equation for a common stock option equal to right-hand side of this equation for a fixed cost security option and solving for EBIT will give the indifference point, that is, the level of EBIT at which EPS will be the same for both alternatives. To Illustrate:

$$\overset{\textbf{Debt}}{\frac{(EBIT - 150)(1 - .5) - 200}{250}} = \overset{\textbf{Common}}{\frac{(EBIT - 100)(1 - .5) - 200}{300}}$$

$$EBIT = \$800,000$$

	Debt	Common
EBIT	$800	$800
Interest	150	100
EBT	$650	$700
Taxes	325	350
EAT	$325	$350
Less preferred	200	200
EATCS	$125	$150
No. of common shares outstanding	250	300
EPS	$ .50	$ .50

At any EBIT level above $800,000, EPS would be higher under the debt option; at any EBIT level below $800,000, EPS would be higher under the common stock option.

The indifference point between the preferred and common stock options is $1.04 million.

	Preferred	Common
EBIT	$1,040	$1,040
Interest	100	100
EBT	$ 940	$ 940
Taxes	470	470
EAT	$ 470	$ 470
Less preferred	245	200
EATCS	$ 225	$ 270
No. of common shares outstanding	250	300
EPS	$ .90	.90

Finally, there is no indifference point between debt and preferred stock because the fixed after-tax dollar cost is different for each option at all levels of EBIT.

The instructor cautioned us against being misled by the term *indifference point*. It refers only to the level of EBIT at which EPS is the same for two (or possibly several) financing possibilities. It does *not* represent the EBIT level at which the manager will be indifferent between the two financing choices. In other words, the financing choice is based on several factors and not just on the choice's effect on EPS.

5. RISK

This factor is concerned with the ability to service debt (or preferred stock). Many approaches are used to evaluate debt capacity. For example, a popular measure is the earnings coverage standard, which is defined as follows:

$$\text{Earnings coverage} = \frac{\text{EBIT}}{i + \left(\dfrac{\text{SF}}{1 - \text{T}}\right)}$$

where EBIT = earnings before interest and taxes
   i = dollars of interest
   SF = sinking fund payments
   T = tax rate

Since a sinking fund payment is not an expense, it is not tax deductible. Hence we divide the amount of the sinking fund by 1 minus the tax rate to convert it to a before-tax amount. This ratio compares the size of the firm's earnings with the size of its debt service. Generally, a ratio of 2 or 3 or even more is desired to provide for an adequate margin of safety. As Donaldson pointed out in his classic article, earnings and cash flow are not the same thing. Since debt payments are made with cash, he recommended comparing the size of the debt service with the size of the firm's cash flow. He suggested that the firm should estimate what its cash flows would be under unfavorable conditions in judging how much debt it can service.

The instructor pointed out that Donaldson's approach was basically an application of pro forma analysis. He concluded by noting that measuring debt capacity is a most important task. A firm has many goals, a primary one being to maximize the market value of the firm's common stock. However, it is obvious that a manager's top priority must be to assure the firm's survival.

6. VALUE

As noted, a primary goal of management should be to maximize the market price of the firm's common shares. Thus, in making a financing decision, the manager must evaluate what impact the choice will have on the market value of the firm's common shares. As we saw, different financing alternatives will produce different levels of EPS. The choice might also have an effect on the multiple (that is, price-earnings ratio) that investors are willing to pay for a firm's earnings. Investors don't like risk. Since debt creates financial risk, investors might penalize the firm's price-earnings ratio, and thus it is possible for the price of the firm's common shares to decline by using debt even if debt produces a higher level of EPS. On the other hand, if the firm is using moderate amounts of debt, the choice of debt might not reduce the price-earnings ratio and could possibly increase it. The reason is that the use of debt or preferred stock magnifies the rate of change of EPS. Thus, if EBIT is growing, EPS will grow at a greater rate by using fixed cost securities. If the growth effect outweighs the risk effect, the price-earnings ratio might increase.

Obviously, it is extremely difficult to evaluate the impact on the price-earnings ratio. Nonetheless, it is an important consideration that cannot be ignored.

Cost-of-Capital Illustrations

"I hope the cost-of-capital illustrations work," said Professor John Moore to a colleague as they were walking back to their offices from lunch at the faculty dining room. He had just given the assignment for the next day's class on the cost of capital to the participants in the Executive Development Seminar. This was the second summer that he was teaching the finance portion of the seminar. The previous year, the class on the cost of capital was poorly received, and he was determined to make this year's session on the topic interesting and useful.

John Moore was a faculty member of a leading business school in the Southwest. Each summer for the past five years, the school offered a two-week management development seminar. A session each day was devoted to financial management. During the prior summer, Professor Moore was invited to teach the finance portion of the seminar. The topics he selected were all well received, with the notable exception of the cost of capital. During the session, he had focused on explaining that the cost of capital was the cost of a firm's sources of funds, and that, if a firm were to earn more than its cost of capital, the market value of its common stock would increase. Approximately half the executives indicated that, although they had heard of the concept, their firms did not use it and Professor Moore's presentation did not convince them to do so. Of the remainder, several told him that they had considered using the cost of capital in making investment decisions, but that they had difficulty applying the models recommended by academicians. Consequently, they continued to rely on an arbitrarily determined cutoff rate when analyzing investment decisions. Finally, a small number of participants whose firms did rely on the cost of capital indicated that Professor Moore's presentation of the subject was reinforcing.

For the current year's seminar, Professor Moore put in a great deal of time preparing teaching materials. He developed a series of illustrations based on actual data for firms. They would be distributed to the participants the day before the class on the cost of capital. Each illustration required calculations, and the class would be devoted to a discussion of the participants' calculations.

The illustrations are presented in the appendix.

APPENDIX
Illustrations on the Cost of Capital

ILLUSTRATION 1

Exhibits 1 and 2 present data on two utilities. The first, Compo, Inc., was a large firm with a national scope. Bay, Inc., was a much smaller, regional utility. Estimate the cost of equity for each firm and the weighted average cost of capital. (You may assume that the income tax rate is 50 percent.)

EXHIBIT 1
Compo, Inc.

		% of Total Capital Structure
Capital structure	Debt	54.5
	Preferred stock	5.4
	Equity	40.1
Before-tax costs	Debt	6.44
	Preferred stock	7.72
	Equity	?

Year*	Dividends per Share	Earnings per Share	Market Price per Share (range)
1	$2.20	$3.67	63–49
2	2.20	3.79	62–49
3	2.40	3.74	58–48
4	2.40	4.00	58–48
5	2.60	3.99	53–40
6	2.60	3.99	53–40
7	2.65	4.34	53–41
8	2.80	4.98	55–45
9	3.16	5.27	53–39
10	3.40	5.13	52–44

* Year 10 indicates the most recent fiscal year.

EXHIBIT 2
Bay, Inc.

		% of Total Capital Structure
Capital structure	Debt	53.4
	Preferred stock	10.1
	Equity	36.5
Before-tax costs	Debt	7.4
	Preferred stock	7.34
	Equity	?

Year*	Dividends per Share	Earnings per Share	Market Price per Share (range)
1	$ .88	$1.27	21–15
2	1.00	1.58	21–18
3	1.10	1.42	25–19
4	1.16	1.39	22–15
5	1.16	1.37	19–13
6	1.18	1.72	20–15
7	1.22	1.67	20–16
8	1.24	1.70	16–12
9	1.24	1.77	15–8
10	1.28	1.71	13–8

* Year 10 indicates the most recent fiscal year.

ILLUSTRATION 2

Exhibit 3 presents data on Century Corporation, a large chemical manufacturer. Professor Moore, while performing a consulting assignment for this firm, heard an interesting debate concerning the cost of equity capital. One member of the firm's financial analysis department argued that book value per share should be used to calculate the cost of equity instead of market price per share. In his view, market price per share was just too erratic. Earnings per share and dividends per share had grown continuously, and this was reflected in the continuous growth in book value per share. Market price per share, on the other hand, had on occasion declined despite increases in earnings and dividends.

Estimate the cost of equity and the weighted average cost of capital for Century Corporation. (You may assume an income tax rate of 50 percent.)

EXHIBIT 3
Century Corporation

		% of Total Capital Structure
Capital structure	Debt	41.9
	Preferred stock	—
	Equity	58.1
Before-tax costs	Debt	6.4
	Equity	?

EXHIBIT 3 (continued)

Year[1]	Dividends per Share	Earnings per Share	Book Value per Share[2]	Market Price per Share (range)
1	$.34	$ .68	$ 4.78	13–8
2	.36	.73	5.18	15–10
3	.39	.75	5.57	14–11
4	.41	.79	5.96	13–10
5	.44	.73	6.08	12–9
6	.45	.85	6.60	19–12
7	.45	1.04	7.24	26–19
8	.48	1.47	8.29	34–23
9	.53	3.18	10.67	35–25
10	.73	3.33	13.22	47–26

[1] Year 10 indicates the most recent fiscal year.
[2] These figures represent book value per share at the end of the year.

ILLUSTRATION 3

Exhibit 4 presents data on Burger Kingdom, a fast-food chain. A member of this firm, who participated last summer, indicated that her firm had considered using the cost of capital as the discount rate when analyzing capital investments. Unfortunately, the models recommended in most textbooks were not relevant for a firm like Burger Kingdom, which had never paid a dividend and did not expect to pay a dividend in the foreseeable future. Using earnings per share in the model instead of dividends per share produced ridiculous results: consequently, her firm decided to continue to use an arbitrarily determined cutoff rate.

Estimate the cost of equity for Burger Kingdom and then calculate the weighted average cost of capital. (Assume a tax rate of 53 percent.)

EXHIBIT 4
Burger Kingdom

		% of Total Capital Structure
Capital structure	Debt	.2
	Preferred stock	—
	Equity	99.8
Before-tax costs	Debt	7.9
	Equity	?

EXHIBIT 4 (continued)

Year*	Earnings per Share	Market Price per Share (range)
1	$ .14	3-1
2	.20	8-2
3	.28	11-5
4	.39	14-8
5	.48	15-9
6	.69	39-14
7	.94	77-37
8	1.31	76-44
9	1.70	63-21
10	2.17	60-26

* Year 10 indicates the most recent fiscal year.

ILLUSTRATION 4

The capital-asset pricing model can be used to estimate the cost of equity capital for a firm.

$$K_e = R_F + (R_M - R_F)\beta$$

where K_e = cost of equity

R_F = the expected rate of return for a risk-free security

R_M = the expected rate of return on the market

β = a measure of the variability of the rate of return of the firm's common stock, relative to the market rate of return

Exhibit 5 presents the quarterly rates of return for the Cobra Company for the past five years, quarterly rates of return for the Standard & Poor's stock index of 500 securities (which will be our market proxy) for the past five years, and the interest rate on three-month Treasury Bills (which will be our risk-free rate proxy) for the same period. Although monthly data for the previous five years are often used to calculate a security's beta, we will rely on quarterly data.

The model requires estimates of the risk-free rate and the market rate of return. You may assume that the averages of the previous five years provide reasonable estimates.

Calculate the cost of equity for the Cobra Company. What is the desired relationship between the cost-of-equity estimate derived from the use of the capital-asset pricing model and the estimate derived from the use of the dividend valuation model?

EXHIBIT 5
Cobra Company

Year	Quarter	Quarterly Rate of Return* Cobra Company	Market Index	Quarterly Risk-free Rate
1	1	(.077)	.017	.015
	2	.018	(.016)	.015
	3	(.06)	(.024)	.018
	4	(.129)	(.050)	.018
2	1	.184	(.018)	.020
	2	(.164)	(.047)	.016
	3	(.18)	(.147)	.016
	4	(.132)	.145	.015
3	1	(.025)	.124	.011
	2	.018	.106	.010
	3	.081	(.031)	.014
	4	(.116)	(.01)	.011
4	1	(.006)	.102	.009
	2	.049	.01	.009
	3	.141	.036	.010
	4	.095	.064	.012
5	1	.186	.033	.014
	2	(.128)	(.055)	.016
	3	(.086)	.049	.020
	4	.164	.098	.018

* Figures in parentheses indicate negative amounts.

ILLUSTRATION 5

An interesting debate occurred at the Early Company. This firm was considering a $10 million expansion program. If it were accepted, it would be financed by a $10 million issue of 7.8-percent debt. The firm's existing capital structure was as follows:

	Before-tax Cost (%)	Amount
Debt	7	$30 million
Preferred stock	8	5 million
Common equity	10.5	80 million

The debate concerned the appropriate discount rate to use in analyzing the proposal. There were three positions:

1. An after-tax rate of return of 3.9 percent should be required, which was the after-tax cost of the debt. (The firm's tax rate was 50 percent.) Since the project was being financed entirely with debt, earnings per share would increase if more than 3.9 percent were earned on the investment.

2. The fact that debt was being used was irrelevant. The weighted average cost of capital should be used as the discount rate in evaluating the proposal.

3. It would be incorrect to use either the debt rate or the weighted average cost of capital. Since the firm was increasing its proportionate use of debt, it was estimated that the cost of equity would increase to 12 percent. This factor must be taken into account in choosing the discount rate.

What rate should the Early Company use to evaluate the $10 million expansion program?

ILLUSTRATION 6

At last year's seminar, two executives, one from a commercial bank and one from a fire and casualty insurance company, noted that most articles they had read about the cost of capital referred to industrial corporations. Since the class on the topic also focused on industrial companies, they wondered whether the concept of the cost of capital was irrelevant for other types of firms.

Exhibit 6 presents data for a commercial bank, and Exhibit 7 presents data for a fire and casualty insurance company. Estimate the weighted average cost of capital for each firm, relying on the models used to calculate the weighted average cost of capital for an industrial firm. Is the weighted average cost of capital relevant for these firms? Why? (You may assume an income tax rate of 40 percent.)

EXHIBIT 6
Metropolis Bank of Tuscaloosa
Income Statement
For the Year Ended 12/31
(000 omitted)

Interest and other fees on loans	$ 788,335
Interest on securities	109,650
Other income	236,000
Gross operating income	$ 1,133,985
Salaries	220,000
Interest expenses	517,340
Other expenses	258,000
Depreciation	40,000
Total operating expenses	$ 1,035,340
Operating income	98,645
Taxes on income	39,458
Net income	$ 59,187

EXHIBIT 6 (continued)
Balance Sheet at 12/31
(000 omitted)

Assets

Cash and due from banks	$ 2,973,117
U.S. government securities	1,003,000
State and municipal obligations	899,390
Other securities	58,416
Loans, net of loan loss reserve	8,404,717
Direct lease financing	311,148
Bank premises and equipment, net	350,132
Other assets	131,671
Earned interest receivable	507,000
Total assets	$14,638,591

Liabilities and Stockholders' Equity

Deposits

Demand	$ 4,035,801
Savings (4.71%)	2,213,770
Time (7.14%)	4,117,743
Foreign office (7.60%)	1,831,524
Federal funds purchased and securities sold[1] (5.78%)	1,062,946
Notes payable (7.83%)	276,750
Other liabilities	432,287
Common stock and surplus	459,891
Undivided profit	207,879
Total liabilities and stockholders' equity	$14,638,591

[1] Under agreement to repurchase.

Selected Financial Data

Year[1]	Earnings per Share	Dividends per Share	Market Price per Share (range)	Book Value per Share[2]
1	$2.09	.77	30–22	$19.49
2	2.19	.83	32–22	20.28
3	2.51	.89	40–24	21.45
4	2.77	.98	39–27	22.77
5	2.82	1.07	33–23	24.24
6	2.64	1.17	34–27	25.22
7	2.81	1.28	37–27	26.50
8	2.99	1.34	33–20	27.39
9	2.73	1.40	26–13	28.33
10	3.16	1.40	20–14	31.82

[1] Year 10 indicates the most recent fiscal year.
[2] These figures represent book value per share at the end of the year.

EXHIBIT 7
Oxford Fire and Casualty Insurance Company
Income Statement
For the Year Ended 12/31
(000 omitted)

Premium earnings	$1,798,043
Investment income	164,000
Other income	155,500
Total revenue	$2,117,543
Insurance operating expenses	1,926,464
Other expenses	136,250
Total expenses	$2,062,714
Total operating income	54,829
Income tax credit	15,264
Deferred income tax	17,525
Net income	$ 87,618

Balance Sheet at 12/31
(000 omitted)

Assets	
Bonds and stocks	$2,751,909
Cash	139,904
Premiums receivable	271,664
Other accounts receivable	548,536
Real estate	101,156
Other assets	914,000
Total assets	$4,727,169
Liabilities and Stockholders' Equity	
Unearned premium[1]	$ 807,938
Unpaid claims[2]	1,434,548
Other accounts payable	450,000
Policy reserve[3]	377,000
Notes payable (7%)	701,400
Preferred stock (4%)	5,515
Stockholders' equity	950,768
Total liabilities and stockholders' equity	$4,727,169

[1] This amount represents premium revenues that have not been earned. For example, if a firm sold a three-year fire insurance policy for $6,000 on January 1, $4,000 of this amount would be unearned premium at December 31 of that year.

[2] This amount represents loss claims owed to policyholders.

[3] This amount represents an estimate of losses incurred by the end of the year that were not reported as of the year end.

EXHIBIT 7 (continued)
Selected Financial Data

Year	Earnings per Share	Dividends per Share	Market Price per Share (range)
1	$2.15	1.27	33–27
2	2.46	1.39	35–29
3	2.18	1.91	59–29
4	2.55	1.68	56–33
5	2.39	1.82	41–25
6	3.70	1.91	47–33
7	4.72	2.00	48–37
8	5.22	2.28	43–34
9	3.46	2.45	41–23
10*	3.29	2.60	45–32

*Year 10 indicates the most recent fiscal year.

American Forge Corporation

In early 1983, John Axelrod, treasurer of the American Forge Corporation ("AFC"), was busily reviewing a series of financing options he intended to present to the company's board of directors. Numerous options had been explored with potential lenders and investment bankers, and Mr. Axelrod had narrowed the choices to four: a 5-year private placement of debt, a 10-year public debt issue, a 10-year public issue of convertible debt, and a common stock issue.

The proceeds would be used to finance plant and equipment construction, working capital, tooling, and start-up expenses for a new aluminum engine that the company had developed and was anxious to market. The expansion would require an initial investment of $10 million. Ten-year projections for the new engine indicated that the project's rate of return would be close to 20 percent (Exhibit 1).

BACKGROUND OF THE COMPANY

AFC had net sales of $117 million in 1982 on total assets of $94.6 million. (Recent balance sheets and income statements are contained in Exhibit 2.) Net income for the year of $4.8 million, although considerably improved over the previous year, resulted in a return on equity under 8 percent. Even so, Mr. Axelrod thought the only significant foreseeable increase in earnings would come from the aluminum engine project, though no revenues would be generated until 1984. In 1983 he expected earnings before interest and taxes (EBIT) from existing operations to total $10 million.

From its beginning, AFC was a producer of forgings for use in industry. (Forgings are semifabricated metal components used in a wide variety of equipment and structures, including automobiles, trucks, airplanes, missiles, space equipment, and nuclear reactors.)

After a long history of sales and profit growth, the company began to experience difficulty in maintaining sales volume and profitability. Sales dropped off slightly during the year, from $124.8 million in 1977 to $123.7 million in 1978, but pre-tax income dropped by 37 percent, from $9.3 million in 1977 to $5.9 million in 1978. Profitability declined even farther in 1979 in the face of a severe raw material price inflation, despite a $17.5 million increase in sales. Pre-tax profits declined to $2.8 million during 1979. During 1980, the company suffered its first loss in its long history. The volume of sales dropped more than 13 percent, to $122 million (the lowest sales volume since 1975), and pre-tax income fell to a loss of $600,000.

In 1981, AFC returned to profitable operations, although sales declined once again, to $121.3 million. Net income improved to $2.7 million, but return on equity averaged only 4.9 percent for the year.

Mr. Axelrod attributed the profit improvement to greater production efficiency, the elimination of unprofitable government contracts, and some price increases put into effect during the year. These improvements were reflected in the firm's gross margin on sales, which increased from 7.4 percent in 1980 to about 13 percent in 1981. The improvement in gross margin alone accounted for the improvement in operating income as a percentage of sales, which increased to 5.6 percent from a deficit of 1.2 percent in 1980.

The improvement continued into 1982, which produced the highest earnings since 1976. Continued weeding out of unprofitable and marginal products was reflected in the drop in sales volume to $117 million and also in the continued improvement in the gross margin, which reached more than 16 percent of sales in 1982. Earnings for the year almost doubled the 1981 level. Mr. Axelrod attributed the higher profitability to a continuation of policies implemented in 1981 and to the realization of other cost savings. However, he believed that further reductions in these areas were unlikely at the current level of activity.

ALUMINUM ENGINE PROJECT

In hopes of reversing its dismal earnings performance and negligible growth prospects, AFC had accelerated development in 1981 of an aluminum engine for small aircraft, which was expected to be superior to existing machines in its cost and design features. By late 1982, AFC's president advised the board of directors that the engine project was ready to launch.

If undertaken, AFC would purchase the factory building and other structures of an airplane manufacturing corporation located nearby. The manufacturer was relocating operations to another part of the country. AFC's engineering and production staff were well acquainted with the manufacturing facility and felt that it could be converted with little difficulty. The factory building, other production facilities, and tooling would cost $7.2 million. Another $900 thousand was thought necessary for additional design and engineering. A railroad spur and loading facilities would also have to be added at an estimated cost of $800 thousand. Working capital requirements were budgeted for approximately $1.1 million. The president informed the board that if financing were arranged quickly the plant could be in operation by early 1984.

Detailed market and engineering analyses indicated that the proposed engine investment of $10 million would yield an internal rate of return of almost 20 percent after taxes for at least 10 years, with projections beyond 10 years subject to substantial competitive and technological uncertainty. Along with the relatively high anticipated rate of return, however, AFC's president cautioned the board that the aluminum project was not without risks, even in the near future. For example, market acceptance, even for such a superior machine, might be more difficult to achieve than anticipated; reaction times of competitors might be faster than anticipated; production costs might well vary significantly from engineered levels; new alloys or designs might quickly make even the aluminum engine obsolete; and so forth. If the aluminum engine project were to fail, AFC could be severely set back.

CURRENT CAPITAL STRUCTURE AND FINANCING OPTIONS

The company presently had $6 million in short-term debt and $8 million in long-term debt backed by $60 million in stockholders' equity. The relatively low debt-to-equity ratio could be attributed to the conservative financial policy of a company that had been closely held for many years, and to the volatile character of the machine tool industry, which made substantial debt servicing requirements hazardous.

The company currently had 1.1 million shares of common stock outstanding. Earnings per share in 1982 reached $4.34. With an average price-earnings multiple of 9.5, AFC's common stock price had averaged over $41 per share during 1982. At January 15, 1983, share price was at an all-time high of $57.50 per share. Mr. Axelrod attributed this in large part to the substantial earnings improvement over 1981 and to expectations about the aluminum engine which the company had announced it might put into production. He noted with some pride the optimism that investors were expressing in the company's future and hoped that they were right. One trade magazine, for example, had predicted that the new engine might revolutionize the industry.

As noted previously, AFC's considerable financial flexibility, despite its recent earnings difficulties, permitted a wide range of financing options. The principal types still under consideration are described below.

Five-Year, 15-Percent Private Placement

The company's investment banker had contacted an insurance company, which indicated its willingness to extend a five-year loan for $10 million at a rate of 15 percent. The loan would be due in full at the end of 1988. Mr. Axelrod thought the rate might be a little high, considering the relatively low level of debt currently in the capital structure and the relatively short maturity of the loan. He was not sure how amenable the insurance company would be to a reduced rate, but he was prepared to suggest a rate of 14 percent or less. He was also concerned that, should things go poorly, AFC might be hard put to pay off the loan in five years and might not be able to receive an extension from the insurance company. In any event, if things did not go well, refinancing could be an expensive and risky undertaking.

Ten-Year, 12½-Percent Debentures

Discussion with the company's investment banker indicated that a public issue of bonds was a realistic possibility. The banker suggested that a 10-year maturity would give AFC maximum flexibility. However, given that the investing public was still unfamiliar with the company and in view of the company's erratic earnings performance, the banker estimated that a 12½-percent coupon might be required.

Mr. Axelrod agreed that a 10-year bond would preserve the financing flexibility he desired, but he was disturbed by the coupon rate, about 4½ percentage points above the company's currently outstanding debt issue. Moreover, a 10-percent prepayment penalty in the first 5 years and 5 percent subsequently raised the prospect of redundant financing if the aluminum project were to go well and the extra financing was not needed. Mr. Axelrod was also concerned that the public issue could cost $250,000 in registration, underwriting, and distribution costs. The relatively large fixed-cost component of issue costs suggested to him that the amount of financing to be raised might not be an economical size for this type of financing. In order to net the company $10 million, $10.25 million of bonds would have to be sold.

Ten-Year, 8-Percent Subordinated Convertible Debentures

The investment banker noted that the coupon rate on the debt issue could be reduced considerably if AFC were willing to offer investors an opportunity for capital gain. A convertible debt issue, for example, could probably be sold with an 8-percent coupon. The debentures could probably be subordinated if the conversion price were sufficiently attractive. According to the investment banker, subordinated convertible debentures were typically carrying conversion premiums above stock prices of about 15 percent. The debentures would have to be made non-callable for at least five years (to protect the capital gain potential). Otherwise, annual sinking fund payments of $1 million would be necessary, beginning in 1984. Typically, the sinking fund requirements could be met through open market purchases.

Mr. Axelrod was concerned with the dilution effects of such an issue and the relatively high flotation costs of $300,000. Thus, $10.3 million in debentures would have to be sold to net AFC $10 million. On the other hand, if things went as expected, the issue would be converted without difficulty. With a conversion price of $62.50, Mr. Axelrod calculated that conversion would result in 164,800 additional shares outstanding. Conversion, of course, would eliminate the $10.3 million debentures while increasing shareholders' equity (and thus financial flexibility) at the same time.

200,000 Common Stock Shares at $52.50 per Share

The final proposal under consideration was an issue of common stock. To ensure the sale of all shares offered, AFC's investment banker advised that underpricing would be necessary. Given a current market price of $57.50 per share, the investment banker suggested an offering price of $52.50 per share. The company would sell 200,000 shares at this price. Issue costs and commissions would be deducted from issue receipts, yielding a net realized price of approximately $50 per share. Mr. Axelrod's principal concern with this option was the earnings dilution it involved. Also, he was worried about weakening the current market price, which he viewed as being supported to some extent by speculative factors.

EXHIBIT 1
American Forge Corporation
Summary of Aluminum Engine Project Data
(\$ millions)

	1983	1984	1985	1986	1987	1988	1989–1993
Revenues		$11.1	$13.3	$15.8	$18.4	$20.0	$22.0/year
EBIT*		2.0	2.4	3.0	3.6	4.0	4.4
Taxes (50% rate)		1.0	1.2	1.5	1.8	2.0	2.2
Net income		$ 1.0	$ 1.2	$ 1.5	$ 1.8	$ 2.0	$ 2.2
Net cash flow**	$(10.0)	$ 2.0	$ 2.2	$ 2.5	$ 2.8	$ 3.0	$ 3.2

*Not including possible financing charges.
**Includes gradual recovery of working capital.

EXHIBIT 2
American Forge Corporation
Statements of Income and Retained Earnings

	Years Ended	
	12/31/82	12/31/81
Sales	$117,445,440	$121,304,089
Cost of goods sold	95,683,429	105,292,730
Depreciation	3,771,649	3,521,468
Selling, general & administrative expenses	5,536,036	5,686,333
Income from operations	$ 9,611,196	$ 6,803,558
Interest expense	1,319,380	1,647,114
Other income	1,170,985	162,961
Profit before taxes	$ 9,462,801	$ 5,319,045
Taxes	4,684,536	2,570,754
Net income	$ 4,778,265	$ 2,748,651
Earnings per share	$4.34	$2.50
Retained earnings, beginning of year	$ 53,448,437	$ 51,559,592
Dividends paid	862,136	859,806
Retained earnings, end of year	$ 57,364,566	$ 53,448,437

Balance Sheets

	12/31/82	12/31/81
Assets		
Cash	$ 1,934,661	$ 1,966,836
Marketable securities, at cost which approximates market	–	2,802,307
Accounts receivable, trade	18,707,920	15,795,495
Accounts and notes receivable, other	513,889	430,776
Inventories	43,030,301	33,666,895
Prepaid expenses	668,191	1,034,499
Total current assets	$ 64,854,962	$ 55,696,808
Noncurrent accounts receivable	1,005,842	1,599,721
Investment in affiliated companies	2,886,630	2,641,853
Property, plant, and equipment, at cost		
Land, buildings, and improvements	22,289,132	22,215,216
Machinery and equipment	49,695,152	49,092,375
Under construction	1,022,674	603,049
	$ 73,006,958	$ 71,910,640
Less accumulated depreciation	48,186,962	45,528,507
Net property, plant, and equipment	$ 24,819,996	$ 26,382,133
Excess of investment in subsidiaries and affiliates over equity in net assets at acquisition	1,007,486	1,034,132
	$ 94,574,916	$ 87,354,647

EXHIBIT 2 (continued)

| | Years Ended | |
	12/31/82	12/31/81
Liabilities		
Bank loans	$ 6,000,000	$ 6,300,000
Long-term loans due within one year	800,000	800,000
Accounts payable		
Trade	7,948,148	4,827,147
Pension fund	2,266,812	2,510,205
Other	1,375,066	1,195,121
Accrued liabilities		
Federal income taxes	1,857,147	1,980,810
Other taxes	1,543,887	776,248
Salaries and wages	2,226,653	1,810,907
Total current liabilities	$ 24,017,713	$ 20,200,438
Long-term loan, 8½%	7,200,000	8,000,000
Deferred federal income taxes	3,087,222	2,788,890
Minority interest in consolidated subsidiary	95,885	107,352
Stockholders' equity		
Capital stock		
Authorized 2,000,000 shares—no par value; issued and outstanding 1,100,000 shares	2,809,530	2,809,530
Retained earnings	57,364,566	53,448,437
	$ 60,174,096	$ 56,257,967
	$ 94,574,916	$ 87,354,647

Children's Memorial Hospital (B)

In late March 1976, the board of directors of Children's Memorial Hospital ("Memorial") was considering a set of refinancing options in an effort to decide which, if any, to present to its bank. The board was particularly concerned with ensuring that it would have adequate financing while avoiding unnecessary financial risk and costs.

The board was especially cautious in its review, owing to the series of almost catastrophic shocks that had recently afflicted the hospital. Of critical importance was the fact that the hospital had defaulted on several installments of its existing bank loan and was substantially in arrears to the Internal Revenue Service for employee withholding taxes. Moreover, Memorial's annual audit had uncovered a number of significant financial reporting errors, and the hospital's auditors had declined to express an opinion on its financial condition or prospects.

THE HOSPITAL AND ITS ENVIRONMENT[1]

Children's Memorial Hospital was founded in Springfield, Massachusetts, in 1949 as a nonprofit voluntary corporation. It specialized in the treatment and rehabilitation of severely handicapped children. Of its 110-bed capacity, 88 were normally assigned to rehabilitative-care patients and 22 to acute-care cases. Rehabilitation for the Children's Memorial Hospital patients was necessarily a long-term process, averaging a stay of almost 140 days. Even the acute-care stay, 8 days, was relatively long at the hospital. The long, intensive hospitalization combined with the high daily cost of health services meant that few families could afford to pay for care directly. Thus children at Memorial were, for the most part, covered by some type of medical assistance from so-called third-party payers—primarily the State Medicaid Program and the Blue Cross Association. Blue Cross coverage normally did not extend to rehabilitation, and thus Medicaid was the principal form of coverage in such cases. Memorial's emphasis on rehabilitation care also meant that Medicaid welfare payments were the hospital's principal revenue source.[2] In fiscal year 1975, state welfare payments accounted for about 56 percent of Memorial's revenues, with another 22 percent coming from Blue

---

1. For additional background, see Children's Memorial Hospital (A).
2. Memorial recently had begun a day care program for severely handicapped children.

Cross. Other insurance plans provided 15 percent of total revenues, and the remainder, 7 percent, represented direct payments and the value of free service.

In fiscal year 1975, ending September 30, the hospital had total assets of almost $6 million (including $5.7 million in "unrestricted" and $.2 million in "restricted" or "earmarked" funds). Total patient revenues for the year were approximately $4.6 million, and the hospital experienced a net loss of more than $750,000, about three times the loss in fiscal year 1974. (See Exhibit 1 for financial statements and the auditor's letter.)

FINANCIAL DIFFICULTIES AND RESPONSES

State Budget Problems

Although the hospital's financial deterioration was substantial during fiscal year 1975, as noted earlier, hospital management was unaware of it. Rather, the pressing problem in the early fall 1975 was the prospect of extensive cutbacks in state spending for medical assistance (Medicaid).

In the summer of 1975, the governor and the state legislature had become so deeply concerned about the pace of health care costs and the impact of medical assistance spending on the state budget that they publicly committed themselves to severely limiting medical welfare payments in the fiscal year 1976 budget. Concern was so widespread that there was strong sentiment for an immediate freeze on such payments. Although this freeze was not implemented, the legislature did unequivocally signal its intentions. For example, the house chamber proposed a limit of $306 million for medical welfare assistance in fiscal year 1976, compared with payments of $510 million in the fiscal year 1975 budget and the governor's proposed budget of $570 million for such assistance in fiscal year 1976. As deliberations proceeded in the senate and in conference, the initial house proposal was revised upward. Ultimately, the legislature enacted, and the governor signed, a budget providing $410 million for welfare assistance—about 20 percent less than the prior year.

Because of Memorial's heavy reliance on state welfare assistance to its young patients and their families, the drastic cutbacks placed the hospital in a precarious situation during all the budget deliberations. It was conceivable to the hospital's board that state welfare payments to the hospital could drop by 90 percent during the coming year. Moreover, even into January 1976, the hospital administrators could not get a firm interpretation of budget policy with respect to the hospital's patients and their families. Because of this uncertainty, the hospital was unable to prepare and install a formal budget for fiscal year 1976 as much as five months into the fiscal year.

To evaluate the impact of a "worst-case" situation—in which medical assistance to Memorial's patients would be eliminated—the hospital's management prepared a tentative contingency plan in October, predicated on complete elimination of medical assistance to Memorial (Exhibit 2). After deducting noncontrollable costs, the projections indicated that only $900,000 would be left for payroll during the year, compared with $3.6 million of payroll expenses during fiscal year 1974. In such an eventuality, the hospital administration believed that shutdown would be unavoidable.

The potentially catastrophic impact of such reductions in the state budget compelled the hospital's administrators to determine as quickly as possible to what extent, if any, the hospital would be affected. The uncertainty necessarily held up formalization of the hospital's budget, and Memorial's management had little recourse but to start cutting back operations and laying off some employees. In addition, by the end of 1975 a moratorium was placed on remodeling and on the purchase of capital equipment, and a freeze was placed on all wages and hiring.

In February 1976 the hospital was finally notified that the budget cutbacks would not directly affect it. However, the hospital's executive director was also advised that sentiment was again building in the state and federal capitals for more stringent control of hospital charges. Retrenchment continued during February. One of the five units (including approximately 20 beds) at the hospital was closed down. The reduction in beds also changed the service "mix." Whereas previously the hospital had operated 88 rehabilitative and 22 acute-care beds, it now had 48 rehabilitative and 42 acute-care beds. Sixteen additional personnel had been laid off. A comparative report revealed that, at September 1974, the hospital had 342 full-time equivalent personnel. By September 1975 the figure was 362, but by March 1 it had dropped to 329. In addition, the hospital petitioned the Rate-Setting Commission for permission to increase rehabilitation and day care program charges.

Blue Cross Problems

As noted before, Blue Cross was Memorial's second major revenue source, principally providing acute-care coverage. In March 1976, Memorial heard from the Blue Cross Association that it was also deeply concerned over the continuing rise in health care costs. The association noted that the cost of its most popular form of coverage, the Master Medical Plan, had reached $1,400 per year in the Boston area, and that this cost would have to double by 1980 to keep pace with hospital charges. The letter pointed out, for example, that the average cost of nonmaternity inpatient claims was in excess of $1,200. Because health care costs were rising more rapidly than Blue Cross could increase its premiums, the association was experiencing substantial losses. Between

January 1974 and 1976, Blue Cross of Massachusetts had lost more than $50 million. The association letter pleaded with hospital administrators to continue cost-reduction efforts; if they didn't, the association might be unable to meet its commitments.

Rate Problems

Currently, Blue Cross—like other third-party payers—closely scrutinized hospital charges and paid for ("reimbursed") only costs that met predefined criteria of allowability. In many instances, full costs were not reimbursed by third-party payers if the costs fell out of the acceptable range. Over and above the control such third-party payers exercised over Memorial's charges, maximum permissible charges were fixed for hospital services by the State Rate-Setting Commission.

Rate-Setting Commission

Maximum rates for Memorial's revenue-generating activities—rehabilitative care, acute care, and day care—were fixed by the Rate-Setting Commission. Such rates were based on a combination of factors, notably the hospital's past costs for providing care and the degree of occupancy experienced and projected.

In September, at the end of Memorial's 1975 fiscal year, the Rate-Setting Commission notified the hospital that maximum allowable per-diem rates for rehabilitative and acute care would change for fiscal year 1976. The hospital's acute care per-diem rates would increase from $147.76 to $175.45. However, its rate for rehabilitative care would be decreased from $105.01 per diem to $95.03. As a consequence of its reduced allowable rates, Memorial's reimbursement from the State Welfare Program and Blue Cross would also change. Overall, for October 1975 alone, Memorial had to make a contractual adjustment of $25,000 in refunds to reflect the altered rates. Hospital administrators believed that this reduction would total $300,000 for the year as a whole. After petitioning the Rate-Setting Commission, the hospital was advised that some rate relief would be forthcoming for rehabilitative care retroactive to February 1, 1976.

Apart from the Rate-Setting Commission, Memorial had also been affected by the mandatory wage-price controls implemented by the Nixon administration between 1971 and 1974. As a result of the stringent controls placed on providers of health care services, the hospital had not been able to increase charges even though costs increased at a rate of 15 percent per year. From time to time, new attempts were being made in Washington, D.C., to regulate all health care providers, especially hospitals, closely.

FINANCIAL REPORTING PROBLEMS

Memorial's sizable and continuing losses severely drained liquidity from the organization. Net working capital, for example, was only $228,000 at year-end 1974. But by the end of fiscal year 1975, the hospital had *negative* net working capital in excess of $280,000. While the erosion of working capital certainly made itself felt in more frequent and greater cash shortages, the true erosion of operating performance was concealed from top management and the board of directors because of significant financial reporting errors.

Throughout the latter half of fiscal year 1975, the hospital board believed that Memorial was recovering rapidly from earlier difficulties, but in fact the hospital was slipping toward bankruptcy. For example, in May 1975 the board was informed that Memorial's year-to-date loss as of April was only $37,000, compared with an anticipated (budgeted) loss of $95,000 and an actual prior year-to-date loss of $211,000. At its September meeting, the board was informed that the August year-to-date loss was $75,000, compared with a prior year-to-date loss of $432,000. At the September board meeting there was a feeling of relief that the previous year's operating reversals had been contained.

In October and November, during the hospital's annual audit by its public accounting firm, some disturbing items surfaced. In the first week of November, the hospital's board was advised that the month of September had actually resulted in a loss of almost $90,000 instead of the breakeven earlier reported. The expected fiscal year loss was raised to at least $243,000. A week later, the auditors advised the board that further errors discovered would result in a loss of at least $570,000 for the year. By November 26, the auditors reported that the fiscal year loss would be more than $700,000 and that the hospital's financial situation should be considered critical. The auditors recommended a preliminary search for a merger partner for Memorial. Two weeks later, the hospital's director of fiscal affairs was fired and the finance function was put under direct control of the hospital's executive director.

The auditor's final report revealed a net loss of $762,000 for fiscal year 1975. Several of the adjustments required are itemized here:

1. *Free Service and Bad Debt Allowance* $165,000
   Although budgeted, a sufficient amount had not been set up in the reserve on a monthly basis to offset the necessary write-offs. The auditors strongly recommended further investigation of outstanding accounts receivable balances due from both welfare and parents, to determine if they were collectible or if a larger reserve should be set up in sufficient amounts to cover their possible write-off.
2. *Interest Adjustment* $130,000
   An adjustment to interest expense was necessary since the hospital accountant had capitalized interest rather than expensing it.

3. *Accounts Payable* $75,000

Department heads made a large number of purchases directly without advising the director of financial control. When the bills arrived for payment, the director simply stuffed them into a drawer unless he had approved the purchase request. This obscured substantial hospital liabilities.

4. *Depreciation Adjustment* $20,000

The hospital accountants had used a useful-life estimate of 50 years rather than the more appropriate basis of $33^1/_3$ years.

As a consequence of these discoveries, stringent financial controls were implemented, along with a new, more competent accounting and financial staff. The director also ordered more frequent and extensive internally developed financial reports. In addition, a financial consultant was hired to assist in financial planning.

CONSTRUCTION LOAN AND PROPOSED REFINANCING

Construction and Financing of New Wing

During fiscal year 1974, the construction of a new wing was completed. The wing had been added in part to accommodate increasing demand for hospital services, but also to conform with Health Department space requirements. It had been constructed with the financial assistance of a construction loan from the Mid-Town Savings Bank. The loan, of which $1.44 million was still outstanding at the end of fiscal year 1975, was collateralized by all the hospital's assets. Although Memorial's books showed the loan as a long-term loan to be amortized over 20 years, it had been understood that the construction loan would be refinanced on completion of the expansion. The exact terms of the construction loan were now somewhat vague, since Memorial did not have a copy of the loan agreement and since all principal parties in the loan negotiation at Memorial and the bank were no longer at either organization. It was clear, however, as the hospital's auditor confirmed, that several loan installments were skipped during fiscal year 1975, technically placing Memorial in default and making the entire loan subject to immediate call by the bank.

The construction of the facility was completed in September 1974 at a cost of approximately $2.5 million. During fiscal year 1975, the hospital representatives and the construction company thoroughly checked out various features of the new facility. To insure performance to requirements, Memorial had held back approximately $100,000 to be delivered to the construction company once the list of items was checked. By January 1976, the "retainage" was due since all construction contract performance had been met.

Mortgage Guarantee and Subsidy

Under the federal Hill-Burton Act, financial assistance was available for hospital construction. The assistance took the form of a mortgage guarantee and a 3-percent interest subsidy. These provisions were available only when the facility was operational and the hospital could certify that it was financially capable and sound enough to maintain operation of the new facility. In Memorial's case, a mortgage guarantee of $1.5 million would be available for a permanent mortgage, along with the interest rate subsidy if the hospital could secure a mortgage and certify its own financial strength.

Obtaining the mortgage was considered possible, even likely, by the hospital's administrators. They reasoned that the bank would definitely prefer a guaranteed mortgage to the current, unguaranteed loan. In fact, they speculated that the bank might even be willing to extend a mortgage of as much as $2.1 million, assuming that the guarantee of $1.5 million was in effect. Since the current bank loan was only about $1.4 million, a $2.1 million mortgage would provide enough working capital to pay some critically overdue obligations and support expected operating losses.

Such an infusion of working capital would also permit Memorial's executive director to certify that the hospital was financially strong enough to maintain the new facility, something not possible now. Major uses of such a working capital infusion would be to catch up on federal withholding tax payments; to pay off the long-standing retainage to the construction company; and to pay accounts payable that had been due since August 1975. (See Exhibit 3.)

Projections

In February 1976, Memorial prepared a projection of cash flow and net income for the fiscal year to end September 1976. (See Exhibits 4 and 5.) In contrast to the $762,000 loss in fiscal 1975, the 1976 projection (Exhibit 5) showed a moderate gain of $62,000. Net patient revenue was projected to grow by about $.5 million, but net operating expenses were actually projected to be slightly lower in fiscal 1976 than they had been in the previous year. The major factor in keeping expenses down was the projected clamp on salaries and wages, which were expected to show negligible growth during fiscal 1976. Although actual results as of January 31 (four months) had shown a loss of $242,000, the projections indicated a return to profitability in February and thenceforth.

The projected cash flow indicated that for the period from March to September 1976, the hospital would face a peak cash shortage of $800,000 in June, assuming payment to IRS of old withholding obligations and other pressing items shown in Exhibit 3. By the end of September 1976, the financing requirement would be down to $637,000, not including proceeds from the proposed refinancing.

Mortgage Proposal

According to calculations prepared by the hospital's financial consultant, the total expansion had a value of $2.5 million if valued at cost and of $2.7 million if valued on a current basis (Exhibit 6). Assuming Memorial could get mortgage financing up to 80 percent of value, the new mortgage would be $2 million if valued at cost and possibly $2.16 million if valued on a current basis. After paying off the existing construction loan of $1.44 million, the refinancing would generate between $560,000 and $720,000 in net working capital.

The consultant prepared three alternative refinancing plans for the hospital's board to consider (Exhibit 7). Since the plans differed in cost, loan maturity, and attractiveness to the bank, the board thought each should be carefully considered.

EXHIBIT 1
Auditor's Report

To the Governing Board of Children's Memorial Hospital, Inc.:

We have examined the balance sheet of Children's Memorial Hospital, Inc. (a nonprofit voluntary corporation organized in Massachusetts), as of September 30, 1975, and September 30, 1974, and the related statements of operations, changes in fund balances, and changes in financial position of unrestricted funds for the two years then ended. Our examination was made in accordance with generally accepted auditing standards, and accordingly included such tests of the accounting records and such other auditing procedures as we considered necessary in the circumstances.

As reflected in the accompanying financial statements, the hospital incurred net losses of $761,630 in 1975 and $252,890 in 1974. Unaudited information subsequent to September 30, 1975, indicates that losses are continuing. At September 30, 1975, the balance sheet reflected a net working capital deficiency of $284,326. The hospital is experiencing and expects to continue to experience significant cash flow problems. As a result of reductions in the level of welfare funds appropriated in the Commonwealth's fiscal 1976 budget and the lack of sufficient information concerning its impact on the hospital, management is unable to project the amount, if any, of the reduction in the level of future payments from the Commonwealth of Massachusetts Department of Public Welfare.

At September 30, 1975, the hospital was in arrears on payment of withheld employee payroll taxes and on principal and interest payments on its 8½-percent construction loan payable to a bank. As a result, the bank has the option to declare the entire sum due and payable. As of November 7, 1975, the bank had not exercised this option. Realization of the investment in plant and equipment ($3,822,896, shown in the accompanying balance sheet) depends on the success of future operations.

In view of the magnitude of the matters discussed in the preceding paragraph (per copy), we are unable to express, and we do not express, an opinion on the accompanying financial statements of Children's Memorial Hospital, Inc.

November 7, 1975

Children's Memorial Hospital
Statement of Operations
For the Years Ended September 30, 1975 and 1974

	1975	1974
Patient revenues		
Inpatient routine care	$2,297,745	$1,800,136
Outpatient charges	239,384	184,845
Ancillary charges	1,999,707	1,299,166
Day care program	416,880	413,592
	$4,953,716	$3,697,739
Less		
Contractual adjustments on agencies, municipalities, and Blue Cross accounts	$ 58,768	$ 76,318
Provision for doubtful accounts and free service to patients	260,170	60,876
	$ 318,938	$ 137,194
Net patient revenues	$4,634,778	$3,560,545
Operating expenses		
Salaries and wages (less physician–returned fees of $153,580 in 1975 and $170,567 in 1974)	$3,482,386	$2,859,006
Supplies and expenses	1,538,070	876,535
Depreciation	225,814	149,718
Interest expense	165,549	31,625
	$5,411,819	$3,916,884
Operating loss	$ (777,041)	$ (356,339)
Other income (expense)		
Cafeteria revenue	$ 33,253	$ 12,805
Unrestricted gifts, bequests, and contributions	20,193	34,468
Unrestricted investment income	36,719	71,049
Other	9,669	14,626
Fundraising expenses	(43,704)	(29,499)
Loss on sale of investments	(40,719)	—
	$ 15,411	$ 103,449
Net loss	$ (761,630)	$ (252,890)

EXHIBIT 1 (continued)
Children's Memorial Hospital
Balance Sheet as of September 30, 1975 and 1974
Unrestricted Funds

	1975	1974
Assets		
Current assets		
Cash in checking accounts	$ 66,959	$ 74,025
Cash in savings accounts	104,685	127,646
Certificates of deposit	260,000	200,598
Accounts receivable—patient care, less allowance of $166,100 in 1975 and $99,400 in 1974	992,952	707,862
Interest and other receivables	28,371	17,045
Inventories, at the lower of cost (first-in, first-out) or market	46,637	45,236
Prepaid expenses	36,683	35,033
Total current assets	$1,536,287	$1,207,445
Investments, at cost	$ 348,293	$ 461,611
Plant and equipment, at cost	$6,744,110	$6,436,406
Less accumulated depreciation	2,921,214	2,695,400
	$3,822,896	$3,741,006
	$5,707,476	$5,410,062
Liabilities		
Current liabilities		
Notes payable to a bank due on demand ($150,000) or by January 26, 1976 ($369,000), interest payable at 1% above prime rate	$ 519,000	$ 250,332
Current maturity of 8½% construction loan	43,700	—
Accounts payable, including construction payables of $110,000 in 1975 and $171,000 in 1974	1,020,329	587,339
Accrued expenses	237,584	141,340
Total current liabilities	$1,820,613	$ 979,011
8½% construction loan payable, in 240 equal monthly installments, less current maturity	$1,414,681	$1,484,014
Due to provincial house	548,703	479,530
Due to restricted funds	58,053	11,919
Commitments and contingencies		
Fund balance	1,865,426	2,455,588
	$5,707,476	$5,410,062

EXHIBIT 1 (continued)
Children's Memorial Hospital
Balance Sheet as of September 30, 1975 and 1974
Restricted Funds

	1975	1974		1975	1974
Assets			**Liabilities**		
Cash	$ —	$ 40,967	Research fund balance	$192,370	$184,669
Cash in savings banks	32,970	32,970	Special purpose fund balance	18,653	15,748
Certificates of deposit	120,000	113,533			
Accrued interest	—	1,028			
Due from unrestricted funds	58,053	11,919			
	$211,023	$200,417		$211,023	$200,417

EXHIBIT 2
Children's Memorial Hospital
Contingency Plan in View of Drastic Cuts in the State Budget
October 3, 1975

Attached is part of the *First Draft of a Contingency Plan*. We will have additional information for you Wednesday, October 8, at the board meeting.

The *income projections* are predicated on the worst coming to pass, namely, complete elimination of medical assistance in the state budget. This is as voted by the House of Representatives. There is still some hope of funds being restored by the Senate. However, this is not certain; and, even if funds are restored, they will still leave the total for this area far below the governor's original budget, which was set at a minimum.

Fixed expenses have been carefully calculated. *Fringe benefits* are stated as accurately as possible; this figure will fluctuate according to the number of personnel laid off.

When these items are deducted from our anticipated income of $2,282,404, there is a remainder of only $1,125,604. Past experience indicates that supplies and other expenses average 20 percent of this amount. Thus only $900,484 is left for payroll. During 1974 and 1975, payroll totaled $3.6 million.

At this point in our analysis, we see no way to cut our payroll by $2,699,516. We would have to close.

However, since we have painted the blackest picture and since we have not yet started to work on means of possibly increasing income by rendering service in a different way, we decided to approach the problem in two steps. *Step 1* would include the following:

1. Moratorium on all remodeling, capital equipment, travel, and education expenses
2. No cost-of-living or merit raises
3. Reduction of the payroll by layoff, thus reducing this expense by approximately $1.35 million

Last evening, we started the analysis to effect number 3. Our first proposals resulted in a reduction of approximately $900,000. This was based on closing two of the rehabilitation units. Today, we started to cut by laying off in public relations, security, and recreational therapy. We will continue to work on this, bringing our recommendations to the board on Wednesday.

Sorry to bring you such bad news; however, we continue to pray, work, and hope.

EXHIBIT 2 (continued)
Children's Memorial Hospital
First Draft of Contingency Plan, 10/1/75

	Actual	Projected	
	1974–1975	1975–1976	Difference
I. Analysis			
A. Income			
Welfare	$2,451,352	$ 245,135	$(2,206,217)
Blue Cross	961,171	1,036,171	75,000
Insurance	651,098	701,098	50,000
Other	324,968	300,000	(24,968)
Total	$4,388,589	$2,282,404	$(2,106,185)
B. Deduct fixed expenses		$ 652,800	
Remainder		$1,629,604	
C. Deduct fringe benefits		$ 504,000	
Remainder		$1,125,604	
D. Deduct supplies and other expenses (20% of C)		$ 225,120	
E. Deduct payroll			
Remainder	$3,600,000	$ 900,484	$(2,699,516)
		0	

II. Plan of action
(Still in progress)

EXHIBIT 3
Children's Memorial Hospital
Proposed Disposition of Net Cash to Be Received from the Refinancing

1. Payment to date of all federal withholding and FICA taxes owed to Internal Revenue Service (approximately)	$392,000.00
2. Payment to HBE* of retainage in full	101,000.00
3. Down payment for new insurance effective March 1976	30,000.00
4. Pay in full all Accounts Payable outstanding through August 1975 and apply balance to September 1975 bills	86,000.00
5. Partial payments of some more current payables	?

* Hospital Building Equipment Company

EXHIBIT 4
Children's Memorial Hospital
Projected Cash Flow
March 1, 1976, through June 30, 1976
(In $000)

	March 1976	April 1976	May 1976	June 1976	Total 3/1/76–6/30/76
Opening cash balance	$201[1]	$ 148	$(548)	$(597)	$ 201
Add receipts					
From operations	426	475	485	275	1,661
Development income	16	40	30	15	101
Physicians' returned fees	14	16	16	16	62
From restricted funds	—	1	2	2	5
Cafeteria income	8	8	8	8	32
Investment income	2	2	2	2	8
Total receipts	$466	$ 542	$ 543	$ 318	$1,869
Total cash available	$667	$ 690	$ (5)	$(279)	$2,070
Free cash					
Less disbursements					
Payroll and payroll taxes	$290	$ 412	$ 273	$ 273	$1,248
Old payroll taxes	—	392	—	—	392
Accounts payable regular	214	300	250	150	914
Accounts payable HBE	—	74	—	27	101
Mortgage payment, net	13	13	14	14	54
Other interest expense	2	2	—	2	6
Capital and contingency	—	—	10	10	20
Total disbursements	$519	$1,193	$ 547	$ 476	$2,735
Closing cash balance	$148	$ (503)	$(552)	$(755)	$ (665)
Less BC/BS "escrow"	—	45	45	45	135
Adjusted cash balance	$148	$ (548)	$(597)	$(800)	$ (800)

1. Excludes $100K of cash in savings account being used as collateral for $100K loan from bank.

EXHIBIT 4 (continued)
Projected Cash Flow
Fourth Quarter 1976
(In $000)

	July 1976	August 1976	Sept. 1976	Total 4th Quarter	Total 3/1/76–9/30/76
Opening cash balance	$(800)	$(635)	$(524)	$ (800)	$ 201
Add receipts					
From operations	638	543	485	1,666	3,327
Development income	5	5	5	15	116
Physicians' returned fees	16	16	16	48	110
From restricted funds	10	10	10	30	35
Cafeteria income	8	8	8	24	56
Investment income	2	2	2	6	14
Total receipts	$ 679	$ 584	$ 526	$1,789	$3,658
Total cash available	$(121)	$(51)	$ 2	$ 989	$3,859
Less disbursements					
Payroll and payroll taxes	$ 283	$ 283	$ 429	$ 995	$2,243
Old payroll taxes	–	–	–	–	392
Accounts payable regular	150	110	130	390	1,304
Accounts payable HBE	–	–	–	–	101
Mortgage payment, net	14	14	14	42	96
Other interest expense	2	1	1	4	10
Capital and contingency	20	20	20	60	80
Total disbursements	$ 469	$ 428	$ 594	$1,491	$4,226
Closing cash balance	$(590)	$(479)	$(592)	$ (502)	$ (367)
Less BC/BS "escrow"	45	45	45	135	270
Adjusted cash balance	$(635)	$(524)	$(637)	$ (637)	$ (637)

EXHIBIT 5
Children's Memorial Hospital
Projected Statement of Operations
First Six Months Ending 3/31/76
(In $000)

	Actual Year to Date 10/1/75–1/31/76	Projected		Total 6 Months to 1/31/76
		Feb. 1976	Mar. 1976	
Revenue				
Routine services	$ 842	$331	$350	$1,523
Special services	724	231	250	1,205
Day care program	178	45	45	268
Gross revenue	$1,744	$607	$645	$2,996
Less				
Contractual adjustments	$ 97	$177	$190	$ 464
Provision for bad debts	38	9	9	56
Free service	37	11	11	59
Total allowances	$ 172	$197	$210	$ 579
Net patient revenue	$1,572	$410	$435	$2,417
Expenses				
Salaries and wages	$1,322	$299	$295	$1,916
Supplies and other	554	120	130	804
Depreciation	80	20	20	120
Interest	69	15	16	100
Total expense	$2,025	$454	$461	$2,940

EXHIBIT 5 (continued)

	Actual Year to Date 10/1/75–1/31/76	Projected		Total 6 Months to 1/31/76
		Feb. 1976	Mar. 1976	
Expense recovery				
Miscellaneous	$ 23	$ 6	$ 6	$ 35
Physicians' returned fees	80	14	14	108
Total recovery	$ 103	$ 20	$ 20	$ 143
Net operating expenses	$1,922	$434	$441	$2,797
Gain or (loss) from operations	$ (350)	$(24)	$ (6)	$ (380)
Other income				
Gain or (loss) on sale of investment	$ 7	$ 5	$ —	$ 12
Investment income	13	2	2	17
Cafeteria income	10	2	2	14
Development income	55	31*	16	102
Miscellaneous	23	4	—	27
Total other income	$ 108	$ 44	$ 20	$ 172
Net income (loss)	$ (242)	$ 20	$ 14	$ (208)

* Includes a one-time special contribution relating to a three-party settlement of old obligations.

424

EXHIBIT 5 (continued)

Projected Statement of Operations

Third Quarter

(In $000)

	Apr. 1976	May 1976	June 1976	Total 3rd Quarter
Revenue				
Routine services	$367	$367	$367	$1,101
Special services	265	265	265	795
Day care program	45	45	40	130
Gross revenue	$677	$677	$672	$2,026
Less				
Contractual adjustments	$190	$190	$180	$ 560
Provisions for bad debts	9	9	9	27
Free service	11	11	11	33
Total allowances	$210	$210	$200	$ 620
Net patient revenue	$467	$467	$472	$1,406
Expenses				
Salaries and wages	$288	$290	$288	$ 866
Supplies and other	134	134	132	400
Depreciation	20	20	20	60
Interest	15	15	15	45
Total expense	$457	$459	$455	$1,371

EXHIBIT 5 (continued)

	Apr. 1976	May 1976	June 1976	Total 3rd Quarter
Expense recovery				
Miscellaneous	$ 6	$ 6	$ 6	$ 18
Physicians' returned fees	16	16	16	48
Total recovery	$ 22	$ 22	$ 22	$ 66
Operating expense	$435	$437	$433	$1,305
Gain or (loss) from operations	$ 32	$ 30	$ 39	$ 101
Other income				
Gain or (loss) on sale of investment	$ —	$ —	$ —	$ —
Investment income	2	2	2	6
Cafeteria income	2	2	2	6
Development income				
Miscellaneous	40	30	15	85
Total other income	$ 44	$ 34	$ 19	$ 97
Net income (loss)	$ 76	$ 64	$ 58	$ 198

EXHIBIT 5 (continued)
Projected Statement of Operations
Fourth Quarter
(In $000)

	July 1976	August 1976	Sept. 1976	Total 4th Quarter	Total Year
Revenue					
Routine services	$367	$367	$367	$1,101	$3,725
Special services	263	263	263	789	2,789
Day care program	–	–	60	60	458
Gross revenue	$630	$630	$690	$1,950	$6,972
Less					
Contractual adjustments	$175	$175	$185	$ 535	$1,559
Provisions for bad debts	9	9	9	27	110
Free service	11	11	11	33	125
Total allowances	$195	$195	$205	$ 595	$1,794
Net patient revenue	$435	$435	$485	$1,355	$5,178
Expenses					
Salaries and wages	$290	$290	$308	$ 888	$3,670
Supplies and other	126	126	131	383	1,587
Depreciation	20	20	20	60	240
Interest	15	15	15	45	190
Total expense	$451	$451	$474	$1,376	$5,687

EXHIBIT 5 (continued)

	July 1976	August 1976	Sept. 1976	Total 4th Quarter	Total Year
Expense recovery					
Miscellaneous	$ 6	$ 6	$ 6	$ 18	$ 71
Physicians' returned fees	16	16	16	48	204
Total recovery	$ 22	$ 22	$ 22	$ 66	$ 275
Operating expense	$429	$429	$452	$1,310	$5,412
Gain (or loss) from operations	$ 6	$ 6	$ 33	$ 45	$ (234)
Other income					
Gain (or loss) on sale of investment	$ —	$ —	$ —	$ —	$ 12
Investment income	2	2	2	6	29
Cafeteria income	2	2	2	6	26
Development income	5	5	5	15	202
Miscellaneous					27
Total other income	$ 9	$ 9	$ 9	$ 27	$ 296
Net income (loss)	$ 15	$ 15	$ 42	$ 72	$ 62

EXHIBIT 6
Children's Memorial Hospital
Alternate Bases of Valuation
New Facilities, Land, and Parking Lot
(Excluding Contents)

	Cost Basis	Current Value
Building only	$2,350,000	$2,520,000
Add 2½ acres at $60,000	150,000[1]	150,000
Add restored parking area	25,000[2]	25,000
Various	(25,000)	5,000
	$2,500,000	$2,700,000

[1] The values listed were based on conversations with the general contractors for the addition under construction at Williams' Hospital. The president of United Construction Corporation has in his possession a formal appraisal for the land near the hospital. Five acres were appraised at $300,000, or $60,000 an acre. The appraisal was made within the last few years.

[2] The president of United Construction Corporation also said that an appropriate value for a reconditioned parking lot would be approximately $25,000, based on the following calculations. Parking for approximately 150 cars requires approximately 550 square yards at $50 per square yard, which equals a total of $27,500. Offset the cost of fencing, curbing, etc., by the fact that restored is not fully equivalent to new; thus use $25,000 as fair value.

EXHIBIT 7
Children's Memorial Hospital
Possible Ways of Restructuring Mortgage Debt
Mid-Town Savings Bank
Plan A
9% for 25 years

	FACTOR	AMOUNT	
Total cost of addition		$ 2,500,000	1
Less Memorial equity	20%	500,000	2
Gross permanent mortgage	80%	2,000,000	3
Construction loan balance		1,440,000	4
Gross proceeds to Memorial		$ 560,000	5
			6
Interest cost only, permanent mortgage: month		–	7
1 year		–	8
2 years		–	9
			10
Amount required to prepay 2 years' interest		–	11
			12
Net proceeds to Memorial		$ 560,000	13
Add back Hill-Burton interest subsidy			14
(2 years at 3% of $1,500,000)		–	15
Net cash benefit to Memorial over 2 years		–	16
			17
Monthly amortization	0.008392	$ 16,784	18
Less Hill-Burton interest subsidy		$ 4,500	19
Net Memorial monthly payment		$ 12,284	20
			21
Present monthly payment by Memorial			22
(as of 11/75, $10,308.39 interest + $3,002.61 principal)		$ 13,311	23
			24
Mid-Town Savings Bank cash position			25
Current construction loan balance		$ 1,440,000	26
Net added cash to Memorial		560,000	27
Adjusted Mid-Town Savings Bank cash position		$ 2,000,000	28
			29
U.S. government mortgage guarantee		$ 1,500,000	30
			31
ASSUMPTION: Convert to 25-year permanent mortgage, amortizing over			32
25 years.			33

EXHIBIT 7 (continued)

Plan B

8½% for 2 years plus 23 years

	FACTOR	AMOUNT	
1	Total cost of addition		$ 2,500,000	1
2	Less Memorial equity	20%	500,000	2
3	Gross permanent mortgage	80%	$ 2,000,000	3
4	Construction loan balance		1,440,000	4
5	Gross proceeds to Memorial		560,000	5
6				6
7	Interest cost only, permanent mortgage: month	0.708333%	$ 14,167	7
8	1 year	8.5%	$ 170,000	8
9	2 years	17.0%	$ 340,000	9
10				10
11	Amount required to prepay 2 years' interest	1.184595	$ 287,000	11
12		rounded		12
13	Net proceeds to Memorial		$ 273,000	13
14	Add back Hill-Burton interest subsidy			14
15	(2 years at 3% of $1,500,000)		90,000	15
16	Net cash benefit to Memorial over 2 years		$ 363,000	16
17				17
18	Monthly amortization, at month 25	0.008261	$ 16,522	18
19	Less Hill-Burton interest subsidy, at month 25		$ 4,500	19
20	Net Memorial monthly payment, at month 25		$ 12,022	20
21				21
22	Present monthly payment by Memorial			22
23	(as of 11/75, $10,308.39 interest + $3,002.61 principal)		$ 13,311	23
24				24
25	Mid-Town Savings Bank cash position			25
26	Current construction loan balance		$ 1,440,000	26
27	Net added cash to Memorial		273,000	27
28	Adjusted Mid-Town Savings Bank cash position		$ 1,713,000	28
29				29
30	U.S. government mortgage guarantee		$ 1,500,000	30
31				31
32	ASSUMPTIONS: Convert to 25-year permanent mortgage paying interest			32
33	only for first two years, amortizing balance over 23			33
34	years. Prepay first two years' interest, taking pre-			34
35	sent value at same interest rate.			35
36				36
37				37
38				38
39				39
40				40

EXHIBIT 7 (continued)
Plan C
9% for 2 years plus 23 years

	FACTOR	AMOUNT
1. Total cost of addition		$ 2,700,000
2. Less Memorial equity	20%	540,000
3. Gross permanent mortgage	80%	$ 2,160,000
4. Construction loan balance		1,440,000
5. Gross proceeds to Memorial		$ 720,000
6.		
7. Interest cost only, permanent mortgage: month	0.750000%	$ 16,200
8. 1 year	9.0%	$ 194,440
9. 2 years	18.0%	$ 388,800
10.		
11. Amount required to prepay 2 years' interest	1.196414	$ 325,000
12.	rounded	
13. Net proceeds to Memorial		$ 395,000
14. Add back Hill-Burton interest subsidy		
15. (2 years at 3% of $1,500,000)		90,000
16. Net cash benefit to Memorial over 2 years		$ 485,000
17.		
18. Monthly amortization, at month 25	0.008593	$ 18,560
19. Less Hill-Burton interest subsidy, at month 25		$ 4,500
20. Net Memorial monthly payment, at month 25		$ 14,060
21.		
22. Present monthly payment by Memorial		
23. (as of 11/75, $10,308.39 interest + $3,002.61 principal)		$ 13,311
24.		
25. Mid-Town Savings Bank cash position		
26. Current construction loan balance		$ 1,440,000
27. Net added cash to Memorial		395,000
28. Adjusted Mid-Town Savings Bank cash position		$ 1,835,000
29.		
30. U.S. government mortgage guarantee		$ 1,500,000
31.		
32. ASSUMPTIONS: Convert to 25-year permanent mortgage paying interest		
33. only for first two years, amortizing balance over 23		
34. years. Prepay first two years' interest, taking pre-		
35. sent value at same interest rate.		

Hammond Publishing Company

In June 1967 Mr. George Hammond, president and principal owner of Hammond Publishing Company, considered several financing alternatives affecting the company's capital structure and possibly its shareholder composition. Hammond Publishing Company had grown rapidly in the several preceding years and its need for funds now outstripped the company's internal supplies. Specifically, Mr. Hammond weighed issuing stock against issuing additional long-term debt. At the same time he wondered whether he should continue to hold the majority of the shares of the company, or indeed any shares at all.

COMPANY DESCRIPTION

Although Hammond Publishing Company was relatively small by industry standards, it carried out the complete range of activities associated with publishing, including the search for and selection of authors, evaluation and editing of manuscripts, design and illustration of publications, and promotion, sale, and distribution of books. Published books fell into four general classes: fiction, nonfiction, school and college texts, and professional books. Company activities were carried out from a modern one-story combined office and warehouse building located in San Mateo, California. Since the company had recently completed a staff and warehouse expansion program, management felt Hammond Publishing could easily handle a higher level of sales than it was then experiencing. Hammond did not own printing or binding facilities. While no long-term agreements for printing or binding services were in effect, it was clear that through careful advance scheduling the company could arrange for the provision of adequate services.

The company employed about 310 people. Of these, 21 were executives and department heads; approximately 30 were engaged in editorial work; about 50 were in sales, promotion, and publicity; approximately 130 were in clerical and office work; and approximately 80 were engaged in shipping and warehousing activities. The company was governed by no collective bargaining agreements. On the whole, the company's employee relations were good. Authors were compensated by royalties at various rates on books sold. In accordance with standard industry practice the company extended royalty advances to authors while manuscripts were being prepared or revised.

Hammond Publishing Company was established by Mr. Hammond's father late in the 1800s. Growth was slow through its early years, most occurring after World War II. For many years Hammond's publications consisted primarily of fiction and nonfiction works of broad interest for both adults and children that reached the public through retail book stores and libraries. In the late 1950s the company expanded into the elementary, high school, and college market, primarily through the development of a series of related books for elementary schools and the development of supplemental information books for use with standard high school and college textbooks.

The greater part of the company's works of fiction and nonfiction and a portion of its children's books were sold directly through the company's retail sales force through wholesalers to retail book stores and department stores throughout the country. Sales to local school boards and libraries were made by a second segment of the company's sales force and also by an independent sales agency. The third part of the company's sales force was composed of "travelers." These men were responsible for the selling of both college textbooks and college supplementary books. As a large part of the job they also solicited manuscripts and maintained relationships with college book authors.

EXPECTED GROWTH

Hammond Publishing Company expected to continue growing faster than the industry, and expected sales to increase by over 30 percent in 1967. This sales growth would be due both to the capture of sales of other firms and to the broadly based rise in book sales. No reason for future slackening in company growth was foreseeable, although a 30 percent annual rise could not be sustained indefinitely.

Between 1965 and 1966 total book sales in the nation rose 15 percent to 2.3 billion dollars. A similar jump was expected for 1966–1967 with a large part of this growth expected to come in textbooks, the most important segment of the industry. Since the rise in school and college enrollments was expected to continue for at least the next ten years (see Exhibit 1) with the trend to the future toward more general and larger educational exposure per person, and since per capita annual book expenditures in 1966 were $5.92 in grammar school, $10.16 in high school and $36.49 in college, it was easy to conclude that textbook sales would increase faster than the 20 percent figure attained in 1965–1966.

The public mood encouraged such feelings. In 1966 federal expenditures for educational purposes reached unprecedented levels. Sales of books other than textbooks were also on the upswing, benefiting from libraries and schools having new buying power from federal funds. Sales were also stimulated by population growth, upgraded reading tastes, and higher disposable incomes.

THE NEED FOR EXTERNAL FUNDS

The company's need for funds derived from sales growth. (See Exhibit 2 for income statements for 1964-1966.) Between the years 1964 and 1965 sales grew by over 30 percent. In 1966 sales growth was 35 percent. Mr. Hammond was convinced that growth in the neighborhood of this rate would continue. The principal need for funds was to finance growth of accounts receivable and inventory supporting increasing sales, but funds were also used for printing plates and royalty advances. (Exhibit 4 shows sources and uses of funds for 1964-1965 and 1965-1966.) Year-end figures in the exhibits do not reflect seasonal influences. Accounts receivable and inventory were higher in the summer and autumn due to the larger percentage of sales made at this time of year. Some 62 percent of company sales took place in the months of June, July, August, and September. Traditionally, the seasonal need for funds had been met through short-term borrowing.

A large part of the additional funds requirements in 1965 and 1966 were financed by deferral of royalty payments. Under the provisions of federal income tax law, it was to the advantage of authors to spread the income received from a publication over a period of years. The maximum period permissible was three years. When such deferrals were made the company was enabled, in essence, to finance a portion of its requirements thereby. If the allowable period of deferral were ever reduced, or if for some reason a substantial number of authors demanded their royalty payments at one time, fund outflows would be occasioned, possibly in large amounts.

During 1966 funds supplied by deferral of royalties dropped from the preceding year's level, and partly in consequence the company was forced to borrow over $1.5 million in short-term loans from the Valley Trust Company. These notes were due on September 1, 1967. Although the loans could possibly be renewed this was not a permanent answer. It seemed unlikely that internal sources could provide the needed funds. Inventories were as low as could be comfortably tolerated. Accounts receivable had been increased relative to sales as a competitive necessity. Profit margins in the industry would not change appreciably in the foreseeable future, and at a level of about 35 days' purchases the company's accounts payable were extended about as far as could be expected. Thus, it seemed that it would be necessary to tap external sources of permanent funds.

POSSIBILITIES OF ADDITIONAL EQUITY

One possible means of raising equity was through an underwritten public stock flotation. In recent stock flotations of other publishing firms (see Exhibit 5) the total of the underwriter's spread (the difference between the amount raised by the underwriter of an issue and the amount remitted to the issuing company) and the "out-of-pocket" costs involved in the flotation varied between 5.3 percent and 8.3 percent of the total issue. Most of this total, perhaps 80 percent, was made up of the underwriter's spread. The remaining direct costs involved in an issue, such as printing, registration, and legal fees, were partially variable and might well total $40,000 on a $4 million public issue. Market price per share at issue in the publishing flotations shown in Exhibit 5 ranged between $15 and $34. Price/earnings ratios at issue varied between 14 and 26.

Some preliminary discussions took place with Mr. Harry Cameron, a senior partner in the underwriting and brokerage firm of Riley and Liggett. From these discussions, it was apparent that a number of warrants equal to 20 percent of the number of shares in an initial public offering would almost certainly be required by the underwriter in return for his support of the "after-market." The warrants would be exercisable for five years at the offering price of the first issue. Support for the after-market would be desirable in the case of Hammond Publishing shares since the company would almost certainly have its shares traded over-the-counter. In the first few months of such trading the market might prove to be a "thin" one and it is here that the underwriter could help maintain the market by being willing to buy and sell for his own account. In supporting the after-market, an underwriter, in effect, becomes an active participant in stock trading in order to preserve an active market in the stock being supported. Through his actions, drastic swings in stock prices are avoided in the period immediately following the stock issue.

Several months would be required for preparation of the issue by the underwriter and registration of the issue with the Securities and Exchange Commission.

A second alternative in raising equity was to use an underwriter's help in finding a private party or parties able to supply a suitable amount of funds, for example a pension fund. In this case the company would remain closely held. Such an alternative had several advantages. A private issue could be carried out faster and would be cheaper than a public issue. There would be an underwriter's fee of perhaps half a point. Potential dilution of the warrants would be eliminated. Also, private placement might reduce subsequent problems of stockholder relations since there would be fewer stockholders involved.

Mr. Hammond owned 15,000 of the 25,000 outstanding shares of the company. With most of his personal estate invested in Hammond Publishing he could not invest any further sizable sum in the company. The remaining 10,000 shares were held among Mr. Hammond's relatives. These holdings represented a large part of the wealth of the various individuals in most instances.

The most compelling argument for public sale involved Mr. Hammond's personal estate. Since he was nearing 60 years of age such matters were of increasing importance to him. In addition to providing for his wife in the event of his death, Mr. Hammond was desirous of establishing a trust fund for his grandchildren. From tax data (see Exhibit 6) he concluded that a public market in Hammond Publishing shares would almost certainly reduce the Internal Revenue Service valuation of his estate by a substantial amount. A lower valuation would reduce estate taxes.

A public market would also provide Mr. Hammond with liquidity for his holdings. At the present time there was no established value for Hammond Publishing shares and no trading in its shares. By longstanding agreement shareholders sold to the company when divesting themselves of holdings of Hammond stock. The price involved in such transactions was the book value per share. The book value of Mr. Hammond's shares was about $2.5 million.

In the past the company declared dividends at irregular intervals. A declaration was usually made when one or more of the shareholders had large fund needs. Hammond's management felt that if a public market in Hammond Publishing shares were made the company would establish some consistent dividend policy and could not be as arbitrary as heretofore.

An alternative that combined the advantages of a public offering for the company and provided liquidity directly for present shareholders was to combine the sale of new shares with currently outstanding shares in a public sale. If some of the shares now closely held were added to new ones in a public flotation, the size of the public market would be increased. The sale of some of his shares would provide funds for Mr. Hammond's retirement or, in the event of his death, for the payment of estate taxes that would then fall due.

OTHER POSSIBILITIES

Floating long-term debt was a practicable alternative to raising new equity. From informal conversations with executives of other publishing firms of approximately the same size, Mr. Hammond was certain that he could negotiate a loan of about $2 million, assuming the bank notes had been paid off, without additional equity funds being added. Such loans were often made by the small loan departments of life insurance companies and other institutional lenders. A loan larger than $2 million would be improbable without the sale of new company stock and certainly would be much more expensive if it could be raised at all. Apparently, most lenders would insist that about $2 of equity be added for each dollar of long-term debt above the $2 million level. A total long-term debt ceiling of about $4 million would apply. Likely provisions in connection with a loan in the region of $2 million would be an annual amortization of about $300,000 starting within one year, an interest rate of about 7.5 percent, reflecting the high interest rates still in effect following the 1966 "credit crunch," a net working capital restriction requiring the maintenance of $1 million minimum, and a partial restriction on dividends. The condition most likely to be imposed was a restriction that dividends could be paid on only 35 percent of the net earnings subsequent to the date of the loan.

Yet another alternative was the merger of Hammond Publishing into a larger concern. Mr. Hammond had been approached about a corporate merger several times during the preceding five years, but he resisted each effort, feeling that he wanted to "run his own show." However, the increasing premiums being paid for publishing companies gave him a pause. During the past few years many publishing companies merged into electronic giants and some of the latter were known to be still actively searching for publishing acquisitions. Two recent examples of such acquisitions (see Exhibit 7) were RCA's purchase of Random House in which two dollars were paid for each dollar of assets, and International Telephone and Telegraph's payment of $50 a share for Howard Sams, although at that time Sams sold for $30 on the open market. Other merger possibilities were with larger publishers. One offer still open to him was made by the publisher of a large national weekly news magazine. In exchange for all outstanding shares of Hammond, the larger company offered to provide an amount of its common stock with a market value of approximately $24.2 million.

Merger offered several advantages. First, the transaction would be tax-free if carried out by means of an exchange of shares. Second, since the exchange would presumably be made with a large company whose shares were listed on a national exchange, valuation and liquidity problems connected with Mr. Hammond's estate would be eliminated. Finally, a merger would solve the problem of management succession and a buyer for Hammond Publishing Company in one transaction and at a time favorable to Mr. Hammond. Other owners of the company were willing to participate in a merger if the price was satisfactory.

On the other hand, there were several disadvantages to a merger. The plans might miscarry after the expenditure of much time and effort. Mr. Hammond remembered the comments he had read concerning the cancellation of a merger, agreed to two months before, between a publisher of business and economics texts and a very large periodical publisher. The president of the larger concern said, "[The smaller company's officials] ran into some difficulties in trying to agree on how their operations would be carried on as a division of [the larger company]. I think this is understandable in a company which has been developed largely by one man and has been run as a privately operated organization for most of its history." The chairman of the board of the smaller company, on the other hand, said in his letter to the stockholders that the merger was called off as "not being in the best interest of [the] employees or stockholders." Also, he said, contrary to some reports regarding the proposed merger, 'the . . . firm is not a family-owned corporation operated by just one individual. . . .''

Merger would mean the loss of control of the company by its present owners. A merger might not be successful and might result in the subsequent resale of Hammond Publishing to a second buyer. Whether successful or not, a merger might well result in a restructuring of the company and the release of long-term loyal employees.

EXHIBIT 1
Hammond Publishing Company
Projected Educational Enrollment in U.S.
1966–1975
(In thousands)

Year	Projected Fall Enrollment in Grades K–12 of Regular Day Schools	Projected Fall Degree Credit Enrollment in All Institutions of Higher Education
1966	49,700	6,055
1967	50,700	6,541
1968	51,500	6,923
1969	52,000	7,050
1970	52,300	7,299
1971	52,600	7,604
1972	52,600	7,976
1973	52,800	8,335
1974	53,100	8,684
1975	53,600	8,995

SOURCE: Projections of Educational Statistics to 1975–76, U.S. Dept. of Health, Education and Welfare, 1966.

EXHIBIT 2
Hammond Publishing Company
Income Statements
Years Ended Dec. 31, 1964–1966
(Dollar Figures in Thousands)

	1964		1965		1966	
Sales		$8,562		$11,437		$15,648
Less returns and discounts		945		1,257		1,425
Net sales		$7,617		$10,180		$14,223
Cost of sales						
Royalties	$1,368		$1,775		$2,585	
Other	2,374	3,742	3,343	5,118	4,346	6,931
Gross profit		$3,875		$ 5,062		$ 7,292
Expenses						
Selling	$ 862		$1,141		$1,402	
Administrative	1,683		1,938		2,299	
Other	836	3,381	1,222	4,301	1,908	5,609
Operating profit		$ 494		$ 761		$ 1,683
Interest expense		12		14		62
Income before taxes		$ 482		$ 747		$ 1,621
Federal income taxes		181		304		803
Net income		$ 301		$ 443		$ 818

EXHIBIT 3
Hammond Publishing Company
Balance Sheets
As of Dec. 31, 1964–1966
(Dollar Figures in Thousands)

	1964	1965	1966
Assets			
Cash	$ 596	$ 627	$ 846
Accounts receivable, net	841	1,854	3,427
Inventory	2,190	2,820	3,774
Prepaid expenses	74	91	157
Total current assets	$3,701	$5,392	$ 8,204
Plant and equipment	2,183	2,370	2,637
Less reserve for depreciation	371	435	515
Net plant and equipment	$1,812	$1,935	$ 2,122
Plates at amortized cost	395	532	718
Royalty advances	678	894	1,239
Miscellaneous assets	680	757	754
Total other assets	$1,753	$2,183	$ 2,711
Total assets	$7,266	$9,510	$13,037
Liabilities and stockholders' equity			
Notes payable	$ 30	$ 35	$ 1,575
Accounts payable	317	478	671
Other accruals	215	363	868
Royalties due in current year	1,059	1,644	2,189
Total current liabilities	$1,621	$2,520	$ 5,303
Mortgage notes less current portion	1,099	1,047	995
Royalties due after one year	1,562	2,504	2,463
Deferred taxes	42	54	73
Total long-term liabilities	$2,703	$3,605	$ 3,531
Common stock, $15 par value, authorized 25,000 shares, issued and outstanding 25,000 shares	375	375	375
Retained earnings	2,567	3,010	3,828
Stockholders' equity	$2,942	$3,385	$ 4,203
Total liabilities and stockholders' equity	$7,266	$9,510	$13,037

EXHIBIT 4
Hammond Publishing Company
Funds Flows
1965–1966
(In Thousands of Dollars)

	1965	1966
Operations		
Net operating income	$ 761	$1,683
Change in accumulated depreciation	64	80
Funds from operations	$ 825	$1,763
Tax flows		
Tax accrued	(304)	(803)
Tax deferred	12	19
Funds required by taxes	$ (292)	$ (784)
Asset account changes		
Net working capital (excluding cash)	(761)	190
Capital assets	(187)	(267)
Other assets	(430)	(528)
Funds required for investment	$(1,378)	$ (605)
Funds profile before financing	$ (845)	$ 374
Financing		
Interest expense	(14)	(62)
Reduction of mortgage	(52)	(52)
Change in royalties due after one year	942	(41)
Net funds provided and used by financing	$ 876	$ (155)
Net changes in cash	(31)	(219)
Net change in financing and cash	$ 845	$ (374)

EXHIBIT 5
Hammond Publishing Company
Selected Equity Flotations of Publishing Firms
1960–1967

Company Name	Issue Date	Size of Issue ($000)	Number of Shares Involved	Underwriting Cost ($000) (Underwriter's Spread and "Out-of-pocket" Costs)	Total Underwriting Cost per Share as % of Total Issue Cost	Market Price at Issue ($)	Price/ Earnings at Issue	Proportion of Issue Representing New Financing (%)
Harper & Row*	Feb. 1960	2,470	157,346	217	8.3	15.00	14.3	10
Richard D. Irwin	Aug. 1961	2,560	160,000	204	8.0	16.00	25	20
Addison Wesley	Mar. 1965	2,010	60,000	129	6.4	33.50	14	0
John Wiley	Apr. 1962	2,625	150,000	164	6.25	17.50	21	0
	Apr. 1967	3,400	100,000	200	5.9	34.00	26	50
G. P. Putnam's Sons	May 1967	8,047	309,126	447	5.6	26.00	20.7	0
Houghton Mifflin	May 1967	19,873	662,440	1,060	5.3	30.00	25.9	40

* Incorporated as Row Peterson and Company. Present title adopted May 1, 1962, on merger with Harper and Brothers.

EXHIBIT 6
Hammond Publishing Company
Tax Provisions Relevant to Estates and Closely-Held Stock

Para. 120,011.   Excerpts from Table for Computation of Gross Estate Tax:

(A) Taxable Estate Equal to or More Than ($)	(B) Taxable Estate Less Than ($)	(C) Tax on Amount in Col. (A) ($)	(D) Rate of Tax on Excess Over Amount in Col. (A) (%)
100,000	250,000	20,700	30
250,000	500,000	65,700	32
500,000	750,000	145,700	35
750,000	1,000,000	233,200	37
1,000,000	1,250,000	325,700	39
1,500,000	2,000,000	528,200	45
2,000,000	2,500,000	753,200	49
3,000,000	3,500,000	1,263,200	56
5,000,000	6,000,000	2,468,000	67
8,000,000	10,000,000	4,568,000	76

Para. 120,312.   Valuation of Unlisted Stocks:

"If there have been bona fide sales, much the same procedure is followed in the case of unlisted stock as is followed with listed stocks (i.e., the fair market value is used). If there have been no sales some of the factors to be considered in arriving at the fair market value are the following: the bid and asked prices for the unlisted stock; the company's net worth; the dividend capacity of the company, and its earning power; value of securities of a like corporation engaged in a similar business whose securities are listed on an exchange."

Para. 120,312.1   Basis of Valuation of Stock of Close Corporations:

"It is obvious that where an estate owns the stock of a close corporation, it is taxed ordinarily on a much higher basis than that of an estate owning listed securities. In the latter case the value is definitely established by actual quotations, and experience has shown that sales of such stock are usually made at a much lower price than the theoretical fair market value determined as in the case of closely-held stock by an examination of financial data and the application of the usual methods of valuation."

Source: Reprinted with permission of the Publisher, *Federal Taxes, Estate & Gift Taxes,* Vol. 1966, Prentice-Hall, Inc., Englewood Cliffs N.J. 07632. Note: The above information, in effect in 1966, has since been superseded.

EXHIBIT 7
Hammond Publishing Company
Selected Mergers of Publishing Firms 1964–1967

Year and Purchasing Company	Sales Level ($000)	Earnings after Tax Last Complete Year ($000)	Publishing Firm Merged	Sales Level ($000)	Earnings after Tax Last Complete Year ($000)	Price*
1964 Encyclopedia Britannica	125,000	n.a.	G & C Merriam Company	n.a.	n.a.	$18.0 million cash
1966 Radio Corporation of America	2,042,001	101,161	Random House	32,000	973	Common stock of RCA worth $37.7 million
1966 International Telephone & Telegraph Corp.	1,639,143	76,110	Howard Sams	17,241	1,179	Convertible preferred and common stock of ITT worth $33.8 million
1966 Scott, Foresman	47,817	11,730	Wm. Morrow and Company	5,400	n.a.	Convertible preferred stock of Scott, Foresman worth $7.0 million
1966 Encyclopedia Britannica	140,000	n.a.	Frederick A. Praeger	2,975	n.a.	$2.5 million cash
1966 McGraw-Hill	216,198	18,151	Standard and Poor's	n.a.	n.a.	Convertible preferred stock of McGraw-Hill worth $50.0 million
1966 International Publishing Corporation	366,735	30,618	Cahners Publishing Corporation (40% of shares)	20,000	n.a.	$12.5 million cash
1967 McGraw-Hill	307,606	28,579	Ipma Publishing Company	1,946	141	Common stock of McGraw-Hill worth $2.0 million

* Stock values quoted at announcement-day values.
n.a.—not available.

PODER Industries

On March 28, 1970, Michael James, senior loan officer of the Second National Bank of Commerce in Los Angeles County, was reviewing a unique proposal submitted by PODER, a community-based, minority group organization. PODER requested an unsecured, subordinated $20,000 loan with which to start a wood pallet-making business. The $20,000 loan was being sought to enable PODER to supply the $30,000 required to obtain a Small Business Administration (SBA)-guaranteed loan of $170,000 from a large insurance company. PODER's investment would thus be $10,000 and would support $190,000 of loans. With income projected to be $36,000 net of interest and taxes in the first year and totaling $478,000 by the end of the fifth year (see Exhibit 1), the proposal appeared sound to PODER. Cash flow projections for the five years indicated that further loans to finance operations would not be necessary (Exhibit 2).

The uniqueness of the loan proposal lay in the fact that the bank had never before extended, or even considered extending, unsecured loans for the formation of "high-risk" minority-owned businesses. Mr. James was considering the proposal in this case because of his familiarity with the personalities involved and the history of the project, and because of his realization that his bank was virtually the last resort for the project. As he had promised to make a decision that afternoon, he decided to review the entire proposal thoroughly once again.

Mr. James was concerned with six general areas of analysis. First, he wondered about the riskiness of the loan requested and the soundness of the income and cash flow projections. Second, were there alternative financing arrangements including a consortium of lenders that might take some of the risk burden off Second National? For example, he thought it might be possible to strengthen the capital base with more equity from private sources. He knew that PODER had sought equity, but he thought he might be able to attract other private sources if he had more time. Third, he considered what restrictions he should place on the loan if he did grant it. He would have to determine such items as the duration of the loan, an appropriate and reasonable interest rate, and the amortization schedule. Fourth, he thought the issue of control would prove the most difficult if the loan were granted. He decided that close monitoring of the company's financial conditions would be essential. Cash management, uses of funds, use of earnings, budgeting, and production costs would be of direct concern to the bank. Yet, Mr. James realized that the threat of "outside control" was a highly sensitive issue in minority businesses. He would somehow have to protect the bank's interests without appearing to try to run the business. Fifth, he realized that if the loan should default and he should have to call it in, much more harm might be done to the bank's goodwill than if he were to reject the loan now. Finally, more generally, Mr. James wondered whether he might be setting a precedent that would be difficult to avoid in the future. For the longer term, he thought there might be vehicles for such investments and decided to investigate them when he had more time.

Mr. James was also troubled that he might be imputing more risk to the venture than was warranted because of possible biases he might unknowingly have against minority-owned ventures, a charge minority groups frequently levied against banks. After all, the product was fairly simple to manufacture. The manager, Mr. Timmons, had considerable experience in the industry. The letters of intent to purchase pallets were encouraging. He remembered that a major life insurance company was willing to commit $170,000 of its own money on the basis of financial statements drawn up by a major accounting firm, which had also agreed to devise the accounting system. The business had received extensive support from a national business assistance organization and from the Economic Development Center, part of Community Action Agency (CAA), which was the local Office of Economic Opportunity (OEO) agency. For these reasons, he wanted to review the proposal as objectively as possible before taking into account the social importance of his decision.

BACKGROUND

The Second National Bank of Commerce was the largest bank in the city, with assets in 1968 over $500 million. The bank had experienced phenomenal growth since its founding in 1959. Bank officers attributed this success to its excellent image of progressive, personal service to the burgeoning metropolitan area. To reinforce its image, the bank had encouraged its personnel to become involved in community activities and had often officially supported community improvement programs in the area. An analysis of the bank's commercial and personal accounts revealed that it serviced a broad area, including all parts of Los Angeles County.

In September 1969, a preliminary feasibility study by the Economic Development Center (EDC) for a wood pallet-making company in East Los Angeles had projected a first-year, after-tax profit of $36,000 from an initial investment of $200,000. The intensive studies that followed projected detailed income and cash flow statements five years into the future and indicated that the venture could be extremely profitable.

Sales were estimated at $700,000 the first year. Since these sales would be generated from reputable national businesses in the area, it was thought that accounts receivable would not age very long and would be highly secure. The product line was simple to manufacture (see Exhibit 3 for a general example) and had a fairly stable industry demand from a wide variety of users. The low-skill requirements would assist in the training of hard-core, unemployed workers, a primary objective of the company. In addition, the related product lines (such as cabinets, caskets, and chairs), which could ultimately be developed at higher and higher skill levels, not only would provide more sales volume but also would gradually increase the employees' skills.

The proposed company, PODER Industries, was sponsored by PODER, a community organization based in East Los Angeles and composed primarily of Mexican-Americans, some of whom had prison records.

The project had encouraged the hopes of John Marshall, head of the Economic Development Center and a prime backer of the proposal. Still, the project faced what Mr. Marshall considered the major problem of minority business development: how people who historically were prevented by whatever reason from accumulating capital could fund new business ventures. The dimensions and reality of this problem of poverty in East Los Angeles had been documented by an internal study just completed by the EDC (see Appendix A). This study about the urgency of the problem virtually at the bank's "front door" had impressed Mr. James deeply.

THE PROBLEMS OF ECONOMIC DEVELOPMENT

Mr. Marshall's commitment to the potential of urban economic development grew out of his long experience in Latin American rural development. He had come to realize the urgency for such concepts and programs in the ghetto areas of U.S. cities through his employment in the CAA, which was the largest OEO agency in Los Angeles County. That experience had led him to conclude that economic development could never work without an agency or fund that could provide equity capital to disadvantaged businesses and thus allow them to obtain the funds available from government agencies and more private sources.

The EDC had been formed in March 1969, with the objective of developing an integrated program of community-wide economic development. To accomplish this goal, the EDC used its connection with CAA to establish credibility among community groups in South Central and East Los Angeles as well as with the business sector in the Los Angeles area. Linkages were developed with community organizations by Ted Starr, who had an extensive knowledge of the area. The EDC

then looked to major corporations in the area to provide various resources. Ultimately, commitments of a minimum of 100 hours of
technical services per year per corporation were obtained from 110
corporations and formed into a Technical Assistance Pool available to
minority businesses through the EDC. This management-community
relationship helped the EDC play an important role in the formation
and funding of over 40 minority businesses in the period of a year. Mr.
Marshall still considered the major obstacle to be the general requirement of 10- to 15-percent equity participation in large, potentially
viable projects. He thought the equity participation would be critical
in higher-risk, low-return projects.

To supply this equity, Mr. Marshall proposed the formation of an
Economic Development Fund, which would be capitalized at a minimum of $300,000 with donations from corporations. The fund then
would provide long-term, subordinated loans at 9½-percent interest.
This interest rate was meant to maintain the self-perpetuating nature
of the fund and would be reallocated as received. The fund's operation
and potential, as envisioned by Mr. Marshall, are detailed in Appendix B.

In March 1970, one year after the formation of the EDC, Mr. Marshall
returned to Latin America and Ted Starr became director of the EDC.
Mr. Starr inherited a skeleton organization seriously weakened by the
federal government's cutback of poverty funds to the CAA. Although
the resources of the CAA staff members and other people were generally available, Mr. Starr was the only full-time member of the EDC.

Mr. Starr shared Mr. Marshall's conviction that equity capital remained the major problem of minority business, citing as an example
the need to raise $30,000 for the proposed total PODER Industries
investment of $200,000. In such cases, the proposed fund would supply
the $30,000 subordinated to all other loans at the rate of 9½ percent
per year amortized over five years. The $30,000 could then support an
additional $170,000 of guaranteed loans to the venture. All ownership
in the business would be held by PODER, the organization.

Mr. Starr strongly believed in organization-oriented businesses as
opposed to individual enterprises for the benefit of one person or a
small group of people. He said, "It is not sufficient to help people
become entrepreneurs because there is no guarantee that they will do
any more for the ghetto than any other bourgeois entrepreneur. There
is a need to help organizations rather than individuals because organizations in the community have a natural constituency, and when organizations become viable and effective, they have direct impact on the people
they serve and people who are members of the organizations. Community development means organizational development because the
urban scene consists of interorganizational rather than interpersonal
transactions. Business can subsidize organizations, making them self-
reliant and more effective. Business development thus can contribute
directly to community action."

With this philosophy in mind, EDC had worked closely with PODER Industries from its inception and first proposal for forming an upholstery business. A preliminary feasibility and market study by the EDC had shown this project to be ultimately unprofitable. In the process of investigation and discussions including the EDC, PODER personnel, and representatives from the National Business Assistance League, the idea of a wood pallet business emerged. From among the Technical Assistance Program members, the EDC had generated letters of intent to purchase wood pallets made by PODER Industries totaling $700,000 worth of sales in the first year (see Exhibit 4).

However, SBA-guaranteed funding, if available, would be a source for only 85 percent of the required capitalization. This assistance was in the form of a guarantee to some institution with the inclination actually to allocate the funds. While this was considered significant in itself, problems with stringent SBA requirements and strained relations among EDC, PODER Industries, and the SBA administrator for the district—as well as the lack of the "high-risk" 15-percent equity—slowed the project.

What perplexed Mr. Starr was the realization that sources of equity funding would have to be developed if economic development were to be possible. His views of economic development were almost ideally represented in the PODER Industries project. Its relationship with an active, viable, community organization was deep; its potential for success seemed excellent. But the EDC had been unable to arrange the critical funding.

Problems of communication and understanding between EDC and PODER, compounded by the difficulty in breaking the funding stalemate, caused PODER to pursue other sources of help. Its relationship with Juan Romero of the National Business Assistance League had been good. As a Mexican-American, Mr. Romero operated and communicated effectively with PODER personnel. Because of his intensive personal assistance, the stalemate was broken and hopes for the project were renewed. In the following six months, Mr. Romero pursued business contacts of the league and was successful in persuading a major insurance company to extend PODER an SBA-guaranteed loan for $170,000. In addition, he had been instrumental in bringing the project to Mr. James's attention.

Through its contact with the National Business Assistance League, the Second National Bank had been kept aware of PODER Industries' plans and problems. When the request for funding was submitted, Mr. James realized that time was running out on the project. If no solution to the equity problem was found, the increasing frustration among the people who had invested effort in the project could seriously affect the prospects of future economic development schemes. Against that he had to weigh the best interests of the bank's depositors and shareholders.

Mr. James thought especially significant Mr. Romero's observation: "Whoever is going to run PODER Industries will not be a traditional PODER-type member but will be independent. The original idea of running PODER Industries out of the front office of the PODER organization day by day has been rejected. In this respect, PODER officers have become more hard-nosed toward the inevitable problems of superfluous hirings and the problems of discipline necessary to maintain production schedules. There has been a big change in philosophy; PODER Industries is now viewed as a wholly autonomous operation. Anyway, if the bank does lend the money, it will almost certainly prohibit any distribution of earnings for several years."

EXHIBIT 1
PODER Industries
Projected Income Statement for 1970–1974[1]

	1970 Quarters				1970 Total	1971	1972	1973	1974
	I	II	III	IV					
Sales @ $4/unit	$125,000	$195,000	$210,000	$170,000	$700,000	$900,000	$1,100,000	$1,300,000	$1,500,000
Discounts and allowances (1%)	1,250	1,950	2,100	1,700	7,000	9,000	11,000	13,000	15,000
Net sales	123,750	193,050	207,900	168,300	693,000	891,000	1,089,000	1,287,000	1,485,000
Cost of goods mfg.	104,695	148,135	158,625	132,235	543,690	678,830	802,740	945,710	1,076,600
Gross margin	19,055	44,915	49,275	36,065	149,310	212,170	286,260	341,290	408,400
Operating expenses	11,320	12,720	13,020	12,220	49,280	54,180	63,625	73,700	83,340
Depreciation	2,100	2,100	2,100	2,100	8,400	8,400	8,400	8,400	8,400
Profit before interest and taxes	5,635	30,095	34,155	21,745	91,630	149,590	214,235	259,190	316,660
Interest[2]	4,750	4,750	4,750	4,750	19,000	16,900	14,800	12,700	10,600
Taxes @ 50%	442	12,673	14,702	8,498	36,315	66,345	99,717	123,245	153,030
Profit after taxes	$ 443	$ 12,672	$ 14,703	$ 8,497	$ 36,315	$ 66,345	$ 99,718	$ 123,245	$ 153,030

[1] Prepared by National Business Assistance League.
[2] Includes interest at 10 percent on 10-year insurance company loan ($170,000) and on proposed 5-year bank loan ($20,000). PODER calculated interest at 10 percent of the loans outstanding at the beginning of the year.

EXHIBIT 2
PODER Industries
Projected Cash Flow for 1970 and 1971–1974

	1970 Quarters				1970 Total	1971	1972	1973	1974
	I	II	III	IV					
Receipts									
Opening cash balance		$ 47,343	$ 31,965	$ 38,968		$ 57,015	$ 93,210	$ 163,828	$ 258,073
Loan proceeds[1]	$ 90,000				$ 90,000				
Receivables collected[2]	83,800	168,150	203,350	181,000	636,300	873,450	1,072,500	1,270,500	1,468,500
Total	173,800	215,493	235,315	219,968	726,300	930,465	1,165,710	1,434,328	1,726,573
Disbursements									
Cash outlays[3]	$120,765	$165,605	$176,395	$149,205	$611,970	$749,910	$ 881,165	$1,032,110	$1,170,540
Taxes @ 50%	442	12,673	14,702	8,498	36,315	66,345	99,717	123,145	153,030
Loan amortization	5,250	5,250	5,250	5,250	21,000	21,000	21,000	21,000	21,000
Capital equipment	$ 37,600								
Leasehold improvement	28,150								
Beginning inventory	44,250								
Working Capital[1]	90,000								
	200,000								
Total	126,457	183,528	196,347	162,953	669,285	837,255	1,001,882	1,176,255	1,344,570
Ending cash balance	$ 47,343	$ 31,965	$ 38,968	$ 57,015	$ 57,015	$ 93,210	$ 163,828	$ 258,073	$ 382,003

[1] Working capital investment portion of initial capitalization.
[2] Assumes 1/12 of year's net sales accrued into following year.
[3] Cost of goods + interest + operating expenses.

EXHIBIT 3
PODER Industries
Sample Wood Pallet

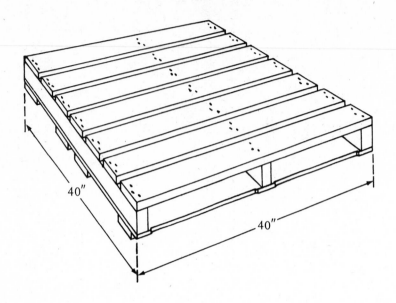

40″

40″

EXHIBIT 4
Metro-Markets, Inc.

Metro—Markets, Inc., Los Angeles, California 90620

September 30, 1969

Mr. Ted Starr
Economic Development Center
Community Action Agency
814 South Spring Street
Los Angeles, California 90014

Dear Mr. Starr:

Enclosed, per our recent conversation, are two copies
of the plan and specifications for our pallets. As we
discussed, we would have to see a sample of PODER Industries' product built to these specifications.

To give you some idea of our usage of pallets, we order from 1,000 to 3,000 about once every three months.
To date this year, we have purchased 15,000 pallets
from our present supplier. We are now paying $4 per
pallet, which is the total cost including taxes and
delivery charges.

When PODER Industries is prepared to submit a bid and
present a sample, please have them contact Glenn Davis
here in Los Angeles. He is already aware of our discussion and your program.

If you require additional information, please do not
hesitate to contact Mr. Davis.

Very truly yours,

METRO—MARKETS, INC.
SOUTHERN REGION

Richard E. Simpson, Jr.
Personnel Manager

EXHIBIT 4 (continued)
Aeroscape Corporation

AEROSPACE CORPORATION
Burbank, California 91503

October 24, 1969

Mr. Ted Starr
Economic Development Center
Community Action Agency
814 South Spring Street
Los Angeles, California 90014

Dear Mr. Starr:

We are pleased to acknowledge your recent letter addressed to E. G. Michaels and wish to advise that it
has been referred to me for reply.

With respect to your need for letters concerning PODER
Industries' opportunities, we are pleased to advise as
follows.

It appears that our requirements for wooden pallets
run somewhere between 700 to 1,000 per year. Specifications for standard stake pallet and pallet stacking
support are enclosed. We will, of course, be glad to
include PODER Industries on bids for requirements in
this line, pursuant to their representation and bidder
qualification. Further information about what we expect of our suppliers is contained in the enclosed
Small Business Profile and Supplier Guide.

Should PODER representatives wish to contact buying
personnel, Pat Marsh is the buyer. Mr. Marsh is located in Building 40 at Hollywood Way and Empire Ave.,
Burbank. He may be reached at 847-6148. To aid you
in reaching facilities you may wish to visit, a map of
our plant layout is enclosed.

Please let me know if I can be of further help.

Very truly yours,

AEROSPACE CORPORATION

Warren K. Dunn
Small Business Administrator

EXHIBIT 4 (continued)
Integrated Industries

INTEGRATED INDUSTRIES
Los Angeles, California 90058

October 30, 1969

Economic Development Center
Community Action Agency
814 South Spring Street
Los Angeles, California 90014

Attention: Mr. Ted Starr

Gentlemen:

Confirming our recent conversations, Integrated Industries is prepared, under a competitive situation, to
place orders with your agency to the total sum of
$50,000 per year.

Such orders would be for pallets and related wooden
products.

Very truly yours,

John J. Crawford
Manager of Material

EXHIBIT 4 (continued)
Consolidated Chemical Corporation

CONSOLIDATED CHEMICAL CORPORATION

October 2, 1969

Mr. Ted Starr
Economic Development Center
Community Action Agency
814 South Spring Street
Los Angeles, California 90014

Re: PODER--Wooden Pallets

Dear Ted:

Consolidated Chemical Corporation is most interested
in doing business with minority groups.

In the year 1970, PODER will be given the opportunity
to quote on our wooden pallets requirements.

Sincerely,

E. W. Varnish
Purchasing Agent

EXHIBIT 5
PODER Industries
Greater Los Angeles Area

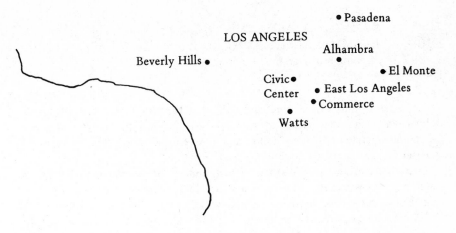

EXHIBIT 6
PODER Industries
Organizational Interrelationships

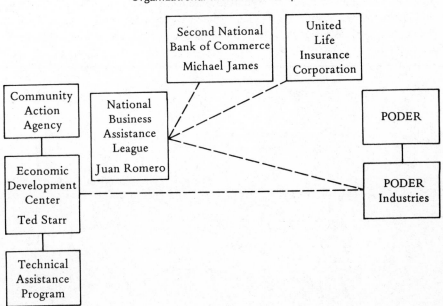

APPENDIX A
PODER Industries
Interoffice Memorandum

TO: Mando Zorra, Executive Director, CAA
FROM: John Marshall, Director, EDC
SUBJECT: Planning Study on East Los Angeles Target Area
DATE: March 20, 1970

An in-depth study of the target area, which we have just completed, documents our conviction that the area is on the verge of crisis. Unless positive programs are begun immediately with high visibility and long-term value, what may happen in the near future is certainly anybody's guess.

Interviews and surveys in the area indicate that dissatisfaction is widespread and has been growing. Residents in the area appear to be united in their demand for change *now* and are becoming increasingly vocal.

It is beyond question that an all-out effort to make substantive improvements in the target area will require the dedication and resources of all concerned citizens and organizations, particularly since recent federal cutbacks have affected the area significantly and there does not appear to be much hope for massive federal aid to the area.

We are currently scheduling briefings to present our findings to all Technical Assistance Program members, as well as to other contacts we have in the private and public sectors, as soon as possible. If they have arranged funding for PODER, we hope to use it as a model of the type of involvement that is needed from them.

APPENDIX B
PODER Industries
Proposed Economic Development Fund*

The fund will make venture capital available to minority entrepreneurs in the form of *high-risk* investments that will be subordinated to SBA guarantees and other major loans for the acquisition of established businesses by minorities, for the expansion of existing minority businesses, and for financing new businesses in the disadvantaged areas of Los Angeles.

The fund will lend money for five-year periods at 1 percent over the prime rate (currently 8½ percent) or at reasonable rates of interest at the time of such loans. The fund will not necessarily require conventional collateral for its investments. Clients will use the management and technical assistance and sales support provided by the EDC, depending on the needs of the business for a period not to exceed the duration of the loan.

Genuine poverty-area business development requires that controlling ownership be in the hands of local people. Therefore the fund will not assume an equity position in any business that it assists. A basic requirement will be that any ventures assisted must be at least 51-percent owned by minority or poverty-area individuals or groups. We contend that equity capital investments of this type would provide the catalyst needed to secure additional financing from conventional lending institutions.

The fund will act as a guarantor of equity positions. Through leverage on its funds, it may be able to guarantee the additional financing acquired by minority entrepreneurs from financial institutions.

FUND STRUCTURE

It is proposed that the fund be formed with donations from major corporations in the Los Angeles–Southern California area. The fund is designed to be a nonprofit, self-generating entity under the umbrella of a large nonprofit organization, and therefore donations to it will be tax deductible. Corporations will be asked to donate in $10,000 units. The initial goal set for the fund is a minimum of $300,000. Additional contributions will continue to be accepted after this goal is reached.

With each unit donation, the corporation will be given a position on the board of trustees, which will approve an executive committee to implement the fund's general guidelines regarding minority business development as presented in this proposal. The committee will be composed of five members, people from the professional business community and from the disadvantaged areas of the city. It will review and approve all proposals for fund investments, and copies will be provided to the board of trustees for observations and recommendations

---

*Prepared by John Marshall, Director, Economic Development Center, Community Action Agency, January 1970. This proposal was generated for internal planning.

OPERATIONS

The fund is designed to be a nonprofit, self-perpetuating entity. Therefore money derived from repayment of the principal and the interest on outstanding loans will be earmarked for future investments for minority business development. The amount of the reserve available for such additional loans will depend on the probabilities for investment losses. Reference should be made to the projected analysis of the operations (attached as Exhibit B-1).

Loans will be sought to enable the fund to increase the amount of the reserve of funds in order to provide additional financial services to minority entrepreneurs. The fund will use loan guarantees provided by the SBA and also those provided by churches and private groups.

The fund will investigate the possibilities for participating in the new program called Minority Enterprise Small Business Investment Companies (MESBIC) as further leverage for increasing the total investment capability in minority business development.

POTENTIAL IMPACT ON MINORITY COMMUNITY (ASSUMING DIRECT LOANS ONLY)

1. Approximately 65 businesses will be developed over the first 10-year period of the fund's operation, of which a percentage can be expected to fail. However, the fund's earnings from investments will allow for such losses.

2. The total valuation of the successful businesses developed at the end of the 10-year period (including a 10-percent growth rate) will be $8.4 million. For each $10,000 unit donated to the fund, new business valuation of $280,000 will be generated in 10 years. This is a multiplying factor of 28 on the original donation.

3. Even more impressive is the fund's effect on gross community product, the total movement of dollars in minority communities over the projected 10-year period. The fund will generate $169 million in gross community product, which represents a growth factor 560 times each original donation of $10,000.

4. In terms of generation of minority employment, the cumulative valuation of $8.4 million in 10 years will create more than 84,000 new and permanent jobs. This figure is based on Department of Commerce data, which indicates that one job is created for every $10,000 in business valuation. One may safely assume that most of these jobs will be for minority citizens. In terms of the total gross community product and its effects on local employment, this figure might well be multiplied by 10.

EXHIBIT B-1
PODER Industries

Analysis of Economic Development Fund Ten-Year Cash Flow Schedule

Year	Cash Balance Investments, Beginning of Yr.[1]	Less New Loans, Beginning of Yr.[1]	No. of Business Developments[2]	Net New Loans[3]	Loans Receivable Before Yearly Repayment	Repayment of Loan at 20%[4]	Interest Earnings on Loan O/S @ 9½%[5]	Excess Earnings of Cash Fund on Other Inventory @ 7%[6]	Total Cash in Bank
1	$300,000	$150,000	10	$135,000	$ 135,000	$ 27,000	$ 12,825	$10,500	$ 200,325
2	200,325	150,000	10	135,000	243,000	54,000	23,085	3,523	130,933
3	130,933	105,000	7	94,500	283,500	72,900	26,933	1,815	127,581
4	127,581	75,000	5	67,500	278,100	86,400	26,419	3,680	169,081
5	169,081	75,000	5	67,500	259,200	99,900	24,624	6,586	225,190
6	225,190	75,000	5	67,500	226,800	86,400	21,546	10,513	268,650
7	268,650	75,000	5	67,500	207,900	72,900	19,750	13,555	299,856
8	299,856	90,000	6	81,000	216,000	70,200	20,520	14,690	315,266
9	315,266	90,000	6	81,000	226,800	72,900	21,546	15,769	335,480
10	335,480	90,000	6	81,000	234,900	75,600	22,316	17,184	360,579
		$975,000	65		$2,311,200	$718,200	$219,564	$97,815	$2,432,941

[1] New loans issued at beginning of year.
[2] Based on $15,000 per business developed.
[3] Net new loans equal gross new loans less 10-percent reserve for losses (interest on 10-percent reserve is also assumed lost).
[4] Net new loans amortized evenly over five years.
[5] Principal and interest payments received at end of year.
[6] Calculated at 7 percent of cash at beginning of year less gross new loans issued for year.

Frecter Company

In late March 1982, Mr. John Rosten, controller of the Frecter Company, was about to evaluate which of two alternatives for financing computer equipment and software was cheaper. Numerous financing alternatives had been discussed over the past several months and all but two had been eliminated. The final two were:

1. A five-year term loan at the firm's commercial bank
2. A financial lease with the leasing subsidiary of a commercial bank at which the firm had no existing relationship

BACKGROUND

Frecter Company was a wholesale supplier of industrial supplies. Sales and profits had grown over the past several years reaching record levels of approximately $1.5 million and $65,000, respectively, for the year ended December 31, 1981.

Mr. Rosten joined the firm in October 1978 as manager of the accounting function which was administered by a bookkeeper, a part-time billing clerk, and himself. At the time, none of the firm's record-keeping functions were performed by a computer. In early 1979, Mr. Rosten was asked to investigate various possibilities, including the option of relying on a service bureau. The controller spent considerable time studying the products and services of various vendors.

At a meeting with Mr. Stone, the firm's president, and other key personnel in mid-1979, Mr. Rosten gave a progress report. He presented four options and noted that his opinion was that all except the one involving an arrangement with a service bureau were feasible. Everyone agreed that the service bureau option should be rejected. However, the other three alternatives also were rejected, at least for the next six months. Mr. Stone felt that it would be worthwhile to explore other possibilities. Another individual noted that his opinion was that the expected benefits were just not worth the cost.

The issue was raised again in early 1980. Mr. Stone suggested that they select a smaller machine (than those considered the previous year) that was flexible in the sense that additional capacity could be added. His idea was to put just the bookkeeping functions on it for now and then add inventory in later years. Everyone agreed that this was a good idea and Mr. Rosten was given the task of performing the necessary investigation.

Toward the end of 1980, Mr. Rosten made a proposal consistent with the guidelines described above. The cost for the hardware and the necessary software was slightly less than $30,000. The proposal was rejected for the following reasons:

1. The firm had more pressing needs for capital expenditures during 1981.
2. The argument was made that recent advances in technology suggested that the cost to the firm would decrease substantially if the firm waited one more year.

As it turned out, the cost did decrease in the latter part of 1981, and Mr. Rosten proposed at a meeting early in 1982 an option that would cost about $14,000 and do almost as much as the alternative considered the previous year. The controller was surprised to see so much opposition. Some argued that the firm had more pressing needs for 1982. One manager recommended that the firm wait one more year because for the same price tag the firm likely would be able to acquire much more computing power. At that point in the meeting, Mr. Stone said that he felt strongly that the firm should wait no longer and he urged approval. The proposal was accepted.

ORIGINAL FINANCING PLAN

Prior to reaching the decision to purchase a computer, Mr. Rosten made inquiries at the firm's bank regarding possible financing arrangements. He was assured that the bank would be happy to lend up to 90 percent of the cost of the equipment on a five-year-term basis either to the firm or to Mr. Stone.

Mr. Rosten had been advocating for some time that it probably would be best to have Mr. Stone buy the equipment and software and lease it to the firm. To him this option was clearly superior to having the firm borrow and purchase. (Earlier they had discussed leasing from the vendor and the option of using equity, but these were rejected.) The firm and Mr. Stone could borrow at the same interest rate. However, the president's marginal tax rate was 55 percent and the firm's was only 35 percent. Thus, the tax shields from depreciation and interest would be greater if Mr. Stone owned the asset.

Mr. Rosten used an example like the following to clarify his point. Suppose depreciation the first year was $100. If Mr. Stone owned the asset, his taxes would be reduced by $55. If the firm was the owner, its taxes would be reduced by $35. By properly structuring a lease transaction, both the firm and Mr. Stone would benefit. The tax reduction would be $55. The firm, in effect, would retain the $35 benefit it would obtain if it owned the asset plus part of the extra $20. In other words, the firm and the president would share the extra $20 in some equitable manner. Normally, the portion going to the actual owner is determined by how much risk he or she is incurring and the administration cost incurred. In this case, there was virtually no risk and the firm would handle all the administrative matters.

The controller concluded his point by noting that when final details were available regarding cost, etc., he would perform an analysis. However, he was confident that this approach would be best. The president agreed.

In early March an agreement was signed with a vendor to acquire computer and software for $12,660. There would also be a sales tax of $633 which would bring the total cost to $13,293. (For purposes of computing the ITC and depreciation, sales tax would not be included as part of total cost. The tax was deductible in the year of purchase.) Payment was due 30 days after delivery which was expected during May.

Once the costs were known, Mr. Rosten was able to analyze the plan to have Mr. Stone buy the equipment and then lease it to the firm. To his amazement, the deal was not a good one. It would produce a savings to the president of less than $500 over the next five years. Of course, this was an excellent return on a zero investment. However, it was not worth the trouble. A document would have to be prepared outlining the terms of the lease and the controller would have to spend more time studying the laws so that the transaction would qualify as a lease. More importantly, he feared that the lease would raise a "red flag" on the president's tax return which might lead to an audit.

Mr. Rosten spoke with a friend who was quite knowledgeable about such transactions. He confirmed the controller's view that it was not worth the effort. The expert noted that "the deal" was just too small.

LEASE VERSUS BORROW AND BUY

The controller decided to borrow the funds and purchase the equipment and software. He happened to be talking to the firm's auditor on another matter and mentioned the plan. The auditor told him about a leasing subsidiary of a bank that was offering very attractive terms. The auditor's firm had just purchased some equipment and the analysis showed that leasing was much more attractive. The controller decided to pursue this possibility and compare the two options.

Borrow and Buy

As noted above, the total cost was $13,293, including the sales tax of $633. The Investment Credit would be $1,266 and annual depreciation charges over its five-year life would be as follows:

Year	Depreciation Expense
1	$ 1,899
2	2,787
3	2,658
4	2,658
5	2,658
Total	$12,660

The firm would have to purchase insurance and pay for the maintenance contract. However, since these costs would also be borne under the lease option, Mr. Rosten planned to ignore them in this analysis. He also intended to exclude excise taxes even though this expense would not be incurred in the lease option. The reason was that the amounts would be so small.

The firm would borrow $12,000 to finance the purchase. This equals the total cost less the ITC which would be recouped on the next tax payment date in April.

Computer and software	$12,660
+ Sales tax	633
− ITC	1,266
Cash required	$12,027

The loan would require five equal annual payments of principal of $2,400, with the first payment due in one year. Interest due would also be paid once each year on the same date as the principal payment.[1] The interest rate on the loan would vary with the bank's prime lending rate, and would be 1½ percent above that rate. For example, in March 1982 the bank's prime was 17%, so the firm would pay 18½ percent. If the bank's prime rate decreased to 16 percent, then the interest rate on the term loan would fall to 17½ percent.

Most "experts" were predicting lower interest rates. Mr. Rosten shared this view but was a bit skeptical because in the recent past "the

---

1. Casewriter's note: The loan agreement called for 60 monthly payments of principal of $200 plus monthly payments of interest. Moreover, the lease arrangement that will be discussed also called for monthly payments. The casewriter has converted the two financing alternatives to annual arrangements to reduce the calculations required.

experts" had been wrong. Consequently, he thought it would be best to use a conservative figure and decided to assume a constant interest rate of 18½ percent for the five-year period.

Lease Option

Under the lease option, the lessor would "pass through" the ITC. That is, the firm would be allowed to claim the credit on its own tax return. Annual lease payments would be as follows:

End of Year	Lease Payment
1	$3,960
2	3,960
3	3,960
4	3,960
5	3,960

There would be no option of canceling the lease during the five-year period.

The firm would be given the option to purchase the computer and the software at the end of five years. The price would be the lesser of the fair market value at that time or 10 percent of the original cost. In other words, the maximum price the firm would have to pay in five years was $1,266.

The firm's marginal tax rate (state plus federal) was projected at 35 percent for 1982. The firm's plan called for increasing levels of income in subsequent years which could cause the marginal rate to increase. Mr. Rosten decided to ignore this possibility and to assume a constant rate of 35 percent in conducting the analysis.

Mr. Rosten was anxious to complete the evaluation and make the final decision. He had spent considerable time on this project, much more than he thought he should have, and he was looking forward to its completion.

Brenco Corporation

In late October 1977, John Giordan, a senior financial analyst of the Brenco Corporation, was about to evaluate a report received from the Capital Leasing Company. The report included an offer of a leasing arrangement along with a comparison of the cost of the lease versus the cost of another financing option the firm was considering. After evaluating the report and performing any additional analysis he thought may be appropriate, Mr. Giordan would recommend which financing alternative should be selected.

BACKGROUND

The Brenco Corporation was a manufacturer of machine tool parts. In September 1977, top management approved a request submitted by the data processing department to purchase $1 million of computer equipment. The manufacturer of the equipment promised delivery in early January 1978. The source of financing would be determined by Mr. Sheehan, the firm's treasurer.

After considering the firm's total financing requirement for the next year, Mr. Sheehan had tentatively decided to use $250,000 of available internal funds and to borrow $750,000 from the firm's commercial bank. The annual interest rate would be 10 percent, and the loan would be repaid in seven equal annual installments commencing December 31, 1978.[1] (These loan payments would include interest and principal.)

Mr. Sheehan was at a chamber of commerce meeting in late September 1977, where he met Mr. Dalton, a vice president of the Capital Leasing Company. During their conversation, Mr. Sheehan mentioned that his firm was going to purchase computer equipment and that he intended to finance 75 percent of the purchase price with debt. Mr. Dalton asked him if he had considered leasing. When Mr. Sheehan said no, Mr. Dalton said he believed that any time a firm was going to borrow it should consider a financial lease as an alternative to debt, because

---

1. Casewriter's note: The $750,000 loan agreement called for monthly payments over seven years. Moreover, the lease agreement that will be discussed also called for monthly payments. The casewriter has converted the two financing alternatives to annual arrangements to reduce the calculations required.

leasing might be cheaper and because it provided 100 percent financing. Mr. Sheehan suggested that they have lunch the next day so they could discuss the matter at greater length.

THE LUNCHEON MEETING

At lunch, Mr. Dalton began by saying that the Capital Leasing Company was basically a financial underwriter. That is, it arranged financing and received a fee for its services. The firm had numerous contacts with wealthy individuals, corporations, and financial institutions that were interested in investing in "leasing deals." The investor, who would become the lessor, would purchase the equipment. Typically, anywhere from 10 percent to 30 percent of the purchase price of the equipment would be invested by the lessor as equity and the remainder would be borrowed from a financial institution such as a life insurance company or a commercial bank. (This type of arrangement is called a leveraged lease.)

Mr. Sheehan asked Mr. Dalton to outline the advantages to the lessor and lessee. Mr. Dalton said that generally the investor (lessor) was primarily interested in obtaining the tax benefits that ownership of the asset created. Indeed, very often the lease payments are set so that they just cover the loan payments on the debt portion of the deal. Suppose, for example, that Joe Jones buys $100,000 of equipment that has a five-year life and leases it to Firm A. Joe invests $20,000 of his own money and obtains a five-year term loan for $80,000. Suppose further than the interest rate on the loan is 12 percent and the loan requires five equal annual payments (interest plus principal) of $22,192. Joe might require five annual lease payments of $22,192. (Actually, a firm like Capital Leasing normally would help to arrange the debt, set lease terms, etc.)

What's in it for Joe Jones? Because he is the owner of the asset, he is entitled to the ITC and to deduct depreciation expense on his own tax return. Moreover, he is entitled to the asset's salvage value, if any. Even if the salvage value is zero, the tax benefits alone often are sufficient to provide a good return on his equity investment. Putting it another way, the equity investment is the cash outlay for Joe and the tax benefits are the cash inflows. Very often, the cash inflows from taxes alone are sufficient to provide a positive NPV.

Mr. Sheehan responded by noting that Firm A loses the cash inflows from the tax benefits. Mr. Dalton said that Mr. Sheehan just got to the heart of the matter. The crucial issue is: How much are the tax benefits worth to Firm A? Generally, the investor's tax bracket is such that his or her marginal tax rate is at least 50 percent. So a depreciation deduction of $100 produces a tax savings of $50. If Firm A's marginal tax rate is also 50 percent, a depreciation deduction of $100 is worth $50 to the firm. However, if Firm A's marginal rate is less than 50 percent, then the savings would be less than $50 and it is especially in these cases that leasing is attractive.

In general, the lower the firm's marginal tax rate, the less valuable are the tax benefits of ownership. By leasing the firm would be trading the tax benefits to the lessor who can take full advantage of them, and the lessor would give back part of the benefit in the form of a low effective interest rate. Mr. Dalton quickly added that even if a firm's effective tax rate were at the maximum (as was Brenco's rate), leasing might still be cheaper than debt. Leasing firms, like Capital, do a substantial amount of business with financial institutions, and thus they have more bargaining power than many firms. This factor, plus the fact that the deals often call for the financial institution to receive part of the residual value of the equipment, often produces an effective interest rate that is lower than what a firm could arrange on its own.

Mr. Dalton proceeded to explain that in evaluating the cost of the lease, the lessee must consider the loss of the residual value because the lessor owns the asset at the end of the lease period. Mr. Sheehan said that this was not an issue here because the computer equipment the firm was going to acquire would most likely have an insignificant economic value in seven years.

Mr. Sheehan then inquired about Mr. Dalton's views concerning the effect of leasing on a firm's debt capacity. Mr. Dalton said that leasing was equivalent to debt. A financial lease creates a legal obligation to make lease payments just as debt creates an obligation to make interest and principal payments. He then said that a recent accounting pronouncement made a financial lease debt anyway.[2] That is, a financial lease must be capitalized and recorded as debt.

At the conclusion of lunch, Mr. Sheehan said he agreed that he should certainly consider a leasing arrangement. Mr. Dalton responded by saying he would put a deal together and send Mr. Sheehan an analysis comparing its cost with the cost of the debt arrangement the firm was considering.

The report arrived a week later. Mr. Sheehan looked it over and then sent it to Mr. Giordan, a senior financial analyst. He asked Mr. Giordan to evaluate the report, to perform any additional analysis he thought was necessary, and to recommend which financing alternative should be accepted. (The report is presented in Exhibit 1.)

---

2. Casewriter's note: Mr. Dalton was referring to the Financial Accounting Standard Board's Statement #13 (FASB 13), which required that financial leases be capitalized on a firm's balance sheet.

EXHIBIT 1
Report from Capital Leasing Company
Proposal for Brenco Corporation

October 1977

Mr. Robert Sheehan
Treasurer
Brenco Corporation

Dear Mr. Sheehan:

I have assembled a leasing arrangement, which I am sure you will agree is most attractive. Enclosed is a financial analysis that shows that this lease arrangement has a much lower cost than the financing option you are considering.

Thank you for permitting me the opportunity to present the enclosed material. I look forward to any questions or comments and to your early decision. Your interest in Capital Leasing is greatly appreciated.

Very truly yours,

Ronald Dalton
Vice President

EXHIBIT 1 (continued)

LEASE-VERSUS-PURCHASE ANALYSIS

Tax Parameters

Federal tax rate	48.0000%
State tax rate	3.8461%
Composite tax rate	50.0000%

Discount Rate Assumed

Annual before-tax rate	18%
Annual after-tax rate	9%

Lease Payments

Annual for four years commencing 12/31/78	$120,000
Annual for three years commencing 12/31/81	$204,372

Debt Assumptions

Borrow $750,000 at 10 percent—Annual payments of $154,054, commencing 12/31/78

Depreciation Data[1]

Residual Value Assumption

Given the nature of the equipment, we believe a zero residual value is a reasonable assumption.

The calculations follow.

---

1. Casewriter's note: This section described the method of computing the annual depreciation amounts presented later in this exhibit. The section was not reproduced because the method is no longer employed for the purposes due to revisions in the tax laws since 1977.

EXHIBIT 1 (continued)
Purchase Cash Flows

| | Depreciation | | | Taxable Income | | Tax Liability | | | Debt | Total Cash |
	Federal	State	Interest	Federal	State	Federal	State	Total	Payments	Flow
Initial outlay										$-150,000[1]
Year										
1	$285,714	$285,714	$75,000	$-346,841	$-360,714	$-166,484	$-13,873	$-180,357	$154,054	26,303
2	204,082	204,082	67,095	-260,747	-271,177	-125,159	-10,430	-135,589	154,054	-18,465
3	145,772	145,772	58,399	-196,318	-204,171	-94,233	-7,853	-102,086	154,054	-51,968
4	105,773	105,773	48,833	-148,660	-154,606	-71,357	-5,946	-77,303	154,054	-76,751
5	79,330	79,330	38,311	-113,116	-117,641	-54,296	-4,525	-58,821	154,054	-95,233
6	52,886	52,886	26,737	-76,561	-79,623	-36,749	-3,062	-39,811	154,054	-114,243
7	126,443[2]	126,443[2]	14,005	-135,046	-140,448	-64,822	-5,402	-70,224	154,054	-83,830
Present value @ 9%										-411,784

1. Down payment of $250,000, less investment tax credit of $100,000.
2. Under prior tax law, total depreciation charges would have been $900,000 and, thus, the equipment's book value would be $100,000 at the end of year 7. Given the zero residual value assumption, the firm would have been able to take a tax loss of $100,000, the residual value of zero minus the book value of $100,000, in year 7. The $126,443 figure includes the depreciation charge of $26,443 in year 7 plus the $100,000 loss. The total was deductible for tax purposes.

EXHIBIT 1 (continued)
Lease Cash Flows

End of Year	Lease Payment	Taxable Income		Tax Liability			Net
		Federal	State	Federal	State	Total	Cash Flow
1	$120,000	$-115,385	$-120,000	$-55,385	$-4,615	$-60,000	$ -60,000
2	120,000	-115,385	-120,000	-55,385	-4,615	-60,000	-60,000
3	120,000	-115,385	-120,000	-55,385	-4,615	-60,000	-60,000
4	120,000	-115,385	-120,000	-55,385	-4,615	-60,000	-60,000
5	204,372	-196,512	-204,372	-94,326	-7,860	-102,186	-102,186
6	204,372	-196,512	-204,372	-94,326	-7,860	-102,186	-102,186
7	204,372	-196,512	-204,372	-94,326	-7,860	-102,186	-102,186

Present value @ 9%   -377,623

EXHIBIT 1 (continued)
Summary

Present Value Cost

	% Equipment Cost	Amount
Lease	37.76	$377,623
Purchase	41.17	$411,784

Interest Cost to Lessee

Effective interest rate: 2.03%[1]

Breakeven Residual Value

Given the 9-percent discount rate, the present value of the after-tax lease cash flow is less than the present value of the after-tax debt cash flows as long as the residual value is less than 12½ percent of the initial cost of the equipment.

Additional Analysis

The present value analysis used an after-tax discount rate of 9 percent. The selection of an appropriate discount rate is a matter in which there is considerable disagreement. Some argue that the firm's cost of capital should be used, and this is our view. However, a case can be made for using a lower rate; for example, many argue that the after-tax interest rate should be used as the discount rate. Therefore we calculated the present value of the cash flows for each alternative using a range of rates. As shown, in each case the present value of the cash flows for the lease alternative is lower.

	Present Value	
	Debt	Lease
2%	522,516	500,714
5%	469,177	441,697
10%	399,452	363,760
15%	347,395	304,697

---

1. This is the rate that makes the present value of the before-tax lease payments equal to $1 million.

Quality Hardware, Inc.

"It's one problem after another," thought Peter Gentry, vice president of Quality Hardware, Inc. It was June 8, 1978, and he was about to work on estimating the value of the firm's common shares. The president, Arthur Brady, had recently received a note from Yolanda Toner, a minority stockholder, which upset him very much. The note formally requested that the firm change its agreement regarding the repayment of a loan the firm owed her. In his response, the president suggested that she consider selling her stock. Since he thought that he might run into her at a party on Saturday, June 10, he wanted to be prepared to discuss numbers, so he asked Mr. Gentry to develop these numbers for him.

BACKGROUND

Quality Hardware, Inc., was a wholesale distributor of hardware products located in Boston, Massachusetts. Sales for the year ended December 31, 1977, were $874,000 on assets of $420,000. (Exhibit 1 presents selected financial data for the 1966–1977 period.) The firm had nine full-time employees, including three executives. The names, titles, and the stockholdings of the three executives follow:

Name	Title	Common Shares Owned at 12/31/78
Arthur Brady	President	67
Philip Sun	V.P.—marketing	7
Peter Gentry	V.P.—administration and finance	6

There were two other stockholders, Yolanda Toner and Thomas Zinter. Each owned 10 shares of the common shares outstanding. These two stockholders were cousins of Arthur Brady as well as close personal friends. They purchased their shares when the firm was founded in the late 1940s. One of them, Ms. Toner, had been the firm's bookkeeper until September 1977.

In the late 1960s it was decided that the firm should be more aggressive in pursuing sales growth. Mr. Brady told the other stockholders that experienced personnel would be needed to manage the growth. Moreover, he told them that approximately $60,000 to $70,000 would be required to finance the growth. (At this time Mr. Gentry and Mr. Sun were not employed by the firm, and Mr. Brady owned 80 of the 100 common shares outstanding.) Ms. Toner and Mr. Zinter agreed with Mr. Brady's view, but they were opposed to additional common stock investments, especially since the level to dividends up to that time had been disappointing. It was decided that the stockholders would loan the firm $60,000 of interest-free funds. The loan amount of each individual was proportional to stock ownership, as shown:

	Loan Amount
Brady	$48,000
Toner	6,000
Zinter	6,000
Total	$60,000

They readily agreed to an interest-free loan because they believed that these loans would be of short duration. It was expected that increased profits would enable the firm to repay this debt quickly.

In 1970 and 1971, poor profitability prevented the loans from being reduced. In subsequent years, higher profits were achieved, but they were needed to support the higher sales level. The minority stockholders appreciated the financial requirements, but they made it clear to Mr. Brady that they wanted and needed their money. To complicate the situation, Mr. Brady strongly believed that these loans should not be converted to interest-bearing debt.

Mr. Brady hired Philip Sun in 1970, and Peter Gentry joined the firm in 1972. They were attracted by offers of stock,[1] but more importantly by the firm's growth potential. Mr. Brady also desired growth, and the three executives often discussed ways to accelerate the rate of growth. More rapid growth meant a greater need for funds and thus conflicted with the stockholders' desire to have the loans repaid as rapidly as possible.

This conflict was resolved in late 1975 when the executives decided that the repayment of stockholder loans and the eventual resumption of dividends would be one of the firm's major goals. Agreement (verbal) was reached that stockholder loans would be reduced by at least $5,000 per year. If only $5,000 were paid, the minority stockholders would each receive $1,000 and Mr. Brady would receive $3,000. Amounts in excess of $5,000 would be distributed as follows:

---

1. Mr. Brady donated seven shares to Mr. Sun and six shares to Mr. Gentry.

	% of Amount in Excess of $5,000
Brady	80%
Toner	10%
Zinter	10%

All agreed that no dividends would be paid until the stockholder loans were eliminated. The rationale was that loan repayments were tax-free distributions, whereas dividends represented taxable income to the shareholders.

FRICTION CONTINUES

The friction caused by the failure to repay the loans was minor in comparison to the problem created by Ms. Toner's performance as a bookkeeper. The firm's accounting system had originally been designed to satisfy tax requirements. Low priority had been given to the value of accounting information as a decision-making tool. This practice had been followed through 1971, when the firm incurred a loss. A careful analysis revealed that an inadequate management information system was one of the major causes of the loss. Moreover, it was determined that profitable growth was impossible without an improved accounting system.

Mr. Brady's first attempt at solving this problem occurred in 1972, when he was about to hire his second new executive. He chose Mr. Gentry because his experience included some accounting work. Mr. Gentry's responsibilities included supervising Ms. Toner. Because of his many other duties, however, he did not have much time to devote to accounting. The result was not satisfactory. Although Ms. Toner tried, she just could not make the necessary adjustment. Finally, in September 1977, she was replaced.

Although the termination did not create immediate business problems, it did create personal problems. As noted, Mr. Brady and Ms. Toner were cousins and also close friends. The friendship ended, and this change hurt both of them a great deal.

1978—A YEAR OF PROBLEMS

As 1978 began, the firm looked forward to a year of record sales. Profit before income taxes was expected to be only $30,000, however, because the firm had to increase operating expenses to generate higher sales. In fact, it was anticipated that profits would remain at this level for 1979 also, but that thereafter they would grow at least as fast as sales. (The plan was to have real growth in sales of 4 percent per year.[2])

In January 1978, an employee problem arose when wage increases were announced. Joseph Santenello, a key assistant to Mr. Sun, was very unhappy about his raise. Moreover, he was unhappy about the firm's disorganized manner of operations and his own level of responsibility.

Mr. Sun suggested that he discuss these matters with Mr. Brady. The president met with Mr. Santenello and patiently listened to what he had to say. He then asked for time to think about the financial issue but promised to deal with some of the operational issues. The major one was the clarification of each employee's duties and responsibilities.

FEBRUARY 1978 — A NEW PROBLEM

Work on the organizational problem was postponed because of a serious snowstorm in early February 1978. Everyone's top priority was to minimize the financial impact. (The firm was shut down for six days because of the storm, and Mr. Brady paid salaries to all full-time employees for this period.) Despite the efforts, sales were less than $180,000 for the quarter ended March 31, 1978, and the firm incurred a $5,000 loss for the three-month period. Moreover, because of storm-related difficulties the firm's customers encountered, accounts receivable increased from $100,000 on December 31, 1977, to $130,000 on March 31, 1978. The result of the loss and the increased receivables was that the firm's term loan with the bank was increased from $18,240 on December 31, 1977, to $30,000 at March 31, 1978. In addition to the term loan, the firm had a $30,000 line of credit with the same bank and was borrowing $25,000 on this line at March 31, 1978.

The firm had maintained a line of credit with its bank for a number of years, and it frequently relied on this line for several months during the early part of each year. However, it was rare to use the line to the extent it was used on March 31, 1978.

The increase in debt was a minor worry in comparison to the prospect of a $25,000 before-tax loss. This estimate was prepared by Mr. Gentry and was based on the assumption that monthly sales for April–December would rebound only to 1977's level. Since management believed that this might indeed happen, a "disaster plan" was prepared. Monthly sales would be carefully monitored and, if certain predetermined levels were not achieved, cutbacks would be made. It was

---

2. "Real growth" refers to growth at constant prices. In other words, the physical volume of sales would increase by 4 percent per year. Price increases would make the growth in sales dollars higher.

described as a "disaster plan" because it called for cutbacks in vital areas. Putting it another way, these cutbacks would upset growth plans for a number of years.

APRIL THROUGH MAY 1978—WEATHER CHANGES, PROBLEM CHANGES

April turned out to be a good month, and May was even better. (Sales for these two months were well above sales for April and May 1977.) Moreover, although the term loan and the line of credit still stood at $30,000 and $25,000, respectively, management hoped to reduce the line of credit by $5,000 or $10,000 by June 15.

Whereas it looked as though June would be another excellent month, management was not ready to conclude that everyone would live "happily ever after." July was considered the key month. If July's sales were also above average, management was confident that pre-tax profits would be $20,000 for the year without implementing the disaster plan, and that the line of credit would be zero by December 31, 1978.

During April and May, the executives worked on the issues raised by Mr. Santenello. They had discussions with two other employees whose responsibility levels were similar to his. They learned that these two people were also dissatisfied, not because of their salaries but because of the firm's manner of operation. Specifically, they felt "shut out" of things and thus concluded that they did not have the opportunity to grow with the firm.

To deal with this problem, the following actions were taken:

1. A meeting was held to explain the financial side of the business.
2. The three employees were allowed and encouraged to request any financial information they desired, except for individual salary data.
3. They were made middle managers, which meant more responsibility, an opportunity for advancement, and inclusion in the bonus system designed for the three executives.
4. Mr. Santenello was given an 8-percent raise on top of the 8-percent raise that he had been given in January 1978. Mr. Brady and Mr. Sun were opposed to this raise, but Mr. Gentry talked them into it.

By early June it appeared that these actions were partially successful in solving the employee problem. Two of the three new middle managers were working quite hard and their performance was excellent. But Mr. Santenello's performance had not improved at all, and Mr. Gentry suggested that perhaps Mr. Santenello was not given proper direction. He suggested that the three executives meet to discuss possible courses of action. The meeting was scheduled for June 7, 1978 at 4:00 P.M.

MEETING AGENDA UPSET

On June 5 Mr. Brady received a letter from Yolanda Toner, who requested that her loan be converted to interest-bearing debt or else repaid. (See Exhibit 2.) Mr. Brady told Mr. Gentry and Mr. Sun that the letter did not upset him. They did not believe him and were convinced when they saw his response. He not only indicated that he would repay the debt, but he also suggested that Ms. Toner consider selling her stock. (See Exhibit 3.) He never made major decisions like this one without consulting his two fellow executives. It was clearly an emotional response.

At the June 7 meeting, the Santenello issue was the first item on the agenda. It was decided that the three executives would work with him to help him learn how to carry out his new responsibilities. The second and final agenda item was the exchange of letters between Mr. Brady and Ms. Toner. The following discussion took place:

Sun: This could be a blessing in disguise. If they sell their stock, we will no longer have to be concerned about their interests.

Gentry: Yes, it would be nice not to have to worry about their interests, but the timing is bad. My guess is that a bank will not go with debt to get rid of equity. As you know, we have set aside cash each year to build reserves and we now have $10,000 set aside. We could use this fund to repay the debt, but I hate to eliminate this vital reserve. It and our shaky profits are all the support we have for our more than $100,000 of debt and emergencies.

Where do we get the money to buy back the stock? Perhaps we could offer debt for the stock. We could put a 10-percent coupon on it.

Brady: Bull —— ! This will be a cash deal. If it's over, it's over. This will be the last check she gets from this company. I will mortgage my house if I have to.

Gentry: No. That would be unfair to you.

Sun: Maybe we could put off paying Tom [Zinter] and offer Yolanda 10K for her debt and stock.

Gentry: That's $600 per share. Book value is about $2,700 per share. Yolanda will probably argue for book value.

Brady: No way. If she comes back with book, I'll tell her to forget it. The firm will not pay dividends until stockholder loans and bank debt are repaid.[3] It will take about six years and thus

---

3. Casewriter's note: Mr. Brady was referring to the $30,000 term loan with the bank.

	the stock is not worth much until then. Pete [Gentry], doesn't the value of stock depend on dividends?
Gentry:	Yes, but they will still argue for book value if a dividend approach produces a number lower than $2,700. Also, they might request an independent valuation, which could be expensive.
Brady:	I'm attending a party on Saturday evening, and Yolanda will probably be there. If she raises the issue, I want to have numbers in mind. Pete, push some numbers and come up with a value for me.
Gentry:	Wait a minute, placing a value on the shares is a complex process. Even if I could devote full time to it between now and Saturday, which I can't, there is no way that I could do the job properly.
Brady:	I appreciate that it is a complex process and that you don't have the time to do a thorough job. But I can't take the pressure any more. If she says something on Saturday night, I want to respond with a number. Please do the best you can.
Gentry:	Okay.

Gentry had a social engagement that evening that he had to attend. The next day was so busy that he did not even have a chance to think about the problem. By 6:00 P.M. everyone had gone home, and he finally had some time to devote to the task.

EXHIBIT 1
Quality Hardware, Inc.
Selected Financial Data, 1966–1977[1]

Year	Net Sales	Cost of Goods Sold	Depreciation Expense	Profit before Federal Income Taxes[2]	Total Assets	Net Worth	Debt due to Stockholders	Bank Debt
1966	$432,462	$371,691	$2,161	$24,999	—	$142,710	$ 0	$ 0
67	456,784	335,760	2,260	23,977	—	152,061	0	0
68	457,665	322,393	2,681	21,904	—	169,146	0	0
69	517,570	369,571	3,249	31,784	—	193,666	0	0
70	518,142	380,249	3,951	11,386	—	202,547	60,000	9,600
71	511,203	380,304	4,172	(7,194)	—	196,936	60,000	16,320
72	566,767	417,551	3,576	27,350	—	218,175	60,000	14,400
73	591,438	422,438	3,132	30,178	—	241,506	60,000	14,400
74	733,808	522,520	2,374	47,669	$350,905	227,392	60,000	18,240
75	756,238	524,816	3,395	36,078	369,404	215,862[3]	60,000	18,240
76	814,099	555,423	3,920	37,855	410,807	248,650	55,000	18,240
77	874,283	606,955	3,388	22,701	419,642	269,343	50,000	18,240

[1] Income statement data are for the year ended December 31, and balance sheet data are at December 31.
[2] The federal income tax rate in early 1978 for corporations was 20 percent on the first $25,000 of taxable income, 22 percent on the second $25,000 of taxable income (that is, $25,001 to $49,999), and 48 percent on income above $50,000.
[3] The decrease is due to an adjustment to retained earnings to reflect an adjustment of previous income taxes.

484

EXHIBIT 2
Letter from Ms. Toner

June 1, 1978

Dear Arthur:

I am writing regarding my loan to the company. As you know, my husband recently quit his job and we have had to reevaluate our income requirements. I can no longer afford to earn zero interest on the funds that I have tied up in the loan. If you cannot see your way clear to paying interest on this debt, would you see what you can do to pay off the loan in its entirety.

I was hoping to speak with you personally about this, but since you have not called a stockholders' meeting, I did not have the opportunity. Thank you for your consideration.

Sincerely,

EXHIBIT 3
Letter from Mr. Brady

June 6, 1978

Dear Yolanda:

I just received your formal request, and I hope to take the latter option even though we verbally agreed that $1,000 would be paid each year. Since you are dissatisfied, would you consider selling your stock? I will have to go for long-term money to repay your loan, and it would be easier to do it all at once.

I will have to make the same offer to Thomas and, if he accepts, it will mean even more financing. It will take time to arrange and I ask you to be patient.

Sincerely,

Basic Industries, Inc.

In early 1982, Joseph Marks, financial vice president of Basic Industries, Inc. ("Basic"), was considering what alternative to recommend with respect to the company's annual dividend for 1982 and thereafter to the firm's board of directors. Initial projections of funds flows and profitability for 1982 indicated that the current annual dividend rate of $0.70 per share declared the previous year would prove difficult to maintain in light of planned capital expenditures and debt reduction. This was particularly troublesome because of $0.70 level itself represented the first dividend reduction ever made by the firm, and the reduction had been accompanied by a decline in the company's common stock price-earnings ratio.

BACKGROUND

Basic was formed in 1965 through the merger of the Universal Potash Company with the Pacific Cement Corporation. Shortly after the merger, both companies became divisions of a new entity, Basic Industries. On a combined basis, sales for 1981 were about $156 million on assets of approximately $193 million (Exhibit 1). The potash division contributed about 16 percent of total revenues and about 31 percent of pretax income in 1981.

The potash division, one of the major producers of potash in the world, operated one mine in the United States and a larger one in Peru. Sales of potash went principally to agricultural markets, where the chemical was used as an essential ingredient in the manufacture of chemical fertilizers.

Demand for potash was highly seasonal, with the majority of annual sales and earnings generated in the first five months of the year. Good weather during the spring planting period created an increase in the use of fertilizer and thereby better demand for potash. Poor weather could cause dramatic declines in potash sales from one year to the next.

The cement division's revenues depended on construction in three general market areas: residential housing, public works, and industrial construction. These markets were strongly affected by overall economic conditions and by the particular monetary and fiscal policies of the federal government. For example, restrictive monetary policy depressed residential housing construction by tightening mortgage credit markets and raising interest costs. Restrictions on government expenditures like-wise tended to reduce funds available for public works projects such as highway programs and dams. Depressed economic conditions also re-stricted private capital expenditures for new plant construction, thereby decreasing demand for cement. Conversely, expansionary policies and rapid economic growth generated strong demand in these markets.

For these reasons, cement demand was highly cyclical. In addition to the volatility of cement demand, the industry was at times plagued with periods of excessive expansion of productive capacity. The excess capacity in the industry had at times led to price competition so intense and potentially ruinous that Basic chose to set minimum prices and to withhold product from the market at prices below those levels.

The situation in the potash division was sometimes worse, as it, too, experienced the twin problems of cyclical demand and excessive expan-sion of productive capacity. For example, excess capacity in the potash industry became so acute in the 1970s that the Peruvian government announced a plan to develop price supports by guaranteeing a minimum price per ton, but requiring pro-rata reductions in the manufacture and sale of potash. The potash division, with substantial operations in Peru, was allocated a quota equivalent to 62 percent of its operating capacity.

The financial results for 1979 were poor for Basic, with a slight de-cline in cement earnings and a collapse in potash income. Earnings per share dropped from $1.09 in 1978 to $0.70 in 1979. Problems in both divisions continued during 1980. Although total sales increased by $10 million during the year, net income declined further. Earnings per share fell to $0.58 in 1980.

Throughout 1981, industry dynamics in both cement and potash were steadily improving. Potash production, aided by the Peruvian sys-tem of production quotas, was being kept more in line with market demand. In the cement industry, the poor profitability resulting from long-lasting overcapacity, severe price competition, increasing costs for antipollution equipment, rapidly rising fuel costs (a major cost compo-nent), fuel shortages, and reduced capital expenditures for capacity expansion served to reduce the level of industry productive capacity.

Results for 1981 were much improved. Net income exceeded $11 million, yielding a return on stockholders' equity of 15 percent. Earnings per share rose to $0.87.

OUTLOOK FOR 1982 AND BEYOND

From trends evident in late 1981, it appeared that 1982 would con-tinue the recovery in both the cement and the potash divisions. Mr. Jones believed that net income could increase by $5 to $7 million over 1981. If so, earnings per share would exceed $1.25.

Offsetting his optimistic forecast for profitability was Mr. Jones's projection that funds requirements would be large during 1982 and thereafter (Exhibit 2). Capital expenditures since 1977 had been minimal, in large part because of industry overcapacity problems and weak profit performance. However, almost $153 million in capital expenditures were planned over the next five years. Of this amount, $141.2 million was going to be needed for plant replacement and capacity expansion, and another $11.8 million would be needed for pollution-abatement projects. In addition, approximately $5 million would be needed in 1982 to meet a maturing note over and above the $4.8 million required to meet debt service on continuing obligations. Although some of this debt could be refinanced, Basic's board of directors thought that the firm was already above its maximum prudent debt usage.

DIVIDEND CONSIDERATIONS

Until 1981, Basic had never decreased its annual dividend. Basic's board members believed that dividend stability was important to the company's stockholders. Basic did not consider itself a high-growth company, and its board members had been advised by the company's investment banker that shareholders were likely to be seeking dividend income rather than capital gains. Even so, the company's common stock had received favorable price-earnings multiples in the market—reaching a high of 13 times earnings in 1979 (Exhibit 3).

Because of the perceived importance of dividend stability, Basic's dividend was not reduced in years when earnings were relatively poor. The company's board members believed that dividend policy should reflect long-term expectations rather than short-term factors. In 1978, Basic's dividend payout represented over 90 percent of earnings for the year. In 1980, dividends exceeded earnings by more than $5 million. In fact, from 1977 to 1980, dividends per share totaled $4.00 compared with earnings per share of $3.66. To meet dividend requirements and carry out needed capital improvements, Basic had had to raise substantial amounts of debt.

During 1980, an explosion at one of Basic's cement plants created an immediate and unexpected cash drain on the company. The company's bankers, with whom it had long-standing and positive relationships, readily extended $5 million on a note due in 1982. In so doing, however, the bankers noted that Basic's ratio of total liabilities to net worth of 1.52 was more than double the range that they considered reasonable for the company. They felt that the high debt usage was particularly incongruous in light of the high dividend payout ratios experienced.

In 1981, Basic's board became persuaded that its bankers were right and ordered a reduction in the dividend level to $0.70 per share—equal to about 80 percent of earnings per share for the year. The dividend reduction was unfavorably received in the stock market, and Basic's price-earnings multiple declined from 12 times earnings in 1980 to 8 times earnings in 1981 (Exhibit 3). In addition, the board requested a study of alternatives with respect to dividend policy over the foreseeable future.

In preparing his study for the board, Mr. Marks began by developing estimates of major sources and uses of funds over the next five years. He considered these projections only tentative, however, as he was well aware how rapidly and dramatically things could change for Basic.

Still, Mr. Marks was faced with the prospect that in 1982 only $1.7 million (approximately $0.13 per share) would be available for dividends. At the current dividend rate of $0.70 per share, dividends would total $9.1 million. He thought the major options were: (1) reduce planned capital expenditures, (2) postpone the scheduled reduction of debt through a refinancing of maturing amounts, (3) decrease the cash dividend, (4) institute a stock dividend in place of all or part of the cash dividend, or (5) some combination of any of these options. He felt there was little prospect that the board would even consider a new issue of equity in order to pay dividends.

EXHIBIT 1
Basic Industries, Inc.
Summary of Income Statement Items
Year Ended December 31, 1981
($000)

Sales & other revenues	$155,582
Cost of sales & other expenses	109,028
Depreciation & depletion	23,109
Interest	3,997
Income taxes	8,100
Net income	$ 11,348
No. of common shares (000)	13,004
EPS	$0.87

EXHIBIT 1 (continued)
Consolidated Balance Sheet
December 31, 1981
($000)

Assets

Current assets

Cash	$ 5,500
Temporary invest	3,849
Accounts receivable, net	19,562
Inventories	13,463
Other	635
Total current assets	$ 43,009
Operating property, net	141,304
Other assets	8,907
Total assets	$193,220

Liabilities & stockholders' equity

Current liabilities

Notes payable	$ 5,000
Current portion long-term debt	4,800
Accounts payable & accrued expenses	4,129
Taxes payable	1,177
Total current	$ 15,106
Long-term debt	89,400
Deferred taxes	12,000
Common stockholders' equity	76,714
Total liabilities & stockholders' equity	$193,220

EXHIBIT 2
Basic Industries, Inc.
Sources and Uses of Funds Projections for 1982–1986
($ millions)

	1982	1983	1984	1985	1986
Sources					
Net income	$16.0	$19.0	$21.0	$23.0	$26.0
Depreciation	23.5	24.0	26.0	27.0	28.0
Subtotal	$39.5	$43.0	$47.0	$50.0	$54.0
Uses					
Capital expenditures	$28.0	$29.0	$31.0	$32.0	$33.0
Debt amortization	9.8	4.8	4.8	4.8	4.8
Subtotal	$37.8	$33.8	$35.8	$36.8	$37.8
Net sources (uses)	$ 1.7	$ 9.2	$11.2	$13.2	$16.2

EXHIBIT 3
Basic Industries, Inc.
Selected Common Stock Data, 1965–1981

	EPS	DPS	Div. Payout (%)	Average P/E
1965	$1.07	$ .45	42	5
66	1.33	.63	47	9
67	1.44	.63	44	7
68	1.22	.67	55	10
69	1.42	.67	47	9
70	1.58	.80	51	12
71	1.22	.80	66	11
72	1.48	.80	54	10
73	1.43	.80	56	9
74	1.35	1.00	74	9
75	1.38	1.00	72	9
76	1.52	1.00	66	7
77	1.29	1.00	78	7
78	1.09	1.00	92	8
79	.70	1.00	—	13
80	.58	1.00	—	12
81	.87	.70	80	8

Dunkin' Donuts Incorporated

In early March 1977, Mary Kelley, a member of the board of directors of Dunkin' Donuts, was about to review a memorandum submitted to the board by Robert Rosenberg, the firm's president. The memorandum presented management's recommendation to pay a cash dividend for the first time in the firm's history. The board was going to meet the next week to decide whether to accept or reject management's recommendation.

BACKGROUND

Dunkin' Donuts was an outgrowth of a catering business established by William Rosenberg in 1946. A substantial portion of the catering firm's growth in sales and profits was due to the sale of coffee and donuts. Because of this success, Mr. Rosenberg opened a roadside shop in 1950 devoted to the sale of coffee and donuts. At that time, his objective was to have his firm become a major factor in the retail sale of coffee and donuts.

The roadside shop did quite well, and Mr. Rosenberg decided to expand. To grow as rapidly as possible, he decided to license independent shops to franchise owners, and the first independent Dunkin' Donuts shop was opened in 1955. Franchise owners were given the right to use the firm's trademark and system as well as assistance in opening shops and continuing advisory assistance. In turn, the firm received an initial fee of a set dollar amount and a continuing fee based on sales. Although a franchisee was encouraged to develop the property on his or her own, the firm frequently became involved in financing the land and/or the building. It would either purchase the land and/or the building and lease them to the franchisee or lease the property and sublet it to the franchisee. In either case the firm's policy was to earn a profit from this activity. Finally, the firm also frequently was involved in financing equipment needed, but in this activity the policy was just to cover costs.

In 1961 the firm began to franchise Howdy Beefburger restaurants, which were designed to be drive-in restaurants offering a standard menu of inexpensive items such as hamburgers, cheeseburgers, fish sandwiches, fried clams, fried chicken, french fries, desserts, and beverages. The franchise agreement was of the same basic type as that for the Dunkin'

Donuts shops. That is, the firm received a fee for services provided. Moreover, the firm became involved in the financing, and its policy was the same as that for the Dunkin' Donuts shops.

Sales and profits grew, reaching a record high of $9.2 million and $1.2 million, respectively, for the fiscal year ended October 30, 1967. (The sales figure primarily represents revenues earned in connection with franchising activities. Less than 20 percent of the firm's sales and profits for fiscal year 1967 were derived from shops that the company owned and operated.) In February 1968, the firm went public at $10 per share (as adjusted for a 2-for-1 stock split in March 1969).[1] One of the major reasons for going public was to provide the capital and the access to capital needed to accelerate the rate of growth. The strategy for this growth was to focus on adding new shops via franchising rather than company-owned and -operated units. The goal was to grow as rapidly as possible to capture a major share of the market.

1968–1973: "WE'RE NUMBER ONE"

Between 1968 and 1973, the firm expanded rapidly and became a major factor, if not the major factor, in the retail sale of coffee and donuts. Table 1 presents a summary of selected operating and financial data for 1967 through 1973. As the data show, the growth was successful at first, but then problems developed and a substantial loss was incurred for the fiscal year ended 1973. (A significant portion of the 1973 loss, approximately $1.5 million, was due to a change in accounting policy. Through fiscal 1972, the firm recorded losses on permanently closed shops as they were incurred. Commencing with fiscal 1973, the firm instituted the policy of calculating the present value of future losses and recording this amount in the year the shop was closed. Prior statements were not adjusted. That is, the $1.5 million figure represents the present value of future losses on all shops permanently closed up through fiscal 1973. Also, up through fiscal 1972, the firm capitalized certain research and development costs, and in fiscal 1973, $500,000 of these costs were written off and the firm instituted a policy of expensing all research and development costs as incurred.)

Management carefully diagnosed the situation and concluded that the following factors were the primary causes of the problems that created the loss. First, there just was not sufficient depth in management to handle such rapid expansion. Second, too much emphasis was placed on expanding the number of units at the expense of focusing on

---

1. As of March 1977, the Rosenberg family owned approximately 40 percent of the common shares outstanding.

TABLE 1
Dunkin' Donuts
Selected Operating Data
Fiscal Years Ended Last Saturday in October
(Dollar Figures in Thousands except EPS and Stock Price Data)

	1967	1968	1969	1970	1971	1972	1973
Total systemwide sales							
Dunkin' Donuts*	$31,292	$44,142	$58,567	$80,360	$99,593	$120,260	$135,269
Howdy Beefburgers	4,742	5,530	6,004	7,008	6,719	6,433	6,488
Total	$36,034	$49,672	$64,571	$87,368	$106,312	$126,693	$141,757
Average sales per unit							
Dunkin' Donuts*	$ 140	$ 149	$ 163	$ 170	$ 176	$ 185	$ 195
Howdy Beefburgers	$ 186	$ 210	$ 238	$ 265	$ 277	$ 285	$ 323
No. of units in operation—year end							
Dunkin' Donuts*	267	334	426	543	651	698	736
Howdy Beefburgers	26	27	26	26	25	22	20
Company revenues	$ 9,269	$10,859	$14,273	$17,594	$ 17,676	$ 22,251	$ 23,993
Net income before taxes	1,226	2,033	2,980	3,474	1,866	2,042	(2,829)
Earnings per share	.41	.52	.72	.91	.50	.55	(.82)
Price range of common (high-low)		27¾-15	33¼-18	26¾-9½	21½-10⅛	17-6¼	8-2½

* In July 1970 the firm entered into a licensing agreement that gave the licensee the right, subject to the fulfillment of certain conditions, to operate or franchise Dunkin' Donut shops in Japan. Total sales, sales per unit, and number of unit figures do not include the shops in Japan. Company revenue and income data do include fees earned and expenses incurred in connection with these shops.

the expansion of sales at existing locations. Third, in opening new shops, the firm focused on new markets rather than established markets. Fourth, errors were made in selecting franchisees. That is, some of these people were just not capable of managing a business. In many of these cases, they permitted the business to deteriorate and then decided on a new occupation. In these instances the firm either operated the business until a new owner was found, temporarily closed the shop until a new owner was found, or permanently closed the shop. In either case the firm generally incurred substantial losses. (Management recognized that it was only natural to make errors in selecting a franchisee, but it believed that the number was too high and that many of these errors could have been avoided.) Fifth, the firm should have been more involved in owning and operating shops. In the late sixties it established a policy of franchising all new shops, and by fiscal 1973 only 10 percent of the firm's revenues were from company units. Sixth, it was an error to expand into drive-in restaurants. Management's competence was in the coffee and donut business, and consequently more profits would have been earned had the firm focused on this activity.

The final problem diagnosed was the biggest of all. Even though $2 million was raised by selling common stock in August 1972 (at $11^7/_8$ per share), the firm was too heavily in debt. At October 27, 1973, long-term debt was $22.3 million and equity was $10.5 million. The principal payments due on this debt for the next five years were as follows:

Fiscal Year	Principal Payments
1974	$3.1 million
1975	2.8 million
1976	2.8 million
1977	2.4 million
1978	1.9 million

Moreover, the firm's practice was not to capitalize financial leases. (Lease payments for the year were recorded as lease or rent expense on the firm's income statement. Also, information regarding future lease payments was provided in the footnotes to the balance sheet.) The minimum amounts to which the firm was legally committed for the next five years were as follows:

Fiscal Year	Lease Commitment[2]
1974	$6.5 million
1975	6.2 million
1976	6.1 million
1977	6.0 million
1978	5.9 million

2. As noted, the firm leased many locations and sublet them to franchisees. Sublease rental revenues relating to financing leases have historically exceeded rental expense.

Finally, the firm was contingently liable at October 27, 1973, for $4.9 million under conditional sales contracts covering the sale of store equipment to franchise owners.

To make matters worse, several lawsuits were pending against the firm. Although management was confident that these cases would be won, it was not a certainty at that time.

Despite the enormity of the challenge, management was confident that it could solve its problems and at the same time continue the firm's growth. A plan was developed that included the following policies. First, the firm reorganized its management structure and recruited a number of new executives. The purpose was to give management more control over operations and to enable it to manage future growth better. Second, there would be a temporary slowdown in the rate of growth in the number of new units to give management time to gain more control over operations and to focus more on existing shops. The new shops that would be opened would be located in established markets, and the firm would own and operate a significant proportion of these new shops. Third, the firm would focus on increasing sales and profits at existing locations. To aid this effort, an increased level of resources would be committed to the development of new products. Fourth, the drive-in restaurant segment of the business would be deemphasized. No new shops would be opened, and existing shops would not be replaced as they closed. Fifth, there would be a reduction in the proportionate use of debt and an overall improvement in the firm's financial position.

1974-1976 IMPLEMENTING POLICIES

Table 2 presents a summary of selected operating and financial data for 1974 through 1976. As the data indicate, the policies were effectively implemented and worked. Sales continued to grow, and there was a dramatic turnaround in profitability. Fiscal 1976 was a record year for both sales and profits. (Exhibit 1 presents financial statements for 1975 and 1976.) The firm was the pre-eminent donut and coffee shop chain in the world. In effect, what McDonald's was to hamburgers, Dunkin' Donuts was to donuts.

At the end of fiscal 1973, the firm owned and operated 25 units; this number increased to 98 by the end of fiscal 1976. Looking at it another way, only 64 percent of the firm's revenues were from franchising activities for fiscal 1976, versus 90 percent for fiscal 1973. The company shops were doing quite well, and the intention was to continue to increase the proportion of company-owned and -operated shops. For example, the firm planned to add 60 new shops during fiscal 1977, 26 of which would be company shops.

TABLE 2
Dunkin' Donuts
Selected Operating Data
Fiscal Years Ended Last Saturday in October
(Dollar Figures in Thousands except EPS and Stock Price Data)

	1974	1975	1976
Total systemwide sales			
Dunkin' Donuts*	$163,278	$187,717	$205,350
Howdy Beefburgers	6,196	6,147	5,183
Average sales per unit			
Dunkin' Donuts*	$ 219	$ 237	$ 241
Howdy Beefburgers	$ 317	$ 336	$ 320
No. of units in operation—year end			
Dunkin' Donuts*			
Franchise shops	744	753	753
Company shop	36	67	98
Howdy Beefburgers	20	17	15
Company revenues	$ 26,719	$ 34,465	$ 43,256
Net income after taxes	1,311	1,881	2,492
Earnings per share	.63	.90	1.19
Price range of common (high–low)	3–1⅝	6⅜–1⅝	7½–4⅛

* Excludes shops in Japan. Company profit data include revenues earned and expenses incurred in connection with these shops.

The new executives and the new structure proved quite effective. One of the major benefits was lower losses because of permanently or temporarily closed shops. Overall, management had operations under control.

The increase in the sales-per-unit figure understates the progress that was made in that area. Management rated the product development program a major success. For example, during fiscal 1974, Munchkins were introduced. These were donut "holes," which were designed to be an inexpensive item that would be especially appealing to children. Also, the firm began to test-market a line of soups during fiscal 1976. The purpose was to sell an inexpensive meal that would attract new customers at times when the shops were less busy selling coffee and donuts. The results of the test-marketing campaign were very encouraging, and the firm intended to introduce the product in all shops during fiscal 1977.

Turning to financial position, the following are the principal payments and lease commitments that were due for the five years subsequent to fiscal 1976:

Fiscal Year	Principal Payments	Lease Commitments
1977	$2.7 million	$7.2 million
1978	2.4 million	7.0 million
1979	2.1 million	6.9 million
1980	1.9 million	6.9 million
1981	1.6 million	6.8 million

As the data show, the required debt service was still onerous. However, substantial progress was made. First of all, lease commitments increased, but this was because of the increase in the number of shops and the focus on established markets. Second, at the end of 1976, long-term debt was $17.7 million and equity was $16.1 million. (At the end of fiscal 1973, long-term debt was $22.3 million and equity was $10.5 million.) Third, the firm was contingently liable for $3.8 million at the end of fiscal 1976 (versus $4.9 million at the end of fiscal 1973) for equipment sold to franchise owners. Fourth, the firm was in a better position to service debt. Cash plus marketable securities was $5.4 million at the end of fiscal 1976, versus $2.3 million at the end of fiscal 1973.

Management was quite pleased with its accomplishments. It was now the major factor in the retail sale of coffee and donuts, and its most recent five-year plan called for a continued increase in market share. Moreover, management was confident that it would achieve its objective of continued improvement in profitability and financial strength.

Management was disappointed, however, in the price performance of the firm's common stock. Because of the problems just discussed, the market price per share fell to $1\frac{5}{8}$ but did not respond as expected with the improved performance. Not only was this performance preventing access to equity financing, but it was also preventing shareholders from earning the rate of return that management thought they deserved. Consequently, during 1976, management began to consider paying a cash dividend to provide a return to shareholders and to improve the price of the firm's stock.

Management considered alternative amounts and decided that $.20 per share per year was all that could be paid, given the desire to reduce debt. Moreover, management thought that, once a dividend was established, it should not be cut. Thus a level was chosen that management believed could be maintained. (It was also believed that a firm should try to establish a record of steadily increasing dividends. However, given the firm's investment and debt-reduction programs, no increases were considered for the foreseeable future.)

Once the amount was set, alternative means of payment were considered. Quarterly payments of $.05 per share was one option. Others were a $.02, $.03, or $.04 quarterly dividend with an extra at year-end. Finally, management decided that it was best to pay $.05 per quarter.

While these difficult choices were being considered, the issue was raised at board of directors' meetings to obtain the opinions of the directors and to obtain an idea of how they would react to a dividend recommendation. Views were mixed. Those in favor of a dividend basically agreed with management's position (as outlined in the appendix). Those opposed believed that the primary reason that the stock price had not rebounded as anticipated was that the firm had a large amount of financial leverage. Consequently, if the cash used to pay dividends were used to reduce the proportion of debt more rapidly, the impact on the firm's stock price would be more favorable than the possible favorable effect of a dividend.

When Ms. Kelley received her copy of the memorandum (see the appendix), she planned to study it carefully. Because of her background in the securities business, she realized that her views and recommendation would carry a great deal of weight in the final decision.

EXHIBIT 1
Dunkin' Donuts Incorporated and Subsidiaries
Statement of Consolidated Income

	Fiscal Year Ended	
	October 30, 1976	October 25, 1975
Gross revenues		
Sales by Company-operated units	$17,535,000	$10,610,000
Rental income	14,106,000	13,329,000
Continuing franchise fee income	9,260,000	8,701,000
Initial franchise fee income	577,000	503,000
Gain on sales of property, plant and equipment at existing locations	505,000	401,000
Interest and other income	1,273,000	921,000
	$43,256,000	$34,465,000
Costs and expenses		
Company-operated units		
Food and paper	5,629,000	3,700,000
Depreciation and amortization	400,000	203,000
Interest expense	278,000	169,000
Rent and other operating expenses	9,172,000	5,408,000
	$15,479,000	$ 9,480,000

EXHIBIT 1 (continued)

	October 30, 1976	October 25, 1975
Rental properties		
Rent	5,746,000	5,746,000
Depreciation and amortization	1,362,000	1,281,000
Interest expense	2,195,000	2,415,000
Provision for estimated future losses associated with permanently closed locations	165,000	612,000
Other expenses	166,000	486,000
	$ 9,634,000	$10,540,000
Selling, general, and administrative expenses	12,869,000	10,674,000
Total costs and expenses	37,982,000	30,694,000
Income before income taxes	5,274,000	3,771,000
Provision for income taxes	2,782,000	1,890,000
Net income	$ 2,492,000	$ 1,881,000
Net income per share of common stock	$1.19	$.90

Consolidated Balance Sheet

Assets	October 30, 1976	October 25, 1975
Current assets		
Cash (including $3,237,000 of certificates of deposit in 1976; $2,755,000 in 1975)	$ 4,821,000	$ 2,789,000
Short-term investments, at cost (which approximates market)	2,400,000	2,600,000
Accounts receivable, principally from franchise owners, less allowance of $305,000 in 1976 and $290,000 in 1975 for doubtful accounts	2,319,000	3,136,000
Notes receivable—portion due within one year	241,000	304,000
Food, supplies and equipment inventories	514,000	391,000
Prepaid rent, deposits and other current assets	875,000	1,256,000
Construction costs reimbursable under financing arrangements	244,000	310,000
Total current assets	$11,414,000	$10,786,000
Property, plant and equipment, at cost		
Land	6,239,000	6,363,000
Buildings	25,427,000	25,380,000
Leaseholds and leasehold improvements	4,212,000	3,818,000
Restaurant and other equipment	5,217,000	3,899,000
	41,095,000	39,460,000
Less accumulated depreciation and amortization	9,357,000	7,690,000
	$31,738,000	$31,770,000

EXHIBIT 1 (continued)

	October 30, 1976	October 25, 1975
Other assets		
Notes receivable, principally from franchise owners—portion due after one year	322,000	501,000
Lease acquisition costs	1,431,000	345,000
Other	261,000	222,000
	$ 2,014,000	$ 1,068,000
	$45,166,000	$43,624,000

Liabilities and stockholders' equity

	October 30, 1976	October 25, 1975
Current liabilities		
Note payable to bank	$ 250,000	$ 250,000
Accounts payable	4,028,000	3,661,000
Accrued expenses	902,000	777,000
Income taxes	2,418,000	1,217,000
Current portion of long-term debt	2,739,000	3,248,000
Current portion of estimated future losses	135,000	497,000
Total current liabilities	$10,472,000	$ 9,650,000
Long-term debt, less current portion	$14,952,000	$16,601,000
Deferred liabilities and credits		
Estimated future losses associated with permanently closed locations	1,810,000	1,984,000
Income taxes	504,000	438,000
Income on notes receivable	420,000	453,000
Security deposits by lessees	866,000	871,000
	$ 3,600,000	$ 3,746,000
Stockholders' equity		
Common Stock, par value $1		
Authorized—4,000,000 shares		
Issued—2,100,212 shares in 1976; 2,091,738 shares in 1975	2,100,000	2,092,000
Capital in excess of par value	2,325,000	2,310,000
Retained earnings	11,815,000	9,323,000
	16,240,000	13,725,000
Less cost of 46,800 shares of treasury stock	98,000	98,000
	$16,142,000	$13,627,000
Commitments, pending litigation, and contingent liabilities		
	$45,166,000	$43,624,000

APPENDIX 1

TO: The Board of Directors of
        Dunkin' Donuts Incorporated
FROM: Robert M. Rosenberg
RE: Recommendation for $.05 per quarter
        ($.20 per year) dividend

At each of our last several board meetings, we have discussed the advisability of cash dividends to our stockholders. However, as you know, we have always decided to conserve the cash and maintain the strongest balance sheet possible. However, for the reasons cited below, I would now like to recommend a $.05 per quarter ($.20 per year) per share dividend to our shareholders, effective with the quarter ended April 30, 1977. The reasons for this recommendation are as follows:

CURRENT STOCKHOLDERS' YIELD

The latest bid price on our stock (February 24, 1977) was 5½, or 4.6 X 1976 earnings. At the same time a year ago, the bid price was 6½, or 7.2 X earnings. Thus, not only has the stock market not recognized our substantially improved performance and prospects for the future with an increased multiple, but in fact our multiple is 36 percent lower than it was a year ago. Assuming a $6-per-share purchase price, the $.20 dividend would give our shareholder a 3.3-percent yield. Attached as Exhibit 1-A you will find a recent White, Weld survey concerning yields of certain leading growth stocks.

COMPARISON OF COMPANY PERFORMANCE TO INDUSTRY ACHIEVEMENTS

For the past three years we have had steady earnings growth, along with substantial improvement in our balance sheet. Attached as Exhibit 1-B you will find a copy of the latest Media General survey, which compares the company's performance with other food service companies in certain areas, including P/E Ratio, Profit Margin, Return on Equity, and EPS Change Last Reported. You will note that we rank ninth in Profit Margin, fifteenth in Return on Equity, eighth in EPS Change Last Reported, *but twenty-seventh in P/E Ratio* — followed only by a company that lost money. Until this point, we thought that our progress would be recognized and would finally result in market appreciation for our stock. In fact, as you know, for about a year we engaged in a substantial outside financial public relations program, including various luncheon meetings and special programs. However, the ranking in P/E Ratio shows that our progress just has not been recognized, and in fairness to our stockholders we must give them a return in another way, through a dividend.

CURRENT WALL STREET AND STOCKHOLDER ATTITUDES TOWARD DIVIDENDS

There appears to be an increasing focus on Wall Street on dividend-paying companies, with the so-called growth stocks falling out of favor. I have attached a recent *Wall Street Journal* article that is very much on point concerning this trend.[1] In addition, at most of our financial public relations meetings the question of dividends came up during the formal question-and-answer periods and usually afterward during individual discussions with brokers. Also, we are regularly questioned by stockholders concerning when we are going to pay a dividend. Attached you will find a copy of the most recent inquiry.[2]

STOCKHOLDER PROFILE

We have determined that the prime prospects for the purchase of Dunkin' Donuts stock are individuals and very small funds. Because of the small size of our float (1 million shares), we are not an attractive institutional purchase. In addition, we are also considered a second-tier food service company; and, because of tightening research budgets in the major brokerage firms, only first-tier companies are being actively followed by the leading analysts. Thus our audience includes the retail brokers and their customers. These brokers have told us that the dividend will help sell new people on the stock and keep existing stockholders in the stock.

AFFORDABILITY AND EFFECT ON BALANCE SHEET[3]

This section of the report discussed the firm's most recent five-year plan. Included was an analysis of what the firm's debt ratios would be with and without the payment of dividends. It showed a small difference, and management concluded: "we will still be able to achieve improvement in important balance sheet indices, while at the same time providing a return to our stockholders." Management also made the following statement:

> In our opinion, if a prospective stockholder or institutional lender was concerned about our leveraged position, the approximate —— %[4] effect of a dividend would not affect the decision to buy the Company's stock or lend it money.

---

1. This article is not reproduced here. It discussed how investors were currently favoring the stocks of companies that paid dividends.
2. The inquiry is not reproduced here. A stockholder sent a copy of a *New York Times* article that discussed how many firms were raising dividends to attract investors. On the copy of the article the stockholder wrote the following: "2/20. Robert: A further *subtle* hint—not from me, but from the *New York Times*." The stockholder's signature followed the message.
3. Because of the sensitive nature of the information presented, this section of the memorandum is not reproduced.
4. Reference was made to the actual difference in the ratio of long-term debt to total capital.

[Finally, it is important to recognize that the dividend would not affect the level of capital expenditures that was planned. If dividends were paid, the funds used would be diverted from the payment of debt. In other words, the firm's plan called for a reduction in the proportionate use of debt used and, if a dividend were paid, the debt ratio would be reduced at a slower rate.]

EXHIBIT 1-A
White, Weld & Co., Incorporated
Yields of Leading Growth Stocks

	2/3/77		
	Price	Dividend	Yield
American Home Products	$ 29	$ 1.10	3.8%
Avon	46	2.00	4.4
Coca-Cola	74	2.65	3.6
Eastman Kodak	72	2.10	2.9
IBM	271	10.00	3.7
Procter & Gamble	85	2.60	3.1
Texas Instruments	84	1.32	1.6

EXHIBIT 1-B
Executive Stock Report
By Media General Financial Services, Inc.
Ranked as of Feb. 18, 1977

For: Mr. R. J. Crawford, Jr.
Dunkin' Donuts Incorporated
P. O. Box 317
Randolph, Massachusetts

Market Value ($ Millions)		Revenue ($ Millions)	
1 McDonald's Corp	1,861.1	1 McDonald's Corp.	1,175.9
2 Holiday Inns Inc.	342.9	2 Holiday Inns Inc.	965.6
3 Howard Johnson	227.5	3 Howard Johnson	457.0
4 Sambo's Restaurants Inc.	211.9	4 Saga Corp.	445.5
5 Pizza Hut Incorporated	182.6	5 Denny's Inc.	392.2
6 Denny's Inc.	179.4	6 Pizza Hut Incorporated	295.3
7 Morrison Inc.	125.8	7 Gino's Inc.	255.3
8 Church's Fried Chicken	124.2	8 Host International	230.5
9 Jerrico Inc.	84.7	9 Hardee's Food Systems	188.1
10 Friendly Ice Cream Corp.	82.7	10 Sambo's Restaurants Inc.	174.4
11 Taco Bell	79.3	11 Church's Fried Chicken	174.1
12 Host International	57.4	12 Morrison Inc.	168.9
13 Saga Corp.	54.7	13 Friendly Ice Cream Corp.	166.7
14 Shoney's Incorporated	53.0	14 Ponderosa System Inc.	160.1

EXHIBIT 1-B (continued)

Market Value ($ Millions)		Revenue ($ Millions)	
15 Gino's Inc.	39.7	15 Jerrico Inc.	159.9
16 Steak 'N Shake Inc.	35.8	16 Collins Foods Intl.	125.6
17 Hardee's Food Systems	28.8	17 Bonanza Intl. Inc.	101.2
18 Collins Foods Intl.	27.7	18 Shoney's Incorporated	95.3
19 Ponderosa System Inc.	27.4	19 Taco Bell	78.4
20 Spartan Food Systems Inc.	21.3	20 Steak 'N Shake Inc.	70.8
21 Furr's Cafeterias Inc.	19.4	21 Frisch's Restaurants Inc.	70.6
22 Valle's Steak House	16.6	22 Furr's Cafeterias Inc.	61.8
23 Pizza Inn Inc.	16.0	23 Spartan Food System Inc.	60.0
24 Bonanza Intl. Inc.	14.1	24 Pizza Inn Inc.	57.0
25 Frisch's Restaurants Inc.	11.9	25 Specialty Restaurants	51.2
26 Dunkin' Donuts Inc.	**10.7**	26 Valle's Steak House	46.0
27 Specialty Restaurants	7.7	**27 Dunkin' Donuts Inc.**	**43.3**
28 Chicken Unlimited Enterp.	2.2	28 Chicken Unlimited Enterp.	13.5

Net Income ($ Millions)		Profit Margin (%)	
1 McDonald's Corp.	110.1	1 Sambo's Restaurants Inc.	11.2
2 Holiday Inns Inc.	39.7	2 Taco Bell	9.9
3 Howard Johnson	28.7	3 McDonald's Corp.	9.4
4 Pizza Hut Incorporated	20.2	4 Church's Fried Chicken	8.6
5 Sambo's Restaurants Inc.	19.6	5 Jerrico Inc.	7.4
6 Denny's Inc.	18.4	6 Pizza Hut Incorporated	6.8
7 Church's Fried Chicken	15.0	7 Howard Johnson	6.3
8 Jerrico Inc.	11.8	8 Friendly Ice Cream Corp.	6.0
9 Friendly Ice Cream Corp.	10.0	**9 Dunkin' Donuts Inc.**	**5.8**
10 Morrison Inc.	9.5	10 Spartan Food Systems Inc.	5.8
11 Host International	8.5	11 Shoney's Incorporated	5.7
12 Taco Bell	7.8	12 Morrison Inc.	5.6
13 Saga Corp.	7.5	13 Valle's Steak House	5.2
14 Shoney's Incorporated	5.4	14 Denny's Inc.	4.7
15 Gino's Inc.	5.1	15 Furr's Cafeterias Inc.	4.7
16 Collins Foods Intl.	4.4	16 Steak 'N Shake Inc.	4.4
17 Hardee's Food Systems	4.2	17 Pizza Inn Inc.	4.2
18 Spartan Food Systems Inc.	3.5	18 Holiday Inns Inc.	4.1
19 Steak 'N Shake Inc.	3.1	19 Host International	3.7
20 Furr's Cafeterias Inc.	2.9	20 Collins Foods Intl.	3.5
21 Dunkin' Donuts Inc.	**2.5**	21 Specialty Restaurants	3.1
22 Valle's Steak House	2.4	22 Frisch's Restaurants Inc.	2.7
23 Pizza Inn Inc.	2.4	23 Hardee's Food Systems	2.2
24 Frisch's Restaurants Inc.	1.9	24 Gino's Inc.	2.0
25 Specialty Restaurants	1.6	25 Saga Corp.	1.7
26 Ponderosa System Inc.	.9	26 Bonanza Intl. Inc.	.7
27 Bonanza Intl. Inc.	.7	27 Ponderosa System Inc.	.6
28 Chicken Unlimited Enterp.	−2.4	28 Chicken Unlimited Enterp.	−17.8

EXHIBIT 1–B (continued)

Return on Equity (%)		% E.P.S. Change Last Reported	
1 Taco Bell	34.4	1 Hardee's Food Systems	+172
2 Church's Fried Chicken	26.8	2 Bonanza Intl. Inc.	+144
3 Pizza Hut Incorporated	24.8	3 Taco Bell	+77
4 Sambo's Restaurants Inc.	23.2	4 Collins Foods Intl.	+67
5 McDonald's Corp.	21.0	5 Specialty Restaurants	+57
6 Pizza Inn Inc.	20.8	6 Church's Fried Chicken	+56
7 Shoney's Incorporated	20.6	7 Shoney's Incorporated	+36
8 Morrison Inc.	20.3	**8 Dunkin' Donuts Inc.**	**+32**
9 Jerrico Inc.	20.1	9 Pizza Hut Incorporated	+32
10 Denny's Inc.	19.5	10 Jerrico Inc.	+29
11 Spartan Food Systems Inc.	19.2	11 Sambo's Restaurants Inc.	+27
12 Steak 'N Shake Inc.	18.6	12 Saga Corp.	+26
13 Friendly Ice Cream Corp.	16.8	13 McDonald's Corp.	+25
14 Saga Corp.	15.7	14 Spartan Food Systems Inc.	+22
15 Dunkin' Donuts Inc.	**15.2**	15 Morrison Inc.	+21
16 Collins Foods Intl.	14.3	16 Denny's Inc.	+19
17 Furr's Cafeterias Inc.	12.9	17 Howard Johnson	+18
18 Hardee's Food Systems	12.7	18 Frisch's Restaurants Inc.	+11
19 Howard Johnson	12.6	19 Friendly Ice Cream Corp.	+5
20 Valle's Steak House	10.9	20 Pizza Inn Inc.	+5
21 Gino's Inc.	10.7	21 Valle's Steak House	+2
22 Frisch's Restaurants Inc.	10.1	22 Furr's Cafeterias Inc.	−3
23 Specialty Restaurants	9.7	23 Holiday Inns Inc.	−5
24 Holiday Inns Inc.	8.1	24 Steak 'N Shake Inc.	−10
25 Ponderosa System Inc.	2.4	25 Ponderosa System Inc.	−32
26 Bonanza Intl. Inc.	NE	26 Gino's Inc.	−35
27 Host International	NE	27 Host International	NE
28 Chicken Unlimited Enterp.	NE	28 Chicken Unlimited Enterp.	NE

P/E Ratio		Price vs. 52 Week High (% under)	
1 Ponderosa System Inc.	30.6	1 Friendly Ice Cream Corp.	56.1
2 Bonanza Intl. Inc.	22.1	2 Jerrico Inc.	55.4
3 McDonald's Corp.	17.0	3 Gino's Inc.	53.5
4 Morrison Inc.	13.8	4 Ponderosa System Inc.	52.9
5 Steak 'N Shake Inc.	11.6	5 Chicken Unlimited Enterp.	44.4
6 Taco Bell	10.2	6 Pizza Inn Inc.	44.2
7 Shoney's Incorporated	10.0	7 Holiday Inns Inc.	40.4
8 Denny's Inc.	9.7	8 Howard Johnson	40.3
9 Sambo's Restaurants Inc.	9.3	9 Frisch's Restaurants Inc.	38.8
10 Pizza Hut Incorporated	9.2	10 Furr's Cafeterias Inc.	35.8
11 Holiday Inns Inc.	9.0	11 Bonanza Intl. Inc.	34.3
12 Church's Fried Chicken	8.8	12 McDonald's Corp.	32.5
13 Friendly Ice Cream Corp.	8.3	13 Pizza Hut Incorporated	29.9
14 Howard Johnson	7.9	14 Host International	28.8
15 Gino's Inc.	7.9	15 Valle's Steak House	27.1
16 Saga Corp.	7.3	**16 Dunkin' Donuts Inc.**	**23.6**
17 Jerrico Inc.	7.2	17 Morrison Inc.	23.5
18 Valle's Steak House	6.9	18 Denny's Inc.	16.8
19 Hardee's Food Systems	6.8	19 Saga Corp.	16.0
20 Pizza Inn Inc.	6.8	20 Spartan Food Systems Inc.	15.8

EXHIBIT 1–B (continued)

P/E Ratio		Price vs. 52 Week High (% under)	
21 Furr's Cafeterias Inc.	6.8	21 Collins Foods Intl.	15.6
22 Host International	6.8	22 Taco Bell	15.5
23 Collins Foods Intl.	6.3	23 Hardee's Food Systems	15.0
24 Frisch's Restaurants Inc.	6.3	24 Specialty Restaurants	14.8
25 Spartan Food Systems Inc.	5.7	25 Sambo's Restaurants Inc.	14.8
26 Specialty Restaurants	5.0	26 Shoney's Incorporated	13.8
27 Dunkin' Donuts Inc.	**4.4**	27 Church's Fried Chicken	10.5
28 Chicken Unlimited Enterp.	NE	28 Steak 'N Shake Inc.	5.0

Price vs. 52 Week Low (% over)		$ Volume This Week ($000)	
1 Pizza Inn Inc.	39.6	1 McDonald's Corp.	11,782
2 Specialty Restaurants	39.4	2 Pizza Inn Inc.	2,755
3 Church's Fried Chicken	36.0	3 Holiday Inns Inc.	2,583
4 Taco Bell	35.8	4 Taco Bell	2,156
5 Morrison Inc.	33.3	5 Howard Johnson	2,052
6 Collins Foods Intl.	30.0	6 Pizza Hut Incorporated	1,548
7 Spartan Food Systems Inc.	29.5	7 Friendly Ice Cream Corp.	1,522
8 Steak 'N Shake Inc.	29.5	8 Jerrico Inc.	1,356
9 Sambo's Restaurants Inc.	29.4	9 Sambo's Restaurants Inc.	1,305
10 Saga Corp.	28.2	10 Denny's Inc.	1,258
11 Host International	27.3	11 Church's Fried Chicken	791
12 Hardee's Food Systems	25.9	12 Morrison Inc.	507
13 Bonanza Intl. Inc.	21.1	13 Saga Corp.	295
14 Denny's Inc.	15.9	14 Furr's Cafeterias Inc.	217
15 Shoney's Incorporated	12.0	15 Ponderosa System Inc.	182
16 Furr's Cafeterias Inc.	9.4	16 Gino's Inc.	177
17 Holiday Inns Inc.	9.4	17 Host International	132
18 Gino's Inc.	8.1	18 Shoney's Incorporated	127
19 Howard Johnson	7.8	19 Steak 'N Shake Inc.	124
20 Dunkin' Donuts Inc.	**7.7**	20 Bonanza Intl. Inc.	113
21 Friendly Ice Cream Corp.	4.4	21 Hardee's Food Systems	110
22 McDonald's Corp.	3.9	22 Collins Foods Intl.	84
23 Jerrico Inc.	3.9	23 Spartan Food Systems Inc.	81
24 Ponderosa System Inc.	2.1	**24 Dunkin' Donuts Inc.**	**69**
25 Pizza Hut Incorporated	.6	25 Valle's Steak House	36
26 Frisch's Restaurants Inc.	.0	26 Specialty Restaurants	19
27 Valle's Steak House	.0	27 Frisch's Restaurants Inc.	11
28 Chicken Unlimited Enterp.	.0	28 Chicken Unlimited Enterp.	0

EXHIBIT 1–B (continued)

Price Change This Week ($)		Price Change This Week (%)	
1 Taco Bell	+.88	1 Pizza Inn Inc.	+8.1
2 Pizza Inn Inc.	+.63	2 Furr's Cafeterias Inc.	+7.7
3 Furr's Cafeterias Inc.	+.63	3 Bonanza Intl. Inc.	+4.5
4 Friendly Ice Cream Corp.	+.50	4 Friendly Ice Cream Corp.	+4.4
5 Sambo's Restaurants Inc.	+.50	5 Taco Bell	+3.9
6 McDonald's Corp.	+.38	6 Sambo's Restaurants Inc.	+3.1
7 Howard Johnson	+.25	7 Howard Johnson	+2.5
8 Host International	+.25	8 Host International	+2.4
9 Steak 'N Shake Inc.	+.25	9 Specialty Restaurants	+2.2
10 Bonanza Intl. Inc.	+.13	10 Steak 'N Shake Inc.	+1.8
11 Gino's Inc.	+.13	11 Gino's Inc.	+1.5
12 Specialty Restaurants	+.13	12 McDonald's Corp.	+.8
13 Ponderosa System Inc.	.00	13 Ponderosa System Inc.	.0
14 Chicken Unlimited Enterp.	.00	14 Chicken Unlimited Enterp.	.0
15 Dunkin' Donuts Inc.	**−.13**	15 Church's Fried Chicken	−.8
16 Morrison Inc.	−.13	16 Spartan Food Systems Inc.	−1.0
17 Frisch's Restaurants Inc.	−.13	17 Morrison Inc.	−1.1
18 Spartan Food Systems Inc.	−.13	18 Holiday Inns Inc.	−1.1
19 Holiday Inns Inc.	−.13	19 Frisch's Restaurants Inc.	−1.8
20 Church's Fried Chicken	−.25	20 Saga Corp.	−2.0
21 Saga Corp.	−.25	21 Pizza Hut Incorporated	−2.2
22 Collins Foods Intl.	−.38	**22 Dunkin' Donuts Inc.**	**−2.3**
23 Jerrico Inc.	−.50	23 Jerrico Inc.	−2.3
24 Pizza Hut Incorporated	−.50	24 Denny's Inc.	−2.9
25 Hardee's Food Systems	−.50	25 Collins Food Intl.	−4.4
26 Valle's Steak House	−.50	26 Shoney's Incorporated	−5.1
27 Denny's Inc.	−.63	27 Hardee's Food Systems	−5.6
28 Shoney's Incorporated	−.75	28 Valle's Steak House	−7.5

P/E Ratios
February 17, 1977

Stocks by P/E Ranking	Composite		NYSE		ASE		OTC	
	Now	52 Weeks Ago	Now	52 Weeks Ago	Now	52 Weeks Ago	Now	52 Weeks Ago
Top 5%	20.3	28.8	18.5	28.5	22.9	31.9	22.9	28.4
10%	15.4	20.1	15.3	20.6	14.6	19.2	16.6	20.8
15%	13.1	16.4	13.2	17.0	12.3	14.9	13.4	17.3
20%	11.5	14.2	11.8	14.8	10.5	13.0	12.1	14.5
25%	10.5	12.5	10.9	13.1	9.4	11.5	10.6	12.4
30%	9.8	11.3	10.2	12.0	8.5	10.2	9.9	11.0
35%	9.2	10.5	9.6	11.1	8.5	10.2	9.9	11.0
40%	8.8	9.7	9.3	10.5	7.3	8.6	8.8	9.4
45%	8.2	9.0	8.9	9.8	6.9	7.9	8.3	8.8

EXHIBIT 1-B (continued)

P/E Ratio Ranges	Composite		NYSE		ASE		OTC	
	Now	52 Weeks Ago	Now	52 Weeks Ago	Now	52 Weeks Ago	Now	52 Weeks Ago
50%	7.9	8.4	8.5	9.1	6.4	7.4	8.0	8.1
55%	7.5	7.9	8.1	8.7	6.1	6.9	7.7	7.6
60%	7.1	7.4	7.9	8.2	5.7	6.3	7.4	7.1
65%	6.7	7.0	7.5	7.8	5.2	5.9	6.9	6.7
70%	6.3	6.4	7.1	7.3	4.8	5.3	6.6	6.3
75%	5.8	6.0	6.8	6.7	4.3	4.4	6.1	5.9
80%	5.2	5.3	6.3	6.3	3.4	NE	5.6	5.4
85%	4.4	3.9	5.7	5.3	NE	NE	5.1	4.8
90%	NE	NE	4.6	2.3	NE	NE	4.1	2.5
95%	NE	NE	NE	NE	NE	NE	NE	NE

P/E Ratio Ranges	Composite		NYSE		ASE		OTC	
	Now	52 Weeks Ago	Now	52 Weeks Ago	Now	52 Weeks Ago	Now	52 Weeks Ago
Under 2*	10.7%	13.3%	7.5%	9.9%	18.6%	21.2%	7.2%	10.0%
2- 2.9	.3	.6	.1	.5	.7	.5	.4	.8
3- 3.9	1.9	1.3	.9	.9	3.5	1.6	1.9	1.4
4- 4.9	5.2	3.4	3.2	2.3	8.7	4.4	4.6	4.1
5- 5.9	8.4	6.3	5.6	3.7	12.0	7.6	8.9	9.6
6- 6.9	11.5	10.2	10.5	9.3	12.6	10.3	12.2	12.0
7- 7.9	13.1	10.5	14.5	10.7	10.0	10.0	14.3	10.7
8- 8.9	11.2	9.0	13.9	10.9	8.0	7.2	12.9	7.8
9- 9.9	9.3	7.2	12.7	8.0	5.4	5.2	8.0	8.1
10-11.9	9.8	11.0	11.7	13.8	7.3	8.5	9.5	8.7
12-13.9	6.0	6.8	6.7	8.0	4.3	5.7	6.4	5.8
14-15.9	3.6	4.8	4.5	4.9	2.7	4.9	3.0	4.2
16-17.9	2.3	3.2	2.7	3.6	1.5	2.0	2.5	3.9
18-19.9	1.4	2.4	1.7	3.0	1.1	1.6	1.3	2.3
20-24.9	1.8	3.5	1.7	3.6	1.4	3.2	2.7	3.9
25-29.9	.9	1.9	.5	2.6	1.1	.7	1.3	2.3
30-39.9	.9	1.8	.7	2.0	1.3	1.5	.8	1.8
40-49.9	.4	.7	.2	.8	.2	.7	.8	.6
50 and over	.6	1.4	.3	1.1	.9	2.1	.7	.9
Negative earnings	10.5	13.1	7.4	9.7	18.1	20.9	7.0	9.6
No. of Companies	3,357		1,508		1,019		830	

Present rank based on day preceding week's close.
* Includes companies with negative earnings.

How To Read This Table

Included in this table are all stocks on the New York and American exchanges, plus 830 OTC stocks, and the composite for all three.

With this table, you can put your own or any other P/E ratio in immediate perspective.

Simply find where the ratio falls in any column in the top portion of the table, and note the figure at the beginning of that row. This is the percent of stocks in that category with a higher P/E ratio, with all others having a lower ratio.

The middle (or 50%) ratio is the median for all stocks in each category, with one-half of the stocks above and the other one-half below that level. This median may tell you more about the status of the market as a whole than any other single figure.

The lower portion of the table shows distribution of all stocks in P/E ratio brackets.

Media General
Financial Services, Inc.
Box 26991, Richmond, Va. 23261, Tel. (804)-649-6436

It is not the purpose of the material in this report to be advisory in nature, or to recommend specific securities, but rather to provide factual data on such securities as a basic reference source. Needless to say, actual stock prices reflect the complex interplay of the forces of supply and demand, and thus reflect many subjective and intangible factors not subject to statistical measurement of any kind. All information is based on sources believed to be reliable, but its accuracy is not guaranteed. Every effort will be made to correct errors, when discovered, in future reports.

PART VI
COMPREHENSIVE CASES

Megansett Corporation

Alden Hanson assumed the duties of vice president for financial management of the Megansett Corporation in early 1983. Although he had left a similar position with the Monterey Corporation, which was about a third the size, Mr. Hanson expected his new job to be a personal and professional challenge. For the first time in his career, he would have the opportunity to overhaul and redesign a corporate financial system completely. He viewed the challenging opportunity with particular satisfaction because he had followed Megansett's progress (though as an industry rival) for many years and had often wondered why the company had fallen into a steep, protracted decline in profitability and marketing aggressiveness.

Mr. Hanson had speculated that Megansett's rapid deterioration was linked to the retirement, in 1976, of the firm's domineering chairman, Mr. Smith, who also had held the positions of president and chief executive officer. Mr. Smith's failure to develop a strong management group to succeed him became evident after his departure. Following his retirement, the company had gone through a series of managers in key positions.

Shareholder resentment and dissatisfaction steadily increased and, in a special election called in mid-1981, an insurgent slate of directors was voted in with a commitment to revitalize management and operations.

Shortly after the new management group was installed, Mr. Hanson received an offer to join the company as chief financial officer. Megansett's new president, Mr. Russell, had personally made the offer and had assured Mr. Hanson that he would be responsible for a complete overhaul of the firm's financial organization, policies, and plans. Mr. Russell made it clear that he would be receptive to proposals for improvement and would strongly support those with which he agreed.

Mr. Hanson's managerial success had been founded on attention to detail and completeness. It was in this manner that he undertook a review of Megansett's financial operations. He began by assembling all available financial documents of the corporation and scheduling a meeting with Mr. Barnum, Megansett's treasurer, who was scheduled to retire in 1983.

Mr. Barnum proved a valuable source of information, with a clear, detailed recollection of Megansett's financial history, which he had accumulated in his 35 years with the firm. Because Mr. Hanson already had extensive knowledge of Megansett (gained from outside the

513

company) and had often speculated about its financial policies and strategies, he thoroughly enjoyed the "inside look" his four-hour session with Mr. Barnum provided.

GUIDING PRINCIPLES OF FINANCIAL POLICY

Mr. Barnum began by noting that the company's financial policy had been established principally by Mr. Smith. Mr. Barnum stated that Mr. Smith's gift for innovative, almost adventurous, marketing strategies was not carried over into financial management. Indeed, Mr. Smith had had almost a fixation on financial safety. Although this might seem paradoxical at "first glance," Mr. Barnum confided that he had come to recognize an inherent logic in Mr. Smith's perspective: lush financial reserves could be crucial to the exploitation of marketing advantage. The overriding preoccupation with financial safety and liquidity had permeated all financial activities and, increasingly, Mr. Barnum thought, had relegated financial management to a relatively passive responsibility. In fact, Mr. Barnum believed that Mr. Smith would have forcefully opposed financial innovation and change. Mr. Barnum thought this was the principal reason financial management had not been able to "contribute to maximum improvement in the value of the firm."

Mr. Barnum attributed the "safety first–safety only" role for financial management in Mr. Smith's scheme to three factors:

1. As mentioned before, it provided a counterbalance to somewhat radical marketing initiatives.
2. Mr. Smith's lack of financial expertise had raised his perceptions of financial risk.
3. Mr. Smith had had a traumatic experience as a young man, when he witnessed the effect of bankruptcy and ruin on his father's business.

This preoccupation with financial safety was evident in the firm's financial policies with respect to working capital management and investment, debt, and in dividend policies. Mr. Hanson asked Mr. Barnum to elaborate on financial practices in these areas.

WORKING CAPITAL MANAGEMENT

Mr. Barnum remarked that Mr. Smith had viewed with pride the firm's large cash balances and its ready access to credit (Exhibit 2). Mr. Barnum had gradually persuaded Mr. Smith to put some of the firm's unneeded cash into short-term, interest-earning securities (now yielding an average of 12 percent per annum) as a way of reducing "borrowing costs," although Mr. Smith had expressed concern about offending the company's bankers by reducing the "healthy" bank balances. Mr. Smith had considered banking relationships particularly crucial since they could assist the firm during an emergency. Moreover, he had thought that the balances themselves might yield some strategic value since competitors would be less inclined to provoke Megansett if it had sufficient reserves to undertake an extensive marketing counterattack. Consistent with this thinking, Mr. Smith had sought increases in lines of credit from banks whenever possible.

Megansett currently had a revolving line of credit with a syndicate of five banks. Total commitments amounted to $80 million. The distribution of these lines among banks is shown in Exhibit 3. Except for the Chart Bank, which had compensating requirements of 20 percent of use and 20 percent of availability (that is, deposit balances equal to 20 percent of the amount borrowed plus 20 percent of the unborrowed credit line), Megansett's compensating arrangement was 15 percent of use and 15 percent of availability. Recently, Megansett had borrowed up to $20 million. Mr. Smith had been considerably pleased that the company had consistently received preferential treatment from its bankers: it had always received the capital it needed and had received money at the prime rate of interest.

Although Megansett's bankers were willing to count the company's average normal operating ("working") balances toward the required compensating balance, any shortfall by the end of the year would be treated as a de facto loan. Thus, for example, Megansett's compensating balance requirement of $750,000 at the Grey bank meant that, on the average, $750,000 would have to be on deposit every working day of the year. If the average daily balance Megansett maintained during the year turned out to be only $500,000, the bank would charge Megansett interest (at the prime rate) on an assumed loan of $250,000 for a full year.

Cash Collection

Mr. Hanson inquired about the firm's monitoring of cash. The treasurer told him that this was integrated into the company's overall credit system to minimize the chance of error. Payments were received in the mailroom, where they were sorted and forwarded to the accounts receivable department. There the payment was analyzed and payments were credited to ledger accounts. The ledger was updated and the checks were sorted for delivery to the bank. The checks processed that day were then sent to the company's banks. When the checks cleared the bank, Megansett was informed by mail that the collected funds had been added to the company's operating account. When available, some of the funds would be transferred by wire to the several banks.

Credit Policy

Megansett sold goods on terms of 45 days, consistent with industry practice. Considerably different from industry practice, however, was its policy of not granting discounts for early payment (allowing it to underprice competitors). Mr. Smith had been opposed to discounts, believing that they implied that quoted prices were overstated.

Megansett was also more patient with slow payers, as evidenced by its average collection period in excess of 60 days compared with an average collection period of 30 days for the industry overall. Mr. Smith felt that a more tolerant credit policy not only offset the absence of a discount for early payment but also helped sales to poorly capitalized customers who would otherwise not be able to buy as much—although the sales impact of this policy had never been estimated.

Mr. Smith had not believed in paying early to take the industry discount (2/10 net 30) either, since he had considered such credit a costless loan—that is, a substitute in certain cases for bank credit, but one that had no interest cost.

INVESTMENT PROGRAM

Mr. Barnum informed Mr. Hanson that the emphasis on safety and liquidity was also present in the firm's investment policy. With one class of exception, no investment was acceptable if its cash flows could not recoup the investment within six years. The only exceptions to this "hurdle" were investments classifiable as "defensive" or "strategic." Projects classified in this group were viewed as absolutely necessary to maintain current activities (and did not include either new projects or expansions of current programs). Exhibit 4 shows the 1983 capital budget presented to the board in late 1982. The capital proposals totaled approximately $43 million, of which $9 million would constitute reinvestment, or defensive, expenditures. Exhibit 5 contains an abbreviated description of cash flow information developed for all investment proposals. However, the total available budget was currently set at $33.8 million.

"Have you been using any discounted cash flow analysis for the proposals?" asked Mr. Hanson.

"You mean *beta*?" Mr. Barnum asked with a chuckle. "Mr. Smith was very, shall we say, 'skeptical' of that kind of approach. He thought that being too technical meant ignoring critical intangibles. One year we hired an MBA fresh out of one of those fancy schools. The MBA circulated a memorandum suggesting that our cost of capital was 15 percent after taxes given our beta, which he estimated to be 1.0. Somehow Smith got a look at the memo; beta became a standard joke around here. The MBA, poor guy, took off soon after."

DEBT POLICY

Corporate policy was opposed to the use of long-term debt. This financial source, along with short-term debt, was viewed as a reserve that should be maintained. Mr. Smith had believed that the use of long-term debt increased the riskiness of the firm, not only by adding fixed financial requirements but also by reducing the available borrowing power. This reasoning applied equally to the use of long-term financial leases, which Mr. Smith had believed weakened market mobility. Adherence to this policy meant that debt and financial leases (whenever possible) were paid off if they appeared in the capital structure of an acquired company. For example, one recent acquisition entailed repayment of $4 million in 5¾-percent debentures and a repayment of $3 million in recently issued 9-percent debentures (plus a prepayment penalty of 5 percent). Megansett liquidated an additional $2 million of leases by buying the underlying assets outright.

Mr. Hanson whistled. "And we thought 35-percent debt was low."

Mr. Barnum responded, "I know what you're thinking, but everyone pretty much bought Smith's flexibility argument. He believed it gave us marketing and productive strength and flexibility. Of course, if we had ever really had to, we would have run debt out to the limit. In fact, an in-house 'what if?' projection showed that we could handle a 45-percent debt ratio. People really thought it was an edge. Obviously, we were giving up that 'EPS' boost but, hell, Smith never had any intention of issuing more stock. In fact, he wanted to buy a lot of it back. Smith was not exactly the most shareholder-oriented guy in the world—as you well know."

DIVIDEND POLICY

Megansett's dividend policy was straightforward. All earnings were retained as long as acceptable investments (as described previously) were available. More specifically, no dividends were paid if acceptable investment proposals exceeded or equaled profits plus depreciation. In this sense, dividends were a simple residual—a mere "detail" of the investment/financing decisions. This approach led to more volatile dividends per share than was typical for the industry. Exhibit 5 contains certain earnings, dividend, and price per share information for Megansett and a typical firm in the industry.

Mr. Smith had believed that it simply wasn't reasonable to pay out capital that could be profitably invested, and he had found it ludicrous that some firms actually had to borrow, in essence, to pay dividends. He had believed that firms that did that were trying to "have their cake and eat it too." He had thought they were just delaying "the inevitable," since sooner or later they would have to get the money back from shareholders (directly through a subsequent stock issue or indirectly through profits or depreciation to repay the debt). "They delay the inevitable and in the meanwhile lose investment money, financial reserves, and greater profits," he used to say.

At the year-end board meeting, the estimated investible funds were compared with the set of acceptable projects. If there were more investible funds than acceptable projects, the difference was paid out on a per-share basis.

In closing, Mr. Barnum remarked, "Granted, Smith did some unorthodox things from a financial perspective. But you know as well as I do that Megansett was considered a 'Rock of Gibralter' financially. I'm convinced that the company's overall financial strength allowed it to get away with things that were astounding. Who else, for example, could have sat out that five-year development of holographic paper that has created so much excitement in the industry? And who else could have—or *would* have—committed $10 million in two years to develop instant-copy paper while market acceptance was still questionable? From a product development and market-share standpoint, Megansett usually had two or three times as many profitable projects to choose from as anyone else. Exploitation of new technology, market niches, acquisition candidates—all this was possible with a speed no one else could match."

EXHIBIT 1
Megansett Corporation
Income Summary 1973–1982

	Sales ($ million)	Net Income ($ million)	Return to Net Worth (%)
1973	$209.3	$ 10.3	4.8
1974	231.4	16.0	6.9
1975	304.2	26.3	10.2
1976	308.1	34.8	12.8
1977	354.1	25.4	9.0
1978	367.0	23.4	7.9
1979	415.0	18.0	5.7
1980	453.3	(10.6)	(3.5)
1981	504.3	12.7	4.0
1982	498.3	24.3	7.1

EXHIBIT 2
Megansett Corporation
Balance Sheet
December 31, 1982
($ Millions)

Assets		Liabilities & Stockholders' Equity	
Cash	$ 15.0	Bank debt	$ 20.0
Treasury Bills	20.0	A/P	40.7
A/R	85.0	Other current liabilities	10.0
Inventory	50.0	Current	70.7
Current	170.0		
P & E (net)	213.0	Shareholders' equity	340.3
Other long-term	28.0	(10 million shares outstanding)	
Total	$411.0	Total	$411.0

EXHIBIT 3
Megansett Corporation
Credit Arrangements
As of February 1983
($ Millions)

	Total	Bank				
		Chart	Marvel	Federal	Silver	Grey
Line	$80	$20	$15	$30	$10	$5
Use	5	2	0	3	0	0
Working balance*	20	0	5	10	0	5

*Average daily balance in accounts, year-to-date

EXHIBIT 4
Megansett Corporation
Proposed Capital Investments

Proposal	Amount ($ millions)	Type	Payback
A	$ 5.0	Strategic	
B	4.0	Defensive	
C	7.8	New	4.6
D	11.0	New	5.3
E	15.0	New	6.1
	$42.8		

EXHIBIT 5
Megansett Corporation
Cash Flow Estimates
($ Millions)

Project	Year 1	Year 2	Year 3	Year 4	Year 5	Year 6	Years 7–10
A	.25	.25	.25	.25	.25	.25	.25/yr.
B	.35	.35	.35	.35	.35	.35	.35/yr.
C	1.0	1.0	2.0	2.0	3.0	3.0	1.0/yr.
D	1.0	2.0	2.0	2.5	2.5	3.0	8.5/yr.
E	1.0	2.0	2.0	2.0	2.0	5.0	10.0/yr.

EXHIBIT 6
Per Share Data for Megansett Corporation and a Typical Competitor

Year	Megansett Corporation			Competitor		
	EPS	DPS	Price*	EPS	DPS	Price*
1973	$1.03	$0.50	$ 7.00	$2.03	$1.20	$14.00
1974	1.60	-0-	5.00	2.60	1.32	21.00
1975	2.63	0.10	16.00	3.63	1.45	29.00
1976	3.48	2.00	31.00	4.48	1.60	45.00
1977	2.54	1.50	20.00	3.54	1.76	39.00
1978	2.34	1.00	12.00	3.34	1.93	33.00
1979	1.80	-0-	7.00	2.80	2.13	22.00
1980	(1.06)	-0-	7.00	(0.06)	2.34	20.00
1981	1.27	-0-	6.00	2.27	2.57	20.00
1982	2.43	-0-	17.00	3.43	2.83	34.00

*Average of annual high and low prices per share of common stock.

Winco Distribution Company

In early June 1965, the directors of Winco Distribution Company were faced with two major financial decisions that would have a long-run impact on the future of the firm. The first was the possible acquisition of Taylor Markets, Inc. The second was a major overhaul of the long-term capital structure of the company.

The first part of this case will present in summary form background information about Winco Distribution Company, stressing its growth and financing in the years immediately preceding 1965. Thereafter the information relevant to the acquisition of Taylor Markets and to alternative methods of reconstructing Winco's long-term capital structure will be summarized.

GROWTH OF WINCO DISTRIBUTION COMPANY

Winco was founded in 1907 to sell supplies to cotton plantations in the vicinity of Memphis, Tennessee. Through the years it expanded and underwent several changes in the nature of its business. By the end of World War II it had evolved into a grocery wholesaler with headquarters in Memphis servicing grocery stores in 10 states; it also owned and operated a chain of 18 retail food stores in Nashville, Tennessee.

Winco grew steadily from 1945 until 1965. The number of affiliated stores increased from 300 in 1945 to 1,350 in 1965 (Exhibit 1). This growth was also reflected in its operating statements and balance sheets for recent years (Exhibits 2 and 3). By 1965 the company's distribution system had expanded from the original single warehouse to a network of eight distribution points and three marine terminals from which it supplied ships calling in port.

In 1965 Winco was by far the larger of the two independent wholesale grocers in Memphis. It provided a wide range of ancillary services for affiliated retail stores. Stores could operate under their own names with standard brands or under a wide variety of advertising groups sponsored by Winco. Winco's staff was available to help plan all aspects of store operations from advertising to insurance and renovations. Financial support was also available to its retail associates. This support was given in the form of direct loans to 180 stores; of guarantees by Winco of liabilities of affiliates or suppliers; and of leases for prime store space signed by Winco and then sublet at cost to its retail affiliates. Management believed that these arrangements were basically quite secure and that they did not expose Winco to major financial risks.

Despite heavy competition from national chains such as A&P, Kroger, and National Tea, Winco's management believed that the sales volume of its own stores and its affiliates was equal to or larger than that of any chain or similar wholesale group in its area of operation. Independent studies by brokerage houses confirmed the ability of Winco and several large grocery wholesalers in other parts of the country to compete effectively with the national chains.

BACKGROUND INFORMATION ON ACQUISITIONS PRIOR TO 1965

Part of the rapid expansion of Winco during the 1961–65 period was accounted for by acquisitions rather than by internal growth.

Certain assets of the Henstock Company, a wholesale grocery business operating in southeastern Texas and southwestern Louisiana, were acquired in July 1962, for $700,000 in cash and common stock of Winco valued at $1.4 million (108,655 shares with a market price at the time of acquisition of about $13). Henstock's after-tax earnings were about $175,000 in the most recent year before acquisition. The book value of the assets acquired, after the deduction of certain liabilities assumed, was $1.7 million. The financial statements for Winco shown in Exhibits 2 and 3 have not been adjusted for the years prior to fiscal year 1963 to show the operations of the combined companies because the transaction was a purchase of assets rather than a merger.

In May, 1964, Winco acquired the principal operating assets of the Warrilow Corporation, a closely held wholesale grocery business and retail store chain operating in Nashville, Tennessee, and nearby areas. Winco paid the owners of Warrilow slightly over $12 million. Payment was made in three parts: (1) $4.8 million in cash; (2) $5 million of 6% cumulative preferred stock (described in more detail in the next section); and (3) the assumption by Winco of $2.4 million of the liabilities of Warrilow. The price paid was estimated by Winco's management at approximately 13 times Warrilow's earnings after taxes. The assets purchased had been carried on Warrilow's books at about $2 million less than the net price Winco paid for them. Most of this amount was assigned to individual asset accounts on Winco's books on the basis of an independent professional appraisal of the acquired assets. The remainder was carried as goodwill.

FINANCING IN CONNECTION WITH THE
WARRILOW ACQUISITION

As previously indicated, Winco issued $5 million of 6% cumulative pre-
ferred stock to the owners of the Warrilow Corporation as partial payment for this acquisition. The terms of the preferred stock provided for
the retirement of the entire issue in May, 1968, although Winco was
given the right to call at par part or all of the issue for retirement prior
to that date. If the preferred stock were not retired by May, 1968, the
preferred stockholders would be entitled to elect a majority of the
board of directors. Furthermore, the holders of the preferred stock
could require redemption of their shares on 30 days' notice if the paid-
in surplus and retained earnings of Winco should fall below $5.5 million.

The management of Winco did not expect to be able to generate
funds from its own working capital position to cover all the $4.8 million
cash payment and the $2.4 million in increased liabilities assumed in the
Warrilow Corporation purchase. It did anticipate, however, that a
smaller amount of current assets would be required to operate the combined businesses than the sum of their current assets before the acquisition. Inventory duplications could be eliminated, and other efficiencies
were expected to reduce somewhat the need for working capital. Because the Winco management was uncertain about the exact amount of
funds required to finance the expanded scale of operations, it decided
to seek interim financing rather than longer-term debt.

The cash required for the Warrilow acquisition was therefore raised
mainly through an intermediate-term loan negotiated in June, 1964,
with banks in Memphis and Nashville. The banks gave Winco a revolving
line of credit at 5¼% in addition to the balance outstanding on a 5¼%
loan previously made to Winco in 1963. The new loan was granted with
the understanding that it would be paid off or replaced by longer-term
debt when a more precise estimate of the company's financial requirements could be made. On June 27, 1964, the end of Winco's 1964
fiscal year, $5 million of the new line of credit had been drawn down.
By the end of fiscal year 1965, Winco was only borrowing $1.9 million
under this arrangement.

FUTURE PLANS

Except for the possible acquisition of Taylor Markets, Inc. which will
be discussed below, the management of Winco knew of no future possible acquisitions of retail or wholesale grocery firms. Moreover, in the
foreseeable future the management did not expect to commit funds to
integrate operations backward into processing, packaging, and manufacturing. No major additions were planned for Winco's physical plant;
funds generated from depreciation charges would be sufficient to cover

construction of whatever new fixed assets might be required. Growth was expected to come primarily from an increased volume of business in existing market areas. The region served by Winco was attracting industry at a significant rate; standards of living were rising and population was increasing. Moreover, as previously noted, the management of Winco was confident of its ability to compete effectively with the national chains. It anticipated a probable growth rate of sales of about 13 percent for the foreseeable future and set the likely boundaries on the range of this growth rate as 10% and 16%. The existing physical plant, with relatively minor additions, was more than adequate to accommodate this rate of growth for some years to come.

TAYLOR MARKETS, INC.

The management of Winco knew of only one prospect for expansion by acquisition in the foreseeable future. It had recently learned that the owners of Taylor Markets, an aggressive retail chain of 10 stores in Memphis, were willing to sell their chain to Winco if suitable terms could be negotiated. The Taylor chain had grown from a single store opened in 1947 to its current size. An independent market survey conducted early in 1964 indicated that Taylor had 18 percent of the Memphis food store business.

Winco had maintained a long and close relationship with Taylor Markets, which had been a member of Winco's voluntary plan since the first Taylor store was opened. The Taylor management had been very impressive, generating sufficient profits to open new stores with a minimum of financial assistance from Winco. Taylor Markets paid approximately $261,000 annually for the properties it leased. Many of these properties had been subleased from Winco and thus were already contingent liabilities of Winco.

The only severe difficulty Taylor Markets had encountered was caused by a labor dispute growing out of an acquisition the chain had made in 1961. As a consequence the company had shown losses for several years, but the issue had been completely resolved by 1965. The management of Winco regarded Taylor Markets' earnings of $220,000 in fiscal year 1965 as reasonably reflecting its true earning power. This figure was also considered a reasonable estimate of Taylor Markets' earning capacity on its existing stores over the next several years. (Recent earning statements of Taylor Markets are shown in Exhibit 4. Its estimated balance sheet for June 26, 1965, is given in Exhibit 5.)

The owners of Taylor Markets wished to continue operating the business after its sale. For tax reasons they preferred to sell by means of an exchange of stock rather than for cash. A sale for cash would involve immediate heavy capital gains taxes whereas an exchange of stock would qualify as a tax-free transaction.

A merger with Taylor Markets might be considered as containing seeds of conflict with the independent retail affiliates of Winco. The Winco management, however, had found no ill will generated from its acquisition of the Warrilow stores in Nashville. All retailers, including wholly owned stores, were given the same terms and treatment. Management had concluded that under these circumstances there was little difference between supplying, on the one hand, a wholly owned store and its independent competitor and, on the other hand, two independent retailers who were competing with each other.

LONG-TERM FINANCING

Winco's long-term debt structure as of June 26, 1965, can be summarized as follows:

Current maturities on long-term debt	$ 300,000
Balloon maturity due in 1968 on 5¼% note of 1963	2,000,000
Amount outstanding on revolving 5¼% loan in connection with Warrilow acquisition	1,900,000
Other long-term debt (about half of which was scheduled to mature during or prior to 1968)	1,400,000
	$5,600,000

In addition to the long-term debt owed by Winco, Taylor Markets had $650,000 outstanding in short-term notes payable. If Taylor was acquired $650,000 would be required to pay off these notes.[1]

In reviewing its debt position the management of Winco had definitely decided to refinance $5.0 million of its existing debt ($5.65 million if Taylor was acquired). An insurance company had expressed a willingness to share a loan of this size with Winco's banks. The interest rate on the outstanding balance would be between 5% and 5¼%. The principal of the loan would be amortized at an even rate over a 20-year period. If the loan was for $5.0 million, the banks would loan $1.25 million and the insurance company $3.75 million. The loan would be paid off at the rate of $250,000 a year, with the full amount going to the banks for the first five years and the remainder to the insurance company for the last 15 years. The covenants on the new loan would be less restrictive than those on the company's existing indebtedness.

Refinancing the $5 million of preferred stock along with the outstanding debt was also under consideration. The lending institutions

---

1. Winco also had contingent liabilities and lease obligations for its affiliates and suppliers amounting to $900,000, and it leased property in its own name involving annual rental payments of $850,000. Neither of these items was shown on its balance sheet.

had indicated that they would be willing to increase the size of the new 20-year loan to a maximum of $7.5 to $8.0 million on the same terms except for a proportionate increase in the annual payments needed to retire the principal of the loan in 20 years. An $8.0 million loan, however, was the maximum amount that they would grant at this time.

In addition to these needs for long-term or equity funds, Winco required seasonal financing each year. Peak needs occurred during the fall months and had amounted to about $1 million in recent years. These funds were borrowed through Winco's Memphis bank, where a 90-day line of credit of $3.5 million was maintained for seasonal financing. No change was expected in this arrangement for seasonal financing.

In its consideration of the restructuring of its long-run financing, Winco's management was considering two other sources of funds to refinance part or all of its needs above the amount that it expected to borrow on a 20-year basis.

POSSIBLE ISSUE OF COMMON STOCK

The first was a public issue of common stock. Winco stock, which was traded over the counter, had recently reached an all-time high of $28\frac{7}{8} a share, bid. (Exhibit 6 shows the range of Winco stock prices to June 10, 1965.) The bid price had only declined to about $28 during the recent softening of the stock market in the second quarter of 1965. During the same period the Dow-Jones average of 30 industrial stocks had declined from 920 to 875.

The company's investment banker had indicated that a new issue of up to $5 million of common stock could probably be sold at a price of about $25 a share to the public provided that the price of Winco common stock did not decline any further. The management of Winco did not want to price the stock so high as to "crowd the market" for fear that the stock might perform unfavorably thereafter. Fees and expenses were estimated at about 7 percent of the gross receipts of a $5 million issue and, because of the fixed costs involved, at a somewhat higher percentage of a smaller issue.

Winco common stock had first been made available to the public in July, 1961. At that time the company had sold 115,500 shares to raise funds to retire debt and for general purposes; members of the founder's family had sold 201,000 shares of their personal holdings at the same time. In order to minimize the cash drain from dividends during the first years of public ownership, the family had converted some of the shares they retained into a Class A common stock. The Class A stock was identical with the regular common stock except that it did not participate in dividends. It was convertible share for share into regular common stock according to a fixed schedule. After converting

the remaining 109,638 shares of Class A stock on July 1, 1965, the
founder's family would own about 437,000 shares of common stock.
Other officers and directors owned about 90,000 regular common
shares.

Management considered the public stock issue a success. It was
priced at $12 a share and subsequently rose to a high of $18½ before
the stock market decline in April, 1962. At that time the price fell
back to about $12.

By 1965 Winco had 1,373 registered stockholders located in 37
states. Some of the stock was held in "street names," the ultimate
owner having left the stock in the name of his bank or brokerage
house. Some mutual and pension funds had taken positions in the
stock. Nevertheless, the number of round lots (100-share lots) held
by the public was still small.

An investment banking firm with a special interest in the leading
wholesale grocers had noted the limited marketability, the relatively
small capitalization, and the lack of listing of these stocks as drawbacks. It expected, though, that these problems would diminish in
intensity during the next several years for the larger wholesale
grocers such as Winco. Exhibit 7 includes some financial statistics for
several large wholesale grocers.

POSSIBLE ISSUE OF CONVERTIBLE DEBENTURES

The management of Winco had also discussed the possibility of issuing
a subordinated convertible debenture to the public. Its investment
banker had indicated that a company like Winco could raise roughly
$5 million by issuing a 15-year or 20-year subordinated convertible
debenture bearing interest at a rate of between 4% and 4½%. This
rate was lower than Winco could obtain on a straight debt issue because of the potential value of the convertible feature to the lender.
The conversion price would be set about 20% above the market price
of the common stock at the time the debenture was sold, or at about
$34 a share on the basis of the $28 market price. In other words, each
$1,000 bond would be convertible into 29.41 shares of common stock.
Fees and expenses would be 3½% to 4% of gross funds raised. The
banks and insurance company that had offered to lend up to $8 million
on a 20-year amortization basis had indicated that they would not object to an issue of convertible debentures provided that these debentures were subordinated to the 20-year loan.

It was normally expected that the price of the common stock of a
growing company would rise sufficiently within a few years to make a
conversion privilege attractive, thereby enabling the company to force
conversion by calling the debenture issue for redemption. Consequently

it was not customary to require a sinking fund for the first few years of a convertible debenture's life. If Winco should issue a 20-year convertible debenture, for example, the repayments on principal would be scheduled to begin after five years and to be sufficient to retire the debt over the remaining 15 years, assuming that it had not been converted in the meantime.

TIMING OF ISSUE OF COMMON STOCK OR CONVERTIBLE DEBENTURES

Although an issue of stock or debt could be canceled at the last minute if the market proved extremely unfavorable, a public issue had to be planned several months in advance so that the necessary registration information could be compiled and filed with appropriate authorities. The nature of the information would differ depending on whether management had decided tentatively to issue stock or debt. A decision to shift from one type of issue to the other after planning was well under way would require a substantial revision of the preparatory paper work. The date of issue would be delayed, and an additional investment in management time and in legal and accounting fees would be necessary. For this reason, if a public issue of Winco securities was selected, management was anxious to choose a form of security that would not have to be changed because of moderate changes in stock market conditions during the next several months.

With the preceding facts in mind, the management of Winco had to decide (1) what action to take with respect to the merger with Taylor Markets; (2) whether to raise more than the $5 million it had already decided to secure by an issue of bonds; and (3) if so, the amount and the source of these additional funds. Management had prepared the forecasts shown in Exhibit 8 as background information for these decisions.

EXHIBIT 1
Winco Distribution Company
Number of Client Stores

	Fiscal Year				
	1961	1962	1963	1964	1965
Number of stores, beginning of year	747	767	774	797	1,197
Number of stores added	53	64	41	418*	161*
Number of stores dropped	33	57	18	18	8
Number of stores at year end	767	774	797	1,197	1,350

* Of the 418 stores added in fiscal year 1964 and the 161 stores added in 1965, 376 and 128 respectively were formerly served by the Warrilow Corporation and became affiliated stores of Winco as a result of the acquisition of Warrilow or by affiliation with Winco after the acquisition.

EXHIBIT 2
Winco Distribution Company
Income Statements for the Fiscal Years 1961–1965
(Dollar figures in millions)

Fiscal Year Ended:	June 24, 1961		June 30, 1962		June 29, 1963		June 27, 1964		(Preliminary) June 26, 1965	
Net sales and service fees*	$74.4	100.0%	$86.3	100.0%	$121.4	100.0%	$138.7	100.0%	$211.8	100.0%
Cost of sales less discounts	69.5	93.4	80.6	93.4	112.6	92.8	128.1	92.3	192.0	90.7
Gross profit on sales and service fees	$ 4.9	6.6%	$ 5.7	6.6%	$ 8.8	7.2%	$ 10.6	7.7%	$ 19.8	9.3%
Operating expenses										
Warehouse and delivery	$ 1.7		$ 1.9		$ 2.8		$ 3.1		$ 4.9	
Selling, general, and administrative	1.9		2.3		3.9		5.2		10.6	
Total operating expenses	$ 3.6	4.8	$ 4.2	4.9	$ 6.7	5.5	$ 8.3	6.0	$ 15.5	7.3
Income from operations	$ 1.3	1.8%	$ 1.5	1.7%	$ 2.1	1.7%	$ 2.3	1.7%	$ 4.3	2.0%
Add: Other income (expenses) net	0.1		0.1		0.1		0.1		(0.2)***	
Less: Interest	0.1		0.1		0.2		0.2		0.4	
Income before taxes	$ 1.3	1.8%	$ 1.5	1.7%	$ 2.0	1.6%	$ 2.2	1.6%	$ 3.7	1.8%
Provision for income taxes	0.7	1.0	0.8	0.9	1.0	0.8	1.1	0.8	1.8	0.9
Net income after tax	$ 0.6	0.8%	$ 0.7	0.8%	$ 1.0	0.8%	$ 1.1	0.8%	$ 1.9	0.9%

* In fiscal year 1964 includes $10.3 million in sales and a negligible amount in net profits from Warrilow for the period May 4, 1964–June 27, 1964. For the full fiscal year 1965, Warrilow contributed sales of $70.0 million and income from operations of $1.5 million.

EXHIBIT 2 (continued)

Fiscal Year Ended:	June 24, 1961	June 30, 1962	June 29, 1963	June 27, 1964	(Preliminary) June 26, 1965
Preferred dividends	—	—	—	—	0.3
Net income applicable to common shares	$ 0.6	$ 0.7	$ 1.0	$ 1.1	$ 1.6
Number of shares of common stock outstanding at end of each period**	704,411	819,911	928,566	932,901	938,393
Net income per share**	$0.85	$0.86	$1.07	$1.21	$1.66
Dividends per share paid on common shares only	$0.04	$0.26	$0.34	$0.41	$0.50
Depreciation (millions)	n.a.	n.a.	$0.4	$0.5	$0.9

** Includes both classes of common stock.
*** Includes $0.3 million loss on abandonment of equipment in the Warrilow operation.

EXHIBIT 3
Winco Distribution Company
Balance Sheets as of End of Fiscal Years 1961–1965
(Dollar figures in millions)

	June 24 1961*	June 30 1962	June 29 1963	June 27 1964	(Preliminary) June 26 1965
Assets					
Current assets					
Cash	$1.0	$ 1.6	$ 2.4	$ 4.2	$ 2.5
Receivables (net)	1.8	3.3	4.7	8.5	10.2
Inventories of merchandise and supplies	4.3	4.5	7.0	12.7	13.0
Total current assets	$7.1	$ 9.4	$14.1	$25.4	$25.7
Investments, advances to affiliates, and other assets	$1.2	$ 0.5	$ 1.8	$ 1.7	$ 1.8
Property and equipment					
Property and equipment	$2.2	$ 2.5	$ 3.5	$ 7.0	$ 6.9
Less: Accumulated depreciation	0.7	1.0	1.3	2.1	2.4
Net property and equipment	$1.5	$ 1.5	$ 2.2	$ 4.9	$ 4.5
Goodwill, deferred charges and other assets	—	—	0.1	0.8	0.8
Total assets	$9.8	$11.4	$18.2	$32.8	$32.8
Liabilities					
Current liabilities					
Notes payable, bank	$1.5	$ 0.5	$ —	$ 0.1	$ 0.4
Current maturities, long-term debt	0.1	0.1	0.3	0.3	0.3
Trade accounts payable and other accruals	2.2	2.8	4.7	8.6	10.0
Income taxes payable	0.6	0.6	0.8	0.9	1.4
Total current liabilities	$4.4	$ 4.0	$ 5.8	$ 9.9	$12.1

EXHIBIT 3 (continued)

	June 24 1961*	June 30 1962	June 29 1963	June 27 1964	(Preliminary) June 26 1965
Long-term debt	$0.9	$ 0.8	$ 4.1	$ 8.8	$ 5.3
Stockholders' equity					
4% preferred stock, noncumulative	$0.4	$ 0.4	$ —	$ —	$ —
6% preferred stock, cumulative, due 1968	—	—	—	5.0	5.0
Common stock, $1 par value**	0.4	0.5	0.6	0.7	0.8
Common stock Class A, $7 par value**	0.3	0.3	0.3	0.2	0.1
Paid-in surplus	0.5	1.8	3.1	3.1	3.2
Retained earnings	2.9	3.6	4.3	5.1	6.3
Total stockholders' equity	$4.5	$ 6.6	$ 8.3	$14.1	$15.4
Total liabilities and stockholders' equity	$9.8	$11.4	$18.2	$32.8	$32.8

* The statement as of June 24, 1961 has not been restated to allow for certain subsidiaries consolidated in 1962 and subsequent years. The assets of these subsidiaries totalled about $350,000.
** Total number of shares outstanding in each period shown in Exhibit 2.

EXHIBIT 4
Taylor Markets, Inc.
Income Statement
(Dollar figures in thousands)

Fiscal Year Ended	June 29, 1963		June 27, 1964		(Preliminary) June 26, 1965	
Net sales	$16,463	100.0%	$18,504	100.0%	$18,162	100.0%
Cost of sales	13,270	80.6	14,833	80.2	14,379	79.2
Gross profit on sales	$ 3,193	19.4%	$ 3,671	19.8%	$ 3,783	20.8%
Operating expenses						
Direct store expenses	$ 2,041	12.4%	$ 2,203	11.9%	$ 2,176	12.0%
Selling, general and administration	1,112	6.8	1,238	6.7	1,100	6.0
Total operating expenses	$ 3,153	19.2%	$ 3,441	18.6%	$ 3,276	18.0%
Income from operations	$ 40	0.2%	$ 230	1.2%	$ 507	2.8%
Other income	19	0.1	46	0.3	3	—
	$ 59	0.3%	$ 276	1.5%	$ 510	2.8%

EXHIBIT 4 (continued)

Fiscal Year Ended	June 29,1963		June 27, 1964		(Preliminary) June 26, 1965	
Other expenses						
Interest	$ 70		$ 71		$ 66	
Other	15		2		5	
Total other expenses	$ 85	0.5%	$ 73	0.4%	$ 71	0.4%
Net income (loss) before taxes	$ (26)	(0.2%)	$ 203	1.1%	$ 439	2.4%
Provision for state and federal income taxes	—	—	95	0.5	219	1.2
Net income (loss)	$ (26)	(0.2%)	$ 108	0.6%	$ 220	1.2%

EXHIBIT 5
Taylor Markets, Inc.
Preliminary Balance Sheet as of June 26, 1965
(Dollar figures in thousands)

Assets

Current assets		
Cash		$ 884
Accounts receivable		10
Inventory		600
Prepaid expenses		116
Total current assets		$1,610
Cash value of life insurance		16
Total property and equipment	$1,659	
Less: Depreciation	808	
Net property and equipment		851
Deferred charges		1
Total assets		$2,478

EXHIBIT 5 (continued)

Liabilities

Current liabilities

Note payable	$ 650
Current maturities, long-term debt	125
Accounts payable and miscellaneous accruals	501
Accrued state and federal taxes	219
	$1,495

Long-term debt

4% note payable	42
5% note payable	130
	$ 172

Stockholders' equity

Common stock, $100 par, 536 shares outstanding	54
Paid-in surplus	71
Retained earnings	686
Total stockholders' equity	$ 811
Total liabilities	$2,478

EXHIBIT 6
Winco Distribution Company
Market Price of Common Stock*

Calendar Years	High	Low
1962: First quarter	$18½	$16½
Second	15¾	12¼
Third	14¼	12½
Fourth	13½	13
1963: First	14	13⅜
Second	17⅝	14¾
Third	17⅛	17
Fourth	17⅜	16⅜
1964: First	17	16½
Second	21⅝	19
Third	21½	21⅜
Fourth	24	21½
1965: First	25	24
Second (to June 10)	28⅞	24

* Bid price in over-the-counter market.

EXHIBIT 7
Winco Distribution Company
Financial Statistics, Four Grocery Wholesalers

	Winco Distribution Company	Fleming Company	Scot Lad Foods	Super Value Stores
Most recent fiscal year ended	June 1964	Dec. 1964	June 1964	Dec. 1964
Most recent fiscal year				
Sales (millions)	$139	$313	$183	$466
Profit after taxes (millions)	$ 1.1	$ 2.6	$ 1.4	$ 3.2
Gross margin (%)	7.7%	6.6%	11.8%	6.2%
Common dividends as a percentage of profit after taxes	25.5%*	47.5%	21%	43.8%
Stock price, fiscal 1964 range	16⅜-21⅝	22¼-28½	19⅝-27¼	27⅛-35½
Price-earnings ratio (based on average price for fiscal year 1964)	15.7	18.5	12.3	18.3
Yield (fiscal 1964 figures)	2.2%	2.6%	1.7%	2.4%
Quoted bid price, June 11, 1965	$ 28¼	$ 29¾	$ 24¾	$ 33½
Capitalization				
Long-term debt	38.3%	25.6%	38.5%	22.3%
Preferred stock	21.8	3.4	—	8.6
Common stock and surplus	39.9	71.0	61.5	69.1
	100.0%	100.0%	100.0%	100.0%
Five-year compound growth rate				
Sales	15.0%	11.6%	21%	17.2%
Profits after taxes	13.3	12.6	28	15.5
Earnings per share	8.4	8.8	18	9.8

* Based on dividends actually paid on the common stock. If dividends at the same rate had been paid on both the regular common and the Class A common stock, dividends would have been 34.8% of profit after taxes.

EXHIBIT 8
Winco Distribution Company
Pro Forma Projections, Fiscal Years 1966 through 1968
(Dollar figures in millions)

	Actual 1965	Projected, 1966–1968		
		1966	1967	1968
1. Sales and Earnings				
Sales—13% annual growth	$211.8	$239.3	$270.4	$305.6
Earnings before interest and taxes	4.1	4.4	4.9	5.6
2. Projected Balance Sheet Data**				
Current Assets and Advances to Affiliates				
Cash	$ 2.5	$ 3.6	$ 4.0	$ 4.6
Receivables (net)	10.2	11.0	12.4	13.9
Inventories	13.0	14.6	16.4	18.5
Advances to affiliates	1.8	1.9	2.0	2.1
Total	$ 27.5	$ 31.1	$ 34.8	$ 39.1
Current Liabilities				
Accounts payable	$ 10.0	$ 10.8	$ 12.2	$ 13.7
Income taxes payable	1.4	1.5	1.7	2.0
Other	0.7	0.7	0.7	0.7
Total	$ 12.1	$ 13.0	$ 14.6	$ 16.4
Net working capital and advances to affiliates	$ 15.4	$ 18.1	$ 20.2	$ 22.7
Incremental funds required for NWC and advances to affiliates	—	2.7	2.1	2.5
Cumulative increase in funds required for NWC and advances to affiliates	—	2.7	4.8	7.3
3. Minimum Financial Charges Following the Proposed $5 Million Refinancing**				
Interest on the $5 million of long-term debt	—	$ 0.25	$ 0.24	$ 0.22
Interest on other remaining long-term debt	—	0.04	0.03	0.03
Debt repayment—$5 million of long-term debt	—	0.25	0.25	0.25
Debt repayment—other remaining long-term debt	—	0.09	0.09	0.09

Note: The projections in this exhibit do *not* include any adjustments to reflect the possible acquisition of Taylor Markets currently under consideration by the management of Winco.

** The balance sheet data in this section include only current assets and current liabilities with the single exception that "advances to affiliates" is classified here with current assets. As stated in the text, expenditures on fixed assets were expected to be about equal to depreciation expenses.

*** These charges are computed on the assumption that $5 million of new long-term debt is borrowed at an interest rate of 5% with repayments of principal of $250,000 per annum. If more than $5 million of long-term debt were borrowed, then charges related to long-term borrowings would have to be increased proportionately.

Electricircuit, Inc.

In late May 1964, Mr. Vito Rappasadi, Treasurer of Electricircuit, Inc. was considering the company's future investment and financing program. Anticipated normal growth, introduction of a new product line, and modification of the company's present inventory control system, together would require substantial external financing. The opportunities for such financing were severely restricted, however, by the company's present financial condition.

COMPANY BACKGROUND INFORMATION

Electricircuit, Inc. had been founded on Long Island and incorporated in New York in 1954 by four young electrical engineers. At the outset stock in the company had been wholly owned by this group of four. Later stock options had been granted to three particularly desirable managers as an inducement to join the company. These options had been exercised, and in 1964, the entire equity was owned by the seven men, in approximately equal blocks. The seven also held all of the top management positions and comprised the board of directors.

In the period from formation through 1963 Electricircuit had enjoyed considerable success. The product line had been expanded from one original product to include several lines of proprietary items sold as components for digital systems. In the form of packaged circuits (modules), these products performed decision control, storage, and ancillary functions as components of digital systems. They were primarily produced for off-the-shelf sale to customers who used them in systems of their own design and manufacture. Company profit came principally from the sale of these proprietary products.

As the company had expanded, it had also begin the manufacture-to-order of a variety of special purpose systems which applied digital techniques to computing, information handling, control tasks, and data processing. The systems were used in space equipment, navigation and positioning systems, signal processing, data converters, and a variety of other end uses associated directly or indirectly with government expenditures for military and nonmilitary purposes. This business accounted for roughly one-fourth of Electricircuit's billings. The company profited from the inclusion of its products in these systems, but little, if any, additional profit had been gained from the provision of engineering services.

Electricircuit's proprietary products were subject to a high rate of obsolescence in an extremely competitive market. Although protected by patents, these items were always exposed to the competition of alternatively engineered products performing the same function. Typically the company's new products had achieved about three-fourths of their highest sales level in the year in which they were introduced. Peak volumes had been reached and maintained in the second and third years, but these years normally had been followed by steep decay and virtual worthlessness by the sixth or seventh year. This six-to-seven-year cycle had been cut short by competitive developments for about 10 percent of the new products which the company had introduced during the past ten years, and on those occasions Electricircuit had been forced to absorb substantial inventory writeoffs.

Thus, the danger of being leapfrogged technically was a very real one. It had been met by unstinting expenditures on research and development to improve existing product lines and add new ones. Company officials had been successful in recruiting and holding a strong research group, and this group, supported by ample budgetary allocations, had created enviable market respect for the quality of the company's products. The seven owner-managers were determined to maintain that reputation.

Over the years continuing expansion had led to a number of changes in Electricircuit's internal organization. Sales outlets had been established in Southern California, and late in 1962 a plant had been constructed there for the design and production of systems for the West Coast space industry. Earlier, production of proprietary products had been shifted from Long Island to a wholly owned subsidiary in North Carolina, largely because of the availability in that area of a low-wage labor force. Production operations at the subsidiary consisted almost entirely of hand assembly and wiring of modules and allied components. Other managerial offices remained at the original site on Long Island.

In the period after 1960, rapidly widening product acceptance had almost trebled the company's sales (Exhibit 1), and its investment in current assets had expanded accordingly (Exhibit 2). Short-term loans, secured by the pledge of receivables, had been obtained from Electricircuit's Long Island bank to support this growing requirement. With isolated exceptions, the bank had been willing to lend 85% of the face amount of the receivables, and this banking arrangement had proved generally satisfactory until early 1964. At that time an officer of the bank had made it clear that Electricircuit had reached the limit of the credit line which the bank was willing to extend in the absence of some improvement in the company's capital structure. New equity of junior debt financing would qualify Electricircuit for a larger loan, if the company so desired and the requisite security were available, but the loan limit would continue to be set in terms of the ratio of bank debt to junior claims (equity plus subordinated debt, if any) which existed at the end of 1963. This assumed no deterioration in earnings or financial condition.

As 1964 had worn on and sales had continued to increase, the company had been forced to cut its cash balance sharply to meet its growing financing needs. Positive earnings had been realized in approximately the same proportion of sales as in 1963, but the retention of these earnings had failed to alter the bank's stand on additional financing. When approached in April, the loan officer had been reluctant to extend additional credit on the basis of unaudited interim statements, but more importantly, he had pointed out that the growth of equity had produced only a modest change in the company's debt/equity ratio. Moreover, about one-half of the earnings had been invested in highly specialized equipment, and to that extent the bank had not benefited either from replenishment of the company's deposit balance or, as a creditor, from the increased protection which investment in more liquid assets might have provided.

GROWTH PROSPECTS

In late May, Mr. Rappasadi prepared the following forecast of Electricircuit's year-end current asset position, to help in assessing the company's immediate financing problems.

Cash		$ 135,000
Receivables		2,720,000
Inventory		
Raw materials	$436,000	
Work-in-process	529,000	
Finished goods	311,000	1,276,000
		$4,131,000

The forecast assumed a year-end sales rate of $13.6 million and a corresponding cost-of-goods-sold figure of $8.1 million. Actual sales for the year were estimated at $12.0 million. These estimates had been employed with some confidence in projecting working capital requirements since sales in recent months and impressions of customers' production plans for the balance of the year pointed unmistakably toward continued growth. Receivables had been estimated at 20% of sales, and raw materials and work-in-process at a four-weeks rate of usage. Finished goods, on the other hand, had been projected at little more than a two-weeks supply.

During preceding months finished goods inventory had been deliberately reduced in relation to sales as other cash requirements had mounted. Mr. Rappasadi believed that continued curtailment of investment in finished goods inventory was likely to be costly, but lacking other immediate sources of funds, he also felt that the stock of finished goods would have to be held to the projected level if the company were to avoid an acute cash emergency. As it was, cash had been projected at merely its current level.

Beyond 1964, the marketing manager had estimated that sales of the company's current products would reach $16 million in 1965. Without major product innovation, he thought that sales could probably be maintained at that level in 1966, but if past patterns prevailed, he expected that the following year would see a decline which might amount to as much as $4 million or $5 million. The exact forecast for 1965 was based primarily on the marketing group's knowledge of government appropriations for ongoing defense and space programs. It could be upset by project cancellations, but that was considered highly unlikely for the projects concerned. On the other hand, the plateau and descent pattern of the more distant estimates emphasized the importance of maintaining Electricircuit's technical pre-eminence.

INVESTMENT POSSIBILITIES

Mr. Rappasadi saw two possible opportunities for investment which might improve the projected sales pattern and its profit consequences in the future. One involved the introduction of a major new product line and the other, a revision of the company's finished goods inventory control system.

The new product line, which had been under development for the past two years, performed comfortably to military specifications and was believed to possess technical qualities which would give it significant competitive advantages. All of the items making up the line were in a late stage of development, and the line was currently scheduled for introduction at the turn of the year. Market reception was difficult to estimate with any degree of precision, but the marketing manager was confident that the line would contribute sales of at least $2.0 million in 1965 and a further increment of at least $0.5 million in 1966. The line would be priced to give the same coverage of costs as was provided by the company's other proprietary products.

To put the line into production in the North Carolina plant would require about $100,000 for specialized equipment. That plant had been built to accommodate more growth than had yet been realized, and therefore no additional outlays were anticipated for production facilities. However, the marketing manager had estimated that a budget allocation of $35,000 would be needed to introduce and promote the line if it were to achieve its full potential.

The second investment possibility—that of increasing stocks of finished goods—grew out of widespread feeling that economizing in that direction had already been pushed far beyond justifiable limits. Expediting had become commonplace in juggling production schedules, with costly consequences, and orders had been lost to competitors with disturbing frequency when customers had been notified of long but necessary delivery delays. Mr. Rappasadi, therefore, had ordered a review of the company's entire inventory control system.

The area of concern, as a result of that study, had been narrowed to the finished goods segment of total inventory. Some improvements seemed possible in balancing raw material stocks, but it was not thought that this would lead to any appreciable change in the relationship of total raw material inventory to production volume. Lead time required by the purchasing department and limited interchangeability of parts among product lines combined to fix the required total at roughly a four-weeks supply level. Work-in-process inventory seemed similarly intractable. Allocation of shop labor, timing of lot starts, schedules, and so on, were already being decided on grounds of optimum production arrangements, as the production manager saw them. Technical changes, necessitating work stoppages, often had to be introduced during the in-process stage, and therefore the production manager, and the engineering group as well, attached considerable value to the flexibility allowed by a four-weeks production period.

By contrast with its approval of current raw material and in-process control practices, the report recommended complete revamping of the system being used to determine finished goods inventory levels. The present system, in brief, was based on specific item-by-item sales forecasts for the coming quarter. Given those forecasts, goods were scheduled into production in quantities which would raise the level of existing stocks to the anticipated sales requirement. Recently, as noted above, financial circumstances had made it necessary to cut stocks below the target levels which would have been set in more normal circumstances, but the report's condemnation of the system was independent of that experience.

Its basic criticism centered on the system's dependence on quarterly sales forecasts and the invariable inaccuracy of such estimates. Replacement demand could be predicted with tolerable margins of error but the same was not true of new orders. They were typically received at erratic intervals. Moreover, they comprised a large part of the total demand for most products.

To cope with the problem the report urged adoption of a system of buffer stocks which would be set with more careful regard to the costs, returns, and risks associated with inventory maintenance. To that end data had been compiled on five possible inventory-sales levels representing substantially different inventory policies (Exhibit 3). In each case the lost-sales estimate had been derived from computer simulations (using appropriate reorder points and reorder quantities) of the demand experience of major product lines.

Since Electricircuit was currently operating with lower finished goods stocks than those contemplated by any one of the five policies, Mr. Rappasadi was particularly impressed by the magnitude of the lost-sales figures. On the other hand, he was also impressed by the inventory investment which would be required to cut those losses by appreciable amounts. Any significant change in inventory policy would therefore tend to enlarge the financing problems which already lay ahead.

FINANCING ALTERNATIVES

As noted earlier, those problems had come to a head at the beginning of 1964 when Electricircuit's bank had refused to increase its line of credit in the absence of some prior strengthening of the company's capital structure. That development had not been completely unanticipated. In 1963 Mr. Rappasadi had begun to explore the possible issuance of subordinated long-term debt with several investment bankers and representatives of lending institutions. The discussions had all been unsuccessful, however, and Electricircuit had been forced as a result to finance the acquisition of a new headquarters building and its West Coast plant with sale-and-leaseback financing. The two buildings together had been constructed at a cost of $950,000 and had been leased by Electricircuit for a ten-year period at a combined annual rental of $280,000. The leases contained ten-year renewal options at the same annual rentals, but no repurchase option. Mr. Rappasadi, at the time, had estimated that the two plants probably would be worth half their original cost at the end of ten years and little or nothing at the end of twenty. Both deals had been arranged with a private group of wealthy New York investors.

The same group had also indicated its willingness to lend the company an additional $500,000 to $1,000,000 at any time at an annual interest rate of 18%. While the loan would be subordinated to bank debt and would permit an increase of the type of secured financing which the bank was currently providing, it would not be without its own restrictive covenants:

1. Cash dividend payments and company purchase of its own stock would be prohibited.

2. No additional debt would be allowed other than bank borrowing and other short-term liabilities arising in the normal course of business, or long-term debt specifically subordinated to this loan.
3. Current assets would have to exceed the sum of current liabilities and all long-term debt by at least $800,000.
4. Default on any provision would automatically accelerate the due date of principal and accrued interest, to the date of default.

Interest payments would be payable semiannually but the principal would not become due for five years. Prepayment in full would become permissible at the end of three years at a penalty of 10% and at the end of four years at 6%, but only with funds from operations.

Concern about weakening of control and earnings dilution made a public sale of common stock seem highly questionable to some of the company's owner-managers. They felt that earnings would continue to improve and cited the company's recent growth record as evidence of the possible cost of bringing in outside shareholders at an inopportune point in the company's development. On the other hand, Mr. Rappasadi had found that underwriters repeatedly expressed the opinion that Electricircuit's only hope for adequate long-term financing was additional common stock. That meant a public offering since none of the present stockholders had additional funds to invest.

Increasingly tight financial straits during 1964 had pressed Mr. Rappasadi to pursue the subject. Expressions of interest had been obtained from several underwriters, but only one, Bayles and Bayles, had expressed willingness to underwrite a stock issue. After many conversations, company visits, and a preliminary study of Electricircuit's financial records, the senior partner of Bayles and Bayles had indicated to Mr. Rappasadi that an issue of common stock to net the company up to $1,000,000 would probably be feasible in early autumn. Offering price to the public would be about $10.50 per share. The brevity of Electricircuit's history of good earnings would be a drawback, but Mr. Bayles explained that he counted on the company's unusual growth record to make that price attainable. The net proceeds to Electricircuit, however, would be closer to $8. The spread between the two prices would cover the underwriter's compensation and risk and all costs of preparing the issue. In addition the company would agree to sell warrants to Bayles and Bayles for $10,000 to purchase 10,000 shares of stock. The warrants would be exercisable after one year at a price of $13.50 per share.

If the terms of a deal were finally agreed, Bayles and Bayles would attempt to assemble a syndicate for which it would act as lead underwriter. The syndicate would be organized to provide wide geographic dispersion and insure a distribution of shares which would pose no threat to existing management. For a period of a year or so after the sale Bayles and Bayles would make an informal market for Electricircuit's stock in limited quantities. Although the firm was not an active over-the-counter dealer, it sometimes made an "after market" in issues which it had originated, largely for the benefit of customers who might be forced to dispose of their stock in emergency circumstances.

Mr. Rappasadi found it difficult to evaluate the terms of this offer. Inquiries addressed to acquaintances in the financial community uncovered some opinion that the company should hold out for a higher price. These sources cited a number of recent growth issues which had sold in the 30 times price-earnings range. In addition they noted that the economy showed strong signs of extending its longest postwar boom and that the stock market was currently at a record high.

Although Mr. Rappasadi realized that of all the firms approached Bayles and Bayles had been the only one to express any interest in underwriting a new issue, he decided to review the above opinions with Mr. Bayles. While Mr. Bayles agreed that both the economy and stock market were unusually strong, he interpreted these developments as cause for apprehension concerning the new-issues market. He was uncertain about how long these favorable conditions could continue, and foresaw a possible break in the market at any time. In a sharply falling market an unseasoned over-the-counter stock such as Electricircuit's was apt to fare much worse than average. In pricing Electricircuit's proposed issue, the underwriter therefore had tried to allow both for some immediate capital appreciation and for the fact that it would be selling the issue to its customers at or near the top of a particularly strong market. Bayles and Bayles was particularly mindful of the second fact because of its agreement to maintain an informal market for Electricircuit common stock. As for the price of so-called comparable issues, the firm disagreed with the critics. The issues referred to were generally smaller, often had a small cash dividend to provide downside price support, and had been sold two or three months earlier in quite different market conditions. For all these reasons, Bayles and Bayles declined to reconsider the offering price.

An alternative to external equity financing was continued reliance on the plowback of earnings with no payment of dividends. Mr. Rappasadi thought that the outlook for expansion and the profitability of contemplated funds commitments probably threw doubt on the wisdom of that policy, but he was uncertain about the amount, and/or types, of outside financing to recommend to his fellow shareholders.

EXHIBIT 1
Electricircuit, Inc.
Income Statements
1961–1963
(thousands of dollars)

	1961	1962	1963
Net sales	$3,616	$5,544	$10,637
Cost of goods sold*	2,368	3,758	6,325
Gross profit	$1,248	$1,786	$ 4,312
Research and development expense	422	529	1,097
Selling, general, and admin. expense**	782	1,105	2,376
Interest expense	30	40	93
Income from operations	13	112	746
Other income	2	7	20
Other deductions	(7)	(9)	(92)
Income before tax	$ 8	$ 110	$ 675
Federal income tax	3	45	329
Net income	$ 5	$ 65	$ 346

Notes:

* *Included in cost of goods sold*

Depreciation, amortization and			
maintenance	$ 31	$ 52	$ 117
Rental charges	40	80	210
State and local taxes (excl. payroll)	1	1	4
Total	$ 72	$ 133	$ 331

** *Included in selling, general, and
administrative expense*

Depreciation, amortization and			
maintenance	$ 11	$ 18	$ 40
Rental charges	19	39	101
State and local taxes (excl. payroll)	10	17	66
Total	$ 40	$ 74	$• 207

EXHIBIT 2
Electricircuit, Inc.
End of Year Balance Sheets
1961–1963
(thousands of dollars)

	1961		1962		1963	
Current Assets						
Cash		$ 279		$ 303		$ 347
Accounts receivable		693		1,260		2,255
Inventories						
Raw materials	$128		$337		$372	
Work-in-process	187		373		537	
Finished goods	244		311		407	
Total inventory		559		1,022		1,317
Prepaid expenses		8		13		24
Total current assets		$1,539		$2,598		$3,943
Fixed Assets						
Gross fixed assets	$212		$298		$537	
Less: accumulated depreciation	72		120		153	
Net fixed assets		140		178		382
Total assets		$1,679		$2,776		$4,325
Current Liabilities						
Notes payable*		$ 541		$1,072		$1,804
Trade accounts payable		159		401		484
Accrued expenses		129		246		240
Provision for taxes		9		56		383
Other		20		102		160
Total current liabilities		$ 858		$1,876		$3,072
Stockholders' Equity						
Common stock, stated value 50¢		318		328		360
Paid-in surplus		486		489		464
Retained earnings		17		83		429
Total stockholders' equity		$ 821		$ 900		$1,253
Total liabilities and capital		$1,679		$2,776		$4,325
Number of shares outstanding		636,086		655,122		719,746

* Secured by the pledge of all receivables.

EXHIBIT 3
Electricircuit, Inc.
Selected Financial Data on Possible Inventory Policies
(thousands of dollars)

Alternative	Ratio Inventory to Cost of Goods Sold*	Total Investment in Finished Goods Inventory*	Annual Sales Loss Because of Stockouts	Annual Combined Setup, Warehouse, Handling, and Insurance Costs**
A	4.9% (18 days sales)	$ 381	$495	$21
B	6.5 (24 days sales)	505	301	25
C	8.9 (32 days sales)	692	150	30
D	11.8 (42 days sales)	917	56	35
E	14.2 (51 days sales)	1,103	17	37

* Based on forecast annual cost-of-sales rate of $8.1 million. Inventory valued at direct cost.
** Interest expense and/or other financing costs are not included.

EXHIBIT 4
Electricircuit, Inc.
Balance Sheet, April 30, 1964
Unaudited
(thousands of dollars)

Current Assets		
Cash		$ 135
Accounts receivable		2,510
Inventories		
Raw materials	$410	
Work-in-process	506	
Finished goods	310	1,226
Prepaid expenses		30
Total current assets		$3,901
Fixed Assets		
Gross fixed assets	$612	
Common stock, stated value 50	168	
Net fixed assets		444
Total Assets		$4,345
Current Liabilities		
Notes payable*		$1,795
Trade accounts payable		530
Accrued expenses		246
Provision for taxes**		245
Other		143
Total current liabilities		$2,959
Stockholders' Equity		
Common stock, stated value 50		360
Paid-in surplus		464
Retained earnings		562
Total stockholders' equity		$1,386
Total liabilities and capital		$4,345
Number of shares outstanding		719,746

* Secured by the pledge of receivables.
** Tax liabilities as of April 30 reflect a large, first-quarter adjusting payment. At year end "Provision for taxes" normally equals the federal corporate income tax for the year just ended, plus approximately $75,000 state and local tax accruals.

Incoterm Corporation

In June 1976, John Clifford, senior vice president and treasurer of Incoterm, was about to re-evaluate his firm's financial strategy. While he was proud of his accomplishment and welcomed the challenge confronting him, he realized that his task would be difficult.

In his view, a primary role of the financial manager is continually to ensure that a high level of financial flexibility and strength will exist. Since the environment in which a firm operates changes, the firm's financial strategy must be continuously reevaluated to determine whether the firm's financial policies need revision. In explaining his views to the casewriter, he made a comparison to a boxer: "A good fighter should be able to take several solid body blows and still fight effectively. A well-managed firm should be able to absorb several solid financial blows and still compete and operate effectively. My job is to make sure that my firm can take several solid blows."

COMPANY BACKGROUND

Incoterm Corporation was formed in February 1969 by Jean Tariot and James Upton. The firm designed, developed, manufactured, and serviced electronic data computer terminals, related equipment, and software.

A computer terminal is one of the three major elements of an electronic data processing system. The three elements are the central-site computer and associated equipment, the communications lines, and the remote computer terminals.

The terminal equipment manufactured by Incoterm was of a type generally known as an intelligent terminal. Such terminals use their own small computer and are more versatile than "nonintelligent" terminals in performing various diverse functions—such as editing, validating, and preprocessing data—that may be needed by customers at the remote locations. In addition, intelligent terminals can be programmed to communicate with more than one central computer and with various types of central computers. The local processing capability of intelligent terminals optimizes the use of central computer facilities and communication lines. The price of intelligent terminal systems varies, depending principally on computation power, memory size, and extent of peripheral devices. Although generally higher-priced than nonintelligent terminals, intelligent terminal systems provide operating cost savings over nonintelligent terminals in some applications. From a manufacturing standpoint, an advantage of the intelligent terminal is that the same basic unit, by changes in programs and accessory items, can be adapted with minimal changes in hardware for use by many different customers with varying needs and with access to different types of central computers. Disadvantages of the intelligent terminal are the need for programming and potentially greater maintenance costs, as well as the generally higher initial cost.

MARKETING STRATEGY

Incoterm's principal marketing strategy was to emphasize solutions of customer's remote terminal and communication problems in a few carefully chosen industries. After choosing an industry to be so emphasized, Incoterm had a policy of attaining in-depth familiarity with the fundamental operations and systems applications of the given industry. This was a major element in planning the required marketing and product development approaches.

Prior to fiscal 1974, Incoterm's customer base was heavily concentrated in the airline industry. As a result of a long-term market diversification program, this customer base had been significantly broadened. The change in mix of product sales is shown in Table 1.

Through the fiscal year ended February 29, 1976, Incoterm's sales of equipment had been made to five major industry segments: airlines, railroads, government, banking, and insurance and securities.

TABLE 1
Incoterm Corporation
Product Sales Mix
($ Millions)

	FY 1973		FY 1974		FY 1975		FY 1976	
	$	%	$	%	$	%	$	%
Airlines	7.8	74	6.2	41	6.8	37	4.4	16
Railroads, government, banks, insurance, securities and other industries*	2.8	26	8.8	59	11.5	63	23.0	84
Total	10.6	100	15.0	100	18.3	100	27.4	100

* Includes sales for foreign licensees and distributors who may have resold equipment to airlines.

Airlines

At the time of Incoterm's founding, the airline industry provided the largest market then available for Incoterm's terminals. Accordingly, Incoterm emphasized sales to this industry in its first years of existence. Incoterm's first major contract was with British Airways in 1970; since then, "major" contracts (involving more than $250,000 business) were received from 13 foreign and domestic airlines. The typical airline industry use of the terminals supplied by Incoterm was for inquiry and response for reservation systems, although the terminals were also used in connection with diverse other functions, such as baggage handling, ticket printing, and check-in. Incoterm's management believed that Incoterm was a major supplier of intelligent terminals to airlines, but the field was highly competitive, and there could be no assurance that Incoterm would retain this position.

Railroads

Incoterm had delivered and installed major orders from Burlington Northern and MoPac. These railroads used Incoterm's equipment to manage and control freight cars. Incoterm had also filled an order from Amtrak for terminals for use in Amtrak's passenger reservation system. These railroad orders totaled approximately $8 million. Other railroads had also purchased Incoterm equipment in less substantial quantities.

Government

The two principal government areas in which Incoterm equipment had been used were drivers' license applications and police information systems. The Registry of Motor Vehicles for the State of Ohio had taken delivery of equipment to process drivers' licenses in over 200 outlets throughout Ohio. This system gave the state more control over both the issuance of licenses and the issuing outlets.

Within the federal government sector, Incoterm had delivered equipment to the Federal Aviation Administration, the Department of Agriculture, and other agencies.

Banking

Incoterm had sold equipment for several years to commercial and thrift banking institutions. Major customers included First National Bank and

Trust Company of Lincoln, Nebraska; Midland National Bank,
Milwaukee, Wisconsin; Great Western Savings and Loan; and Mellon
Bank, N. A., which accounted for equipment sales aggregating $2.8
million. Since Incoterm introduced the Series 7000 On-Line Banking
System early in 1975, three orders were received from major banks.
Security Pacific Bank placed an order for $6.3 million and Mellon Bank
ordered $5.5 million of Series 7000 equipment and services. Subject to
performance and other factors, deliveries of equipment to these banks
under these contracts were expected to amount to approximately $6.6
million by the end of fiscal year 1977. The Seattle First National Bank
made an initial Series 7000 commitment of $1.1 million.

The Series 7000 had compact terminals for the tellers and larger
administrative terminals for the supervisor, assistant branch manager,
and/or branch manager. The on-line terminal at the teller's window
enabled the teller to perform traditional functions such as checking
and savings account balance checks, account record changes, and loan
payments. The administrative terminals handled more complicated
functions such as opening new accounts, installment loans, mortgages,
lines of credit, and bank credit cards.

Insurance and Securities

In the insurance industry, the company had substantially completed
two contracts, aggregating $1.5 million, to provide terminal equipment
to Occidental Life of California and to Northwestern Mutual Life Insurance Company. Occidental Life used Incoterm equipment for the
on-line update of its life policies and for servicing Medicare policies
for the Department of Health, Education and Welfare. Northwestern
Mutual Life used Incoterm display equipment with supporting
peripheral units for update and inquiry of its life-insured master file.
In the securities industry, a major order was received for terminal
equipment from Blyth Eastman Dillon & Company, Inc., for trans-
mission of orders, retrieval of in-house quotations, and data communications management in its branch offices throughout the United States.
A major order was completed for the Philadelphia-Baltimore-
Washington Stock Exchange in 1974.

Other

The company has also made sales for use in other industries, including
hospitals, manufacturers, service industries, and freight forwarders.

International Business

The company realized a substantial portion of its revenues from customers in foreign countries. For the fiscal year ended February 29, 1976, the approximate amount of international product sales was $13.1 million, constituting 48 percent of total product sales as compared with international product sales of $6.4 million, or 35 percent of total product sales in fiscal 1975. In both years, the gross profit contribution as a percentage of sales made to foreign customers was comparable to that from sales made to domestic customers. The company directly handled the marketing of its products to overseas customers in some countries, through distributorships in Hong Kong, Spain, Sweden, and Japan and through wholly owned subsidiaries in the United Kingdom and Canada.

A key element of the firm's marketing strategy was customer service. Management believed that maintaining its products with a strong customer service organization was essential to customer satisfaction and was the key to the organization's future success. Consequently, in each year the expenses incurred to maintain and expand customer service were greater than the service revenue generated. The policy of operating the service segment of the business at a loss was expected to continue.

The firm offered its products for sale, lease, or rental. Through fiscal 1976, emphasis was on outright sales. For example, only 3 percent of product sales revenues for the fiscal year ended February 29, 1976, was financed by third parties through full-payout leases. Although the firm intended to continue to emphasize outright sales, management realized that it would have to become more involved in financing in order to remain competitive. Consequently, during fiscal 1976, to provide future full-payout, nonrecourse lease financing for its customers, the firm made arrangements with four bank-related leasing companies under which the firm could arrange customer lease financing under certain stipulated conditions. In management's view, these arrangements represented a suboptimal solution, for two reasons. First, they were for full-payout leases and did not help with operating leases. (A full-payout or financial lease is one that the lessee normally cannot terminate. An operating lease is one that can be canceled.) Second, the banks were obtaining the benefits of the investment tax credit and the tax shields from depreciation. Putting it another way, Incoterm was not taking advantage of those benefits.[1] And the loss of these benefits was especially significant since the firm's effective income tax rate was now close to 48 percent.

---

1. By establishing a finance subsidiary to handle the leasing, the firm could take advantage of the tax benefit. Moreover, management believed that it would be possible for the subsidiary to raise substantial amounts of debt and that the parent would not have to guarantee this debt.

PRODUCT DEVELOPMENT

The company's original product, the SPD® 10/20, first sold in May 1970, represented one of the first intelligent terminal systems to be successfully marketed. Since that time the firm had developed new products and refined the SPD® 10/20 to meet the needs of its expanding customer base.

Continuous product development was a necessity. The industry within which the firm operated was characterized by rapid technological change. (It was management's view that actual and potential change in technology constituted the major risk confronting the firm.) The useful commercial life of any computer terminal design could be short, and substantial research and development efforts were required to prevent product obsolescence. To fill this need, the firm maintained an engineering, research, and development program directed to developing new products and systems, improving and refining its present products and systems, and expanding their uses and applications. For this effort, the firm spent $1.815 million during fiscal 1975 and $2.302 million during fiscal 1976.

ACQUISITION POLICY

During 1973, management instituted a policy of conducting a continual search for suitable acquisition candidates. The primary purpose was to consider candidates that would strengthen the firm's competitive position. Although several possibilities were explored, no firms had been acquired as of June 1976.

Incoterm had been approached by several firms interested in taking it over. Management considered these but concluded that the offers were unattractive. Although management would consider future offers, it would not actively seek them. (Management was not concerned about an unfriendly takeover, for two reasons. First, management controlled about 25 percent of the common stock. Second, management believed that an acquirer would not buy the firm unless the management of Incoterm approved the offer.)

FINANCIAL PERFORMANCE

Exhibits 1 and 2 present a summary of operating results and financial position for 1971 through 1976. (For the fiscal year ended February 28, 1970, the firm had zero revenues and incurred a pretax loss of $571,000.) Sales and profits grew in each year except for the fiscal year ended February 28, 1975. A number of factors caused the decline in 1975. The primary ones were the following:

1. The fuel crisis caused a sharp decline in sales to the airline industry.

2. The firm relocated its manufacturing activities, and the expenses involved in doing this were considerable.

3. The decision was made to continue the program to increase the research and development effort and to increase the managerial staff. In other words, the decline in profits could have been reduced considerably by making cutbacks in these areas. Management decided, however, to sacrifice short-term profits to strengthen these areas, which were key to the organization's future success.

FINANCIAL STRATEGY

Management's objective was to maintain financial strength and financial flexibility at all times. This was to be accomplished by instituting conservative policies and by having these policies determine growth opportunities. Putting it another way, management would sacrifice growth if doing so was necessary to maintain financial strength and financial flexibility.

To understand the policies instituted, it is necessary that one appreciate the competitive environment in which the firm operated. When the firm was organized in 1969, there were four classes of competitors:

1. Independent producers of intelligent terminals, including divisions of large diversified electronics companies
2. Manufacturers of minicomputers
3. Suppliers of large computer systems such as IBM, Honeywell, and Univac
4. Manufacturers of semiconductors

Although the competitors in the third category did offer intelligent terminals as part of their packages, these "main frame" companies were not interested in focusing on this aspect of the business, at least not in 1969.

In 1969 the size of the intelligent terminal market was small. The founders of Incoterm believed that it would grow. Since no firm had a dominant position and none of the major firms seemed interested in pursuing it, the founders believed that they could establish a foothold. The focus on selected industries would enable them to be in a better position to protect their market share.

While the giants' apparent lack of interest provided hope, competing against the independent manufacturers was considered to be no easy task. Moreover, the founders realized that, as the intelligent terminal market grew, it was likely that the manufacturers of minicomputers would respond. (The intelligent terminal market would reduce the potential size of the minicomputer market.) In the face of this competition and the prospect of potential competition from the giants, management realized that it would take several years to develop an organization capable of capturing and maintaining a share of this market.

To permit the proper development of the organization, the firm established the following financial policies:

1. To rely primarily on equity financing
2. To pay no dividends on common stock
3. To maintain large cash balances
4. To maintain reserve borrowing capacity

The firm's initial financing came primarily from a private placement of convertible preferred stock with the Prudential Insurance Company. A total of $3,375,000 was raised from this source. In addition, shortly after these funds were raised, a $1 million revolving line of credit was obtained from the Shawmut Bank of Boston, and a $700,000 revolving line of credit was obtained from the Prudential Insurance Company. The intention was to rely on these lines primarily as financial reserves.

When these financings were arranged, it was estimated that they would be sufficient to enable the firm to develop into a profitable operation. The estimate proved to be good. The firm had experienced two profitable quarters and had a sizable backlog of orders before the need for additional permanent financing occurred. Moreover, during this period the firm had to rely on the revolving credit lines for only short periods, and the amounts were always less than $500,000.

To obtain a maintainable foothold with these policies, the firm had to gain access to additional sources of equity. Fortunately, the demonstration of profitability in a relatively short period enabled the firm to go public in October 1973. Five million dollars was raised. The firm used $1.7 million to retire the debt outstanding on its revolving line of credit, which at that time had a limit of $2 million. (It should be noted that management decided to use this proportion of the line only after the public offering was arranged with the underwriter.) The remainder of the $5 million was used to finance further growth.

Although the suitability of the financial policies was continuously evaluated, they were maintained with only minor modifications over time. For example, shortly after the public offering, the decision was made to use $800,000 of long-term debt to help finance the construction of a new manufacturing facility. As confidence in management increased and the firm's equity base grew, the size of the revolving line of credit grew. By June 1976, it was $5 million with two commercial banks. Although it had been used more frequently in recent years, the intention still was to rely on it primarily as a financial reserve.

Mr. Clifford, through discussions with bankers and other financial institutions, was continuously able to assess the firm's ability to raise funds. As of June 1976, he estimated that, if necessary, he could increase his revolving line of credit to $10 million. Moreover, he believed that he could raise another $5 million with an issue of convertible subordinated debentures or convertible preferred stock.

EVALUATION OF STRATEGY

While Mr. Clifford believed that the financial strategy and policies were sound, two aspects of them concerned him. First, would conservative financial policies hinder the firm's effort to obtain a sustainable foothold? If the firm were to use more debt, it could grow more quickly and thus obtain a greater share of the market. Second, as competition intensified, there would be pressure on prices. Because of its emphasis on quality and in-depth knowledge of customer's system needs, it was expected that the firm's products would not be the cheapest alternative for a customer, at least not initially.[2] (The selling point was that the higher initial cost would be offset by greater operating cost savings.) Nevertheless, Mr. Clifford realized that the excess liquidity and conservative debt policies made the firm less price competitive; consequently, he wondered how this would hinder the marketing effort as competition became more intense.

Two factors made these concerns more relevant and made Mr. Clifford wonder whether the existing financial policies would continue to ensure financial strength and financial flexibility. First, the price performance of the firm's common stock had been poor. (See Exhibit 3.) Thus the firm's ability to raise additional equity was impaired. The possibility of instituting a cash dividend to bolster the price of the stock was suggested to management.[3] Management believed that it was unrealistic for Incoterm to pay a dividend. Approximately 70 percent of the common stock outstanding was private, that is, owned by Prudential, other institutions, and officers and directors of the company. These investors were interested in capital gains and not in dividends.

Second, the expected intensification of competition materialized. Although the "main frame" companies did not make a major entry into this market, they did enter. For example, during fiscal 1976, IBM

---

2. Although the firm emphasized custom design, there was some synergy. Thus, as it continued, its products would become cheaper, and, consequently, it could compete more effectively for business where the needs of the customer were largely standard. At the moment, the firm could not compete for this business effectively.

3. During 1976 many companies, including growth companies, were increasing their dividends or paying dividends for the first time. This activity was receiving considerable coverage in the financial press.

entered the market with several intelligent terminal systems, including one that competed directly with the firm's products designed for the banking industry.

What would the giants do? Although several lawsuits were pending against IBM, Mr. Clifford guessed that, at least with respect to the market for intelligent terminals, IBM would not be constrained. He thought that IBM was motivated not to enter the business for custom-designed products in a big way because, if it did, it would have to give up standard business somewhat, which was very important. Despite this opinion, Mr. Clifford believed that he had to prepare for the worse situation and develop a strategy and institute policies that would ensure financial strength and financial flexibility even if IBM were to enter in a major way.

EXHIBIT 1
Incoterm Corporation and Subsidiaries
Six-Year Summary of Operations
(Dollar Amounts, except Per-share Data, in Thousands)

	For the Fiscal Years					
	1976	1975	1974	1973	1972	1971
Revenue						
Product sales	$27,399	$18,313	$15,040	$10,622	$4,662	$ 322
Lease, rental and service	5,297	3,091	1,544	980	113	39
	$32,696	$21,404	$16,584	$11,602	$4,775	$ 361
Cost of sales and other revenue	16,603	12,602	8,545	6,262	2,637	336
Gross profit	$16,093	$ 8,802	$ 8,039	$ 5,340	$2,138	$ 25
Gross profit percentage	49.2%	41.1%	48.5%	46.0%	44.8%	6.9%
Customer service expense	$ 3,391	$ 1,678	$ 920	$ 544	$ 431	$ 65
Engineering, research, and development expense	2,302	1,815	1,706	911	781	551
Selling, general, and administrative expense	6,619	4,865	3,652	2,499	1,557	1,109
	$12,312	$ 8,358	$ 6,278	$ 3,954	$2,769	$ 1,725

EXHIBIT 1 (continued)

	For the Fiscal Years					
	1976	1975	1974	1973	1972	1971
Income (loss) from operations	$ 3,781	$ 444	$ 1,761	$ 1,386	$ (631)	$(1,700)
Interest income (expense)	(160)	(99)	(16)	(111)	(68)	87
Other income	74	—	—	—	—	—
Income (loss) before taxes and extraordinary item	$ 3,695	$ 345	$ 1,745	$ 1,275	$ (699)	$(1,613)
Income taxes	1,471	195	679	585	—	—
Income (loss) before extraordinary item	$ 2,224	$ 150	$ 1,066	$ 690	$ (699)	$(1,613)
Extraordinary item	276	175	541	480	—	—
Net income (loss)	$ 2,500	$ 325	$ 1,607	$ 1,170	$ (699)	$(1,613)
Percent net income to total revenues	7.6%	1.5%	9.7%	10.1%	(14.6%)	(446.8%)
Preferred dividends	$ 121	$124	$ —	$ —	$ —	$ —
Net income per common share—primary						
Income (loss) before extraordinary item	$1.10	$.02	$.61	$.50	$(2.23)	$(5.16)
Extraordinary item	.14	.10	.31	.35	—	—
Net income (loss)	$1.24	$.12	$.92	$.85	$(2.23)	$(5.16)
Number of common shares used to compute earnings per common share	2,008,400	1,692,700	1,747,614	1,368,980	313,040	312,520

EXHIBIT 2
Incoterm Corporation
Year-end Position

	1976	1975	1974	1973	1972	1971
Working capital	$ 8,451	$ 8,477	$ 7,900	$ 3,567	$ 265	$ 836
Ratio of current assets to current liabilities	2.9-1	2.5-1	3.9-1	3.1-1	1.1-1	2.8-1
Total stockholders' equity	$12,345	$ 9,948	$ 9,742	$ 3,034	$ 380	$1,077
Book value per common share	$ 6.25	$ 4.96	$ 4.85	$ 1.22	$(9.55)	$(7.34)
Total assets	$18,358	$16,445	$12,488	$ 5,789	$3,547	$1,535
Long-term debt	$ 1,336	$ 832	$ 33	$ 1,047	$ 395	$ —
Orders received	$41,908	$26,804	$21,033	$13,524	$7,757	$1,108
Order backlog	$24,712	$15,500	$10,100	$ 5,651	$3,729	$ 747
Number of employees	750	606	421	331	244	120

EXHIBIT 3
Incoterm Corporation
Common Stock Price Performance
October 1973–May 1976

Date	High	Low
October 1973–November 1973	14*	7½
December 1973–February 1974	7¾	5
March 1974–May 1974	6⅞	3⅝
June 1974–August 1974	5	2¾
September 1974–November 1974	3	1½
December 1974–February 1975	3	1¼
March 1975–May 1975	6⅞	2¾
June 1975–August 1975	12¼	6⅜
September 1975–November 1975	10½	7⅛
December 1975–February 1976	18	7½
March 1976–May 1976	20⅛	10½

* The offering price to the public was $14 per share.

Phillips Bakeries, Inc.

In early July, Henry Phillips, founder and president of Phillips Bakeries, was confronted with what many managers would consider a pleasant problem. He had just received the firm's financial statements for fiscal 1976 (Exhibit 1). As expected, the annual sales growth goal of 20 percent, the profit after taxes to sales target of 4 percent, and the return on equity target of 25 percent had been achieved. The problem was that if the 20-percent annual growth goal were maintained and the debt and dividend policies were not changed, excess cash would be generated; consequently, the firm would be unable to continue to achieve its 25-percent return on equity goal. Phillips knew that his fellow stockholders would argue for greater sales growth, probably 30 percent per year. They would point to the fact that opportunities were certainly available. The firm's growth-by-acquisition program, begun only in 1972, had attracted such attention in the industry that the firm had been contacted by over 100 potential acquisition candidates in 19 states during fiscal 1976. While Mr. Phillips agreed that opportunities were available, he was not convinced that the 20-percent target should be changed.

PHILLIPS BAKERIES, INC.

Henry Phillips, formerly an accountant with an industrial firm in Framingham, Massachusetts, was 31 when he opened his first retail bakery in 1968. He had long wanted to go into business for himself, and, after a careful study of various opportunities, he concluded that the baking industry presented some very favorable profit opportunities, and it was a field he could enter even with his limited personal savings. Retail baking might lack the glamour of some high-technology companies, but Phillips was convinced that he had discovered the formula for making money in the business.

The key to Phillips's original plan was bakery location. He found that retail bakeries located next to supermarkets in shopping centers could generate a sales volume of between 5 percent and 7 percent of the gross volume of the supermarkets themselves. A large number of executives in the supermarket industry believed that retail bakeries so located helped build their own store volume. Moreover, many of these executives preferred to rely on an independent bakery, like Phillips, rather than operate their own bakery.

In selecting locations, Phillips had to be aware of two critical factors. The first was the competitive environment in which the supermarkets operated. If the supermarket became involved in a tough, competitive battle and lost some of its volume, the bakery located next to it would also suffer. The second factor was competition from other bakeries. A tough, competitive environment could prevent a supermarket bakery from achieving the normal percentage of the supermarket's volume. A bakery located next to a supermarket was protected from competition within the shopping center. However, well-managed bakeries located within the community, especially those with low rental costs, could compete quite effectively with bakeries located within shopping centers. (Phillips found that many bakery owners learned, to their dismay, that people were indeed willing to shop in a supermarket, ignore the bakery located next to it, and drive several miles to purchase their bakery products.) Fortunately, Phillips's study of the industry revealed that there were many areas with a favorable competitive environment.

Phillips calculated that with cash equal to about 1 percent of sales, inventory of 5 percent, equipment and fixtures of 28 percent, and accounts payable and accruals of approximately 9 percent and 1 percent respectively, such sales volume could be supported. If he could find lenders willing to sustain a long-term debt to equity ratio of 50 percent, profit after taxes (PAT) for such an operation would equal 4 percent on sales, and return on equity would equal 25 percent (assuming a 9-percent interest rate and a 50-percent tax rate). Phillips's commercial banker advised that if management kept careful control over costs and profit margins, the bank would be willing to supply term debt equal to 50 percent of equity.

Budgeting and cost control were Phillips's specialties, and he was confident that all his targets were feasible. And so they were in the first operation; he attained sales of $150,000 in his first year, and although after-tax profits were below the desired 4-percent level for the first two years, the target was surpassed in the third year, when after-tax profits reached $7,500. The lower profit levels for the first two years were a result of Phillips's lack of experience. It took two years of very hard work to learn the bakery business, to experiment with his fresh bakery product mix, and to develop appropriate controls, advertising and promotion programs, and personnel policies.

EXPANSION BEGINS

The experience Phillips accumulated in his first three years of operation could be used, he believed, to expand the scope of his operations far beyond a single location. Stringent control over costs and capital requirements, so essential to the success of his first store, could be exercised in many other locations. Rather than attempt to develop additional locations on a start-up basis, Phillips believed it possible to acquire existing bakeries already operating near supermarkets in shopping centers.

In late 1971, Phillips approached several wealthy private investors, demonstrated the bakery volume/supermarket volume relationship he had discovered, showed how he had managed to earn a handsome return on equity through careful cost and capital controls, and persuaded two of them to buy into his business. In return for 45 percent of the young company, Phillips was able to expand his equity base substantially and receive his commercial bank's assurance that it would be willing to support the firm in its expansion efforts. Because of the investors' high tax brackets, they were interested in capital gains rather than dividends. Thus it was decided that no dividends would be paid initially, and that a primary goal would be to take the company public in the early 1980s.

Phillips was interested in going concerns that promised the 4-percent PAT target he had established earlier. Every expense category of potential acquisitions was carefully scrutinized. Lease expenses—a very important category—received special attention, since leases on store locations generally had to be signed for 10-year or longer periods. Phillips believed that a lease expense to projected sales ratio of 3.1 percent was acceptable and that less favorable ratios would not permit him to reach his desired 4-percent PAT target. Acquisition candidates with such unfavorable ratios were immediately eliminated from further consideration.

For the bakeries Phillips began acquiring in 1971, the firm sought area managers experienced in cost accounting and budgeting. Rigid adherence to budgets established monthly for each store was essential to attainment of the firm's overall profit and return on investment goals, and area managers were expected to move rapidly to correct unfavorable budget variances. Strong and capable area store management was essential, Phillips believed, because the acquisitions made in the first five years were geographically dispersed in Massachusetts and New Hampshire. The skilled bakers operating individual stores seldom had the management talents he required, and Phillips knew that further growth would require a capable management base.

When expansion was initially undertaken in 1971, Phillips planned to change the names of the purchased bakeries to his company's name. This had not always been possible or desirable, however, since some bakeries had such a strong local identification that a renaming might have an unfavorable impact on sales. By 1976, with 14 stores in 12 different cities and with an overall sales volume running at an annual rate of $2 million, the company hired a marketing manager to address problems of identification, advertising, and promotion for the full chain of bakeries. Phillips believed, however, that his flexible identification policy had served the company well and could be maintained.

SCREENING ACQUISITION CANDIDATES

Although Phillips Bakeries, Inc., had been approached by several supermarket chains regarding its interest in entering new shopping center developments, Phillips management had rejected these opportunities as being relatively more risky than acquiring going concerns next to established supermarkets. And although Henry Phillips believed his business concept had some national potential, and although he had been approached by candidates from 19 different states, he believed that, for the immediate future, he should limit expansion to the New England region. Even with its regional target for development, he believed the company had more than enough suitable candidates for consideration. Indeed, so many were beginning to seek him out that he did not need to conduct a very vigorous search on his own.

When a potential acquisition was identified, Phillips would first perform a thorough investigation of the competitive environment. Given that the environment was favorable, he would then determine the supermarket's annual volume and multiply this amount by 5 percent to estimate the bakery's potential. (Obtaining the supermarket's volume was not usually difficult.) As noted previously, 5 percent to 7 percent of the supermarket's volume was considered attainable; thus using 5 percent produced a conservative estimate. He would then determine how much, if any, additional inventory and equipment would be needed. If total inventory plus equipment needed exceeded the capital requirement targets, he would not consider the acquisition further. The next step was to construct a pro forma income statement for the bakery. If it appeared that it would be difficult to achieve the 4-percent net profit to sales target, Phillips would not consider the acquisition further.

Once these initial screening tests were met, determining the value—and hence the maximum offering price—was simple. The price was set so that a 25-percent return on equity could be achieved. Since Phillips would offer to purchase the inventory, fixed assets, and trade name, but not assume the trade credit or other liabilities, the offering price could be calculated as follows:

> Supermarket volume
> times five percent
> equals bakery volume
> times asset requirements target
> equals assets needed for bakery

less cash required
less additional inventory and/
or additional equipment needed
equals maximum offering price

For example, suppose the supermarket had an annual volume of $3 million and that $5000 of new equipment would be needed:

Supermarket volume	= $3,000,000
times five percent	X .05
equals bakery's volume	= $ 150,000
times asset requirements target	X 34%
equals assets of bakery	= $ 51,000
less cash required	− 1,500
equals potential offering price	= $ 49,500
less additional equipment and/ or inventory required	− 5,000
equals maximum offering price	= $ 44,500

Occasionally, certain liabilities were assumed. In these cases, the amount of the debt was subtracted in arriving at the maximum offering price.

Phillips did not believe in playing the negotiating game. If the owner asked for less than the maximum offering price, Phillips would immediately accept. If the owner asked for more, Phillips would immediately counter with his maximum price. For the most part, this screening-and-negotiating approach worked well. However, some bakery owners thought that Phillips's offer was unreasonably low and were surprised to learn that he had no interest in negotiating further.

BEYOND 1976

Phillips realized that the 25-percent return on equity target could not be maintained given the existing debt and dividend policies if annual sales growth were to continue at 20 percent. He knew his fellow stockholders would push for faster sales growth since they were anxious to take the company public. He guessed that they would recommend annual sales growth of 30 percent or more. Phillips was not sure whether sales growth of 30 percent would solve the excess cash problem. However, even if it did, he was hesitant to increase the annual rate of growth of sales above 20 percent because it would require that he delegate responsibility sooner than he considered desirable.

Since its inception in 1968, Phillips Bakeries, Inc., had been a good example of how to make money in the bakery business. However, Henry Phillips was aware of many examples of how easy it was to lose money in the business. In addition to managing the day-to-day operations of the business, there were three critical tasks:

1. Selection of acquisitions
2. Transition to Phillips's style of operation
3. Management development

Phillips personally performed these tasks. For example, when a new bakery was purchased, Phillips would spend between 50 and 75 percent of his time at the new location for two or three months. He realized that, even with 20-percent growth, he would soon have to delegate some of these tasks, and he had a plan for doing it. The firm was scheduled to recruit and train one area manager during fiscal 1977. Phillips intended to recruit two people, and, after proper training— which typically required 12 to 18 months—he would select and train one of his existing area managers to assist in the performance of the tasks. An annual growth rate of 30 percent would accelerate the process, and that worried him.

EXHIBIT 1
Phillips Bakeries, Inc.
Income Statement
Fiscal Year Ended 6/30/76
($000)

Net sales	$2,016
Cost of goods sold	1,409
Gross profit	$ 607
Rent	60
Advertising and promotion	23
Salaries of store clerks	198
General and administrative	166
Operating profit	$ 160
Income taxes	69
Net income	$ 91

Phillips Bakeries, Inc.
Balance Sheet
Fiscal Year Ended 6/30/76
($000)

Cash	$ 37	Accounts payable trade	$177
Marketable securities	39	Accruals	27
Inventory	102	Bank debt	181
Fixed assets, net	567	Net worth	360
Total	$745	Total	$745

Meditronics, Inc.

In late March 1982, Mr. Domenic Venuti, financial vice president of
Meditronics, Inc., was preparing for a meeting with the firm's treasurer,
controller, investor relations manager, and several members of their
staffs. The meeting would be devoted to evaluating the firm's policy regarding the size of liquidity balances (i.e., cash plus marketable
securities).

This issue had been raised at the end of a previous meeting of this
group. Ms. Diane Stearns, an assistant treasurer, said that she believed
an alteration was in order, and several people seemed to agree with her.
Mr. Robert Kiley, the investor relations manager, argued that the policy
should not be changed. Mr. Venuti then noted that the issue would be
considered in depth at the next meeting. He asked Ms. Stearns to be
prepared to propose a specific alternative and Mr. Kiley to be prepared
to defend the existing policy.

COMPANY BACKGROUND

Meditronics, Inc. was founded in 1964 by Mr. White, a scientist, to
capitalize on a piece of medical equipment he had recently invented.
The new equipment represented a major technological advance. It not
only enabled doctors to make a more accurate assessment of whether
patients had certain diseases, but it also enabled them to perform these
tasks in less time. Thus, the promised result was an improvement in
health care and at the same time a lowering of medical costs.

This product was an instant success, and it was just the first of many
successful products developed by Meditronics for the health care industry. Products had also been introduced for use in the research
laboratories of a variety of industries, particularly the drug and photo-
graphic industries, and for several government agencies.

Losses were incurred for the first two years because sales were not
sufficient to cover the large research and development (R&D) expenditures. Profits were earned in 1966, and after that they increased by
more than 10 percent per year and frequently reached 15 percent; sales
grew at about the same rate. In 1976 several innovative products were
introduced that gained broad market acceptance. For each of the next
five years, growth in sales and profits exceeded 20 percent per year, the
net profit margin was more than 10 percent, and the ratio of net

income to owners' equity averaged a little over 16 percent. (See Exhibit 1 for selected financial data for 1977 to 1981.)

The firm's plan called for sales and profits to grow by 20 percent in 1982, and management was confident that this target would be achieved. Management believed that sales and profit growth would decline after 1982 to 10 to 15 percent per year. Competition had intensified in the past couple of years and management felt that the firm would not continue to be immune to poor economic conditions, should they continue.

FINANCING

Unlike so many new businesses. Meditronics began with ample resources. In talking with venture capital firms, Mr. White insisted on raising enough money to provide for operations for the first two years, and his proposal included a healthy allocation for R&D. Moreover, he insisted that the form of financing be straight common stock rather than convertible debt or debt with warrants. Mr. White was able to achieve his financing objectives because of his excellent reputation as a scientist and as a creative manager, and because of the potential of the new product.

Mr. White wanted his firm to grow rapidly and to accomplish this goal he recruited numerous talented managers and engineers. Mr. Venuti was one of the first managers hired. He played a key role in arranging the initial financing, and he and Mr. White developed the financing policies described below.

The basic financing principle from the start was to avoid debt financing. The rationale was that the firm possessed considerable operating risks and so risk should not be increased by debt financing. Hence, the policy was to rely on retained earnings and new issues of common stock to fund growth. The firm did maintain a revolving line of credit, and in 1982 the limit of the line was $200 million. However, the policy was to rely on the line principally as a financial reserve and to use liquidity balances to finance unexpected requirements. Reliance on the line was rare and the firm had never borrowed more than $50 million. As of March 1982 the firm had not borrowed for more than two years.

Mr. White and Mr. Venuti realized that there were advantages to debt financing. However, they had always been reluctant, and still were in 1982, to alter a policy that had served the firm so well. The price performance of the stock was often cited to support this view. For example, in early 1982, Mr. Venuti made the following statement.

If someone purchased our stock when we first went public in 1966 and held it through December, 1981, this person would have earned a compounded rate of return which averaged more than

21 percent per year. While the days of consistent increases in sales and profits of over 20 percent are numbered, growth will be substantial. Why should we jeopardize this potential for the small benefit that debt might provide?

To maximize the amount available from operations, the firm had originally instituted a policy of paying no dividends. Mr. Venuti had always believed the firm should not pay dividends. However, since so many prestigious growth firms paid dividends, he relented; in 1975 the firm paid a small quarterly dividend, the first of an uninterrupted series of regular quarterly dividends. Although dividends increased each year, the proportion of earnings distributed had always been less than 10 percent and the policy was to keep the payout ratio below 10 percent.

As noted above, the firm issued stock publicly for the first time in 1966, and there had been numerous issues since then. The market had always been receptive and Mr. Venuti believed that this was due in part to the firm's timing strategy. The policy was to issue stock before the funds were actually needed to avoid temporary difficulties in the financial marketplace. In addition, the firm entered the market no more than once in a given twelve-month period.

In developing and evaluating financial policies, Mr. Venuti always analyzed the financial policies of competitors. In his view, relevant comparisons had become more difficult because as the firm diversified, there were substantial differences with respect to product categories between Meditronics and any other firm. Nevertheless, firms with over-lapping product lines and that were roughly the same size as Meditronics in terms of annual sales and total assets relied on debt financing. Long-term debt to capital (i.e., sum of long-term debt plus owners' equity) ratios for these firms ranged from 10 percent to 30 percent. Moreover, while these firms maintained ample liquidity, Meditronics's cash plus marketable securities balance was generally much larger than the balances of most of these firms.

LIQUIDITY POLICY

The firm's policy with respect to how much liquidity to maintain was an essential part of its business strategy. Cash plus marketable securities was kept at a level sufficient to fund day-to-day operations and unexpected needs. For the past 10 years, the policy had been to have cash plus marketable securities equal about 6 percent of sales for the next year. For example, the sales target for 1982 was almost $2.1 billion and this called for a liquidity level of about $126 million at December 31, 1981. (Exhibit 1 shows that cash plus marketable securities was $213.5 million at December 31, 1981. This was due to timing strategy for stock issues. Funds were raised months before they were needed and invested temporarily in marketable securities.)

To understand how the 6 percent figure was derived, one must first appreciate how the amount of external equity financing was determined. Table 1 shows the procedure for estimating the amount needed for the next year. To this amount a rough estimate of how much would be needed for the next couple of years would be added. Sometimes the firm would raise enough for the next two or three years to avoid too frequent stock issues and to gain the transaction cost savings that come with the increasing size of an issue.

Because sales were not seasonal and because of the timing of cash receipts and disbursements each month, the amount of liquidity needed for day-to-day operations was not great. For example, in 1982 it was estimated that if liquid balances were maintained only for day-to-day operating requirements, less than $5 million would be needed. Thus, most of the balance was for unexpected expenditures and increases in inventories and receivables.

Given the nature of the business, it was virtually impossible to make an accurate assessment of how much would be required for additions to plant and equipment, even for the next year. Sometimes a breakthrough occurred sooner than expected and capital expenditures were necessary to exploit the opportunity. At the current level of operations, it would not be surprising to see actual capital expenditure for the year exceed the planned amount by as much as $20 million.

Unanticipated increases in receivables and inventories was the factor that caused the greatest need for liquidity. The firm had just been unable to control the level of these current assets effectively, and the problem with inventories was especially serious. Improvements had been made, but Mr. Venuti believed that there was still considerable cause

TABLE 1
Procedure For Estimating External Equity Requirements

Step 1
    Uses of funds for the next year:
        Planned additions to fixed assets
        Anticipated increases in current assets other than cash
    Sources of funds for the next year:
        Funds provided by operations minus dividends
        Anticipated increase in trade payables and accrued expenses

Step 2
      Total estimated used
    − Total estimated sources
    = Estimate of amount of new equity required

for concern. He indicated that at the current level of operations there could be unanticipated increases in inventories and receivables as large as $75 million and $10 million, respectively.

Based on the above considerations, Mr. Venuti had set the level at about 6 percent of the next year's sales in the early 1970s, and although he reviewed the figure periodically, he had never made a change. It should be added that the figure was based primarily on Mr. Venuti's subjective assessment of the factors described above rather than on any sophisticated quantitative analysis.

FINANCE STAFF MEETING, FEBRUARY 1982

Mr. Venuti encouraged the finance people to question policies. Although they questioned many, particularly the no-debt policy, they had seldom questioned the policy on liquidity until late 1981, when several individuals talked to him about it. At the end of a staff meeting in February 1982, he raised the issue, which was not on the agenda, to obtain a sense of the opinions of the group.

Ms. Diane Stearns, an assistant treasurer, said that while she was not prepared to defend her view at that time, she believed that 6 percent was much too high. She indicated that the firm had a vastly improved control system, especially for inventory, and so the large unanticipated increases of the past were unlikely. She added that even if they did occur, the firm could abandon its no-debt policy, at least temporarily, to fund vital expenditures.

Mr. Venuti inferred from the facial expressions of several people that they agreed with Ms. Stearns. However, Mr. Robert Kiley, the investor relations manager, did oppose her point of view. He said that he, too, was not prepared to discuss the topic, but he indicated that they should keep the shareholders in mind. The firm's shareholders were probably very comfortable with the existing financing policies and might object to a change. He certainly had not received any complaints about the firm's policies. Indeed, the firm's strong financial position was frequently mentioned in the press and in reports of security analysts. Mr. Kiley concluded by saying that he was not convinced that the control systems were that effective. Previous systems were supposed to have solved the problems, but they never had.

Mr. Venuti did not want to spend more time on the issue at this meeting because it was already past the planned ending time. Thus, he said that the liquidity policy would be discussed in more depth at the next meeting. He asked Ms. Stearns to be prepared to propose a specific alternative to the 6 percent policy and Mr. Kiley to be prepared to defend the 6 percent figure. (Mr. Venuti frequently assigned opposing viewpoints to ensure that options received proper attention. Debates were often lively but they were always friendly.) Mr. Venuti concluded by saying that they should all conduct their own reviews.

EXHIBIT 1
Meditronics, Inc.
Selected Financial Data*
(In millions)

	1981	1980	1979	1978	1977
Net sales	$1,732.3	$1,428.1	$1,181.3	$968.3	$800.9
Net income after taxes	187.1	154.3	127.6	106.1	85.7
Depreciation expense	58.9	44.3	40.2	35.8	23.2
Capital expenditures	133.9	141.4	73.2	122.0	88.1
Cash plus marketable securities	213.5	104.2	226.8	72.9	113.7
Accounts receivable	708.4	553.4	419.3	338.2	291.5
Inventory	872.7	697.4	549.8	447.1	326.3
Short-term debt			50.0	—	41.0
Accounts payable and accruals	419.2	341.5	264.7	207.9	173.5

*Income statement and capital expenditure data are for the years ended December 31; balance sheet information is at December 31.

APPENDIXES

APPENDIX A

Present Value of $1
at Discount Rate k for n Years

	1%	2%	3%	4%	5%	6%	7%	8%	9%	10%	11%	12%	13%	14%	15%
1	.9901	.9804	.9709	.9615	.9524	.9434	.9346	.9259	.9174	.9091	.9009	.8929	.8850	.8772	.8696
2	.9803	.9612	.9426	.9246	.9070	.8900	.8734	.8573	.8417	.8264	.8116	.7972	.7831	.7695	.7561
3	.9706	.9423	.9151	.8890	.8638	.8396	.8163	.7938	.7722	.7513	.7312	.7118	.6931	.6750	.6575
4	.9610	.9239	.8885	.8548	.8227	.7921	.7629	.7350	.7084	.6830	.6587	.6355	.6133	.5921	.5718
5	.9515	.9057	.8626	.8219	.7835	.7473	.7130	.6806	.6499	.6209	.5934	.5674	.5428	.5194	.4972
6	.9420	.8880	.8375	.7903	.7462	.7050	.6663	.6302	.5963	.5645	.5346	.5066	.4803	.4556	.4323
7	.9327	.8706	.8131	.7599	.7107	.6651	.6228	.5835	.5470	.5132	.4817	.4524	.4251	.3996	.3759
8	.9235	.8535	.7894	.7307	.6768	.6274	.5820	.5403	.5019	.4665	.4339	.4039	.3762	.3506	.3269
9	.9143	.8368	.7664	.7026	.6446	.5919	.5439	.5002	.4604	.4241	.3909	.3606	.3329	.3075	.2843
10	.9053	.8204	.7441	.6756	.6139	.5584	.5084	.4632	.4224	.3855	.3522	.3220	.2946	.2697	.2472
11	.8963	.8043	.7224	.6496	.5847	.5268	.4751	.4289	.3875	.3505	.3173	.2875	.2607	.2366	.2149
12	.8874	.7885	.7014	.6246	.5568	.4970	.4440	.3971	.3555	.3186	.2858	.2567	.2307	.2076	.1869
13	.8787	.7730	.6810	.6006	.5303	.4688	.4150	.3677	.3262	.2897	.2575	.2292	.2042	.1821	.1625
14	.8700	.7579	.6611	.5775	.5051	.4423	.3878	.3405	.2993	.2633	.2320	.2046	.1807	.1597	.1413
15	.8614	.7430	.6419	.5553	.4810	.4173	.3625	.3152	.2745	.2394	.2090	.1827	.1599	.1401	.1229
16	.8528	.7284	.6232	.5339	.4581	.3936	.3387	.2919	.2519	.2176	.1883	.1631	.1415	.1229	.1069
17	.8444	.7142	.6050	.5134	.4363	.3714	.3166	.2703	.2311	.1978	.1696	.1456	.1252	.1078	.0929
18	.8360	.7002	.5874	.4936	.4155	.3503	.2959	.2502	.2120	.1799	.1528	.1300	.1108	.0946	.0808
19	.8277	.6864	.5703	.4746	.3957	.3305	.2765	.2317	.1945	.1635	.1377	.1161	.0981	.0829	.0703
20	.8195	.6730	.5537	.4564	.3769	.3118	.2584	.2145	.1784	.1486	.1240	.1037	.0868	.0728	.0611
21	.8114	.6598	.5375	.4388	.3589	.2942	.2415	.1987	.1637	.1351	.1117	.0926	.0768	.0638	.0531
22	.8034	.6468	.5219	.4220	.3418	.2775	.2257	.1839	.1502	.1229	.1007	.0826	.0680	.0560	.0462
23	.7954	.6342	.5067	.4057	.3256	.2618	.2109	.1703	.1378	.1117	.0907	.0738	.0601	.0491	.0402
24	.7876	.6217	.4919	.3901	.3101	.2470	.1971	.1577	.1264	.1015	.0817	.0659	.0532	.0431	.0349
25	.7798	.6095	.4776	.3751	.2953	.2330	.1842	.1460	.1160	.0923	.0736	.0588	.0471	.0378	.0304
26	.7721	.5976	.4637	.3607	.2812	.2198	.1722	.1352	.1064	.0839	.0663	.0525	.0417	.0332	.0264
27	.7644	.5859	.4502	.3468	.2678	.2074	.1609	.1252	.0976	.0763	.0597	.0469	.0369	.0291	.0230
28	.7568	.5744	.4371	.3335	.2551	.1956	.1504	.1159	.0896	.0693	.0538	.0419	.0326	.0255	.0200
29	.7493	.5631	.4244	.3206	.2429	.1846	.1406	.1073	.0821	.0630	.0485	.0374	.0289	.0224	.0174
30	.7419	.5521	.4120	.3083	.2314	.1741	.1314	.0994	.0754	.0573	.0437	.0334	.0256	.0196	.0151
31	.7346	.5412	.4000	.2965	.2204	.1643	.1228	.0920	.0692	.0521	.0394	.0298	.0226	.0172	.0131
32	.7273	.5306	.3883	.2851	.2099	.1550	.1147	.0852	.0634	.0474	.0354	.0266	.0200	.0151	.0114
33	.7201	.5202	.3770	.2741	.1999	.1462	.1072	.0789	.0582	.0431	.0319	.0238	.0177	.0133	.0099
34	.7130	.5100	.3660	.2635	.1903	.1379	.1002	.0731	.0534	.0391	.0288	.0212	.0157	.0116	.0086
35	.7059	.5000	.3554	.2534	.1813	.1301	.0937	.0676	.0490	.0356	.0259	.0189	.0139	.0102	.0075
36	.6989	.4902	.3450	.2437	.1727	.1227	.0875	.0626	.0449	.0324	.0234	.0169	.0123	.0089	.0065
37	.6920	.4806	.3350	.2343	.1644	.1158	.0818	.0580	.0412	.0294	.0210	.0151	.0109	.0078	.0057
38	.6852	.4712	.3252	.2253	.1566	.1092	.0765	.0537	.0378	.0267	.0190	.0135	.0096	.0069	.0049
39	.6784	.4620	.3158	.2166	.1492	.1031	.0715	.0497	.0347	.0243	.0171	.0120	.0085	.0060	.0043
40	.6717	.4529	.3066	.2083	.1420	.0972	.0668	.0460	.0318	.0221	.0154	.0107	.0075	.0053	.0037
41	.6650	.4440	.2976	.2003	.1353	.0917	.0624	.0426	.0292	.0201	.0139	.0096	.0067	.0046	.0033
42	.6584	.4353	.2890	.1926	.1288	.0865	.0583	.0395	.0268	.0183	.0125	.0086	.0059	.0041	.0028
43	.6519	.4268	.2805	.1852	.1227	.0816	.0545	.0365	.0246	.0166	.0113	.0077	.0052	.0036	.0025
44	.6454	.4184	.2724	.1781	.1169	.0770	.0509	.0338	.0226	.0151	.0101	.0068	.0046	.0031	.0021
45	.6391	.4102	.2644	.1712	.1113	.0727	.0476	.0313	.0207	.0137	.0091	.0061	.0041	.0027	.0019
46	.6327	.4021	.2567	.1646	.1060	.0685	.0445	.0290	.0190	.0125	.0082	.0054	.0036	.0024	.0016
47	.6265	.3943	.2493	.1583	.1010	.0647	.0416	.0269	.0174	.0113	.0074	.0049	.0032	.0021	.0014
48	.6203	.3865	.2420	.1522	.0961	.0610	.0389	.0249	.0160	.0103	.0067	.0043	.0028	.0019	.0012
49	.6141	.3790	.2350	.1463	.0916	.0575	.0363	.0230	.0147	.0094	.0060	.0039	.0025	.0016	.0011
50	.6080	.3715	.2281	.1407	.0872	.0543	.0340	.0213	.0135	.0085	.0054	.0035	.0022	.0014	.0009

Munn and Garcia, *Encyclopedia of Banking and Finance*, 7th ed. (Boston: The Banker's Publishing Co., 1973), pp. 464-467.

APPENDIX A (continued)

	16%	17%	18%	19%	20%	21%	22%	23%	24%	25%	30%	35%	40%	45%	50%
1	.8621	.8547	.8475	.8403	.8333	.8264	.8197	.8130	.8065	.8000	.7692	.7407	.7143	.6897	.6667
2	.7432	.7305	.7182	.7062	.6944	.6830	.6719	.6610	.6504	.6400	.5917	.5487	.5102	.4756	.4444
3	.6407	.6244	.6086	.5934	.5787	.5645	.5507	.5374	.5245	.5120	.4552	.4064	.3644	.3280	.2963
4	.5523	.5337	.5158	.4987	.4822	.4665	.4514	.4369	.4230	.4096	.3501	.3011	.2603	.2262	.1975
5	.4761	.4561	.4371	.4190	.4019	.3855	.3700	.3552	.3411	.3277	.2693	.2230	.1859	.1560	.1317
6	.4104	.3898	.3704	.3521	.3349	.3186	.3033	.2888	.2751	.2621	.2072	.1652	.1328	.1076	.0878
7	.3538	.3332	.3139	.2959	.2791	.2633	.2486	.2348	.2218	.2097	.1594	.1224	.0949	.0742	.0585
8	.3050	.2848	.2660	.2487	.2326	.2176	.2038	.1909	.1789	.1678	.1226	.0906	.0678	.0512	.0390
9	.2630	.2434	.2255	.2090	.1938	.1799	.1670	.1552	.1443	.1342	.0943	.0671	.0484	.0353	.0260
10	.2267	.2080	.1911	.1756	.1615	.1486	.1369	.1262	.1163	.1074	.0725	.0497	.0346	.0243	.0173
11	.1954	.1778	.1619	.1476	.1346	.1229	.1122	.1026	.0938	.0859	.0558	.0368	.0247	.0168	.0116
12	.1685	.1520	.1372	.1240	.1122	.1015	.0920	.0834	.0757	.0687	.0429	.0273	.0176	.0116	.0077
13	.1452	.1299	.1163	.1042	.0935	.0839	.0754	.0678	.0610	.0550	.0330	.0202	.0126	.0080	.0051
14	.1252	.1110	.0986	.0876	.0779	.0693	.0618	.0551	.0492	.0440	.0254	.0150	.0090	.0055	.0034
15	.1079	.0949	.0835	.0736	.0649	.0573	.0507	.0448	.0397	.0352	.0195	.0111	.0064	.0038	.0023
16	.0930	.0811	.0708	.0618	.0541	.0474	.0415	.0364	.0320	.0281	.0150	.0082	.0046	.0026	.0015
17	.0802	.0693	.0600	.0520	.0451	.0391	.0340	.0296	.0258	.0225	.0116	.0061	.0033	.0018	.0010
18	.0691	.0592	.0508	.0437	.0376	.0324	.0279	.0241	.0208	.0180	.0089	.0045	.0023	.0012	.0007
19	.0596	.0506	.0431	.0367	.0313	.0267	.0229	.0196	.0168	.0144	.0068	.0033	.0017	.0009	.0004
20	.0514	.0433	.0365	.0308	.0261	.0221	.0187	.0159	.0135	.0115	.0053	.0025	.0012	.0006	.0003
21	.0443	.0370	.0309	.0259	.0217	.0183	.0154	.0129	.0109	.0092	.0040	.0018	.0008	.0004	.0002
22	.0382	.0316	.0262	.0218	.0181	.0151	.0126	.0105	.0088	.0074	.0031	.0014	.0006	.0003	.0001
23	.0329	.0270	.0222	.0183	.0151	.0125	.0103	.0085	.0071	.0059	.0024	.0010	.0004	.0002	.0001
24	.0284	.0231	.0188	.0154	.0126	.0103	.0085	.0070	.0057	.0047	.0018	.0007	.0003	.0001	.0001
25	.0245	.0197	.0160	.0129	.0105	.0085	.0069	.0056	.0046	.0038	.0014	.0005	.0002	.0001	.0000
26	.0211	.0169	.0135	.0109	.0087	.0070	.0057	.0046	.0037	.0030	.0011	.0004	.0002	.0001	.0000
27	.0182	.0144	.0115	.0091	.0073	.0058	.0047	.0037	.0030	.0024	.0008	.0003	.0001	.0000	.0000
28	.0157	.0123	.0097	.0077	.0061	.0048	.0038	.0030	.0024	.0019	.0006	.0002	.0001	.0000	.0000
29	.0135	.0105	.0082	.0064	.0051	.0040	.0031	.0025	.0019	.0015	.0005	.0002	.0001	.0000	.0000
30	.0116	.0090	.0070	.0054	.0042	.0033	.0026	.0020	.0016	.0012	.0004	.0001	.0000	.0000	.0000
31	.0100	.0077	.0059	.0045	.0035	.0027	.0021	.0016	.0013	.0010	.0003	.0001	.0000	.0000	.0000
32	.0087	.0066	.0050	.0038	.0029	.0022	.0017	.0013	.0010	.0008	.0002	.0001	.0000	.0000	.0000
33	.0075	.0056	.0043	.0032	.0024	.0018	.0014	.0011	.0008	.0006	.0002	.0001	.0000	.0000	.0000
34	.0064	.0048	.0036	.0027	.0020	.0015	.0012	.0009	.0007	.0005	.0001	.0000	.0000	.0000	.0000
35	.0055	.0041	.0030	.0023	.0017	.0013	.0010	.0007	.0005	.0004	.0001	.0000	.0000	.0000	.0000
36	.0048	.0035	.0026	.0019	.0014	.0011	.0008	.0006	.0004	.0003	.0001	.0000	.0000	.0000	.0000
37	.0041	.0030	.0022	.0016	.0012	.0009	.0006	.0005	.0003	.0003	.0001	.0000	.0000	.0000	.0000
38	.0036	.0026	.0019	.0014	.0010	.0007	.0005	.0004	.0003	.0002	.0001	.0000	.0000	.0000	.0000
39	.0031	.0022	.0016	.0011	.0008	.0006	.0004	.0003	.0002	.0002	.0000	.0000	.0000	.0000	.0000
40	.0026	.0019	.0013	.0010	.0007	.0005	.0003	.0002	.0002	.0001	.0000	.0000	.0000	.0000	.0000
41	.0023	.0016	.0011	.0008	.0006	.0004	.0003	.0002	.0002	.0001	.0000	.0000	.0000	.0000	.0000
42	.0020	.0014	.0010	.0007	.0005	.0003	.0002	.0002	.0001	.0001	.0000	.0000	.0000	.0000	.0000
43	.0017	.0012	.0008	.0006	.0004	.0003	.0002	.0001	.0001	.0001	.0000	.0000	.0000	.0000	.0000
44	.0015	.0010	.0007	.0005	.0003	.0002	.0002	.0001	.0001	.0001	.0000	.0000	.0000	.0000	.0000
45	.0013	.0008	.0006	.0004	.0003	.0002	.0001	.0001	.0001	.0000	.0000	.0000	.0000	.0000	.0000
46	.0011	.0007	.0005	.0003	.0002	.0002	.0001	.0001	.0001	.0000	.0000	.0000	.0000	.0000	.0000
47	.0009	.0006	.0004	.0003	.0002	.0001	.0001	.0001	.0000	.0000	.0000	.0000	.0000	.0000	.0000
48	.0008	.0005	.0003	.0002	.0002	.0001	.0001	.0001	.0000	.0000	.0000	.0000	.0000	.0000	.0000
49	.0007	.0005	.0003	.0002	.0001	.0001	.0001	.0000	.0000	.0000	.0000	.0000	.0000	.0000	.0000
50	.0006	.0004	.0002	.0002	.0001	.0001	.0001	.0000	.0000	.0000	.0000	.0000	.0000	.0000	.0000

APPENDIX B

Present Value of an Annuity of $1
at Discount Rate k for n Years

	1%	2%	3%	4%	5%	6%	7%	8%	9%	10%	11%	12%	13%	14%	15%
1	.9901	.9804	.9709	.9615	.9524	.9434	.9346	.9259	.9174	.9091	.9009	.8929	.8850	.8772	.8696
2	1.9704	1.9416	1.9135	1.8861	1.8594	1.8334	1.8080	1.7833	1.7591	1.7355	1.7125	1.6901	1.6681	1.6467	1.6257
3	2.9410	2.8839	2.8286	2.7751	2.7232	2.6730	2.6243	2.5771	2.5313	2.4869	2.4437	2.4018	2.3612	2.3216	2.2832
4	3.9020	3.8077	3.7171	3.6299	3.5459	3.4651	3.3872	3.3121	3.2397	3.1699	3.1024	3.0374	2.9745	2.9137	2.8550
5	4.8534	4.7135	4.5797	4.4518	4.3295	4.2124	4.1002	3.9927	3.8897	3.7908	3.6959	3.6048	3.5172	3.4331	3.3522
6	5.7955	5.6014	5.4172	5.2421	5.0757	4.9173	4.7666	4.6229	4.4859	4.3553	4.2305	4.1114	3.9976	3.8887	3.7845
7	6.7282	6.4720	6.2303	6.0021	5.7864	5.5824	5.3893	5.2064	5.0330	4.8684	4.7122	4.5638	4.4226	4.2883	4.1604
8	7.6517	7.3255	7.0197	6.7328	6.4632	6.2098	5.9713	5.7466	5.5348	5.3349	5.1461	4.9676	4.7988	4.6389	4.4873
9	8.5660	8.1622	7.7861	7.4353	7.1078	6.8017	6.5152	6.2469	5.9953	5.7590	5.5371	5.3282	5.1317	4.9464	4.7716
10	9.4713	8.9826	8.5302	8.1109	7.7217	7.3601	7.0236	6.7101	6.4177	6.1446	5.8892	5.6502	5.4262	5.2161	5.0188
11	10.3676	9.7868	9.2526	8.7605	8.3064	7.8869	7.4987	7.1390	6.8052	6.4951	6.2065	5.9377	5.6869	5.4527	5.2337
12	11.2551	10.5753	9.9540	9.3851	8.8633	8.3839	7.9427	7.5361	7.1607	6.8137	6.4924	6.1944	5.9177	5.6603	5.4206
13	12.1338	11.3484	10.6349	9.9857	9.3936	8.8527	8.3577	7.9038	7.4869	7.1034	6.7499	6.4235	6.1218	5.8424	5.5832
14	13.0037	12.1062	11.2961	10.5631	9.8986	9.2950	8.7455	8.2442	7.7862	7.3667	6.9819	6.6282	6.3025	6.0021	5.7245
15	13.8651	12.8492	11.9379	11.1184	10.3797	9.7123	9.1079	8.5595	8.0607	7.6061	7.1909	6.8109	6.4624	6.1422	5.8474
16	14.7179	13.5777	12.5611	11.6523	10.8378	10.1059	9.4467	8.8514	8.3126	7.8237	7.3792	6.9740	6.6039	6.2651	5.9542
17	15.5623	14.2919	13.1661	12.1657	11.2741	10.4773	9.7632	9.1216	8.5436	8.0216	7.5488	7.1196	6.7291	6.3729	6.0472
18	16.3983	14.9920	13.7535	12.6593	11.6896	10.8276	10.0591	9.3719	8.7556	8.2014	7.7016	7.2497	6.8399	6.4674	6.1280
19	17.2260	15.6785	14.3238	13.1339	12.0853	11.1581	10.3356	9.6036	8.9501	8.3649	7.8393	7.3658	6.9380	6.5504	6.1982
20	18.0456	16.3514	14.8775	13.5903	12.4622	11.4699	10.5940	9.8181	9.1285	8.5136	7.9633	7.4694	7.0248	6.6231	6.2593
21	18.8570	17.0112	15.4150	14.0292	12.8212	11.7641	10.8355	10.0168	9.2922	8.6487	8.0751	7.5620	7.1016	6.6870	6.3125
22	19.6604	17.6580	15.9369	14.4511	13.1630	12.0416	11.0612	10.2007	9.4424	8.7715	8.1757	7.6446	7.1695	6.7430	6.3587
23	20.4558	18.2922	16.4436	14.8569	13.4886	12.3034	11.2722	10.3711	9.5802	8.8832	8.2664	7.7184	7.2297	6.7921	6.3988
24	21.2434	18.9139	16.9355	15.2470	13.7987	12.5504	11.4693	10.5288	9.7066	8.9847	8.3481	7.7843	7.2829	6.8352	6.4338
25	22.0232	19.5234	17.4132	15.6221	14.0940	12.7834	11.6536	10.6748	9.8226	9.0770	8.4217	7.8431	7.3300	6.8729	6.4641
26	22.7952	20.1210	17.8768	15.9828	14.3752	13.0032	11.8258	10.8100	9.9290	9.1610	8.4880	7.8956	7.3717	6.9061	6.4906
27	23.5596	20.7069	18.3270	16.3296	14.6430	13.2106	11.9867	10.9352	10.0266	9.2372	8.5478	7.9425	7.4086	6.9352	6.5135
28	24.3165	21.2813	18.7641	16.6631	14.8981	13.4062	12.1371	11.0511	10.1161	9.3066	8.6016	7.9844	7.4412	6.9607	6.5335
29	25.0658	21.8444	19.1885	16.9837	15.1411	13.5908	12.2777	11.1584	10.1983	9.3696	8.6501	8.0218	7.4701	6.9831	6.5509
30	25.8077	22.3964	19.6005	17.2920	15.3725	13.7649	12.4091	11.2578	10.2737	9.4269	8.6938	8.0552	7.4957	7.0027	6.5660
31	26.5423	22.9377	20.0005	17.5885	15.5928	13.9291	12.5318	11.3498	10.3428	9.4790	8.7331	8.0850	7.5183	7.0199	6.5791
32	27.2696	23.4683	20.3888	17.8736	15.8027	14.0841	12.6466	11.4350	10.4062	9.5264	8.7686	8.1116	7.5383	7.0350	6.5905
33	27.9897	23.9885	20.7658	18.1477	16.0026	14.2303	12.7538	11.5139	10.4644	9.5694	8.8005	8.1353	7.5560	7.0483	6.6005
34	28.7027	24.4986	21.1319	18.4112	16.1929	14.3682	12.8540	11.5870	10.5178	9.6086	8.8293	8.1565	7.5717	7.0599	6.6091
35	29.4086	24.9986	21.4872	18.6646	16.3742	14.4983	12.9477	11.6546	10.5668	9.6442	8.8552	8.1755	7.5856	7.0701	6.6166
36	30.1075	25.4888	21.8323	18.9083	16.5469	14.6211	13.0352	11.7172	10.6118	9.6765	8.8786	8.1924	7.5979	7.0790	6.6231
37	30.7995	25.9694	22.1673	19.1426	16.7113	14.7368	13.1170	11.7752	10.6530	9.7059	8.8996	8.2075	7.6087	7.0868	6.6288
38	31.4847	26.4406	22.4925	19.3679	16.8679	14.8461	13.1935	11.8289	10.6908	9.7327	8.9186	8.2210	7.6183	7.0937	6.6338
39	32.1631	26.9026	22.8082	19.5845	17.0171	14.9491	13.2650	11.8786	10.7255	9.7570	8.9356	8.2330	7.6269	7.0998	6.6380
40	32.8347	27.3555	23.1148	19.7928	17.1591	15.0464	13.3317	11.9246	10.7574	9.7791	8.9510	8.2438	7.6344	7.1051	6.6418
41	33.4997	27.7995	23.4124	19.9931	17.2944	15.1381	13.3941	11.9672	10.7866	9.7991	8.9649	8.2534	7.6410	7.1097	6.6450
42	34.1581	28.2348	23.7014	20.1857	17.4232	15.2246	13.4525	12.0067	10.8134	9.8174	8.9774	8.2619	7.6469	7.1138	6.6478
43	34.8100	28.6615	23.9819	20.3708	17.5459	15.3062	13.5070	12.0432	10.8380	9.8340	8.9886	8.2696	7.6522	7.1173	6.6503
44	35.4555	29.0799	24.2543	20.5489	17.6628	15.3833	13.5579	12.0771	10.8605	9.8491	8.9988	8.2764	7.6568	7.1205	6.6524
45	36.0945	29.4901	24.5187	20.7201	17.7741	15.4559	13.6055	12.1084	10.8812	9.8628	9.0079	8.2825	7.6609	7.1232	6.6543
46	36.7273	29.8923	24.7755	20.8847	17.8801	15.5244	13.6500	12.1374	10.9002	9.8753	9.0161	8.2880	7.6645	7.1256	6.6559
47	37.3537	30.2866	25.0247	21.0430	17.9810	15.5891	13.6916	12.1643	10.9176	9.8866	9.0235	8.2928	7.6677	7.1277	6.6573
48	37.9740	30.6731	25.2667	21.1952	18.0772	15.6501	13.7305	12.1891	10.9336	9.8969	9.0302	8.2972	7.6705	7.1296	6.6585
49	38.5881	31.0521	25.5017	21.3415	18.1687	15.7077	13.7668	12.2122	10.9482	9.9063	9.0362	8.3010	7.6730	7.1312	6.6596
50	39.1961	31.4236	25.7298	21.4822	18.2559	15.7619	13.8008	12.2335	10.9617	9.9148	9.0416	8.3045	7.6753	7.1327	6.6605

Munn and Garcia, *Encyclopedia of Banking and Finance,* 7th ed. (Boston: The Banker's Publishing Co., 1973), pp. 464–467.

APPENDIX B (continued)

	16%	17%	18%	19%	20%	21%	22%	23%	24%	25%	30%	35%	40%	45%	50%
1	.8621	.8547	.8475	.8403	.8333	.8264	.8197	.8130	.8065	.8000	.7692	.7407	.7143	.6897	.6667
2	1.6052	1.5852	1.5656	1.5465	1.5278	1.5095	1.4915	1.4740	1.4568	1.4400	1.3609	1.2894	1.2245	1.1653	1.1111
3	2.2459	2.2096	2.1743	2.1399	2.1065	2.0739	2.0422	2.0114	1.9813	1.9520	1.8161	1.6959	1.5889	1.4933	1.4074
4	2.7982	2.7432	2.6901	2.6386	2.5887	2.5404	2.4936	2.4483	2.4043	2.3616	2.1662	1.9969	1.8492	1.7195	1.6049
5	3.2743	3.1993	3.1272	3.0576	2.9906	2.9260	2.8636	2.8035	2.7454	2.6893	2.4356	2.2200	2.0352	1.8755	1.7366
6	3.6847	3.5892	3.4976	3.4098	3.3255	3.2446	3.1669	3.0923	3.0205	2.9514	2.6428	2.3852	2.1680	1.9831	1.8244
7	4.0386	3.9224	3.8115	3.7057	3.6046	3.5079	3.4155	3.3270	3.2423	3.1611	2.8021	2.5075	2.2628	2.0573	1.8830
8	4.3436	4.2072	4.0776	3.9544	3.8372	3.7256	3.6193	3.5179	3.4212	3.3289	2.9247	2.5982	2.3306	2.1085	1.9220
9	4.6065	4.4506	4.3030	4.1633	4.0310	3.9054	3.7863	3.6731	3.5655	3.4631	3.0190	2.6653	2.3790	2.1438	1.9480
10	4.8332	4.6586	4.4941	4.3389	4.1925	4.0541	3.9232	3.7993	3.6819	3.5705	3.0916	2.7150	2.4136	2.1681	1.9653
11	5.0286	4.8364	4.6560	4.4865	4.3271	4.1769	4.0354	3.9019	3.7757	3.6564	3.1474	2.7519	2.4383	2.1849	1.9769
12	5.1971	4.9884	4.7932	4.6105	4.4392	4.2785	4.1274	3.9852	3.8514	3.7251	3.1903	2.7792	2.4559	2.1965	1.9846
13	5.3423	5.1183	4.9095	4.7147	4.5327	4.3624	4.2028	4.0530	3.9124	3.7801	3.2233	2.7994	2.4685	2.2045	1.9897
14	5.4675	5.2293	5.0081	4.8023	4.6106	4.4317	4.2646	4.1082	3.9616	3.8241	3.2487	2.8143	2.4775	2.2100	1.9932
15	5.5755	5.3242	5.0916	4.8759	4.6755	4.4890	4.3152	4.1530	4.0013	3.8593	3.2682	2.8254	2.4839	2.2138	1.9954
16	5.6685	5.4053	5.1624	4.9377	4.7296	4.5364	4.3567	4.1894	4.0333	3.8874	3.2833	2.8337	2.4885	2.2164	1.9970
17	5.7487	5.4746	5.2223	4.9897	4.7746	4.5755	4.3908	4.2190	4.0591	3.9099	3.2948	2.8397	2.4918	2.2182	1.9980
18	5.8179	5.5338	5.2732	5.0333	4.8122	4.6079	4.4187	4.2431	4.0799	3.9279	3.3037	2.8443	2.4941	2.2195	1.9986
19	5.8775	5.5845	5.3163	5.0701	4.8435	4.6346	4.4415	4.2627	4.0967	3.9424	3.3106	2.8476	2.4958	2.2203	1.9991
20	5.9289	5.6278	5.3528	5.1009	4.8696	4.6567	4.4603	4.2786	4.1103	3.9539	3.3158	2.8501	2.4970	2.2209	1.9994
21	5.9732	5.6648	5.3837	5.1268	4.8913	4.6749	4.4756	4.2915	4.1212	3.9631	3.3199	2.8519	2.4979	2.2213	1.9996
22	6.0113	5.6964	5.4099	5.1486	4.9094	4.6900	4.4882	4.3021	4.1300	3.9705	3.3230	2.8533	2.4985	2.2216	1.9997
23	6.0443	5.7234	5.4321	5.1669	4.9245	4.7025	4.4985	4.3106	4.1371	3.9764	3.3254	2.8543	2.4989	2.2218	1.9998
24	6.0726	5.7465	5.4510	5.1823	4.9371	4.7128	4.5070	4.3176	4.1428	3.9811	3.3272	2.8550	2.4992	2.2219	1.9999
25	6.0971	5.7662	5.4669	5.1952	4.9476	4.7213	4.5139	4.3232	4.1474	3.9849	3.3286	2.8556	2.4994	2.2220	1.9999
26	6.1182	5.7831	5.4805	5.2060	4.9563	4.7284	4.5196	4.3278	4.1511	3.9879	3.3297	2.8560	2.4996	2.2221	1.9999
27	6.1364	5.7975	5.4919	5.2152	4.9636	4.7342	4.5243	4.3316	4.1541	3.9903	3.3306	2.8563	2.4997	2.2221	2.0000
28	6.1521	5.8099	5.5016	5.2228	4.9697	4.7390	4.5281	4.3346	4.1566	3.9923	3.3312	2.8565	2.4998	2.2221	2.0000
29	6.1656	5.8204	5.5098	5.2292	4.9747	4.7430	4.5312	4.3371	4.1585	3.9938	3.3317	2.8567	2.4998	2.2222	2.0000
30	6.1772	5.8294	5.5168	5.2347	4.9789	4.7463	4.5338	4.3391	4.1601	3.9950	3.3321	2.8568	2.4999	2.2222	2.0000
31	6.1873	5.8371	5.5227	5.2392	4.9825	4.7490	4.5359	4.3407	4.1614	3.9960	3.3324	2.8569	2.4999	2.2222	2.0000
32	6.1959	5.8437	5.5277	5.2431	4.9854	4.7512	4.5376	4.3420	4.1624	3.9968	3.3326	2.8569	2.4999	2.2222	2.0000
33	6.2034	5.8493	5.5320	5.2463	4.9878	4.7531	4.5390	4.3431	4.1632	3.9975	3.3328	2.8570	2.5000	2.2222	2.0000
34	6.2098	5.8541	5.5356	5.2490	4.9899	4.7546	4.5402	4.3440	4.1639	3.9980	3.3329	2.8570	2.5000	2.2222	2.0000
35	6.2154	5.8582	5.5386	5.2512	4.9915	4.7559	4.5411	4.3447	4.1644	3.9984	3.3330	2.8571	2.5000	2.2222	2.0000
36	6.2201	5.8617	5.5412	5.2531	4.9930	4.7569	4.5419	4.3453	4.1649	3.9987	3.3331	2.8571	2.5000	2.2222	2.0000
37	6.2243	5.8647	5.5434	5.2547	4.9941	4.7578	4.5425	4.3458	4.1652	3.9990	3.3332	2.8571	2.5000	2.2222	2.0000
38	6.2278	5.8673	5.5453	5.2561	4.9951	4.7585	4.5431	4.3461	4.1655	3.9992	3.3332	2.8571	2.5000	2.2222	2.0000
39	6.2309	5.8695	5.5468	5.2572	4.9959	4.7591	4.5435	4.3464	4.1657	3.9993	3.3332	2.8571	2.5000	2.2222	2.0000
40	6.2335	5.8713	5.5482	5.2582	4.9966	4.7596	4.5438	4.3467	4.1659	3.9995	3.3333	2.8571	2.5000	2.2222	2.0000
41	6.2358	5.8729	5.5493	5.2590	4.9972	4.7600	4.5441	4.3469	4.1660	3.9996	3.3333	2.8571	2.5000	2.2222	2.0000
42	6.2377	5.8743	5.5503	5.2596	4.9977	4.7603	4.5444	4.3471	4.1662	3.9997	3.3333	2.8571	2.5000	2.2222	2.0000
43	6.2394	5.8755	5.5511	5.2602	4.9980	4.7606	4.5446	4.3472	4.1663	3.9997	3.3333	2.8571	2.5000	2.2222	2.0000
44	6.2409	5.8765	5.5518	5.2607	4.9984	4.7608	4.5447	4.3473	4.1663	3.9998	3.3333	2.8571	2.5000	2.2222	2.0000
45	6.2422	5.8773	5.5523	5.2611	4.9986	4.7610	4.5448	4.3474	4.1664	3.9998	3.3333	2.8571	2.5000	2.2222	2.0000
46	6.2432	5.8781	5.5528	5.2614	4.9989	4.7611	4.5450	4.3475	4.1665	3.9999	3.3334	2.8571	2.5000	2.2222	2.0000
47	6.2442	5.8787	5.5533	5.2617	4.9991	4.7613	4.5450	4.3475	4.1665	3.9999	3.3334	2.8571	2.5000	2.2222	2.0000
48	6.2450	5.8792	5.5536	5.2619	4.9992	4.7614	4.5451	4.3476	4.1665	3.9999	3.3334	2.8571	2.5000	2.2222	2.0000
49	6.2457	5.8797	5.5539	5.2621	4.9994	4.7615	4.5452	4.3476	4.1666	3.9999	3.3334	2.8571	2.5000	2.2222	2.0000
50	6.2463	5.8801	5.5542	5.2623	4.9995	4.7615	4.5452	4.3477	4.1666	3.9999	3.3334	2.8571	2.5000	2.2222	2.0000

INDEX OF CASES

Addison Electric Company	196	Javits Company	324
American Forge Corporation	400	Jenkins Plumbing Company	308
Ankh Corporation	37	J. H. Company	184
Basic Industries, Inc.	486	Meditronics, Inc.	569
Bolton College Food Service	105	Megansett Corporation	513
Breau Company (A)	60	Metchler Corporation	340
Breau Company (B)	70	Midwest Grain Company	209
Brenco Corporation	469		
Brown Furniture Company, Inc.	171	National Credit Company	174
Budin Company (A)	112	Note on the Capital Asset	
Budin Company (B)	188	Pricing Model (CAPM)	310
Capitol Corporation	18	Paducah Portrait	96
Carroll Company Incorporated	100	Palazolo Manufacturing	
ChemCo, Inc.	56	Company	363
Children's Memorial Hospital (A)	154	Phillips Bakeries, Inc.	563
Children's Memorial Hospital (B)	408	PODER Industries	446
Chou Canning Company	287		
Cost-of-Capital Illustrations	390	Quality Hardware, Inc.	477
Daily Ledger, The	292	Super Sounds	58
Delicious, Inc.	377	Swanson Corporation	236
Dunkin' Donuts Incorporated	492		
		Teague Corporation	370
Electricircuit, Inc.	537	Tesco, Inc. (A)	77
Etech, Inc.	265	Tesco, Inc. (B)	83
		Thermo Rubber, Inc.	296
Filtron Corporation	334		
Frecter Company	464	United Chemical Company	294
Fulton Flying Lessons, Inc.	9		
Fund for Government Investors	144	Valuation Exercise	322
		Valu-Hi Drug Stores (A)	25
Gansett Furniture Company (A)	129	Valu-Hi Drug Stores (B)	33
Gansett Furniture Company (B)	350		
		Winco Distribution Company	521
Hammond Publishing Company	433	Winston College	88
Hollowville National Bank	39		
		Xenon, Inc.	71
Incoterm Corporation	549		